1995 YEARBOOK
EVENTS OF 1994

NEW

FOR CONGRE

NEWT
FOR CONGRESS

Congrat-
ulation's
NEWT

Republican Congressman
Newt Gingrich celebrates
his—and the GOP's—
election victory in
November.

1995 FUNK & WAGNALLS NEW ENCYCLOPEDIA YEARBOOK

LEON L. BRAM
Vice-President and
Editorial Director

NORMA H. DICKEY
Editor in Chief

Funk & Wagnalls Corporation

Publishers since 1876

MEMBERS OF THE STAFF

CONTENTS

FOREWORD: THE WORLD IN 1994

It was a hard year for U.S. President Bill Clinton. His dream of reforming the national health care system died in Congress, and then Congress itself fell to the Republicans in the November elections. (The details of the GOP triumph are reported in an article in the Events of 1994 section of the Yearbook.)

Clinton scored a foreign policy success, however, when he presided over the return to power of exiled Haitian President Jean-Bertrand Aristide under the protection of U.S. troops.

Elsewhere, the year brought both hope and horror. South Africa held its first all-race elections; the presidency went to Nelson Mandela, a prisoner under the country's previous regime. But in Rwanda ethnic hatreds exploded into genocide. Two million Rwandans flooded refugee camps in bordering nations, and many died of disease and starvation.

The civil war in Bosnia-Hercegovina seemed to quiet down toward the end of the year, but bitter conflict broke out between the Russian government and the would-be independent republic of Chechnya. Mexico lived through political assassination and peasant rebellion; a newly elected president was sworn in only to see the country sink into economic crisis.

On a happier note, the spectacular collision of a comet with Jupiter delighted scientists and science buffs alike. When the comet hit the giant planet, the resulting splash exceeded the watchers' wildest hopes. One of our feature articles tells that story and takes a look at the awe and fear such celestial wanderers have inspired in people through the ages.

It was a good year not only for sky watchers but for scandal watchers as well. Figure skater Nancy Kerrigan was clubbed just weeks before the Winter Olympics, prompting allegations that rival skater Tonya Harding had been somehow involved in the attack. Kerrigan brought home the silver medal, and Harding was subsequently barred from the sport for life. A special article in the Events in 1994 section gives a wrap-up of Olympic events.

The media uproar caused by the Kerrigan attack paled next to the scrutiny trained on ex-football star O. J. Simpson after he was charged with the murder of his former wife and a friend of hers. A police chase of Simpson, televised live, drew millions of viewers.

But not even the pursuit of O. J. Simpson could match the global interest accorded soccer's World Cup, played in the United States in the summer. One of our feature articles tells exactly what happened at the tournament, which drew the largest television audience in history—some 2 *billion* viewers.

Another feature casts a nostalgic and discerning eye on small towns—those enduring yet evolving foundation stones of American life.

The Yearbook begins with a photo feature that collects in one place many of the most unforgettable images of 1994.

THE EDITORS

1994 IN PICTURES

U.S. troops on patrol in Haiti in September, shortly after arriving under an agreement intended to restore democratic rule.

Representative Dan Rostenkowski (D, Illinois) was forced to resign his powerful committee chairmanship after being indicted in May for alleged misuse of federal funds. Then, in November, he lost his bid for reelection.

Members of Congress look over a "Street Sweeper" on Capitol Hill. Congress passed an assault weapons ban in August as part of a major anticrime bill.

In April, at her first press conference as first lady, Hillary Rodham Clinton answers questions about the Clintons' involvement in the Whitewater affair.

Ex-football great O. J. Simpson led police on a chase in a white Ford Bronco before being arrested and charged with murdering his ex-wife and a male friend of hers. (Inset, Simpson with lawyer Robert Shapiro.)

President Clinton presses for health care reform, his primary domestic initiative for 1994. Though the issue was hotly debated in Congress and in the nation, no major legislation was enacted.

A powerful earthquake hit the Los Angeles area on January 17, killing more than 50 people and causing heavy damage, as illustrated by the collapsed roadway above and the row of smashed cars at right.

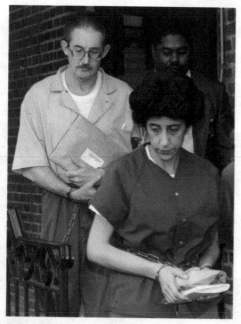

CIA official Aldrich Ames and his wife, Rosario, pleaded guilty in April to selling secrets to the Soviet Union and Russia.

ELECTION '94

The Virginia Senate candidates debate on Larry King Live: (left to right) King; incumbent Charles Robb (D), who bucked the Republican tide and won reelection; ex-Governor L. Douglas Wilder (I), who later dropped out of the race and endorsed Robb; Marshall Coleman (I); and Iran-contra figure Oliver North (R).

Republicans ended Election Day in control of the governor's mansions in seven of the eight largest states. In California, incumbent Pete Wilson (right) won a second term. In Texas, George W. Bush, son of the former president, ousted Democratic incumbent Ann Richards.

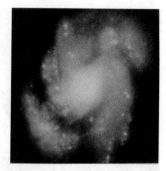

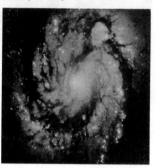

Very different photos of a remote galaxy, taken by the Hubble Space Telescope before (top) and after it was repaired by astronauts.

Queen Elizabeth II and French President François Mitterrand at the official inauguration of the Channel Tunnel, May 6 in Calais, France. Behind them is a huge tunnel-boring machine.

Vice President Al Gore, Jr., in January, holds the first White House electronic news conference, responding via computer and modem to questioners from around the world.

REMEMBERING D DAY

Fifty years after the Allied invasion of Normandy on June 6, 1944 (above, a photo of the landing on Omaha Beach), veterans (right) and other visitors returned to pay tribute to those who fell in combat and are buried there (below).

TRANSITIONS

On May 19, Jacqueline Kennedy Onassis, widow of President John F. Kennedy and one of the most elegant and admired first ladies in U.S. history, died at the age of 64.

The death of Richard Nixon on April 22 revived contrasting memories. Above, President Nixon, with his wife, Pat, visits the Great Wall of China. At left, after resigning because of Watergate, he takes leave of the American people, August 9, 1974.

CHANGE IN SOUTH AFRICA

Voters line up in large numbers
(above) to cast ballots in South
Africa's first election open to all
races. At left, Nelson Mandela,
whose African National Congress
won the most votes, is sworn in on
May 10 as the nation's president.

WORLD EVENTS

Rwanda's capital was littered with corpses (below) after massive ethnic violence broke out in April. Hundreds of thousands fled across the border to face hunger and disease in refugee camps in Zaire (inset).

North Korean strongman Kim Il Sung (left) died July 8 at age 82, leaving a son, Kim Jong Il, as his chosen heir.

Cuban refugees aboard makeshift rafts sight a U.S. Coast Guard helicopter. In August and September 1994, the Coast Guard intercepted more than 20,000 Cubans attempting to reach U.S. shores, before a new U.S.-Cuban immigration accord took effect.

Ultranationalists, such as Vladimir Zhirinovsky (left, in bulletproof vest), and pro-Communist hard-liners posed challenges to reformers in Russia.

As the Mideast peace process continued, self-rule began in occupied territories (at right, Palestinian police enter Jericho in May), and Jordan and Israel ended the state of war between them and signed a peace treaty (below, Jordan's King Hussein and Israel's Yitzhak Rabin shake hands at the White House in July).

ARTS AND ENTERTAINMENT

Kurt Cobain, leader of the rock group Nirvana, died April 5 of a self-inflicted gunshot wound.

Perhaps the most talked-about TV show was the gritty police drama NYPD Blue. *The original cast included, at right, David Caruso (who later left the series) and Dennis Franz.*

Beauty and the Beast, *with Susan Egan and Terrence Mann in the title roles, was Disney's Broadway debut—and, at $11.9 million, the most expensive Broadway musical ever.*

Steven Spielberg (inset) picked up best director and best picture Oscars March 21 for Schindler's List, a moving film about the Holocaust, starring Liam Neeson (below, left) and Ben Kingsley.

Russian writer Aleksandr Solzhenitsyn returned to his homeland after 20 years of exile; here he walks with his wife, Natalya, in Vladivostok.

Returning to the concert circuit after more than 20 years, Barbra Streisand, shown performing at London's Wembley stadium in April, proved she was still a superstar.

19

SPORTS HIGHLIGHTS

MVP Emmitt Smith (carrying the ball) helped the Dallas Cowboys defeat the Buffalo Bills on January 30, 1994, and take the Super Bowl for the second year in a row.

Scotty Thurman sinks a shot to help Arkansas overcome Duke on April 4 to win the NCAA championship.

The New York Rangers won the Stanley Cup for the first time since 1940, defeating the Vancouver Canucks in a seven-game championship series.

Houston Rockets MVP Hakeem Olajuwon goes up for a shot during the NBA finals, in which the Rockets beat the New York Knicks to win their first title.

Pete Sampras triumphed at Wimbledon in July, becoming the first man to win back-to-back titles there since Boris Becker in 1986.

Dunga scores the winning penalty kick for Brazil in a shoot-out against Italy for soccer's World Cup on July 17 at the Rose Bowl in California.

Though fans showed signs of distress, major league baseball players went out on strike in August.

21

THE WINTER OLYMPICS

The Olympic torch is passed to a ski jumper at the opening ceremonies for the XVII Winter Olympics on February 12 in Lillehammer, Norway.

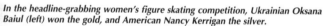

In the headline-grabbing women's figure skating competition, Ukrainian Oksana Baiul (left) won the gold, and American Nancy Kerrigan the silver.

COMETS
MYSTERIOUS VISITORS FROM OUTER SPACE

by RONALD A. SCHORN

Comets have fascinated people for millennia, but until 1994 no one had ever had the chance to witness their destructive power firsthand. Then, from July 16 to 22, fragments of Comet Shoemaker-Levy 9 smashed into Jupiter, creating a series of spectacular fireballs in the giant planet's atmosphere.

The string of explosions was awesome, yet the discovery that comets can wreak havoc would not have surprised our distant ancestors. Widely different cultures have regarded comets with fear and dread. Comets' unpredictable appearances were believed to be omens, or even causes, of wars, revolutions, plagues, and other calamities. When Halley's Comet appeared in 1066—the year William the Conqueror, the ruler of Normandy, won the British crown by defeating King Harold II—frightened courtiers reported the evil omen to Harold. The episode is vividly illustrated in the medieval Bayeux Tapestry, which tells the story of the Norman conquest.

Modern scientists may not believe in omens, but they have come to realize that comets, which are only mountain-sized bodies, are capable of causing worldwide disasters as terrible as any that were imagined of old—and paradoxically might also be responsible for our very existence.

Exotic Visitors

When observed from Earth, a typical comet may show a starlike or fuzzy nucleus inside a surrounding coma, which is a hazy blob of

Ronald A. Schorn, former chief of ground-based astronomy for NASA, is a planetary astronomer and historian for Intaglio, Inc., a private firm in College Station, TX, that specializes in researching and writing social, economic, technical, and scientific histories.

ISTI MIRANT STELLA

HAROLD

In ancient times comets were often seen as bearers of bad tidings. In the medieval Bayeux Tapestry, courtiers view the appearance of Halley's Comet in 1066 and rush to warn England's King Harold II, who indeed lost his life that year.

light that can appear as large as the Moon. The nucleus and coma together—or the coma alone—are often called the head. The tail issues from the coma and usually is brightest nearest the head, gradually dimming along its length. Comet tails come in a wide variety of shapes and must be extremely rarefied, for stars shine through them without a trace of dimming. The tail generally points away from the Sun and in rare cases may span a good fraction of the sky.

Not every comet shows all these features. Some never show a nucleus, but only a coma, while others display just a starlike nucleus. In the latter case they resemble asteroids, the miniplanets that orbit the Sun mainly between the paths of Mars and Jupiter. Many faint comets never develop a tail but come and go merely as ghostly comas.

Comets in the past have been described in such terms as "brilliant," "awesome," or "spectacular," so it might seem surprising that most people today have never seen one. But even so-called great comets are usually not all that bright. The tail of a typical comet has roughly the same surface brightness as the Milky Way or even less, and the head is not much brighter. Even a first-quarter or last-quarter Moon will wash out much of the show, and today most people live in urban areas, where lights and smog spoil the view.

A great comet is indeed a noble sight when seen in a truly clear, dark sky. But only on extremely rare occasions do circumstances conspire to produce a spectacle that is capable of riveting the attention of even the most casual viewer: a startlingly bright object—perhaps brighter than the Moon—visible above the western horizon just after sunset or above the eastern horizon at sunrise.

Ancient Puzzle

Ancient astronomers could predict solar, lunar, and planetary movements and positions accurately, but comets left them baffled. Unlike the Sun, Moon, and planets (which are restricted to the rather narrow belt called the zodiac), comets can appear anywhere in the sky, and they can move in any direction at weirdly variable speeds with respect to the background stars. Moreover, different comets have different shapes, which can change almost whimsically over time. Perhaps most terrifying to the ancients was the fact that comets appeared and disappeared unpredictably. For millennia it was thought that comets might be special messengers of God or the gods.

For some 2,000 years Western ideas on the nature of comets were essentially those of the ancient Greek scientist and philosopher Aristotle. In Aristotle's view the starry heavens above were changeless; the planetary, solar, and lunar regions below could change, but they were subject to strict laws. Only in his lowest sphere (Earth's atmosphere in the broad sense) could there be unpredictable changes of any sort. He reasoned, therefore, that comets were fairly close to us, exhalations of some sort from the Earth that caught fire as they rose up near the moving heavens.

A recurring fear has been that a comet could destroy the Earth. This French cartoon of 1857 predicted that such a disaster would soon occur.

25

British astronomer Edmond Halley was the first to show that a comet could make regular, periodic appearances.

So matters stood until the 16th century, when the Danish astronomer Tycho Brahe (1546-1601) proved from observations that the great comet of 1577 had to be farther from the Earth than the Moon and thus was a heavenly body. The nature and motions of comets were still hotly argued, but astronomers gradually swung around to the view that they were celestial objects that passed by or around the Sun in some kind of orbit. More than a century later, the English astronomer Isaac Newton (1642-1727) provided the key to such orbits. His 1687 book *Principia Mathematica* laid out the law of gravity and the laws of motion for all material bodies—laws that were essential to explaining how the Sun's gravitational force affected the movements of celestial bodies.

It was Newton's close friend Edmond Halley (1656-1742), however, who made comets full-fledged members of the solar system. Halley was able to show that the comets of 1531, 1607, and 1682 had the same orbit—a very elongated ellipse with a period (the time required to make one complete revolution about the Sun) of about 76 years—and thus were actually the same comet. Halley predicted that his comet would

It is now generally accepted that the comet depicted at the top of Giotto di Bondone's Adoration of the Magi *is Halley's Comet. It appeared in 1301, about three years before the completion of the fresco, where it serves as the Star of Bethlehem.*

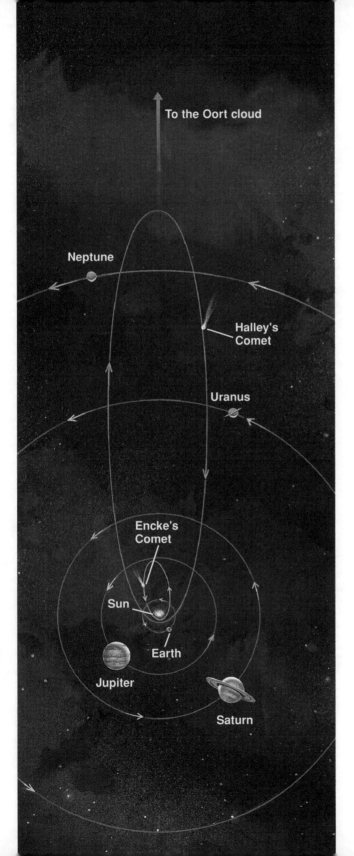

To the Oort cloud

Neptune

Halley's
Comet

Uranus

Encke's
Comet

Sun

Earth

Jupiter

Saturn

Known comets generally spend the majority of their time in the more distant parts of their orbits, periodically returning to dash around the Sun. Most comets, however, are thought to reside in the so-called Oort cloud, beyond the orbits of the planets.

return in 1758 or 1759, and he was right. It has been known ever since as Halley's Comet.

Halley was very lucky, for the comet named after him is the only bright predictable one known in the entire solar system. Subsequent calculations were able to verify earlier recorded appearances of Halley's Comet as far back as 239 B.C. It is now generally accepted that Halley's is the comet rendered (with notable accuracy) in the *Adoration of the Magi* by the great Italian painter Giotto di Bondone. The fresco has been dated to around 1304, three years after Halley's Comet streaked across the sky.

Surprising Discoveries

The 19th century saw several unexpected developments in cometary astronomy. The curious history of Comet Encke is an example. First spotted in 1786, it was seen again in 1795, in 1805, and in 1819, when its orbit was calculated by German astronomer Johann Franz Encke. In fact, accounting for times when it was badly placed for observation from the Earth, it had a period of just over three years, an incredibly short time for a comet— more like an asteroid. But a comet it was, with tail and all. It was the first known short-period comet, one with an orbit more nearly circular than those of such objects as Comet Halley.

However, Encke's Comet had an even greater surprise in store, for astronomers learned that the interval between its appearances was still shortening. Some theorized that there was a "resisting medium" slowing its motion and causing it to spiral toward the Sun. The German astronomer Friedrich Bessel (1784-1846) suggested the cause might be the "rocket effect" of erupting jets of gas from the sunward side of a cometary

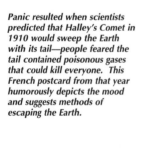

Panic resulted when scientists predicted that Halley's Comet in 1910 would sweep the Earth with its tail—people feared the tail contained poisonous gases that could kill everyone. This French postcard from that year humorously depicts the mood and suggests methods of escaping the Earth.

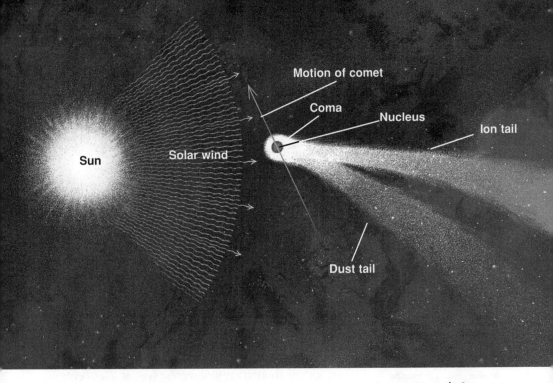

Sun

Solar wind

Motion of comet

Coma

Nucleus

Ion tail

Dust tail

As a comet nears the Sun, sunlight heats the nucleus, surface ices evaporate, and gas and dust escape. The dust is pushed away by the pressure of sunlight, and the gas molecules are swept up by the solar wind. As a result, the comet may have two tails.

nucleus. Bessel was right, but it took more than a century to prove it.

A different case was the demise of Comet Biela, which astronomers in 1845 and 1846 saw split into two pieces. The pair—more widely separated than before—were observed again in 1852 and did not reappear. But the year 1872 saw a spectacular meteor shower whose components all had the same orbit as that of the missing comet. By then the annual Leonid meteor shower had been shown to be due to debris from Comet Swift-Tuttle. Evidently both Comet Biela and Comet Swift-Tuttle had disintegrated into cosmic rubble.

These showers taught scientists something very important about the makeup of comets, for of all the billions of such shower meteors seen to enter our atmosphere, not one is known to have reached the Earth's surface. Thus the stuff of comets must be weak and fragile indeed (although, traveling as fast as they do, they can still pack a wallop).

At about the same time, the newly invented spectroscope (a device that analyzes matter by spreading out into a rainbow the light that it emits, absorbs, or scatters) showed that the light of comets comes partly from sunlight reflecting from small particles and partly from glowing gas, with the ratio between the two varying from comet to comet—and sometimes from day to day for the same object. However, in most cases the only gas that could be definitely identified was molecular carbon (a molecule made of two carbon atoms), a situation that remained unchanged until the 20th century. Two exceptions were comets that passed very close to the Sun in 1882 and displayed evidence of sodium and even iron vapor.

In the 19th and early 20th centuries scientists generally believed that a comet's nucleus was a swarm of small, separate particles following the same orbit around the Sun. This "flying gravel bank" or "flying sandbank" view was supported by the connection between comets and meteor showers, but astronomers now know that, at least in some cases, it is wrong.

Modern Insights

The 1910 appearance of Halley's Comet caused a worldwide sensation. But after all the excitement had subsided, it turned out that scientists had learned relatively little that was new. The next few decades saw scientific knowledge about comets grow slowly, if steadily, although public interest was at a low ebb.

Improved equipment and better physics helped astronomers identify a number of simple molecules— ionized carbon monoxide, for example—in the spectra of comets. (When an atom or molecule is ionized, it

This diagram reveals the path Comet Shoemaker-Levy 9 followed to its destruction. Passing close to Jupiter in 1992, it was broken into fragments by the giant planet's gravitational pull. These continued in the comet's orbit and then plummeted down to Jupiter in July 1994. The relative position of the Earth can be seen as it circles the Sun at right.

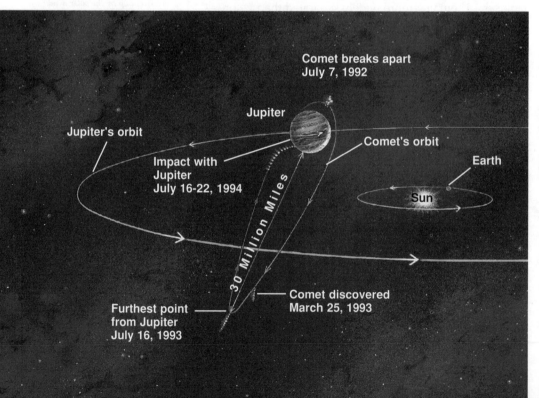

Comet breaks apart
July 7, 1992

Jupiter

Jupiter's orbit

Comet's orbit

Impact with
Jupiter
July 16-22, 1994

Earth

Sun

30 Million Miles

Furthest point
from Jupiter
July 16, 1993

Comet discovered
March 25, 1993

A false-color image, made in 1994, of the "string of pearls"—comet fragments—resulting from the breakup of Shoemaker-Levy 9.

gains or loses one or more electrons, thereby acquiring an electric charge.) Since these substances are short-lived, it was conjectured that they may be produced when ultraviolet light from the Sun breaks up more complex "parent" molecules driven off from the comet's nucleus. The "daughter" molecules are "excited" by sunlight and then give off light as they return to a "deexcited" state. But the search for the parents was a long one.

A real advance came in the mid-20th century when Fred L. Whipple, a professor of astronomy at Harvard University, published his "icy conglomerate," or "dirty snowball," model of a comet's nucleus. In this view the nucleus is a solid body a few miles across, composed of assorted ices and shot through with grains of a metallic and stony nature much like the stuff meteorites are made of.

When far from the Sun, a comet is only an inert lump of frozen material, but as it approaches our star, sunlight heats the nucleus. The surface ices evaporate, releasing gas and dust that easily escape the snowball's feeble gravity. The dust is pushed away from the Sun by the pressure of sunlight, while the gas molecules, broken apart and ionized by solar ultraviolet light, are swept up by the "solar wind," a stream of ionized particles flowing outward at high speed from the Sun. Because of these two different processes acting on two different kinds of materials, a comet can have two separate tails. Generally, the "dust" tail is shorter and more curved, while the "ion" tail is longer and straighter.

Whipple suggested that such common substances as methane, ammonia, and especially water, were the parent molecules that formed the ices. In addition, he

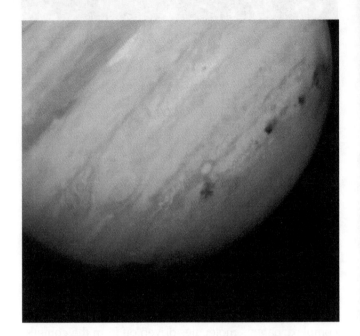

proposed that as a comet ages it develops a dark covering of dust that is not swept away with the gas, like a dirty crust of snow left behind after a springtime thaw. Finally, he revived Bessel's old "rocket" idea, suggesting that sunlight produces jets of gas and dust by heating isolated, exposed areas of surface ice.

Whipple has been proved correct on every major point, and his ideas on the nature of a comet, with some modifications, are the ones that scientists hold today. Still, recent observations have again raised the possibility that the nucleus, rather than being a single solid dirty snowball, may be composed of many smaller bodies held together loosely by gravity. This might explain how Shoemaker-Levy broke apart so easily under the influence of Jupiter's powerful gravitational pull when it passed by the giant planet in 1992.

Halley Returns

As 1986 approached, scientists were determined to learn more than had been discovered from the 1910 appearance of Halley's Comet, and they made extensive preparations for its return. By 1986 there were more tools available for research. Since World War II, infrared and radio astronomy had been developed. Space vehicles—able to soar above Earth's obscuring atmosphere and study comets at *all* wavelengths—had come next. Space probes were now able to fly by a comet and take close looks.

Spurred by the fiasco of Comet Kohoutek in 1973 and 1974, when tremendous publicity over the "comet of the century" was followed by a dismal flop of a spectacle, astronomers took great pains to warn the public not to expect stunning views of Halley.

Scientifically, however, things went well. Close-up images of Comet Halley's nucleus showed a solid, potato-shaped body mostly covered with a coal-black crust, with jets of gas and dust erupting from a few active areas of exposed ices. This comet, at least, has a solid nucleus. The most prominent parent molecule proved to be ordinary water, along with carbon monoxide and carbon dioxide. The presence of methane and ammonia was inferred, and hydrocyanic acid was confirmed. Surprisingly, formaldehyde was detected in the form of polymers, or complex chains forming very complex molecules. This finding might hold some very important clues regarding the origin of life on Earth.

The Origins of Comets

The jury is still out on when, where, and how comets are formed. Most scientists assume comets formed when the rest of the solar system did, some 4.5 billion years ago. But this raises a problem: if comets are that old, Comet Halley and the short-period comets that frequently pass near the Sun would have been long gone by now—evaporated—if they had always been in their present orbits.

It is clear that comets must have been formed in a cold place far from the Sun for they are mostly made up of water ice and of other ices that evaporate at even lower temperatures. In fact, most known comets spend most of their time loitering near the most distant part of their orbits, making periodic dashes toward, around, and then away from the Sun in what is for comets a relatively short time. Astronomers have concluded, from computing many comets' orbits, that not one has come from outside the solar system.

Two infrared images of the fireball that flared and subsided when fragment K of the comet hit Jupiter. In the photograph above, taken 13 minutes after impact, the fireball is about 20,000 kilometers (over 12,000 miles) in diameter. The collisions occurred on the side of Jupiter not visible from Earth, but Jupiter's rapid rotation soon brought the sites into view.

It appears that most comets today are in the so-called Oort cloud, a shell of some 100,000 million comets that surrounds the Sun and is located at the far reaches of the solar system. The cloud is named after the Dutch astronomer Jan H. Oort (1900-1992), who proposed its existence in 1950. In the Oort cloud, comet nuclei can last almost indefinitely, except for those that are lost to the solar system because of the gravitational pulls of nearby stars and the Milky Way. However, sometimes

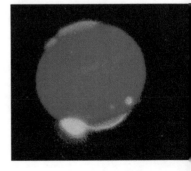

The spacecraft Galileo *(above, in an artist's conception), had a direct view of the Shoemaker-Levy collisions with Jupiter in July 1994. Astronomers hoped that the spacecraft would eventually yield detailed images of the event (its pictures are transmitted very slowly).*

gravitational forces can change the orbits of comet nuclei in the Oort cloud so as to cause them to pass close to the Sun. Those are the comets we see on Earth; the rest move in their orbits dark and unnoticed.

The connection of comets with asteroids remains a mystery. At the beginning of the 20th century, astronomers were convinced that comets died by disintegrating into clouds of small particles, as did Comet Biela. But things are not that simple. If a comet is far from the Sun, for example, it is just a small body that shines by reflected sunlight, indistinguishable from an asteroid. Are "asteroids" in the outer solar system— which astronomers have been discovering recently—just dormant comets? No one knows. Closer to Earth are "asteroids" that may be the remains of short-period comets. It may take a space probe that can analyze samples of such an object to decide whether that theory is correct.

Comets and Collisions

The prospect of a comet colliding with the Earth was taken seriously in the 18th and 19th centuries but was dismissed in later years as far-fetched. Today the possibility is again attracting concern. Geologists have proved that the Earth has undergone sudden catastrophes in its long history. Encounters with comets and asteroids have been blamed for episodes of mass extinctions of life on our planet, including the demise of the dinosaurs.

But there is another side to the story. Had dinosaurs not been eliminated, mammals—and, in particular, humans—might never have had the chance to come to the fore. So we might owe our very existence to a comet. To go back even further, the Earth formed relatively close to the Sun, where volatile substances such as water and organic matter would find it hard to condense. Comets may have brought such material to the Earth from the outer reaches of the solar system. Thus, comets might have made it possible for life to get started on Earth.

Jupiter Jolted

The collision of Comet Shoemaker-Levy 9 with Jupiter in July 1994 provided the first opportunity for scientists to study such an event as it happened. Moreover, astronomers had over a year to prepare, so observatories around the world—along with satellites and space probes—had their instruments pointed toward the giant planet at the right times.

Sensibly, astronomers were cautious in their predictions, pointing out that Jupiter's enormous nonsolid bulk (its atmosphere is mostly hydrogen gas, and its interior mostly liquid hydrogen) might simply

David Levy (left) and Carolyn and Eugene Shoemaker (center and right) pose with the 18-inch Schmidt telescope at Palomar Observatory in California that they used to find the comet named after them. Indefatigable sky watchers, the Shoemakers hold the record for most comets found.

Comet West, one of the brightest comets in decades, as seen in March 1976. The comet takes about 500,000 years to traverse its orbit.

swallow the comet fragments, without anything much being visible from Earth. What actually happened exceeded even the most optimistic forecasts.

All the impacts were at about the same latitude on Jupiter but at different longitudes. They all occurred just before sunrise on Jupiter, and all on the side of the giant planet away from Earth. The explosions were enormous by earthly standards—perhaps equivalent to millions of megatons of TNT. By contrast, the biggest thermonuclear device, or "H-bomb," ever tested was about 60 megatons. Some of the fireballs were as big as the Earth, and some expanded so far that telescopic images showed them flaring past Jupiter's limb—the edge of the planet as seen from Earth.

Jupiter's rapid spin soon brought the impact sites into view, revealing dark spots so large they could be seen from Earth with an amateur telescope. That the impact sites were dark was not completely unexpected, for astronomers knew that the white areas visible on the planet are clouds that are at higher altitudes than those of the darker regions. But the spots proved to be surprisingly durable. Although strong winds quickly began to distort and tear them apart, they were expected to remain visible for a year or more.

Questions Remain

Spectroscopic observations after the collisions revealed the presence of elements and compounds not otherwise found in Jupiter's upper atmosphere; these substances presumably came from the comet itself and from material dredged up from lower layers of Jupiter's atmosphere. But the presence of water vapor was not confirmed, even though it is known to exist on the planet. Perhaps there was no water in the comet, or perhaps the fragments did not penetrate deep enough to reach the layers in the planet's atmosphere where water vapor exists. Evidently the pieces of Comet Shoemaker-Levy 9 exploded relatively high up in Jupiter's atmosphere. That would be consistent with the spectacular fireballs.

Some scientists question, though, whether Shoemaker-Levy 9 really was a comet. All of its pieces had tails, just like normal comets, but these shone only by reflected sunlight, indicating that they were made of dust particles. There was no trace of the glowing gas— glowing because of the effects of energetic ultraviolet radiation from the Sun—that is given off by most comets. Could this have been some unusual sort of asteroid, made up perhaps of rock and metal? If it was, why would it disintegrate and shed fine material so far from the Sun? The most fascinating possibility was that it was an entirely new type of object, one that seldom comes close to the Sun.

New Challenge

Whatever the nature of Comet Shoemaker-Levy 9, its spectacular demise had some very concrete results. The incident showed plainly that life on our planet could be wiped out by such an impact. We now have the technology to avert such a disaster (a rocket armed with a nuclear device that would presumably be able to change the object's course) but no way to track a potential killer before it strikes. Fortunately, at the very moment that the fireballs were exploding on Jupiter, the Science Committee of the U.S. House of Representatives voted to require the National Aeronautics and Space Administration to track any comets or asteroids that pose a real threat to Earth. Soon afterward NASA named a study panel to examine the feasibility of an early-warning system that would survey the inner solar system in search of such objects.

The wheel has come full circle, but with a vengeance, for now we know for certain that comets and their ilk can indeed be the agents of our doom. Not as omens, as was thought in the past, but in a very dramatic, direct, and drastic way.

Soccer's Big Show Comes to the United States

by PAUL GARDNER

It's known simply as the World Cup—so universally popular that there is never any need to define it further. Soccer's world championship is the most popular sporting event on Earth, a monthlong gala that all but paralyzes the normal life of the globe. The 1994 tournament, with 52 games, was the first ever played in the United States, and it drew the greatest number of fans in history. A television audience of 2 billion— about one out of every three people alive—watched Brazil defeat Italy for the world title.

Indeed, soccer is bigger than politics. The sport's international governing body, FIFA (Fédération Internationale de Football Association), has a membership of 191 countries—more than the United Nations! Worldwide, FIFA estimates, there are over 120 million active soccer players on organized teams.

And the sport keeps growing. Just 13 teams made up the field for the first World Cup in 1930. More than 100 nations vied to enter the 1994 finals, and regional qualifying games took nearly two years to narrow the field down to 24 finalists. In 1998, when the World Cup is to be held in France, there will be 32 finalists.

The Lure of the United States

Americans' seeming lack of interest in soccer has long puzzled fans of the sport, and it is even felt to be a challenge to soccer's claim to be the world's number

---

Paul Gardner is a freelance writer specializing in soccer and the author of The Simplest Game *and* Nice Guys Finish Last: A Study of Sport in American Life. *He has served as a soccer commentator for all three major U.S. television networks. His column, "SoccerTalk," appears each week in* Soccer America.

one game. If only Americans could see the sport at its best, the United States Soccer Federation (USSF) reasoned, if only they could experience firsthand the color and the passion of a packed soccer stadium, feel the drama of real, do-or-die games—that, surely, would turn the nation on to soccer. In 1988, FIFA agreed to hold the 1994 World Cup in the United States.

There were many doubters, both overseas and within the United States. Some U.S. sportswriters compared holding the World Cup in the United States with staging baseball's World Series in India—how could there be any local interest? Foreign critics felt that money was the sole reason for FIFA's decision—after all, soccer was big business, and major corporate sponsors were interested in opening up the U.S. market.

Around the world, the rumors flew: FIFA was going to enlarge the goals. It would allow time-outs (unheard of in the sport) to accommodate U.S. television. The game would be played in quarters instead of the traditional halves. And if those changes *weren't* made, well, the Yanks would cheapen the sport in another way, ruin it by smothering the World Cup with brash, tacky showbiz hype. And who ever heard of soccer played under a roof, as the Americans proposed to do in the Silverdome in Pontiac, MI?

Then there was the summer heat and humidity, which would surely make it impossible to play. Jack Charlton, Ireland's coach, later expressed the fear that "players would die out there." On top of all that, how could U.S. security be expected to cope with those dreaded English hooligans, those loutish traveling fans who regularly caused problems no European police force had yet solved?

In the end the doomsayers were confounded at every turn. Even the hooligans stayed home: England, against all expectations, failed to qualify.

And those who predicted a lack of interest were quickly proved wrong. The World Cup Organizing Committee received applications from 27 cities that wanted to stage games. Nine sites were selected—the Silverdome and stadiums at Foxboro, MA; East Rutherford, NJ; Washington, DC; Orlando, FL; Palo Alto and Pasadena, CA; Dallas; and Chicago. A $2 million turf grass installation in the Silverdome met FIFA's "no artificial turf" requirement.

Overwhelming proof that World Cup '94 would succeed came when the first ticket sales were announced in early 1993. The qualifying games were

still going on, and only two of the 24 finalists were known—Germany (as holder of the trophy won in 1990) and the United States (as the host country). Yet the first ticket allocations were heavily oversubscribed.

By December 1993 the whittling down was done among the teams that were World Cup hopefuls. The 24 finalists were divided into six groups of four teams each at a ceremony in Las Vegas; each team would play the other three in its group. The top two teams from each group, plus the four best third-place teams, would advance to the second round of the tournament, which would then become a single-game elimination event. Tied games would be settled by 30 minutes of overtime; if that did not produce a winner, a penalty kick shoot-out would be used. In this, players from each team would take five alternate shots at the goal from the 12-yard penalty spot, with only the opposing goalkeeper to beat. If the score remained tied after these ten shots, the shoot-out would continue on a sudden-death basis.

The sky above Soldier Field was filled with balloons at the festive opening ceremonies of the 1994 World Cup in Chicago as enthusiastic fans flocked to see the first game of the monthlong tournament.

Molding the American Team

A big question mark hung over the American team, long a weakling in the international field. The United States didn't even have a major professional league. But no host nation in the history of the World Cup had ever

41

The heartening success of the U.S. team was in great measure due to Serbian-born coach Bora Milutinovic, seen above with his players at their training camp in California. Below, the coach demonstrates the proper method of making a play.

failed to advance to the second round of the tournament.

The task of making sure that the United States got at least that far fell to Bora Milutinovic, a Serbian coach who had led Mexico to a quarterfinal berth in the 1986 tournament and Costa Rica to the second round in Italy in 1990. But the United States was another story. The best American players had gone overseas, mostly to Europe, to get playing experience, and many of the rest were barely out of college. The USSF set up a permanent base for 20 of them in Mission Viejo, CA, where Milutinovic picked the players who would complement the stars still in Europe.

The naysayers predicted the United States would be put in an "easy" group for fear that the American public would lose interest if their team made an early exit. But the United States ended up with Romania, Switzerland, and Colombia—certainly no pushovers. "If it were fixed," said USSF President Alan Rothenberg, "I don't think Colombia would be in our group."

The Games Begin

Colombia was an early favorite, having shown its strength by thrashing Argentina, 5-0, in Buenos Aires during the qualifying round. No less an expert than Pelé, the retired Brazilian star often called history's greatest soccer player (now a television commentator), had named Colombia as a team that could win it all. But Colombia began poorly, as Romania concentrated on defense, breaking away three times to score in sudden counterattacks. The Colombians lost, 3-1.

Colombia's second game was against the United States, which had opened with a 1-1 tie against Switzerland. Coach Milutinovic cautiously relied on a packed defense of Marcelo Balboa, Alexi Lalas, Paul Caligiuri, and either Cle Kooiman or Fernando Clavijo, plus midfielders Tom Dooley, John Harkes, and Mike Sorber playing primarily defensive roles. This emphasis on defense severely limited playmaker Tab Ramos's effectiveness, but he did provide forward Ernie Stewart with a brilliant assist on a goal that proved to be the winning one.

The 2-1 upset was the Americans' first World Cup victory since 1950. The United States advanced to the Cup's second round, while Colombia—along with Greece, Bolivia, Morocco, Norway, Russia, Cameroon, and South Korea, all of which lost in the first round— went home.

But the U.S.-Colombia game was overshadowed by tragedy. Even before the game, Colombian coach Francisco Maturana and his staff were threatened with death if player Gabriel Gómez took the field. Gómez was left on the bench. Then the first U.S. goal was scored by the Colombian defender Andres Escobar, when he inadvertently put the ball into his own net. On July 2, soon after arriving back in Colombia, Escobar

Colombian defender Andres Escobar (below) falls down in shock after inadvertently putting the ball into his own net, thus scoring a goal for the United States. He was later murdered in Colombia, a senseless act that was mourned by soccer fans (inset) bearing a commemorative banner.

Much of the color of the tournament was provided by the spectators. Here, an Irish fan shows off his colors.

was killed outside a Medellín restaurant, apparently in reprisal for the team's poor showing.

Some of the smaller teams in the first round (notably Bolivia, Morocco, and South Korea) played enterprising soccer—especially the South Koreans, who, trailing the Germans, 3-0, fought back brilliantly to 3-2 and were threatening to tie the game when time ran out. But Cameroon proved a faint shadow of the team that had so delighted four years earlier in Italy. And Norway's crude long-ball style endeared it to no one; its early exit was mourned by few.

Soccer politics virtually ensured Russia's failure—a number of top players had refused to play for coach Pavel Sadyrin. But the previously unheralded Oleg Salenko, who plays for Valencia in Spain and who did not join the Russian squad until October 1993, set a World Cup single-game goal-scoring record by hitting five goals in a 6-1 win over Cameroon.

This feat did not make Salenko the talk of the first round, however. That distinction went to Argentina's captain, Diego Maradona—for a positive drug test. Maradona's career had already seen a 15-month suspension for cocaine use. Traces of a banned substance, ephedrine, and four related drugs were found in his urine after the game against Nigeria. Maradona withdrew from the tournament, and FIFA later imposed a 15-month worldwide ban on a man who had been

One of the World Cup's stunning moments came when Saeed al-Owairan of Saudi Arabia (No. 10) dribbled half the length of the field before scoring.

one of the game's greatest players and had led Argentina to the world title in the 1986 World Cup.

The Second Round

Even without Maradona, Argentina was still considered a potential World Cup winner. It moved into the second round, there to face Romania. Argentina played some of the best soccer of the tournament against a staunch Romanian defense and was desperately unlucky to lose, 3-2, in an exhilarating game. The tournament had lost its most lively team, one of the few unreservedly devoted to attacking soccer. Another such team was Brazil, by now being viewed as the most likely winner. Never noted for defensive solidity, Brazil surprised everyone by giving up only one goal in the first round. Up front was the more traditional Brazilian strength: Romário and Bebeto, two of the most skillful forwards of the tournament.

It was the bad luck of the United States to face Brazil in the round of 16. The game was played on July 4, before a capacity crowd of 84,147 in Stanford Stadium in Palo Alto and a nationwide television audience. The Americans lost, 1-0, as Romário fed Bebeto perfectly for the game's only goal. The contest, however, was not as close as the final score suggests. Brazilian domination was almost total. Milutinovic was aiming for a tie and a penalty-kick tiebreaker, which the United States had as much chance of winning as Brazil. Even in the second half, playing with only ten men after defender Leonardo was ejected for elbowing American Tab Ramos in the face, the Brazilians were in command.

Milutinovic's cautious, almost defeatist tactics against

Italy's Roberto Baggio (right) puts an overtime penalty kick past Nigerian goaltender Peter Rufai to give his team a 2-1 victory and keep it alive in the tournament. Baggio had earlier tied the game by hitting a goal with only two minutes remaining.

Brazil meant that his squad did not exactly go out in a blaze of glory. Milutinovic's strategy showed that the tiebreaker invited teams to stall, producing dull games. Since the sluggish 1990 World Cup in Italy, FIFA had introduced rule changes to encourage offensive play. The changes, plus a refereeing clampdown on foul play, helped to increase goal scoring from the all-time low average of 2.2 per game in 1990 to 2.7 in 1994. But many teams still relied on cautious, defensive play. The same message came from Bulgaria. Its game against Mexico went into overtime tied at 1-1. After 30 minutes of boring overtime play, Bulgaria took the penalty kick shoot-out, 3-1.

The most surprising of the second-round teams was Saudi Arabia. Its 1-0 win over Belgium featured highly entertaining soccer and a magnificent goal from Saeed al-Owairan. He dribbled half the length of the field and had the Belgian defenders falling over themselves before he beat goalkeeper Michel Preud'homme and put the ball into the net. "It was the best goal I ever scored in my life," he said later. The disheartened Belgian coach, Paul Van Himst, commented, "To be able to run through half the field and come to the goalkeeper like that—it's not normal." But later, against the Swedes, Saudi Arabia gave up a goal after only five minutes and lost, 3-1.

Meanwhile, Germany and Italy, both three-time winners of the title, were making rather lackluster progress. Germany had been lucky to beat Bolivia, 1-0, in the tournament's opening game and had then survived that scare from South Korea. Against Belgium in the second round the Germans squeaked through by a 3-2 score—but only after the referee had inexplicably failed to call a blatant penalty kick against Germany when defender Thomas Helmer bumped Belgian striker Josip Weber, who was heading toward the goal.

Italy, as always, seemed determined to make its own life difficult. After losing, 1-0, to Ireland, it had to face Norway. Disaster struck after only 21 minutes when goalkeeper Gianluca Pagliuca was ejected after a foul on Norwegian forward Oyvind Leonhardsen—the first goalkeeper ever ejected in the World Cup. Playing with ten men and a reserve goalkeeper, Italy suffered another setback when captain Franco Baresi left the field with an injury. But then Dino Baggio headed a splendid goal to give the Italians a 1-0 victory.

Italy's opponent in the second round was Nigeria. Strong, fast, and skillful, the Nigerians came within two minutes of knocking Italy out of the competition. That was how much time was left when Roberto Baggio (FIFA's 1993 World Player of the Year, and no relation to teammate Dino Baggio) scored to equalize Emmanuel Amunike's 27th-minute goal for Nigeria. Baggio scored a second goal (from a penalty kick) in overtime. Italy had survived yet again. Completing the eight

One of the tournament's outstanding players was Bulgaria's Hristo Stoichkov; his penalty-kick goal over Germany's defensive wall helped knock the Germans out of the World Cup.

quarterfinalists were the Netherlands (a 2-0 victor over Ireland), and Spain (3-0 over Switzerland).

Quarterfinals and Semifinals

Sweden versus Romania was, predictably, one of the tournament's worst games, featuring, as it did, two teams content to lie back and let the other set the pace. Boredom reigned until Tomas Brolin scored for Sweden after 78 minutes. Florin Raducioiu replied for Romania ten minutes later, and the game went first to overtime and then to penalty kicks. Sweden triumphed because its goalkeeper, Thomas Ravelli, made saves on two of Romania's attempts.

With his receding hairline and protruding eyes, the 34-year-old Ravelli, Sweden's oldest player, turned out to be one of the more colorful participants in the tournament. In the game to determine the World Cup third-place winner, the irrepressible Ravelli enlivened the Swedes' 4-0 victory over Bulgaria with a second-half display of somersaults and dances. "I heard the Swedish crowd yelling that I should dance," he said, "so I danced a little bit."

In the quarterfinal match between Brazil and the Netherlands, Brazil's opponent once again opted for defensive caution. But the 0-0 halftime score was cracked when Romário volleyed home a Bebeto pass

Eighty minutes into a scoreless game, Brazil's celebrated forward Romário (No. 11) scored this improbable header over the much taller Swedish players. The goal enabled a 1-0 Brazil win and put the victors into the championship match against Italy.

ROUND OF 16 RESULTS

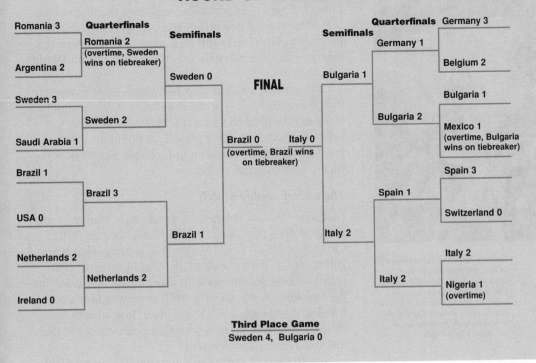

Round of 16	Quarterfinals	Semifinals	Final	Semifinals	Quarterfinals	Round of 16

Romania 3

Argentina 2

Romania 2
(overtime, Sweden wins on tiebreaker)

Sweden 0

Germany 3

Germany 1

Belgium 2

Bulgaria 1

Sweden 3

Saudi Arabia 1

Sweden 2

Bulgaria 1

Bulgaria 2

Mexico 1
(overtime, Bulgaria wins on tiebreaker)

FINAL

Brazil 0   Italy 0
(overtime, Brazil wins on tiebreaker)

Brazil 1

USA 0

Brazil 3

Spain 3

Spain 1

Switzerland 0

Brazil 1

Italy 2

Netherlands 2

Ireland 0

Netherlands 2

Italy 2

Italy 2

Italy 2

Nigeria 1
(overtime)

Third Place Game
Sweden 4, Bulgaria 0

seven minutes into what turned out to be a dazzling second half. Bebeto himself scored ten minutes later, and Brazil appeared to be well in command. But at last the Dutch woke up and began to play. Dennis Bergkamp made it 2-1, and Aron Winter tied it up with a superb header. Eighty-one minutes into the seesaw battle, fullback Branco scored for Brazil with a spectacular 30-yard left-footed free kick. This time the Brazilians kept the lead, for a 3-2 win. More late heroics from Roberto Baggio saw Italy past Spain by a score of 2-1. Baggio's winning goal was scored, once again, with only two minutes left in the game.

The shock of the tournament occurred at New Jersey's Giants Stadium, where Germany's faltering progress finally staggered to a halt. Unfancied Bulgaria came back from a goal down to beat the Germans with two goals in the space of three minutes. The first was a left-footed free kick that Hristo Stoichkov spun over the six-man German defensive wall; the second was a flying header from the balding Yordan Lechkov. "Today, God is a Bulgarian," said Stoichkov after the game.

But the achievement seemed to satisfy the Bulgarians.

Exultant Brazilian fans celebrate in the streets of Pasadena, CA, after their team defeated Italy in the championship match and won the World Cup for a record fourth time. Below, Dunga, the Brazilian team captain, raises the trophy in triumph.

Against Italy in the semifinal, they played with much less verve. The Italians won, 2-1, on two fine goals from Roberto Baggio. Stoichkov complained that the referee had twice turned down Bulgarian appeals for penalty kicks. "Today, God is still Bulgarian," he said, "but the referee was French." Italy was through to its fifth World Cup final.

Its opponent was Brazil, a 1-0 winner over Sweden in the other semifinal. For the Brazilians, it was a familiar story as they tried to find a way past a tenaciously defensive Sweden. They played for 80 minutes before the 5'6" Romário scored an improbable header over the much taller Swedish defenders.

The Championship Match

Brazil versus Italy promised a great final. Had not these two countries produced a classic final back in 1970? On that occasion Brazil—with Pelé leading what many still regard as the greatest of all World Cup champion teams—came out on top with an emphatic 4-1 win. But the freedom of attack of the 1970 team was long gone; the Brazilian team of 1994 was much less adventurous, its midfield made up of workers and runners rather than the creative artists of the past.

Nevertheless, if for nothing else the final was notable for matching the two most prominent players of the World Cup—Brazil's Romário and Italy's Roberto Baggio. Romário was one of the most flamboyant players on the scene. When he was married he held his wedding on the penalty spot in a huge stadium before a live TV audience. He had acquired a reputation as one of the world's most skilled and instinctive players; a renowned striker, his coach called him king of the penalty area (the area just in front of the goal), where he dominated, waiting for the slightest opportunity and then using his quickness and skill to score.

Baggio was hailed as an offensive genius, able to score from seemingly impossible angles. Reporters, ever on the alert for the unusual, made much of his ponytail (the Italians called him Il Divino Codino, or "the divine pigtail") and the fact that he had converted from Catholicism to Buddhism, an act of considerable consequence in a country that is 95 percent Catholic. Baggio had begun the tournament slowly and had even been benched during the game against Norway, but his late goals against Nigeria and Spain reminded everyone of just how effective he could be. He scored two more in the semifinal against Bulgaria but also suffered a pulled muscle. Baggio played in the final but was clearly not at his best.

In the end, however, it was not the players who dictated the course of the final, but the two coaches, Carlos Alberto Parreira for Brazil and Arrigo Sacci for Italy—two men who had never played the game at the top level but who were strong on the theory of coaching and tactics. It was more like chess than soccer. Brazil, at least, tried to attack, though the Italian defenders countered every move. There was no score at 90 minutes, and no score after the 30 minutes of overtime. The first-ever scoreless World Cup final thus became the first final to be decided by the penalty kick tiebreaker. Italy's two biggest stars—Baggio and Baresi—missed their kicks. Brazil took the shoot-out, 3-2, and became the first four-time World Cup champion. It was an immensely unsatisfactory conclusion to what had been an exciting tournament.

Controversy and Profit

Despite controversy over the use of the shoot-out to decide such an important match, for Alan Rothenberg and his U.S. organizers the news was almost all good. Media coverage was extensive, and television ratings topped expectations, with the final reaching over 10 million U.S. households. The total stadium attendance of 3,567,415 for the 52 games was over 1 million more than the previous record. The fans behaved impeccably throughout—a big plus in the United States, where soccer's image had been marred by its reputedly savage fans in other countries.

The World Cup had been one huge party—and a very profitable one. A surplus of $40 million was paid into a foundation that would oversee its use for the promotion of the sport in the United States. A separate initiative was the formation of a professional major league, building on the excitement created by the World Cup. FIFA had insisted that this was a principal reason for holding the tournament in the United States. The MLS was to be the proof that the United States had joined the worldwide community of soccer-playing nations.

In June 1994 it was announced that the new league, to be called Major League Soccer (MLS), would begin in April 1995. But the organizers, headed by Rothenberg, ran into problems raising the $100 million in capital they needed. In November 1994 came the announcement that the launching of the MLS would be delayed. Play would not begin until April 1996.

LEFT BEHIND

SMALL TOWNS
FACE CHANGE

by STEVE TURNER

Photographs by
LIONEL DELEVINGNE

Both fire and flood have chewed away parts of Idanha (that's Eye-DAN-uh), and the residents of this shrinking Oregon town might reasonably wonder when the plague of locusts will arrive.

But it's not accidents that have depressed Idanha—officially a city, even though barely 300 people live there—into a condition that one local official describes as "hitting bottom." Instead, it is the dynamics of social and economic change that have forever altered the role of the small town in U.S. and Canadian life.

Small towns survive—often as harbors for urban flight, or as economic shadows of their former selves, or even, for some, as self-sufficient places—but they collectively have lost their muscular place in history. Urban growth has overwhelmed the role they played in the past: seedbed of the political values and national conscience of both the United States and Canada. In many minds, small towns remain the grounding place of social values—the self-justifying homeplace of nostalgic patriotism. The idealized rural village as the supposed wellspring of solid families, neighborliness, decent incomes, and friendly merchants remains deeply embedded in the U.S. and Canadian psyche. Nostalgia overlooks the copious accounts of the shortcomings of small town life—the pecking order, the rigidities, the cycles of poverty, the cruelties toward those who lived on the wrong side of the tracks—and what stays with us in these times of urban troubles is the sanitized image of civility, order, and peace and quiet.

Basically, most of these places have been left behind by the growth of urban factories, developments in technology, regionalization of retailing and education, or the exhaustion or restriction of the natural resources that brought these settlements into being.

In Idanha's case it's a natural-resource problem, and that resource is timber. Due to previous overcutting and new environmental regulations, much of the remaining forest depended on by the town's loggers and millworkers has been put off limits. Two of the three big plywood veneer mills have closed. Wageworking families have left town. The manager of the sole remaining mill says that the only hope of staying open is the importation of logs from Mexico and the third world.

Different reasons have brought similar outcomes to a wide range of other small towns. Some have simply died out; others have been absorbed by the amoeba-like spread of suburbs. Many, formerly self-sufficient from farming, fishing, mining, or milling, have simply withered. Lately, an increasing number are seeing their former wageworkers' housing filling with computer commuters, retirees, and others weary of urban stress who are looking for the fabled "simple life." Helplessly, the nature of these towns changes as their economies shift from the former interplay of pay and profits into the more sedate framework of pensions and out-of-town salaries.

A Sense of Place

Once upon a time most of the inhabitants of the United States and Canada lived in small towns. But that dominance began to wane after the turn of the 20th century. The industrial revolution was mostly to blame, creating the factory cities that became the destination for most newly arriving workers. In 1900, 60 percent of the population of the United States lived in places with a population of 3,000 or less. By 1970 that figure had shrunk to 27 percent. Canada's pattern of decline is the same: in 1901, 65 percent of Canadians lived in places with 1,000 or fewer residents, with another 10 percent in places with between 1,000 and 5,000 residents. By 1976, Canada's rural village figures had declined to 24 percent of the total population. In the United States the trend reversed somewhat during the 1970s but shifted back in the 1980s to what may be a stable division of the population: roughly three-quarters in larger towns or cities, one-quarter in the remaining villages.

Partly, of course, it was the swift, enormous growth of the urban areas, rather than the shrinkage of the small towns, that caused this dramatic shift. But as the century rolled along—particularly as machines replaced human labor on the farms and as small farms began to be absorbed into larger and larger spreads—many people left rural villages to go to cities where there was work. Nor was it just the changes in farming that caused this exodus. Played-out mines left ghost towns in such areas as Nevada, British Columbia, and Canada's maritime provinces. Factory fishing fleets—and consequent overfishing—rendered many small-boat villages on both coasts obsolete.

Nevertheless, small towns still offer themselves as

Steve Turner is a freelance journalist and member of the National Writers Union whose articles have appeared in more than 50 newspapers and magazines.

places that individual residents can comprehend entirely, where life is predictable and, to a large extent, safe. Where a lack of privacy (Arlie Ellis, Idanha's volunteer Fire Chief, notes, "If you sneeze here, pretty soon the whole town knows it") is matched by a surplus of community concern.

A Town Hits Bottom

Idanha fits this mold. Despite years of economic downslide, the city retains an identity, and a network of interactions among its residents, that longtimers particularly cherish. The surroundings are of nature-photo quality. Idanha stretches along the rushing North Santiam River among spectacular mountains of Oregon's Cascade Range. Big, beautiful Detroit Lake, a hydroelectric reservoir, is nearby. Elk graze on the ball field and in backyards.

The city's history began with a resort hotel built after the railroad arrived in the late 1890s. Timbering, however, quickly eclipsed tourism (the hotel is long gone). The town grew around its sawmills, shingle mill, and, finally, three veneer mills—which peel big boles of Douglas fir into thin sheets for the sandwiching of plywood. At its peak Idanha had several taverns and boardinghouses, two restaurants, a grocery and a dry goods store, a movie theater, an auto repair shop, and a gas station.

But the shingle mill burned, and so did the grocery store and one of the taverns. The river, accidentally dammed by a log jam in 1964, broke free and took 13 houses. As work petered out, the dry goods store

55

closed. So did the theater, the other taverns, the cafés, the car repair shop, and the gas station. And when the two huge, rambling veneer mills closed, they were removed lock, stock, and barrel, leaving lonely-looking, field-size expanses of bare earth. Today, there is only the post office, one recently reopened café, and the one mill—which is working shortened hours. Idanhans believe it will soon close. The influx of unemployed welfare recipients, drawn by the available housing and low rents (a trend seen also in other economically distraught small towns), is viewed by old-timers as further evidence of the city's deterioration.

But even though there is civic as well as economic depression, a core of activists who want to save the place remains—Mayor Donald Spier, for instance, a millwright with 22 years of seniority at the remaining veneer plant; Darrlene Mann, a 30-year resident who owns a restaurant in nearby Detroit; City Clerk Rosemary Wilson, whose husband, laid off in the mill closings, now works as a long-haul trucker; and a sprinkling of others who remain dedicated to the once and future Idanha.

"It's like in any small town, there's just a handful of people who get active," says Mayor Spier. "But you've got to take responsibility, because no one else will do it." Encouraged by recent inquiries about homesites for vacation and retirement, the goal of these leaders is to shift the city's economy to recreation and travel services. Mayor Spier estimates it will take at least four years; pessimists say ten.

If those service jobs do come, the wages will be much

lower than the mill's. The population and the character of the city will change. But what else to do? "I don't think it's going to get worse than it is," says City Clerk Wilson. "It can only go up from here."

Where the Past Is Not Forgotten

In the lexicon of how small town economies rise and fall, railroads often appear. A railroad began Idanha. Railroads also built Eagle Bridge, NY, on the Hoosic River, at a place where geography offered a good junction point for north-south and east-west lines. And it was the railroads, also, as they evolved, that brought about the town's decline.

Eagle Bridge had its agriculture, and, later, its renown: famed "primitive" painter Mary Robertson ("Grandma") Moses was born nearby, and her family's land is still in crops there. But it was the intersection of three rail lines in the late 19th century that gave the little village its warehouses and other depot structures, the creamery, the lumber yard, the passenger station, two hotels, an opera house, and shops. At its peak, Eagle Bridge may have had nearly 300 residents. Eventually, the consolidation of railroads, the development of long-haul engines, the advent of paved roads and trucking, and the cessation of passenger service took away from Eagle Bridge—as from many other small waypoints—the purpose that the more rudimentary railroad technology had brought. Eagle Bridge's last hotel became a bookstore. Today, commercial activity is otherwise reduced to an auto repair shop and the Moses family farm stand. The population is, perhaps, 200.

The last surviving lumber mill in Idanha (left) provides employment for a few workers, but as the defunct gas station in the heart of town—with its ironically optimistic sign—reveals (right), it is barely enough to keep the town going.

Six or so miles upstream from Eagle Bridge sits the village of Hoosick Falls, another town left behind for yet another reason. Like many other places on smaller streams during the waterpowered phase of the industrial revolution, it became essentially a one-factory town. A farming settlement well before the American Revolution, the town's waterpower attracted early grist mills and some small woolen and cotton manufactories.

The economic anchor of the village, however, was the Walter A. Wood Company ("Wherever Grass and Grain Is Grown, Walter A. Wood Machines Are Known"), once the largest U.S. producer of horse-drawn mowing and reaping equipment. The Wood Company's operation expanded Hoosick Falls from a population of about 1,200 in 1860 to some 10,000 at the turn of the century. But the company failed to make the shift to mechanized equipment, and World War I cost it its major European markets. It closed in 1925.

Smaller industries helped sustain Hoosick Falls until the 1970s. But the closing of a shoe factory, which moved to Barbados, only emphasized the town's decline by fire and creeping decrepitude. Sites of some of the fires are now vacant lots. Other old-time buildings have been boarded up. One historic mansion has been replaced by a convenience store. Trains pass through the village without stopping now; both depots have been decommissioned. Three small manufactories occupy the former site of the Wood Company mills, which also burned down.

The population of Hoosick Falls has dropped to 3,500, more than half of whom are retirees. Indeed, with its senior housing projects and two expanding nursing homes, Hoosick Falls is an example of a town turning for its future toward the increasingly elderly portion of the population. So it is appropriate that in this place the past is not forgotten. At the rebuilt gazebo in the village park, volunteer musicians directed by longtime bandmaster William Gaillard give a concert each Wednesday evening during July and August, continuing a tradition begun in the late 1870s. Further downtown, a mural on a leftover wall from a demolished building displays an expanded version of a painting by Grandma Moses, who is buried uphill in the Maple Grove Cemetery. Her grave marker (she died in 1961, aged 101) appropriately notes that her paintings

Despite its decline, Hoosick Falls carries on a venerable tradition of band concerts in the village park.

"captured the spirit and preserved the scene of a vanishing countryside."

Saved by Seniors

The tendency of once wageworking small towns to become retirement centers appears on both sides of the U.S.-Canadian border. In Riondel (REE-on-dell), British Columbia, population just under 400, the transition literally saved the town.

Riondel took its economic fall in the mid-1970s. The culprit was the Bluebell Mine, which was shut down when its access to blended lead, zinc, and silver ores played out.

Like Idanha, Riondel features tremendous scenery. Laid out in neat rows terracing down the last, gentle slope of Bluebell Mountain, the town sits on a low bluff above fjordlike Kootenay Lake. The memory of the European settlers who set out orchards there still flourishes in the cherry trees that grow in many residents' yards.

The first mine was opened before the turn of the century and closed in 1927. The second mine, the Bluebell, was opened by the Cominco mining conglomerate in 1947. Cominco built dormitories for single miners and loaned money for houses to those who were married (some of the families spent their first two years on the site in tents or scrapwood shacks). Next came the school, the store, the restaurant, and the curling rink. The population increased to a peak of 700. But the Bluebell encountered powerful water seepage as it burrowed under the lake, and it closed in 1972.

"After Cominco pulled out," recalls Frank Downing, one of the original miners who stayed on, "Riondel was a ghost town. They were advertising houses for sale for $5,000." Cominco had sweetened the situation by making land available for a golf course and a campground. Frank and his wife Leslie held on and watched the semivacant town become a target of opportunity for outsiders.

The era of cheap housing prices brought in a sampling of younger working families—including the Downings' daughter, Val, who grew up there, and her husband, Henry Antonius, a contractor. Val now operates a Riondel-based ambulance service that covers a wide territory in the Kootenay region. Some others who came were recipients of social assistance. But most were older couples from the plains of Alberta, who snapped up the cheap houses for recreation and retirement.

Its mines have closed, and Riondel in British Columbia now attracts retirees drawn by its scenery (right). The Downing family (above), however, has lived there for years. From left to right: Henry and Val Antonius, Frank and Leslie Downing, and Carl Downing. In front: Mr. Pickwick.

Bluebell Manor, a small retirement home, was built. The school was converted into a community center, and the town earned itself the nickname "wrinkle city."

Terry Turner, a member of Riondel's governing council, estimates that the town's population is almost two-thirds retirees and seasonal residents who may retire there. With the town having been "found" by bargain hunters, housing prices have spiked up. Anyone moving into Riondel in the near future, says Turner, is going to have to be economically self-sufficient.

So, without changing physically—Riondel has avoided the curse of fire—the town has become another town. The muscle and blood of mining have given way to the calmer pursuits of residents who do not have to punch a time clock.

Government ownership of surrounding land blocks further housing growth. Some Riondellians, however, look covetously at the wide swath of tree-covered lake shoreline still owned by Cominco. If the mine debris there were cleaned up and the land sold, it could become a resort area. But retired mining engineer Ray Nelson and his wife, Edith, apparently speak for most residents when they say, "We don't want development that would radically change the town."

Riondel, once headed for oblivion, has become a modern-day Brigadoon.

A Different Fate

Other small mining towns have not been so fortunate. After the P & M Coal Company shut its excavation in West Mineral, KS, in 1974, the town's population dropped from some 2,000 to near 200. The commercial sector shrank accordingly. The most substantial thing left was a huge mining shovel nicknamed Big Brutus. This behemoth has become a tourist attraction of sorts, but the nearest motels and restaurants are in Columbus, 12 miles away.

Springhill, Nova Scotia, has done better. Known from a famous folk song about one of its underground disasters, Springhill has fended off the worst results of its mines' closings by opening a miners' museum and a showplace dedicated to a superstar native daughter,

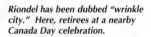

Riondel has been dubbed "wrinkle city." Here, retirees at a nearby Canada Day celebration.

singer Anne Murray. A budding geothermal energy
project, an offshoot of the area's mining explorations,
adds further hope to the recovery.

Friendly Places

Arguably, there *is* a higher level of civility among
residents in small towns. One can find that quality also
in the encounters of "regulars" with small businesses in
city neighborhoods. But in the villages, as in Lind, WA,
the friendliness and reassurance of residents
encountering residents and dealing with familiar
merchants permeates the downtown, too, and the feeling
of closeness lasts all day long.

Dust and drought have withered Great Plains farming
settlements from Texas to Alberta. But it is not the
climate that has afflicted Lind, which still is surrounded
by an abundance of wheat fields. Lind's shrinkage—as
in the corn belt and some dairy regions—is due to labor-
saving technologies.

The fields around Lind have been farmed since the
19th century—since the days when a harvesting
machine was pulled by a team of some 20 mules or
horses, requiring a large crew as well as stable hands.
In the century's early years, Lind had not only grain
elevators but three grocery stores, two barber shops, a
hotel, two pool halls, a movie theater, gas stations, a
drugstore, and several restaurants. But today, one self-
propelled combine harvester, driven by one operator,
can do the work of many of those earlier machines.
Moreover, a substantial number of local acres have been
put into subsidized, soil-saving grass crops.

Lind itself has shrunk from a population of over 700 to
450 today—and the small staffs of the town's still-active
grain elevators and farm machinery dealership do not
contribute economically to Lind the way the former
gangs of farm workers did. Nor do the retirees, long-
range commuters, and welfare recipients who have
snapped up the town's housing vacancies. The fixed-
income spending of many of the new residents—
particularly with a regional shopping center just 30
miles away—is not enough to revitalize Lind's
commercial center. The result is that of all the former
retail businesses, only one café, one tavern, and one
grocery store remain.

"The town is drying up," says Mayor Larry Koch. "We
tried like hell to get a state prison sited here, but we
failed." He adds, "The only thing we can do now is try
to get some developer to come in and build some

[market rate] housing for us, to attract people [with spendable incomes] to live here."

While the town is waiting for a renaissance, however, the Lind spirit lives on. The morning coffee klatsch of active and retired farmers at the Golden Grain Café continues. A walk on the downtown streets, even when they're relatively deserted, still gives the feeling of being in a homeplace. In honor of the past, an expansion of the county historical museum is in the works. And there's every indication that Myra Horton speaks for many others when she says, "There's no place else I'd rather live."

A Continuing Presence

The United States and Canada will always have at least some villages—the smallest dots on the map, reminders of the source of many undying cultural mainstays. Reminders, too of just how quirky village life can be. Urban growth will never erase the likes of Herman, MN, which advertised for women to balance its surplus of single men; Rockingham, VT, where townspeople, finding that the gas station attendant had quit in mid-shift, left more than the required amount of money for the fuel they pumped; Riverside, WA, which adopted an ordinance requiring every household to have a gun and ammunition (exempting those who opposed the idea); and Dixville Notch, NH, where the 34 resident voters purposefully go to the polls at 12:01 A.M. in presidential primaries and elections to maintain the town's claim to the earliest tally in the United States.

But even as so many of these shrinking small places fill up again with the current census bulge of older citizens, it's necessary to remember that they are repositories of the past, rather than—as once they were—generators of the future.

The forlorn townscape of West Mineral, KS, vividly demonstrates what can happen when a small town loses its economic base. After the local coal mining company closed, the population declined from some 2,000 to about 200.

1995 YEARBOOK
EVENTS OF 1994

A

ACCIDENTS AND DISASTERS. Among the major disasters that occurred during 1994 were those briefly described below.

Jan. 3, Russia: A Russian airliner experienced engine failure and crashed in the wilderness in Siberia, killing all 111 passengers and nine crew members, as well as one person on the ground.

Jan. 15, India: A ferry carrying religious pilgrims sank in thick fog after ramming another boat near the mouth of the Ganges River; more than 100 people died.

Jan. 17, California: An earthquake measuring 6.6 magnitude hit Southern California, killing over 50 people. The quake's epicenter was in the town of Northridge, northeast of Los Angeles. Damage estimates neared $30 billion.

Jan. 23, Argentina: Twenty-five apprentice firefighters, some of them teenagers, were killed when they attempted to extinguish a brush fire near Puerto Madryn in Patagonia.

Jan. 25, India: A fire broke out in the state-owned New Kenda coal mine, near the town of Asansol, trapping and killing 55 miners inside.

Feb. 16, Indonesia: An earthquake of 7.2 magnitude rocked Sumatra, leaving more than 200 dead.

Feb. 25, Peru: An Expresso Aereo airliner crashed in the Peruvian jungle near the Brazil border. The 31 people on board were not found.

Mar. 8, South Africa: At least 63 people were killed and 370 were injured when a speeding commuter train derailed outside the town of Durban.

Mar. 22, Russia: An Aeroflot Airbus 310 fell 32,000 feet to earth in Siberia; all 75 people on board were killed. An investigation concluded that a crew member's children had been at the controls when the plane went down.

Mar. 23, North Carolina: An F-16 fighter jet and a C-130 cargo plane collided in midair over Pope Air Force Base; both pilots thought they had been cleared for landing. The pilots and crews escaped without injury, but wreckage from the F-16 hit an Army training unit on the ground; 23 paratroopers died, and more than 80 were injured.

A lesson in tragedy. A flurry of aviation accidents in Russia in 1994 raised serious questions about airline safety standards in the former Soviet Union. Shown here is the crash of a Russian-operated Airbus 310 in Siberia in March; all 75 people on board were killed. The pilot had apparently been giving a flying lesson to two children in the cockpit.

Mar. 27, Southeast United States: More than 40 people were killed as Alabama, Georgia, North and South Carolina, and Tennessee were hit by a series of tornadoes.

Apr. 1, Peru: A bus carrying Easter celebrants swerved to avoid another vehicle and plunged down a steep cliff near Izcuchaca; 44 people were killed.

Apr. 5, China: Two ferries crowded with schoolchildren collided and capsized in the Yanmenxiang Reservoir in Chekiang Province, killing 43 students.

Apr. 14, Iraq: Two U.S. UH-60 Blackhawk helicopters carrying members of an international coalition to protect Kurds were mistakenly shot down by two U.S. F-15 fighters over a no-fly zone in northern Iraq. All 26 people on board died.

Apr. 26, Japan: A China Airlines jetliner caught fire and crashed while attempting to land in Nagoya; 263 people were killed.

Apr. 29, Kenya: More than 270 people drowned when an overcrowded commuter ferry capsized and sank near Mombasa.

May 2, Bangladesh: A cyclone carrying heavy winds and rain caused severe flooding in southeastern coastal areas; the storm appeared to hit land near Cox's Bazar. More than 300 people died.

May 23, Saudi Arabia: At least 250 Muslim worshipers died during the annual pilgrimage to Mecca when a crowd stampeded during a "stone the devil" ritual at a sacred cavern in Mina.

June, China: Typhoon Russ arrived via the South China Sea on June 8 and stayed over land for weeks, inundating six provinces. More than 800 people drowned, including at least 200 in Guangdong Province alone. The storm's fierce rains caused $100 million in damage from flooding.

June 2, Scotland: A Royal Air Force CH-47 Chinook helicopter crashed in heavy fog near the Mull of Kintyre cliffs; all 29 people on board, most of them officials from Northern Ireland, were killed.

June 6, China: A China Northwest Airlines jet on its way to Guangzhou crashed soon after takeoff from Xi'an; all 160 people on board were killed.

June 6, Colombia: An earthquake and subsequent mudslides in the Cauca and Huila regions claimed the lives of 1,000 or more people and rendered thousands homeless.

June 12, Gulf of Aden: About 50 Somalis, former refugees, were feared dead when their ship sank en route from Yemen to Somalia.

July, Georgia: Tropical Storm Alberto caused nearly two weeks of torrential rains and flooding in southern Georgia and northern Alabama and Florida, forcing the evacuation of entire towns and ruining thousands of acres of crops. More than 30 deaths were reported.

July, Spain: Wildfires ravaged the Mediterranean coast for a week in early July, damaging an estimated 360,000 acres and killing 21 people, including some firefighters.

July 1, Mauritania: An Air Mauritania Fokker 28 passenger plane crashed in Tidjikdja during a sandstorm, killing 94 of the 101 people on board.

July 2, North Carolina: A USAir DC-9 carrying 52 passengers and five crew members crashed shortly after an aborted landing in Charlotte, resulting in 37 deaths. The accident appeared to have been caused by a sudden rainstorm.

July 3, Texas: In a deadly day on Texas highways 14 people were killed when an 18-wheeler hit a van from behind outside Weatherford. Near Snyder a tractor-trailer slammed broadside into a pickup truck, killing three adults and nine children. Another six people died when their car collided with a tractor-trailor that had overturned near Ballinger.

July 6, Colorado: A mountain wildfire suddenly blew out of control near Glenwood Springs, burning more than 2,000 acres and trapping and killing 14 firefighters.

July 9, China: As many as 49 people drowned when their overloaded bus slid off a ferry and sank in the Yangtze River near Yichang.

July 13, Cuba: A tugboat carrying 63 people sank after it collided with—or was rammed

67

by, according to some reports—a boat that was pursuing it north of Havana; more than 30 passengers drowned.

Aug. 5, Russia: Forty-seven people were killed when a military transport plane crashed on its approach to the Bada military base in Siberia.

Aug. 18, Algeria: An earthquake measuring 5.6 magnitude hit northwestern Algeria, killing at least 170 people and leaving thousands homeless.

Aug. 20, Bangladesh: An overloaded ferry capsized in the Meghna River near Chandpur; more than 300 people drowned.

Aug. 21, China: Typhoon Fred brought torrential rains and caused flooding in the coastal province of Chekiang in eastern China, leaving more than 700 people dead. Damage to property and industry was estimated at $1.16 billion.

Aug. 21, Morocco: A Royal Air Maroc aircraft crashed in the Atlas Mountains soon after takeoff from Agadir. All 44 people aboard died; among them was a Kuwaiti prince.

Aug. 29, Philippines: A methane gas explosion in a coal mine in the town of Malangas on the island of Mindanao caused the deaths of at least 82 miners.

Sept. 8, Pennsylvania: A USAir Boeing 737 crashed just outside Pittsburgh as it prepared to land; all 132 people aboard were killed. It was the worst air disaster in the United States in seven years.

Sept. 22, Angola: A train carrying granite derailed, killing 300 people and injuring 147 as it plunged into a ravine near Tolunda in the province of Huila. The crash was blamed on faulty brakes.

Sept. 28, Baltic Sea: The *Estonia*, en route from Tallinn, Estonia, to Stockholm, Sweden, capsized when rough waves broke through improperly sealed cargo doors. More than 800 people died.

Oct. 16-24, Texas: Heavy rains caused flooding around Houston; 19 people died and 48 counties were declared state disaster areas.

Oct. 31, Indiana: An American Eagle commuter plane en route to Chicago crashed in high winds and heavy rain in a field near Roseland. All 68 people on board died.

Nov. 2, Egypt: A river of flames flooded through the town of Durunka in the Nile Valley, killing more than 500 people and destroying buildings and property, when a fuel oil spill was set ablaze by electrical wires during a torrential rain.

Nov. 5, Italy: Torrential rains in the Piedmont, Liguria, Valle d'Aosta, and Lombardy regions caused at least 64 deaths and possibly up to $6.6 billion in damage. The storms also caused damage and deaths in France, Morocco, and Spain.

Nov. 10-11, Haiti: Tropical Storm Gordon caused flash floods that killed at least 829 people (officials said the death toll could be as high as 2,000), as well as ruining houses and roads and wiping out crops and livestock.

Nov. 23, India: An estimated 130 people were killed when a stampede broke out during a massive protest rally being held in the city of Nagpur by tribes demanding greater opportunities.

Nov. 27, China: When a fire broke out in a crowded dance hall in the town of Fuxin in the northeastern province of Liaoning, 233 people were killed.

Dec. 2, Philippines: The *Cebu City,* an inter-island ferry carrying over 600 people, collided with a freighter near Rosario in Manila Bay. More than 34 drowned, and more than 100 were reported missing.

Dec. 4, Bangladesh: At least 36 people drowned when a cargo ship and a ferry collided on the Bolai River near the town of Sunamganj.

Dec. 8, China: A fire in a theater in Karamay—where more than 800 people, mostly schoolchildren and teachers, were watching a variety show—caused at least 385 deaths and left 115 other people critically injured.

Dec. 13, North Carolina: An American Eagle commuter plane flying from Greensboro to Raleigh-Durham crashed in rain and fog as it prepared to land; 15 of the 20 people aboard were killed.

Dec. 14, Mozambique: Two trucks traveling on a highway north of Maputo had a head-

on collision, causing barrels of oil on one
of the trucks to burst into flame; 45 people
died and dozens were wounded.

Dec. 28, Venezuela: A passenger bus
slammed into another bus on a mountain
highway, shoving it into an oil pipeline that
exploded; at least 30 people died.

Dec. 29, Turkey: A Turkish Airlines jet
carrying mostly military personnel crashed
in Van when it tried to land in a
snowstorm; 55 people were killed.

Dec. 31, Burma: A passenger train derailed
and plummeted into a ravine near the town
of Wuntho, killing 102 people.

A.A. & K.E.K.

AFGHANISTAN. War over Kabul, Afghanistan's capital, became more fierce in 1994.
Faction leaders Gulbuddin Hekmatyar and Abdul Rashid Doestam, formerly enemies,
launched a joint assault on January 1 on districts of Kabul held by President Burhanuddin
Rabbani's government troops. As of late fall,
an estimated 19,000 people, mostly civilians,
had been killed in interfactional fighting in
Kabul since April 1992, when rebel groups
toppled the Soviet-backed government then in
power. A half million residents had fled Kabul
since the rebel takeover—more than a third of
the city's population.

Under the military command of Ahmad
Shah Mausood, a faction leader allied with
Rabbani, government forces continued to hold
much of Kabul late in the year, but fighting
continued in the area. Meanwhile, in northern
Afghanistan, seesaw fighting continued between Doestam's and Mausood's armies. In
the Tajikistan border region, a low-intensity
war, involving Russian Army units, also continued between Tajikistan government forces
and Islamic rebels who had taken refuge in
Afghanistan.

By summer, there were numerous calls for
peace generated by war weariness, the urgent
need to resettle millions of refugees, and the
delay in repairing the devastation left by the
Soviet-Afghan war. Yet a diplomatic settlement proved elusive; indeed, in the autumn
United Nations representatives declared they
had been unable even to bring the opposing
factions to the negotiating table. Meanwhile,
in Jalalabad, the prominent faction leader Yu-

Peacemaker. *Hamid al-Gabid, secretary-general of
the Organization of the Islamic Conference, visits
Afghan President Burhanuddin Rabbani (left) in
Kabul in July. The OIC was attempting to negotiate
peace between warring factions in Afghanistan.*

nis Khalis declared himself president in June.
The following month Ismael Khan, controlling
western Afghanistan, convened a supreme
shura, or assembly, of more than 1,000 secular
and religious leaders in Herat. The assembly
created a political process to establish an interim national government in October. Rabbani, who refused to leave office when his
term expired in June, said that he would resign
October 23 and not seek reelection.

Rabbani did not step down, and at the end
of October, Hekmatyar's forces launched a
fresh assault on Kabul. Meanwhile, UN negotiator Mahmoud Mestiri had presented a peace
plan to the various warring factions.

Iran, Pakistan, Saudi Arabia, and the former
Soviet Central Asia republics formally supported peacemaking efforts, but all were
deeply involved in Afghan politics. Iran supported Shiite leaders opposed to the Kabul
government. Islamic extremists and elements
of the Pakistani Army supported Hekmatyar.
Saudi Arabia supported both sides in the struggle for Kabul and promoted its Wahhabi form
of Islam among Afghans. Doestam was closely
aligned with the leadership of Uzbekistan, and
Ismael Khan had close relations with Turkmenistan.

See STATISTICS OF THE WORLD.

N.P.N. & R.S.N.

Africa

The year 1994 saw the first election in South Africa's history in which all races were allowed to vote. African National Congress leader Nelson Mandela was elected president in a relatively peaceful transition to majority rule. But civil conflict caused deep hardship elsewhere. In Rwanda hundreds of thousands of people were slaughtered, and massive numbers of refugees fled to neighboring countries.

Two contrasting events framed 1994. South Africa's April election of Nelson Mandela as president in the country's first nonracial balloting symbolized hope, while in the same month Hutu extremists in the Rwandan government began a campaign of genocide against the minority Tutsi and Hutu moderates. The subsequent military victory by the predominantly Tutsi opposition produced an unprecedented outflow of refugees. Peaceful elections were held in Botswana, Guinea-Bissau, Malawi, Mozambique, Namibia, Uganda, and elsewhere, but transitions to democracy remained stalled in key countries such as Nigeria and Zaire. The Angolan government and rebel movement Unita signed a new peace treaty in November, but civil war continued in Liberia. Economists projected modest increases in growth rates for the continent that were insufficient to check declining per capita incomes.

OAU, Economic Developments. A record 42 heads of state attended the Organization of African Unity summit conference in Tunisia in June, where South Africa was admitted as the 53rd member. The summit strengthened the conflict prevention mechanism set up in 1993. The OAU also played a leading although unsuccessful role in trying to encourage negotiations in the Rwandan crisis and helped to avert escalation of conflict in Congo and Burundi.

The Economic Commission for Africa estimated that, since 1990, African economies had grown by only 1.3 percent a year, equivalent, with population growth, to a yearly fall in per capita income of 1.7 percent. Growth was uneven within the continent, however, with 11 countries (20 percent of the population) achieving growth rates of 5 percent or more in 1993. Modest increases in commodity prices

in 1994 were expected to bring some improvement, and growth rate estimates for the year ranged from a low of 2 to 2.5 percent to a high of 3.9 percent. But overall, the economic prospect was still precarious. South Africa's economic recovery held possible long-term benefits, particularly for southern Africa, but faced an enormous backlog of social needs within South Africa itself.

Southern Africa. Despite threats of disruption, South Africa's first nonracial election was held as scheduled in April. The African National Congress (ANC), headed by Nelson Mandela, won 252 of the 400 seats in the National Assembly, with 62.7 percent of 19.5 million votes. The National Party, led by outgoing President F. W. de Klerk, won 82 seats with 20.4 percent of the vote. Chief Mangosuthu Gatsha Buthelezi's Zulu nationalist Inkatha Freedom Party won 43 seats with 10.5 percent of the vote.

The ANC carried seven of the nine provinces, winning control of the provincial governments. But the National Party won in the Western Cape, where it successfully exploited fears by "Coloured" (mixed-race) voters that the predominantly black ANC would discriminate against the relatively privileged Coloureds. In a negotiated deal after charges of massive fraud and intimidation in Inkatha-controlled areas, the ANC conceded victory in KwaZulu/Natal to Inkatha. For the government of national unity mandated by the interim constitution, Mandela chose the ANC's Thabo Mbeki as first vice president; de Klerk automatically became second vice president.

South Africa joined the regional Southern Africa Development Community as its 11th member. The seven-member Frontline States alliance (Angola, Botswana, Mozambique, Namibia, Tanzania, Zambia, and Zimbabwe) was also transformed into a counterpart association of the SADC states for dealing with security issues, bringing in previously uninvolved SADC members Lesotho, Malawi, and Swaziland as well as South Africa.

In May, Malawi held its first free elections since independence, resulting in a plurality for the opposition United Democratic Front headed by Bakili Muluzi and ousting incumbent strongman Hastings Kamuzu Banda. Regularly scheduled elections in Namibia and Botswana gave victories to the incumbent South West Africa People's Organization party and the Democratic Party, respectively, although Botswana's opposition National Front also made gains. In Lesotho, conflict between the Army and the elected government was contained by strong diplomatic action by regional states, including South Africa, Botswana, and Zimbabwe.

Peaceful elections in Mozambique in October, with a large UN presence, resulted in a national victory for incumbent President Joaquim Chissano and his Frelimo party, but former South African-sponsored rebel leader Afonso Dhlakama won majorities in several provinces in central Mozambique.

In Angola an agreement was signed in November that was designed to end a brutal war that had been ignited after the opposition party Unita lost elections in 1992. The agreement granted a share of power to Unita and was backed by plans to deploy UN peacekeeping troops within Angola.

East Africa. Famine primarily due to drought threatened more than 8 million people in Eritrea and Ethiopia during the year, eliciting a relatively prompt response from international agencies. Both countries continued at peace. Ethiopia held an election for a constituent assembly in June, but the election was boycotted by most opposition groups. In Somalia, despite the failure to reestablish central government authority or a stable peace, U.S. troops withdrew in September, and the remaining UN troops were scheduled to leave by April 1995. The civil war in Sudan continued unabated, despite negotiations sponsored by Sudan's neighbors, amid catastrophic conditions for at least 2 million southern Sudanese.

On April 6 the airplane carrying Presidents Juvénal Habyarimana of Rwanda and Cyprien

Fleeing for their lives. After Rwanda's and Burundi's presidents were killed in a plane crash, extremists in Rwanda belonging to the country's Hutu majority massacred members of the Tutsi minority as well as Hutu moderates. By midsummer hundreds of thousands of people had been killed. Below, Rwandan refugees streaming to camps in Zaire in July.

Cooling things off. *King Letsie III of Lesotho (right) confers with South African President Nelson Mandela (center) and South African Home Affairs Minister Mangosuthu Buthelezi (left) in Pretoria, South Africa, in late August. A constitutional crisis had developed in Lesotho as a result of the king's threat to dissolve the country's democratically elected government, along with conflict between the government and the Army. The tension, however, was defused by diplomatic action by regional states, including South Africa, Botswana, and Zimbabwe, and Letsie agreed to abdicate in favor of his father.*

Ntaryamira of Burundi crashed at the Kigali airport as the two presidents returned from a peace conference in Tanzania. Burundi, despite delicate relations between its Tutsi-dominated Army and predominantly Hutu government, managed to avoid a new explosion of ethnic violence. In Rwanda, however, Hutu extremists in the military, charging the Tutsi opposition with responsibility, immediately launched a campaign to eliminate Hutu moderates and all Tutsis. Most informed observers suspected that the military extremists themselves had shot down the plane in order to avoid a compromise peace settlement with the opposition party of the Tutsi-dominated Rwandan Patriotic Front (RPF). It was estimated that as many as 500,000 people were killed over the next three months until the RPF took control of Kigali in July.

Millions of Hutu refugees flooded neighboring Tanzania and Zaire. Although the international community responded with massive aid, critics charged the UN and major Western powers with failure to respond to the initial genocide and continued reluctance to act to prevent a new eruption. The small UN force in Kigali was reduced after the plane crash and only reinforced months later with African troops. France, accused of backing the former Rwandan government, intervened in July and August to avert an even more massive flow of

refugees to Zaire. In November the UN voted to establish a tribunal to judge war crimes in Rwanda. But the new government was fragile and unable to control reprisals by its own forces. The former Rwandan Army led by Hutu extremists controlled most refugee camps, and observers feared a new escalation of violence at any moment.

West and Central Africa. In Nigeria protest intensified against the military regime's annulment of the June 1993 election. Hundreds of opponents of the regime were arrested or harassed. Chief Moshood Abiola, who had won 59 percent of the vote, was charged with treason in June after proclaiming himself president. He was still being detained at year's end. Leaders of the Ogoni people, who had been protesting environmental destruction and loss of their lands to oil production, were arrested in May, part of ongoing governmental repression involving hundreds of killings and arrests. A strike by oil workers that began in July was broken in September after the military regime arrested key union officials. Also in September, three leading newspapers were banned for six months; the ban was later extended indefinitely.

In Liberia implementation of the 1993 peace agreement stalled as rival armed groups repeatedly missed deadlines to disarm. The nominal interim government was unable to organize elections scheduled for September, and countries contributing troops to the West African peacekeeping force began to plan partial withdrawals.

In the Gambia, West Africa's smallest nation, the government of President Dawda Jawara was overthrown in July. Lieutenant Yahya Jammeh took power; he survived a November countercoup attempt.

President Mobutu Sese Seko of Zaire, the most prominent of Africa's longtime authoritarian rulers, gained a new lease on power from international efforts to support Rwandese refugees in Zaire. A new prime minister, Kengo wa Dondo, chosen by the transitional Parliament despite a boycott by supporters of incumbent Prime Minister Etienne Tshisekedi, won recognition by most Western countries.

North Africa. Conflict between incumbent governments and violent Muslim fundamentalist groups remained a central political issue in both Algeria and Egypt. In September the Algerian military government released several leaders of the Islamic Salvation Front, which was banned on the eve of its expected election victory in 1992. Despite such signs of compromise, the violence—government repression as well as Islamic extremists' assassinations of officials, intellectuals, and foreigners—continued. According to some estimates, by late 1994 the total number killed had reached 10,000. Similar conflict on a lesser scale also continued in Egypt, where extremists wounded Nobel Prize-winning novelist Naguib Mahfouz in October.

See separate articles on many of the individual countries mentioned and STATISTICS OF THE WORLD. W.M.

AGRICULTURE AND FOOD SUPPLIES. Agriculture saw some promising technological developments in 1994, and world harvests were projected to be generally higher than in 1993, with record corn and soybean crops in the United States.

Technological Developments. Agricultural researchers reported two of the most promising breakthroughs in food production in a generation. Philippine plant breeders said they had developed a variety of rice that will eventually produce about 25 percent more food than existing varieties. The new variety was said to re-quire less fertilizer than existing strains. Scientists in the United States said they had isolated and cloned the so-called iaglu gene, a plant characteristic that regulates a growth hormone. The breakthrough could someday lead not only to plants that yield far greater food volume but also to plant sizes that require less costly harvesting methods.

Sale of a milk production stimulant known as bovine somatotropin began in the United States in February. Dairy farmers reported cows produced as much as 20 percent more milk after biweekly injections. In October the Monsanto Company, developer of the synthetic hormone, said it had been used in 7 percent of U.S. dairy herds and that cow health effects were minuscule. However, public concerns about human health risks prompted a number of grocery chains and dairy cooperatives to refuse to accept milk produced by treated cows. Canada and the European Union continued to prohibit the hormone's use altogether.

World Output. A record rice crop was projected for 1994, but rising consumption led to a projected ratio of stocks to use at year-end

An Olde Drink

Back in 1494 the Scottish Exchequer Roll Number 305 listed "Delivery of eight bolls of malt to Friar John Cor wherewith to make aquavitae." This is believed to be the first official record of Scotch whisky.

Consequently, the Scotch Whisky Association proclaimed 1994 the 500th anniversary of the "spirit of Scotland." A special logo was designed and plastered on bottles, and enthusiasts imbibed at celebratory tastings. One company even re-created medieval Scotch (aging in wood was then unknown). The result was deemed "a bit grassy" but certainly suitable for warming up on a frosty Scottish evening.

Scotch is consistently among Great Britain's top five export goods, topping £2 billion (nearly $3 billion) in 1993. But the smoky potable is more to Scots than a source of cash. Consider the tale of the Scotsman with a flask of the stuff in his pocket who fell in the snow. As he felt a liquid running down his leg, he said, "Man, I hope that's blood."

that was the lowest since 1973. Wheat production was expected to be down slightly from 1993, well below the recent growth trend. Largely because of a substantial increase in corn production over the flood-reduced 1993 U.S. crop, world production of feed grain was projected to be up 9 percent. Crops were larger in the United States, India, Eastern Europe, and Argentina, but smaller in China, the European Union, the former Soviet Union, Canada, and Brazil. Although grain production in low-income, food-deficit countries was 1.5 percent higher than in 1993, per capita output was off 0.8 percent.

Food Aid. Severe food shortages in the Horn of Africa led the Food and Agriculture Organization (FAO) of the United Nations to project a near doubling in grain import needs from 1993, to nearly 4.7 million metric tons. Most of that need was met by donations. The FAO called the food deficit massive at about 1 million metric tons in Rwanda and critical or serious in Tanzania and Uganda. Iraq's food situation remained critical, in large part because of an international trade embargo. Haiti's shortages appeared to ease in late fall after the

Hot tomato. The "Flavr Savr" tomato, marketed under the brand name MacGregor, in May 1994 became the first genetically engineered whole food to be approved by the U.S. Food and Drug Administration for sale. Developed by the biotechnology company Calgene, the tomato is genetically altered to slow the natural ripening process and has a three-week shelf life and, it is claimed, a better flavor. Some consumer groups, however, were wary of the new technology and said that they would boycott the tomato.

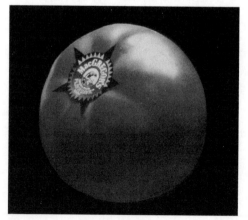

return of the elected government and resumption of large-scale U.S. food aid.

U.S. Developments. Secretary of Agriculture Mike Espy resigned October 3, effective at year's end, after fighting all summer against allegations that he had accepted gifts from companies that stood to profit from decisions made by the U.S. Department of Agriculture (USDA). An independent counsel was appointed to bring criminal charges if an investigation showed any violations of the law.

In October, President Bill Clinton signed into law a bill passed by Congress, at Espy's urging, to reorganize the USDA and cut its staff by about 7,500 employees (from more than 110,000) over five years. The bill merged the three agencies that administered price support, farm credit, and crop insurance programs and upgraded the status of the USDA's meat and poultry inspection program. Congress also approved legislation to reform the crop insurance program and repeal a $1.5 billion annual agricultural disaster assistance program that, auditors reported, had been abused by farmers.

The USDA proposed legislation to stiffen standards at meat and poultry plants to prevent bacterial contamination blamed for recent incidents of food poisoning. Congress was expected to consider the USDA request in 1995. The Food and Drug Administration implemented a new inspection system for seafood, and the USDA said in December that it would require a similar system for meat and poultry.

Record production of corn, soybeans, rice, and cotton was forecast for 1994. Corn, the nation's largest crop, was expected to yield 133.8 bushels per acre, the most ever, while the soybean yield was forecast to exceed 40 bushels per acre for the first time. The harvest, the largest ever for U.S. corn and soybeans, taxed storage capacity and depressed per-unit prices, but overall farm income was expected to remain at or near record levels because of strong volume.

Farmers' income increased over 1993; grain prices were elevated after the 1993 flood, but federal payments were lower. Livestock prices declined because of rising supplies. USDA analysts expected 1994 net cash income to decline some 4 to 6 percent from the 1993 record of $58.5 billion. Exports were projected to reach $43 billion, the highest level in a decade.

Europe and Former Soviet Union. European Union production-restraint programs began to succeed in holding down output of grain and livestock products while production rebounded from postprivatization declines in most of the former Eastern bloc countries. Western analysts predicted continued shortfalls in grain and meat production in the former Soviet Union. Compared with the output for 1992, which had been a record year, grain production was forecast to be off by approximately 18 percent.

Asia. Japan's rice crop recovered from the disastrous 1993 harvest, which had required major imports for the first time in decades, to create a slight rebound in Asian rice production despite a small decline in China's rice output. Drought in Indonesia cut rice production, requiring imports for the first time in years. Rice production continued to recover in Vietnam but lagged in Burma. A smaller corn crop in China curtailed exportable supplies, in contrast with rising feed grain output in other parts of Asia.

Western Hemisphere. While the wheat production of Canada was forecast down about 15 percent from 1993, Latin American output was projected to be up, led by a 5 percent gain in Argentina, the continent's leading food grain producer. Feed grain output in South America was projected to set a record 54.9 million metric tons.

Fisheries. The world's commercial fishing catch in 1992 was 98.1 million metric tons, down from a peak of 100.2 million metric tons in 1989. Destructive fishing practices have reduced the sustainable maximum from many popular stocks. The recent U.S. total catch has been estimated to be only about two-thirds of the maximum sustainable with good management. Future markets will increasingly need to be satisfied through substantially improved government management of fishing and by aquacultural production.

In 1993, in an effort to minimize overfishing, the U.S. Congress ordered that new rules be drawn up to limit takes of many species in shallow inshore waters—in particular, inshore waters of the Atlantic coast. The Georges Bank fishing ground was declared off-limits for commercial fishing for the first few months of 1994. In December 1994 the U.S. Commerce Department issued an emergency order closing the U.S. portion of the Georges Bank as well as other waters off New England—a total of some 6,000 square miles—to most commercial fishing for at least three months. The fishing grounds were near depletion, with the haddock catch having fallen by 75 percent in the preceding ten years and landings of other catches down dramatically as well.

The top five species groups in 1992 world catches were herrings, sardines, and anchovies at 20.4 million metric tons; cods, hakes, and haddocks at 10.5 million metric tons; redfishes, basses, and congers at 5.9 million metric tons; carps, barbels, and other cyprinids at 7.0 million metric tons; and tunas, bonitos, and billfishes at 4.4 million metric tons.

The top five fish-producing countries during 1992 were China at 15.0 million metric tons, Japan at 8.5 million metric tons, the countries of the former Soviet Union at 5.6 million metric tons, Peru at 6.8 million metric tons, and Chile at 6.5 million metric tons.

W.F.R. (Fisheries) & J.C.W.

ALABAMA. *See* STATE GOVERNMENT REVIEW; STATISTICS OF THE WORLD.

ALASKA. *See* STATISTICS OF THE WORLD.

ALBANIA. During 1994, Albania continued to make discernible progress in strengthening its economy, but its successes in this area were overshadowed by political strife at home and abroad. The ongoing conflict between the ruling Democratic Party and its major opposition, the Socialist (former Communist) Party, intensified following the conviction and imprisonment in April of Socialist Party leader and former Prime Minister Fatos Nano for misappropriation of state funds. In July, Albania's last Communist president, Ramiz Alia, was jailed after being convicted of having abused his authority and violating the rights of Albanian citizens. These trials, along with those of others from the ousted Communist elite, appeared to have resulted from pressure within the Democratic Party to settle the score with the nation's former rulers. The bitter partisan conflict that engulfed Albania following the trials delayed the ratification of the new

Berbers on the march. *Over 100,000 Berber demonstrators take to the streets of Tizi-Ouzou, a regional capital east of Algiers, in October. They were demanding the recognition of their language by Algeria and the release of Lounes Matoub, a popular Berber singer, who had been abducted by Muslim militants. Matoub's mother, center, displays her son's picture.*

democratic constitution. A referendum on the constitution was finally held on November 6; it was voted down.

Tensions between Greece and Albania heightened in April following the killing of two Albanian soldiers during a raid on an Albanian military post by members of the pro-Greek Northern Epirus Liberation Front. Relations between the two countries further deteriorated in September after conviction of five ethnic Greek Albanian activists on espionage charges. Greece retaliated by expelling some 70,000 of the estimated 300,000 Albanian economic immigrants within its borders. One of the activists was later freed; the others' sentences were reduced.

Albanian-Yugoslav relations, already antagonistic, were further strained in 1994 by Yugoslavia's support of Greece in the latter's dispute with Albania, as well as by Yugoslavia's steadfast refusal to consider any changes in the political and legal status of ethnic Albanians in its Kosovo region. Albania and Macedonia, however, drew closer, owing to their mutual differences with Greece and Yugoslavia. Albania continued to give priority to strengthen-

ing relations with the United States and Western Europe, and in February it joined the Partnership for Peace, a new NATO program intended to promote military cooperation with former Communist bloc countries (and Finland and Sweden).

A cholera outbreak that began in the fall had caused at least a dozen deaths by year's end. *See* STATISTICS OF THE WORLD. N.C.P.

ALBERTA. *See* CANADA; STATISTICS OF THE WORLD.

ALGERIA. In 1994, Algeria's military-backed regime experienced a third year of turmoil and brutality, with violence between government forces and armed insurgents approaching the level of a guerrilla war.

On March 10, insurgents stormed the Lambèse prison near Batna, enabling an estimated 1,000 prisoners to escape. In September the Armed Islamic Group (GIA), a virulent band of extremists, threatened the safety of high school and university students, delaying the opening of the school year by two weeks. In late September, Islamic militants killed one popular Berber singer and kidnapped another. These attacks caused outrage among Algeria's 8 million Berbers, and on October 2 more than 100,000 Berbers massed in protest in Tizi-Ouzou. In December, GIA militants hijacked an Air France jet in Algiers, killed three passengers, and flew on to Marseilles. There, the militants were killed by French commandos after the French government learned of their intention to blow up the plane and its passengers over Paris.

The GIA retaliated by killing three French priests and a Belgian priest, carrying out yet again the death threat it had issued in 1993 against foreigners in Algeria. Nearly 90 foreigners—many of them French citizens—were killed in 1994. Estimates of the number of Algerians killed since the imposition of military rule in January 1992 ranged widely from a conservative 3,000 to 30,000.

The five-member High State Committee (HCE), through which the military ruled, had late in 1993 extended its mandate to the end of January 1994. A halfhearted attempt at a national dialogue in early 1994 collapsed when the HCE refused to let the Islamic Salvation Front (FIS), banned in 1992, participate, and other political parties either refused to participate or walked out. On January 31, the regime installed the minister of defense, retired General Liamine Zéroual, as Algeria's new president.

Faced with an ever-worsening security situation, Minister of the Interior Salim Saadi announced on March 23 an all-out offensive to eradicate the Islamic insurgency. Throughout the spring and summer, Zéroual explored contacts with the opposition and in late August held talks with several political parties. On September 13, Zéroual transferred FIS leader Abassi Madani and his deputy, Ali Belhadj, from Blida prison to house arrest and freed three members of the FIS executive bureau. These limited gestures toward conciliation ended abruptly on October 31, when Zéroual denounced the FIS as "murderers, traitors, and mercenaries." Shortly thereafter, Madani and Belhadj were returned to prison. By year's end, hard-liners in the military had prevailed over Zéroual, the president had abandoned the prospect of a dialogue with the opposition, and the regime had decided to have elections a year early, in 1995, without the FIS.

In April, Algeria signed an economic reform plan, supported by the International Monetary Fund, calling for structural reforms to move Algeria's heavily centralized economy toward a market-oriented system. Algeria was able to reschedule its $26 billion foreign debt on favorable terms, reducing its repayment obligations for 1994 from $9.4 billion to $5.06 billion. This offered some relief to a beleaguered economy further weakened by poor harvests.

See STATISTICS OF THE WORLD. J.D.

AMERICAN SAMOA. *See* STATISTICS OF THE WORLD.

ANDORRA. *See* STATISTICS OF THE WORLD.

ANGOLA. The Angolan government and the rebel National Union for the Total Independence of Angola (Unita) signed a peace agreement on November 20, 1994, following a year in which the United Nations mediated talks between the two sides and the Angolan Army made major gains on the battlefield. The agreement called for a cease-fire, power sharing between the two sides, and a UN peace-keeping force of 7,000 to provide security. Although Unita leader Jonas Savimbi did not appear at the signing ceremony, in protest against Angolan government military advances immediately preceding the cease-fire, fighting declined significantly after the signing. Despite mutual accusations of cease-fire violations, uncertainties about the arrival of the UN forces, and doubts about Savimbi's role in the future government, there was increasing confidence that the agreement would hold.

The talks had begun in November 1993, after the UN Security Council imposed an oil and fuel embargo on Unita. Although they resulted in agreement on procedures for troop demobilization, a second round of presidential elections, and other issues, the talks became stalemated over the division of power between the government and Unita, which had returned to war after losing elections in September 1992.

In March 1994 the mediation team proposed a compromise giving Unita three of 18 provincial governorships, seven vice-governorships, and a number of national and local government posts. The government agreed in May, but Unita held out for the provincial governorship in Huambo, its headquarters, and for a vice presidency for Savimbi. In June the Security Council threatened to impose additional sanctions on Unita unless it accepted the compromise by July 31. Implementation of the threat was repeatedly postponed as negotiations continued.

Although deaths due to the war were less than the 1,000 a day estimated by relief agencies in 1993, for much of 1994 relatively secure conditions were confined to coastal cities under government control. Most of the interior was inaccessible even to relief agencies. Shortages of food and medicine were pervasive. The UN estimated that at least 3.3 million of Angola's population of 10 million were severely affected by war and drought, with 2.1 million needing immediate food aid. With the cities overcrowded with displaced people and inflation exceeding 1,000 percent, virtually all of Angola faced both a health crisis and economic desperation.

Government forces retook the provincial capital of Ndalatando in May and a key diamond-producing zone in Lunda Norte in July. A large illegal shipment of automatic weapons and ammunition from South Africa apparently fell through in August when Unita was unable to pay for it. In an offensive launched in the fall, government troops overran numerous Unita strongholds, including Huambo, and took back a major oil center, Soyo.

International interest in Angola's oil continued to run high. Chevron announced plans to invest $2.8 billion to expand production. In 1993, Angola ranked seventh among U.S. oil suppliers.

See STATISTICS OF THE WORLD.   W.M.

ANTHROPOLOGY. The discovery of a new hominid species—claimed to be the oldest human ancestor ever found—made headlines in anthropology in 1994. Newly found bones from an already known species—*Australopithecus afarensis*—prompted reconsideration of how that species lived, and a new date for previously discovered Indonesian fossils led to revised theories about the rise of tool use in Africa and elsewhere.

The Missing Link? The new species, whose discovery was announced in September, is said to be the oldest yet found in the genus *Australopithecus,* which most anthropologists consider to be a direct ancestor of modern human beings. The identification was based on fossils found along the Aramis River, near the Awash (also known as Hawash) River in Ethiopia. The species is called *Australopithecus ramidus* (*ramid* means "root" in the local Afar language). Teeth and bones from a total of 17 individuals were collected by a research team led by anthropologist Tim D. White of the University of California at Berkeley.

The fossils were found to be 4.4 million years old—half a million years older than the earliest *Australopithecus afarensis* fossils yet discovered. The *afarensis* species, whose existence was established in 1978, had been the oldest generally accepted known human ancestor. It lived from 3 million to 3.9 million years ago in a range of habitats that included both dry grasslands and wetter, forested areas. A partial *afarensis* skeleton nicknamed Lucy, discovered in 1974, is its most famous example. But the *ramidus* fossils, found less than 80 kilometers (50 miles) south of the site where Lucy's remains were unearthed, are more than a million years older than Lucy.

White indicated that the *ramidus* fossils, mostly teeth, were significantly more primitive than those of previously known australopithecine species. The canines, or eyeteeth, and the elbow region of an arm bone show that *ramidus,* though apelike in many features (like other *Australopithecus* species) was also distinctly humanlike and had already split off from the ape lineage. The *ramidus* fragments were found along with some 600 fossils of ancient monkeys, elephants, bats, and other animals, some of which were woodland-loving species. This could indicate that humans' ability to walk upright evolved in a forested environment, rather than on relatively treeless grasslands and open savanna plains, as many anthropologists think. Because the *ramidus* fossils were all from the upper body, it was not known whether the species could walk upright, but another expedition was scheduled to begin late in the year in hopes of finding pelvic, knee, and foot bones.

Scientists were delighted with the discoveries. "The metaphor of a missing link has often been misused, but it is a suitable epithet," wrote one paleoanthropologist, referring to the long-sought common ancestor of humans and apes whose existence was first suggested by Charles Darwin. Indeed, if the new species truly is the oldest fossil hominid yet discovered on the main line of human evolution, it would be the closest yet found to the separation of humans and apes, but more research will be needed before the claim is generally accepted.

Son of Lucy. Meanwhile, new fossils of *Australopithecus afarensis* were prompting anthropologists to reconsider their views of how members of the species lived and what males and females looked like. The fossils were found in the Hadar Formation near the Awash River in Ethiopia.

The bones included a reasonably complete skull, dubbed Son of Lucy. The skull was the first ever found for *afarensis,* and it was the largest yet unearthed for any species in the genus *Australopithecus.* Yet it was primitive enough to reinforce an emerging view in anthropology that the australopithecine brain was more apelike than humanlike. The upper arm, or humerus, and a complete lower arm bone, an ulna, suggest that the newly found *afarensis* both climbed trees and walked upright on two legs. Unlike modern chimpanzees and gorillas, however, it lacked the ability to walk on all fours.

The possibility that this young male *Australopithecus afarensis* was a part-time arborealist as well as a part-time walker challenged the prevailing viewpoint in physical anthropology that human ancestors walked on two legs during the australopithecine phase of their evolution. This viewpoint has also been called into question by recent research on inner ears indicating that australopithecine posture was not yet fully upright. The slightly curving finger bones of Lucy suggest a climbing ability.

The notion that smaller and larger australopithecines belonged to different species has been seriously challenged by the Son of Lucy. According to the researchers who found the skull, *afarensis* males were considerably bigger and heavier, and had thicker, more robust skeletons than the females. Such physical differences between the sexes—a phenomenon known as sexual dimorphism—are present in living great apes, too, and to a lesser extent in modern human beings.

Older Age for Java Man. Fossil remains of the immediate ancestor of modern *Homo sapiens,* known as *Homo erectus* or, informally, Java Man, were redated in 1994 to be more than half a million years older than previously thought. Using a technique involving two types of argon, scientists dated the layer of volcanic sediments thought to have embedded the fossil remains of three *Homo erectus* specimens collected in 1936 and the 1970s from the Indonesian island of Java.

The specimens were crudely estimated at the time of their collection to be about 1 million years old. The new age, based on measurement of the gradually changing ratios of stable argon to unstable, radioactive argon in the sediments, is 1.6-1.8 million years, making Java Man the oldest known species of *Homo* yet discovered outside Africa.

The new date is significant because it suggests one possible reason why scientists have failed to find in Indonesia certain relatively advanced stone tools that were in wide use among the African members of *Homo erectus* about 1.4 million years ago. If the new date

Skull-ossal discovery. *In March researchers announced the unearthing in Ethiopia of the first fairly complete skull of the species* Australopithecus afarensis, *a hominid ancestor of modern human beings. Together with other newly found fossil bones, it caused anthropologists to reconsider their views of how members of the species lived and what males and females looked like.*

holds up, it will mean that *Homo erectus* of Java must have left Africa 800,000 years earlier than previously thought, well before these advanced tools—such as the hand ax or the two-faced stone cleaver—appeared in Africa. The oldest *Homo erectus* yet discovered in Africa dates to 1.8 million years ago. The new date for Java Man also raises the possibility that the Indonesian group of *Homo erectus* could represent a distinct lineage in hominid evolution.

Thumbs Up. A U.S. researcher proposed in 1994 a test for humanlike precision grasping—that is, the enhanced ability to manipulate tools—based on the structure of a thumb bone. Using the test, the researcher concluded that all hominids of about 2 million years ago were likely to have used tools. It appears, however, that *Australopithecus afarensis* was able to grasp tools only between palm and thumb, index finger, and middle finger.   D.B.G.

ANTIGUA AND BARBUDA. See CARIBBEAN BASIN; STATISTICS OF THE WORLD.

ARABIAN PENINSULA. See KUWAIT; PERSIAN GULF STATES; SAUDI ARABIA; YEMEN.

ARCHAEOLOGY. A newly discovered ceremonial site in the Great Plains of the United States, a revised date for a Minoan volcanic eruption, and new techniques for diagnosing ancient diseases dominated the news in archaeology in 1994.

Wichita Intaglios. A vast ceremonial site with embankments, shallow trenches, causeways, and animal figures was found near Wichita, KS, in spring 1994 after a landowner burned off the fields into which they were carved. The animal figures, called intaglios, included a serpent 27 meters (nearly 90 feet) long and a turtle. Two others were unidentifiable, and a fifth may have been destroyed by construction. Only two other sites with intaglios have been found in the Great Plains; each contains a single serpent intaglio. Archaeologists speculated that the causeways at the newly discovered site, which lead from a nearby spring, were used for religious processions and that some features have astronomical alignments. The site was likely built by ancestors of the Wichita tribe, who probably also carved the intaglio at one of the other sites prior to 1541.

Making a Mummy. Beginning in May two scientists mummified a donated human body with the embalming procedures of ancient Egyptians. Using replicas of ancient tools, they extracted the brain through the nostrils with a bronze hook and removed the abdomen's contents via an incision made with an obsidian blade, placing organs in replicas of ancient jars. They washed out the body cavity with palm wine and with a solution of pounded spices and then packed the body with myrrh and natron—essentially a natural baking soda used to dehydrate the tissue—and placed the entire body in natron. After 35 days they again washed out the body and wrapped it in linen smeared with resin.

Based on this experiment, the researchers now believe that a bronze instrument identified almost a century ago as an embalmer's knife was instead a razor for daily use. They also determined that bodies probably contained some moisture when wrapped by ancient embalmers. The researchers planned to take tissue samples periodically from various parts of the body in order to study the effects of natron on cell preservation.

Turkey Strikes Back. Turkey continued its aggressive policy to recover stolen antiquities. A Roman-era sarcophagus, smuggled out of Turkey in the mid-1980s, was returned to Istanbul in April. Known as the Garland Sarcophagus for the sculpted decoration on its sides and ends, the sarcophagus, dated A.D. 150, had been purchased by a New York collector for a reported $1 million. In 1993, Turkey won a six-year struggle with New York City's Metropolitan Museum of Art, which returned 363 pieces of sixth-century B.C. gold and silver jewelry, vessels, and other objects known collectively as the Lydian Hoard.

Turkey continued to seek the return of Byzantine objects from the Dumbarton Oaks Museum in Washington, DC, as well as the top half of a statue of Hercules, which matches a bottom half still in Turkey, from the Museum of Fine Arts in Boston. Turkey was also seeking the return of the Great Altar of Pergamon from Germany. Discovered in 1871, the altar, erected by Eumenes II of Pergamon (197-159 B.C.), shows a battle between the gods and giants. As of the end of 1994 there had been no response from the German government.

Bronze Age Upset. By studying a core of ice from northern Greenland, scientists determined that the Santorin, or Thira, volcano eruption, which buried the Minoan town of Akrotiri, occurred in about 1628 to 1625 B.C. The old Aegean chronology had placed the eruption around 1500 B.C. or even later, meaning that the dates archaeologists assigned to the first half of the Late Bronze Age were off by more than a century.

Eruptions can be identified in ice cores from elevated levels of sulfate from sulfuric acid spewed into the atmosphere. Because precipitation varies by season, it is possible to count annual layers in the ice core that are similar to the growth layers in trees. The ice core had sulfate peaks corresponding roughly to 1600 B.C., 1621 B.C., and 1667 B.C. However, carbon dates reported in 1976 suggested Akrotiri was buried by volcanic ash around 1625 B.C., and in the 1980s studies of annual growth rings of trees in the United States and Europe indicated that there had been climatic disturbances about 1628 B.C.

Colonization of the Americas. Researchers continued to seek evidence of colonization of the Americas before 10,000 B.C., the earliest definite date.

After comparing grammatical features that change slowly in some 200 language families, linguist Johanna Nichols concluded in 1994 that humans reached the New World 35,000 to 40,000 years ago, and that if all the world's languages are descended from a single ancestor, that language was spoken more than 100,000 years ago. Of the world's 300 language families, 130 are in the western hemisphere. Nichols believes there must have been about ten separate infusions of new language groups into the New World to create so much diversity in a period of just 35,000 years.

Emory University scientists reported in 1994 that they believe humans have been in the New World for 23,000 to 29,000 years. Researchers studied the DNA of 22 Native American tribal populations and ten Siberian groups in hopes of learning how long the groups have been isolated from one another. They based their conclusions on the assumption that DNA mutations occur at a steady rate.

Further support for an early date came from studies of radiocarbon dates of lichen, pollen, charcoal, and fungi found on stone tools from the Mojave Desert in California and on petroglyphs (carvings or inscriptions on rocks) from the Petrified Forest in Arizona. Researchers obtained dates of 12,000 and 26,000 years for the tools and 16,000 to 18,000 years for the petroglyphs.

Ancient Scrolls From Petra. At least 50 charred papyrus scrolls were discovered near a sixth-century church at Petra in Jordan in December 1993. In A.D. 551 an earthquake evidently caused the church to collapse. The scrolls were found in a room adjacent to the church, under and between the charred remains of the shelving on which they had been stacked. Five scrolls had been examined by the end of 1994. They included a listing of the property of a deceased man named Obodianus, the will of a severely ill man, and a document concerning the division of inherited property. The scrolls constitute the largest group of written material from antiquity ever found in Jordan.

Ancient Diseases. Archaeologists excavating a cemetery outside Rome where at least 47 children were buried around A.D. 450 said the children may have died in a malaria outbreak.

Tiny victim. *Archaeologists announced the excavation of a cemetery dating to around* A.D. *450 on the grounds of an ancient villa near Rome At least 47 children were buried there, and it is believed they died in a malaria outbreak. One of the infant skeletons is seen here.*

The large number of fetuses and the pattern of burial, plus what is known about the history of the region, all pointed toward a malaria epidemic. No skeletons of adults were found.

Using DNA replication and matching techniques, two University of Minnesota scientists announced in March that they had identified the bacterium that causes tuberculosis in tissue from a 900-year-old Peruvian mummy. Tuberculosis had been only tentatively identified in the pre-Columbian New World on the basis of bone lesions. M.R.

ARCHITECTURE. U.S. architecture in 1994 remained in a state of aesthetic flux, with leading architects continuing to shun stylistic labels. Accordingly, in the tradition of Frank Lloyd Wright (the subject of a major retrospective at New York City's Museum of Modern Art early in the year), the best buildings of 1994 were often idiosyncratic responses to program and site, reflecting the fact that good architecture transcends any one particular style.

The representative works of the 1990s continued to be institutional and civic commissions—museums, libraries, fire stations, performing arts centers, university buildings, and sports facilities. These types of buildings, whether large or small, offer more flexibility for architects to explore diverse stylistic and programmatic solutions.

ARCHITECTURE

Global Profession. Architecture continued to be a global profession. Many of the most celebrated buildings of the year were designed by architects based thousands of miles away. The American Center in Paris, designed by Los Angeles architect Frank O. Gehry, opened to rave reviews in June. Planned as the cultural centerpiece of a redeveloped district overlooking the Parc de Bercy, the 198,000-square-foot (18,400-square-meter) center, with its assemblage of disparate forms and curvilinear ribbons of limestone and metal, is characteristic of Gehry's aesthetic ideology. (In October, Gehry was awarded the first Dorothy and Lillian Gish Prize. The award, worth $250,000, was established to recognize an individual for an outstanding contribution to the arts.)

In neighboring Luxembourg, Richard Meier of New York City continued to hone his restrained brand of rationalism with a branch office for Hypobank International, a Munich-based commercial bank. Another variation on Meier's consistent theme, the bank building has a facade of meticulously crafted granite and signature white enamel panels.

Major Urban Projects. Back in the United States work continued on San Francisco's ambitious downtown Yerba Buena urban renewal project. A major new cultural center was established with the opening late in 1993 of Yerba Buena's Center for the Arts Theater, by James Stewart Polshek and Partners of New York City, and Center for the Arts Galleries and Forum, by Japanese architect Fumihiko Maki. The buildings are arranged around the 5.5-acre (2.2-hectare) Yerba Buena Gardens, designed by MGA Partners with Romaldo Giurgola. Next to the Esplanade, an oval walkway at the center of the gardens, is a memorial to Martin Luther King by sculptor Houston Conwill, architect Joseph De Pace, and poet Estella Conwill Majozo. Construction on the neighboring new Museum of Modern Art, designed by Swiss architect Mario Botta, was completed during 1994, and parts of the building were opened to the public in the fall. The formal opening of the museum was scheduled for January 1995.

In Los Angeles, a city not known for its urban amenities, a refurbished Pershing Square opened in February. Architect Ricardo Legorreta and landscape architect Laurie Olin transformed the crime-infested square into an urban plaza with a purple campanile, hot pink columns, and a cascade of water.

Universities Host New Projects. Beginning with Thomas Jefferson's University of Virginia, college campuses have long been a fertile proving ground for architecture, and in 1994 innovative buildings by leading architects appeared on campuses around the United States. The talented young Atlanta firm Scogin Elam and Bray completed a bold new law library at Arizona State University. The 68,000-square-

Looking up to nature. The iconoclastic architect Antoine Predock drew inspiration from the nearby mountains and Indian tepees to create a highly praised design for the American Heritage Center and Art Museum at the University of Wyoming at Laramie. The concrete cone shown here is copper sheathed and steel framed and houses research rooms, offices, and a five-story atrium.

Frank Lloyd Wright Remembered

Admirable abode. *Fallingwater, a summer home cantilevered over a waterfall in Bear Run, PA, is the best-known work of Frank Lloyd Wright's middle period. Some critics consider it the finest house of the 20th century.*

No fewer than four New York exhibitions in 1994 were devoted to Frank Lloyd Wright, the man who called himself America's greatest architect (many others agree).

Wright (1869?-1959) grew up mostly in Wisconsin and apprenticed with Chicago architect Louis Sullivan. Beginning in the 1890s, Wright built a series of houses in a new design idiom called the prairie style—low-slung, horizontal buildings that hug the landscape. Unique in scale, proportion, detail, and ornament, Wright's buildings "broke out of the box" to create continuous and flowing spaces, not as a series of rooms but as a sculptural whole.

One of Wright's best-known buildings is Fallingwater (1936), which is cantilevered over a waterfall in Bear Run, PA. It is now open to the public as a museum. Wright's last major building is the Guggenheim Museum in New York City. Although it has been criticized as a difficult place to view paintings, the Guggenheim, with its ascending spiral ramp, is a stunning work of art in itself.

The most ambitious of the four Wright shows was at New York City's Museum of Modern Art, which traced Wright's career with more than 500 exhibits. The Metropolitan Museum of Art explored Wright's contributions as a decorative artist, while Columbia University presented a show based on his famous "Wasmuth folios" (1910-1911), photographs and drawings of his buildings. And at Manhattan's Lobby Gallery, Wright's flamboyant personality was captured in photographs by Pedro E. Guerrero.

The exhibitions demonstrated clearly that Wright was a genius as well as an innovator, challenging conventional wisdom on the aesthetics of design.   E.L.N.

foot (6,300-square-meter) facility is a collision of forms and materials, with a central reading room, shaped like a fragmented trapezoid, sandwiched between a three-story rectangular tower topped with a steel barrel vault and a pie-shaped wedge clad in galvanized steel.

The iconoclastic architect Antoine Predock, best known for his innovative Southwestern designs, won acclaim for the American Heritage Center and Art Museum at the University of Wyoming at Laramie. Evoking mystical images, from a tepee to a pueblo to a UFO, the museum features a copper-sheathed, steel-framed cone set askew atop a plinth constructed of sandblasted concrete blocks.

Fields of Dreams. Two years after Hellmuth, Obata & Kassabaum's winning design for Baltimore's Oriole Park at Camden Yards, other cities followed the lead with brand new, old-fashioned baseball parks. In Cleveland, HOK hit another grand slam with the Indians' Jacobs Field, which boasts a distinctively industrial

Terror in Buenos Aires. The old Jewish quarter of Argentina's capital city was the scene of devastation after a bomb went off on July 18 at the headquarters of the Argentine Jewish Mutual Association, the heart of Argentina's Jewish community. The bombing was later attributed to Islamic fundamentalists backed by Iran. Above, rescue workers dig through the rubble in a frantic search for survivors.

aesthetic that evokes the steel bridges spanning the Cuyahoga River.

Rather than hire one of the well-known baseball park specialist firms, the Texas Rangers sponsored a limited competition and invited a roster of star architects to take a swing. David M. Schwarz/Architectural Services of Washington, DC, in association with HKS of Dallas and HNTB Sports Architecture Group of Kansas City, was selected. The Rangers' 49,000-seat Ballpark in Arlington opened for the 1994 season. The Rangers' owners, reportedly, had liked the romantic de-

sign of Baltimore's Camden Yards and wanted a traditional ballpark with a "Texas" twang. Schwarz delivered a lively blend of tradition—grass, sky, an asymmetrical outfield—and the required modern amenities, such as luxury suites, and unobstructed sight lines.

Sustainable Design. The numbers of architects embracing sustainable design principles continued to grow. "Green" architects, who are motivated by a commitment to sound ecological practices, can call on a wide array of technological advances that minimize energy consumption; they also employ commonsense approaches such as passive heating and cooling strategies, and they use recycled, reused, or renewable materials in order to conserve natural resources.

A project completed late in 1993 in Portland, OR, was a model for construction recycling. For the new headquarters for Metro, the public agency that directs solid-waste management for the city, architects Thompson Vavoida & Associates converted an abandoned Sears store. They salvaged tons of materials from the existing building and used recycled products whenever possible in the new building's construction. E.L.N.

ARGENTINA. A terrorist attack directed against Argentina's Jewish community and agreement on a new national constitution were the major events of the year 1994.

Terrorist Bomb. On July 18 a car bomb exploded outside the community center of the Argentine Jewish Mutual Association in Buenos Aires, the nation's capital, marking the 30th time in 20 years that Argentine Jews faced terrorist violence. About 100 people were killed and hundreds more were injured. Government officials later linked the blast to Iranian-backed Islamic fundamentalists.

Three days after the blast up to 150,000 people marched through the streets of Buenos Aires in a show of concern. President Carlos Saúl Menem announced plans for a new Secretariat of Security and Community Protection to coordinate the efforts of police and security forces during times of emergency.

New Constitution. Elections were held on April 10 to select representatives for a convention to draw up a new constitution. Congressional members of the two leading parties, the ruling Peronists and the opposition Radical Civic Union, had voted for such a convention following a late 1993 deal between their leaders, Menem and former President Raúl Alfonsín, that had, in effect, set out the broad outlines of a new constitution.

When the convention election returned a working majority of Peronists and their allies, it became clear that Menem would gain his key objective: the right to run for reelection in May 1995. The new constitution, approved by the convention on August 24, also gave Alfonsín much of what he had sought, including new congressional powers to reject presidential decrees and a 50 percent increase in the size of the Senate, with the extra seats going to opposition parties.

The Presidency. Corruption charges continued to plague Menem's administration, which by March had already weathered more than 20 scandals. In August, Menem ended compulsory military service for 18-year-old males selected by annual draft. Labeled a cost-cutting measure, the plan seemed to observers to be aimed at building popular support among young Argentinians.

Economic Ups and Downs. Economy Minister Domingo Cavallo announced on August 31 that all remaining government-owned industries would be privatized within 16 months. Inflation remained low (estimated at below 5 percent), and the economy continued to grow. But most of the growth continued to be confined to a few major cities, and the economy in most of the 23 provinces was stagnant. Further, unemployment was on the rise, reaching an estimated 10.8 percent in July.

Planned cuts in provincial payrolls, salaries, and programs had prompted thousands to demonstrate in La Rioja and Santiago del Estero provinces during December 1993. Over the next four months similar disturbances occurred in the provinces of Catamarca, Jujuy, and Salta.

In July 1994 unions and opposition parties organized a protest march through Buenos Aires that drew more than 60,000 participants, and farmers associated with the Argentine Agrarian Federation initiated a ten-day work stoppage in August to protest government economic and trade policies.

In response, the government announced that it would resist the suggestion of the International Monetary Fund to cut public spending even more. Earlier, Menem had announced the creation of a multiyear, multibillion-dollar program to fight poverty and create jobs.

See STATISTICS OF THE WORLD.   D.Le.

ARIZONA. *See* STATE GOVERNMENT REVIEW; STATISTICS OF THE WORLD.

ARKANSAS. *See* STATISTICS OF THE WORLD.

ARMENIA. The year 1994 in Armenia saw a marked decrease in support for the government of President Levon Ter-Petrosyan. Although widespread evidence of gross governmental corruption was a factor, the dissatisfaction was largely the result of the government's inability to relieve the economic hardships caused by neighboring Azerbaijan's blockade of Armenia as the two countries

A time to mourn. An Armenian woman grieves over a casualty of Armenia's war with Azerbaijan over Mountainous Karabagh (also known as Nagorno-Karabakh). In the spring Russia mediated a cease-fire in the conflict, which had been going on since 1988.

fought over Mountainous Karabagh (also known as Nagorno-Karabakh), a mostly Armenian region within Azerbaijan.

By January 1994, Mountainous Karabagh Armenian forces had gained control of all of the region and a considerable amount of Azerbaijani territory to its north and south. In the spring Russia succeeded in mediating an unofficial cease-fire, which, despite minor violations, held remarkably well. In December the Conference on Security and Cooperation in Europe decided to send a multinational peacekeeping force to Mountainous Karabagh once a formal cease-fire was agreed on.

Meanwhile, the Armenian national currency, the dram, introduced in November 1993, proved to be very unstable, and serious inflation gripped the country. Imports continued to exceed exports, unemployment increased dramatically over 1993, and it was estimated that 85 percent of the population was either at or below the poverty line. Serious malnutrition was clearly visible in photographs taken in all parts of the country. Over 10 percent of the population were refugees, and at least another 10 percent had left the country, most of them for Russia. There were some bright spots: The privatization of 80 percent of the land since independence in 1991 had led to an increase in agricultural products, and there had been a marked increase in industrial production.

In the summer President Ter-Petrosyan visited the United States and met with President Bill Clinton. The two countries signed a bilateral military agreement, conditional upon a permanent end to the Mountainous Karabagh conflict. At the same time Armenia took steps to alleviate the energy crisis caused by the blockade, negotiating with Turkmenistan for the building of a high-voltage power line and with Iran for the import of natural gas. In September, Armenia signed an agreement with Russia for financial and technical aid that would hasten plans for reactivating the controversial Mezamor nuclear plant.

See STATISTICS OF THE WORLD.   R.H.H.

ART. As 1994 ended, the Vatican's Sistine Chapel looked almost as good as new, impressionism was being rediscovered, thousands of Warhols had roosted in Pittsburgh, and a new

Cy-chology. The Museum of Modern Art in New York mounted a retrospective of the work of Cy Twombley, an American long resident in Italy. Among the works shown was Summer Madness, from 1990. Although Twombley's international reputation is great, he has had less recognition in his native land.

director for the Museum of Modern Art in New York City had finally been found.

Sistine Rejuvenated. The completion of the 14-year cleaning of Michelangelo's frescoes in the Sistine Chapel was marked by a papal mass before the newly luminous *Last Judgment,* a 1,700-square-foot panorama of sinners and saved cowering before Christ. Occupying the altar wall of the chapel, it was completed in 1541, some 25 years after Michelangelo painted the Sistine's famous ceiling frescoes. After a majority of scholars approved the results of a controversial cleaning of the ceiling undertaken in the 1980s, similar work on *The Last Judgment* began in 1989. Conservators not only removed centuries' worth of grime but also eliminated some of the prudish overpainting that had marred the fresco since 1564, when churchmen scandalized by the nudity of its many figures ordered the addition of 40 drapes and loincloths. Several of Michelangelo's figures have been returned to nakedness, but conservators chose to leave others—including the Virgin Mary—modestly draped for now.

Impressionism Revisited. On both sides of the Atlantic audiences flocked to "Origins of Impressionism," a chronicle of avant-garde painting in France in the 1860s. As the show moved from the Grand Palais in Paris to New York City's Metropolitan Museum, the lineup of around 170 pictures changed somewhat, but both versions of the exhibit featured textbook exemplars by such luminaries as Courbet, Degas, Manet, Monet, Renoir, Pissarro, and Cézanne.

Other exhibits took up smaller slices of the impressionist enterprise: A show of landscapes by Degas at the Metropolitan Museum highlighted an overlooked aspect of that renowned figure painter's oeuvre; and at the Musée des Beaux Arts in Rouen, France, the centenary of Monet's *Rouen Cathedral* suite (1892-1894) occasioned a reunion of 16 works from the series, a painterly meditation on the ways in which natural effects of light and atmosphere visually transform a static human construct into an ever-changing spectacle of color and texture.

Flemish Master Reexamined. In Bruges, Belgium, the art center of 15th-century Flanders, a retrospective of the work of Hans Memling marked the quincentennial of his death. Since his rare and fragile panel paintings seldom travel, the exposition provided a unique opportunity to see dozens of Memlings assembled in his adopted hometown.

Modern Masters Reprised. The haunting work of Odilon Redon—an artist idiosyncratic enough to practice an art of fantasy in the era of impressionism—was given long-overdue attention in a retrospective organized by the Art Institute of Chicago. Redon's free-floating heads and eyeballs, winged horses, and anthropomorphic plants eventually gave way to the tame floral still lifes of his last years.

A much more celebrated oddball, Salvador Dalí, was recalled in an exhibition devoted to the artist's early years that traveled from London to New York and Madrid.

The exhibit documented Dalí's belated embrace of cubism in the early 1920s and subsequent explorations of monumental classicism and precisionist realism. The show then moved on to consider the Spanish-born painter's alliance with the surrealist movement in Paris, and the birth, in 1929, of Dalí's trademark style, which combined Miró-like whimsy, biomorphism, and boundless space

Where it all began. *One of the year's most popular shows was "Origins of Impressionism," which was seen at the Grand Palais in Paris and the Metropolitan Museum in New York. One of the works on display was* On the Beach at Boulogne *(1868) by Edouard Manet.*

with obsessive detail, steamy eroticism, and a taste for putrefaction.

Dalí's most famous compatriot was the subject of a thematic exhibition in 1994, "Picasso and the Weeping Women," organized by the Los Angeles County Museum. Focusing on his depictions of female subjects from 1927 to 1942, the show suggested that Picasso's renderings of his wives and lovers should be read not only as barometers of the artist's psychosexual disposition but also as reflections of his political convictions and frustrations. The show's centerpiece was a series of pictures of grief-stricken wailers whose histrionics are thought to mirror the artist's own anguished response to events of the Spanish civil war.

Contemporary Art. The recent work of Louise Bourgeois, which formed the U.S. exhibit at the Venice Biennale in 1993, was reassembled in 1994 for an expanded retrospective at the Brooklyn Museum in New York. Using found objects and multiple media, the artist had spent the preceding decade crafting sculptures and installation pieces that evoke a shadow world of memories and dreams, wherein childhood anxieties and longings mingle with explosive adult desire. At once erotic, eerie, humorous, and fearsome, they not only conjure up a deeply felt personal history but speak to a broad range of contemporary artistic and societal concerns.

On the occasion of his 90th birthday, Willem de Kooning was feted with a chronological overview of his career that opened at the National Gallery in Washington, DC. The show charted his oeuvre from cubistic black and white paintings to increasingly colorful abstract expressionist figuration—including the well-known *Woman* series inaugurated in the 1950s—and lyrical late-life abstractions.

A similarly inclusive chronicle of Cy Twombley's artistic development was presented by an exhibition at New York's Museum of Modern Art. Twombley, an American resident in Italy, is best known for works in which calligraphic and graffitilike marks are deployed. In Twombley's works scribbles, doodles, and numbers mingle with effects of erasure as well as discernible words and phrases—most of which are tied to the artist's deep affection for Mediterranean culture.

The career of Cleveland native R. B. Kitaj—a founder of the pop movement in England and longtime resident of London—was the subject of a show mounted by the Tate Gallery. Abounding in literary, art-historical, and filmic references, Kitaj's work also touches on his own Jewish heritage, and when the exhibit elicited some negative reviews, the outraged artist publicly branded his British critics anti-Semitic, anti-American, and anti-intellectual. The show moved on to Los Angeles and was slated to be seen in New York in 1995.

The largest survey ever of postwar Japanese art (200 objects) documented that culture's love-hate relationship with Western art and lifestyles. "Japanese Art After 1945: Scream Against the Sky" included Japanese spins on Euro-American vogues and artistic responses to the rampant commercialism and cultural imperialism of Western nations. It began its run in Yokohama, traveled on to New York, and was scheduled to be shown at two California venues in 1995. Meantime, postwar art and design trends in Italy were charted in "The Italian Metamorphosis, 1943-1968." That exhibit, at the Guggenheim Museum in New York City, comprised painting, sculpture, architecture, photography, film, and fashion.

A polemical show at New York's Whitney Museum of American Art focused on myths of African-American manliness. "Black Male: Representations of Masculinity in Contemporary American Art"—an examination of a particular stereotype, based on race and gender, and its promulgation, ridicule, and putative transformation in the visual arts since 1960—presented more than 100 works by 25 artists, including Jean-Michel Basquiat, Robert Colescott, Jeff Koons, Adrian Piper, Gary Simmons, and Lorna Simpson.

Art Market. The art market continued soft in 1994, with buyers unusually cool to impressionist offerings. The keenest disappointments came at Christie's spring sales of impressionist, modern, and contemporary art; 50 percent of offered works—including a Cézanne and two Monets—failed to sell. The most surprising successes of the spring sales were scored by Sotheby's, where Gustav Klimt's *Lady With a Fan* (1917 to 1918) brought $11.6 million (while a Degas and a Monet went unsold) and a pristine late Mondrian fetched $5.6 million—almost double the price that had been anticipated. In October another unexpectedly lucrative sale resulted when James Tissot's *Garden Bench* was put on the block; composer-collector Andrew Lloyd Webber paid almost $5.3 million for this middling work by a quasi-realist on the fringe of the impressionist circle. The recent enthusiasm for Latin American art continued, with works by Rufino Tamayo being the top sellers at both Sotheby's and Christie's auctions of Latin American art.

Scream Stolen. Edvard Munch's *Scream,* the quintessential image of psychic pain, was stolen from the National Gallery in Oslo in February. A bizarre hoax was later attempted when an abortion opponent claimed that the painting would be returned if Norwegian national TV aired an antiabortion film called *The Silent Scream,* but as it turned out, antiabortionists had no part in the crime. *Scream* was recovered undamaged in May when two men demanding a ransom of more than $400,000 were apprehended.

Museums. The National Museum of Beirut began a $4.5 million restoration effort; years of civil strife had left its building intact but badly damaged.

In April the Metropolitan Museum in New York opened its Florence and Herbert Irving Galleries for the arts of South and Southeast Asia—the result of a seven-year, $10 million renovation. Its 16 rooms were planned to display 1,300 objects from a dozen countries.

A $35 million shrine to Andy Warhol—the largest single-artist museum in the United States—opened in his hometown of Pittsburgh in May. Playing on the "art factory" idea that so intrigued Warhol, the new interior of the renovated warehouse (built in 1911) features industrial materials and a bare-bones look. It houses a permanent collection that includes 900 paintings, 1,500 drawings, 400 photos, 77 sculptures, and a wealth of films, videos, and archival materials.

Kansas City's new facility, the Kemper Museum of Contemporary Art and Design, opened in October. Also in October, the Joslyn Museum in Omaha, NE, unveiled a 58,000-square-foot wing with a show of contemporary Navajo weaving, and the Baltimore Museum of Art opened a 36,000-square-foot wing to house its renowned Cone Collection, which features works by Cézanne, Van Gogh, Matisse, and Picasso.

New York's Museum of Modern Art spent the year in search of a director after Richard Oldenburg stepped down at the end of 1993 (he agreed to stay on temporarily). The long search ended in November, when Glenn D. Lowry, director of Toronto's Art Gallery of Ontario, was chosen to fill this high-visibility post. He was to take over in July 1995.

See PHOTOGRAPHY.   J.Su.

ASTRONOMY. The biggest astronomical event of 1994 was the collision of the fragments of Comet Shoemaker-Levy 9 with the planet Jupiter (*see the feature article* COMETS: MYSTERIOUS VISITORS FROM OUTER SPACE). Less spectacular but far more significant were the first results from the *Hubble Space Telescope* concerning the age of the universe.

Hubble Puzzle. Observations made with the *Hubble Space Telescope* indicated that the

The Game of the Name

The Big Bang was the explosion that most astronomers believe marked the beginning of the universe. But some regard the name as disrespectful for an event so grand. Indeed, it was devised as a term of ridicule by skeptical astronomer Fred Hoyle in 1950.

In 1994, *Sky & Telescope* magazine sponsored a contest to find a more fitting appellation. It received 13,099 entries from 41 countries. "Creation," "Cosmogenesis," and "Genesis" got the most votes. Then the fun started. Also suggested were "START" (Some Trivial Acronym Regarding Time), "Big TOE" (Theory of Everything), and "MOM" (Mother of Matter). Then there were "Bertha D. Universe," "Origin of the Space-ies," "God's Log-on," and "The Big Boot." Other tries were "Spark in the Dark," "Jurassic Quark," "God Fodder—Part 1," and "What Happens If I Press This Button?" Among serious entries was the Greek word "Panarche" (beginning of all things).

The winner? Fred Hoyle! No entry, the judges decreed, "is a worthy successor to Hoyle's original."

Ida's moon. In March astronomers announced that the spacecraft Galileo, while passing the asteroid Ida, had discovered that Ida has a tiny moon. The color-enhanced image at left shows both Ida and its moon. The image above, also enhanced, provides an enlarged view of the moon, which is about 1.5 kilometers (roughly 1 mile) in diameter and orbits Ida at a distance of some 100 kilometers.

universe is only some 8-12 billion years old. If true, this estimate poses a stunning paradox, for astronomers have strong reasons to believe that some stars are 14-18 billion years of age.

Astronomers can calculate the age of the universe because it is expanding. Knowing the distance of a galaxy and the speed at which it and our own Milky Way are fleeing from each other, one can determine how long ago the two, and indeed all galaxies, were in the same spot. This time in the past is the starting point of the Big Bang. Measuring the line-of-sight velocity is relatively easy, but the distance is another matter. This is a particularly serious obstacle because the method works better for galaxies that are more distant.

To determine distances, scientists using the *Hubble Space Telescope* relied on observations of "Cepheid variables," stars whose brightness changes in regular ways in a matter of days or weeks, and over periods that repeat as precisely as the beat of a clock. A vital characteristic of Cepheids is that the longer their periods, the greater their intrinsic brightness. Thus, measuring a star's period leads to a knowledge of its intrinsic brightness. Knowing that, an astronomer can calculate how far away that star must be to have its observed apparent brightness. One of the main reasons for building the *Hubble Space Telescope* was to study Cepheids in distant galaxies, but a flawed optical system prevented scientists from attempting to do so until the satellite was repaired in late 1993.

Scientists studied a score of Cepheids in a spiral galaxy known as Messier 100 and came up with a distance of 56 million light-years (a light-year is the distance light travels in one year), by far the most remote application of the Cepheid method. This distance implies a relatively young age for the universe. On the other hand, scientists believe that at least some stars in globular clusters, huge balls of stars associated with the Milky Way, have been shining for almost 20 billion years.

This paradox is not something new. There have been many estimates of the universe's age over the past several decades, and some of them have led to the same apparent contradiction. What makes the *Hubble Space Telescope*'s result different is that it is more precise than earlier efforts, and cannot be easily dismissed as the result of observational errors. This leaves two possibilities. Either scientists' knowledge of how stars age is seriously wrong, or their ideas on how the universe evolved are profoundly in error. Both of these prospects pose major challenges to theoreticians.

Other Planets? Planets orbiting other stars have been "discovered" for many decades, only to prove illusory. Astronomers may finally have found two bodies with a mass roughly similar to Earth's circling the pulsar PSR 1257+12 in the constellation Virgo. One has a period of revolution of 67 days and the other 98 days. There also may be another, Moon-sized body orbiting every 25 days. If so, this would be an unlikely location for planets, as pulsars (extremely dense, small, and rapidly rotating stars made of neutrons) are believed to be the remnants of titanic supernovae explosions. Life would be impossible in such locations because of the tremendous concentration of ionizing radiation. On the other hand, an earlier report of a planet with a period of 1.1 years in the same system seems to be spurious.

Indirect evidence suggests that a planet may be orbiting Beta Pictoris. This star is somewhat hotter, larger, and more massive than the Sun, but is known to have a disk of dust orbiting it. There are indications that the inner part of the disk has been depleted, and this could be done by a planet going around the star every 70 years or so at a distance some 20 times greater than the distance from the Earth to the Sun.

New "Neighbors." Astronomers discovered two galaxies that lie relatively close to our own. Despite their nearness, they are difficult to observe because of intervening clouds of dust in the Milky Way. One was found by radio studies. It is a large spiral galaxy known as Dwingeloo 1, similar to ours but about one-fourth the size, that lies some 10 million light-years away in the direction of the constellation Cassiopeia. The other was ferreted out by optical means. It is a dwarf spheroidal system that lies on the other side of the Milky Way from us. This galaxy is only some 50,000 light-years from the center of the Milky Way, far closer than the Clouds of Magellan, and thus appears to be our system's closest neighbor. Such a close approach to our own, much more massive galaxy should tear this satellite apart in the near future in astronomical terms.

Gamma Ray Bursts. For decades, artificial satellites from Earth have been detecting bursts of gamma rays that are distributed at random over the sky and last but a few seconds. Not one has been positively identified with a celestial object observed at any other wavelength, and scientists are at a loss as to what the bursts are due to, or even if they are relatively close to us or at vast distances. There are recent indications that they are at enormous distances, which would make them more powerful than supernovae and would pose a severe problem for theoreticians trying to explain the phenomenon.

In 1994, however, there were two intriguing glimpses into the enigma. In March a burst came from close to the direction of one recorded in July 1993. If the two events did indeed come from the same object, that would be proof that the source of the radiation was not destroyed in the process. Another development is even more surprising. It appears that the brightest such event is only ten times more intense than the faintest. This is an incredibly small range, for at X-ray, optical, and radio wavelengths sources differ in brightness by millions or even billions of times. At present there is no accepted explanation for this behavior.

A rare, for there are only three known, type of gamma-ray emitter gives off only "soft" (relatively long-wavelength) emission and consistently repeats. This year it was discovered that one of them, SGR 1806-20 in Sagittarius, lies in the same place as a supernova remnant. If the identification is correct, it raises the question as to why so few supernovae remnants are "soft gamma-ray repeaters."

See SPACE EXPLORATION.   R.A.S.

AUSTRALIA. The year 1994 began ominously with wildfires burning some 1.5 million acres (370,000 hectares) in New South Wales, ultimately reaching the outer suburbs of Sydney. Almost 200 homes were destroyed, but only four people died—a tribute to thousands of mostly volunteer firefighters. The year ended with most of New South Wales and Queensland stricken by drought and Victoria, South Australia, and Western Australia headed toward drought conditions.

Good News for the Economy. The nation seemed finally to have emerged from a prolonged recession. In the budget for the July 1994 to July 1995 financial year, Treasurer Ralph Willis predicted that by mid-1998, Australia's real output would rise by 22.5 percent and that growth would accelerate to 4.5 percent—driven, Willis said, by a 14.5 percent increase in business investment. Unemployment, Willis said, would fall from 10.5 percent to 9.5 percent by June 1995 and inflation would rise from 1.75 percent to just 2.25 percent. Willis's optimistic projections proved conservative. By midyear, consumer confidence had reached highs not seen since the late 1980s. Lending for houses reached record levels. By September, unemployment had fallen to 9.1 percent, and business investment was up almost 15 percent and still climbing.

Concerned that the economy might overheat, the Reserve Bank twice raised interest rates sharply, to 6.5 percent by the end of October. Consequently, mortgage rates rose from around 8.5 percent to 10 percent. The current account deficit also increased much faster than anticipated as imports surged and exports, affected by the drought, stayed stagnant. Indeed, agricultural economists estimated the drought would cost Australia more than Aus$2 billion in export income in the 1994-1995 financial year. It was becoming clear that Australia could not sustain a growth rate approaching 5 percent without danger of a trade deficit, a fall in the dollar's value, and as a result, a big hike in interest rates that would almost certainly choke off economic growth.

New Gains for Labor. Overall, it was a good year for Prime Minister Paul Keating and his Labor Party. Having won a federal election in March 1993 that virtually everyone believed Labor would lose, Keating was presiding over a surging economy.

The election's losing candidate, John Hewson, was clearly a leader under siege throughout the first months of 1994. Nothing he could say or do could unite the liberal and conservative factions of his Liberal and National parties' coalition. They were divided on whether Australia should become a republic, on legislation to deal with aboriginal land claims, on racial vilification laws, and on legislation to override Tasmanian laws making homosexual sex a crime. By May, opinion polls showed Hewson trailing Keating as the preferred prime minister by 53 percent to 29 percent.

Then, in May, the shadow treasurer, Alexander Downer, and the shadow attorney-general Peter Costello (the minority party members

Ring of fire. *In January wildfires swept along the coast of New South Wales, Australia, destroying parkland and grazing country and coming within miles of downtown Sydney.*

who would hold such positions if their party were in power), both threw their hats into the leadership ring. Hewson's fate was sealed. In a party leadership ballot on May 24, Downer was elected leader and Costello deputy leader.

Downer, who came from a distinguished Liberal Party family, was seen as a pragmatist and a consensus builder. But a series of political blunders—including misfires in his attempts to appeal to a broad range of party members—sent Downer's rating from an early high of 60 percent to 20 percent by October—a low point that even Hewson had not reached. Meanwhile, the coalition's infighting intensified. By year's end, Downer's leadership was in grave trouble.

Victims of Violence. In what appeared to be the nation's first political assassination, John Newman, a Labor Party MP for the New South Wales state parliament seat of Paramatta in Sydney's western suburbs, was shot dead outside his house after attending an evening meeting of his local branch of the Labor Party. The assassination was believed to be connected to Newman's campaign against Asian crime gangs in his area. Late in the year, Newman's killer or killers had not been caught.

In July, Khmer Rouge guerrillas in Cambodia took as hostages an Australian, a Frenchman, and an Englishman who were traveling on a train held up by the Khmer Rouge. The three were eventually killed by their captors, prompting calls for aid to be cut off from Cambodia. Foreign Minister Gareth Evans, however, insisted that Cambodia needed aid to be able to get its Army into shape to take on the Khmer Rouge.

Accusations, Gaffes, and Outrages. The former prime minister, Bob Hawke, released his long-awaited autobiography. In it Hawke accused Keating, his successor, of calling Australia the "arse end of the world" in 1990 and of saying he would not stay in "this joint" if Hawke refused to relinquish the prime ministership and hand over power to him. Many readers thought Hawke was embittered over losing the prime ministership to Keating in a party ballot in December 1991.

In the states, Victoria's premier, Jeff Kennett, got involved in the dispute between Greece and the former Yugoslav republic of Macedo-

Paul Keating

Australian Prime Minister Paul Keating marked 1,000 days in office in September, and even his opponents agreed he was in a class of his own among Australia's politicians.

In 1994, Keating promoted his goals of internationalizing Australia's economy and ending the country's status as a constitutional monarchy. In April he visited Vietnam and said the time had come to put the Vietnam War behind the two nations. In June, after the 50th anniversary of D day, Keating told British Prime Minister John Major that Australia could no longer have a British monarch as its head of state. Keating then met with President Suharto of Indonesia—and was criticized in Australia for failing to point out Indonesia's human rights abuses.

Perhaps Keating's greatest international triumph in 1994 was helping set a timetable for creating a regional free-trade zone at the Asia-Pacific Economic Cooperation forum summit held in November. APEC government leaders agreed to aim for the year 2020.   M.G.

nia by traveling to Greece and by calling Australia's recognition of the state of Macedonia a betrayal of Greeks. The numerically smaller Macedonian-Australians were outraged by Kennett's remarks. There was serious friction between the Greek and the Macedonian communities in Australia, with firebombings of cultural centers and churches.

In New South Wales, the minister for police in the conservative government of Premier John Fahey quit his post after female staff members alleged that he had sexually harassed them. Terry Griffiths admitted that he sometimes kissed and cuddled his female staff members but insisted that these signs of affection had no sexual connotations. Fahey told the state parliament that Griffiths had behaved appallingly and should also resign from parliament and from the Liberal Party. Griffiths refused to quit the party but said he would quit parliament at the next election.

See STATISTICS OF THE WORLD.   M.G.

AUSTRIA. After long negotiations a popular referendum was called for June 12 on the Austrian government's application to join the European Union. The Social Democrats (SPO) and People's Party (OVP)—the governing coalition—urged a yes vote, as did the fledgling Liberal Forum (LF). The Green Party opposed the measure, but the clear leader of the opposition was the mercurial Jörg Haider, leader of the Freedom Party (FPO). To almost everyone's surprise, the yes vote was 66.6 percent. Following parliamentary elections later in the year, the new Parliament ratified Vienna's accession treaty to the European Union in a 141-40 vote on November 11.

In the elections, held on October 9, the two dominant parties made their worst showing in 50 years, while the opposition made significant gains. Official results of the election (with changes from 1990 in parentheses) were: SPO 35.2 percent (–7.6), OVP 27.7 percent (–4.4), FPO 22.6 percent (+6.0), Greens 7.0 percent (+2.2), and LF 5.7 percent. The final seat allocation was SPO 65 (80 in 1990), OVP 52 (60), FPO 42 (33), Greens 13 (10), and LF 11. Opinion polls showed the number of undecided voters increasing over the course of the rather listless campaign. A crucial last-minute support shift from SPO to FPO occurred two weeks before the vote, when Haider revealed that some officials of the SPO-dominated Chamber of Labor were drawing salaries above $200,000. Franz Vranitzky, chairman of the SPO, was sworn in as chancellor on November 29.

In provincial elections in Carinthia, Salzburg, and Tyrol in March and in Vorarlberg in September, the SPO lost ground, while the FPO gained somewhat. In Carinthia, Haider held up postelection negotiations for three months in an unsuccessful attempt to reclaim the governorship from which he had been ousted in 1991 because of a pro-Nazi remark.

Economic indicators during the first eight months of 1994 were generally positive. Inflation held at 3 percent and unemployment fell to just above 4 percent, bringing the misery index (unemployment plus inflation) down to about 7 percent, from about 10 percent in 1993. However, Austria's national debt climbed to $100 billion, with a deficit of about $7 billion expected. Largely because of a slump in tourism, an overall negative balance of payments was expected for 1994.

See STATISTICS OF THE WORLD.   F.C.E.

AUTOMOBILE INDUSTRY. The automobile industry continued to rebound in 1994. Sales in the United States increased for the third straight year, and earnings of the U.S. Big Three automakers totaled a record $13.9 bil-

TV star. *To build consumer awareness of its Mercury Mystique sedan, Lincoln-Mercury launched a media advertising blitz to coincide with the automobile's debut in late September. The highlight was a promotion on the NBC television network in which a Mystique was given away on seven successive weeknights.*

Keep on truckin'. The 1995 Dodge Ram Club Cab pickup truck from Chrysler Corporation featured a backseat for passengers. Chrysler had a banner year, with its new products garnering great acclaim.

lion. Two of the Big Three—Ford Motor Company and Chrysler Corporation—earned record profits during the second, third, and fourth quarters. Europe bounced back from its deepest recession since World War II. And Japan finally shook a three-year sales slump.

Chrysler's Glory. Chrysler Corporation, the number three automaker in the United States, ranked as the nation's—if not the world's—top auto success story. Indeed, Chrysler seemed to hit a home run with each new product. The Neon small car—*Automobile* magazine's 1994 Car of the Year—took off so well that Chrysler quickly scrambled to expand production. In the 1994 model year (October 1993 through September 1994), the company sold more vehicles—2.1 million—than in any previous year.

About six of every ten Chryslers sold were classed as "trucks" (most of them Jeeps and minivans), which are more profitable than cars. Two new cars, the Dodge Stratus and Chrysler Cirrus, drew rave reviews in their preliminary showings, proving again that Chrysler knew how to excite buyers at first sight. Quality, though, loomed as a nagging concern. The company consistently scored below average on the industry's best-known quality scorecards, and executives urgently sought to bring about improvement.

Sales and Production. Sales of cars and light trucks increased again during the 1994 model year. The U.S. market rose 6.8 percent, to 14.6 million cars and trucks, nearly matching the gains that had been made a year earlier.

Most everyone shared the wealth. General Motors enjoyed the biggest increase among the Big Three, and Nissan stood out among the Japanese winners. European automakers also fared well. Luxury brands like BMW, Volvo,

Jaguar, and Mercedes-Benz seemed to have regained some bounce after being stunned in the late 1980s by Japan's new luxury divisions.

U.S. factories worked overtime to keep up with demand. Toyota began production at a second plant in Kentucky, and BMW opened the Europeans' only auto assembly plant in the United States. For the most part, though, automakers shied away from building new plants. They did not want to be left with too much production capacity the next time sales declined. Chrysler, for example, turned to around-the-clock work shifts in Detroit to keep up with demand for its Grand Cherokee sportutility vehicle.

In Europe sales rose about 5 percent after a disastrous 1993. Japan finally turned around after three losing years in a row. Canada snapped a five-year sales slump. Mexico, newly linked to Canada and the United States because of the North American Free Trade Agreement, rebounded too. Much of its sales growth came from U.S. imports, which flooded into Mexico after Nafta eased that nation's trade barriers.

Product. U.S. automakers showed more signs of a product renaissance. Oldsmobile brought out a stylish new entry, called the Aurora, that promised to rival Japanese and European luxury sedans. Chrysler followed the Cirrus sedan with a pair of sporty coupes, the Sebring and Avenger. And Ford introduced a new front-wheel-drive minivan, the Windstar, that seemed capable of challenging Chrysler's industry leaders.

The foreign competition did not stay still. Honda unveiled its first minivan ever, the Odyssey. Toyota's Lexus division brought out a new LS 400 sedan. The previous edition had risen from $35,000 to over $50,000 in just five years. But Lexus held the price on its 1995 model at $51,200.

Prices. At the start of the 1995 model year the Big Three raised prices an average of $369 over final 1994 prices. The Japanese raised their U.S. prices $458. The gap was not as wide as it had been a year earlier, but Japanese vehicles were still generally much more expensive than U.S. products.

As a result, the Japanese pushed leases; lease customers tend to "shop" monthly payments, not sticker prices. Some European automakers took dramatic steps to make their products stand out. Germany's Audi sliced an average of $4,200 off the price of each of its 1995 U.S. models. And Porsche shaved $12,000 from the price of its Carrera 4.

Earnings. The strong yen battered profits for most Japanese manufacturers. Nissan, for example, suffered its first back-to-back annual loss in the postwar era. Mazda and Fuji Heavy Industries (the maker of Subaru) also lost money. In Europe, however, automakers showed signs of regaining financial health.

In the United States each of the Big Three performed much better than in 1993. Ford earned $5.3 billion, more than twice as much as in 1993, while GM nearly doubled its earnings, to $4.9 billion; Chrysler earned $3.7 billion (its 1993 loss of almost $2.6 billion reflected a one-time accounting charge).

Yet the gains masked some wide differences in productivity and efficiency. Chrysler, for example, earned about $1,000 in the third quarter on every car and truck it made in North America. General Motors, in contrast, lost about $295 per vehicle.

Global Jockeys. Automakers' battles for superiority spanned the globe. Germany's BMW bought Britain's Rover Group. Renault of France and Volvo of Sweden, meanwhile, canceled plans to merge. Each of the Big Three, in one way or another, pushed global strategies. In the most ambitious example, Ford moved to streamline overlapping product plans for 200 countries into a single, global product strategy.

U.S. and Japanese trade negotiators failed to find ways to ease the huge U.S. trade deficit in autos and auto parts. While the governments quarreled, Japanese automakers continued to buy U.S. auto parts, and U.S. automakers sold more cars in Japan. Still, trade friction was apparent in a new U.S. law that required automakers to list a vehicle's "North American content" on window stickers of each new vehicle. In a victory for U.S. flag wavers, the United States built more vehicles than Japan for the first time since 1980.   D.V.

AVIATION. Large aerospace firms with diverse product lines turned to consolidation to cope with shrinking military budgets and overcapacity, while manufacturers of commercial aircraft felt the effects of the airlines' continuing financial hardships.

Commercial Aerospace. The U.S. aerospace industry underwent further transition in 1994. In two major developments, Northrop acquired Grumman in April, and in late August, Lockheed proposed consolidation with Martin Marietta, to take effect in early 1995. The major commercial aircraft manufacturers—Boeing, McDonnell Douglas, and Airbus Industrie—suffered through their fourth consecutive year of flat or declining orders in 1993. There was, however, hope for the future based on a projected growth in world air travel of 5.2 percent annually between 1993 and 2013, new orders from Asian-Pacific countries, and orders for replacements for aging aircraft and those that cannot be retrofitted to accommodate noise regulations. These predictions, however, were dependent to a large extent on how well manufacturers could improve their operating margins through increased revenues, stringent cost-cutting, and other measures to improve productivity in a highly competitive market environment.

Military Business. Military markets for major aerospace manufacturers have grown smaller as a result of the end of the cold war and the call for reduced spending by the administration of U.S. President Bill Clinton. The effects of the Bottom-Up Review, a far-reaching assessment of Pentagon needs conducted in 1993, continued in 1994. The BUR is intended to limit the size and structure of military forces, forecast the types of equipment necessary to meet certain contingencies (especially the ability of the United States to deal with two major regional conflicts at the same time), and determine the chronology of the

Fatal journey. *The wreckage of a USAir Boeing 737, as seen on a television monitor, rests in a wooded ravine near Pittsburgh. The September crash, which killed all 132 people aboard, was the fifth fatal accident involving a USAir plane within five years.*

Courtesy WPXI

phases that would bring about these changes. An important development in 1994 was a Defense Department memo targeting nine military programs for elimination or delay, including deferral of the Air Force's F-22 fighter project. The Air Force, however, was adamant that such action would damage its modernization programs and preferred to cut costs through force reductions and consolidation of roles and missions.

General Aviation. The general-aviation sector of the industry—manufacturing small piston-engine aircraft—has been in the throes of recession for more than a decade. There was some optimism that it would be helped by the General Aviation Revitalization Act, signed into law in August, which reduced the period of time in which lawsuits can be brought against a manufacturer for product liability from 40 years to 18. Another bright spot was the National Aeronautics and Space Administration's General Aviation/Commuter Element, a $63 million program designed, in the words of a NASA official, to "produce technology in response to industry's stated needs for revitalization and competitiveness."

Airlines. The airline industry experienced its fourth consecutive year of operating losses in 1993, and analysts predicted very modest growth for 1994. The industry was caught in a major dilemma: how to lower prices to match the competition while operating profitably to meet stockholder demands. Among many cost-cutting initiatives were the elimination of unprofitable routes and a possible transition away from the expensive hub-and-spoke routing system back to the traditional point-to-point system, used effectively by Southwest Airlines. Southwest was the model that all the major airlines seemed to want to emulate because of its low fares and steady profitability, but it too seemed to have hit some turbulence. By mid-September its stock had plunged 33 percent, although there was improvement later in the year. Meanwhile, American Airlines, the industry's leader, planned to trim a billion dollars from its budget, mostly by reducing labor costs.

After a number of fatal crashes in 1994, including two commuter plane crashes in six weeks, the U.S. government ordered a safety review of every U.S. airline and a speeding of new safety rules for commuter planes.

International Picture. European aerospace manufacturers faced the same woes that beset their American counterparts: shrinking military budgets and declining civil aircraft sales. One panacea, privatization of the nationalized European aerospace industry, was hindered by the firms' precarious financial situations, because governments were reluctant to lose money by privatizing before their companies were profitable. In commercial airline developments, members of the European Community's "Wise Men Committee" issued a report on Europe's airline crisis early in 1994. The report criticized the carriers' slowness to adapt to changing global air transportation conditions and rejected a delay in achieving European airline deregulation.   D.A.P.

Gunfight. *Azeri soldiers fire an artillery piece at their Armenian foes near the town of Fizully in January. Azerbaijan was trying to reclaim territory captured by Armenia during their six-year war, but the winter campaign cost the Azeri forces dearly.*

AZERBAIJAN. President Haidar Aliyev of Azerbaijan walked a tightrope in 1994 between Russian demands and opposition insistence on retaining Azerbaijan's independence.

Aliyev, who came to power after a 1993 military coup, continued to maintain pressure on the political opposition. Rallies were broken up by baton-wielding police, and a number of opposition leaders were arrested. In October 1994, Aliyev removed a former ally, Prime Minister Surat Huseinov, from office, saying he had been preparing a coup.

During 1993, Armenian forces had occupied all of Mountainous Karabagh (also known as Nagorno-Karabakh), an ethnically Armenian region within Azerbaijan, plus adjacent Azerbaijani territory. In May 1994 an informal cease-fire agreement was accepted by all parties, including those of the self-proclaimed Mountainous Karabagh Republic. Unlike previous cease-fires, this one seemed to be holding. Efforts to find a lasting settlement had foundered on the question of the status of Karabagh. Armenia demanded recognition of the region as, at least, a separate entity in negotiations or, at most, an independent state. Azerbaijan insisted that Armenian troops be withdrawn from specific strategic areas before such discussions commenced.

Asserting its role as "peacekeeper" in former Soviet republics, Russia sought to supplant the efforts of the Conference on Security and Cooperation in Europe, which had led efforts toward peace since 1992. Moscow moved from criticism of the negotiation process to demands that mostly Russian troops from the Commonwealth of Independent States be deployed as peacekeepers under CSCE or United Nations auspices. At a CSCE summit meeting in December, it was agreed that a multinational peacekeeping force would be sent once a formal cease-fire was in place.

The coup that brought Aliyev to power came just as his predecessor, President Abulfez Elchibey, was about to sign an agreement with a seven-company oil consortium comprising U.S., British, Norwegian, and Turkish firms. Aliyev renegotiated the pact, quickly bringing in Russia's Lukoil, which would receive 10 percent of Azerbaijan's share, a move widely believed to have been a result of Russian pressure. A new agreement was signed on September 20, 1994.

See STATISTICS OF THE WORLD.   A.L.A.

B

BAHAMAS. *See* CARIBBEAN BASIN; STATISTICS OF THE WORLD.

BAHRAIN. *See* STATISTICS OF THE WORLD.

BANGLADESH. Politics in Bangladesh during 1994 were highlighted by two events: the Taslima Nasreen affair, in which a woman writer was accused of heresy and threatened with death, and opposition party demands for new general elections under a neutral caretaker government.

Nasreen, who was trained as a physician, had written a number of novels about life in Bangladesh. Her 1993 novel *Lajja (Shame)*, about the anti-Hindu riots in Bangladesh following the destruction of a mosque in Ayodhya, India, in 1992, was seen by Islamic fundamentalists as blasphemous. After she was interviewed by an Indian newspaper in May 1994, the newspaper reported that she had questioned the validity of the Koran—revered by Muslims as the revealed word of God (Allah)—and had suggested that it needed revision. Nasreen denied this, stating that she said only that Islamic law, called the sharia, should be restudied and revised. The law is not considered revealed by most Muslims, but fundamentalists often accord it status approaching that of the Koran itself.

A warrant for Nasreen's arrest was issued on June 4, but she went into hiding. It seemed clear that the governing Bangladesh Nationalist Party (BNP) would have much preferred that the issue simply go away. Nasreen surrendered on August 3, was granted bail and freedom to travel, and fled to Sweden on August 10. Her trial on charges of "hurting the religious sentiments" of Muslims was originally scheduled for December but was postponed until 1995.

The other major political event, the demand by opposition parties for early elections overseen by a caretaker government, arose mainly from accusations of rigging by the government in a key by-election. (The next regularly scheduled elections were due in February 1996.) The call was spearheaded by the three principal opposition parties, the Awami League, the Jatiya Party, and the Jamaat-i-Islami—a group of parties that usually opposed each other on matters of policy. Insisting that the constitution be amended to meet their demand, they boycotted sessions of Parliament

Speaking loudly, carrying big sticks. A host of Islamic militants gathered in Dhaka in late July to demand the death of fugitive Bangladeshi author Taslima Nasreen, whose writings, they charged, had maligned Islam.

Taslima Nasreen

Bangladeshi feminist writer Taslima Nasreen has been compared to Salman Rushdie for her plight. A physician, poet, novelist, and columnist who advocates equal rights for women, Nasreen was accused of blasphemy in 1994 and condemned to death by Islamic religious fundamentalists.

Married and divorced three times, Nasreen smokes and wears her hair in a Western style—and the graphic sexual images found in her poems have shocked many conservative Bangladeshis.

Nasreen, who fled to Sweden in August, responded to her persecution by attacking not only Islamic fundamentalists but reformers in Bangladesh for doing too little. Even some sympathetic to her cause have questioned her judgment in excoriating her enemies and making self-serving statements. But her plight has made her something of an international cause célèbre; she was awarded the European Parliament's Sahkarov Prize for freedom of thought in November.   C.R.

Prime Minister Begum Khaleda Zia agreed to opposition demands that she resign before the next election.

The Bangladesh economy did not grow as rapidly as anticipated, the rate being 4.5 percent for the 1993-1994 fiscal year. Export targets were not met in several key areas such as garments, jute, and tea. Per capita income continued to be among the lowest in the world at about $220. Bangladesh has been lauded for its population control program, with a predicted 1.8 percent growth for the remainder of the 1990s. Because of pressure from fundamentalists, however, Zia canceled a scheduled trip to the September UN-sponsored population conference in Cairo.

See STATISTICS OF THE WORLD.   C.B.

BANKING AND FINANCE. The U.S. banking industry continued to prosper in 1994, as low (but rising) interest rates and a growing economy combined to produce the most profitable year ever. Banks elsewhere had a much more stressful year.

U.S. Banks. It was hard to overstate just how profitable U.S. banks had become. In the first nine months of 1994 the industry recorded earnings of $34 billion—a record. Much of the story was written by consumers who continued to take advantage of low interest rates to buy homes or refinance their mortgages. During those same nine months mortgage lending at banks grew by $48 billion, to a total volume of $971 billion. That was almost half the industry's total $2.2 trillion in loans.

But even as bank profitability soared, regulators began raising caution flags, warning that they were starting to see evidence of a growing laxity in lending standards. At the American Bankers Association's annual convention, Federal Reserve Board Chairman Alan Greenspan and Comptroller of the Currency Eugene Ludwig expressed concern that banks were extending credit to borrowers who would have been turned away in earlier years. Moreover, Greenspan said, banks were not charging high enough rates to compensate for the risks they were taking.

One sign of trouble for the future could be discerned in the steady rise of interest rates. After nudging rates up a quarter-point at a time for the first part of the year, the Fed demon-

and mounted demonstrations to promote their cause. While the government functioned with only the BNP present in Parliament, it was clear that the debate required under a parliamentary system was not taking place. Formal talks to resolve the impasse began in October. On December 28 most of the opposition members of Parliament resigned. The following day

strated on May 17 that it meant business in the battle against inflation. On that day the Fed hiked the federal funds rate—the rate banks charge for overnight loans—by a half-percent, and also raised the largely symbolic discount rate. Another hike, this time of three-quarters of a percent, came on November 15. The prime rate, which determines the interest charged to many businesses, began the year at 4.75 percent and ended it at 8.5 percent.

In stark contrast, central banks outside the United States kept rates low. Through the first ten months of the year short-term rates held steady in Japan and actually fell in Germany. Still, the dollar took a pounding all year long in the international currency markets. U.S. interest rates, while higher in nominal terms than those of Japan or Europe, were actually low when adjusted for inflation. As a result, foreign investors preferred Japanese yen and German deutsche marks to dollars.

Derivatives usage increased markedly during the year as well. Use of the controversial instruments—called derivatives because their value is calculated, or "derived," from an underlying security, such as stocks or currencies—increased to truly mind-boggling levels. Veribank, a research firm based in Wakefield, MA, estimated the face value of outstanding derivatives contracts at $15.3 trillion by midyear.

Helping direct attention to bank derivatives activity was the collapse of a bank-owned money market mutual fund that had relied heavily on the volatile instruments. All of the investors in the fund, U.S. Government Money Market Fund, were small banks. Representative Jim Leach (R, Iowa), who had taken a leading role on Capitol Hill on the derivatives issue, said that Congress should not overreact to the failure of a single, small fund, but warned that it was "impossible not to note that the failure is in the context of accumulating losses at very substantial, sophisticated institutions." His comment called to mind earlier episodes in which Bank of America, among others, had been forced to pump money into one of its own mutual funds to offset losses from derivatives. Although Leach and House Banking Committee Chairman Henry B. Gonzalez (D, Texas) sponsored legislation designed to tighten regulation of derivatives, the bill never really got a serious hearing. In December, in what some observers saw as a signal from the Fed that it was willing and able to supervise banks' derivatives activities without new legislation, the Fed reached a settlement with Bankers Trust, a prominent derivatives dealer, requiring the bank to make the risks of derivatives clearer to its customers. (In the same week Orange County, CA, filed for bankruptcy after its investment fund lost $1.5 billion because of investment strategies tied to derivatives; the figure was later revised to some $2 billion.)

Among a number of high-profile prosecutions of banks on fair-lending grounds, the case that awoke the industry like a firebell in the night was the Department of Justice's prosecution of Chevy Chase Federal Savings Bank. In that case, Justice unveiled a new theory: that Chevy Chase was guilty of discrimination not because of the way it treated customers, but because of where it chose to locate branches. In October the savings and loan industry's top regulator, Office of Thrift Supervision Director Jonathan Fiechter, attacked the Justice Department for employing "untested theories" in

A matter of interest. Alan Greenspan, chairman of the Federal Reserve Board, testifies on interest rates before the House Banking Committee in February. With the U.S. economy heating up, the Federal Reserve raised short-term interest rates several times during 1994 in an effort to ward off inflation.

bringing fair lending cases. And the industry's principal trade group, the Savings and Community Bankers of America, set up a $100,000 fund to help institutions fight Justice.

U.S. Banking Legislation. U.S. banking enjoyed a banner year on Capitol Hill. Most significantly, Congress passed an interstate banking law permitting banks to make acquisitions anywhere they please starting in September 1995. While interstate banking had already been permitted to some extent, the new law struck down existing requirements that interstate organizations be maintained as a patchwork quilt of individual institutions. Starting June 1, 1997, large interstate organizations such as BankAmerica Corporation and NationsBank would be able to realize huge cost savings by consolidating their individual banks into a single network.

Consumers could benefit as well, particularly those located in any of the multistate regions such as metropolitan New York or Washington, DC, in which individuals live in one state and work in another. Interstate branching will sweep away the old restrictions that made it illegal for a bank headquartered in New Jersey to accept a deposit through an affiliate in New York. Still, consumer groups warned that interstate banking would leave small communities at the mercy of large, out-of-state organizations that they said would sweep up deposits locally but lend elsewhere. Analysts agreed that the interstate banking law would lead to significant consolidation in the industry.

But interstate was only the tip of the iceberg for bank legislation. In the final days of the 1994 legislative session, Congress passed an omnibus bill that eased burdensome regulations on banks, rewrote money laundering laws, and made $382 million available for community development banks. The legislation fulfilled a major campaign promise for President Bill Clinton, who had vowed in 1992 to create a network of community development banks that would revitalize poor communities and give a boost to small business everywhere.

Another section of the community development bank bill did away with regulatory and accounting impediments that some lawmakers believed stood in the way of a secondary market in small business loans. Senator Alfonse M. D'Amato (R, New York), principal sponsor of the secondary market law, said it would make credit more readily available to small businesses by giving banks a new outlet in which to sell the loans.

International. While banks in the United States prospered, institutions elsewhere found themselves under considerable stress. In Japan the nation's trust banks suffered under a crushing burden of bad loans. At the government's urging, Mitsubishi Bank took over Nippon Trust, inheriting an estimated $5 billion in bad loans. Elsewhere, Mitsui Trust's bad loans stood at 8.1 percent of assets, while Yasuda Trust held nonpaying loans equal to 8.5 percent of assets—uncommonly high levels. The nation's big commercial banks were also burdened by bad loans—more than 6 percent of assets, according to the estimates made by private analysts.

The process of deregulation—known in Japan as "liberalization"—took a number of significant steps in 1994. In October the last of the interest rate controls was lifted. At the same time five commercial banks were granted licenses to offer investment management services.

Germany's central bank, the Bundesbank, engaged in a little financial deregulation as well. In May it announced that it would finally allow money market funds, the investment instruments which for years have made it possible for small savers in the United States to earn market rates of interest. In the United States the introduction of money market funds disrupted relations between banks and their customers, as families began buying the funds which, initially, were only offered by securities firms. In Germany, however, banks will control the money market funds.

The taming of inflation in Brazil clipped earnings at banks that had grown accustomed to dealing with rapidly rising prices. The nation's six state-owned banks were in bad shape and the government was forced to rescue three of its wards in October. The banks in the private sector remained in better shape, though they suffered from ties to the public sector institutions.

State-owned banks suffered elsewhere as well. In France government-owned Crédit Lyonnais announced in late September that it had lost some $850 million during the first half of the year, putting to rest its confident predictions of a turnaround. Despite the assistance of a government recapitalization, the bank was still so hamstrung by bad loans that it just barely met minimum capital requirements.

Mexican banks, privatized in the early 1990s, also found themselves struggling in 1994, turning in their worst earnings performance since they were cut free from government ownership. Banamex, the country's largest bank, saw its earnings drop by more than 50 percent in the second quarter, compared with the same quarter in 1993, and other banks reported similar results.

Encouraging signs. *Japanese stock dealers flash hand signals as they trade at the Tokyo stock exchange on February 1; the preceding day the Nikkei index, buoyed by optimism that the government was at last confronting Japan's economic distress, posted its fourth-largest one-day gain.*

But one of 1993's banking disasters shaped up as one of 1994's success stories. Spain's Banco Español de Credito, better known as Banesto, began to turn around under new ownership. Banco Santander had purchased the failed institution after its rescue by the Bank of Spain in 1993.

Meanwhile, foreign bank assets in the United States dropped for the first time in a decade. The trade newspaper, *American Banker,* reported in August that foreign bank assets fell 1.6 percent in 1993 (the latest period for which data was available). The decline reflected in part a drop in loan demand but also, more importantly, a decision by the banks to deemphasize lending in favor of fee-based, capital market services. R.M.G.

STOCK MARKETS

The world economy kicked into gear in 1994, but stock markets were battered, after a year of relatively easy money in 1993. The main culprit: rising interest rates, which lured investors to fixed-income investments, devalued corporate earnings and dividends, and increased borrowing costs for companies.

United States. The Dow Jones industrial average reached a high of 3,978 on January 31, 1994. Just a few days later the Federal Reserve hiked the federal funds rate, a key short-term interest rate, by a mere one-quarter of a percentage point, to 3.25 percent—the first of six increases in short-term interest rates that brought the federal funds rate to 5.5 percent by mid-November. The February rate hike, though modest, triggered a sell-off in stocks and bonds. Stocks recovered somewhat, but bonds did not. And as bond prices tumbled, long-term interest rates soared, causing stocks to fall again. By early April, after a second interest-rate hike, stocks had fallen 10 percent from the high.

Good corporate profits helped offset some of the damage of higher rates, and stocks ground their way higher for the next eight months. Aiding the move up was a boom in companies buying or merging with other companies. The dollar value of mergers and acquisitions was $339.4 billion, a fractional increase over the previous record year, 1988. However, shortly before Thanksgiving the market was hit by a sell-off that sent the Dow down 167 points in four days. The downturn was followed by a partial recovery. By the end of December the Dow was at 3,843, a 2.14 percent gain for the year. The Dow was an exception; all other U.S. market indexes were down some 1.5 to 3.5 percent.

The Americas. The Canadian stock market was bolstered by energy, metals, and forest products, but rising interest rates, a weakening currency, and separatist sentiment in Québec took a toll. By early November the Toronto Stock Exchange 300 Index had dropped 3.3 percent.

The once-hot Mexican stock market cooled as the economy slowed, interest rates rose, and political unrest rocked the country. Then, in late December, Mexico's currency, the peso, collapsed in the foreign exchange markets, losing some 30 percent in value against the dollar. Though Mexican stocks managed to contain their losses to 8.7 percent in local currency, U.S. investors in Mexico lost some 40 percent. The big winner in the Americas was Brazil, where foreign investors rushed in, impressed by economic reforms. In dollar terms the market was up 56 percent.

Europe. The economic recovery in Europe was just getting rolling when interest rates started to climb there, too. Only one of Europe's stock markets had a double-digit gain: Finnish stocks were up 16 percent. Europe's largest markets slumped—with the United Kingdom down 10.5 percent, Germany down 8.5 percent, and France down 17.1 percent.

Asia. In the first half of 1994 the Japanese market rose about 20 percent, largely on investments made by non-Japanese betting on an end to the bear market. Stock prices fell later, but still, at year's end the Nikkei 225 average was up 12.7 percent.

Hong Kong stocks plunged 31 percent during 1994. The standout performers in the Far East were South Korea, up 18.6 percent, and Taiwan, up 17.1 percent.   J.M.L.

BARBADOS. *See* CARIBBEAN BASIN; STATISTICS OF THE WORLD.

BEHAVIORAL SCIENCES. Research published in 1994 considered the relationship between aging and memory and the possibility that there may be universal standards of beauty, among other subjects.

Memory Loss and Old Age. Most Americans believe that losing one's memory is an inevitable part of getting old. A 1994 study that compared memory ability in young and old members of three distinct cultures suggested that this stereotype is a self-fulfilling prophecy. Harvard researchers found that in cultures with a negative attitude toward aging, the elderly tend to have more memory loss than in cultures that hold their old people in high esteem.

The researchers compared mainstream, hearing Americans, who often view the elderly as forgetful and cranky, with two groups that have more positive attitudes toward aging: Americans who see themselves as part of the American deaf culture and mainland Chinese. Americans who grow up deaf are less exposed than hearing Americans to negative attitudes toward aging from sources such as radio and television, and, as a community, they tend to regard their aged members highly. Chinese people, deriving values from Confucianism, respect the elderly and even practice ancestor worship.

The researchers recruited 30 participants from each group. Half of each group was younger adults (aged 15-30) and half was older adults (aged 59-91). Each volunteer took a series of memory tests. In one test, for example, a researcher gave volunteers ten seconds to memorize a pattern of dots on a grid. Then the volunteer was asked to reproduce the dot pattern on a blank grid. Young participants from all three cultures performed about the same on the memory tests. Among the older volunteers deaf Americans and Chinese scored higher than the hearing Americans.

What Makes a Face Beautiful. Beauty is more than an individual judgment of the beholder, according to a study published in 1994. Certain face shapes seem to be universally attractive, and the features of faces considered most beautiful differ in important ways from average-looking faces, reported British and Japanese researchers.

The researchers created a composite picture of a woman's face from photographs of 60 white British women between 20 and 30 years old. A second composite was made from the 15 photos rated most attractive by a panel of 36 male and female British adults. The researchers then generated a third picture by exaggerating the distinguishing characteristics of the second composite. A new panel of volunteers judged the second composite more attractive than the first and the exaggerated picture most beautiful. When the researchers made similar composites of photographs of young Japanese women, both British and Japanese observers found the exaggerated picture most attractive. Some features that distinguished the exaggerated composites from the average were higher cheekbones, a thinner jaw, and larger eyes relative to the size of the face. The researchers concluded that such cross-cultural agreement on the aesthetics of facial beauty may help explain the evolution of human face shape.

Defining Mental Disorders. A new edition of the psychiatrist's bible—the *Diagnostic and Statistical Manual of Mental Disorders,* or *DSM-IV*—was published in 1994 by the American Psychiatric Association. Distinguishing mental illness from eccentricities within the range of normal human behavior is more than tricky business; it can also be highly political. The fourth edition of the manual will be used for a decade to determine diagnoses, and whether a diagnosis can be made from the manual determines if insurers will pay for a pa-

tient's psychiatric care. Under new guidelines, diagnoses being considered for addition to the fourth edition had to be supported by more empirical findings than was required for earlier editions. For example, the authors determined that not enough evidence existed to list extreme symptoms of premenstrual syndrome as a diagnosis. The authors also placed more stress on the need to understand diagnoses in their social and cultural contexts and tried to make the book accessible to a wide array of mental health professionals.   B.H.

BELARUS. Belarus saw dramatic political changes in 1994. In January the Supreme Soviet voted to remove Stanislau Shushkevich from his post as its chairman (a position equiv-

Hey, good lookin'. A study found that certain face shapes seem to be universally attractive and that the features of beautiful faces differ from average features in important ways. The researchers made composite pictures of faces of British (top) and Japanese (bottom) women. The faces at left were rated average, and the center ones attractive; the ones at right deliberately exaggerate the attractive characteristics. Both British and Japanese observers rated the exaggerated pictures the most attractive, suggesting that aesthetic judgments of faces are similar across different cultures.

alent to head of state). Since his election soon after Belarus announced its independence from the Soviet Union in August 1991, Shushkevich had failed to create a solid political base for his program of moderate reform and political distance from Russia. After his removal the Supreme Soviet moved quickly to adopt a new constitution, which took effect in March. The presidential election provided for by the new constitution was held in June. Almost all observers felt that Prime Minister Vyacheslau Kebich was a shoo-in, but in a stunning upset Kebich was defeated by Alyaksandr Lukashenka, who received a decisive 80 percent of the vote in a second-round face-off with Kebich. Lukashenka was a political outsider who achieved notoriety through vague accusations of corruption.

These political changes had little immediate effect on the continually gloomy economic situation. Since the disruption of economic ties with Russia, the old Soviet-style economy was no longer viable, yet Belarus had refused to undertake market reforms. Industrial production had fallen by 10 percent in 1993 and was projected to fall more than twice as much by

Surprise winner. *In a stunning upset, Alyaksandr Lukashenka was chosen as the first president of Belarus in a July runoff election. An outsider and a decided underdog, Lukashenka campaigned on a platform of rooting out corruption and establishing closer ties to Russia.*

the end of 1994. At the same time inflation had reached as much as 40 percent in some months. The only solution seemed to be closer economic union with Russia. Soon after his election Lukashenka met with Russian President Boris Yeltsin and obtained some short-term concessions. In the fall he announced to a skeptical Supreme Soviet a market-oriented "program of urgent measures" to end the economic crisis. In November, Lukashenka rolled back some recently introduced liberalization measures, saying they were too hard on the poor. Under pressure from the International Monetary Fund, he later pledged to go ahead with market reforms.

See STATISTICS OF THE WORLD.   L.T.L.

BELGIUM. Belgium's federal coalition government headed by Jean-Luc Dehaene and the Walloon regional government was affected early in 1994 by the resignations of several ministers reportedly involved in a bribery scandal. All the ministers belonged to the Socialist Party (PS) of the French-speaking Walloon region and were implicated in a deal with an Italian helicopter manufacturer. One of those implicated was Guy Spitaels, longtime leader of the Walloon PS and chief minister of the Walloon region; he resigned from both positions. In the June elections to the European Parliament the Christian Democrats won seven seats; the Socialists and Liberals captured six seats each; and the right-wing Vlaams Blok and National Front won two seats and one seat, respectively. Later in the month Dehaene's anticipated nomination to the presidency of the European Commission was derailed by a British veto.

The process of decentralizing the country continued during 1994. Agreement was reached on May 31 on the division of state properties, pensions, the public workforce, and outstanding debts after Brabant Province was divided along linguistic lines. Brabant was the last of the nine Belgian provinces to give up its unitary administration.

Belgian paratroopers were sent to Rwanda in April to protect Belgian nationals there who were caught up in a renewed flare-up of the Rwandan civil war. After the loss of both civilians and military personnel the paratroopers were withdrawn. Diplomatic involvement continued, not least because of Belgium's special ties to the country, which prior to its independence had been part of a UN trust territory under Belgian administration.

The Belgian government exchanged diplomatic missions with the former Yugoslav republic of Macedonia in February. Relations with Libya were strained when Libyan embassy bank accounts were blocked by the Belgian government in accordance with UN sanctions related to the downing of Pan Am flight 103 over Lockerbie, Scotland, in 1988. In October, Belgian Foreign Minister Willy Claes took over as secretary-general of NATO.

Overall, Belgium's economic and fiscal situation showed improvement for much of the year. October projections put gross domestic product growth for 1994 at 1.7 percent. Inflation had slowed to about 2.8 percent, and the budgetary shortfall was less than anticipated. Unemployment, however, was high, reaching nearly 13 percent. Arms continued to be a major export item. France, Germany, and the Netherlands continued to be Belgium's primary trading partners.

See NETHERLANDS, THE; STATISTICS OF THE WORLD.   F.G.E.

BELIZE.   See STATISTICS OF THE WORLD.

BENIN.   See STATISTICS OF THE WORLD.

BHUTAN.   See STATISTICS OF THE WORLD.

BIOLOGY.   Among developments in biology that made news in 1994, seafloor tube worms were discovered to have an extraordinarily fast rate of growth, convincing evidence was reported for the existence of bacteria beneath the Earth's surface, and new research was published on biodiversity.

Fast Growth Near Hot Vents.   Marine tube worms, which live near hydrothermal vents (through which hot, mineral-rich water emerges from the seafloor), were found to grow much faster than scientists thought possible. Marine biologists who had been monitoring deep hot vents at a Pacific Ocean site found that since 1991, when an earthquake shook the area, tube worms were able to colonize the region in thickets and grow as long as 1.5 meters (5 feet). Meanwhile, "chimneys" formed from minerals in the vent water grew as tall as 10 meters (over 30 feet).

The findings indicate that tube worms, curious creatures that have neither eyes nor digestive tracts nor means for locomotion, are the fastest-growing marine invertebrates. Apparently, scientists' time schedules for change deep beneath the sea—long thought to be a region of slow development because of cold temperatures and high pressure there—will have to be altered.

Such hot vents, first discovered in 1977, occur on the ocean floor above volcanic fissures. They are difficult to study because they occur at great depths, but scientists were able to reach the site, which is roughly 800 kilometers (500 miles) southwest of Acapulco, Mexico, to the west of Costa Rica, in the research submarine *Alvin*.

New Ideas From Old Bones.   Two partial dinosaur skeletons from Africa found by researchers in Niger suggest that geologists' theories of continental drift may need review. The bones were from a plant-eating sauropod over 15 meters (50 feet) long and a meat-eating theropod that was roughly 8 meters (over 25 feet) long. The researchers dubbed the theropod *Afrovenator abakensis,* or "African hunter from In Abaka," after the place where the bones were found. The sauropod was left unnamed pending the discovery of a more complete skull.

Both dinosaurs lived roughly 130 million years ago, during Earth's Cretaceous period. The scientists were consequently surprised to find that the two dinosaurs closely resembled the *Allosaurus* and the *Camarasaurus,* two dinosaurs that lived in North America about 150 million years ago. Scientists have long believed that 200-300 million years ago there existed a giant landmass, called Pangaea, from which the continents of today were formed. About 170-180 million years ago, it is thought, Pangaea separated into a southern landmass and a northern landmass (including North America). During the Cretaceous period the African continent was still joined to the South American continent.

According to the traditional time schedule for continental drift, African dinosaurs of the Cretaceous period should more closely resemble dinosaurs from South America. But scientists say the newly discovered African dinosaurs differ markedly from the South

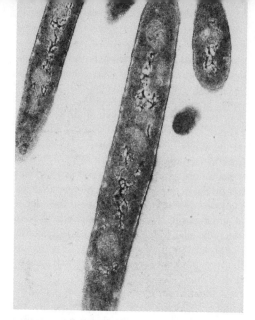

The lower depths. The discovery deep in the Earth of microbes cut off from other life on the planet for millions of years came as exciting news. Shown here (magnified thousands of times) are examples of a bacterium found nearly 2 miles below the Earth's surface. The microbe's proposed name: Bacillus infernus ("bacillus from hell").

The presence of bacteria below the Earth's surface demonstrates that decomposition of organic matter extends much deeper than had previously been suspected. These findings greatly increase the size of the biosphere—the portion of the Earth inhabited by living organisms. The fact that some of the species found in these samples are new to biologists indicates that these habitats, too, contribute to the diversity of life on Earth.

New Mammal Species. In July a new kangaroo species was reported. It was found in a remote mountainous region of central Irian Jaya, the Indonesian region of the island of New Guinea. The animal, a tree kangaroo, has long black fur over most of its head and back. Its front is white, and there are two streaks of white across its black muzzle and a white star in the middle of its forehead. Although the animal appears to be adapted to life in the trees, it apparently spends a great deal of its time on the ground. Members of this species are as big as a medium-sized dog, with a large adult male standing 1 meter (about 3 feet) tall and weighing approximately 15 kilograms (30 pounds). Its tail is about half a meter in length, the shortest, relative to body size, of any known kangaroo.

American dinosaurs of that period. The findings suggest that North America had a connection with Africa for a much longer period of time than previously thought.

Deep Life. Drilling in an area of Virginia called the Taylorsville Basin revealed bacteria 2,800 meters (9,200 feet) below the surface of the Earth. Rock at the site, one of six under exploration by the U.S. Department of Energy, was formed from sediment dating back 230 million years to the Triassic period, when early dinosaurs appeared. Scientists isolated and cultured about a hundred types of subterranean microbes that may be descendants of microbes from that era; they were sealed off from oxygen in temperatures up to 75°C (about 170°F). The drilling program, in existence since the mid-1980s, had isolated more than 5,000 microbes overall. Meanwhile, British researchers discovered bacteria in ocean sediments to depths greater than 500 meters (close to 2,000 feet) below the floor of the Pacific Ocean in the Sea of Japan. The scientists believed that bacteria are present at still greater depths.

The discovery of another new mammal species was announced in April—the giant muntjac or barking deer of Vietnam. The deer is distinct from the Vu Quang ox, discovered in 1992 in the same remote area, the Vu Quang Nature Reserve, which is located in northern Vietnam near the Laos border. The giant muntjac weighs 90 to 110 pounds, is larger than any other muntjac deer, and has a red grizzled coat. Scientists working in the area also reported evidence of two new bird species and a new tortoise species with a bright yellow shell.

Biologists working in Africa discovered what appear to be new species among the great apes. Analysis of DNA (deoxyribonucleic acid), the basic genetic material, from chimpanzees indicates that the West African chimpanzee is so different from the other chimp populations that it may be considered as belonging to a separate species. Similar work with gorilla DNA indicates that the West African lowland gorilla may belong to a different species from that of East African gorillas. In both cases researchers noted that further work on behavior, physiology, and other characteristics would be needed before classification into new species would be warranted, and the new findings indicated how much there is still to learn about even such well-studied species as the apes.

The chimps were studied using a particularly ingenious method to obtain samples for DNA testing. To avoid anesthetizing the animals to get tissue samples, they used chimp hair collected from the nests the animals build in trees. Chimpanzees usually use a nest for only one night, so it is relatively easy to examine recently used nests when the biologist knows the identity of the animal that slept in it.

Besides indicating the genetic differences between chimpanzee populations, the study also yielded information on the relationships among animals within a single group. The males in a group turned out to be more closely related to each other than were the females, a finding that correlates well with observations on behavior. Males are much more likely to cooperate with each other and assist each other than are females. By aiding animals related to him, a male chimpanzee is increasing the survival chances of individuals genetically related to him, and thereby, indirectly, of his own genes.

Cooperative behavior by a female chimpanzee would not provide her with as much of a genetic advantage, because the females she would be aiding would probably not be closely related to her.

Colorful Offspring. While the significance of some chimpanzee behavior has been explained, the significance of a newly discovered element in bird behavior is still a mystery. In studies on the American coot reported in 1994, Canadian biologists found that parents are more likely to feed offspring with bright plumage than those without this decoration. It has puzzled biologists that day-old coot chicks have bright orange ornamental plumes; the color would seem to be a liability, making the chicks much more obvious to predators. To see if the bright color influenced parental behavior, the researchers trimmed the colored feathers on half the chicks in each of several coot nests. They found that the parents fed the chicks with the colorful plumage in preference

Sex Differentiation Gone Batty

Since the dawn of the women's movement, men have come a long way in improving their reputation as parents. Few now doubt that fathers can change diapers and mash bananas as capably as Mom. Breast-feeding, however, remains a strictly female domain.

Except, perhaps, among bats. In February 1994, scientists reported capturing in Malaysia several male Dayak fruit bats with visibly swollen breasts. When gently squeezed, the breasts produced small amounts of milk.

Could the bats have evolved in such a way that males can nurse babies? No male bats were seen feeding their young, and the scientists suggested that milk production could result from an unusual diet or exposure to pollutants. But pollutants have been blamed for causing reproductive defects, and the bats' reproductive systems appeared normal.

Will bat fathers prove to be as nurturing as bat mothers? The researchers planned to investigate further.

to their experimentally altered and duller nestlings.

While it has long been known that bright ornamentation in males can influence the mate choice of females in many bird species, this is the first identified case of ornamentation influencing parental care.

It may be that the bright feathers indicate the healthiest chicks, which are most likely to benefit from feeding, or the brightest feathers may belong to the youngest chicks and thus be a way for parents to identify the offspring most in need of food.

Magnetic Migrations. Scientists are homing in on the ways some animals use the Earth's magnetic field to help them find their way when migrating over long distances. In 1994 there was reported compelling evidence that after hatching on Florida or Caribbean beaches, loggerhead turtles navigate to feeding grounds in the Sargasso Sea by way of an internal magnetic compass. After five to seven years they use their magnetic compasses to return to the beaches on which they hatched.

Several years ago scientists discovered particles of the magnetic mineral called magnetite in turtles' brains. In the new study, to test the hypothesis that loggerheads use the Earth's magnetic field to orient themselves, the researcher placed the hatchlings in a tank of water surrounded by a magnetic coil and put the hatchlings in harnesses tethered to a swivel arm that was in turn connected to a computer that recorded where the turtles swam. He found that he could get the turtles to change direction by turning the magnetic coil and thus reversing the magnetic field. The study shows that it is very plausible that when the hatchlings reach the Gulf Stream, they ride the current and rely on their magnetic inclination compasses to tell them when to turn south.

The researcher also found that the young turtles oriented themselves magnetically according to the light they first see. Previous work suggested that when the hatchlings emerge from nests at night, they are drawn to the sea by an attraction to the moonlight or starlight reflecting off the water. In the new research, if the light in the experimental tank first came from the east, the turtles swam east; if it was first from the west, the turtles swam west. Initially, however, the turtles swam into waves, no matter which direction the waves came from. The researcher believes that swimming into waves is a strategy for heading offshore and that the magnetic compass takes over once the turtles reach the open sea, where the waves come from all directions.

In a study of magnetoreception in the honeybee, biologists from Taiwan have found the cells that appear to be responsible for the insect's ability to detect a magnetic field and use it for homing. In honeybees, trophocytes surrounding the insect's abdominal sections are the only cells that contain iron granules. The researchers found that the magnetite crystals within the trophocytes are organized into lattices that can be permanently magnetized. They also discovered that the trophocytes are in contact with nerve cells so that it is possible that information on magnetic orientation can be transmitted from the trophocytes to the nervous system.

Honeybee Population Declines. While some researchers are trying to unlock the mysteries of honeybee navigation, others are attempting to stem the decline in the honeybee population in the United States. Besides economic factors that make beekeeping and honey making less financially attractive, a major cause of the decline is the introduction of two parasitic mites. One mite species invades the respiratory system and kills by suffocating the bee, and the other consumes the insect's circulatory fluid, or hemolymph. Besides the threat these parasites pose to honey production, they also

Sense of direction. *Scientists reported a breakthrough in understanding how loggerhead sea turtles navigate large areas of ocean. It seems that the animals carry a sophisticated magnetic compass in their heads that helps them sense direction, as well as how far north or south they have traveled. The loggerhead shown here swimming in a tank is wearing a harness connected to recording equipment that monitors its movements.*

threaten agriculture, since honeybees are needed to pollinate many crops, including almonds, apples, pumpkins, and alfalfa.

Cleanup. One form of pollution that seems to be alleviated by nature is atmospheric PAHs, polycyclic aromatic hydrocarbons produced by incomplete combustion. Researchers reported that over 40 percent of PAHs can be removed from the atmosphere by vegetation. When the vegetation dies at the end of the growing season, the PAHs are then incorporated into the soil and thus are permanently removed from the atmosphere. While there has been a great deal of discussion about the importance of vegetation for the removal of carbon dioxide from the atmosphere, this study indicates that vegetation may also be important in controlling other forms of pollution as well.

Diversity and Productivity. Many ecologists accept the idea that biodiversity is good, that ecosystems with more species are better than those with few, but it has been difficult to gather evidence to support this idea. In April, however, scientists at Britain's Ecotron facility reported on an experiment that suggested plant productivity increases when the biodiversity of the plant community is increased. The Ecotron contains environmental chambers where light, temperature, humidity, and other factors can be carefully controlled and where life processes such as respiration and decomposition can be measured. In the chambers the researchers established communities of plants and animals with 9, 15, or 31 species.

The chambers with the most species turned out to be the most productive. In fact, plant productivity increased twofold to threefold as biodiversity increased twofold to threefold—perhaps in part because of the increased amount of light intercepted and used, since more plant species in the same plot can fill the three-dimensional space more completely than fewer species can.

Meanwhile, a study of grassland plots in the United States supported the idea that diversity increases the resilience of an ecosystem—that is, its ability to bounce back after a disturbance. Researchers compared plots of grassland containing different numbers of species. A drought in 1987 and 1988 reduced productivity in all the plots, but those with the greatest number of species had smaller reductions and recovered in one season, as opposed to more than four seasons needed in the plots with five or fewer species. The researchers also found, however, that the greatest gains in stability came with the first additions of species to the plots. Further additions had markedly less effect.

Pollination Puzzle Solved. A scientific question dating back to the days of Darwin seems to have been answered. Botanists long wondered why some plants can fertilize themselves and others must rely on cross-pollination with other plants of the same species. Researchers, working with the genes of petunias, recently reported finding direct evidence of a self-incompatibility gene in plants that cannot pollinate themselves.

According to the researchers, the gene, called an S gene, is designed to let a plant's pistil recognize pollen produced by itself. The gene for self-recognition is turned on in some plants but not in others. To test their hypothesis, researchers altered the petunias' self-recognition gene, inserting so-called antisense DNA, which mirrors normal DNA. The modified petunias were able to fertilize themselves. The discovery could be useful in commercial agriculture. M.C.F.

BLACKS IN THE UNITED STATES. See MINORITIES IN THE UNITED STATES.

BOLIVIA. In January 1994, Bolivian President Gonzalo Sánchez de Lozada sent to Congress proposed legislation to authorize the privatization of a number of government-owned enterprises, such as the oil and power companies. Congress passed the legislation in March. It provided for 50 percent of the stock in privatized companies to be distributed equally among adult citizens, with the other 50 percent to be put up for sale to private investors.

In April the main labor organization, the Central Obrera Boliviana, launched a general strike. The main demands were a doubling of the minimum wage and larger raises for public employees than the 8 percent across-the-board increase offered by the government. There were several weeks of hunger strikes, demonstrations, and roadblocks, and military units were deployed. On May 7 the government agreed to an increase in the minimum wage and to raises of 6 to 12 percent for public employees.

Ex-President Jaime Paz Zamora retired from politics in March after officials began investigating his alleged involvement with drug traffickers. Meanwhile, farmers from the coca-growing Chaparé region demonstrated against planned government eradication of coca plantations. In September, after 3,000 growers had marched 300 miles to La Paz to protest the government's coca policy, the president agreed to reassess it. (Earlier in the year it had been reported that coca paste and the cocaine extracted from it accounted for 13 to 15 percent of Bolivia's gross domestic product.)

In August, Sánchez de Lozada predicted a GDP increase of 4.2 percent for the year. Nontraditional (that is, other than tin) exports rose 78 percent in the first half of 1994, and annual inflation was about 7 percent. The country received new loans earmarked for education, mining, and upgrading tax administration from the Inter American Development Bank and the World Bank, among others.

See STATISTICS OF THE WORLD. R.J.A.

BOOK PUBLISHING. The financial condition of U.S. book publishers improved moderately in 1994 as savings from previous years' staff and title cutbacks began to take effect.

Sales. Book sales in 1993 rose 6.4 percent, to $17.993 billion from $16.918 billion the previous year, according to figures released by the Association of American Publishers. Continuing trends of past years, the adult hardcover category jumped 14.9 percent, to $2.5 billion, while children's paperback titles rose 12.9 percent, to $369 million. The largest drop was in children's hardcover, down 9.8 percent. This was attributable in part to customer price resistance. Another drop was in mail order, down 4.6 percent, reflecting the erosion of book club business. Sales by the top ten U.S. book publishers increased 9 percent during 1993, to $3.9 billion, according to *Publishers Weekly.*

Nonfiction. "Instant books"—books written and published within weeks—tied to murder, mayhem, and scandal became ever more popular and successful in 1994. O. J. Simpson, accused of murdering his ex-wife and a friend of hers, provided the most grist for the instant-book mill. Within hours of the June 12 slay-

Low fat, high sales. In the Kitchen With Rosie, *a collection of low-fat, low-sugar, low-salt recipes from Rosie Daley, personal cook for television talk-show host Oprah Winfrey, became one of the fastest-selling books in U.S. history, with half a million copies moving off the shelves in the first five weeks after publication. At left, Daley with some of her creations.*

Profitable prophecy. James Redfield's Celestine Prophecy—*a parable, about an ancient manuscript, that was touted as able "to change lives forever"—shot to the top of the fiction best-seller lists in 1994.*

ings, St. Martin's Press commissioned an instant book on the murder. The paperback book, *Fallen Hero* by Don Davis, was published in July. In the weeks following Simpson's arrest, other titles were signed up, including one by Joe McGinniss, author of several true-crime titles.

The Simpson book making the biggest splash was *Nicole Brown Simpson: The Private Diary of a Life Interrupted* by her friend Faye Resnick, released in October. Although some observers doubted Resnick's claim that the book was based on a diary as told by Nicole, the title hit the lists running. The book received one of the most effective, unintentional plugs ever when the judge slated to preside over the Simpson trial, Lance Ito, forbade potential jurors to read it.

During the year several best-selling books chronicling the lives of Britain's royal family caused such scandal that some people questioned whether the monarchy would survive. First came *Princess in Love* by Anna Pasternak (great-niece of Russian poet and novelist Boris Pasternak), in which a former British Army officer alleged that he and Diana had had a four-year affair. Several weeks later the royals took another hit when a biography of Prince Charles (written with his cooperation) ap-

peared. In *The Prince of Wales* by Jonathan Dimbleby, the prince said his marriage was a sham and that his father had pressured him to wed Diana.

The single most effective promoter of books was Oprah Winfrey, whose casual mention of a book on her talk show could result in hundreds of thousands of additional sales. Although she backed out of writing her memoirs in 1993, she became involved in another huge best-seller in 1994: *In the Kitchen With Rosie: Oprah's Favorite Recipes* by her cook, Rosie Daley. After Oprah plugged the book on the show, it boiled to the top of the charts.

In what was probably the largest advance offered during the year, Alfred A. Knopf paid Pope John Paul II more than $6 million for *Crossing the Threshold of Hope.* The book crossed the threshold of best-sellerdom, reigning at the top of the lists for weeks. This was the first of the pope's books to be aggressively marketed to a general audience.

As always, political books were a strong category. Several politicians with presidential aspirations wrote books during the year. William J. Bennett, the former Reagan-Bush appointee, came out with a surprise best-seller, *The Book of Virtues,* readings and commentaries on living the correct life according

113

to Bennett. Former Vice President Dan Quayle's memoir *Standing Firm,* promoted in an author tour that some analysts said was a rehearsal for a presidential campaign in 1996, stood firmly on the best-seller lists for weeks.

Among other political memoirs that appeared on best-seller lists, Barbara Bush's memoirs drew an attentive audience. Titles by two political figures linked by Watergate—both of whom had died recently—also made the lists: Richard Nixon's *Beyond Peace* and H. R. Haldeman's *The Haldeman Diaries.* Several titles analyzing the Clinton presidency appeared in 1994. Bob Woodward's book *The Agenda* was the most popular of these titles, soaring onto the lists after publication.

Considerable controversy was sparked by at least two political and historical works. In *The Bell Curve: Intelligence and Class Structure in American Life,* Richard J. Herrnstein and Charles Murray explored class, ethnicity, and differences in intelligence. *Strange Justice* by Jane Mayer and Jill Abramson rehashed the controversies surrounding Supreme Court Justice Clarence Thomas and generally supported Anita Hill's allegations.

Nonfiction medical books making it onto the lists later in the year included *The Hot Zone* by Richard Preston, about a contagious virus that kills people by liquefying their organs. *Listening to Prozac* by Peter Kramer apparently tapped into a needy market.

In the biggest fad category of the year were books depicting stereographs—images that pop into 3-D after a few moments of staring. *Magic Eye* by Thomas Baccei started the trend. It was followed by *Magic Eye II* and *Magic Eye III* as well as by *Another Dimension, Do You See What I See?,* and *Stereogram.* Each book sold hundreds of thousands of copies.

Fiction and Poetry. In January, Michael Crichton showed his magic touch yet again: His *Disclosure,* about a man who both suffered sexual discrimination and was falsely accused of it, jumped to the head of the best-seller lists upon publication. The most popular author of the past several years, John Grisham, recaptured the top spot for part of the year with his legal thriller *The Chamber.*

Early in the year the PBS *American Playhouse* production of *Tales of the City* by Armistead Maupin pulled the 1970s story collection back onto the best-seller lists. In a similar way, the popularity of the quirky movie *Forrest Gump* propelled the novel on which it was based onto the lists. In an unusual twist, *Gump* spawned several other titles. One by *Gump* author Winston Groom, called *Gumpisms,* was a collection of Gump wit and wisdom. Another was the *Bubba Gump Shrimp Co. Cookbook.*

E. Annie Proulx showed the power of literary awards when her *Shipping News* sailed onto the lists after she won the National Book Award and Pulitzer Prize. Joseph Heller's sequel to *Catch 22,* called *Closing Time,* hit a catch-22 of its own: Most fans of the original book liked it so much that they saw no need for a follow-up—and didn't flock to this one.

Thrillers and mysteries by familiar names crowded onto the best-seller lists. Robin Cook scared readers with *Fatal Cure,* a medical thriller. Despite its title, V. C. Andrews's posthumously published *Ruby* was in the black. Dick Francis raced to success with *Driving Force,* while Frederick Forsyth smashed onto the lists with *The Fist of God.* Readers were kept awake by Stephen King's *Insomnia. A Debt of Honor* was Tom Clancy's offering.

Romance continued to be a strong category. Danielle Steel showed success was no accident with her *Accident* and followed that success with *The Gift,* a short retrospective novel that some observers thought resembled *Bridges of Madison County. The Gift* sold at a faster rate than any of Steel's preceding best-selling novels.

A still-unfinished novel by a 44-year-old British screenwriter, Nicholas Evans, set two records. Robert Redford's studio agreed to pay $3 million for the movie rights to *The Horse Whisperer,* and Dell Publishing offered a $3.15 million advance for the manuscript (due to be completed by year's end). The advance was thought to be the largest ever for North American rights to a first novel, and the Redford bid was apparently an all-time record for such a work. J.M.

BOSNIA-HERCEGOVINA. In 1994 two new plans to end the war in Bosnia-Hercegovina were introduced. The balance of power among Muslims, Croats, and Serbs shifted during the year, but by year's end the advantage seemed to lie with the Serbs.

The Washington Agreement. Talks between the warring parties on a plan, first proposed in 1993, to end the hostilities in Bosnia-Hercegovina by partitioning the country into three ministates, for Serbs, Muslims, and Croats, resumed in January 1994. The talks were mediated by representatives of the United Nations and the European Union. The only apparent obstacle to agreement was a dispute between the Serbs and Muslims over 3 percent of Bosnia's territory. However, the Muslim-dominated Bosnian government, never fully satisfied with the plan, refused to accept it after a new and more favorable American initiative was launched in February.

The Washington agreement, as the U.S. initiative came to be known, was accepted by the Muslims and the Croats in March. It sought to preserve the unity of Bosnia-Hercegovina by shifting the balance of power. The agreement's main feature was the ending of hostilities between the Croats and Muslims, accomplished through the creation of a Muslim-Croat federation within Bosnia-Hercegovina, to be followed by a parallel confederation between the new federation and Croatia. Although the agreement initially left out the Serbs, it envisioned that the Serbs would be either encouraged or pressured to join the federation. The Serbs, however, never really indicated that they seriously thought about joining.

The Bosnian government accepted the Washington agreement because it effectively ended the war with the Croats, thus allowing them to concentrate their forces against the Serbs, and because it sought to preserve the country's territorial integrity.

However, the agreement was not fully implemented, as both sides displayed more interest in consolidating their hold on territories within their control than on integrating into a true federative system.

Contact Group Plan. Hoping to build upon the Washington agreement, a "contact group" of great powers offered in July yet another plan to end the war. The United States, Russia, France, Britain, and Germany created a map that would divide Bosnia-Hercegovina along ethnic lines, giving the Muslim-Croat federa-

tion 51 percent and the Serbs 49 percent of the country. The group also proposed constitutional principles that would at least formally preserve the sovereignty and territorial integrity of Bosnia-Hercegovina in a loose federation in which the Serbs were promised the right to strong ties with Serbia.

The Bosnian government and the Bosnian Parliament halfheartedly accepted the contact group plan. The Bosnian Serb leader Radovan Karadzic and the self-styled Bosnian Serb Parliament rejected it, even following intense pressure from Serbian President Slobodan Milosevic, the dominant political figure in

War and peace. In Sarajevo, Bosnia, two men carry a wounded person from the marketplace after it was hit by a mortar shell; 68 people were killed.

neighboring Yugoslavia, and other Yugoslav government officials, who were eager to have international sanctions against their country eased. In late August, in an effort to avert a rift between Serbs, the Bosnian Serbs held a referendum on the contact group's plan; 96 percent of the voters rejected it. Meanwhile, on August 4, seeking to avoid a dramatic tightening of sanctions against Yugoslavia, Milosevic ordered the closing of Serbia's borders to all goods going to the Bosnian Serbs, except for food and medicine.

Fighting Continues and Escalates. On February 5 some 68 people were killed when a mortar shell exploded in a Sarajevo market. A few days later, after hastily called talks between the Bosnian government and Bosnian Serbs, a cease-fire began. Later in the month, following a NATO ultimatum to the Bosnian Serbs, a heavy-weapons exclusion zone went into effect around Sarajevo, ending the Serbs' shelling of the city. Also in February, NATO planes shot down four suspected Bosnian Serb jets on February 28 after they violated the no-fly zone (a ban on military flights) over Bosnia-Hercegovina imposed by the United Nations in 1992, the first such action by NATO. Late in March, Serbian forces attacked the Muslim enclave of Gorazde, a UN-protected area. NATO planes hit Serbian positions near that city on April 10 and 11. Faced with a NATO ultimatum, the Serbs began to withdraw two weeks later.

During the summer the Army of Bosnia-Hercegovina launched a series of probing attacks, mostly small-scale actions designed to exhaust Bosnian Serb forces and ammunition. The Bosnian government imported large quantities of small arms and ammunition through Croatia. Army units were trained and redeployed from the Sarajevo area, where the cease-fire mostly held, to front lines in northern and central Bosnia. The Army was also able to defeat rebel Muslim forces loyal to Fikret Abdic in the Bihac enclave, another UN-protected area.

In October the Army launched major offensives from Bihac, the Kupres Plateau, and the southeast part of the Sarajevo protected area. The attacks seemed to catch the Bosnian Serbs unprepared and gave the mostly Muslim Army its greatest victories of the war. Within one week, however, the Bosnian Serbs managed to take back all the territory they had lost around Bihac, and in late November they attacked the town itself, with help from forces from the Serb-held Krajina region in Croatia. In retaliation, NATO planes bombed an airfield in Krajina and three Serb-controlled missile sites near Bihac. On November 27, as the Serbs tightened their noose on Bihac, the Bosnian government accepted a UN plan for a cease-fire in the area. As the long-standing dispute between the UN and NATO over the use of force against the Serbs came to a head, virtually eliminating the air strike option, initial UN attempts to get both sides to accept a three-month truce for Bihac and for Bosnia-Hercegovina as a whole were a failure.

Three members of the contact group—Russia, Britain, and France—pressed for an amendment to their peace plan that would allow the Bosnian Serbs to federate with Serbia. The United States and Germany opposed this. Meanwhile, the Bosnian Serbs brought UN operations to a halt by, among other actions, taking UN peacekeepers as hostages.

Earlier, some countries had talked of withdrawing their troops from the UN Protection Force if large quantities of weapons began to reach the Bosnian Army after the United States ended its enforcement of the UN-mandated arms embargo in November. By December there were suggestions that the UN might withdraw from Bosnia-Hercegovina altogether. In an unexpected turn of events in mid-December former U.S. President Jimmy Carter got the Bosnian government and the Bosnian Serbs to agree to a seven-day cease-fire, followed by a cessation of hostilities that began on January 1, 1995. The cessation of hostilities was supposed to last four months. During these four months, it was hoped, peace talks would begin under the auspices of the contact group. But it was clear that there were still major differences between the government and the Bosnian Serbs, including differences over the status in the proposed negotiations of the contact group's peace plan.

See Statistics of the World. O.K.

BOTSWANA. *See* Africa; Statistics of the World.

BRAZIL. In 1994, in one of the most dramatic turnarounds in its history, Brazil elected Fernando Henrique Cardoso president. Inroads were made by a program to curb inflation, and the whole country went wild when its soccer team won the World Cup in July.

A Remarkable Election. In the presidential election on October 3, former Finance Minister Fernando Henrique Cardoso polled 53 percent of the vote, enough to avoid a runoff against his nearest challenger, Luis Inacio ("Lula") da Silva. Cardoso had spent years during the military dictatorship of 1964-1985 in exile, lecturing at prestigious U.S. universities. A member of the center-left Social Democratic Party, he won the support of business leaders for the tough anti-inflation program he had authored as finance minister and for his promise to renew efforts to privatize state companies and maintain a foreign debt accord he had negotiated.

Cardoso's victory was even more remarkable given that, at the end of June, he had only 17 percent support in the opinion polls to Lula's 40 percent. The victory, accompanied by significant gains by centrist political parties in Congress and state governorships, created a surge of optimism that replaced the resignation Brazilians felt for much of the year. His inauguration took place on January 1, 1995.

Corruption and More. In 1994, as in 1993, the country was plagued by corruption scandals. In April, after a yearlong investigation of the popular numbers racket, *jogo do bicho,* it was revealed that 150 prominent officials were on the take, including ex-President Fernando Collor de Mello (who fared better in December when he was acquitted of the corruption charges that had led to his resignation in 1992) and even Herbert de Souza, the popular leader of the national antihunger crusade. Also in April, Congress expelled some of the 18 members implicated in a budget committee kickback scheme.

Adding to the disillusionment, rumors of military plots against the government surfaced, there were shoving matches in Congress, and the lack of quorums stalled efforts to reform the constitution.

The Sporting World. In May the nation mourned the death of idol and three-time For-

One more vote. Brazilian presidential candidate Fernando Henrique Cardoso casts his ballot in the October election. Cardoso, the designer of Brazil's economic stabilization plan, won easily.

mula One world champion Ayrton Senna after a crash in a race in Italy. In July there was national rejoicing when Brazil defeated Italy to win an unprecedented fourth World Cup soccer championship, its first since 1970. (*See the feature article* WORLD CUP '94: SOCCER'S BIG SHOW COMES TO THE UNITED STATES.)

An Improving Economy. Economic news was mostly good. The gross domestic product was projected to grow by 5 percent in 1994, about the same as in 1993. The government reduced tariffs on 13,000 products, including medicines, cleaning products, and appliances; the resulting surge in imports was accompanied by a tremendous increase in exports to the United States, despite weather-related problems with the coffee and orange crops.

Cardoso's dramatic election victory was mirrored by his equally dramatic attack on inflation, which had soared to over 2,000 percent in 1993 and continued to be a major problem through much of 1994. In February, while still finance minister, Cardoso introduced a new plan to cut inflation drastically and eliminate the huge budget deficit. Under the plan, prices were gradually converted from the cruzeiro real to a newly introduced Unit of Real Value. The URV, which was pegged to the U.S. dollar, took the place of a number of indexes used to adjust wages, rents, and the like. The URV was transformed in July into a new currency—the sixth in 13 years—the real. Following the introduction of the URV there was an initial wave of strikes protesting the erosion of purchasing power.

By September, however, monthly inflation, which stood around 45 percent in June, had

Everyone's favorite shrink. *NBC's successful sitcom* Frasier, *in which Kelsey Grammer expanded the role of psychiatrist Frasier Crane that he played on* Cheers, *won the Emmy as best comedy series, while Grammer took the top actor award. The cast included (left to right): David Hyde Pierce, Peri Gilpin, Grammer, Jane Leeves, and John Mahoney, with Moose, in front, as Eddie.*

fallen to below 2 percent. There was also a stock market boom.

The improved economic outlook led to a tremendous increase in foreign investment and in the number of U.S. firms doing business in Brazil, including fast-food operations and retailers. New investment from corporations such as Fiat, IBM, and Union Carbide, which were already in the country, also surged.

In February the United States dropped its threat to impose trade sanctions against Brazil and ended a long-standing dispute over intellectual property protection. In April, Brazil reached an agreement with its creditor banks to reschedule some $50 billion of its commercial debt.

Foreign Affairs. Outgoing President Itamar Franco urged Latin American nations to end the U.S.-led embargo of Cuba and also criticized the sending of U.S. troops to Haiti in October. Brazil continued its commitment to Mercosur, its free-trade pact with Argentina, Paraguay, and Uruguay; on January 1, 1995, the four countries ended tariffs on 95 percent of the goods traded between them and adopted common tariffs for goods from non-Mercosur countries.

See STATISTICS OF THE WORLD.   W.M.W.

BRITISH COLUMBIA. *See* CANADA; STATISTICS OF THE WORLD.

BROADCASTING. After years of speculation about the survival prospects of television broadcasting networks in the United States, suddenly, in 1994, it seemed as if everybody wanted to own, merge with, or start one. A proposed merger of CBS and QVC, a home-shopping network, fell through, but by year's end CBS was exploring the possibility of merging with the Walt Disney Company. Time Warner and NBC were talking about merging. Fox, after picking off a dozen network affiliates in a single deal that stunned the broadcast industry, continued its aggressive efforts to lure ABC, CBS, and NBC stations into its growing fold. Meanwhile, Warner Brothers and Paramount lined up independent stations to form what were to become the fifth and sixth commercial broadcast networks early in 1995.

Networks became hot properties largely because of changes in Federal Communications Commission regulations. The FCC all but eliminated its financial interest and syndication rules, which barred networks from syndicating shows. The FCC also said it might end altogether its already diluted rules barring broadcast networks from owning cable systems. The other factor making networks more attractive was the improved economy. Advance sales of commercial time for the 1994-1995 prime-time season hit a record figure of $4.4 billion.

Violence. The hot issue of 1993, video violence, cooled in 1994 after broadcast and cable industry representatives agreed to independent monitoring of violent program content. The networks chose as their monitor the University of California at Los Angeles Center for Communications Policy. The Center was to focus on the context of violence rather than simply counting "acts of aggression."

Concern about violence showed up in other areas. Following the lead of CBS-owned WCCO in Minneapolis, a number of local stations introduced "family sensitive" early newscasts that minimized videos of crime and accident scenes.

Late-night TV. *Late Show With David Letterman* continued to be CBS's smartest investment since it hired Walter Cronkite. Letterman's success drove the syndicated *The Arsenio Hall Show* out of the late-night competition, but there was no shortage of new challengers. New syndicated efforts included *The Jon Stewart Show,* featuring a cool former MTV personality; a current-affairs parody series called *The Newz;* and *Last Call,* a pop-cultural equivalent of the political roundtable *McLaughlin Group.*

NBC replaced *Later* host Bob Costas with Greg Kinnear, who came to attention as host of E! Entertainment Television's snide digest of the daily talk shows, *Talk Soup.* And CBS, encouraged by Letterman, named Tom Snyder, who moderated NBC's wee-hours *Tomorrow* show in the 1970s, to host a new series that would follow *Late Show.*

Direct Broadcast Satellite. Cable and traditional broadcasting got a new competitor with the introduction of GM Hughes Electronics' DirecTV and Hubbard Broadcasting's United States Satellite Broadcasting (USSB). Offering digital sound and picture, both new services

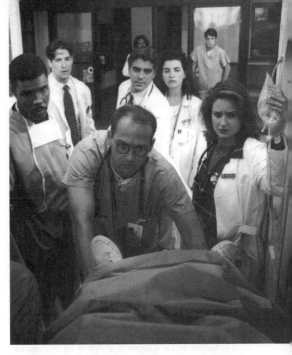

To the rescue. One of the fall season's top-rated new shows was NBC's drama ER, about the emergency room of a Chicago hospital. The cast included (front row, left to right) Eriq LaSalle, Anthony Edwards, and Sherry Stringfield, along with (back row, left to right) Noah Wyle, George Clooney, and Julianna Margulies.

beam previously cable-only channels, as well as a large number of pay-per-view options, directly to an 18-inch dish that can be mounted on the side of a house. The dishes were retailing for $699. Dish owners also pay a monthly bill, much as they would pay a cable company. Initial marketing was aimed at rural homes not served by cable.

1993-1994 Season. CBS won the September to April prime-time ratings crown for the third year in a row. CBS averaged a 14.0 rating, ABC a 12.4, and NBC an 11.0. Fox, with fewer affiliates, had a 7.2. (Each rating point represents 942,000 households.) But the key to CBS's victory was the tremendous success of its coverage of the Winter Olympic Games in February. The network had only two series in the top ten, both of them long-established hits.

The highest-rated series was ABC's *Home Improvement,* a comedy starring Tim Allen as the star of a TV how-to show. It averaged a 21.8 rating. ·The rest of the top ten slots were taken by *60 Minutes* (CBS); *Seinfeld* (NBC);

Roseanne (ABC); *These Friends of Mine* (ABC); *Grace Under Fire* (ABC); *Coach* (ABC) and *Frasier* (NBC), tie; *Murder, She Wrote* (CBS); and *NFL Monday Night Football* (ABC).

The 1993-1994 season marked the last gasp for several long-running network series: *L.A. Law, Evening Shade,* and *In the Heat of the Night.* In addition, Paramount halted production of *Star Trek: The Next Generation,* still a huge hit in syndication, so that it would not compete with a new *Star Trek* series planned as the cornerstone of the forthcoming Paramount network.

The season was unusual in that three new shows made the top ten. *These Friends of Mine,* aimed at the same young adults who make up the core audience for *Seinfeld,* revolved around comic Ellen DeGeneres; it re-turned in the fall renamed *Ellen. Grace Under Fire,* based on the comedy routines of its star, Brett Butler, was about a blue-collar single mother trying to start life over after escaping an abusive marriage. *Frasier* gave Kelsey Grammer the opportunity to expand the supporting character he played on *Cheers:* psychiatrist Frasier Crane.

The Emmy for best dramatic series went to CBS's *Picket Fences,* for the second year in a row. *NYPD* costar Dennis Franz won the award for best dramatic actor, and Sela Ward of NBC's *Sisters* was named best actress in a dramatic series. *Frasier* and its star won in the comedy category, along with *Murphy Brown* star Candice Bergen.

HBO again had the Emmy-winning movie: *And the Band Played On,* based on Randy

A grand night for Klingons. *Fronted by Monika Deol of Toronto's CITY TV, Canadian fans of the television show* Star Trek *party hearty on the occasion of the final episode of* Star Trek: The Next Generation. *The free event, which attracted more than 35,000 people, was billed as the largest* Next Generation *farewell in North America. Although Paramount halted production on the show, Trekkies did not have to despair, since plans were under way to replace it with a new* Star Trek *series.*

Shilts's book about the beginning of the AIDS epidemic. Other notable TV movies included a remake of the musical *Gypsy,* starring Bette Midler; *Breathing Lessons,* based on an Anne Tyler novel; and *Prime Suspect 3,* the third British TV film to star Helen Mirren as London police inspector Jane Tennison.

1994 Fall Season. NBC's *ER,* a Michael Crichton creation about a Chicago hospital's emergency room, quickly became an audience favorite. CBS initially counterprogrammed *ER* with another hospital show, *Chicago Hope,* but moved it to another slot a few weeks into the season.

The most talked-about face-off, however, was between two returning hits. NBC shifted *Frasier* to Tuesday nights to challenge ABC's *Roseanne.* ABC responded by switching *Roseanne* to Wednesday and top-ranked *Home Improvement* to Tuesday. The reigning ratings champ maintained its number one status, but while *Frasier* suffered some loss of audience, it improved NBC's Tuesday performance dramatically.

Other new series included NBC's *Madman of the People,* starring Dabney Coleman as an irascible magazine columnist, and *The Cosby Mysteries,* in which Bill Cosby played a criminologist; CBS's *The Five Mrs. Buchanans,* a sitcom about four sisters-in-law and their fearsome mother-in-law; and ABC's *All American Girl,* the first network series with a predominantly Asian cast. The season's most acclaimed new series, ABC's *My So-called Life,* a drama about a teenage girl from the creators of *thirtysomething,* did abysmally in the ratings.

Fox Broadcasting. After outbidding CBS for the rights to the NFL's National Football Conference games and aggressively wooing new affiliates, Fox seemed poised to make tremendous improvements in its prime-time ratings. But football did not boost Fox's Sunday night lineup, which included the new series *Fortune Hunter,* inspired by the James Bond movies, and *Wild Oats,* a risqué comedy. Fox also struck out with *M.A.N.T.I.S.,* the first series about a black superhero. Its best-received new show was *Party of Five,* a drama about a family of orphaned children.

Public Television. For the centerpiece of its season, PBS turned to *Civil War* documentar-

---

The BBC It's Not

In early 1994, Britain's Channel 4 presented *United States of Television,* six shows composed of weird and zany television clips the likes of which most Britons had never seen.

But then, most Yanks probably hadn't seen all the stuff either. Among the excerpts was an evangelical exercise program—in which the instructor cited Biblical chapter and verse while firming up those thighs—and a bit of *Cowboy Cookin' With Bruce Wood,* who announced, "A lot of people don't like fat these days. I like it." Viewers also took in an episode from the *Joan Rivers Show* starring people who claimed they were vampires, a Geraldo Rivera piece on young Hitler admirers, and a candid talk with a male prostitute.

"A Niagara of fluent drivel," harrumphed the *Evening Standard.* The producers, however, claimed their "clipumentary" showed that British television is not, as commonly believed, the world's finest.

---

ian Ken Burns for *Baseball,* an 18½-hour series that used the history of baseball as a microcosm of the country's development. It was a success, though not as highly rated as Burns's war epic.

PBS's ongoing anthology of history documentaries, *The American Experience,* impressed critics with *FDR,* a biography of Franklin Roosevelt; *Telegrams From the Dead,* about the mid-1800s heyday of spiritualist religion; and *Midnight Ramble,* which recalled movies made exclusively for black audiences in the 1920s and 1930s. PBS introduced its first game show, *Think Twice,* which tested thinking skills as well as information recall, and *Future Quest,* a dazzling science series.

PBS also began testing on selected affiliates *Ready to Learn,* a daylong educational schedule for children that included old favorites such as *Sesame Street* and new series such as *Bill Nye the Science Guy.* The goal was to contribute toward having children better prepared for school by the year 2000.

Cable Television. USA Network was the most watched cable network for the fourth year in a row, followed by TBS, TNT, and

ESPN. Nevertheless, USA announced a major overhaul of its programming, saying it would have a greater emphasis on original series, such as the satirical *Duckman,* and less on reruns of broadcast series.

Turner Pictures' *Gettysburg,* a drama about the Civil War battle, became the highest-rated movie ever shown on a basic cable channel. It was seen by 23 million viewers on TNT. Turner Broadcasting cable outlets combined forces for the most ambitious cable project of the year: *The Native Americans* included three, two-hour movies about American Indian history on TNT; a six-hour history documentary from an Indian perspective on TBS; and a 20-part CNN series, *The Invisible People,* about issues facing modern Indians.

In hopes of stemming erosion of ratings that had peaked during the 1991 Persian Gulf War, CNN launched an innovative, high-tech talk show, *Talk Back Live,* that offered people an opportunity to participate by phone, fax, or online personal computer in daily discussions in the style of a town meeting. What really reinvigorated CNN's ratings, however, was the network's extensive coverage of the O. J. Simpson murder case.

Several new cable channels began service in 1994, among them Fox's F/X, the Independent Film Channel, the commercial-free Turner Classic Movies, the all-talk America's Talking, and Adam & Eve, a channel devoted to sexy merchandise and programs. Additional new channels were announced, including the Classic Sports Network and also the Popcorn Channel (devoted to movie listings and coming attractions previews).

News and Public Affairs. The O. J. Simpson case dominated national TV news. Not only did Court TV and CNN cover the pretrial hearings gavel-to-gavel, so did ABC, CBS, and NBC, even though it meant preempting the daytime soap operas for days on end. The real beneficiaries of the case, however, were the talk, tabloid, and general interest magazines, from *Geraldo* to *Hard Copy* to *Prime Time Live,* which fed on the case for months.

The impact of tabloids on mainstream TV news had been evident earlier in the year in the networks' dogged pursuit of the assault case involving rival figure skaters Nancy Kerri-

gan and Tonya Harding. CBS co-anchor Connie Chung did little but follow Harding during the Winter Olympics.

ABC's *World News Tonight* was the top-rated evening newscast of the 1993-1994 season, averaging a 9.6 rating. CBS was second, with 8.7. NBC was third, with 7.8.

The most inventive steps in TV news came on the local level. WSJV-TV in South Bend, IN, provided an 800 number for viewers to vote for certain optional stories on its early evening news. In Minneapolis, WCCO, the station that introduced "family sensitive" news, also experimented with *News of Your Choice.* The station bought time on another, independent station to run an alternative version of its 10 P.M. news, giving viewers the option of choosing, for instance, more local news instead of a long weather report. It was a rousing success.

New Faces at the FCC. Two new commissioners were named to the FCC in March: Rachelle Chong, a Republican, and Susan Ness, a Democrat.   N.W.H.

BRUNEI. See STATISTICS OF THE WORLD.

BULGARIA. During 1994 the Bulgarian government accepted the invitation of the North Atlantic Treaty Organization to join the Partnership for Peace, a program launched by NATO in January to promote military cooperation with 19 former Communist bloc countries and Finland and Sweden. Agreements on the standardization of arms followed, as did Bulgarian participation in Black Sea naval maneuvers with NATO forces. Bulgaria continued to adhere to the United Nations embargo against neighboring Serbia, despite the economic hardship this caused.

On September 2, having survived 19 months in office and seven votes of no confidence, the government of Prime Minister Lyuben Berov announced its resignation. Leaving office, Berov pointed to his government's successful completion of negotiations with Western banks for the rescheduling of debts inherited from the Communist era, which removed a major obstacle to the expansion of foreign trade and foreign investment in Bulgaria. On the negative side, Berov had been embarrassed when the military command, backed by the Bulgarian Socialist Party (BSP), openly opposed his defense minister's plan to retire several hundred officers.

After Bulgaria's two largest parliamentary blocs, the BSP and the Union of Democratic Forces, each declined to attempt to form a government, President Zheliu Zhelev called on a newly formed bloc of deputies, New Choice, headed by Dimitur Ludzhev. Ludzhev was unable to form a government, however, and in elections on December 18 the BSP won a majority of seats in the Parliament.

Privatization of state enterprises lagged, but the Berov government did adopt a new privatization law before it left office. However, the clouded political situation made quick implementation unlikely. Inflation continued to be a problem, and the value of the lev declined by 88 percent against the dollar.

See STATISTICS OF THE WORLD.   J.D.B.

BURKINA FASO. *See* STATISTICS OF THE WORLD.

BURMA. In 1994 the military remained in firm control of the government of Burma (officially Myanmar). The National Convention, an assembly of delegates chosen by the military, continued to draft a new constitution. The new constitution was expected to perpetuate the military's administrative and legislative power, although military officials promised that a multiparty political system would evolve.

Hostilities continued between the government and the Mong Tai Army, the sole significant opposition force remaining from among several ethnic guerrilla groups that once resisted the regime. The MTA, led by drug-running warlord Khun Sa, apparently gained strength during the year as former Shan dissidents and members of the Karenni and Wa ethnic groups joined or forged alliances with it. Although most of the fighting occurred along the border between Thailand and Burma, some battles took place hundreds of miles from the border in Shan State.

Responding to cuts in foreign aid, the government attempted to quell international condemnation of its poor record in human rights by allowing nonfamily members, among them a U.S. congressman, to visit Nobel Peace Prize laureate Aung San Suu Kyi—leader of the National League for Democracy, who was under house arrest—and by broadcasting pictures on local television of Suu Kyi meeting with top military commanders. The meeting took place just as the 49th UN General Assembly opened in September.

Indonesia, Malaysia, Singapore, and Thailand continued to trade extensively with and invest in Burma, and Burma attended the July Association of Southeast Asian Nations (Asean) meeting in Bangkok as a guest of Thailand. Thailand and other Asean states have advocated "constructive engagement" with the military regime.

The economy continued to grow, although there were disputes about the rate. Inflation was officially about 30 percent, but some observers believed it was as high as 40 percent. Visits by tourists were projected to top 100,000 in 1994 and reach a half million in 1996, which the government had designated Visit Burma Year. Late in 1994, 17 new hotels were being built by foreign investors in Rangoon alone.

See STATISTICS OF THE WORLD.   D.I.S.

BURUNDI. In April 1994, Burundian President Cyprien Ntaryamira and Rwandan President Juvénal Habyarimana were killed when Habyarimana's plane was shot down by unknown forces. An ethnic bloodbath ensued in Rwanda which, like Burundi, had a Hutu majority and a Tutsi minority. Although Burundi saw bloodshed, the country's Hutus and Tutsis managed to reach a shaky state of accommodation and to avoid an all-out disaster. Ethnic fighting was never out of the picture, however, and Rwanda's battles posed constant threats to Burundi. Burundian Tutsi exiles reportedly fought alongside the victorious Rwandan Patriotic Front, leading to fears that they might try to repeat their exploits at home. There was also fear that defeated Rwanda Hutu forces might link up with Hutu extremists in Burundi. Incidents of ethnic violence increased throughout the year, especially in the north near Rwanda. In September a pitched battle was fought between the Tutsi-dominated Army and Hutu irregulars in the northern suburbs of the capital, Bujumbura, and violence continued around the city in October.

One stabilizing development was a power-sharing agreement signed in September. The

Hutu-led Front for Democracy in Burundi (Frodebu) would control the presidency and Ministry of Foreign Affairs while the Tutsi-dominated Unity and National Progress Party—(Uprona) the country's former single-party minority rulers—got the premiership and Interior Ministry. The Defense and Justice ministries would go to "neutral" figures. Presidential decisions would have to be countersigned by the prime minister. The interim president, Sylvestre Ntibantunganya of Frodebu, was confirmed in his post on September 30. In December, however, Uprona withdrew from Parliament and the government to protest the election as parliamentary speaker of a Hutu whom they accused of having incited violence against Tutsis. It was eventually agreed he would step down.

See STATISTICS OF THE WORLD.　　　T.E.T.

BYELARUS. See BELARUS.

C

CABINET, UNITED STATES. See UNITED STATES OF AMERICA: The Presidency.

CALIFORNIA. See STATISTICS OF THE WORLD.

CAMBODIA. Early in 1994 the situation in Cambodia looked promising. The UN had withdrawn the last of its troops and advisers, humanitarian assistance and foreign investment had surged, and in March the international community promised millions of dollars in development aid. But hopes were soon dashed. Corruption and factionalism weakened the ability to govern of the uneasy coalition elected under UN auspices in May 1993. Hostilities between the Cambodian Army and

Exiled. *Prince Norodom Chakrapong of Cambodia is led by an armed guard on July 3 to an airplane bound for Malaysia. The prince, the estranged son of Cambodian King Norodom Sihanouk and former deputy prime minister, had been implicated in an abortive coup attempt.*

the Khmer Rouge, who had boycotted the elections and who still controlled parts of northern and western Cambodia, continued. In March government troops took control of the Khmer Rouge base town of Pailin, only to lose it a month later. Pitched battles were fought for Battambang, and raids and ambushes intensified around Siemreab, near Angkor Wat. Both sides were accused by human rights groups of having carried out indiscriminate assassinations, kidnappings, and extortion; up to 50,000 refugees fled over the border to Thailand within just a few months.

King Norodom Sihanouk, the head of state, favored trying to bring the Khmer Rouge into the coalition. The joint prime ministers—Prince Norodom Ranariddh, leader of the royalist United National Front for an Independent, Peaceful, and Cooperative Cambodia (and Sihanouk's son), and Hun Sen, leader of the Cambodian People's Party and premier of the Vietnam-installed government of 1979-1993—did not. Responding to an appeal from Sihanouk, however, the government agreed to talks with the Khmer Rouge. The talks began in May but by mid-June had reached deadlock, and soon afterward the government closed down the Khmer Rouge's office in Phnom Penh. On July 3 there was an apparent coup attempt, reportedly led by Prince Norodom Chakrapong, another of Sihanouk's sons (who had allied himself with the Khmer Rouge after being expelled from the Hun Sen government for his part in a 1993 coup attempt). Four days later the National Assembly approved legislation outlawing the Khmer Rouge.

Hostilities escalated almost immediately. An American aid worker and her two local assistants were kidnapped, as were 16 passengers on a train ambushed by the Khmer Rouge in Kampot. Among the passengers were three backpackers from Australia, England, and France. After a confusion of ransom demands by many bogus intermediaries, some kidnap victims were released. The backpackers were found murdered in November. Ransom demands for the three had included requests first for money and then for an end to military aid to the Cambodian government by Australia, England, and France.

See STATISTICS OF THE WORLD.　　　G.B.H.

CAMEROON. *See* STATISTICS OF THE WORLD.

CANADA. As has been the case so often in Canada's 127-year history as a nation, 1994 was marked by sharply contrasting displays of unity and discontent. On one hand, Prime Minister Jean Chrétien, elected to power with his Liberal Party in October 1993, finished his first year in office with the highest approval rating of any prime minister in Canadian history. Opinion polls showed that 75 percent of respondents approved of his personal performance in office; 60 percent said they would vote for the Liberals in an election. At the same time, the debate over whether Chrétien's home province of Québec would remain within Canada returned to the forefront. On September 12, Québecers voted out the profederalist provincial Liberal Party and elected the prosovereigntist Parti Québécois. The PQ, under new Premier Jacques Parizeau, promised to hold a referendum on the province's future place in or out of Canada within "eight to ten months" of the election—although Parizeau later revised that promise to say the referendum would take place sometime in 1995. (Late in the year Canadians of all political stripes joined in sympathy for Lucien Bouchard, the prosovereigntist leader of the official opposition at the federal level, whose left leg had to be amputated above the knee after he was stricken with necrotizing fasciitis, a rare flesh-eating disease. He was otherwise expected to recover completely, although it was unclear whether he would return to politics.)

Canadians had many things to concern themselves with in addition to the country's constitutional future. Although Canada continued to rebound from the economic recession of the early 1990s—with strong growth and a drop in the unemployment rate—the year ended amid warnings from the federal government that strong measures would be taken to reduce the country's expensive network of social programs as part of a widespread program of deficit reduction. The country's business community also took several decisive steps, including a merger that created the largest multimedia company in Canada's history, and a history-making sales trip to China headed by Chrétien and nine of

Split decision? *Jacques Parizeau, leader of the Parti Québécois, is sworn in as Québec's premier in September. The election of Parizeau, who had pledged to hold a referendum on sovereignty, gave new hope to those favoring independence for the province.*

the ten provincial premiers. Other important events included landmark decisions by Canadian courts on issues including euthanasia and the right to use excessive intoxication as a defense in criminal cases. There was heated debate over plans by Canada's justice minister to include sexual orientation in a bill defining hate crimes and over another planned bill that would require all gun owners in the country to register their weapons. Finally, Canada won some unwelcome international attention on two fronts: revelations concerning Canadian spy agencies, and a bizarre mass suicide and murder saga involving a religious cult alternately based in Canada and Switzerland.

There was little solace to be found on the troubled sports scene. The baseball strike that prematurely ended the major league season was particularly frustrating for Canadians because the Montréal Expos—who had not won a pennant since their inception in 1969—had the best record in baseball at the time the strike began. Similarly, a lockout imposed by National Hockey League owners on players deprived Canadians throughout the fall and early winter of their favorite sport—and threatened the entire NHL season.

Conflicting Signals. Fourteen years after Québecers voted in a referendum to reject a proposal that would have led to their becoming a sovereign country, they elected a party

committed to the same proposition. But the result was fraught with all the ambiguity that has come to characterize Québecers' feelings about Canada. Despite the PQ's comfortable majority, their victory total in actual votes—out of some 3.9 million ballots cast—was only 15,000, or less than half a percentage point better than the Liberals. And in the months following the PQ's election, a series of opinion polls showed that support for sovereignty had dropped to as low as 33 percent in one poll—which led to talk within the PQ of delaying the referendum.

Another Canadian province undertook a revolution of a different kind. Alberta Premier Ralph Klein, in his first year in office, led a government cost-cutting campaign aimed at reducing the province's Can$2.5 billion deficit to nothing by 1997 without raising taxes. To do so, Klein imposed major spending cuts in almost all areas, including education, health care, and welfare. Although he was accused by political opponents of gutting the province's social safety programs, polls showed that his popularity actually increased after the measures were announced.

New Government. On the federal level, the new Liberal government's first year in office was characterized by a much more cautious approach. The Liberals launched several studies of what to do in major policy areas—such as tax reform, restructuring of social programs, and debt reduction—with the promise of action to come later. Still, there was no mistaking the government's long-term goals. Human Resources Minister Lloyd Axworthy unveiled a discussion paper in early October that called, among other things, for sweeping changes and reductions in Canada's unemployment insurance system, new incentives to encourage welfare recipients to accept jobs that might pay them less than they currently receive, a cut in grants for postsecondary education, and a transfer of powers to give the provinces more control over welfare and social services. An internal government document leaked to the media appeared to suggest the government was aiming for Can$7.5 billion in savings.

Finance Minister Paul Martin, on the other hand, was very specific about his intention to sharply reduce government spending. In October, Martin said that the budget he would present in February 1995 would include a total of Can$6.3 billion in new spending cuts or tax increases over the next two years. The aim was to reduce the federal deficit from the 1994 total of Can$39 billion to Can$25 billion by the 1996-1997 fiscal year. The steps necessary to achieve that, said Martin, bleakly, "will be felt by all Canadians." Still, some critics, such as the opposition Reform Party, charged that the cuts were insufficient, considering the fact that the overall federal debt was approaching Can$550 billion by the end of 1994. The C. D. Howe Institute, an independently financed and highly respected think tank, urged Martin to take far more dramatic action that would involve cutting Can$14.6 billion at once and more later, in order to reduce the deficit to Can$11 billion by 1996-1997.

Orders From the Courts. While politicians put off several important decisions to another year, the same could not be said of the country's jurists, who produced a number of decisions with potentially important effects on the lives—and deaths—of ordinary Canadians. The most controversial of those decisions was a ruling by the Supreme Court of Canada in September in which it said that extreme drunkenness may be used as a defense in certain criminal cases, including rape. Although the

Jean Chrétien

Politics, Jean Chrétien used to say, "must be the only profession in the world where people consider experience a handicap." But despite Chrétien's 30 years in the game, the folksy Canadian prime minister notched up the highest approval ratings in Canadian history in late 1994: around 70 percent.

Chrétien showed impressive élan for a 59-year-old man who has boasted about his small-town roots. Visiting China, he commandeered a bicycle and rode down one of Shanghai's busiest streets. At home, he would drop in at Ottawa bars to chat and sometimes slipped into movie theaters with his wife, Aline.

Critics claimed Chrétien's success was one of style over substance. But Canadians tired of a bloated federal budget cheered Chrétien's "Chevrolet government." Chrétien pared the size of the cabinet to a two-decade low—and furnished most of his official residence with leftovers from Canadian embassies.

But the prime minister's hardest task—to keep Canada united—lay ahead; a referendum on the status of Québec was slated for 1995.   A.W.

ruling emphasized that the accused must be in a state similar to insanity or automatism and, thus, the defense could be used only rarely, it became the basis for acquittal in at least two subsequent cases in the following months. The ruling caused a public outcry, and Justice Minister Allen Rock said he would introduce a new law to counteract the extreme drunkenness defense. The legislation was expected to be introduced in 1995.

Another case involving a lower court evoked equal amounts of controversy but much more sympathy for the defendant. In November, the Saskatchewan Court of Appeal found Robert Latimer, a 41-year-old farmer, guilty of second-degree murder in the mercy killing of his severely disabled 12-year-old daughter. Latimer, who was sentenced to life imprisonment without possibility of parole for ten years, acknowledged that he killed his daughter by feeding carbon monoxide into a truck compartment where she slept. He said he did so because her illness, the most severe form of cerebral palsy, caused her constant pain. The decision, which was appealed, led to pressure on Rock to introduce a law dealing specifically with mercy killings—although Rock said he was opposed to doing so. Still, the House of Commons was likely to stage a "free" vote in 1995—meaning that members of Parliament would not have to vote on party lines—on the issue of whether euthanasia should be considered a criminal act.

Rock also faced controversy from within his own party on two issues that were of his own making. Faced with a growing public belief that Canadian society was becoming more Americanized and violent, Rock said he would introduce legislation to force all gun owners to formally register their weapons. That caused a storm of protest in rural areas, where hunters viewed the move as discriminatory. A demon-

And the winner is . . . The roulette wheel spins at the new Casino Windsor in Windsor, Ont. In 1994, Ontario became the third Canadian province to establish legal gaming, as more and more financially strapped local governments were looking to gambling as a source of revenue.

stration on Parliament Hill attracted thousands of angry protesters from across the country—and criticism from some Liberal members of Parliament representing rural ridings. But Rock appeared determined to stick, figuratively, to his own guns, and such legislation was expected to pass. Similarly, some Liberals were opposed to Rock's plan to include sexual orientation in a new bill that would impose tougher sentences on crimes motivated by hate. Opponents argued that this measure would create special rights for gays and lesbians. But Rock denied that was the case, and said the measure was necessary because of increased incidences of gay bashing.

Improving Economy. Despite concerns over a falling Canadian dollar and the country's mushrooming debt, the economy grew at a healthy pace in 1994. Late in December economic indicators showed the country's gross domestic product up 4.8 percent over 1993, while industrial production had increased 6.7 percent, retail sales were up 7.3 percent, and the unemployment rate—while still high at 9.6 percent—was down from 11.1 percent in 1993. Another positive factor was a low inflation rate of less than half a percent in consumer prices.

The generally healthy state of the economy contributed, not surprisingly, to a renewed sense of buoyancy in the business community. A significant move came in March, when Edward (Ted) Rogers, the head of Rogers Communications Inc., led his company to a Can$3.1 billion takeover of Maclean Hunter Ltd. The acquisition move, which Rogers described as a merger, gave his company tentative control of the largest range of communications properties in the country. That included cable television operations, cellular telephones, long-distance telephone services, radio and television stations, and a network of some of the country's largest newspapers and magazines, including the *Sun* chain, the *Financial Post* newspaper, and *Maclean's,* a weekly newsmagazine. The final hurdle to the deal was approval by the Canadian Radio-Television and Telecommunication Commission and the U.S. Federal Communications Commission; their decision was expected sometime in 1995.

Going out in style. *Canadian gymnast Stella Umeh capped her career by winning four medals at the 1994 Commonwealth Games, held in Victoria, British Columbia, in August. The 19-year-old said she planned to retire from the sport after the competition and pursue a career as a sportscaster.*

Another noteworthy venture came as a result of unprecedented cooperation between the federal and provincial governments and the business community. In November, Chrétien led a delegation that included all of the premiers except Parizeau and close to 400 business executives on a weeklong selling mission to Beijing and Shanghai that resulted in the signing of about Can$10 billion in formal or tentative deals. Among the contracts signed by the delegation, which dubbed itself Team Canada, was a tentative agreement to sell the Chinese two Canadian Candu nuclear reactors worth more than Can$2.6 billion.

Spy Versus Spy. Canada's usually publicity-shy intelligence agencies came in for a dose of unwelcome attention in 1994. The Canadian

Security Intelligence Service, the government-run counterintelligence agency, was racked by allegations that a paid informer for the group had played a key role in controversial acts that ranged from spying on the opposition Reform Party to working with neo-Nazi groups that gave the names of prominent Jewish community activists to similar groups in the United States. There were also allegations in a book published late in the year by veteran Ottawa journalist Michel Gratton that members of another government intelligence agency had, among other things, spied on sovereigntist groups in Québec and eavesdropped electronically, at former British Prime Minister Margaret Thatcher's request, on conversations between two cabinet ministers whom she considered to be disloyal.

Apocalypse Abroad. A mysterious set of suicides and murders in Switzerland turned out to have a domestic angle. In October, Swiss police were shaken by the discovery of 48 bodies in two locations who had been, they later determined, either shot, smothered, or, possibly, poisoned in most cases. Another five bodies were found in Morin Heights, Québec. It was established that the dead were members of the Order of the Solar Temple, a cult alternately based in Switzerland and Québec and made up largely of residents of the two countries. One of the cult's leaders was Luc Jouret, a charismatic Belgian who divided his time between homes in Europe and Canada; he was among the dead. Although it was not possible to immediately identify all the dead, the bodies of 11 Canadians were identified. At year's end police were still investigating the killings.

See STATISTICS OF THE WORLD.   A.W.

CAPE VERDE. See STATISTICS OF THE WORLD.

CARIBBEAN BASIN. The year 1994 was eventful in the Caribbean, highlighted by a host of elections and the ripple effect of political turmoil in Cuba and Haiti. A new trading group was formed, and there was a major international conference on sustainable development for small island nations.

Dominican Republic. In the Dominican Republic, Joaquín Balaguer, 88, won a narrow victory in a disputed May 16 vote over his leading challenger, José Francisco Peña Gómez. Pressured by the United States and other countries to call new elections immediately, Balaguer did agree to set an early vote for November 16, 1995. However, a pro-Balaguer constitutional assembly subsequently changed the date to May 16, 1996.

Barbados. In Barbados the opposition Barbados Labor Party won 19 of 28 parliamentary seats in a September 6 election. Owen Arthur, a 44-year-old economist, became the new prime minister. Ousted Prime Minister Erskine Sandiford of the Democratic Labor Party had been forced to call the elections two years ahead of schedule after losing a parliamentary vote of confidence in June. Former Finance Minister David Thompson, 32, replaced Sandiford as the head of the DLP.

Antigua and Barbuda. In Antigua and Barbuda, Lester Bird succeeded his father and longtime island leader Vere C. Bird—who retired—as prime minister. Bird's Antigua Labor Party won 11 of 17 parliamentary seats in March 8 elections.

St. Vincent and the Grenadines. Prime Minister James Mitchell of St. Vincent and the Grenadines led his ruling center-right New Democratic Party to a third straight victory, winning 12 of 15 parliamentary seats in February 21 elections.

Anguilla. In the British colony of Anguilla, 19 candidates from four political parties and three independents vied for seven House of Assembly seats in March 16 elections. Hubert Hughes, 57, became the new chief minister when his Anguilla United Party formed a coalition with the Anguilla Democratic Party. Each party won two seats, as did the incumbent Anguilla National Alliance.

Netherlands Antilles. A coalition government headed by Miguel Pourier was installed in the Netherlands Antilles following February elections in the five-island Dutch Caribbean possession. Pourier's Antillean Recovery Party won eight of the 14 seats allocated to Curaçao, which is the administrative capital of the federation.

Grenada. In Grenada, Agriculture Minister George Brizan was chosen as the new leader of the governing National Democratic Congress at a party congress in September. Brizan succeeded Prime Minister Nicholas Brathwaite, who announced his resignation as party leader earlier in the year but retained the prime minister's post.

New Trading Group. Perhaps the most significant regional event of the year came on July 24 in Cartagena, Colombia, when government leaders and ministers from 25 Caribbean and Latin American states officially gave birth to the Association of Caribbean States. Cuban President Fidel Castro was among the signatories. The ACS was intended to promote economic integration and functional cooperation among the countries of the Caribbean Basin. It had the potential to become the world's fourth-largest trading bloc.

Sustainable Development. Another major gathering came in the spring when delegates from some 120 nations met in Barbados for the first UN conference on small island developing states. It was agreed that the international community would provide new resources to support sustainable development. However, no specific funds were allocated for this purpose, and the so-called Barbados Declaration issued at the conclusion of the conference made no mention of increased assistance from the more developed countries.

Royal Visit. Perhaps the social highlight of the year came in March with a visit to the region by Britain's Queen Elizabeth II. The three-week tour took her to Anguilla, Dominica, Jamaica, the Bahamas, Guyana, the Cayman Islands, Belize, and Bermuda—all former or present British colonies.

Haiti and Cuba Turmoil. The ongoing crisis in Haiti and a flood of rafters fleeing Cuba during August affected the entire region. Several English-speaking Caribbean countries—among them Antigua and Barbuda, the Bahamas, Barbados, Belize, Guyana, Jamaica, St. Kitts and Nevis, and Trinidad and Tobago—contributed token troop contingents to an international peacekeeping force for Haiti. In Jamaica the government authorized processing of Haitian refugees' asylum claims aboard U.S.-chartered ships anchored in Kingston harbor in June and early July. The Turks and Caicos Islands and Suriname joined other Caribbean Basin countries in authorizing the United States to construct on their territory safe-haven camps for Cuban or Haitian refugees.

The fleeing Cuban rafters posed a major problem for the Cayman Islands. By the end of September the tiny British colony of 30,000 off the south coast of Cuba harbored some 1,200 Cuban refugees, putting a tremendous strain on the islands' resources.

Bloc building. Cuban President Fidel Castro signs the agreement establishing the Association of Caribbean States in July. The pact created a 25-member trading bloc of Latin American and Caribbean nations with a potential market of 200 million people.

Tropical Storm. Tropical Storm Debby—sweeping through the Caribbean in early September—claimed nine lives, left hundreds homeless, and caused heavy damage, much of it in St. Lucia. There, an estimated 75 to 80 percent of the banana crop and 80 percent of the coconut crop were destroyed. Water and electrical supplies were disrupted and extensive road damage inflicted. Banana crops in other eastern Caribbean islands also were hard hit by the storm.

See Cuba; Haiti; Puerto Rico; Statistics of the World. D.B.

CENTRAL AFRICAN REPUBLIC. See Statistics of the World.

CEYLON. See Sri Lanka.

CHAD. See Statistics of the World.

CHEMISTRY. A major theme of chemistry in 1994 was discoveries that could lead to molecular devices replacing electrical circuitry in computers and other applications. Other areas of important developments included laboratory synthesis of promising cancer and AIDS drugs, superconductivity, and safer, more environmentally friendly manufacture of certain chemicals.

Materials Science. A molecular-scale wire that transmits light has been developed. It is made of an array of light-absorbing pigments similar to chlorophyll molecules, which play a key role in photosynthesis. The molecular-scale wire is 100 times smoother than existing computer circuitry. Possible uses include computer circuitry and artificial retinas.

Materials belonging to a new family of solid compounds actually contract rather than expand when they are heated at around room temperature. An example is an oxide of zirconium, vanadium, and phosphorous. When blended with other materials, these compounds could be used to create objects that do not change in size on heating. Possible applications include use in telescopes, laser communications, and circuit boards.

Carbon films strengthen and toughen many ceramics, making them suitable for automotive, aerospace, and nuclear energy applications. The usual methods of making carbon films are expensive and not easily used for coating fibers or powders. Japanese researchers developed an improved method for forming very thin carbon films on silicon carbide fibers, powders, and crystals.

The treatment is performed in water under pressure at 300° to 800° Celsius (about 570° to 1,472° Fahrenheit). The center of a fiber can be completely consumed when the treatment is carried out for a long time or at high temperatures, resulting in a thin, hollow, carbon pipe 10 microns across with a wall thickness of 3 microns. (A micron is one-millionth of a meter; a meter is about 39 inches.) Such tubes, a thousand times larger than carbon nanotubes, may have applications in catalysis—the science of accelerating chemical reactions; catalysts are widely used in oil refineries and in chemical plants.

Catalysis. A pigment used in white paints, titanium dioxide, plus air and sunlight promote a powerful oxidation reaction that kills bacteria in water, as well as removing hazardous metals. Water purified by this method was found to remain disinfected for a couple of hours. This makes the technique unsuitable for large-scale water treatment plants; however, campers, soldiers, and residents of rural areas should find it useful.

Polymers. Each human brain cell is connected to many other cells by cell branches called dendrites. These interconnections make rapid and complex thought possible. Scientists recently reported a method of making polymer dendrites, which might be used to interconnect computer chips in three dimensions as opposed to the two dimensions currently possible. (Polymers are substances whose molecules consist of large numbers of repeated "submolecule" units.) This would enable computers to work more rapidly and process more complex information. The new method involves growing an electrically conducting polymer called poly(3-methylthiophene) in solution in such a way that polymer fibers form interconnecting dendrite branches. According to the researchers, the trick was finding a way to get the fibers to connect properly instead of shorting out or connecting to the wrong thing.

Chemists have long sought to develop a plastic that can record optical patterns and later record another image over the original one. A new polymer material reported in

Fuels rush in. *The 1994 winner of the Nobel Prize in chemistry was George A. Olah of the University of Southern California. Olah was honored for his hydrocarbon research, which is important to the development of new fuels and which has led to technology that gives gasoline a higher octane rating.*

making large amounts of the superconducting material was to add carbon to a melted mixture of the other atoms. The new compounds offer the potential for higher superconducting temperatures and greater current-carrying capacity than superconducting current wires now in use.

Organic Synthesis. The drug taxol shows great promise as a treatment for some types of cancer. However, it is difficult to obtain. Small amounts can be extracted from the bark of certain species of yew trees found in the U.S. Pacific Northwest and certain parts of Asia. Two groups of researchers independently synthesized taxol in their laboratories. The two synthesis methods cannot be used commercially, but they could be used to prepare taxol analogs that are more effective or have fewer side effects.

Also synthesized in the laboratory was a compound called thiarubrine B that, some evidence suggests, may prove useful in treating AIDS. It is found naturally in very small amounts in some species of ragweed and sunflowers. J.K.B.

CHESS. Gary Kasparov held the Professional Chess Association (PCA) world championship title and Anatoly Karpov the World Chess Federation (FIDE) title, and their marathon matches appeared to have come to an end, with each defending his title against a younger challenger.

1994 may have achieved this goal. The material, derived from poly(*N*-vinylcarbazole), is suitable for use in applications such as storage of holograms and optical image processing.

Polycarbonate is a polymer widely used in windows, bottles, and many other applications. Nearly all polycarbonate is made by a process using toxic phosgene and methylene chloride, a solvent that is a possible human carcinogen. Japanese researchers developed a solid-state polymerization process to make polycarbonate without using phosgene and methylene chloride.

Superconductivity. Two different research groups developed a new class of superconductors containing four different types of atoms and called quaternary intermetallic compounds. (Superconductors are substances that at low temperatures offer no resistance to the conduction of electricity.) One group reported synthesis of a superconductor containing yttrium, palladium, boron, and carbon atoms. Working independently, the other group developed similar compounds containing nickel instead of palladium. The trick in

Elimination matches were held throughout the year to determine the challenger for each title in 1995. On the PCA track, Gata Kamsky (United States) annihilated Vladimir Kramnik (Russia) by 4½-1½. Viswanathan Anand (India) beat Oleg Romanishin (Ukraine), 5-2; Nigel Short (Great Britain) beat Boris Gulko (United States), 6½-5½, in a tie-break; and Michael Adams (Great Britain) beat Sergey Tiviakov (Russia), 7½-6½, also on a tie-break. In the ten-game match semifinals, Kamsky crushed Short, 5½-1½, and Anand beat Adams by the same score. Kamsky and Anand were scheduled to face off in March 1995.

In the FIDE matches, Kamsky came back from two games behind to tie Anand, 4-4, and then beat him, 2-0, in the tie-break. Boris Gelfand (Belarus) beat Kramnik, 4½-3½, and Valery Salov (Belarus) beat Jan Timman

(Netherlands), 4½-3½. Karpov, seeded into the semifinals, was slated to play Gelfand, and Kamsky faced Salov. Kamsky, whose performance in the matches was spectacular, could thus become the first American to challenge for the world title since Bobby Fischer and is the only contestant who can challenge for both the PCA and FIDE titles.

Peter Leko of Hungary became the youngest grand master ever at age 14, beating the record of Judit Polgar (also from Hungary) who had gained the title at the age of 15 years and 5 months. At the Madrid tournament, Polgar, 17, finished undefeated ahead of four of the world's top ten players.

Computers threaten, however, to eclipse even these rising young stars. The program Chess Genius 2, which processes 100,000 moves a second, defeated Kasparov, 1½-½, and then drew two 25-minute games before losing to Anand in the last round of the Intel World Chess Grand Prix.

Women's champion Xie Jun (China) easily defended her title against Nana Ioseliani (Georgia), 8½-2½. The United States team headed by Kamsky won the World Team Championship. Ukraine was second, and a Russian team without Kasparov and Karpov third. A Russian team led by Kasparov won the Moscow Olympiad. Alexander Shabalov and Alex Yermolinsky tried for first in the U.S. Championship. Estonians Jaan Ehlvest and Lembit Oll topped the 200-master New York Open field.   J.T.S.

CHILE. On March 11, 1994, Patricio Aylwin handed over the presidency of Chile to Eduardo Frei Ruíz-Tagle, elected as his successor the previous December. Just before Frei took office, Congress ratified a constitutional amendment reducing the presidential term from eight years to six. (Under a special arrangement, Aylwin, the first democratically elected president since the military coup of 1973, had served for four years.)

The New Government at Work. Soon after taking office, Frei faced a showdown with military police chief Rodolfo Stange, implicated by a senior judge in a cover-up of the 1985 murders of three Communists. Since the president could not, under the terms of the 1981 constitution, remove top military officials, he

sought Stange's resignation. Stange refused to resign, however, and later in the year he was cleared of all charges.

Frei announced he would submit to Congress proposals for constitutional reforms, including one that would allow the president to call plebiscites; other proposals concerned changes in the electoral system, the structure of municipal government, and legislative powers and called for the elimination of the nine so-called designated senators appointed by the military (who, in effect, gave the right-wing opposition a Senate majority).

In August the government announced a plan to raise education spending from 5 to 7 percent of gross domestic product over the next few years. This investment in the workforce was expected to help increase productivity and fuel economic growth.

Human Rights. Before leaving office, Aylwin pardoned the remaining four political prisoners from the dictatorship period. At the end of March, 16 people, including 15 former military police officers, were sentenced to jail terms for the murders of three Communists in 1985 (the case Stange had been linked to). In a surprise move the Supreme Court reopened a case involving the alleged death during torture of a Spanish citizen, Carmelo Soria. The case had been closed because the murder took place during the period covered by the amnesty law of 1978.

Terrorism. Five members of the terrorist Youth Lautaro movement, including the group's leader, Guillermo Ossandón, were sentenced to die for killing four police officers.

Economic Developments. Although growth was slower than in previous years (a projected 4.3 percent compared with 6.5 percent in 1993), Chile was still considered a prime Latin America investment. In the first 11 months of 1994 foreign investment rose to $4 billion, a record. Preliminary figures put the annual inflation rate for 1994 at around 9 percent, versus 12.2 percent for 1993. Unemployment, however, was up, at 6.5 percent. Exports for the first eight months exceeded imports by some $319 million, compared with a deficit of $294 million in the same period in 1993.

Foreign Affairs. In December, U.S. President Bill Clinton announced that Chile would be

Frei at last. *Eduardo Frei, newly inaugurated as president of Chile, waves to the crowd as he parades through downtown Santiago in March.*

the next country to enter the North American Free Trade Agreement. Negotiations on Chile's entry were to begin in 1995. The Chilean government announced it would work for formal association with Mercosur, the common market of Argentina, Brazil, Paraguay, and Uruguay due to come into effect in 1995.

See STATISTICS OF THE WORLD. D.W.

CHINA. In 1994, China's economic growth remained very high (at about 12 percent), a good harvest was taken in, and aging paramount leader Deng Xiaoping once again did not die. In foreign relations, Beijing avoided any serious trouble. But there were growing indications of domestic troubles ahead. Inflation was running at 20 percent, corruption rose to new heights, and the Communist Party was losing control over important sectors of society and vast geographic regions. A political succession was imminent, but none of the leadership had a solid grip on power.

The Economy. The Chinese economy remained a qualified success. The Communist Party promulgated reforms in taxes, currency, exchange rates, and banking. The economic boom moved inland to encompass such regional centers as Wuhan in the Yangtze Valley, Chongqing in Sichuan, and Kunming in Yunnan. With the aid of Japanese and Korean investment, Shandong and the three northeast provinces joined the revolution of privatization and double-digit growth.

Oil was discovered and wells were drilled, both offshore and in the Tarim Basin, which had the potential to rival Saudi Arabia in reserves. The massive Three Gorges dam and electrification project, designed to control the upper reaches of the Yangtze River and provide more hydroelectric power than any other such project in the world, was finally initiated.

Abolition of China's dual exchange rate system and a final unification of currency (doing away with so-called foreign exchange certificates) helped calm foreign investors' anger at currency manipulation. A reorganization of futures markets, replacing 40 unregulated locations with 11 controlled arenas, meant that further successful marketization could proceed. In the new PPP (Purchasing Power Parity) international comparative accounting system, the national income of China was calculated at somewhere between $1.7 trillion and $3.4 trillion, making China probably the third—perhaps even the second—richest country in the world.

These gains, however, came at very high costs, including political corruption and an inflation rate that reached 40 percent in some localities. The shift in income distribution in favor of the coast and the southeast at the expense of the inland and western provinces threatened to bring on major civil disruptions. Most remaining state-run industries, accounting for 50 percent of the country's industrial production, operated at heavy losses, which had to be made up by state bailouts. Efforts at reform in the state sector came to a halt. Rural to urban migration continued at a very fast pace, and poor urban living and working conditions were evidenced in a series of disastrous fires and explosions that resulted in thousands of deaths.

In the countryside, where incomes were generally up, the demand for food, especially processed food, increased dramatically. Middlemen emerged to broker food prices and sales, adding costs. Much prime land was taken out of agricultural production because of urban spread. Meanwhile, rural environmental problems increased dramatically; desertification continued, and runoff from farms caused floods and downstream pollution.

Officials estimated it would take some $500 billion of new investment over the next decade to keep up with the infrastructural requirements of rapid economic modernization. It was not clear where such money would come from, as China was finding it increasingly difficult to compete for foreign investment. Already, problems were manifest. The railroads were breaking down, and the airline system was overtaxed, a factor that led to numerous

fatal crashes. Power production, always lagging, threatened to fall even farther behind, despite the coming on line of many new plants.

Society and Culture. Nonetheless, for many, China was an exciting place to live. The party still asserted its right to control the details, as well as the direction, of social and cultural life, but it was increasingly less capable of doing so; hence theater, cinema, and literature were able to flourish. Several Chinese film directors, including Huang Jianxin, Xia Junin, and especially Zhang Yimou, came away with prizes at festivals—although the party banned Zhang from directing international productions for five years. China's rock stars sang verses delivering sharp political criticism, and young people attended rock concerts in large numbers.

In sports, China, dominated the Asian Games in Hiroshima; its swimming team was particularly strong. Critics noted, however, that China had hired several East German coaches and that a dozen Chinese athletes tested positive for use of performance-enhancing drugs.

There was a party crackdown on religious expression, especially on Chinese Pentecostal Protestants. "House churches," where mil-

Warming trend. *Chinese President Jiang Zemin (left) shakes hands with Russian President Boris Yeltsin in September. Jiang's visit to Moscow was the first by a Chinese head of state in nearly four decades and resulted in a series of pacts designed to decrease tension and bolster cooperation between the two countries.*

lions met outside of party control, were banned, as was any purposeful contact with missionaries. China also promulgated "better birth" regulations, aimed at "improving" the population by means of sterilization, prohibiting marriages of the mentally ill, and requiring abortions when mothers had certain hereditary diseases.

Crime was an increasing problem. In March, 32 vacationers, including 24 Taiwanese tourists, were robbed and murdered on Qiandao Lake in coastal Zhejiang Province, possibly by a gang of renegade People's Army soldiers. In September a People's Army lieutenant shot nearly 100 citizens at a major Beijing intersection, killing up to 14. Hong Kong newspapers reported that the soldier was infuriated because his wife had died during a forced abortion, and that he had earlier killed up to ten officers and soldiers at his base.

Politics. Deng, who turned 90 in 1994, was, depending on the source of information, either in relatively good if gradually declining health or barely surviving on medical life-support systems. The various contenders for power— General Secretary Jiang Zemin, Premier Li Peng, National People's Congress head Qiao Shi, and economic czar Zhu Rongji, among others—maneuvered among themselves. But in the end, nothing much changed. At a party meeting in September there was a slight apparent turn toward conservatism and an increase in the military presence.

Foreign Relations. China sought to avoid security crises and prepare the way for an expansion of power and assertiveness consonant with the additional means that economic growth would provide. The balance of payments, the best indicator of China's international economic standing, was nearly even, and overall trade was about $250 billion. Chinese politicians, especially Li Peng, toured abroad, and a stream of foreign visitors—led by the French and Japanese premiers but including U.S. Defense Secretary William J. Perry—came to Beijing.

The regime showed some willingness to negotiate territorial and oil-rights differences in the South China Sea. However, it sent warships to confront Vietnam on the placement of oil rigs, and it arrogated to itself the right to form oil-drilling districts in waters claimed by other nations.

China attended the November summit meeting of the Asia-Pacific Economic Cooperation group at Bogor, Indonesia, as well as a July regional forum sponsored by the Association of Southeast Asian Nations (members are Brunei, Indonesia, Malaysia, Philippines, Singapore, and Thailand) in Bangkok, Thailand. Beijing succeeded in keeping what little influence it still retained in North Korea and furthered its rapprochement with Russia, getting Moscow to agree to the sale of a number of important weapons systems.

China continued to resist outside pressures to improve its human rights record. Perhaps the most significant development in relations with the United States came when the Clinton administration, facing opposition from American business, decided to delink trade and human rights, renewing China's most-favored-nation trading status without any conditions pertaining to human rights.

Overall, U.S. relations were mixed. The military-to-military relationship was restored, the U.S. Export-Import Bank provided a sea of loans to American businesses exporting to China, a textiles agreement was initialed, and yet another agreement curbing the sale of missile and nuclear technology to Pakistan was signed. But the bilateral trade imbalance continued to grow in China's favor. China stonewalled negotiations on carrying out an intellectual property protection pact, and negotiations for China's entry into the General Agreement on Tariffs and Trade broke down. Restrictions of all sorts were levied on American firms, and China regularly violated established agreements and norms.

China took an increasingly hard line regarding Hong Kong, declaring that all democratic reforms and institutions would be replaced upon the colony's reversion to Chinese control in 1997. Beijing did finally reach an agreement on funding of a major Hong Kong infrastructure project, including an expensive airport already under construction on the island of Chek Lap Kok.

Beijing opposed Taipei's increased sense of independence from the mainland, and especially its thus far unsuccessful attempt to join the United Nations as a separate nation. Progress in negotiations on trade ties and other contacts ground to a halt, and China conducted no less than 11 military exercises in areas near Taiwan.

China continued its military modernization with production and purchase of high-technology equipment and practiced how to use it. This assertiveness regarding the military was of much concern to neighbors in the region.

See STATISTICS OF THE WORLD.   T.W.R.

CHINA, REPUBLIC OF. *See* TAIWAN.

CIVIL LIBERTIES AND CIVIL RIGHTS. *See* MINORITIES IN THE UNITED STATES; WOMEN.

COINS AND COIN COLLECTING. During the closing months of 1993, U.S. President Bill Clinton announced his intention to nominate Philip N. Diehl to be the next director of the United States Mint. Confirmed by the Senate as the 35th director in July 1994, Diehl soon announced his intention to end the proliferation of commemorative coin programs.

Good intentions aside, 1994 subsequently saw the rush to commemorate by coin carried to new extremes. New issues approved or issued included a silver dollar for the Bicentennial of the U.S. Capitol, an issue of up to 800,000 silver dollars for the Special Olympics, proof and uncirculated silver dollars dated 1993 and struck a year later recognizing the 250th anniversary of the birth of Thomas Jefferson, and three silver dollars for U.S. veterans groups—prisoners of war, women in the military, and veterans of Vietnam. Approved in 1993 and struck during the year was a three-coin set issued to raise funds for the 1994 World Cup soccer championship, held for the first time in the United States.

The largest issue authorized for 1995 and 1996, 16 different coins for the XXVI Olympic Summer Games in Atlanta in 1996, ran into unexpected problems when Olympic officials rejected the approved designs. Officially, it was reported by the mint that designs failed to conform with their legislated themes; unofficially, it was said that the designs depicted scenes from the ancient games when athletes competed without hindrance of clothes. There would be "no frontal nudity" on Olympic coins, said one U.S. Olympic Committee official. Meanwhile, collectors who were especially interested in Olympic coins greeted the establishment of the United States Olympic Numismatic Association.

To commemorate the 50th anniversary of events in World War II, former Allies and even those on the opposing side struck special coins. Great Britain, France, and the United States marked the anniversary of the D day landings, while Germany issued a ten-mark silver coin noting the 50th anniversary of the attempt to assassinate Adolf Hitler.

In June a Wisconsin-based organization called the Freedom From Religion Foundation filed suit in a Denver federal court to have the motto "In God We Trust" removed from U.S. currency as being a government endorsement of religion. The words first appeared on two-cent pieces in 1864 and were gradually added to all coins. The motto began appearing on paper money in 1955 and is now printed on all U.S. coins and paper money.   E.C.R.

COLOMBIA. Colombia's Liberal government headed by César Gaviria Trujillo finished its term of office in 1994. After an extremely close election, Ernesto Samper Pizano won the presidency and was inaugurated in August. Samper confronted long-standing problems of

Capitol coin. *Despite the U.S. government's declaration that it would try to end the proliferation of commemorative coin programs, a slew of new issues were approved or issued during 1994, including a silver dollar marking the bicentennial of the Capitol.*

Fleeing the quake. *Earthquake survivors from the town of Belalcazar in Colombia struggle to board a rescue helicopter. The June earthquake and subsequent mudslides were estimated to have killed more than a thousand people in the region.*

violence and public security, aggravated by contentious relations with the United States over drug policy; in mid-1994 the Constitutional Court ruled that possession of small amounts of drugs was no longer a prosecutable offense. Meanwhile, Colombia continued to enjoy steady economic growth.

Tight Presidential Race. The race for a successor to President Gaviria, who had reached the constitutional limit of his term in office, was intense. The Liberal torch was passed to Samper, who faced the Conservative candidate Andrés Pastrana Arango and the Democratic Alliance/M19 candidate Antonio Navarro Wolff. In the first round of voting in May, Samper outpolled Pastrana by only 18,000 votes (0.3 percent), while Navarro received less than 4 percent of the vote. No one secured the sim-

ple majority needed to win outright, and in a runoff held on June 19, Samper won by two percentage points.

The 43-year-old Samper indicated he would slow Gaviria's pace of reform, promising to erect an extensive social net to help humanize the reform process. He promised a minimum of 1.5 million new jobs, to be created through industrial assistance, and said revenues from the expanding Cusiana oil fields would be channeled into social programs to help the poorest one-third of Colombians.

The Economy. Although he had, as a Gaviria minister, accepted neoliberalism, Samper's initiatives as president showed that he favored some degree of state intervention. He also indicated he would slowly liberalize trade while combating unemployment and investing in major infrastructure projects. Coming into office with the economy already growing, inflation dropping, and external debt falling, Samper inherited a budget surplus for 1994. In September the government presented its budget to Congress, detailing ambitious programs for social and agricultural assistance. Yet there were repeated assurances that a tight monetary policy would be maintained.

Drugs Policy Causes Stir. The killing of Medellín drug boss Pablo Escobar in December 1993 left a power vacuum. It was filled by the Cali drug cartel, which appeared able to wield influence on government through nonviolent means. Both Samper and Pastrana favored continuing Gaviria's policy of appeasing the cartel with lenient sentences for trafficking rather than allowing the all-out warfare wreaked by the Medellín gang. This approach, the liberalizing of drug laws, and the discovery of a recording of two drug lords purported to be discussing donations to Samper's campaign led to a series of sharp exchanges between Bogotá and Washington. These only served to create a wave of nationalistic anger at the United States, which was regarded as culpable for its role in processing the drugs, providing a market for them, and laundering drug money. Nonetheless, Colombian efforts to curb the drug industry continued, and the Samper administration also announced new initiatives designed to control guerrilla violence and reduce human rights violations. In early November the government said it would submit legislation to Congress that would amend the constitution to forbid drug consumption.

See STATISTICS OF THE WORLD.   J.D.M.

COLORADO. See STATE GOVERNMENT REVIEW; STATISTICS OF THE WORLD.

COMMONWEALTH OF INDEPENDENT STATES. See RUSSIA and other former Soviet republics.

COMOROS. See STATISTICS OF THE WORLD.

COMPUTERS. The U.S. computer industry finally went home in 1994, turning the spotlight on mom, dad, and the kids, as million of home users were bitten by the computing bug.

Industry Highlights. The year saw personal computer vendors build increasingly affordable yet powerful computers based on Intel's Pentium chip and equipped with the latest accoutrements for multimedia computing. These machines, aimed squarely at the burgeoning consumer market, accounted for almost 40 percent of all PCs sold in the United States during the year.

A flaw that was reported in the Pentium late in 1994, however, turned into a public relations nightmare for Intel. The company had discovered the problem—a math error that occurred in rare circumstances—at midyear but had not disclosed it publicly, and in December, IBM suspended sales of all its PCs using the chip. Meanwhile, Apple's new Power Macintosh systems, based on the new PowerPC microprocessor jointly developed with IBM and Motorola, got off to a strong start.

Along with the expansion of the home computer market came a corresponding boom in the popularity of on-line services. Throughout the year there was a stampede to commercialize the Internet, the huge computer network that was once the exclusive electronic domain of the military and scientists.

IBM Rebounds. IBM's tough cost-cutting policies returned the company to solid financial footing after several years of multibillion-dollar losses, layoffs, and declining market share. In a much-anticipated speech to Wall Street analysts in late March, IBM Chairman Louis V. Gerstner, Jr., candidly acknowledged that Big Blue had lagged behind the industry's shift toward PCs and workstations; other companies had undercut IBM's once-popular midrange computer, the AS/400, with cheaper and more powerful desktop machines. IBM's rivals were designing "open systems," letting customers mix and match various computers and software programs. Gerstner de-emphasized IBM's bread-and-butter mainframe business and vowed to concentrate on producing "open" computer products and selling licensing technologies and designs to other computer makers.

IBM was forced to delay the fall introduction of its systems based on the PowerPC microprocessor. The new systems were a cornerstone of Big Blue's strategy for taking back the technical edge from other PC manufacturers, but IBM was slow in developing a version of its OS/2 operating system software that would run on the PowerPC chip.

Start spreading the news. *The 25th anniversary of the founding of what became the Internet, the global computer network, was commemorated with a reunion sponsored by Bolt Beranek and Newman, Inc., one of the original contractors on the project. Here, the original BBN team of developers poses in 1969 with their first message processor.*

Apple Breaks With the Past. In September, Apple agreed to allow other companies to clone its flagship Macintosh computer. Apple had previously refused to license its operating system, which was considered far easier to use than the rival DOS and Windows operating systems. However, more recent versions of Windows had eroded the Macintosh's technical advantage, and Apple needed to make a radical break with the past if it hoped to increase its 11 percent share of the worldwide PC market.

Late in the year Apple broadened the scope of the existing PowerPC partnership by agreeing on a common computing design standard with IBM. Consumers will ultimately be able to buy computers from either company that run many different operating systems, including Apple's Macintosh operating system, IBM's OS/2, Microsoft's Windows NT, and Solaris from Sun Microsystems.

In March, Apple began shipping its new PowerMac systems, free of the technical snafus that had been experienced by IBM. The PowerPC-based systems helped Apple earn $310.2 million for its fiscal year, a figure that was more than three times its profit from the previous year.

Compaq Emerges. Compaq emerged as the number one seller of PCs, surging ahead of rivals IBM and Apple, which were both going through difficult product transitions. Competitors struggled to match Compaq's rapid-fire price cuts. Compaq eventually finished 1994 with nearly $11 billion in sales.

Tensions with Intel, Compaq's major supplier of microprocessors, bubbled to the surface in 1994. Compaq Chief Executive Officer Eckhard Pfeiffer complained that Intel's multimillion-dollar "Intel Inside" ad campaign effectively deemphasized the value of the Compaq brand name. Pfeiffer was also upset at

Intel for selling to other PC makers system boards with the Pentium chip already installed. Compaq, which had previously signed a deal to buy some of its microprocessors from Advanced Micro Devices, threatened to buy still more computer chips from Intel rivals.

Compaq's new Presario line of computers was a huge hit. All the computers in the Presario series, which was targeted at the consumer market, were powered by AMD chips. The Presario line took much of the credit for Compaq's record fourth-quarter sales figures, which were 48 percent higher than those for the fourth quarter of 1993.

Microsoft Dominates. While price wars eroded the profitability of many high-tech companies, Microsoft enjoyed another banner year in the software market. Revenues rose 24 percent, to $4.65 billion, during fiscal 1994, Microsoft's 19th consecutive year of growth since its founding in 1975, and the company earned $1.15 billion, a figure that was up 20 percent from a year earlier.

Microsoft has been known primarily as a supplier of operating system software, such as MS-DOS and Windows. In recent years, however, the company's applications business has soared, rising to about 60 percent of total sales. In addition, Microsoft in 1994 pushed into the consumer software field, announcing a variety of applications for home and education uses.

Merger and Acquisition Fever. The drive for size and diversification could be explained in one word: Microsoft. Bill Gates's juggernaut accounted for close to 40 percent of all PC software sales worldwide. When Microsoft is unable to dominate a market, the company can reach into its very deep pockets to buy its way to the top.

In October, Microsoft announced a stunning $1.5 billion stock deal to acquire Intuit and its Quicken personal finance package. Intuit, despite its smaller size, had consistently outmaneuvered Microsoft in the personal finance software arena. News of the acquisition sparked calls for the federal government to reopen the antitrust investigation of Microsoft that had been settled in July.

In June, Novell, the industry's biggest supplier of network operating-system software, paid $855 million to buy WordPerfect and, in a separate deal the same month, bought Borland's Quattro Pro spreadsheet business for $145 million.

The British publisher Pearson PLC, which hoped to expand into the entertainment and education software market, acquired Software Toolworks for roughly $462 million.

The two leading developers in the desktop publishing field, Adobe Systems and Aldus, also merged. Powersoft and Sybase, two companies that specialize in developing sophisticated database and software tools, agreed to form a union as well.   C.C.

CONGO. *See* AFRICA; STATISTICS OF THE WORLD.

Cracking the Code

In 1977, three mathematicians at the Massachusetts Institute of Technology encoded a message and challenged the world to figure it out. They said it would take 40 quadrillion years.

It took just 17.

The trio—Ronald Rivest, Adi Shamir, and Leonard Adleman—had devised an encryption system, called RSA, based on factoring numbers that are products of extremely large prime numbers. Decoding the message required factoring a 129-digit number. (Prime numbers are divisible only by themselves and 1; when you factor a number you find the prime numbers whose product is that number.)

By 1993, though, computers were faster—and they could be linked in networks. Late in the year, would-be code crackers turned to the Internet. Over 600 volunteers on five continents did an estimated 100 quadrillion calculations on some 1,600 computers, and in April 1994 the secret message was revealed: "The magic words are squeamish ossifrage."

Although RSA is widely used today for encryption, the factoring of RSA-129 does not mean secret information is now an open book. The code cracker's task can be made far harder simply by using larger numbers.

CONGRESS. *See* UNITED STATES OF AMERICA: Congress.

CONNECTICUT. *See* STATISTICS OF THE WORLD.

COSTA RICA. A sense of normality returned to Costa Rica in 1994 following a wave of violence and uncertainty the previous year. The democratic election of a new president and a 57-member Legislative Assembly witnessed the peaceful transfer of power from one political party to another.

The February presidential elections were dominated by Costa Rica's two major political parties. José María Figueres Olsen, son of the founder of the country's democracy, represented the center-left National Liberation Party (PLN). His opponent was businessman Miguel Angel Rodríguez of the ruling conservative Social Christian Unity Party (PUSC).

The electoral campaign was dominated by economic issues. As in other Latin American countries, the major question was how to restructure the economy so as to compete internationally. The PUSC argued for free-market reforms such as the rapid privatization of government-controlled businesses and the reduction of social programs. While the PLN also recognized the need for such reforms, it wanted the changes implemented at a much slower rate. Figueres won the election by a narrow margin and assumed the country's presidency in May.

In April outgoing President Rafael Calderón Fournier signed an important free-trade agreement with Mexico. When ratified, it would become one of the most advanced agreements among Latin American countries, and it would position Costa Rica for early membership in the North American Free Trade Agreement.

Things did not go as smoothly with other foreign policy matters, however. Because Costa Rica was beginning to compete successfully in world markets, the U.S. government called for revision of existing labor laws, which were viewed as depressing local wages. There was also friction over the selection of a new secretary-general to head the Organization of American States. Costa Ricans accused the U.S. government of favoring Colombia's candidate for the post over their own.

See STATISTICS OF THE WORLD.   S.C.R.

CRIME AND LAW ENFORCEMENT. In 1994, U.S. officials on both the federal and local levels attempted to grapple with the issue of violent crime, which opinion polls showed to be high on the public's agenda. Congress passed a sweeping $30 billion crime bill designed to provide additional local police officers, help build new prisons, and support crime prevention programs. A Central Intelligence Agency official whose role as a double agent greatly damaged the country's intelligence operations was sentenced to life in prison. Statistics showed that violent crime among young people was rising dramatically. And in a case that riveted public attention, former football star O. J. Simpson (*see profile in* PEOPLE IN THE NEWS) was arrested and accused of the brutal murders of his ex-wife and a friend of hers.

Getting Tough on Crime. In February the Brady law, which mandated a five-day wait and a background check for gun purchases throughout the United States, went into effect. That same month, Treasury Secretary Lloyd Bentsen announced new restrictions on semiautomatic shotguns, which are often used in drug crimes. Three types of shotguns were reclassified as "destructive weapons," meaning they had to be registered and licensed and the prospective owners fingerprinted and photographed.

Soon thereafter, Congress began the long and divisive political process that would culminate in August with passage of a $30.2 billion anticrime measure. Early in August the bill appeared dead after a procedural move to bring it to the floor of the House of Representatives was defeated. But in a remarkable turnaround that required the defection of dozens of Republicans and much tinkering with the bill itself, the measure was passed by both houses of Congress and signed in September by President Bill Clinton.

A major selling point of the legislation was a program that provided $8.8 billion over six years to help local governments hire 100,000 police officers. An additional $7.9 billion was earmarked for prisons and boot camps, with 50 percent reserved for states that adopt truth-in-sentencing laws requiring violent offenders to serve at least 85 percent of their sentences.

Crime buster. In September, President Bill Clinton signs one of the year's major pieces of legislation, a $30 billion crime bill. Behind him are Vice President Al Gore (left) and Stephen Sposato, whose wife was killed in a San Francisco shooting.

About $1.8 billion was set aside to reimburse states for the cost of incarcerating illegal aliens who commit crimes.

Money in the bill for prevention programs, which critics charged included pork barrel projects, totaled $6.9 billion. That included $1.6 billion to fund a package of new federal penalties and grant programs to combat violence against women and $1 billion for drug courts that sought to rehabilitate first-time or nonviolent drug offenders through alternatives to incarceration. Other provisions of the bill extended the death penalty to dozens of new or existing federal crimes and mandated life imprisonment for a person convicted of a third violent felony involving a federal statute. The most contentious provision banned for ten years the manufacture and possession of 19 types of assault weapons (and copycat models of them) and semiautomatic guns with two or more characteristics associated with assault weapons. The provision exempted more than 650 types of semiautomatic weapons and allowed gun owners to keep guns they already owned legally.

Spy Catching. In February, Aldrich H. Ames, an employee of the Central Intelligence Agency for 32 years, became the highest-ranking CIA officer ever charged with espionage. Court documents alleged that, starting in 1985, Ames was paid more than $2 million by Moscow authorities. They also said that the information he provided led to the deaths of at least ten Soviet and Eastern European double agents working for the United States and revealed the identities of two dozen other U.S. intelligence officers and foreign agents working for the CIA. Ames also exposed some 50 secret operations, the papers said.

Ames agreed to a plea bargain that put him in prison for life without parole in return for leniency for his wife, who was charged with abetting him. At his sentencing, Ames criticized the espionage establishment, saying it spied on friendly nations and gathered information that was "insignificant or irrelevant to our policy makers' needs." Although the CIA reprimanded 11 current or former officials for failing to properly monitor Ames, many observers felt this was insufficient punishment. The criticism was one of the factors leading to the resignation of CIA Director James Woolsey in December.

Crime Statistics. A study released in October revealed that homicide among male American teenagers was rising alarmingly, reaching epidemic proportions and advancing at far higher rates than for any other age group. The study, by the Centers for Disease Control and Prevention, showed that between 1985 and 1991 the annual homicide rate for men 15 to 19 years old rose more than 150 percent, compared with a decrease of 1 percent for men 25 to 29 and 13 percent for men 30 to 34. The study attributed the increase to the use of crack cocaine and the proliferation of guns. The increased rate also meant that men in the 15-to-19 age group were the most likely to be arrested for homicide.

The National Crime Victimization Survey, released by the Bureau of Justice Statistics at the end of October, showed that overall crime in the United States increased only slightly between 1992 and 1993. Violent crime was, however, up 5.6 percent, continuing its steady rise, while property crime remained about the same. A new category, sexual assaults (other than rape), showed that an estimated 173,000 such attacks occurred in the United States during 1993. The victimization study surveyed 100,000 people and included crimes not reported to police.

Federal Bureau of Investigation figures (which cover only crimes reported to the police) published in December showed a 3 percent decline in serious crime in the first six months of 1994. Rapes and burglaries were down 6 percent, robberies 4 percent, and aggravated assaults 3 percent. Homicides were down 2 percent. But for the first time more people were killed by strangers or unknown assailants than by people they knew, and this randomness fueled public fears about crime, for "every American now has a realistic chance" of being murdered.

A survey released in October reported that on June 30 the U.S. prison population passed 1 million for the first time, reflecting tougher sentencing. The report by the Justice Department's Bureau of Justice Statistics found that the U.S. prison population grew by almost 40,000 during the first six months of 1994. In June 1994, the report said, there were 373 people in prison for every 100,000 residents, compared with 139 per 100,000 in 1980. That put the United States second, behind Russia, in imprisonment rates. U.S. rates were four times those of Canada and 14 times those of Japan.

Violent Crime. The most sensational arrest of the year was that of former professional football star and television personality O. J. Simpson, who was charged with murdering his former wife, Nicole Brown Simpson, and her friend Ronald Goldman. Both victims were stabbed to death in a suburb of Los Angeles on June 12. Before surrendering, Simpson led police on a slow chase along Los Angeles freeways, an event that attracted crowds and was broadcast live on national television. At his ar-

raignment Simpson pleaded innocent. Subsequent disclosures before Simpson's trial focused attention both on the issue of domestic violence and on the validity of DNA testing (often the basis of capital convictions) in the courtroom. Samples of DNA found in blood at the crime scene and tested by forensic scientists were the subject of controversy throughout pretrial hearings. The process of selecting a jury of 12 (plus 12 alternates) was completed in December.

Other Murders and Their Aftermath. Legal maneuverings surrounded the case of Colin Ferguson, who was accused of shooting dead six persons and wounding 18 others on a Long Island Railroad train in New York in December 1993. His lawyers wanted him to plead insanity, but he was ruled mentally competent to stand trial and allowed to serve as his own attorney. In January the trial of the Menendez brothers, who admitted to having killed their parents with shotgun blasts in August 1989, ended in a mistrial (a new trial was later set for 1995). And in May, Joel Rifkin, an unemployed landscaper, was found guilty of murder in the first of a series of trials involving six women whom Rifkin was accused of killing (he had originally confessed to killing 17). He was sentenced to 25 years to life by a Long Island, NY, county court judge.

Also in May four men convicted in connection with the February 1993 bombing of the World Trade Center, in which six people were killed, were sentenced to 240 years each. Mohammed Salameh, Nidal Ayyad, Mahmud Abouhalima, and Ahmad Ajaj, the four defendants in the six-month trial, were denied the possibility of parole. The bombing was termed a terrorist attack with Middle East connections.

Early in the year a 30-year-old murder case involving civil rights leader Medgar Evers came to a close with the conviction in Mississippi of white supremacist Byron De La Beckwith. Two trials in 1964 before all-white juries resulted in hung juries and Beckwith's release. But after witnesses came forward in 1989 with statements that Beckwith had bragged about murdering Evers, the case was reopened. In February a jury of eight blacks and four whites found Beckwith guilty of murder; he was sentenced to life imprisonment.

The O. J. Simpson Case

Actor, TV personality, and ex-football superstar O. J. Simpson was probably the biggest celebrity ever to be charged with a capital crime in U.S. history. Certainly few criminal cases had ever provoked as much public attention as this one. Simpson was accused of brutally murdering his ex-wife, Nicole Brown Simpson (above left, with Simpson and their two children), and her friend, Ronald Goldman (right), on June 12 at her Los Angeles-area home (above right).

In November, Jeffrey Dahmer, convicted in 1992 of 15 murders that involved cannibalism and necrophilia, was beaten to death in the Wisconsin prison where he was serving 15 consecutive life terms. One inmate was initially named as the murderer; prison authorities later said they were investigating the possibility of a conspiracy.

Parents Who Kill Children. To the shock of friends and neighbors, Susan Smith of Union, SC, was arrested in early November and charged with the murders of her two sons, aged 14 months and three years. Smith, who is white, had first claimed the children had been kidnapped in her stolen car by a black man but eventually confessed she had strapped them into their car seats and let the car roll into a lake. Also in November, Ronald Rako of Chicago was convicted of killing his three-month-old son by suffocating him with a pillow. After the death, Rako had donated the baby's heart to another child.

Abortion Clinic Violence. In August the Clinton administration sent federal marshals to a dozen abortion clinics around the United States in an effort to end violence against the

146

clinics and their personnel. Separate trials in Pensacola, FL, of two men accused of killing abortion doctors resulted in convictions, one on federal charges under a newly enacted law to combat violence against abortion providers. As the year ended, a gunman fired on two Massachusetts clinics, killing two, and then fired on a clinic in Virginia a day later, after which he was arrested.

Corruption and Fraud. The New York City Police Department came under scrutiny in July after a mayoral commission found that corruption within the department was aided by a "willful blindness" on the part of supervisors. According to the Mollen Commission report, "scores of officers told us that they believed the department did not want them to report corruption, that such information was often ignored, and that their careers would be ruined if they did so. The evidence shows that this belief was not unfounded." The result, said the commission, was the acceptance of highly organized networks of rogue officers who dealt in drugs and preyed on African-American and Hispanic neighborhoods. As if to accentuate the point, 39 officers in a Harlem precinct were arrested during the year and charged with stealing and selling drugs, extortion, tampering with evidence, and perjury.

In the medical field, National Medical Enterprises, a California-based hospital chain, pleaded guilty in June to paying kickbacks and bribes for referrals. It agreed to pay more than $360 million, believed to be the largest settlement between the government and a health care provider. A former company executive, Peter Alexis, pleaded guilty to similar charges and said in court that more than 50 doctors and others had received payments. Investigators had accused National Medical of handling patients who did not need treatment and filing false insurance claims.

Criminal Justice Administration. In October a federal district court judge in California ordered the state to dismantle its gas chamber at San Quentin prison, where almost 200 prisoners had been executed since 1938. Judge Marilyn Hall detailed evidence of dying inmates remaining conscious long enough to experience a pain similar to strangulation or drowning. Meanwhile, executions in other states

continued. A Virginia prisoner became the first person to be executed after a conviction based on DNA-matching technology. Arkansas renewed the practice of executing two and three inmates in the same night. And in Illinois, John Wayne Gacy, 52, convicted 14 years earlier in the sex-related killings of 33 young men and boys, was executed by lethal injection in May.

Around the United States state legislatures introduced and passed laws designed to make prisons more harsh. In Mississippi, for example, prisoners were denied private televisions, radios, computers, and access to weight-lifting equipment. Starting in 1995 they would have to wear striped uniforms with the word "convict" stamped on the back. Louisiana eliminated martial arts training and California allowed prison authorities to bar obscene publications and materials that incite violence.

In Washington, DC, the U.S. Supreme Court ruled in April that during jury selection defense attorneys and prosecutors could not remove prospective jurors solely because of their sex. The decision extended a protection that eight years before had been granted to African-American jurors in civil and criminal cases.

Organized Crime. Russian and Asian crime gangs gained notoriety during 1994. In January the Justice Department elevated the Russian mafia to the highest investigative priority, on a par with the American and Sicilian mafias. Law enforcement officials said Russian gangs had set up headquarters in émigré communities, especially in Brooklyn, NY. The more recent arrivals, they said, were better organized and more violent than those who came during the initial influx of the 1970s. Asian organized groups, already an important target for the Justice Department, saw one of their most wanted members arrested in Hong Kong in September on murder and conspiracy charges. In addition, 14 members of his gang were arrested in New York. FBI officials believed the gang was involved in smuggling illegal aliens into the United States.

Also in September, law enforcement officials in New York and Italy arrested 79 suspects and charged them in connection with a drug ring that imported cocaine from Colombia and exported it to Italy, where it sells for three times the New York price. The group was alleged to have worked out of pizza parlors, cafés, butcher shops, and private homes around New York City, handling tens of millions of dollars worth of cocaine and heroin over the previous three years.   L.S.G.

CROATIA. Late 1994 developments in the civil war in neighboring Bosnia-Hercegovina had possibly profound implications for Croatia. Slight improvements in the economy took place amid internal political turmoil.

Bosnian Quagmire. The government of Croatia scored a major diplomatic success when it played an important part in negotiations that led to the signing of a U.S.-initiated agreement between Bosnia's Croats and Muslims in March. It was hoped that the agreement, which called for Croats and Muslims to link their territories into a federation, would be a milestone on the road to a settlement of the Bosnian civil war. The agreement enabled the Croatian government to end its unpopular and controversial involvement in the war, and it improved Croatia's international standing dramatically.

Developments in the fall changed the picture considerably. After Bosnian Serbs regained land they had lost in an initially successful offensive by Bosnian Croat militia and the Muslim-led Bosnian Army, they crushed the Army in the Muslim enclave of Bihac. They accomplished the latter with the aid of Serbs from the Krajina region of Croatia.

Krajina borders on the Bihac enclave, and the Krajina Serbs, who had declared their independence from Croatia in 1991, bombed Bosnian Army positions around Bihac and then crossed the border into Bosnia to fight on the ground. Tensions between the Croatian government and the Krajina Serbs rose, and the cease-fire between the two sides that had gone into effect in March 1994 was violated numerous times in the following days. (Direct negotiations on Krajina's status had come to a virtual standstill earlier in the fall.) Croatia declared that it would enter the war if Bihac fell to the Serbs.

Economic Developments. On the economic front the first phase of the stabilization program unveiled by Prime Minister Nikica Valentic in October 1993 exceeded the government's expectations in inflation reduction, produced more modest gains with regard to incomes policy, and took steps designed to reinvigorate the market economy.

A new currency, the kuna, was introduced in the spring to great criticism from the international community, which voiced its displeasure at the government's adoption of the name of the currency that had been used by Croatia's profascist puppet government during World War II.

Political Uncertainty. April 1994 saw the much-anticipated split of the ruling Croatian Democratic Union (HDZ) as two leaders of the party's left wing, the speakers of the upper and lower houses of Parliament, Josip Manolic and Stipe Mesic, announced the formation of the Croatian Independent Democrats. This led to a parliamentary crisis over the naming of new speakers, predictions of early elections, and opposition hopes that the HDZ would disintegrate. By the fall, however, President Franjo Tudjman seemed to have both consolidated the HDZ's ranks and boosted his own level of support in the polls.

Controversial cash. *The introduction in May of a new Croatian currency, the kuna, caused considerable debate because the currency of the pro-Nazi Croatian regime in World War II had the same name. This 200-kuna bill bears the portrait of Stjepan Radic, a Croatian nationalist assassinated in 1928.*

International Standing. Croatia made small improvements in its relationship with Serbia, and each country opened an information office in the other. The election of an ultraconservative government in Italy reopened confrontations over Croatia's Istria region. The Slovene Parliament's passage of a new electoral boundaries law in October 1994, which incorporated four Croatian villages into Slovenian voting districts, threatened regional cooperation.

See STATISTICS OF THE WORLD.   O.K.

CUBA. In 1994 the Cuban economic crisis that began with the collapse of the Soviet trading bloc in 1990 intensified. Bad weather and shortages of fertilizers and fuel limited the 1993 sugar crop to only 4 million metric tons (half as much as the 1990 crop). By early 1994 exports had fallen by 80 percent since 1989, and foreign currency reserves were exhausted. As a result, import capacity fell from more than $8 billion in 1989 to under $2 billion. Manufacturing enterprises operated at a fraction of capacity, and unemployment was rising. Inflation, pushed by a budget deficit of 4.2 billion pesos and an excess money supply of 10 billion pesos, continued to increase steadily.

Faced with economic collapse, the Cuban government adopted a limited version of China's strategy of economic reforms without democratic political reform. In late 1993, Cubans had been given the right to use foreign currencies, and limited private enterprise was permitted. During 1994 subsidies to state enterprises were halved, public payrolls were slashed, and central planning was abandoned. Rationing of essential goods at subsidized prices was continued, but prices for other goods and services were freed and rose dramatically. An income tax on the newly self-employed was levied, along with a tax on private property. Foreign investment was encouraged, particularly in the tourism and petroleum industries. Despite optimistic government reports on the economy, Cuba's standard of living continued to fall, and social unrest boiled over.

In early August thousands of Cubans rioted in downtown Havana, protesting the new two-tier economy that benefited those who worked in the hard-currency tourist sector or had ex-iled relatives sending them dollars while other Cubans went hungry. After the attempted flight of a group of Cubans on a stolen ferry boat ended in an armed confrontation with Cuban officials and several deaths, President Fidel Castro said he would not stop those who wanted to leave. More than 20,000 desperate Cubans then tried to cross the Florida Straits on flimsy rafts.

U.S. President Bill Clinton responded by reversing the long-standing policy of granting asylum to all Cuban political refugees and ordering the Coast Guard to intercept the rafters and intern them at the U.S. naval base at Guantánamo Bay, Cuba. He pressured Castro by tightening the decades-old U.S. trade embargo and prohibiting the remission of dollars, worth as much as $500 million annually to Havana, from U.S. citizens to family members in Cuba.

In the negotiations that followed, the United States resisted calls to accept 100,000 Cuban immigrants a year and to loosen the embargo, but did agree to accept 20,000 a year in return for a Cuban crackdown on illegal emigration. In December the Clinton administration said it would consider allowing Cuban children and their families detained in American internment camps into the United States—if the families had full financial sponsorship.

See STATISTICS OF THE WORLD.   P.W.

CYPRUS. Greek and Turkish Cypriots came no closer in 1994 to settling the dispute that had divided the island for 20 years. A 1974 coup by the Greek junta and a subsequent Turkish invasion had split Cyprus into the Greek Republic of Cyprus (ROC) and the Turkish Republic of Northern Cyprus (TRNC).

Confidence-building measures proposed by United Nations negotiators in 1993 to help resolve the long-standing estrangement collapsed in 1994. The main reason for their failure was the July 5 ruling of the European Court of Justice in Luxembourg banning the export of citrus and potatoes from the TRNC to Europe without the permission of the ROC. In addition, export duties of at least 14 percent were to be placed on clothing and textiles exported from the TRNC to Europe. Citrus, potatoes, clothing, and textiles account for 47 percent of the TRNC economy.

In retaliation for the court's ruling, TRNC President Rauf Denktash threatened to make the TRNC an autonomous province of Turkey. The Legislative Assembly of the TRNC gave force to Denktash's statement on August 28 when it voted, 30-16, to revoke all previous resolutions that had envisaged some sort of federation with the Greek south. The TRNC's action reinvigorated the ROC's efforts to seek early membership in the European Union.

There were increasingly rancorous disputes between Turkey and Greece in 1994 over the delimitation of territorial waters, continental shelves, and airspace in the Aegean Sea. These disputes stressed the geopolitical and geostrategic importance of Cyprus in Greek efforts to maintain hegemony in the Aegean Sea region and Turkey's attempts to increase its influence there.

See STATISTICS OF THE WORLD. R.O.

CZECH REPUBLIC. During 1994 the Czech Republic consolidated its position as Eastern Europe's greatest success story; unemployment hovered around 3 percent (the second lowest rate in Europe), and economic growth resumed after a prolonged transitional slump.

The year also saw the completion of the second wave of the innovative Czech program for privatizing state-owned industry. Under this approach, all adult citizens could buy nominally priced vouchers to exchange for shares in newly reorganized enterprises. By year's end it was estimated that as much as 80 percent of economic activity had been transferred to the private sector.

The performance of the governing coalition, led by Prime Minister Vaclav Klaus and his Civic Democratic Party, was supported by nearly two-thirds of the population, according to opinion surveys. The coalition was divided over a Klaus proposal for balanced budget legislation, but more important was the government's continuing inability to reach agreement on two steps mandated by the 1992 constitution: the holding of elections to form an upper house in Parliament and the creation of an intermediate regional authority between the local governments and the central government.

The Czech Republic's citizenship law drew both domestic and international criticism. The law's requirement that citizenship be granted

Laureate. *Philadelphia mayor Edward Rendell presents the Liberty Medal to Czech President Vaclav Havel on July 4; the annual award is given to a person or group contributing to freedom and equality.*

only to those with a clean criminal record for the previous five years was widely regarded as targeted at Gypsy immigrants from Slovakia. In October the Constitutional Court upheld the existing law after a challenge from left-wing Parliament deputies.

The primary objective of Czech foreign policy remained integration into NATO and the European Union as soon as possible. The Czech Republic became an associate member of the European Union in May but chafed under EU trade restrictions in key industries such as steel, textiles, and agriculture.

The government signed on to U.S. President Bill Clinton's Partnership for Peace program of East-West defense cooperation in early 1994, but it continued to press for full NATO membership. In May the government paid off its share of the International Monetary Fund's loan to the former Czechoslovakia and announced that in the future the Czech Republic would meet its borrowing needs in the financial markets.

See STATISTICS OF THE WORLD. C.S.L.

D

DANCE. Russia's most hallowed dance institution, the Bolshoi Ballet, suffered serious internal conflicts in 1994. In the United States, years of belt-tightening led to a flurry of resignations by and dismissals of artistic directors of important companies.

Battles at the Bolshoi. After the end of the Communist era in 1991, Russia's ballet companies suffered a steep drop in financial support. But while the Bolshoi's sister company, the Kirov Ballet in St. Petersburg (formerly Leningrad), renewed itself, the Bolshoi languished, even as the Bolshoi Theater building itself grew ever more dilapidated.

For much of 1994 it appeared that Bolshoi ballet master Yuri Grigorovich would be a casualty of the company's decline. During three decades of directing the Bolshoi, Grigorovich had wielded power as if his three titles—artistic director, chief choreographer, and principal ballet master—were his for life. In the process he garnered many powerful enemies, including star dancer Gedeminas Taranda, whom Grigorovich fired shortly before a performance in February. While Grigorovich shouted for security guards, Taranda walked on the stage and announced to the audience that he had been sacked.

Grigorovich's most powerful enemy, however, seemed to be Vladimir Kokonin, the Bolshoi Theater's chief director. Kokonin succeeded in ejecting the Grigorovich troupe from the theater at one point in the course of the summer. Indeed, battles between Kokonin and Grigorovich delayed the start of the fall season by a week.

In September, Russian President Boris Yeltsin issued a decree to put the Bolshoi's dancers and directors, who once enjoyed lifetime privileges, on shorter-term contracts—evidently one of Kokonin's wishes. Meanwhile, tours intended to provide much-needed funds collapsed. In Australia, six of 26 performances were canceled for lack of ticket sales, and a tour of England was canceled for the same reason. In November the theater announced that Grigorovich would be offered a new contract, but rumors circulated that Grigorovich would

Splendid specter. *Sections of* Chronicle, *a work by Martha Graham from the 1930s, were reconstructed for the series "Radical Graham" at the Brooklyn Academy of Music in October. The opening section, "Specter," was danced by Terese Capucilli.*

Refulgent revival. *Kevin McKenzie, the artistic director of the American Ballet Theater, restored Anthony Tudor's* Echoing of Trumpets, *an antiwar ballet rarely seen since it was created in 1963. The lead couple were doomed partisan Stephen Hyde and the devoted Julie Kent (center).*

step down after a 30-year anniversary celebration in his honor scheduled for January 1995.

European Ballet Companies. Peter Schaufuss became director of the Royal Danish Ballet in 1994, and he immediately replaced the existing production of August Bournonville's classic *La Sylphide* with his own version of the well-known ballet in which, in November, he bade farewell to his distinguished international dancing career.

Patrick Dupond, artistic director of the Paris Opera's ballet company, commissioned a reconstruction of Nijinsky's *Till Eulenspiegel* from dance and art historians Millicent Hodson and Kenneth Archer. The well-received production, danced in February, restored Nijinsky's last ballet, unseen since 1916. Anthony Dowell, director of Britain's Royal Ballet, staged a new production of the company's signature work, *The Sleeping Beauty*, which had its world premiere at the Kennedy Center Opera House in Washington, DC, in April. Though it respected the text of the 19th-century classic, the production's dancing was overwhelmed by the tilting columns that dominated designer Maria Bjornson's decor.

U.S. Budget Troubles. If financial and leadership problems were undermining Russian

ballet, similar problems could be seen in the United States as years of recession-enforced cuts and compromises finally brought artistic directors and boards of directors into open conflict. Robert Barnett, who had directed the Atlanta Ballet for more than 30 years, resigned a year before his scheduled retirement rather than comply with another round of mandated cutbacks. Christopher d'Amboise, who brought national notice to the Pennsylvania Ballet, could not get a budget past his board and resigned, while John McFall, Christopher Fleming, and Dace Dindonis were dismissed by the boards of BalletMet (Columbus, OH), Bay Ballet Theatre (Tampa, FL), and Indianapolis Ballet Theatre, respectively, all in clashes over finances. In November, McFall was named the new artistic director of the Atlanta Ballet.

New Works and Revivals. In May the New York City Ballet presented its second Diamond Project, a biennial workshop that commissioned new ballets en masse. Of the 12 choreographers whose works premiered in the spring, none emerged as outstanding, though Lynne Taylor-Corbett's *Chiaroscuro* and Kevin O'Day's *Viola Alone (With One Exception)* were widely respected. At American Ballet

Theatre, new artistic director Kevin McKenzie revived Antony Tudor's antiwar ballet, *Echoing of Trumpets,* scarcely seen since its creation in 1963. The company's adoption of Lar Lubovitch's *The Red Shoes,* from the unsuccessful Broadway musical of that name, was big box office but artistically disastrous.

The Joffrey Ballet, with a changed profile since the death of founder Robert Joffrey in 1988, had its first New York repertory season in three years. Its reconstruction of Leonide Massine's 1933 antiwar ballet, *Les Présages,* proved a highly stylized, symbol-laden series of group images. Miami City Ballet, directed by Edward Villella, presented a triumphant production of Balanchine's three-act *Jewels* at the prestigious Edinburgh Festival in August.

Modern Dance. The Brooklyn Academy of Music opened its Next Wave Festival in October with a selection of Martha Graham's work from the 1920s and 1930s; the program was entitled "Radical Graham." Several "lost" Graham works were reconstructed from old photographs by company director Ron Protas. Merce Cunningham presented a 90-minute world premiere, *Ocean,* in Brussels in May. During the year he also revived his 1975 masterpiece *Sounddance,* not seen since 1980, and his *Signals* was staged by Mikhail Baryshnikov's modern dance company, the White Oak Dance Project. Also, the Film Society of Lincoln Center screened a retrospective of Cunningham's considerable oeuvre for film and video, "Cunningham on Camera," in April and May.

Dance Personalities. Several dancers, most significantly Adam Luders, retired from the New York City Ballet; meanwhile at American Ballet Theatre, Paloma Herrera, who danced several leading roles at age 18, was called the most outstanding young dancer in decades. Igor Youskevitch, the *danseur noble* of the 1940s and 1950s for whom Balanchine choreographed *Theme and Variations,* died at the age of 82. AIDS took the lives of several dance figures, among them Gregory Osborne, Paolo Bortoluzzi, John Curry, and Jeff Wadlington.

A.F.

DELAWARE. *See* STATISTICS OF THE WORLD.
DEMOCRATIC PARTY. *See* ELECTIONS IN THE UNITED STATES.

DENMARK. The mood of the 1994 political landscape in Denmark was set late in 1993 by local election gains for the right-of-center opposition Liberal Party, whose roots are agrarian but whose platform was pro-European Union and favored fiscal austerity. The June elections to the European Parliament continued the trend. The Liberals gained modestly (one seat), as did the Conservatives (for whom former Prime Minister Poul Schluter won a seat), while parties in the center-left coalition led by Prime Minister Poul Nyrup Rasmussen lost ground. Two strongly anti-European Union parties kept four of Denmark's 16 seats in the European body.

National parliamentary elections on September 21 ended the Rasmussen government's narrow (one-seat) parliamentary majority. The Liberals gained almost 32 percent more seats. Rasmussen's Social Democrats lost 10 percent of their seats; one of his coalition partners, the Christian People's Party, lost all of its seats, and another, the Center Democrats, lost almost half. Although the remaining coalition partner, the Radical Liberals, gained a seat, Rasmussen was left with a minority government. He and his two surviving coalition partners expected to be able to weave a working majority on an issue-by-issue basis, with support from two leftist parties. Perhaps the biggest surprise of the election was the victory won by political humorist Jacob Haugaard without any party affiliation—an exceedingly rare occurrence in Denmark's party-based political system.

At midyear there was a partial resolution of "Tamilgate" when a court issued a suspended jail sentence to ex-Labor Minister Grethe Moeller, implicated in a scheme involving the illegal restriction of Tamil immigrants from Sri Lanka. (Tamilgate's discovery brought the resignation of Schluter's government in early 1993.) The impeachment trial of the scandal's central figure, ex-Justice Minister Erik Ninn-Hansen, was put on hold after he suffered a stroke in June.

Denmark's economic growth accelerated in 1994, reaching about 4.5 percent without rekindling inflation (which stood at 2 percent at year's end) or hurting the positive trade balance. Even so, no progress was made in re-

153

ducing unemployment, which was above 12 percent, or the public budget deficit.

See STATISTICS OF THE WORLD.   E.S.E.

DISTRICT OF COLUMBIA. See STATISTICS OF THE WORLD.

DJIBOUTI.   See STATISTICS OF THE WORLD.

DOMINICA.   See CARIBBEAN BASIN; STATISTICS OF THE WORLD.

DOMINICAN REPUBLIC. See CARIBBEAN BASIN; STATISTICS OF THE WORLD.

EARTH SCIENCES. The year 1994 brought record winter cold in the northeastern United States, record summer heat in western states, and record wet-season rainfall in parts of the Southeast. Scientists were intrigued by an especially deep earthquake of substantial magnitude in Bolivia, and a federal jury reached a verdict on charges resulting from the 1989 *Exxon Valdez* oil spill.

CLIMATOLOGY

While parts of the United States saw unprecedented extremes of cold or heat in 1994, Haiti and eastern China were ravaged by deadly storms that killed hundreds of people in each country.

Harsh Northeast Winter. Record snowfall buried the northern Appalachians from January 4 to March 18 as many sections received nearly 100 inches (2.5 meters) during this ten-week period. The excessive snowpack in the East raised concerns about spring flooding, but an unusually warm and dry April caused a gentle runoff.

A phenomenal cold wave spread into the Ohio Valley and Northeast from January 20-22, forcing schools, businesses, and even government offices to close. Rolling blackouts were implemented to keep the electric power grid that supplies the densely populated cities of the Northeast from collapse. The mercury fell to a state record minimum of –36°F (–38°C) in central Indiana and unofficially to –52°F (–47°C) at Amasa, MI. Many cities across Ohio and Pennsylvania set new all-time minimums, including Harrisburg, PA, at –22°F (–29°C). New York City dropped to –2°F (–18°C), the lowest reading to be recorded since 1968.

Hot Summer in West. Just after the summer solstice a record heat wave developed in the West, and by the end of the season Idaho, Nevada, Utah, Arizona, New Mexico, Colorado, and Wyoming had experienced their hottest and driest summer in the 100 years of regional records. Tucson, AZ, reached 100°F (38°C) on 99 occasions, and a new state maximum temperature of 128°F (53°C) was set. It was even hot in spots that do not usually get hot. Seattle, for example, reached 100°F (38°C) for the first time ever on July 20.

Deluges in Southeast. A series of tropical rainstorms inundated Florida, Georgia, and the coastal Carolinas starting in early July and continuing into early October and November. Tropical Storms Alberto (July 3) and Beryl (August 15) both struck the Florida panhandle. Alberto stalled over Georgia, dumping a state record 21.1 in. (53.6 cm) of rain in 24 hours on Americus, GA. Remnants of Tropical Storm Debby brought more heavy rain to the area in the early fall.

On November 15, after wreaking havoc on Cuba and Haiti, Tropical Storm Gordon hit the United States. The storm, with gusts of 60 miles (100 kilometers) per hour, dropped more than 8 in. (20 cm) of rain on Florida and caused power outages affecting several hundred thousand homes and businesses. Gordon spun off a deadly tornado in Florida and briefly achieved hurricane intensity off the North Carolina coast. Gordon was the deadliest storm of the hurricane season, causing more than 500 deaths, the vast majority of them in Haiti.

Typhoon. Supertyphoon Fred struck Zhejiang Province in eastern China on August 21, killing at least 700 people and causing $1.2 billion damage. It was the worst storm in the region in over a century.

Longest-lived Hurricane. Hurricane John, formed in the eastern Pacific on August 12, was reported as the most intense storm ever in the central Pacific, with winds exceeding 170 mph (275 kph). The storm struck tiny Johnston Island, about 700 miles southwest of Hawaii, and finally dissipated on September 9 in the north Pacific.

Advances in Meteorology. On April 13 the first of a new generation of weather satellites, GOES-8, was successfully launched from the Kennedy Space Center. GOES-8 began operational use in late October, providing both finer resolution and greater frequency of satellite imagery for better short-range forecasts. On May 23 the U.S. National Weather Service installed a Cray C90 supercomputer at its National Meteorological Center in Suitland, MD. The computer's ability to perform 15 billion math operations per second will allow forecasters and researchers to make improved weather predictions for the United States.

P.G.K.

GEOLOGY

In 1994 geologists continued to learn important lessons from earthquakes, while an old controversy resurfaced about the role played by tectonic plates (the segments into which the Earth's crust is divided) in the generation of occasional catastrophic upheavals.

Earthquakes. Among the more than 6 million earthquakes detected by instruments in 1994, two deserve special mention.

An earthquake of magnitude 6.6 struck the San Fernando Valley region of Los Angeles on January 17. It was a disturbing illustration of a "blind thrust" earthquake, which occurs when a thrust fault ruptures but does not break the surface.

Detailed subsurface-fault mapping has, in recent years, revealed a network of similar faults buried in the Los Angeles area, leading geologists to believe that blind thrust earthquakes may pose as great a hazard to the Los Angeles area as the more well-known San Andreas strike-slip fault, along which movement occurs parallel to the direction of the fault.

On June 9 northern Bolivia was shaken by an earthquake of magnitude 8.2. The seismic waves of the quake were felt by people as far away as Toronto. Earth scientists will study the 1994 Bolivian earthquake for years, not because of its size but because of its depth: at

650 kilometers (400 miles) beneath the Earth's surface, it was probably the largest very deep earthquake of the 20th century. The Bolivian event enlivened an already hot scientific discussion of the mechanics of deep earthquakes. Many geologists think that deep earthquakes

Dante's inferno. *Engineers look over Dante II, an eight-legged experimental robot explorer that in late July descended into the scorching crater of an Alaskan volcano. The machine, sponsored by the U.S. National Aeronautics and Space Administration, successfully carried out its primary mission, although it toppled over from a misstep on its way out of the crater. Dante's survival was an encouraging sign that robots will someday be able to explore a variety of environments too hostile for humans.*

Thar she blows! *When a nearby volcano erupted spectacularly in September through two separate cones, the port of Rabaul on New Britain Island, Papua New Guinea, was buried under ash and rock. Over 50,000 people fled the town, which had been a strategic focal point in World War II and more recently was a major commercial center. Left, a cargo ship sails near Rabaul as ash billows into the sky. Above, a satellite view of the eruptions.*

differ fundamentally from shallow earthquakes, which are caused by slippage along a cracklike fault. Deep earthquakes, it is argued, may be caused by "anticracks," or planar collapse zones, along which shearing may also take place. Anticracks are suspected as a cause because deep earthquakes occur at places where cold sinking "slabs" of old oceanic plates descend into the mantle to a depth where minerals are converted by heat and pressure into more compact minerals that take up less space, relieving pressure and causing shearing. But some geologists say that the Bolivian earthquake was so powerful that it must have involved the deformation of a volume of material too large to fit into the descending slab of a cold oceanic plate.

Meteorite Impact. In 1994 evidence was unearthed indicating that Chesapeake Bay owes its existence to a meteorite impact about 35 million years ago. Seismic reflection data suggested that the Chesapeake Bay site and an impact site off the New Jersey coast were centers where large pieces of a meteorite hit. This evidence helps explain and is supported by patterns of unusual rocks ("tektites") found throughout the eastern United States.

Huge Quantities of Volcanic Rock. During certain periods in the Earth's history (notably the Cretaceous period, which lasted approximately from 145 million to 66 million years ago) extraordinarily large quantities of volcanic rocks were produced. One theory has it that the turmoil during the Cretaceous resulted from disturbances deep within the Earth's mantle, near the Earth's core, which started superplumes of extra-hot rock ascending through the mantle. An alternative theory, set forth in 1994, put the blame on a chance rearrangement of plate boundaries during the Cretaceous. According to this theory, thousands of kilometers of spreading centers (where new crustal material rises up from below) along the southwest Pacific were converted into subduction zones (regions where old ocean crust sinks into the mantle), suddenly reorienting the plate motion. Continents were dragged off of long-held positions, which allowed the excess heat that had built up beneath them to escape, causing the voluminous volcanic production.

P.Bo.

OCEANOGRAPHY

Legal battles over the 1989 *Exxon Valdez* oil spill in Alaska's Prince William Sound moved slowly toward a final settlement in 1994. In a three-part trial, a federal jury found in June that Exxon and the *Exxon Valdez*'s captain had both acted recklessly. In August the jury awarded $286.8 million in compensatory damages to Alaskans harmed by the spill, and the following month it awarded the plaintiffs $5 billion in punitive damages, the largest award ever for a pollution case. Exxon appealed the decision in December.

Meanwhile, environmentalists and marine scientists differed over how to spend the $620 million remaining in a $900 million fund Exxon had established in 1991 to settle charges from the spill. Environmentalists wanted to use most of the money to buy forest land otherwise subject to logging, which, they argued, would damage streams in which

salmon breed. Late in the year the fund's trustees approved a plan to set aside money for various restoration activities, including land purchases.

As of December 28, under a 1990 federal law enacted as a result of the *Valdez* spill, tankers were no longer allowed to dock in the United States if they could not demonstrate to the U.S. Coast Guard that they had the financial ability to carry hundreds of millions of dollars of liability insurance to cover accidents and spills.

The year 1994 saw North American surface vessels reach the north pole for the first time, as U.S. and Canadian icebreakers sailed from the Pacific to the Atlantic by way of the pole. The U.S. Coast Guard ship *Polar Sea* and the Canadian Coast Guard ship *Louis St. Laurent*, both with scientists on board, entered the Arctic Ocean through the Bering Strait in late July and reached the north pole on August 22. The event was marked by festivities that included a wedding and a barbecue. Near the pole the ships rendezvoused with a nuclear-powered Russian icebreaker, the *Yamal*.

Scientists found that the Arctic waters were more variable and biologically productive than previously known. A new undersea mountain was discovered by the *St. Laurent*. Analysis of the data gathered during this excursion could change the way scientists view the Arctic and its ice cover.

M.G.G.

Top of the world. *The Canadian icebreaker* Louis St. Laurent *and the U.S. Coast Guard icebreaker* Polar Sea *carve a path through the ice on their way to the north pole. Part of a mission to study, among other things, arctic pollution, in August they became the first North American surface vessels to reach the northernmost spot on the globe.*

ECONOMY AND BUSINESS, U.S. The economic outlook for the United States was bright in January 1994. Economists were predicting confidently that unemployment would continue to drop and wages would rise, interest rates would rise less than 1 percent, and consumer spending would remain in check. At the same time they predicted that inflation would rise only slightly, permitting the Federal Reserve Board to largely continue its loose money policy. By year's end, however, these predictions were in tatters.

Interest rates, rather than remaining stable, had soared as the Fed, in an attempt to slow economic growth, raised the rates it charges its member banks. Thirty-year mortgage rates, which had dropped to 6½ percent in 1993, jumped to more than 9 percent in 1994. True, unemployment had continued to drop, but at a rate exceeding expectations, as the U.S. economy produced thousands of new jobs each month. About the only accurate prediction was the one concerning inflation—it had remained low.

If one looked only at stock market and bond market reactions throughout the year, the economy appeared to be in a shambles. Far from it. After growing 2.8 percent in 1993, the economy grew 4 percent in 1994. Indeed, Laura D'Andrea Tyson, head of the president's Council of Economic Advisers, declared that the economy had not enjoyed such a healthy combination of strong growth and modest inflation in 30 years.

The Fed's increasingly harder taps on the economic brakes in reaction to this rate of growth, which was much higher than its preferred noninflationary rate of 2½ percent, caused fears among some U.S. workers. In November demonstrators marched outside the Marriner S. Eccles Federal Reserve Board Building in Washington, DC, fearful that the Fed's tighter grip on the money supply would cost them their jobs. In a city accustomed to demonstrations, marchers outside the Federal Reserve Building were a surprise. Not since the early 1980s, when tractor-driving farmers blocked traffic in front of the building, had a demonstration accompanied a Fed meeting.

But this was November 1994, and inside the building the bankers who comprise the Open Market Committee, the Fed's top policy-making body, were meeting to decide whether to increase interest rates for the sixth time in less than a year.

The Fed denied charges that it was trying to squelch economic growth with no regard for ordinary Americans. It added, however, that it could not afford to let down its guard against inflation. That said, the Open Market Committee decreed that interest rates were still too low. The economy was growing too fast and inflation fears were real. The bankers boosted the federal funds rate, the rate banks charge each other for overnight loans, to 5½ percent from 4¾ percent, and the discount rate was boosted to 4¾ percent from 4 percent. These were the biggest rate increases in 13 years.

The Fed acted on fears that growth was too hot to prevent price pressures from reaching the boiling point in 1995. The large rate hike suggested that the central bank was admitting to underestimating both the economy's resilience and the interest rate pressure needed to cool growth to a 2½ percent annual rate. The credit crunch, which was blamed for the snail's pace growth of the economy at the beginning of the recovery in 1992, was virtually gone, according to Federal Reserve Chairman Alan Greenspan.

A week after the November increase the stock market plunged nearly 200 points as investors abandoned stocks and sought safety in Treasury bonds. This was a stark change of events from February; then, investors were fleeing bonds after the Fed raised interest rates for the first time in 1994.

The biggest and most-watched average, the Dow Jones Industrial Average, stayed within narrow trading ranges throughout 1994. The average closed out the year up only 2.1 percent at 3,844.44. It was a sorry performance compared to previous years, and it left investors without much to show for 1994 except dividends, which averaged less than 3 percent.

Other less-watched indexes did much worse. The New York Stock Exchange composite index was down 3.1 percent; the Standard & Poor's 500 was down 1.5 percent, and the Nasdaq composite was down 3.2 percent. Getting the blame for the lackluster showing was the Fed.

Trade. Trade continued to flourish throughout 1994 as the full effects of the North American Free Trade Agreement (Nafta), which gradually reduces tariffs between the United States, Mexico, and Canada over 15 years, began settling into place.

The success of Nafta prompted the U.S. Congress to approve in December a new global trade pact negotiated under the General Agreement on Tariffs and Trade (GATT). That pact was designed to force countries worldwide to reduce some of the protectionist barriers that had inhibited trade for years.

President Bill Clinton, seeking to build on the success with Nafta and GATT, said in December at the Summit of the Americas in Miami that he hoped to see Nafta expanded to include other countries in the hemisphere, particularly Chile. Chile has one of the most robust economies in South America.

Better Than Money?

As corporate cutbacks continued in 1994, managers looked for ways to keep workers happy on the cheap. Management consultant Bob Nelson collected some of their ideas in the book *1001 Ways to Reward Employees.* Examples:

• Amway supervisors park employees' cars one day a month

• At Domino's Pizza headquarters, employees may bring their pets to work on Fridays

• Eastman Kodak's "Humor Room" features Monty Python videos, Woody Allen books, and other laugh-making props

• In Bank of America's monthlong Laugh-A-Day Challenge, workers try to make other employees laugh

• Federal Express started putting the name of an employee's child on each new airplane

• AT&T and Ford use employees in national commercials

• The folks at Microage Computer collect fines from people who come late to meetings and give the money to the on-timers

• In Levi Strauss's "Quiet Room," frazzled workers can meditate (or pound the walls)

• Disneyland reserves one night a year for employees, with managers in costume running the rides and concessions

Employment. The jobless rate declined during 1994, dropping by 1.7 percent from January to December. The unemployment rate fell to a four-year low of 5.4 in December, with 256,000 payroll jobs added during the month. This followed an even more impressive November, during which businesses added 488,000 new workers.

The U.S. economy gained 3.5 million jobs in 1994—the best showing in a decade—making a total of 5.6 million jobs added since President Clinton took office in January 1993. Job growth was particularly strong in services as well as in manufacturing, in part reflecting rising demand for high-tech products. But Clinton, who based his 1992 election campaign on the economy, got little credit.

It was a far better showing than expected at the beginning of 1994, when many people predicted that the economy would show an increase of only 4 million jobs over the next two years. The downside was that the growth in jobs was partly responsible for the economy's robust growth rate.

Interest Rates. Strong employment growth was one of the factors that prompted the Federal Reserve to raise short-term interest rates in November for the sixth time.

Still, home buying held up fairly well during the year, despite higher mortgage rates, because buyers largely switched to adjustable-rate mortgages. But those rates also were continuing to rise. The initial rate for a one-year adjustable-rate mortgage in mid-December was 6.59 percent, just about where fixed-rate mortgages were a year earlier.

With affordability more of an issue, demand began sliding. The National Association of Home Builders, which said that over half of its members reported buyer traffic had fallen sharply in October, reported that traffic plunged by more than 10 percent in November and December.

As the Fed's interest rate increases took hold, sales of new homes fell by more than 2.5 percent in November, according to the Commerce Department. The National Association of Realtors said that sales of previously owned homes fell 2.6 percent that same month.

It was the kind of slowdown the Fed had been hoping to induce. Many economists ex-

159

Big deal. *Robert Allen, chairman of AT&T (left), Craig McCaw, chief executive officer of McCaw Cellular Communications, and Jim Barksdale, chief executive office of AT&T Wireless Services, try out their cellular phones at a New York press conference in August. They were announcing progress toward finalization of an agreement under which AT&T would buy McCaw, the largest cellular telephone company in the United States—a deal that would give AT&T a major boost in its effort to create a nationwide wireless communications network.*

pected the Fed to continue raising the rates during 1995.

The rise in short-term interest rates did not just affect housing. For homeowners with adjustable-rate mortgages, the Fed tightening meant higher monthly house payments, so more money had to be put aside for mortgage payments than before. And the boost in banks' prime lending rates lifted the interest cost of small business borrowings, home equity loans, and, most importantly, credit card balances. Less borrowing was part of the Fed's plan to slow the economy and keep inflation in check.

There was a bright side to the Fed's relentless effort to step on the brakes. As it increased interest rates, the savings rates paid by banks finally began inching back up. For senior citizens who used the interest earnings from their savings accounts to help cushion their retirement, the turnaround was a boon. The rate had hovered in the 3 percent range for 2½ years. By the end of 1994 it was approaching 5 percent.

Even with the increases in interest rates, however, retailers expected the 1994 Christmas season to be the best in five years. They were disappointed. For many retailers, although sales were better than Christmas 1993 sales, they fell short of expectations.

Inflation. Despite consumer spending, inflation remained in check throughout the year. But the Fed and Chairman Greenspan insisted

it was lurking around the corner. While consumer prices had not risen appreciably, prices for raw materials and intermediate supplies had accelerated. Fed officials predicted producers could soon attempt to pass along their higher costs if consumer demand remained strong. But because incomes had not been growing that fast, Americans had become bargain shoppers, often preventing manufacturers from passing on increased costs.

At the consumer level, inflation in 1994 rose at an annual rate of 2.7 percent, the same as in 1993. This was one thing Fed critics pointed to when criticizing the bank's increasingly tough stand on ratcheting up interest rates in an effort to control future inflation.

Wages. While jobs were growing, the wages workers received for performing those jobs grew slowly. Because consumers account for two-thirds of U.S. economic activity, the buying power of the average worker is viewed as key to future growth. But wages were kept in check for the year, many economists said, by competition from overseas markets. Normally, as the economy improved in the past, it hit a point at which a shortage of workers pushed up wages and cut into corporate revenue. This did not happen in 1994. The failure of the inflationary spiral to take place created fear among some Fed members and economists that the spiral would come on suddenly when producers begin seeking big price hikes.

Currency Advantage. The foreign trade component was credited, along with consumer spending, with driving the economy. A cheap dollar helped to supply the muscle for U.S. manufacturers in the emerging markets of the world. It gave most manufacturers a price advantage over their major competitors from Japan and Germany. The dollar fell about 11 percent against both the Japanese yen and the German mark from January to December. The currency advantage helped boost overseas demand for U.S.-made goods. But that seemed likely to change in 1995 because of the Fed's persistent increases in short-term interest rates.

Stock Market. The first of the Fed's 1994 increases in interest rates, in February, after 12 years of declining rates, took investors by surprise. The move resulted in a 10 percent slide in the domestic stock market that began in mid-February and bottomed nearly six weeks later. It was the first substantial stock market correction in 41 months. On top of that,

plunging prices on existing bonds led to one of the worst bond markets in decades.

Of the 33 sectors traced by Lipper Analytical Services only two, Japan and financial services, produced positive returns for the first six months. It was even tougher for mutual funds.

But the nation's fixation on high returns, whether it was high company earnings, high earnings in the stock market, or high savings rates, caused more than a few anxious nights at some companies and in some communities. Officials of Procter & Gamble and Gibson Greetings Cards were among the firms to report sharp losses after company treasurers attempted to play the interest rate market, known as the derivatives market, in an effort to win big returns. Many of the companies blamed Bankers Trust New York Corporation for their problems. Bankers Trust subsequently negotiated an agreement with the Federal Reserve on new regulations for the derivatives part of its business.

Kidvid hits. The Mighty Morphin Power Rangers do their stuff as they prepare to kick off a tour of the United States at the end of 1994. The colorful crew, already a megahit on television, was not only putting together a live show but also was making plans to film a movie. The Power Rangers dominated the U.S. market for action figure toys, with sales approaching $1 billion for the year.

Roadside Rhymes

In the days before superhighways, the tedium of driving long hours through rural America was brightened by Burma Shave signs—placards placed 100 feet apart along the roadside that advertised the shaving cream in humorous verse. One ran, "Every shaver / now can snore / six more minutes / than before / by using / Burma Shave." Another was "A chin where / barbed wire / bristles stand / is bound to be / a no ma'ams land."

The signs were the brainchild of Allan Odell, who died in Edina, MN, on January 17, 1994, at age 90. In 1925, he joined his father's firm, which was trying to promote the fledgling brand. His idea came from a row of roadside signs touting a gas station. Once Odell turned to doggerel, sales soared. At one point there were 7,000 sets of signs in 45 states. Odell's own favorite: "Within this vale / of toil and sin / your head grows bald / but not your chin."

Interstate highways and antibillboard laws finally did in the Burma Shave signs, although a set was given to the Smithsonian for posterity. The Philip Morris Company, by then Burma Shave's owner, discontinued the product in 1977.

But the biggest shock came in December, when officials of wealthy Orange County, CA, reported that the county treasurer had lost $1.5 billion betting on fixed-income securities whose value fell as interest rates rose. The estimate of the losses was later raised to $2 billion or more. The county filed for bankruptcy protection, in the largest-ever bankruptcy filing involving a government unit and the first involving a large U.S. county. While Orange County's losses were the highest, officials of San Diego County subsequently said an investment fund they had run with taxpayer money had lost 10 percent of its value, while officials of Auburn, ME, said they had lost 40 percent of the city's funds on bad investments.

J.S.

ECUADOR. During 1994 in Ecuador political disunity and partisanship continued to plague the government of President Sixto Durán Ballén. Minor economic progress was overshadowed by difficulties with proposed state modernization.

Having lost its congressional majority in early 1992, the Durán government underwent further weakening in the May 1 elections. Durán's Republican Unity Party was virtually wiped out, while the Social Christian Party obtained 25 of the 77 seats.

When the unicameral legislature reconvened in August, the Social Christian Party allied with other opposition parties. This development assured defeat for major government programs as well as votes of censure against controversial ministers.

Frustrated by the problems in proceeding toward modernization, Durán sought constitutional reforms by means of a popular referendum. Partisan squabbling repeatedly shifted the terms and timing until a plebiscite was eventually held on August 28.

The plebiscite's provisions included a constitutional strengthening of presidential authority vis-à-vis Congress. The electorate unexpectedly voted in favor of Durán's proposals by a 2-1 margin. While boosting the president's political standing, the vote did little to weaken partisan opposition to his administration and his policies.

There were bitter attacks on such matters as a new agrarian law, which the government initiated in June. This measure was linked to a long-running confrontation that was going on between the administration and the politically vigorous Confederation of Indigenous Nationalities, which Durán increasingly viewed as a threat to his government.

Congressional opposition not only derailed Durán's plans for the reform of the state but also gravely disrupted the drive toward privatization. Such initiatives as projected sales of both the petroleum and telecommunications corporations were blocked. Public austerity and selective tax increases did serve to cut the government deficit, and the growth rate for the full year was projected at 2.5 percent. Attempts to reduce an inflation rate running in excess of 20 percent were not realized, however, and a sharp rise in banana exports provided the only sunlight in an otherwise gloomy economic picture.

See STATISTICS OF THE WORLD. J.D.M.

EDUCATION. Privatization, violence in schools, and school prayer were leading education issues in the United States in 1994. Congress passed the Goals 2000: Educate America Act, designed to help states improve school performance. The states themselves sought new, more equitable ways to finance their school systems.

Privatizing Schools. From Minneapolis to Miami, for-profit companies assumed control of schools and even whole districts under contracts that typically required payment in exchange for meeting performance requirements. In October the Hartford, CT, school board hired Education Alternatives, Inc., to run all facets of the district's schools. Meanwhile, the Edison Project was selected to run three Massachusetts schools under that state's new charter school program and to operate two elementary schools in Wichita, KS, in 1995. And in June the Walt Disney Company reached an agreement with the Osceola County, FL, schools to build and run a public school at its planned 5,000-acre residential development near Walt Disney World.

School Violence. Concern over rising student violence in the nation's schools impelled the U.S. Congress to require states to establish laws that would expel students for one year for bringing a gun to school. The Department of Justice reported in 1993 that 35 percent of high school males in high-crime urban areas carried guns. And the Children's Defense Fund said in January 1994 that homicide had become the third leading cause of death for elementary and middle school students.

School Prayer. Proponents of school prayer made some progress in 1994 as Congress added school prayer language to two education bills. In November, after Republicans had taken control of Congress, they announced plans for a constitutional amendment guaranteeing the right to organized prayer in public schools. Meanwhile, two states—Mississippi and Georgia—joined Tennessee and Alabama in enacting school prayer legislation. In September, however, a U.S. district court judge struck down the Mississippi law, saying it was unconstitutional.

New Education Laws. The federal government became a partner in the effort to improve schools in 1994, enacting the Goals 2000: Educate America Act and renewing the Elementary and Secondary Education Act (ESEA), the largest federal aid program to schools, which serves more than 90 percent of U.S. school districts. Goals 2000 encourages states and school districts to set high curricular content and student performance standards by providing them with money to do so. The renewed ESEA requires the setting of high standards in at least mathematics and science in order for districts to receive federal aid. In May, Congress also passed the School-to-Work Opportunities Act, which was designed to smooth the transition from high school to work for students not attending college.

Goals and Standards. The standards movement was helped by funding from the Clinton administration, and the 11 groups involved in establishing content standards progressed in varying degrees.

Four national arts associations became the first groups to issue standards for what elementary and secondary students should know and be able to do in the arts. According to the standards, students in various grades should be able to create a dance, compose in different musical styles, or demonstrate several kinds of acting techniques. The National Council for History Standards released draft standards for grades K-4, and the National Council for the Social Studies released model standards for grades K-12; health and fitness educators also released model standards.

However, the U.S. Department of Education, which was helping fund the standards-setting efforts, notified the University of Illinois, the National Council of Teachers of English, and the International Reading Association that it would cease to fund their effort to develop English standards. The groups, which had received $960,000 from the department, pledged to continue their work.

School Financing. In the states much attention was focused on attempts to change the way school systems were financed. In Michigan nearly 70 percent of residents voted in favor of a two-cent increase in the sales tax to fund schools, coupled with a dramatic lowering of property taxes. By ending the reliance on property taxes, the new law was designed to ensure that rich and poor school districts would spend about the same amount of money per child.

During the year several states were involved in school finance lawsuits, in which students, parents, and advocates sued to ensure more equitable funding between districts. State supreme courts ruled in favor of plaintiffs in New Hampshire, New Jersey, and Arizona but found in favor of the states in North Dakota, Virginia, and Nebraska.

Student Testing and Performance. Student performance was mixed in 1994. The results of the 1992 National Assessment of Educational Progress in writing found that while most students understood narrative and informational writing, they had a hard time putting their knowledge into practice. On a scale from 1 to 6 no more than 3 percent of the 30,000 students tested scored as high as 5 or 6, and only 25 percent had scores of 4 or above. The Third International Study on Science and Mathematics noted that, compared to schools in 50 other countries, U.S. schools covered more topics but in less depth.

Meanwhile, in 1994 the average Scholastic Assessment Test math score increased by one point, to 479 on a 200-800 scale, continuing a 13-year rise. Women's scores rose three points (to 460), while men's scores dropped one point (to 501). The 41-point gap was the smallest since 1971. The average verbal score was 423 (a one-point drop), with men's scores dropping three points to 425, and women's rising one point to 421.

Average scores on the American College Testing program increased by one-tenth of a percent to 20.8 on a scale of 1 to 36. Again, women narrowed the gap between their scores and men's, with an average of 20.7 compared to 20.9 for men.

Testing itself remained controversial. The U.S. Department of Education's Office for Civil Rights investigated Ohio's high school graduation test following charges of racial bias. While the investigation found no discrimination, Ohio officials agreed to take steps to ensure that all students were adequately prepared for the test.

In September, California Governor Pete Wilson vetoed a bill that would have reauthorized the state's existing learning assessment system, saying it would not have allowed students to obtain individual test scores until at least 1999 and that it did not sufficiently test basic skills. The test, which combined traditional multiple-choice and short-answer questions with newer essays and problem solving, had come under

Trailblazer. *Shannon Faulkner greets the dean of The Citadel, Brigadier General Roger Poole, as she arrives for her first class in January 1994. Faulkner was in the midst of an ongoing battle to become the first woman to join the corps of cadets at the military college, which was founded in 1842.*

fire from critics who said it probed students' values and invaded their privacy.

The Courts. In June, in one of the most closely watched education cases to reach the U.S. Supreme Court, the justices voted, 6-3, to strike down a New York State law that created a special school district for Satmar Hasidic Jews, saying it violated the First Amendment's ban on separation of church and state. According to the Court's majority in *Board of Education of Kiryas Joel Village School District* v. *Grumet,* the 1989 law amounted to "religious favoritism." The Supreme Court also heard arguments in *United States* v. *Lopez,* in which the constitutionality of a federal law that banned gun possession within 1,000 feet of a school was in question.

In another case that reached the High Court, Shannon Faulkner challenged the gender barrier at The Citadel, an all-male, state-supported military college in South Carolina. Faulkner was initially admitted as a cadet, but the college rescinded its offer after learning she was a woman. In January, Chief Justice William Rehnquist let her enroll as a day student pending resolution of her suit; a few months later a federal district judge ordered her admitted as a cadet, but an appeals court stayed the order. The Citadel and the state of South Carolina filed a counterproposal in October to subsidize the military training of Faulkner and other women at other institutions.

Public Opinion. According to the annual Phi Delta Kappa/Gallup Poll, school violence and student discipline topped the list of adults' concerns. Of those surveyed, 54 percent disapproved of school choice, while 45 percent favored it. Meanwhile, a Public Agenda Foundation poll found that a majority of 1,100 Americans surveyed agreed with the setting of higher standards but not necessarily with the methods used to achieve them; education reformers have linked high standards with new forms of assessment, cooperative learning, and the use of calculators in math. Drugs and violence led the list of respondents' concerns, followed by low academic standards.

Adults continued to rate their local schools well, with 52 percent grading schools with an A or a B, according to a study by the American Association of School Administrators. One-third, however, said their own schools needed major reform, while more than 50 percent said schools throughout the United States needed major changes. An Associated Press poll said 62 percent of 1,004 adults surveyed rated their schools good or excellent compared with 53 percent in 1989.

Higher Education. The Clinton administration reversed a Bush administration ruling that race-based scholarships are unconstitutional. Such scholarships would be allowed as a remedy for past or long-standing discrimination, to diversify campuses, and when targeted toward disadvantaged students. In September the Corporation for National and Community Service issued the first grants for national service in a sort of domestic peace corps. The corporation issued about $46 million to 57 service groups run by schools, universities, community organizations, nonprofit organizations, and federal agencies. About 7,000 volunteers were expected to work in areas such as education, public safety, health and homelessness, and environmental protection. M.P.

EGYPT. The struggle between President Hosni Mubarak's government and Islamic extremists seeking to topple it dominated Egypt's political and economic affairs in 1994.

Egypt experienced an unprecedented level of violence in early 1994, as extremists attacked tourists, businesses, and the government. Passenger trains and cruise ships were fired upon, and bombs exploded outside several banks in January and February. In March, Mubarak escaped an assassination attempt by two Islamist-sympathizing Army officers, and one high-ranking police official was assassinated in early April. The Interior Ministry responded with heightened force: Two prominent extremists were killed in police raids in April, and more than 20,000 extremists were incarcerated. Among those arrested in April was a lawyer, Abd al-Harith Madani, accused of abetting the extremists. His death within 24 hours of his arrest provoked accusations that police officials had used torture and culminated in government suppression of a protest march by sympathetic lawyers on May 17.

The government's show of force seemed to seriously weaken the major Islamic extremist organizations—the Islamic Group and Jihad.

Lawyers lash out. *Police arrest an Egyptian lawyer during a demonstration in Cairo in May. Hundreds of lawyers were protesting the death of one of their colleagues while in police custody.*

Both sought dialogue with the government, and many imprisoned extremists appeared on television to renounce the use of violence. Nevertheless, the convening of a world conference on population in Cairo in September provided the backdrop for a new spate of violence in which several people died. Mubarak had hoped the heavily attended conference would serve indirectly to revive tourism; extremists were bent on foiling this hope, as well as on displaying their rejection of the conference's objectives regarding population control, which they perceived as a Western attempt to impose "corrupt values" upon the Islamic world.

Egyptian diplomats were actively engaged as mediators in several regional conflicts. Palestinian-Israeli talks in Cairo finally produced an agreement on how to resolve their differences, and, on July 1, Mubarak escorted Palestinian President Yasir Arafat to Egypt's border with the Gaza Strip for Arafat's historic return to Palestinian territory.

Elsewhere, diplomacy proved more nettlesome. Northern Yemenis accused Egypt of a pro-South Yemen bias, frustrating Egypt's efforts to mediate in Yemen's civil war. Egypt also experienced little success in resolving Libya's crisis with the West over the 1988 bombing of a plane over Lockerbie, Scotland. Egyptian relations with the Sudan remained very strained over Sudanese appropriations of Egyptian assets in Sudan and alleged Sudanese support for Islamic extremists. On a brighter note, Egypt restored diplomatic relations with South Africa on May 10 in recognition of the end of apartheid.

With tourism badly hit by extremist violence, economic growth remained sluggish. Plans for further economic liberalization through privatization stalled because of fears that increased unemployment would provide new recruits to the Islamic fundamentalist camp. Slowed privatization produced friction with the World Bank and International Monetary Fund, since both organizations linked progress toward privatization to the delivery of additional debt relief and economic assistance. Egypt maintained a low rate of inflation and reduced the budget deficit, but government expenditures on low-income citizens were increased to counter the spread of Islamists' influence.

See STATISTICS OF THE WORLD.   K.J.B.

ELECTIONS IN THE UNITED STATES. Call it a sea change, a tidal wave, a tsunami. Whichever metaphor you use (and postelection pundits used them all), the results of the November balloting in the United States left Republicans riding a conservative tide while storm-tossed Democrats huddled in lifeboats.

The GOP won control of the U.S. Senate for the first time since 1986 and captured a majority of state governorships for the first time in more than two decades. The GOP also gained near parity with Democrats in the state legislatures. But it was in the U.S. House of Representatives that the turnabout was most dramatic. Not since 1954—when Dwight Eisenhower was president, a first-class postage stamp cost less than a nickel, and Newton Leroy Gingrich was an 11-year-old Army brat—had Republicans commanded a majority in the House. On Election Day, however, a shift of more than 50 seats toppled this Democratic fiefdom, making it possible for Representative Newt Gingrich (R, Georgia) to become speaker of the House in the 104th Congress, convening in January 1995.

Exit polls found Americans in a sour mood: anti-Washington, anti-Congress, anti-Clinton. According to one nationwide survey, only 45 percent of voters in House races approved of the job President Bill Clinton was doing. Evidence of Democratic weakness buoyed the 1996 presidential prospects of a dozen Republicans, including Bob Dole (Kansas), who became the new Senate majority leader, and newly reelected Governors Pete Wilson (California) and William Weld (Massachusetts).

As pollsters and pundits had predicted, voters took out their fury on incumbents—but only if the incumbents happened to be Democrats. Not a single incumbent Republican senator, House member, or governor was voted out of office. In four key Midwestern states that went for Clinton in 1992, Republican Governors Jim Edgar (Illinois), John Engler (Michigan), George Voinovich (Ohio), and Tommy Thompson (Wisconsin) all won landslide reelection victories.

Among Democrats, dozens of incumbents faced ferocious challenges, and several party leaders were sent packing. Thomas Foley (Washington) became the first sitting House speaker since 1860 to lose his seat. Governor Mario Cuomo (New York) and former House Ways and Means Committee Chairman Dan Rostenkowski (Illinois) also suffered dramatic defeats.

Great day for the GOP. Senator Bob Dole (left) and Representative Newt Gingrich, both Republicans, have plenty to smile about as they meet the press after the November election. With the GOP gaining control of Congress, Dole was slated to become Senate majority leader, and Gingrich to become speaker of the House.

Fine day for Feinstein. *Seeking reelection to the Senate from California, Democrat Dianne Feinstein encourages her supporters at a rally the day before the election. She went on to defeat Representative Michael Huffington (R) in a closely fought contest.*

The Right Stuff. "We got our butts kicked," said Democratic National Committee Chairman David Wilhelm, who stepped down, as scheduled, just after the election. Few political professionals disagreed. The GOP scored significant gains in almost every demographic category but did especially well among some of the most highly motivated voter groups. In House races in 1992, supporters of H. Ross Perot's independent presidential campaign had broken 51 to 49 percent in favor of the Republicans; in 1994 the GOP advantage among Perot voters jumped to 65-35. (Perot had urged his followers to vote Republican this time around except in a few specific cases.) Talk-radio listeners favored Republicans by 64 percent to 36, gun owners went Republican by a 71-29 ratio, and members of the religious right gave Republicans a 90-10 advantage.

The hemorrhage in Democratic support was especially notable among white males, who split their vote between Democratic and Republican congressional candidates in 1992 but swung Republican in 1994 by an almost two-to-one margin.

The GOP shift among white voters, combined with the effects of redistricting and a generally sluggish turnout among blacks (who remained overwhelmingly Democratic), produced major Democratic losses in Southern states. Among the 11 states of the old Confederacy, once counted on by Democrats as the "solid South," Republicans now have about half the House seats and hold majorities of the Senate seats and state governorships.

Nationalizing the Campaign. Republican strategy went a long way toward disproving one of the great American political clichés, former House Speaker Thomas P. ("Tip") O'Neill's dictum that "all politics is local." The GOP congressional leadership pressured incumbents in safe districts to share their campaign funds with candidates in tougher races. Republicans deliberately incorporated national themes into local contests, keeping the focus on the Clintons (both Bill and Hillary Rodham) and on the Democratic Congress.

In September the GOP unveiled its Contract With America, a ten-point platform that more than 300 Republican House members and hopefuls promised, if elected, to bring to a vote. The "contract" called for tax cuts, welfare reform, term limits for members of Congress, a constitutional amendment to balance the federal budget, a beefed-up military, and other proposals, many of proven popularity. Democrats quickly pounced on the document, dubbing it a contract *on* America. They insisted that in order to cut taxes while raising defense spending, Republicans would have to slash benefits to the poor, the elderly, farmers, and the middle class. What Democratic strategists failed to recognize was that in using the final weeks of the campaign to debate the Republican agenda, Democrats were playing to the GOP's strength and their own weakness.

Headline Races. Few results were more poignant for Democrats than Tom Foley's loss to George Nethercutt, a Spokane lawyer who said, "I don't want to be the speaker; I want to be the listener." After his weak showing in the primary election, Foley knew he was in trouble. A 30-year House veteran, he was a very public opponent of term limits—not a popular stance in his increasingly conservative district. Because he had supported a ban on assault weapons, the National Rifle Association, usually an ally, was out gunning for him. Also opposed by Perot, Foley lost a tight race, as he was swallowed up in a Republican tide that turned Washington State's House delegation from an 8-1 Democratic margin to a 7-2 Republican advantage.

In Illinois the embattled Rostenkowski, indicted in May on charges of corruption and embezzlement, lost his bid for a 19th House term to 32-year-old attorney Michael Flanagan (R), a virtual unknown. What made Flanagan's victory all the more astonishing was the fact that he had no professional campaign staff and, until the closing week, very little money. Three other representatives under indictment all held onto their seats without difficulty: Joseph McDade (R, Pennsylvania) and Walter Tucker (D, California), both accused of bribe taking; and Mel Reynolds (D, Illinois), charged with child pornography, statutory rape, and obstruction of justice. In the year's most remarkable (and, some said, least welcome) political comeback, Marion Barry (D), the former mayor of Washington, DC, who emerged from prison in 1992 after serving a six-month sentence for cocaine possession, was reelected to the office he had left in disgrace.

Democratic Disappointments. After 12 years of Mario Cuomo as governor, New York State voters were ready for a change—even if that meant casting their ballots for a little-known state senator named George Pataki, a protégé of controversial U.S. Senator Alfonse D'Amato (R). The incumbent Democrat, who had started way behind in the polls, had seemed to gain ground as Election Day approached. President Clinton, more popular in New York than elsewhere, came in to campaign. New York City Mayor Rudolph Giu-

Maine event. Republican Congresswoman Olympia Snowe smiles at a news conference held after she won the senatorial race in Maine. She defeated Democratic Congressman Tom Andrews to claim the seat being vacated by retiring Senate Majority Leader George Mitchell.

liani (R), a rival of D'Amato's, shocked his own party by endorsing and campaigning for Cuomo, while Ross Perot in this instance supported a third-party candidate. But the endorsements backfired, and Cuomo, one of the Democratic Party's most ardent and eloquent liberals, lost to Pataki by a margin of four percentage points. In a postelection slap at Giuliani, GOP Chairman Haley Barbour said he would recommend that New York City no longer be considered as the site for the 1996 Republican National Convention.

In other key contests, Representative Jack Brooks (D, Texas), the highly partisan chairman of the Judiciary Committee and the second most senior member of the House, lost the seat to which he was first elected in 1952. Representative Neal Smith (D, Iowa), an influential player on the Appropriations Committee, and Representative Dan Glickman (D, Kansas), chairman of the Intelligence Committee, also lost their seats. So, too, did first-term

Representative Marjorie Margolies-Mezvinsky (D, Pennsylvania), targeted by Republicans because in 1993 she had cast the deciding vote in the House for Clinton's deficit reduction plan. In Pennsylvania's U.S. Senate contest, conservative Republican Representative Rick Santorum overthrew incumbent Harris Wofford (D), a champion of health care reform.

Tennessee proved an especially bitter pill for Democrats. Senate Budget Committee Chairman Jim Sasser (D), who had hoped to become majority leader, lost his reelection bid to a political novice, heart surgeon Bill Frist (R), and Vice President Al Gore's old Senate seat went to Fred Thompson (R), an actor and lawyer who made his mark in the early 1970s as minority counsel to the Senate Watergate committee. Representative Don Sundquist (R) won the governorship, and the GOP also picked up a majority of the state's House delegation.

Famous Families. In Texas a well-oiled campaign by George W. Bush (R), son of the for-

By George! On the morning after Election Day, George Pataki, along with his wife, Libby, celebrates his win in the New York governor's race. The Republican's victory ended incumbent Democratic Governor Mario Cuomo's bid to gain a fourth term.

mer president, wrested the governorship from a popular incumbent, Ann Richards (D). George's younger brother, Jeb Bush (R), fell just short of unseating another Democratic incumbent, Lawton Chiles, in the Florida governorship race. Also in Florida, Hugh Rodham (D), brother of the first lady, was swamped in his quixotic effort to dethrone Senator Connie Mack (R). California State Treasurer Kathleen Brown (D), whose father, Pat, and brother, Jerry, had each been governor, stumbled in her attempt to follow in their footsteps when she lost to incumbent Pete Wilson (R).

Facing the roughest election challenge of his 32-year Senate career, Edward Kennedy (D, Massachusetts) outdistanced businessman Mitt Romney (R), son of former Michigan Governor George Romney. The senator's youngest son, Patrick Kennedy (D), won his first House term, representing a Rhode Island district; the senator's nephew, Representative Joseph Kennedy II (D, Massachusetts)—son of Robert Kennedy, was returned unopposed. Robert Kennedy's daughter, Kathleen Kennedy Townsend (D), became lieutenant governor of Maryland when her gubernatorial running mate, Parris Glendening (D), bested Ellen Sauerbrey (R) by a paper-thin margin.

Money Talks—Sometimes. Incumbents enjoyed a huge advantage in fund-raising, especially from political action committees, and nearly all the Democrats who lost their seats had outspent their challengers. On the other hand, Republicans who were seeking to oust incumbent Democrats were generally better funded—often from their own considerable fortunes—than were Democrats opposing Republican officeholders.

Oddly, in two of the nation's nastiest and most expensive races, Democratic incumbents beat back free-spending Republican challengers. In Virginia, Oliver North (R) raised well over $16 million—something like $19 for every vote he got—in a vigorous but unsuccessful effort to unseat Senator Charles Robb (D). Robb, a plodding speaker, was tarnished by scandal and by an ugly feud with former Virginia Governor L. Douglas Wilder (D), while North still bore the scars of his involvement in the Iran/contra arms affair (his 1989 conviction for lying to Congress was over-

turned on a technicality). Not until Wilder gave up his independent candidacy in September did Robb's campaign catch fire, and former first lady Nancy Reagan's accusation that North "lied to my husband and lied about my husband" gave the incumbent a last-minute boost.

Just as bizarre was the U.S. Senate contest in California, where Representative Michael Huffington (R) spent some $28 million of his own money in a bid to replace Dianne Feinstein (D). Blitzed by attack ads, Feinstein was in deep trouble but was aided by press reports focusing on Huffington's wife and her alleged involvement with a New Age cult. The race climaxed with an exchange of charges based on whether either or both candidates had employed undocumented immigrants; in the end Feinstein eked out a narrow victory.

Also on the Ballot. The issue of undocumented aliens was especially sensitive in California, where Proposition 187—which would deny most public services, including education, to illegal immigrants—passed with 59 percent support. Immediately after the election, opponents moved to block Prop 187 in the courts, and a court ruling put it on hold. By overwhelming majorities, California voters buried measures that would have weakened the state's antismoking laws and mandated a taxpayer-funded system of health insurance.

A "three strikes and you're out" proposal requiring life imprisonment for persons convicted of three serious offenses passed in California, and an even tougher "two strikes and you're out" law was enacted in Georgia. Oregon voters approved a measure allowing physician-assisted suicide for terminally ill patients; opponents then sued to block the law. Efforts to limit government protection for homosexual rights failed in Oregon and Idaho.

Term limits for political officeholders passed in seven states—Alaska, Colorado, Idaho, Maine, Massachusetts, Nebraska, and Nevada—and in Washington, DC. With Republicans now controlling the House and Senate, early signs were that GOP support for a constitutional amendment to limit congressional terms was somewhat less enthusiastic than it had been when Democratic incumbents predominated. G.H.

171

ALABAMA

U.S. House Delegation: 4 D, 3 R.
State Government: Gov.: Fob James, Jr. (R); lt. gov.: Don Siegelman (D). Legislature: Senate, 23 D, 12 R; House, 74 D, 31 R.

ALASKA

U.S. House Delegation: 1 R.
State Government: Gov.: Tony Knowles (D); lt. gov.: Fran Ulmer (D). Legislature: Senate, 12 R, 8 D; House, 22 R, 17 D, 1 ind.

ARIZONA

U.S. Senator: Jon Kyl (R).
U.S. House Delegation: 5 R, 1 D.
State Government: Gov.: Fife Symington* (R); sec. of state[1]: Jane Dee Hull (R). Legislature: Senate, 19 R, 11 D; House, 38 R, 22 D.

ARKANSAS

U.S. House Delegation: 2 D, 2 R.
State Government: Gov.: Jim Guy Tucker* (D); lt. gov.: Mike Huckabee* (R). Legislature: Senate, 28 D, 7 R; House, 88 D, 12 R.

CALIFORNIA

U.S. Senator: Dianne Feinstein* (D).
U.S. House Delegation: 26 D, 26 R.
State Government: Gov.: Pete Wilson* (R); lt. gov.: Gray Davis (D). Legislature: Senate, 21 D, 17 R, 2 ind.; Assembly, 40 R, 39 D, 1 ind.

COLORADO

U.S. House Delegation: 4 R, 2 D.
State Government: Gov.: Roy Romer* (D); lt. gov.: Gail Schoettler (D). Legislature: Senate, 19 R, 16 D; House, 41 R, 24 D.

CONNECTICUT

U.S. Senator: Joseph I. Lieberman* (D).
U.S. House Delegation: 3 R, 3 D.
State Government: Gov.: John Rowland (R); lt. gov.: M. Jodi Rell (R). Legislature: Senate, 19 R, 17 D; House, 90 D, 61 R.

DELAWARE

U.S. Senator: William V. Roth, Jr.* (R).
U.S. House Delegation: 1 R.
State Government: Legislature: Senate, 12 D, 9 R; House, 27 R, 14 D.

DISTRICT OF COLUMBIA

U.S. House Delegation: Delegate: Eleanor Holmes Norton* (D).
City Government: Council of the District of Columbia: 11 D, 1 ind., 1 D.C. Statehood.

FLORIDA

U.S. Senator: Connie Mack* (R).
U.S. House Delegation: 15 R, 8 D.
State Government: Gov.: Lawton Chiles* (D); lt. gov.: Kenneth H. ("Buddy") MacKay* (D). Legislature: Senate, 21 R, 19 D; House, 63 D, 57 R.

GEORGIA

U.S. House Delegation: 7 R, 4 D.
State Government: Gov.: Zell Miller* (D); lt. gov.: Pierre Howard* (D). Legislature: Senate, 35 D, 21 R; House, 114 D, 66 R.

HAWAII

U.S. Senator: Daniel K. Akaka* (D).
U.S. House Delegation: 2 D.
State Government: Gov.: Ben Cayetano (D); lt. gov.: Mazie Hirono (D). Legislature: Senate, 23 D, 2 R; House, 44 D, 7 R.

IDAHO

U.S. House Delegation: 2 R.
State Government: Gov.: Philip E. (Phil) Batt (R); lt. gov.: C. L. ("Butch") Otter* (R). Legislature: Senate, 27 R, 8 D; House, 57 R, 13 D.

ILLINOIS

U.S. House Delegation: 10 D, 10 R.
State Government: Gov.: Jim Edgar* (R); lt. gov.: Bob Kustra* (R). Legislature: Senate, 33 R, 26 D; House, 64 R, 54 D.

INDIANA

U.S. Senator: Richard G. Lugar* (R).
U.S. House Delegation: 6 R, 4 D.
State Government: Legislature: Senate, 30 R, 20 D; House, 56 R, 44 D.

IOWA

U.S. House Delegation: 5 R.
State Government: Gov.: Terry E. Branstad* (R); lt. gov.: Joy Corning* (R). Legislature: Senate, 27 D, 23 R; House, 64 R, 36 D.

KANSAS

U.S. House Delegation: 4 R.
State Government: Gov.: Bill Graves (R); lt. gov.: Sheila Frahm (R). Legislature: Senate, 27 R, 13 D; House, 80 R, 45 D.

KENTUCKY

U.S. House Delegation: 4 R, 2 D.
State Government: Legislature: Senate, 2 D, 17 R; House, 64 D, 36 R.

LOUISIANA

U.S. House Delegation: 4 D, 3 R.
State Government: Legislature: Senate, 33 D, 6 R; House, 86 D, 17 R, 1 ind., 1 vacancy.

MAINE

U.S. Senator: Olympia Snowe (R).
U.S. House Delegation: 1 R, 1 D.
State Government: Gov.: Angus King, (I); pres. of the Senate[2]: Jeffrey Butland* (R). Legislature: Senate, 18 R, 16 D, 1 ind.; House, 77 D, 74 R.

MARYLAND

U.S. Senator: Paul S. Sarbanes* (D).
U.S. House Delegation: 4 D, 4 R.
State Government: Gov.: Parris Glendening (D); lt. gov.: Kathleen Kennedy Townsend (D). Legislature: Senate, 32 D, 15 R; House, 101 D, 40 R.

MASSACHUSETTS

U.S. Senator: Edward M. Kennedy* (D).
U.S. House Delegation: 8 D, 2 R.
State Government: Gov.: William F. Weld* (R); lt. gov.: Paul Cellucci*(R). Legislature: Senate, 30 D, 10 R; House, 124 D, 35 R, 1 "unenrolled."

MICHIGAN

U.S. Senator: Spencer Abraham (R).
U.S. House Delegation: 9 D, 7 R.
State Government: Gov.: John Engler* (R); lt. gov.: Connie Binsfeld* (R). Legislature: Senate, 22 R, 16 D; House, 56 R, 53 D, 1 vacancy.

MINNESOTA

U.S. Senator: Rod Grams (IR).[3]
U.S. House Delegation: 6 DFL,[4] 2 IR.
State Government: Gov.: Arne H. Carlson* (IR); lt. gov.: Joanne Benson (IR). Legislature: Senate, 43 DFL, 23 IR, 1 vacancy; House, 71 DFL, 63 IR.

MISSISSIPPI

U.S. Senator: Trent Lott* (R).
U.S. House Delegation: 4 D, 1 R.
State Government: Legislature: Senate, 35 D, 17 R; House, 88 D, 30 R, 2 ind, 2 vacancies.

MISSOURI

U.S. Senator: John Ashcroft (R).
U.S. House Delegation: 6 D, 3 R.
State Government: Legislature: Senate, 19 D, 15 R; House, 87 D, 76 R.

MONTANA
U.S. Senator: Conrad R. Burns* (R).
U.S. House Delegation: 1 D.
State Government: Legislature: Senate, 31, R, 19 D; House, 67 R, 33 D.

NEBRASKA
U.S. Senator: J. Robert (Bob) Kerrey* (D).
U.S. House Delegation: 3 R.
State Government: Gov.: E. Benjamin Nelson* (D); lt. gov.: Kim Robak* (D). Legislature: 25 members elected to the nonpartisan 49-member unicameral Legislature.

NEVADA
U.S. Senator: Richard H. Bryan* (D).
U.S. House Delegation: 2 R.
State Government: Gov.: Bob Miller* (D); lt. gov.: Lonnie Hammargren (R). Legislature: Senate, 13 R, 8 D; Assembly, 21 D, 21 R.

NEW HAMPSHIRE
U.S. House Delegation: 2 R.
State Government: Gov.: Stephen Merrill* (R); pres. of the Senate[2]: Joseph L. Delahanty (R). Legislature: Senate, 18 R, 6 D; House, 286 R, 112 D, 2 Libertarian.

NEW JERSEY
U.S. Senator: Frank R. Lautenberg* (D).
U.S. House Delegation: 8 R, 5 D.
State Government: Legislature: Senate, 24 R, 16 D; General Assembly, 52 R, 28 D.

NEW MEXICO
U.S. Senator: Jeff Bingaman* (D).
U.S. House Delegation: 2 R, 1 D.
State Government: Gov.: Gary Johnson (R); lt. gov.: Walter Bradley (R). Legislature: Senate, 26 D, 15 R; House, 46 D, 24 R.

NEW YORK
U.S. Senator: Daniel Patrick Moynihan* (D).
U.S. House Delegation: 17 D, 14 R.
State Government: Gov.: George Pataki (R); lt. gov.: Betsy McCaughey (R). Legislature: Senate, 36 D, 25 R; Assembly, 94 D, 56 R.

NORTH CAROLINA
U.S. House Delegation: 8 R, 4 D.
State Government: Legislature: Senate, 26 D, 24 R; House, 67 R, 52 D, 1 undecided.

NORTH DAKOTA
U.S. Senator: Kent Conrad* (D).
U.S. House Delegation: 1 D.
State Government: Legislature: Senate, 29 R, 20 D; House, 75 R, 23 D.

OHIO
U.S. Senator: Michael (Mike) DeWine (R).
U.S. House Delegation: 13 R, 6 D.
State Government: Gov.: George V. Voinovich* (R); lt. gov.: Nancy Hollister (R). Legislature: Senate, 20 R, 13 D; House, 56 R, 43 D.

OKLAHOMA
U.S. Senator: James Inhofe (R).
U.S. House Delegation: 5 R, 1 D.
State Government: Gov.: Frank Keating (R); lt. gov.: Mary Fallin (R). Legislature: Senate, 35 D, 13 R; House, 65 D, 36 R.

OREGON
U.S. House Delegation: 3 D, 2 R.
State Government: Gov.: John Kitzhaber (D). Legislature: Senate, 19 R, 11 D; House, 34 R, 26 D.

PENNSYLVANIA
U.S. Senator: Rick Santorum (R).
U.S. House Delegation: 11 D, 10 R.
State Government: Gov.: Tom Ridge (R); lt. gov.: Mark Schwieker (R). Legislature: Senate, 29 R, 21 D; House, 102 R, 101 D.

RHODE ISLAND
U.S. Senator: John H. Chafee* (R).
U.S. House Delegation: 2 D.
State Government: Gov.: Lincoln Almond (R); lt. gov.: Robert Weygand* (D). Legislature: Senate, 40 D, 10 R; House, 84 D, 16 R.

SOUTH CAROLINA
U.S. House Delegation: 4 R, 2 D.
State Government: Gov.: David Beasley (R); lt. gov.: Bob Peeler (R). Legislature: Senate, 29 D, 17 R; House, 62 R, 58 D, 4 ind.

SOUTH DAKOTA
U.S. House Delegation: 1 D.
State Government: Gov.: William J. Janklow (R); lt. gov.: Carole Hillard (R). Legislature: Senate, 19 R, 16 D; House, 46 R, 24 D.

TENNESSEE
U.S. Senators: Bill Frist (R), Fred Thompson (R).
U.S. House Delegation: 5 R, 4 D.
State Government: Gov.: Don Sundquist (R); lt. gov.[2]: John Wilder. Legislature: Senate, 18 D, 15 R; House, 59 D, 40 R.

TEXAS
U.S. Senator: Kay Bailey Hutchison* (R).
U.S. House Delegation: 19 D, 11 R.
State Government: Gov.: George W. Bush (R); lt. gov.: Bob Bullock* (D). Legislature: Senate, 17 D, 14 R; House, 89 D, 61 R.

UTAH
U.S. Senator: Orrin G. Hatch* (R).
U.S. House Delegation: 2 R, 1 D.
State Government: Legislature: Senate, 19 R, 10 D; House, 55 R, 20 D.

VERMONT
U.S. Senator: James M. Jeffords* (R).
U.S. House Delegation: 1 ind.
State Government: Gov.: Howard Dean* (D); lt. gov.: Barbara Snelling* (R). Legislature: Senate, 18 R, 12 D; House, 86 D, 61 R, 2 ind., 1 Progressive Coalition.

VIRGINIA
U.S. Senator: Charles S. Robb* (D).
U.S. House Delegation: 6 D, 5 R.
State Government: Legislature: Senate, 22 D, 18 R; House, 52 D, 47 R, 1 ind.

WASHINGTON
U.S. Senator: Slade Gorton* (R).
U.S. House Delegation: 7 R, 2 D.
State Government: Legislature: Senate, 25 D, 24 R; House, 60 R, 38 D.

WEST VIRGINIA
U.S. Senator: Robert C. Byrd* (D).
U.S. House Delegation: 3 D.
State Government: pres. of the Senate[2]: Earl Ray Tomblin (D). Legislature: Senate, 26 D, 8 R; House, 69 D, 31 R.

WISCONSIN
U.S. Senator: Herb Kohl* (D).
U.S. House Delegation: 6 R, 3 D.
State Government: Gov.: Tommy G. Thompson* (R); lt. gov.: Scott McCallum* (R). Legislature: Senate, 17 R, 16 D; Assembly, 51 R, 48 D.

WYOMING
U.S. Senator: Craig Thomas (R).
U.S. House Delegation: 1 R.
State Government: Gov.: Jim Geringer (R); sec. of state[1]: Diana J. Ohman (R). Legislature: Senate, 20 D, 10 R; House, 47 R, 13 D.

---

* denotes incumbent.

[1] In Arizona, Oregon, and Wyoming the secretary of state is first in the line of succession to the governorship.

[2] In Maine, New Hampshire, New Jersey, Tennessee, and West Virginia the president (or speaker) of the Senate is first in the line of succession to the governorship. In Tennessee, the speaker of the Senate bears the statutory title of lieutenant governor.

[3] IR stands for the Independent-Republican Party.

[4] DFL stands for the Democratic-Farmer-Labor Party.

Nintendo goes ape. *Nintendo brought the venerable 16-bit video-game technology to new heights by reintroducing its famous character Donkey Kong in Donkey Kong Country, which features 3-D animations. At left, Donkey Kong follows a baddie called Kritter along a trail in an exotic world called the Kongo Jungle. Donkey Kong Country takes advantage of enhanced compression technology, and Nintendo used Silicon Graphics workstations to create the computer models for the characters, resulting in details and textures unusual in a 16-bit game.*

ELECTRONICS. Interactivity continued to be the buzzword in the world of consumer electronics in 1994, although there were few significant innovations in this area. Cable TV got some competition from digital broadcast satellite systems, and there was little letup in the home theater trend.

Interactive Systems. While experts continued to argue whether the convergence of the personal computer and the television set would ever happen, several companies, including Apple, Compaq, IBM, and Packard Bell, released PCs that displayed TV or video in a window on the monitor while users performed other on-screen tasks.

No TV-based interactive systems really caught on in 1994, but Panasonic's Interactive Multiplayer, released in 1993, seemed to gather momentum, becoming more accessible as its price dropped below $400; late in 1994, sales had surpassed 200,000. A CD-ROM system that runs video games and other CD software on a TV, the multiplayer uses an operating system developed by 3DO, a licensing company supported by corporate heavyweights such as AT&T and Time Warner. Other companies, including Sanyo and Goldstar, released 3DO multiplayers late in 1994; 3DO multiplayers were also being used in some of the interactive television trials under way in 1994.

Philips's Compact Disc-Interactive (CD-I) player, another type of TV-compatible CD-ROM system, continued to sell, but less than steadily, and Magnavox released a CD-I player. Despite an increase in educational software available for TV-based interactive systems, most such systems continued to be considered as video game players.

Video Games. Meanwhile, video game companies such as Nintendo and Sega prepared to release in 1995 video game systems with processing chips that would outperform many computers.

In November, to bridge the gap until its more powerful Saturn system debuted in 1995, Sega released a 32X add-on that would prolong the lives of its Genesis and CD systems. Atari responded to complaints that there were not enough games for its 64-bit Jaguar system by putting out several at the end of the year.

In response to congressional concern about violence in video games, Nintendo, Sega, and others in the industry developed an industry-wide rating system similar to the one used in rating movies. The first games to be rated appeared in stores in the fall.

Digital Satellite Systems. The cable TV industry got competition: a digital broadcast satellite system that beamed laser-disk-quality video and CD-quality sound directly to homes via a satellite dish the size of a pizza box. Two

Hughes Corporation satellites transmitted more than 150 channels to 18"-satellite dishes made by RCA and receivers made by Thomson Electronics.

After buying the equipment for $700-$900, a consumer would expect to pay monthly programming costs comparable to those of cable. Over 500,000 Digital Satellite Systems were sold in just a few months. However, customers would still need a regular antenna or cable to watch local network affiliates.

DSS also was touted as an alternate route for the so-called information highway, but opponents argued that its interactive capabilities were limited.

TV Developments. More and more households turned on to the home theater trend in 1994. Sales of TV sets rose to more than 24 million; one in five of them had 27-inch screens or larger. Also increasing were sales of stereo videocassette recorders that tap into the Dolby Surround Sound sound tracks built into prerecorded tapes and many TV programs. Digital VCRs were expected to hit the market early in 1995.

Audio Formats. Though professional compact disk recorders have been marketed for several years, the first consumer model was re-leased in late September. A product of Pioneer Electronics, it was priced at $4,000. Two digital recording formats, released in 1992 to replace analog audiocassettes, remained on the market. Most observers agreed that Sony's Mini Disc had a better chance of success than the Digital Compact Cassette that was being championed by Philips and Matsushita.

M.S.

EL SALVADOR. Elections held in 1994 left the conservative National Republican Alliance Party (Arena) still firmly in control of decision making in El Salvador at all levels. Arena candidate Armando Calderón Sol won the presidential race by a margin of more than two to one (68 to 32 percent) in an April runoff contest against Rubén Zamora, a candidate representing a coalition of left-of-center parties. Crime rates were high as El Salvador struggled to change from a wartime to a peacetime economy.

In March mayoral elections, Arena won 80 percent of the nation's 262 municipalities. The centrist Christian Democratic Party won 11 percent, the leftist Farabundo Martí National Liberation Front (FMLN) won 6 percent, and the rightist Partido de Conciliación Nacional (PCN) won 3 percent. Also in March

Thumb's up. *Rightist presidential candidate Armando Calderón Sol shows off his ink-stained thumb after voting in El Salvador's runoff election in April. Calderón won an easy victory, taking 68 percent of the vote.*

elections Arena retained all of the 39 seats in the Legislative Assembly it had won in 1991 (El Salvador has a unicameral legislature with 84 members). The FMLN won 21 seats, the Christian Democrats 18 (down from 26 in 1991), and the conservative PCN four. Two other parties won one seat each. With PCN legislators on their side, Arena was able to control a majority of the assembly, assuring that on most votes the conservative point of view would prevail. The elections marked the first time that FMLN guerrillas, who fought a bruising civil war from 1979 to 1992, had formed a political party and offered themselves as candidates. In December one of the main FMLN factions broke away, charging that the party was too far left to be politically viable.

The rapid shift after 1992 from a wartime to a peacetime economy and the demobilization of both armies (under direct United Nations supervision) left thousands of persons displaced in one way or another, leading to an extraordinary increase in common and organized crime, including gang activity, in some instances supported by U.S.-based drug-related gangs. While peace agreements stipulated that ex-combatants on both sides of the civil war would be eligible for a wide range of benefits including loans and land, by late 1994 nearly one-third had received no benefits at all, less than 1 percent had received land, and none had received credit, as promised, to set up small industries. A severe drought in the eastern region caused a serious food crisis and increased the likelihood of continued crime. The economy as a whole fared better as coffee prices skyrocketed and as the nation's elite began to invest more confidently after the elections guaranteed a fiscally conservative government.

See STATISTICS OF THE WORLD.   J.Z.G.

ENERGY. *See* POWER AND ENERGY.

ENVIRONMENT. A dramatic oil fire on the San Jacinto River in Texas was the most eye-catching environmental story in the United States in 1994. The administration of President Bill Clinton proposed an indoor air-quality regulation that would affect some 6 million workplaces, and the president signed an order aimed at ending so-called environmental racism. Among other developments, an in-

ternational agreement called for the banning of shipments of hazardous wastes from one country to another, and steps were taken to conserve the once-vast Aral Sea in the former Soviet Union.

Environmental Racism. On February 11, President Clinton signed an executive order to combat "environmental racism," the alleged tendency for toxic-waste sites and other environmentally undesirable facilities to be placed in neighborhoods with poor or minority populations. Federal agencies that deal with the environment were directed to establish measures to ensure that such communities were not being singled out for higher-risk projects, such as hazardous-waste incinerators, or being given lower priority in determining which polluted sites would be cleared up first under the federal Superfund Program. An interagency task force, headed by Environmental Protection Agency (EPA) Administrator Carol Browner, was created to supervise implementation of the president's order.

Although a number of studies have suggested the existence of environmental racism, others have questioned such findings. A study released in March by researchers at the University of Massachusetts, for example, analyzed census data from 1970, 1980, and 1990 in 555 areas with commercial hazardous-waste facilities and found no pattern of placement in minority communities.

Indoor Air Pollution. In March, U.S. Labor Secretary Robert Reich spelled out a proposed indoor air-quality regulation that would, among other things, limit smoking in an estimated 6 million workplaces to specially designated areas with separate ventilation systems. The intent was to protect nonsmokers from secondhand smoke. (*See* HEALTH AND MEDICINE.) The regulation, which could be changed before being issued in final form in 1995, would also require employers to inspect ventilation and air-conditioning equipment regularly, overhaul these systems to keep vehicle exhaust and other outdoor pollutants from entering their buildings, and give employees advance notice when potentially hazardous chemicals were to be used in the workplace.

Air Pollution. Swiss voters backed a referendum in February that called for a ban on inter-

Hot water. *An observer on the bank of the San Jacinto River in Texas watches fires caused by the October ruptures of several fuel pipelines running beneath the river.*

national truck traffic through the Swiss Alps by the year 2004. Freight passing through the country would be required instead to move on railroads, thought to be less damaging to the fragile Alpine ecosystem. Nearly 52 percent of voters backed the so-called Alpine Initiative; it was opposed by the Swiss government, which feared it might hurt trade.

Germany and Italy, the nations that rely most heavily on the key St. Gotthard Pass between northern and southern Europe, said the initiative would increase expenses and add to travel times. Some 1,000 long-haul trucks use the St. Gotthard Tunnel each day, but up to 90 percent of international freight that passes through Switzerland is already being carried on trains.

Neighboring Austria, whose roads also draw international freight traffic, won an agreement from the European Union in March that allowed it to limit truck traffic through its Alpine region through 2004. The agreement was part of the negotiations for Austria to join the EU. Rather than falling as expected, however, the number of trucks and cars traveling through Austria's busy Brenner Pass had increased by late 1994.

In the United States the EPA issued a regulation in March that required chemical plants to cut toxic emissions by 88 percent within three years. The regulation was part of the EPA's implementation of the wide-ranging Clean Air Act of 1990. EPA officials estimated the regulation would reduce such emissions by 506,000 tons a year, at a cost to the chemical industry of $450 million initially and an additional $230 million in annual operating costs. The rules apply to 370 plants in 38 states.

After a three-year study the EPA issued a draft report in September that reaffirmed its previous position that dioxin was a probable cancer-causing chemical. The report, which was based on animal studies, also linked dioxin to a variety of other health problems, including hormonal imbalances and weakened immune systems.

The EPA had reassessed its 20-year-old position on dioxin as an especially dangerous toxin following challenges from chemical industry executives and some scientists. The agency had already proposed, or planned to propose, stricter controls on medical, industrial, and municipal waste incinerators, the source of most dioxin emissions.

ENVIRONMENT

Waste Disposal. Following a five-day United Nations conference, most democratic industrialized nations agreed in March to stop exporting hazardous wastes to developing countries, Eastern European nations, and the former Soviet republics. Facing growing opposition to new waste dumps at home, industrialized nations had turned to shipping an increasing amount of their hazardous waste abroad. For their part, cash-strapped countries had taken the wastes, without necessarily having the disposal or recycling facilities to handle them properly.

The agreement tightened the terms of the 1989 Basel Convention, in which industrial nations pledged not to ship hazardous wastes without the written permission of the receiving country. Under the terms of the 1994 agreement, the industrialized nations pledged to end such shipments immediately and to end shipments of recyclable wastes by 1998. The United States was not a party to either the 1989 Basel Convention or the 1994 agreement, but the Clinton administration had previously introduced a bill that would follow the Basel Convention's guidelines.

In July the only remaining U.S. dump for low-level radioactive waste, in Barnwell, SC, stopped accepting waste from all but a handful of states in the Southeast. As a result, waste generators such as nuclear power plants and medical centers in the remaining states had to store low-level waste—contaminated filters, protective clothing, used supplies from medical procedures involving radioactive materials, and so forth—in temporary spaces (for example, in unused buildings on their property). Because of fierce local opposition, attempts to find new places for low-level dumps were running years behind schedule. Waste generators, and medical centers in particular, warned that temporary storage space was inherently less safe than a permanent disposal site.

Two decisions by the U.S. Supreme Court struck down attempts by state or local officials to control the disposal of garbage within their jurisdictions. In April the Court struck down a 1989 Oregon law that imposed higher fees on garbage coming from other states than it did on local waste. The Court ruled, 7-2, that such laws violated the commerce clause of the U.S. Constitution. The following month the Court struck down a popular technique for directing garbage to certain facilities, so-called flow control laws, by which local governments order all garbage generated within their limits to be sent to a particular site. Flow control had become an increasingly popular way for a local government to guarantee that a facility built with municipal bonds has a steady stream of business. But in a case involving Clarkstown, NY, the Court again cited the commerce clause, saying "state and local governments may not use their regulatory power to favor local enterprise."

Oil Spills. On January 7 a barge carrying fuel oil broke loose from the tugboat that was pulling it and ran into a reef a few hundred yards off San Juan, PR. An estimated 750,000 gallons of oil poured into the Atlantic Ocean, fouling several miles of beaches at the height of the winter tourist season. Rough waves on January 13 caused the barge to spill another 168,000 gallons of oil, and the Coast Guard towed the barge out to sea and sank it in the deep Puerto Rican trench to prevent further coastal fouling. At a Coast Guard hearing on the spill, a tugboat crew member testified that the tug's towline had broken and had not been properly repaired.

Following days of torrential rains that flooded the Houston area in October, two pipelines running under the San Jacinto River ruptured on October 20. Leaking oil and fuel exploded into a fire that sent 120 people to local hospitals, mostly for treatment for smoke inhalation. At least two other pipelines under the river also ruptured, including one that carried natural gas. Altogether, an estimated 1.2 million gallons of gasoline, diesel fuel, and crude oil spilled into the river, which empties into the Houston Ship Channel and Galveston Bay. Booms were used to contain the spill and skimmers vacuumed petroleum products out of the water. Texas officials said environmental damage was confined to several oily birds and some blackened marshlands.

Also in October, a U.S. Energy Department official said that a pipeline in the remote Komi region of Russia's Arctic, just south of the Arctic Circle, had been spilling oil for months. Estimates on the amount of oil involved varied

178

widely, from a U.S. figure of more than 80 million gallons to a Russian estimate of around 4 million gallons. The pipeline, which was nearly 20 years old and had been patched many times previously, was leaking in at least seven places, according to a U.S. oil company executive. A makeshift earthen dike had contained the oil until it was damaged by rain; the oil was expected to drift further northward during spring thaws in 1995. Late in the year a new rupture in the pipeline reportedly caused some 3.8 million gallons to flood the tundra about 40 miles north of the city of Usinsk; the oil subsequently caught fire, and reports spoke of blazing oil lakes in the tundra.

Conservation. Five Asian republics of the Commonwealth of Independent States set up a protection committee and a rescue fund for the Aral Sea, which had been reduced to a quarter of its original size after being repeatedly tapped for extensive irrigation projects. As the sea retreated, fertilizer residue on the exposed seabed became a toxic dust. Eighty percent of the women and children in the region were anemic, and life expectancy was low. Four of the five republics—Kazakhstan, Kyrgyzstan, Turkmenistan, and Uzbekistan—pledged to donate 1 percent of their 1994 budgets to a conservation and health care fund. (Tajikistan was excused from paying because of its financial crisis.) As a first step, Kyrgyz President Askar Akayev said his country would accept reductions in the allocation of water from two rivers that feed the Aral Sea.

Restoration of Florida's Everglades became more of a certainty in May when Governor Lawton Chiles signed into law the $700 million Everglades Forever Act. The law calls for

Cleanup time. Workers tackle a massive cleanup job in Russia's Arctic in October. Oil had leaked from a pipeline for months before earthen dikes containing the oil collapsed from heavy rains.

Hot topic. *With efforts to find new sites for nuclear waste dumps in the United States running years behind schedule, Ward Valley in California's Mojave Desert emerged as a test case. Proponents argued that the area's remoteness and geological features made it a logical place to dispose of low-level radioactive waste. Opponents, however, filed lawsuits to block its use. Prominent among opposition groups were local Indians, who paid for the road sign shown here.*

construction of 40,000 acres of marshes around Lake Okeechobee, to be financed by the federal government, the state, and sugar producers; sugar producers dumped water contaminated with fertilizers and agricultural wastes into the Everglades for decades. The new marshland would filter phosphorous, a fertilizer ingredient, out of water before it drained into the Everglades. Also, some drained swampland would be reflooded.

In December a federal judge approved a Clinton plan that would allow up to 1 billion feet of lumber to be logged in the Pacific Northwest, home to the spotted owl and other imperiled species.

To allow depleted stocks of cod, halibut, and haddock to replenish themselves, the United States and Canada announced on the last day of 1993 that the Georges Bank fishing ground off Nova Scotia would be off-limits to fishermen between January 1 and May 31. The U.S. Commerce Department announced in January a longer-term recovery plan that would reduce fishing in U.S. North Atlantic waters by 50 percent over the next five to seven years while providing financial aid to coastal New England towns that stood to be hit hardest by the restrictions. In an effort to save the endangered cod, haddock, and flounder stocks from "economic extinction," the Commerce Department issued an emergency order in December banning for at least three months

most commercial fishing of these species in roughly 6,000 square miles of the Atlantic ocean, including the U.S. portion of the Georges Bank and the waters off southern New England.

Desertification Agreement. In October an international convention involving some 100 countries met in Paris to discuss ways to prevent desertification, in which persistent overuse and erosion turn arid and semiarid land into desert. Worldwide, according to UN estimates, 900 million people are sustained by crops grown on these types of land, but crop yields are decreasing steadily as deforestation, overgrazing, overcultivation, and improper irrigation dry them out. The situation is especially critical in Africa.

The agreement that resulted from the October meeting established a "Global Mechanism" to coordinate conservation projects and to find money to pay for them. The agreement was to become an international treaty when ratified by 50 nations.   S.S.

EQUATORIAL GUINEA. *See* Statistics of the World.

ERITREA. Nation building was the main business of newly independent Eritrea in 1994. In February the third congress of the ruling Eritrean People's Liberation Front (EPLF) adopted a national transitional charter based on principles of national unity, democracy, social justice, and regional and international cooperation. Of the 1,961 delegates attending, 15 percent were women.

The congress elected a 19-member Executive Council headed by President Isaias Afewerki and passed a resolution placing all land under government ownership. Meanwhile, the EPLF officially became the People's Front for Democracy and Justice (PFDJ), Eritrea's first political party since parties were banned by imperial Ethiopia in the early 1960s.

In March the National Assembly approved creation of a cabinet to replace the existing State Council and established a Constitutional Commission. The process of writing a constitution, based on principles spelled out in the national charter, began in April.

In early December, Eritrea broke off diplomatic relations with neighboring Sudan; Eritrea accused Sudan of supporting Islamic fundamentalist Eritreans bent on unseating the PFDJ government. Late in 1994 the main opposition group, Jebha, which had been all but wiped out by the EPLF, was reorganized and armed heavily by Algeria, Morocco, Sudan, and Tunisia. Armed conflicts between Eritrean forces and Jebha were reported to have occurred along the Sudanese border. Meanwhile, relations between Eritrea and Ethiopia continued to be positive.

International donors, including Denmark, Finland, Germany, Sweden, the United States, the World Bank, and various UN agencies, began pumping substantial amounts of foreign assistance into Eritrea. In addition, Eritrea adopted legislation in August to stimulate foreign investment.

See STATISTICS OF THE WORLD. E.K.

ESTONIA. In 1994 the political spectrum in Estonia became increasingly fragmented, and the right-of-center coalition government of Prime Minister Mart Laar, in office since October 1992, fell in September due to a no-confidence vote in Parliament. Andres Tarand, previously the environment minister, formed a

Long good-bye. *Russian soldiers await their return home from Estonia. Troop pullouts from the Baltic states marked the final end of the region's era of incorporation into the former Soviet Union.*

Baltic nightmare. *One of history's worst ferry disasters occurred in September, when the ferry* Estonia *(above), en route from Tallinn to Stockholm, sank at night in stormy seas. More than 800 people died, and fewer than 200 were rescued. At right, a Swedish Navy rescue worker examines bodies found in a life raft from the ship.*

new government in November based on the same political parties as the Laar cabinet. Since regular parliamentary elections were scheduled for March 1995, Tarand clearly headed a transitional government.

After long and heated negotiations Estonia finally reached agreement with Russia at the end of July on the key issue of withdrawal of ex-Soviet troops by August 31. With a few exceptions this deadline was actually met. In return, the Estonian side accepted the principle of "social guarantees" for the slightly more than 10,000 retired Russian military personnel living in Estonia. The retirees were to receive their pensions, paid in Estonian currency, from the Russian Federation, and they were to have

the right to dispose of property acquired in Estonia as they saw fit.

A further agreement, also signed with Russia at the end of July, called for the dismantling of the nuclear training site at the Paldiski submarine base, which is located only 30 miles from Tallinn, by the end of September 1995. The fuel rods from Paldiski's two nuclear reactors were removed to Russia without incident during the fall.

Estonia took steps during 1994 to strengthen its ties with the West. In February it joined NATO's Partnership for Peace, and in May it became an associate member of the Western European Union. In these initiatives Estonia was joined by its two Baltic neighbors, Latvia and Lithuania, with whom it increasingly cooperated in economic and foreign policy. In July the three Baltic states signed a free-trade agreement with the European Union, slated to go into effect for Estonia on January 1, 1995.

See STATISTICS OF THE WORLD.   T.U.R.

ETHIOPIA. In 1994 the Transitional Government of Ethiopia (TGE), dominated by the Ethiopian People's Revolutionary Democratic Front (EPRDF) and led by President Meles Zenawi, continued to go through the motions of building a multiparty democracy. However, it was clear that the EPRDF would continue to control transitional politics, especially after main opposition groups boycotted June elections for a Constituent Assembly to ratify a new constitution. The groups complained that they had not been involved in drafting the proposed constitution, and they objected to provisions for local autonomy and even secession, saying the document was dangerously tipped toward disunity. The EPRDF won 484 of 547 seats in the assembly.

In November the assembly deemed Ethiopia to be a federal democratic republic. It said that the country was to be run parliamentary-style, with a prime minister accountable to Parliament and a president to fulfill mainly ceremonial functions. Most of the articles of the proposed constitution had been passed by year's end, with a new government to be formed after the expected 1995 polls.

Throughout 1994 the Council of Alternative Forces for Peace and Democracy, a broad coalition of EPRDF-opposed groups, pressed for the TGE to dissolve itself and open up the political system. In April five groups merged to form the Ethiopian National Democratic Party, and the All-Amhara Peoples' Organization finally declared itself a political party. But some groups turned to armed struggle; several were engaged in armed conflict with the EPRDF Army or in assassination attempts on officials. The activities carried out by armed opposition groups in border zones caused friction between Ethiopia and its neighbors Kenya and Sudan.

See STATISTICS OF THE WORLD.   E.K.

Food crisis. *Famine struck parts of Ethiopia in 1994; many of the children affected had to be spoon-fed because they had forgotten the sensation of eating. Here, a tiny victim is slowly nourished back to health.*

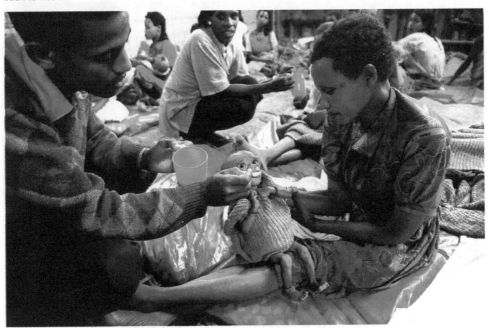

EUROPEAN UNION. Change was the operative word for the European Community in 1994. Not least among the changes was the name of the European Community itself, which, with the coming into force of the Maastricht Treaty, became the European Union, also known as the EU.

Monetary Union. During 1994, Europeans took important steps forward in their efforts to establish a monetary union. Despite currency crises in 1992 and 1993, the relative stability in exchange rates required by the Maastricht Treaty for monetary union was in evidence in 1994. Also, a central bank in the form of the European Monetary Institute was established in Frankfurt, Germany.

Political Developments. The most significant happenings within the European Union in 1994 were political—in particular, two disputes involving member governments.

The first dispute concerned the admission of four countries to the EU (the 12 countries that were already members were Belgium, Denmark, France, Germany, Great Britain, Greece, Ireland, Italy, Luxembourg, the Netherlands, Portugal, and Spain). By mid-March negotiations between the European Union and the governments of Austria, Finland, Norway, and Sweden for accession had been favorably concluded. But Great Britain and Spain did not want their voting power diminished when the Council of Ministers increased in size. In the end, however, London and Madrid were forced to accept a German-backed proposal that instituted the voting arrangement they had initially opposed.

A dispute over the presidency of the European Commission also revealed growing German influence. In May, Jacques Delors announced his intention to retire as president of the European Commission (the EU's executive body). At the EU summit meeting in Corfu, Greece, in June, the British government vetoed the candidate for Commission president supported by the other 11 EU governments, Jean-Luc Dehaene of Belgium, but failed to rally support for its own nominee. German Chancellor Helmut Kohl stepped in, called an emergency EU summit in Brussels in mid-July, and there succeeded in having Luxembourg Prime Minister Jacques Santer named as the new Commission president.

Elections to the 567-seat European Parliament, held in June, yielded ambiguous results.

Jacques Santer

In July 1994, Jacques Santer, the prime minister of Luxembourg, was elected president of the European Commission—in effect, president of the European Union. Santer, dubbed Champagne Jack for his convivial style, took up his post in January 1995.

The EU president-elect was born in 1937 in Wasserbillig, a small town in Luxembourg, and has spent most of his life in that country. He became head of Luxembourg's Social Christian Party in 1974 and was first named prime minister in 1984. He chaired negotiations in 1985 that led to the creation of a single European market, and he has served as vice president of the European Parliament. He speaks fluent French—a qualification the French had insisted upon—and is described as a quiet, behind-the-scenes negotiator.

Santer has said that "the more decentralized Europe is, the stronger it is"—and as prime minister he stood up for his own country's interests against pressures by bigger EU states. W.A.M.

Only 56.5 percent of the EU-wide electorate cast ballots in the elections; relatively few candidates took positions on European-wide issues; and some candidates were professedly against the EU.

Enlargement of the EU. On January 1 the European Economic Area (EEA) came officially into being, uniting the 12 countries of the European Union with all of the countries of the European Free Trade Area (EFTA) except Switzerland.

But the EEA's opening was eclipsed by the fact that several of the EFTA countries—Austria, Finland, Norway, and Sweden—were already slated for full membership in the European Union. The question of joining the European Union was finally put to the electorates of Austria, Finland, Norway, and Sweden in referendums held during the summer and autumn. Austrians, Finns, and Swedes all opted for EU membership by narrow majori-

ties; their countries entered the European Union in January 1995. But in November 1994, despite strong endorsement from the Oslo government, Norwegians voted—52 to 48 percent—to stay out of the European Union. Many Norwegians were apparently concerned about possibly losing national sovereignty.

Poland and Hungary, who were already linked to the EU via specially negotiated "European agreements" of economic association, both formally applied for full membership in April. Meanwhile, a landmark Partnership and Cooperation Agreement (PCA), involving the liberalization of trade and investment and the prospect of a free-trade area by 1998, was concluded between Russia and the European Union at the Corfu summit in June. Similar though less ambitious PCAs were also negotiated with Estonia, Latvia, Lithuania, and Ukraine.   D.J.P.

F

FASHION. The world of couture snapped out two backlashes against black in 1994. Spring collections were pale-hued, with a heavy beige theme; by autumn, electric colors lit up Lurex and fake fur, while designs in mohair and angora showed up in pastels. The fashion world also widened its band of shapes, from plain A-lines to curve-clinging, belt-cinched numbers with shoulder pads, an attempt to make women look more grown-up and glamorous after the year of the waif.

All told, 1994 mixed it up enormously. Alongside the year's undeniable postwar look there were also bare midriffs, slips that were worn as dresses, and corsets that were worn as blouses.

Costume Party Over. After the costume party mood of 1993, spring 1994 found fashion designers in Milan, Paris, and New York "cleaning up [our] act," as Alan Cleaver, half (with Keith Varty) of Milan's Byblos design team, told a *Women's Wear Daily* reporter.

"You can't wear a ruffled blouse and a velvet coat to dinner without getting it in your plate, darling." The paper declared the clean-lined "Plain Jane" look in. Menswear seemed to be going in the same direction, with grunge, punk, and deconstruction giving way to prewashed chinos, unconstructed suits, and comfortable knit shirts.

But not everyone was ready to leave the costume party, least of all Gianni Versace. He not only produced shredded and "distressed" pieces but also revolted against the unrelieved black of the previous season by "going to color heaven."

Others started the color backlash more cautiously—with beige. According to a Strawbridge & Clothier ad for a Liz Claiborne ensemble, "No color feels as right as no color."

Slips made a splash in 1994, too, but were called "slipdresses," and were intended to be seen. Sheer nightgowns masquerading as dresses also graced many runways. The chal-

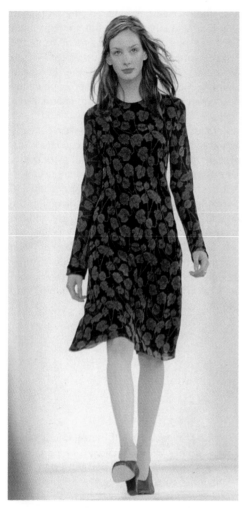

Mom's dress? *A black print dress shown as part of Calvin Klein's 1994 fall collection. Hemlines were taking a dip as designers experimented with skirts that just covered the knee—a length out of fashion for nearly three decades.*

bringing the concept full circle: They'd made the slipdress work by turning it back into a slip.

Fall Colors. With their fall collections, designers let strong colors onto the runways. Marc Jacobs showed Lifesaver colors in his first collection since departing Perry Ellis. Isaac Mizrahi, saying he'd gone "insane with color," mixed periwinkle with turquoise and lilac, and showed a neon-pink slicker lined with Day-Glo orange fake fur. Fake fur, which was cheap, easy to dye, and politically correct, added fun to many a number, as did Lurex, vinyl, and textured wools like mohair and angora, in a hodgepodge of styles from the 1960s and 1970s.

But the defined shapes of even earlier decades reemerged, too. Shoulders, waists, and hips, until recently veiled under flowing layers, reappeared as tailoring made a comeback. Shoulder pads were reinstated and belts, mostly narrow ones, were tightened. And unapologetic undergarments—some displayed as part of the outfit—underpinned nearly every collection and the renewed emphasis on shape. The new generation of foun-

lenge for most designers and wearers of slipdresses was to make them look enough like underwear to be racy, but not so much so as to be unwearable. Designer Vera Wang built underwear into her slipdresses, while Calvin Klein and Ralph Lauren put theirs over white T-shirts. At least three clever young designers—Anne Marie Gabalis, Bradley Bayou, and Lola Faturoti—hit on the same solution to the slipdress dilemma in their autumn shows. They popped chiffon overdresses over them,

Bustlines Get a Boost

"It's a miracle!" proclaimed one ad. "Nothing gives your bust, or your confidence, such a superb boost," cooed another. Call it a feat of engineering or call it marketing, but be sure to call 1994's push-up bra a hit. When the Super-Uplift bra arrived at a New York City department store in March, nearly 500 were sold the first day. Within months the Wonderbra, Miracle Bra, Incredibra, It Must Be Magic Bra, and others were competing to defy gravity.

Whether or not they deliver a psychological uplift, these are no ordinary bras. The Wonderbra boasts 54 different parts, about twice as many as a conventional bra—wires, straps, hooks, elastic, fiberfill pads, and other things, all sewn together to push the breasts up and center to create 1994's favorite fashion accessory: cleavage.

So is this what women really want? Perhaps. Millions of the bras, priced at up to $80, were sold during the year in the United States, Canada, and Great Britain alone.

dation garments included "bodyshapers," "hip slips," and compression shorts, which used Spandex instead of whalebone and tight lacing to reshape the body. Ultra-control-top pantyhose also sold well. Meanwhile, the underwire bra was reborn when the Wonderbra, a push-up, underwire brassiere that supposedly improved cleavage, was introduced in the United States after enjoying years of popularity in Great Britain. In his couture collection for Chanel, Karl Lagerfeld created suits with boned corsets instead of blouses.

Although the winter of 1993-1994 had been the coldest in some time, few designers seemed interested in keeping women warm. The feud between 1994 Olympic figure skaters Nancy Kerrigan and Tonya Harding inspired a brief rash of skating skirts, while a startling number of fall ensembles bared not just the entire leg, but the entire midriff, too.

Navel maneuver. A design from Karl Lagerfeld's fall 1994 collection featuring a pink classic ensemble with an open strapless brassiere and a furlike colored hat. Many of the designs shown in the fall bared the midriff.

Banished by autumn 1994 was the underfed waif look of the previous year, which proved controversial and hadn't sold well. The most infamous waif model of all, Kate Moss, was made to put on grown-up-looking red lipstick; her hair was tidied and streaked blond; and she wore the Wonderbra, giving her a hint of cleavage that spelled the "new glamour" look of 1994. Curves were emphasized with shiny, clingy fabrics and accessorized with spike heels and alarming amounts of makeup.

Meanwhile, hemlines took a decided dip. After the recent years' ultrashort skirts, followed by poor-selling down-to-the-ankle lengths in 1992-1993, Calvin Klein and Miuccia Prada experimented in 1994 with skirts that just covered the knee—the only length left that had been definitively out of fashion since 1965. The controversial "new length" was taken up by some of the fashion avant-garde but derided as dowdy and retro by others.

Suits in Court. Yves Saint Laurent sued Ralph Lauren in a French court, charging Lauren had copied a tuxedo-based evening dress from a Saint Laurent collection, and won $395,000, although Lauren appealed the decision. Copying was again the issue when designer Gianni Versace protested that ABS, the American sportswear house, had knocked off his safety-pin dress and delivered it to stores—including one right next door to Versace's South Beach Miami boutique—before the original had even been manufactured.   P.McL.

FIJI. *See* Pacific Islands; Statistics of the World.

FINLAND. In February 1994, Finnish voters elected career diplomat Martti Ahtisaari to succeed two-term President Mauno Koivisto on March 1. At the same time, negotiations with Brussels for the terms of Finnish membership in the European Union (EU) were wrapped up. In agreeing to the treaty of accession to the EU, set to take effect January 1, 1995, Finland was abandoning the neutrality it had pursued in the cold war era and was expanding its market access. Finnish voters approved the treaty in an October referendum, and Parliament subsequently ratified it in November.

On February 6, Social Democrat Martti Ahtisaari, a former United Nations mediator, was elected president with 53.9 percent of the

Home away from home. *A striking new Finnish embassy building, which was designed by the Finnish architects Mikko Heikkinen and Markku Komonen, opened in Washington, DC, in 1994.*

vote. Finnish Defense Minister Elisabeth Rehn, representing the Swedish People's Party, pulled in 46.1 percent. The race was decided in a second round of voting, in Finland's first French-style, two-stage direct ballot; turnout was 82.3 percent. Although Finnish presidents typically concentrate on foreign affairs, Ahtisaari's victory owed much to his discussion of a painful domestic subject: centrist Prime Minister Esko Aho's government's lackluster record on unemployment, which hovered around 19 percent.

In September the Aho-led cabinet survived its 18th vote of no confidence, sponsored by the Green Party over economic mismanagement. Meanwhile, because of massive state debt and high unemployment, a policy of severe restraint in public sector spending looked set to continue.

An export-led recovery was under way in 1994, however, helped by marked growth in Finnish-Russian trade and a revival in trade with Finland's principal Western European trade partners.

With its 1994 EU referendum the first to be held among the Nordic applicants (Sweden and Norway followed), Finland was considered a bellwether. Although 57 percent of Finns voted in favor of the EU on October 16, there was much opposition throughout the year. In June the Christian League left the ruling center-right coalition (composed of the Center, Conservative, and Swedish People's parties) over the EU issue. And although the EU-Finland accession treaty included various support schemes for the heavily subsidized Finnish farming sector, most farmers strongly opposed EU membership. Nonetheless, Parliament ratified the accession treaty on November 18.

See STATISTICS OF THE WORLD. D.A.

FLORIDA. *See* STATE GOVERNMENT REVIEW; STATISTICS OF THE WORLD.

FORMOSA. *See* TAIWAN.

FRANCE. The highlights of 1994 in France featured nostalgic celebrations of key events in World War II, inauguration ceremonies for the Channel Tunnel, and a renovated Louvre and refurbished Champs Elysées designed to establish an ultramodern image for the country on the brink of the 21st century. The 50th anniversary of the allied assault on the Normandy beaches brought leaders of a dozen nations and more than 50,000 veterans together at the site where Hitler's empire began to crumble. It was a highly symbolic event, not least because of ticklish diplomatic matters. Germany's Chancellor Helmut Kohl was not invited—a snub that left hurt feelings on the other side of the Rhine. France and its wartime allies, however, did not want to awaken old animosities by inviting German soldiers who once served the cause of Nazi occupation.

Another golden anniversary marked the allied liberation of Paris. Although American troops had cleared the way into the capital before allowing Charles De Gaulle and the Free French Forces to make their triumphant entry, the highly patriotic spirit of the anniversary celebration was clearly aimed at bolstering France's fading sense of heroic grandeur. The City of Lights was bathed in a festival of color, music, and fireworks that lasted through the warm August night.

While much of summer was consumed with commemorations of the last world war, France also kept its eyes pointed toward the future. The Channel Tunnel, opened in May by President François Mitterrand and Britain's Queen Elizabeth II, was hailed as the engineering marvel of the century, one that formally marked the end of Britain's physical isolation from the continent. The $15 billion project, featuring twin tubular train tunnels under the English Channel, each some 38 kilometers (24 miles) in length, cost more than twice its original estimate, and some analysts feared it might evolve into a white elephant. Nonetheless, Mitterrand envisioned the project as one of the touchstones of his 14-year presidency, scheduled to end in May 1995.

Mitterrand also glowed in the success of a billion-dollar renovation of the Louvre museum, spearheaded by the gleaming new Richelieu wing that opened in November 1993 to rave reviews by architecture critics.

Jackal jailed. This photo, released by the French Interior Ministry, was said to show the notorious international terrorist Ilich Ramírez Sánchez (also known as Carlos the Jackal) in Sudan before his capture there in August. He was quickly extradited to France, where he was wanted for his role in several murders.

189

Not to be outdone, Paris Mayor Jacques Chirac unveiled a spruced-up Champs Elysées which, he said, would now be restored to its rightful place as "the world's most beautiful and glamorous boulevard." New underground parking banished cars at curbside, the pedestrian zone was doubled in space, and the vast promenade now displays leafy plantain trees and elegant street lamps.

The Touvier Trial.   One of the most dramatic events of the year was the trial of Paul Touvier, former militia chief for the collaborationist Vichy regime in Nazi-occupied France, on charges of crimes against humanity. It was the first time that a Frenchman had ever stood trial on such charges, and it revived a painful argument over the true extent of French collaboration with Nazi occupiers. Touvier's lawyer argued that his client was a scapegoat who was being sacrificed to ease the country's stricken conscience. But in April a nine-member jury gave Touvier the maximum penalty of life in prison, affirming that he was carrying out genocidal policies when he executed seven Jews in a Lyon suburb in 1944 in retaliation for the killing of a Vichy minister by the French resistance. The trial provided vivid evidence of how French citizens actively carried out anti-Semitic purges, often without prompting by the German occupation forces. Indeed, the Vichy regime led by Marshal Henri-Philippe Pétain was shown to have rounded up at least 75,000 French Jews and deported them to Nazi-run death camps; only 2,500 of them survived.

The collaboration debate became even more controversial when a new biography of Mitterrand showed that after escaping from a prisoner of war camp, he served the Vichy regime as a minor functionary before switching sides and joining the resistance. Pierre Pean's book *A French Youth: François Mitterrand 1934-1947* showed that Mitterrand had clearly embraced right-wing views in his youth and was even awarded the Vichy regime's highest honor. The president's Socialist supporters were shocked and dismayed to learn that he had maintained a friendship until the 1980s with René Bousquet, the former Vichy police chief who was assassinated in Paris in June 1993 before he could stand trial for deporting Jewish prisoners.

Politics.   After Mitterrand underwent a second operation in the summer for prostate cancer, speculation was rife that he would not be able to finish out his second seven-year term. Under France's constitution, a special election to choose a successor must be held within 35 days after the death or resignation of a president. The notion that Mitterrand, who turned 78 in 1994, might not survive until the expiration of his mandate in May 1995 inflamed the simmering personal rivalry between leading presidential contenders within the ruling conservative alliance: Prime Minister Edouard Balladur and Gaullist party leader Jacques Chirac. Throughout much of the year Balladur's patrician style and disdain for social confrontation seemed popular with voters, and opinion polls consistently ranked him as the man most likely to become France's next president.

As French magistrates suddenly began to show the same enthusiasm for rooting out corruption as their Italian peers in recent years, however, a succession of scandals within Balladur's cabinet appeared to jeopardize his stature with the electorate. Two ministers, Alain Carignon and Gérard Longuet, were forced to resign on suspicion of influence peddling and tampering with state funds. Both men were key centrist allies whose support was deemed crucial for Balladur's run at the presidency. A third minister, Michel Roussin, resigned after press reports of influence peddling. While Balladur continued to insist that he had not decided whether to run, Chirac announced his candidacy in November.

At the same time, the opposition Socialists were having trouble finding their own candidate. Party leader Michel Rocard was forced to resign his position and drop out of the race after the Socialists were clobbered at the polls during June's elections to the European Parliament, an indication that the Socialists had still not recovered from the poor handling of the economy and the string of corruption scandals that drove them out of government in 1993's national elections.

Jacques Delors, whose term as president of the European Union's executive commission was to end in January 1995, emerged as the most popular candidate in the latter part of 1994. But in December he announced that he

Gallic flair. Christian de Portzamparc (above) became the first French architect to win the Pritzker Architecture Prize, generally considered the highest honor in the field. The formal citation hailed his designs as "bound neither by classicism nor modernism." One of his most notable works is the City of Music, a conservatory in the suburban Parisian park of La Villette (top). The conical structure visible in the center of the complex is the organ recital hall, shown at right in an interior view.

had decided not to run for president, leaving the Socialists scrambling around to find a new candidate.

Economy. After suffering in the doldrums for two years, France's economy showed new signs of vigor as the pace of recovery picked up elsewhere in Europe. The country's trade surplus reached new highs, and the government upgraded growth predictions to 3 percent for the year. Still, unemployment remained stubbornly above 11 percent, with young people hit extremely hard. One in four people under the age of 25 could not find work, and the Balladur government began to worry out loud about the dangers of a social explosion if new jobs could not be found for the young. But economists warned the government that for more jobs to be created, it needed to reduce the burdens on employers, who pay up to 50 percent in supplementary taxes on wages and salaries to fund France's substantial social benefits, such as comprehensive health care and six-week vacations.

Foreign Policy. In June, France demonstrated that it still ranks as perhaps the most influential outside power in Africa when it dispatched 2,500 soldiers to set up a safe zone in western Rwanda, along the Zaire border, and stop the civilian slaughter that left an estimated half-million dead in the brutal civil war that was tearing Rwanda apart.

France's role was greeted with suspicion among the minority Tutsi because they believed that French troops had propped up the government of former president Juvénal Habyarimana, a Hutu, whose death in a plane crash in April triggered the bloody civil war. But French forces avoided any serious clashes with the Tutsi-dominated Rwandan Patriotic Front that defeated the former Hutu government, and their humanitarian rescue role was generally applauded as having saved thousands of lives.

Algeria was another area of grave concern for France, which feared that if Islamic fundamentalists prevailed in their bloody guerrilla war with the Army-backed government, as many as 100,000 Algerians would flee to the former colonial power across the Mediterranean Sea. More than a dozen French citizens living in Algeria were killed in the anti-

foreigner campaign waged by suspected Islamic gunmen, and Paris urged the remaining 2,000 French nationals to leave the country. France pressed its allies to relieve Algeria from its huge debts until oil and gas revenues recovered. But the Balladur government was also suspected of keeping open all options, including secret channels to Islamic militants.

An important dividend was the August arrest and extradition to France of the world's most wanted terrorist, Carlos the Jackal (Ilich Ramírez Sánchez). French authorities had cultivated a dialogue with the Islamic government in Sudan, where Carlos had taken refuge. While serving as a conduit for communications with Islamic fundamentalists in Algeria, Sudan also cooperated in delivering the man wanted for the killing of two French policemen and others in terrorist acts carried out on French territory. Carlos's arrest was hailed as a triumph for Interior Minister Charles Pasqua. In December, Algerian militants hijacked an Air France jet in Algiers and flew it to Marseilles, where it was stormed by French commandos, who rescued some 170 hostages. The militants said they were avenging France's aid to Algeria.

Culture. The year's publishing milestones featured long-hidden works by two of France's most revered authors. Albert Camus's incomplete fourth novel, *The First Man,* soared to the top of best-seller lists within two weeks after hitting the bookstores. The autobiographical novel was found in a briefcase Camus was carrying when he died in a car accident in 1960, and for 34 years it remained a family secret.

A second popular book was kept even longer from the public. In 1863, Jules Verne peered nearly a century into the future and wrote a science fiction work titled *Paris in the Twentieth Century.* It remained hidden until his great-grandson, while moving from the family home, decided to open a locked safe, in which he discovered the manuscript. It had been cast aside after Verne's editor said nobody would believe his prophecies. Yet the book contains remarkably prescient descriptions of many of the givens of modern life, including the fax machine and Parisian automobile traffic.

See STATISTICS OF THE WORLD.   W.D.

G

GABON. *See* Statistics of the World.

GAMBIA, THE. *See* Africa; Statistics of the World.

GEORGIA. The government of Eduard Shevardnadze was largely occupied in 1994 with the secessionist movement in Abkhazia, a formerly autonomous republic in northwestern Georgia. The Abkhazians, though only 18 percent of Abkhazia's population, had earlier evicted the local Georgian population and established an independent Abkhazia with its capital at Gudauta. In April 1994, after several cease-fires between the Georgian government and Abkhazia had failed, a new one brokered by Russia, the Conference on Security and Cooperation in Europe, and the United Nations was arranged. This cease-fire was still generally in force late in the year, although relations were strained. In August trilateral talks opened in the Russian city of Sochi between Russian, Georgian, and Abkhazian negotiators. The following month the three parties and the United Nations signed an agreement meant to govern the safety of ethnic Georgian refugees who wished to return to their homes in Abkhazia.

In the spring and summer protesters taking part in mass antigovernment rallies demanded a stronger hand with Abkhazia, the resignation of the increasingly authoritarian and unpopular Shevardnadze, and the withdrawal of Georgia from the Commonwealth of Independent States, the voluntary federation replacing the former Soviet Union.

Relations with neighboring Armenia remained relatively cordial throughout the year, and the two countries concluded an agreement allowing Armenia to import supplies through Georgian ports. Relations with Azerbaijan were strained by Georgian claims to certain districts in northwestern Azerbaijan inhabited by Georgians and by continued Azerbaijani efforts to disrupt the shipping of fuel to Armenia by blowing up pipelines and trains within Georgia.

The Georgian economy remained in serious condition as economic reforms such as liberalization of prices, undertaken to further the transfer from a communist to a free market, continued to be slowed by the fighting.

See Statistics of the World.   R.H.H.

GEORGIA (U.S. STATE). *See* State Government Review; Statistics of the World.

GERMANY. Germany's economy improved in 1994. Federal elections in October produced another victory for Christian Democratic Chancellor Helmut Kohl and his Free Democratic coalition partners, although their parliamentary majority dropped dramatically from 134 seats to ten.

Economy. After undergoing the worst recession of the postwar era, the German economy surged upward with a real growth rate just under 3 percent in the first half of 1994. At the same time, the rate of inflation dropped to 3 percent in September from 4 percent in September 1993. In eastern Germany, the rate of real growth was 9.0 percent during the first half of 1994.

The German Central Bank attributed the sharp recovery to a boom in construction and to moderate wage agreements and reductions in personnel, which made German exports less expensive and more competitive in international markets. After falling in 1993, exports in 1994 were expected to exceed the 1992 total.

Personnel reductions, on the other hand, contributed to the highest levels of unemployment of the postwar era. More than 4 million were unemployed in January, for a rate of 8.8 percent in western Germany and 17.0 percent in the east. The growing economy, however, began to create jobs, so that by September unemployment rates had dropped to 7.9 percent in the west and 13.8 percent in the east.

Elections Through September. From March to September, elections in five states and for the European Parliament served as previews for federal elections in October. In Lower Saxony in March, with Christian Democrats still bearing the onus of economic recession, the party dropped from 42.2 percent of the vote in 1990 to 36.4 percent. The Social Democrats with 44.3 percent of the vote won 81 of 161 seats, giving them a single-seat majority and

193

Reason to applaud. *Chancellor Helmut Kohl (left) shows his approval during voting by a special electoral college in May for Germany's new president, who turned out to be Roman Herzog (right), a member of Kohl's party. Kohl himself remained in power as a result of elections five months later.*

the ability to govern without their former coalition partners, the Greens.

By June, however, the economy was moving sharply ahead, and the Christian Democrats took 38.8 percent of the vote to 32.2 percent for the Social Democrats in countrywide elections to the European Parliament in Strasbourg. The right-wing Republicans, who polled 7.1 percent in 1989, failed to secure the 5 percent of the vote needed to gain any seats and lost their representation in Strasbourg.

Three summer elections in eastern Germany saw the former Communist party, renamed the Party of Democratic Socialism, increase its voting strength in all three states, to an average of 18.4 percent from 14.2 percent in 1990. The election in Saxony-Anhalt in June resulted in a Christian Democratic/Free Democratic coalition government being replaced by a Social Democratic/Green government with only a minority of seats. The new coalition government was supported, however, by the former Communists. Although not in the government, they allowed it to gain majorities either by abstaining or voting for government bills.

September elections in the other two states were determined by the increased popularity of their minister-presidents during the preceding four-year terms. The vote for the Social Democrats under Manfred Stolpe in Brandenburg went up to 54.1 percent from 38.2 percent in 1990. The vote for the Christian Democrats under Kurt Biedenkopf in Saxony rose to 58.1 percent from 53.8 percent in 1990.

The election in late September in Bavaria resulted in a majority vote for the Christian Democrats. But it was a disaster for the Free Democrats, coalition partners of Chancellor Kohl at the federal level. In a repeat of the other five elections, they failed to surpass the 5 percent barrier and lost their representation in the state parliament. Kohl, ahead in the opinion polls for the October 16 federal elections, campaigned hard for a high voter turnout and asked Christian Democratic voters to give their second vote to the Free Democratic Party. Germans vote twice in Bundestag elections: for a candidate running in their district and for a party list. If the Free Democrats did not surpass the barrier on the party-list vote and the former Communists did, it could mean, as in Saxony-Anhalt, a Social Democratic/Green government either supported by or including the party once led by Walter Ulbricht and Erich Honecker. Although the Social Democratic party leader, Rudolf Scharping, insisted he would not accept support from the former Communists, Kohl made the possibility of such a government a major theme of his campaign.

October Elections. In the federal elections, "borrowed votes"—Christian Democrats giving their second vote to the Free Democrats—

enabled another four-year term for the governing coalition and for Kohl. Countrywide, the Free Democrats took 6.9 percent of the vote while polling an average of only 3.0 percent in three state elections held at the same time. The 1994 vote for the Christian Democrats dropped slightly to 41.5 percent from 43.8 percent in 1990 while that for the opposition Social Democrats increased to 36.4 percent from 33.5 percent.

The Greens, having merged with an eastern party, Alliance 90, almost doubled their vote to 7.3 percent from 3.9 percent. The Democratic Socialists (former Communists) fell short of the 5 percent barrier. Election law, however, allows a party to receive its proportional representation if it wins at least three districts. In eastern Berlin, home to many party and state officials of the former East Germany, the Democratic Socialists won four districts and thus took the 30 seats (up from 17 in 1990) that their 4.4 percent of the vote allowed. The vote for the far-right Republicans was only 1.9 percent, down from 2.1 percent in 1990.

In the three state elections, the Social Democrats again won a majority in the Saar. In two eastern states, Mecklenburg-Vorpommern and Thuringia, Christian and Free Democratic coalitions were turned out of office when the Free Democrats polled, respectively, only 3.8 and 3.2 percent of the vote. With the Democratic Socialists receiving 22.7 and 16.6 percent, two "Grand Coalitions"—governments including the two largest parties, Christian and Social Democrats—were formed.

German Troops Abroad. The Federal Constitutional Court ruled in July that German armed forces may participate in NATO and United Nations military operations mandated by the UN Security Council. The German government, however, had to obtain the approval of the Bundestag before any troops could be assigned. The ruling ended a long-standing controversy among the country's political parties on Germany's international role.

Atomic Smuggling. Top officials of Germany and Russia announced in September a joint effort to combat organized crime in Europe. Its primary objective was to halt an illegal trade in radioactive materials. In the first half of 1994, the government stated, police had discovered some 90 cases of atomic smuggling. Most importantly, at the Munich airport in August, police seized 350 grams of weapons-grade plutonium, suitable for use in a nuclear warhead. German officials have long suspected sales to the Russian Mafia by individuals in Russian military labs and installations.

Right-wing Violence. Although the number of reported crimes by right-wing extremists—8,109—increased in 1993 by 14 percent over 1992, the number of violent crimes—1,814—decreased by 30 percent. Over 70 percent of the violent acts were attacks on foreigners. Other victims included political opponents, Jews, and homeless and handicapped people. Extremists killed eight people and committed 302 cases of arson, about half as many as in 1992 (17 and 708, respectively). The extremists tended to be young, male neo-Nazis and skinheads, often unemployed and rootless.

Mystery of the missing magnate. Officials in Germany were mystified by the disappearance in April of real estate developer Jürgen Schneider. Shortly afterward, his company filed for bankruptcy in what was the largest insolvency in German real estate since World War II.

Dramatic gesture. *A Kurdish protester who set himself afire runs toward policemen during a demonstration near Frankfurt in March (photo from a TV image). The marchers, who blockaded German highways, were demanding an independent Kurdish homeland in Turkey.*

In late September the two houses of Parliament approved a bill that increased the maximum punishments for bodily injury and dissemination of extremist propaganda to five years' imprisonment and gave the Post Office a legal basis to seize neo-Nazi materials sent to Germany from abroad. The bill also allowed organized crime information held by the German Intelligence Service to be passed on to public prosecutors, who were given the right to request more lenient sentences for organized crime informants.

Kurdish Unrest. Kurds living in Germany staged protests, some violent, during 1994 over what they perceived as German support of repressive Turkish policies toward the separatist Kurdish Workers Party (PKK), which had been fighting since 1984 for an independent homeland in southeast Turkey. In April, German officials suspended arms deliveries to Turkey while investigating to see whether German weapons were being used against the Kurds; they lifted the embargo in early May, saying there was insufficient evidence of such use to sustain a ban on arms sales.

See STATISTICS OF THE WORLD.   R.J.W.

GHANA. *See* STATISTICS OF THE WORLD.

GREAT BRITAIN. The year 1994 saw peace in Northern Ireland and an improvement in the nation's economy. But the political year ended with the ruling Conservatives in turmoil, Prime Minister John Major's position as leader in continuing doubt, and his popularity at an all-time low (*see profile in* PEOPLE IN THE NEWS).

A Growing Economy. At first sight, the government's recovery from the trough of recession in 1992 came straight from the textbook. The devaluation of the pound in September of that year enabled British firms to sell more abroad. Interest rates were cut and taxes increased to curb consumption. By 1994 the recession was over, inflation hovered around the 2.5 percent mark, and unemployment had fallen. As the year drew to a close, growth was accelerating to over 4 percent and the trade deficit was narrowing. Moreover, government revenues were higher than forecast, and public expenditures lower.

But politically, the 1992 devaluation was a disaster. The money markets drove the government out of the European Union's Exchange Rate Mechanism and forced devaluation upon it. After that humiliation—known still as "Black Wednesday"—the opposition

Labor Party replaced the Conservatives in the polls as the party best able to handle the economy. In addition, the tax increases of 1993 came too soon after the 1992 election campaign—which the Conservatives won on the promise of reducing taxation.

Toward an Irish Peace. Major's Downing Street Declaration, made jointly with Prime Minister Albert Reynolds of Ireland in December 1993, opened the way for the historic cease-fire finally announced by the Irish Republican Army (IRA) at the end of August 1994. The cease-fire ended 25 years of violence in which more than 3,000 people were killed, over 2,000 of them civilians.

The government's response to the cease-fire—in reality, the recognition by the IRA that the armed struggle had failed—was carefully tailored to reassure Northern Ireland's Loyalist, or Protestant, majority that the cessation of hostilities would not endanger their position. Finally, the Loyalist paramilitaries in turn announced a cease-fire. The unexpected fall from power of the Irish prime minister in November dashed Major's hopes of entering into cross-party peace talks, in which Gerry Adams, president of Sinn Fein, the political arm of the IRA, would have been involved. But lower-level talks between Britain and Sinn Fein and between Britain and the Loyalists did take place in December.

Scandal in the Government. The government entered 1994 committed to Major's "back to basics" moral crusade, but a series of sex scandals in the government undermined Major's attempt to present the Conservatives as the party of the "old core values" of self-help, self-discipline, and social order. Allegations of corruption and cover-ups, many dating from the era of Margaret Thatcher, Major's predecessor as prime minister, did more deep-seated damage. The hearings of the Scott inquiry into the arms-for-Iraq scandal revealed that prominent government ministers were prepared to allow innocent men to go to prison rather than reveal government complicity in arms sales to the Iraqi regime—they had tried to prevent the release in court of official documents proving that ministers had encouraged the exports of arms equipment to Iraq by three businessmen on trial for illegally selling the equipment. Ev-

idence at the inquiry also revealed that ministers and civil servants deliberately misled Parliament over the affair. In May the government was accused of making a deal with Malaysia for that country to buy arms from Britain in exchange for millions of pounds to fund construction of a hydroelectric dam on the Pergau River in 1991. The government's conduct was condemned as a waste of money by the National Audit Office and as illegal by the courts.

The expansion of the paragovernmental agencies and boards known as quangos (quasi-autonomous nongovernmental organizations) also aroused concern. Government ministers claimed to have reduced the number of executive quangos to 358 (from 492 in 1979). But

Why is this man smiling? A British soldier on duty in Belfast, Northern Ireland, is in an uncharacteristically good mood. The reason: it was the first day of a historic cease-fire announced in late August by the outlawed Irish Republican Army.

an independent research body, the Democratic Audit, found that over 5,500 existed, mostly at the local level, and accounted for nearly a third of central government expenditures. The Audit's main concern was that these bodies largely operated in secret and were barely accountable. There was considerable evidence that the government was packing quangos with its own supporters and that its allocation of public positions on bodies of all kinds was linked to business donations to Conservative Party funds.

Public concern about sleaze mounted when, on October 20, the *Guardian* newspaper published allegations by Mohamed al-Fayed, the owner of the prestigious London store, Harrods, that through a parliamentary lobbying firm he had paid two Conservative members of Parliament (MPs) for asking parliamentary questions on his behalf at £2,000 a question from 1987 to 1989. (MPs can ask questions of the prime minister and government ministers, both spoken and written, and in most cases expect a reply.) The lobbying firm was run by Ian Greer, a prominent ally of Major. Both MPs, junior ministers in Major's government, were obliged to resign. To allay growing public disillusionment, Major appointed a special inquiry into the standards of conduct in public life. But the damage to public confidence in British politicians, and to his own party in particular, had already been done. In an October opinion poll 61 percent of those surveyed found the Conservatives "sleazy and disreputable."

Elections, Local and Euro. The Conservatives fared badly on the electoral front. In May, Britain's third party, the Liberal Democrats, received the same share of the vote—27 percent—as the Conservatives in local government elections, while Labor led comfortably with 42 percent. It looked as though the Conservatives would suffer an electoral meltdown in the June election for members of the European Parliament, but the death in May of Labor Party leader John Smith led to significant party realignments. A huge swell of sympathy for Labor increased the party's vote, resulting in Labor's best performance in nearly 30 years and preventing a Liberal Democrat breakthrough. Labor took 62 of the 87 British seats. The Conservatives won only 18 seats with just 28 percent of the vote—their worst performance in a nationwide election since the 1832 Reform Bill.

A Dynamic New Leader. In July the Labor Party elected Tony Blair, a charismatic young former lawyer, as its new leader. Blair, a prominent party "modernizer," carried scarcely any ideological baggage beyond a se-

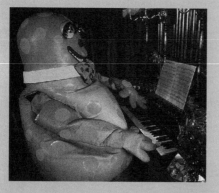

Mr. Blobby

Among the standout public figures in 1994—at least in Great Britain—was a pink, polka-dotted, 7-foot-tall, foam-rubber gentleman with a vocabulary of one word—"blobby."

Mr. Blobby started his rise to fame in 1992 as a minor TV character who embarrassed guests on the BBC's *Noel's House Party* by falling down on stage and ruining their acts. These antics hit the British funny bone, and Blobbymania swept the scepter'd isle, spawning more than 250 Blobby products ranging from dolls to clothing to lunch boxes. *The Blobby Song* was number one on the British charts, and a Blobby video sold 300,000 copies in a month. Mr. Blobby's public appearances drew the level of frenzy that once greeted the Beatles.

In June, Mr. Blobby visited New York as part of a campaign to open new vistas (and markets) for the green-eyed star. His tour included a dance session with eight ballerinas and a visit to Macy's, where he spilled candy and threw a New York Knicks T-shirt on the floor. Asked for his impressions of the United States, he replied diplomatically, "Blobby!"

rious commitment to a fair and just society. In an August poll Blair's appeal gave his party a 34.5 percent lead over the Conservatives—the largest lead ever recorded by the polls in Britain. Blair himself eclipsed both Major and Liberal Democrat leader Paddy Ashdown in popularity; 45 percent of the British public regarded him as the "best potential prime minister" compared to a mere 13 percent for both Major and Ashdown.

Britain and the EU. Major's political weakness and the Conservative Party split over Europe fed off each other. The bitter hostility of 30 to 35 Conservative MPs toward Britain's forging closer ties with the European Union forced Major to play a spoiler's role, which alienated such natural allies as Germany's right-wing Chancellor Helmut Kohl.

In March, Major picked a fight with his EU partners by publicly stating that he would refuse to agree to new proposals that would reduce Britain's ability to block EU decisions within the EU's Council of Ministers. Within weeks Major was publicly humiliated when his fellow heads of government drove the proposals through. Then, in June, Major further angered the Council by vetoing the appointment of Belgian Prime Minister Jean Luc Dehaene to take over as president of the European Commission in 1995, on the ground that Dehaene came from "a tradition of big government and intervention." Later, Major agreed to a compromise candidate, Luxembourg's Jacques Santer—who at once made it clear that he shared Dehaene's views.

Government Crisis. The major issue in the Conservative split was supposedly the EU movement toward a single currency. But the anti-Europeans, known as Euroskeptics, provoked a new government crisis over a November House of Commons vote for a modest increment in Britain's contribution to the European budget. (The increase was agreed to at an EU summit in Edinburgh in 1992 and hailed then as a triumph for Major's diplomacy.) Major and his allies could have won the vote by relying on the support of the Labor and Liberal Democrat parties. Instead, they crushed the rebellion by making the vote a vote of confidence (which, if lost, would have forced Major to resign and brought about an

Tony takes over. *Tony Blair, the new leader of Great Britain's Labor Party, speaks in a church in October. Blair, the youngest leader in the history of the Labor Party, was chosen in July to succeed John Smith, who died in May.*

immediate general election). They then suspended from membership of the parliamentary party the eight MPs who still refused to vote for the government. Another MP voluntarily removed himself from party control to protest these "strong-arm tactics." Since the Conservative majority in the Commons had already been reduced to 14, the loss of nine Conservative MPs seemed to political commentators to be a self-destructive act. Within days, the suspended Tories helped the opposition kill a controversial tax proposal, undermining Major's authority and renewing doubts about his ability to survive.

Month by Month. In January, Britain refused to return the celebrated Elgin marbles, which were taken from Greece by a 19th-century aristocrat, to their country of origin, in defiance of a European Union ruling. In February,

Winning smile. *Jockey Richard Dunwoody's expression says it all after he and his mount, Miinnehoma, won the Grand National steeplechase at England's Aintree race course in April. Miinnehoma, a 16-1 long shot, fought a close battle with Just So to snag the victory as the Grand National, perhaps the most famous horse race in the world, made a successful comeback from its 1993 fiasco, when the race was declared void because of starting problems.*

Parliament voted to reduce the age of homosexual consent from 21 to 18 (the age for legal heterosexual consent is 16). In March the first women priests in the established Church of England were ordained, creating bitter divisions in the church and a modest exodus to the Roman Catholic Church. In May, Queen Elizabeth II and French President François Mitterrand formally opened the Channel Tunnel between Britain and France. In June the first major strike since the epic miners' strike of 1984-1985 broke out after the government intervened to block a pay agreement between the Railtrack company and its 4,600 signal workers. The strike disrupted Britain's railways for 17 weeks, until it was finally settled on terms which scarcely differed from the blocked offer. In August, Parliament voted to allow Sunday retail trading, though with restrictions on the opening hours of large stores. In November, Britain's National Lottery was launched, and Channel Tunnel service between London and both Paris and Brussels finally began. And in December the queen gave an oil exploration company permission to drill under Windsor Castle to see if there was any oil there.

See PEOPLE IN THE NEWS: Princess Diana; STATISTICS OF THE WORLD.   S.W.

GREECE. With Andreas Papandreou and his Panhellenic Socialist Movement (Pasok) back in power since October 1993, 1994 was for Greece a year of political transition as well as strained relations with fellow European Union (EU) members over Macedonian statehood.

On two separate occasions the Socialist majority in Parliament voted that former Premier Constantine Mitsotakis stand trial before a special tribunal, as Papandreou had been forced to do when Mitsotakis and his New Democracy Party were in power. In June, Mitsotakis was charged with involvement in phone tapping when in office. In September he and two of his former ministers were indicted for corruption in the 1992 sale of the giant, state-owned Aget-Herakles cement company to Italian cement producers. The New Democracy deputies boycotted the voting on these measures in protest. On December 31, Papandreou said he would suspend the phone tapping investigation.

In elections to the European Parliament on June 12, Pasok did less well than expected, taking 37.6 percent of the vote and ten seats. The conservative New Democracy won 32.7 percent and nine seats, a Communist-led leftist coalition won 12.3 percent and four seats, and the nationalist splinter group called Political Spring won 8.7 percent and two seats. The Pasok setback was attributed to a sluggish economy and concern about the 75-year-old premier's health.

The ongoing dispute over Macedonian statehood strained the relations of Greece with its Western allies. On February 16, reacting to recognition of the Former Yugoslav Republic of Macedonia by the United States earlier that month and by six members of the EU the previous December, Greece unexpectedly imposed a trade embargo on its northern neighbor. The act was intended to back Athens's already-stated demands that the republic remove the word Macedonia from its official name, the symbol of Alexander the Great from its flag, and clauses from its constitution providing for protection of Macedonians abroad. All three, Greece claimed, implied claims on its northern province of Macedonia.

Greek fears were not allayed by the new republic's offer to instead sign a treaty guaranteeing the existing border between the two countries. By early April the European Commission formally began legal proceedings against Greece for its refusal to lift the embargo. Though Washington disapproved of Greece's trade embargo, the Clinton administration encouraged U.S.-mediated bilateral negotiations between Athens and Skopje. It stopped short of establishing full diplomatic relations with the Macedonian republic and in April received Papandreou for his first White House visit as premier of Greece.

Acknowledging the economy as its greatest challenge, particularly the massive public debt, the Papandreou administration adopted a tight budget for 1994, focusing on revenue gathering and spending reduction. In March consumer price inflation was reported to have fallen, as targeted by the government, from 14.4 percent for 1992 to 12.1 percent for 1993. The public debt was estimated to be approximately 130 percent of Greece's gross domestic product. The European Commission urged the Greek government to cut public spending and raise taxes.

See STATISTICS OF THE WORLD.   J.A.P.

GRENADA. *See* CARIBBEAN BASIN; STATISTICS OF THE WORLD.

GUAM. *See* STATISTICS OF THE WORLD.

GUATEMALA. Ongoing peace talks between the government of Guatemala and the guerrilla movement the Guatemalan National Revolutionary Union went forward in 1994, but even so, little was accomplished toward ending the country's bitter, three-decade-long civil war. Although an agenda for negotiations was set and a human rights accord was signed, few steps were actually taken to fulfill the agreements until November 21, when a United Nations mission that was responsible for verifying human rights agreements was installed in Guatemala City.

Two other agreements, one on resettling uprooted populations and the other establishing a Truth Commission, also failed to effect significant changes. The most positive innovation of the entire process was the coming together of a very broad-based Assembly of Civilian Sectors—which allowed informal participation by civil society—to develop consensus proposals on the major themes under negotiation.

Guatemala received increased international attention in the fall, when American lawyer Jennifer Harbury staged a 32-day hunger strike in front of the presidential palace in an attempt to locate her leftist guerrilla husband. She believed he was being held in military custody, but government officials denied any knowledge of his whereabouts.

Early in 1994 the government of President Ramiro de León Carpio sponsored a referendum, mandating new elections in August for a transitional congress and anticorruption reforms. The government's proposals were approved, but with only 16 percent of eligible voters participating. The most conservative parties triumphed in the August elections—the most notable result being the election of ex-dictator General Efraín Ríos Montt. However, the most significant aspect of the election was 80 percent abstentionism.

Guatemala showed moderate economic growth, thanks to an unexpected coffee boom, but maintained serious disequilibriums. Unable to increase direct taxes, the government implemented budget reductions, provoking protests both in the countryside, over land occupation, and in the capital, over rising bus fares and other austerity measures.

See STATISTICS OF THE WORLD.   S.J.

GUINEA. *See* STATISTICS OF THE WORLD.

GUINEA-BISSAU. *See* STATISTICS OF THE WORLD.

GUYANA. *See* STATISTICS OF THE WORLD.

H

HAITI. Exiled Haitian President Jean-Bertrand Aristide returned to power in October 1994—and the military leaders who had ousted Aristide in a violent 1991 coup stepped down peacefully—in a transition negotiated and enforced by the United States.

Unsuccessful Measures. For most of the year the international community's efforts to restore Aristide to power were ineffective. The economic sanctions imposed by the United Nations in 1993 were tightened in May and expanded by the United States in June, causing runaway inflation, economic paralysis, and widespread suffering among Haiti's poor majority (in a country with a per capita income of only about $250 a year). But the oil embargo proved porous, and Haiti's military rulers and civilian elites profited from their control of a black market in scarce goods.

In late 1993, Haiti's rulers scuttled the July 1993 Governor's Island accords providing for Aristide's restoration. When this led not to for-

Puppet president. In May 1994, Lieutenant General Raoul Cédras, who had declared Haiti's presidency vacant, gave the post to interim President Emile Jonassaint. The photo below shows Cédras (right) and Jonassaint (left) after the latter's inauguration.

eign intervention but to the withdrawal of a U.S. Navy vessel and international peacekeepers, Lieutenant General Raoul Cédras, the Army commander, and Lieutenant Colonel Joseph Michel François, head of the police, ceased to take threats of international intervention seriously. The persecution of Aristide supporters, which had claimed more than 3,000 lives since the coup, intensified. In May 1994 the presidency was declared vacant, and Emile Jonassaint, an 80-year-old Supreme Court justice, was inaugurated as interim president. In July the regime expelled the international human rights monitors named by the UN and the Organization of American States. In August it declared a state of siege, restricted the news media, and increased attacks on political opponents and asylum seekers. By then, it was clear that nothing short of a credible threat of U.S. intervention would persuade the military to step down.

U.S. Action. President Bill Clinton resisted ordering a U.S. intervention that most U.S. citizens opposed, but by September he was prepared to change his policy. One reason was the failure of economic sanctions, broadened in June to include, among other things, a ban on commercial flights to and from Haiti. Another reason was Clinton's fear that a Haiti policy widely viewed as weak and vacillating had called into question the credibility of his foreign policy leadership. Also important was the growing discontent within the African-American community and among liberal Democrats with U.S. inaction on Haiti.

In May these pressures had led Clinton to reverse a long-standing U.S. policy and to process Haitian applications for political asylum, setting off a tenfold increase in Haitian boat people. By September, at least 14,000 Haitian refugees had been picked up by U.S. ships and interned at the Guantánamo Bay naval base, persuading many in Washington that only the ouster of the military and the restoration of Aristide could stop a politically costly rising tide of Haitian boat people.

At the end of July the UN Security Council

authorized the use of military intervention to remove the regime and the deployment of a 6,000-strong UN peacekeeping force once stability was restored. In September, with U.S. forces poised to invade, a delegation including former President Jimmy Carter, former armed forces chief General Colin Powell, and Senator Sam Nunn negotiated a face-saving compromise that permitted U.S. troops to enter Haiti unopposed, allowed for a reduced and retrained Haitian Army and police force, and provided for the resignations of Jonassaint, Cédras, and François and the restoration of Aristide, who returned to Haiti on October 15 under the protection of U.S. troops.

Challenges for Aristide. Aristide inherited a bankrupt treasury, a devastated economy, a stalled educational system, and a deeply divided country, in which his enemies retained many of their weapons and his supporters expected justice to be done. He was dependent on U.S. troops to maintain peace and on international financial assistance, including a promised $555 million in donations being coordinated by the UN. Under U.S. pressure, Aristide appointed centrist businessman Smarck Michel as his new prime minister. Meanwhile, parliamentary elections scheduled for December had to be postponed until at least March 1995 because of a lack of time to prepare the voting apparatus. With his own

Aristide back in office. *UN Secretary-General Boutros Boutros-Ghali (left) visits President Jean-Bertrand Aristide (right) in Haiti in mid-November, a month after Aristide returned to power under the protection of U.S. troops.*

term of office scheduled to expire in early 1996, Aristide had little time left to confront Haiti's troubles.

See STATISTICS OF THE WORLD.   P.W.

HAWAII.   *See* STATISTICS OF THE WORLD.

Jean-Bertrand Aristide

Haitian President Jean-Bertrand Aristide was born in 1953 to a modest provincial family and educated at the Salesian school in Port-au-Prince. He found a religious—and political—calling in a radical wing of the Roman Catholic Church, becoming a Salesian priest in 1982.

Aristide soon emerged as a leader in the popular resistance to Haiti's repressive Duvalier dictatorship and the military-dominated governments of the 1980s. He was expelled from the Salesian Order in 1988 for his political activities, although he did not resign from the priesthood until 1994.

After winning two-thirds of the vote in the 1990 presidential election, Aristide pursued land reform, higher wages, and increased spending on health and education but was accused by his opponents of promoting class conflict. He was ousted in a September 1991 military coup.

During his three-year exile in the United States, Aristide adopted more pragmatic politics and a more conciliatory style. When he resumed Haiti's presidency in October 1994 under the protection of U.S. troops, it was with a message of reconciliation, a conservative economic policy, and the goal of becoming the first elected Haitian president to hand over power to a democratically elected successor.

P.W.

Health and Medicine

During 1994 important advances were made against two major killers, cancer and stroke. A new anti-AIDS drug won approval in the United States, and the war against smoking heated up.

Experts announced that adoption of a new treatment strategy would stop peptic ulcers from recurring. The first published progress report said that gene therapy works. Meanwhile, news reports brought to light the use of falsified data in a major breast cancer study.

Blood-cell Hormone Discovered. U.S. and European researchers announced in June that they had isolated a key hormone in the blood that should prove to be a valuable new drug. The hormone, called thrombopoietin, stimulates the production of platelets, which promote blood clotting. Its discovery is expected to benefit cancer or lymphoma patients who have received chemotherapy or a bone marrow transplant. These patients have low platelet counts, putting them at serious risk of death from bleeding. Currently they are treated with transfusions of platelets, which require time-consuming procedures and many blood donors. Thrombopoietin seems able to increase platelet production to previously unattainable levels.

Surgery Halves Stroke Risk. An operation that removes fatty buildups from a major artery in the neck dramatically lowers the risk of stroke in people who have no symptoms, researchers announced at a news conference in September. Their findings indicate that the surgery, known as carotid endarterectomy, could prevent thousands of disabling strokes each year among people who have severe narrowing of either of the two carotid arteries in the neck yet who have no disease symptoms.

Among 1,662 of such people at 39 medical centers in the United States and Canada, those who underwent the operation had a 1 in 20 chance of having a stroke over a five-year period, compared with a 1 in 10 chance for those who took drugs instead. The risk reduction for men was 55 percent; for women it was much lower at 16 percent, a phenomenon that the researchers could not explain. The researchers said that patients should have the surgery done only when the artery is narrowed by more than 50 percent.

Major Shift in Ulcer Treatment. Almost all people who have peptic ulcers should be treated with antibiotics in addition to conventional antiulcer medications, a panel of experts wrote in July.

The participants in a U.S. National Institutes of Health consensus development conference said nearly all people with ulcers in the duodenum and 80 percent of people with ulcers in the stomach are infected with an organism called *Helicobacter pylori.* This organism can be eradicated by an intensive regimen of antibiotics, reducing the chance of ulcer recurrence to less than 10 percent in the first year. With conventional medications that suppress acid secretion, ulcers usually heal but are more likely to recur.

A number of antibiotic combinations may kill *H. pylori.* The one studied most extensively consists of bismuth subsalicylate (Pepto-Bismol) and the antibiotics tetracycline and metronidazole. One in ten Americans develop ulcers at some time in their lives.

Success in Gene Therapy. The first published report of any benefits from human gene therapy came out in April. U.S. researchers said they had partly corrected a usually fatal cholesterol disorder called familial hypercholesterolemia, which causes early heart attacks. The 29-year-old Canadian woman who received the gene therapy had experienced a heart attack at age 16. Eighteen months after receiving copies of an essential gene she lacked, the woman's low-density lipoprotein ("bad") cholesterol level had fallen almost 20 percent and the concentration of high-density lipoprotein ("good") cholesterol had risen. Her harmful cholesterol level remained dangerously high, at about four times the ideal level, but the research team said the results showed that gene therapy can work.

Lower Cholesterol, Longer Life. Scandinavian researchers showed for the first time that lowering the cholesterol level in the blood prolongs life. The study findings, published in November, probably will convince more doctors to prescribe cholesterol-lowering drugs for people at risk of having a heart attack. Many doctors have been reluctant to prescribe the drugs because even though they reduced deaths from heart attacks, some studies suggested that they increased the rate of deaths from other causes.

The new study included 4,444 people who had heart disease and moderate to high cholesterol levels. After a median of 5.4 years, those who were taking a cholesterol-lowering drug called simvastatin had a 30 percent lower death rate than the people who took dummy pills: 8 percent of the drug group died, compared with 12 percent of the group receiving standard care. There were 111 heart-disease related deaths in the drug group and 189 in the standard care group. Other causes accounted for about the same number of deaths in each group—46 and 49, respectively.

The results suggest, although they do not prove, that people who have no symptoms of heart disease also would benefit from cholesterol lowering.

Hormone Therapy Refined. Findings announced in November showed that a combination of two hormones is better than one in hormone replacement therapy.

Many postmenopausal women take the hormone estrogen to relieve menopausal symptoms and to prevent bone loss and heart disease, all of which are related to reduced estrogen in the body. Because estrogen replacement therapy increases the risk of uterine cancer as much as ninefold, many doctors also prescribe progestin (a synthetic version of the natural hormone progesterone) to counter the adverse effect. However, it was not known whether progestin canceled out estrogen's protective effects on the heart.

The new study, which involved about 900 women, confirmed that a combination of estrogen and progestin or finely ground progesterone had no adverse effects on the uterus. Moreover, the hormone combination, particularly with the finely ground progesterone, showed almost as much heart-protecting benefit as estrogen alone. Both regimens lowered harmful LDL cholesterol and raised protective HDL cholesterol levels.

Eating Habits and Disease Risks. According to findings by the National Center for Health Statistics that were reported in February, Americans' consumption of fats dropped to 34 percent of daily calories in 1990, down from 36 percent in 1978 and 42 percent in the mid-1960s. Consumption of saturated fats, which are closely linked to heart disease and some cancers, dropped to 12 percent of daily calories, down from 13 percent in 1978 and 16 percent in the 1960s.

The declines in fat consumption coincided with a steady drop in blood cholesterol levels. From 1978 to 1990 the average total cholesterol level dropped from 213 milligrams per 100 milliliters of blood to 205 milligrams. The ideal cholesterol level is less than 200 milligrams. In October the U.S. Census Bureau said in its 1994 *Statistical Abstract of the United States* that consumption of red meat and eggs—associated with stroke and heart disease—decreased from 1970 to 1992. The annual per capita consumption of whole milk dropped from about 27 gallons to 10 gallons. At the same time, the per capita consumption of broccoli increased, rising from half a pound to 3.4 pounds.

Despite those trends, researchers from the National Center for Health Statistics reported in July that their survey of 8,260 adults in the period 1988 to 1991 showed an 8 percent increase in the prevalence of overweight individuals compared with the period 1976 to 1980. One-third of U.S. adults—about 58 million—were estimated to be overweight. Being overweight has been linked with hypertension, coronary heart disease, cancer, adult-onset diabetes, and gallbladder disease.

New Nutrition Labels on Foods. By August all processed foods in the United States began carrying standardized nutrition labels, as required by the 1990 Nutrition Labeling and Education Act. The new labels were designed to be less confusing than the old ones and to guide people to more healthful foods. The most important additions to the information on the labels were the percentages of daily value. These figures indicate the contribution that a food serving makes to the recommended daily consumption of fat, saturated fat, cholesterol, sodium, carbohydrate, and fiber on the basis of a 2,000-calorie diet. In another change for the better the serving sizes on the labels are uniform within each food category.

The government also restricted the use of claims on food packaging. For example, terms such as "healthy," "light," and "low-fat" may be used only to describe foods that are low in fat, saturated fat, cholesterol, and sodium. Makers of products regulated by the Food and Drug Administration (FDA) that already use such terms have until January 1, 1996, to comply with the regulation; packagers of meat and poultry have until November 1995.

Breast Cancer Study Scandal. Many women became alarmed in March when U.S. officials confirmed newspaper reports that the findings of a major breast cancer study were based in part on falsified data. The federally funded study, published in 1985, had concluded that lumpectomy (removal of a cancerous lump) followed by radiation was as effective as a mastectomy (total breast removal) in preventing the spread of early breast cancer. The findings helped change the way the disease is treated. But a federal investigation found that

Killer bug? Tabloid newspapers and television shows raised a great to-do about a "flesh-eating" germ, a particularly virulent form of streptococcus A that can cause necrotizing fasciitis, a fast-acting destruction of fat, skin, and muscle. Health officials assured the public, however, that the condition was not new and was very rare. Below left, the Streptococcus pyogenes group A bacterium seen through an electron microscope. Below right, a patient stricken with necrotizing fasciitis is attended by a physician.

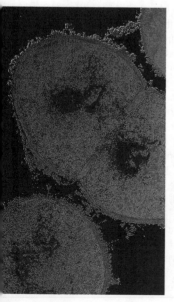
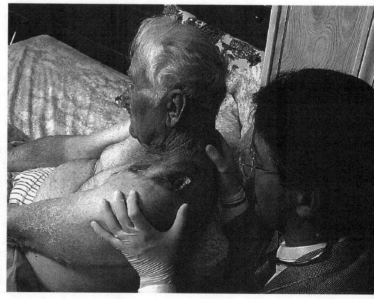

the records of six of the 354 patients enrolled in the study by a Canadian surgeon, Dr. Roger Poisson of Saint-Luc Hospital in Montréal, had been falsified. About 16 percent of the study's patients came from Dr. Poisson's team. Study organizers had known about Poisson's falsifications since 1990 but did not inform the National Cancer Institute (NCI), the study's sponsor, until 1991. After an investigation, Poisson (who admitted to 115 falsifications in 99 patient records in the lumpectomy and other breast cancer studies) was disqualified from receiving U.S. research funds for eight years, but the matter had not been widely publicized and a corrected version of the original study had not been published.

News of the fraud shook many women who had chosen the less disfiguring operation on the basis of the study findings. The University of Pittsburgh, which had coordinated the study, assured women that its conclusions remained the same when the Canadian data were excluded. This assertion was later confirmed by the NCI.

Moreover, a new study rushed to publication in April supported the use of lumpectomy for some women with breast cancer. The new study, which involved the records of more than 5,800 patients, showed that women who had a lumpectomy followed by radiation were at least as likely to survive five years as women who had a mastectomy. Among women over 50, about 90 percent of those who had a lumpectomy and 80 percent of those who had a mastectomy lived at least five years. Among women under 50, the survival rates were about the same with the two treatments.

Another breast cancer study coordinated by the Pittsburgh group also ran into trouble. The study, begun in May 1992, was designed to answer whether the drug tamoxifen can prevent breast cancer in healthy women at increased risk for the disease. The Pittsburgh team had apparently delayed notifying federal health officials that patients in another study of tamoxifen, where it was used to treat breast cancer, had died of uterine cancer. Medical experts had known that tamoxifen could cause a threefold increase in cancer of the uterine lining, but this kind of cancer is not usually fatal. The NCI suspended the tamoxifen prevention trial in the spring. On the basis of treatment studies, the FDA ordered changes in the drug's labeling. The new label warned that tamoxifen poses a risk of uterine cancer that is two to three times higher than the risk in the general population of women. In June a panel of experts recommended that the prevention trial be resumed, with additional monitoring to check for uterine cancer.

Tuberculosis Epidemic. Statistics released in 1994 suggested that the resurgence of tuberculosis that started in the United States in 1985 might be receding. Nationwide, the number of new cases dipped 5 percent, from 26,673 in 1992 to 25,313 in 1993. New York City health officials reported a 15 percent drop in new cases during the same period, from 3,811 to 3,235. New York City has 15 percent of all tuberculosis cases in the United States and 60 percent of drug-resistant cases. Although some health officials thought the decline was due to intensive control efforts, others said it might be due to underreporting and may not be a trend.

Two studies published in June confirmed that there is still cause for concern. Researchers found that a much higher number of cases than previously thought—about a third of cases in San Francisco and New York—were spread in recent years. The fact that so many new cases were newly acquired rather than activations of old infections signified an increased danger of the disease spreading through the general population. The virus spreads through coughing and sneezing.

Meanwhile, health officials tracked the worst outbreak of drug-resistant tuberculosis in a high school ever reported in the United States. By July, 376 students at La Quinta High School, 25 miles from downtown Los Angeles, had tested positive for tuberculosis; 12 of them had active cases of drug-resistant tuberculosis. In April the U.S. Centers for Disease Control and Prevention (CDC) reported that poor ventilation had contributed to the spread of the cases. However, the main problems were slow diagnosis and failure to monitor treatment of the girl who started the outbreak.

Most of the increases in tuberculosis in the United States from 1985 through 1992 occurred among immigrants, people infected with HIV (the virus that causes acquired immunodeficiency syndrome, or AIDS), and medically underserved low-income populations, CDC researchers reported in August.

AIDS Epidemic. AIDS remained a worldwide threat and, with no cure or vaccine in sight, it promised to remain so for years to come. However, researchers did report that AIDS patients were living longer, thanks to improved treatment of an AIDS-related infection.

From the beginning of the epidemic in 1981 through the end of 1994, approximately 442,000 cases of AIDS were reported in the United States. In the 12 months of 1994, 80,691 new cases were reported to the CDC. An estimated 1 million people in the United States are infected with HIV.

Worldwide, the estimated number of full-blown AIDS cases increased 60 percent, from 2.5 million to 4 million, from July 1993 to July 1994. Sub-Saharan Africa had the most cases, but in Asia, AIDS cases increased eightfold, from 30,000 to 250,000. As of July 1994, 17 million people worldwide had been infected with HIV since record keeping began in the early 1980s, 3 million in the 12 months ending in July 1994 alone.

The heterosexual transmission of AIDS increased faster than any other means of AIDS transmission. Of the 84,268 new cases of AIDS that were reported in the United States between July 1993 and June 1994, 10 percent were acquired through heterosexual contact, as compared with only 2 percent in 1985. Partners of intravenous drug users were the largest known risk group. At the same time the proportion of cases from homosexual contact fell to 47 percent, from 67 percent in 1985.

Although there was still no cure for the fatal disease, survival times for AIDS patients were a year longer in 1993 than in 1983. In a study reported in April the median survival time among 761 patients increased by almost 12 months, from 28 months to 40 months. Most of the increase was found in patients with an AIDS-related infection known as *Pneumocystis carinii* pneumonia (PCP), which at one time accounted for most of the deaths caused by the AIDS virus in the United States.

In June the FDA announced approval of a new drug for use when the three other approved anti-AIDS drugs no longer work or cannot be tolerated. Stavudine, or D4T (trade name, Zerit), is an antiviral drug that may delay the onset of symptoms in HIV-infected people. In some it may extend survival. Stavudine was the first drug granted parallel-track status by the FDA, which makes new drugs available to certain patients before they are approved. It had been used by some 11,000 patients since October 1992.

The three drugs approved earlier for treating HIV infection are zidovudine (trade name, Retrovir), didanosine (Videx), and zalcitabine (Hivid). All cause fairly severe side effects. In addition, the benefits from even the best-known therapy against AIDS, zidovudine, last no longer than two years in most people. However, zidovudine dramatically reduces transmission of HIV from infected mothers to their newborns, researchers reported in February. (Of about 7,000 infants born to HIV-infected mothers each year, as many as 2,000 acquire HIV.) In August the FDA approved zidovudine for use in preventing transmission of HIV from pregnant women to their babies.

War Against Smoking. In February the FDA asserted its authority to regulate cigarettes in the United States if sufficient evidence proved that nicotine is addictive and that cigarettes are intentionally sold to satisfy an addiction. The agency then launched an aggressive and widely publicized investigation of tobacco company practices.

In hearings of the House Subcommittee on Health and the Environment in June, FDA Commissioner Dr. David Kessler presented evidence indicating that tobacco companies manipulate the amount of nicotine in cigarettes. He said that Brown & Williamson Tobacco Corporation had developed a genetically engineered tobacco that would more than double the amount of nicotine delivered in some cigarettes. The tobacco industry maintained that cigarettes are not addictive and that companies do not increase the nicotine in cigarettes above what is found naturally in tobacco. However, it did admit that companies could control the amount of nicotine in cigarettes—allegedly for reasons of taste—by changing the types of tobacco and the parts of those plants included in the blend. Earlier in the hearings

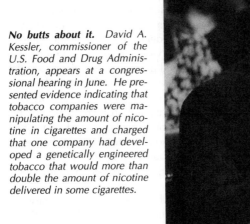

No butts about it. *David A. Kessler, commissioner of the U.S. Food and Drug Administration, appears at a congressional hearing in June. He presented evidence indicating that tobacco companies were manipulating the amount of nicotine in cigarettes and charged that one company had developed a genetically engineered tobacco that would more than double the amount of nicotine delivered in some cigarettes.*

it came out that the Philip Morris Companies had suppressed several studies on the hazards of smoking that had been done in their own laboratories, including one showing the addictiveness of nicotine. And among other disclosures, it was revealed that tobacco companies had discovered ways to make a safer cigarette by the early 1960s but had made the decision not to market them.

In August an advisory panel to the FDA said nicotine was addictive and that it was the main reason why people smoke. The panel's opinion reflected that of leading medical groups and a U.S. surgeon general's report in 1988. That same month the National Academy of Sciences lent more support for FDA regulation of tobacco. The group stated that tobacco use was an addiction that began in youth and the best way to prevent it was to enact strict new federal and state regulations that would make it harder for those under 18 to start smoking.

Smoking causes numerous ailments, including heart disease, lung and other cancers, and respiratory disease. In February two studies involving a total of more than 160,000 people showed that cigarette smoking can also lead to colon cancer and that, unlike with many other cancers, the risk does not diminish after the smoker has quit.

Concern about secondhand smoke continued to mount. The largest study ever of environmental smoke in nonsmokers confirmed that women who do not smoke but are married to men who do have a small but increased risk of developing lung cancer. Among the more than 1,900 women in the study, those whose husbands smoked had a 30 percent higher risk of developing lung cancer over a lifetime than women who had nonsmoking husbands. The U.S. Environmental Protection Agency has said that secondhand smoke kills 3,000 nonsmokers a year from lung cancer alone and in addition causes respiratory ailments like pneumonia and bronchitis, especially in children.

To prevent the health hazards of secondhand smoke, several new smoking bans were announced in the United States. Washington State enacted the toughest statewide ban on workplace smoking in October. The ban prohibits smoking in private offices, restricting it to specially ventilated smoking rooms. A California law banned smoking in any enclosed space that is also a place of employment as of January 1, 1995. The Defense Department

209

banned smoking in workplaces on military bases and ships around the world. In March the Occupational Safety and Health Administration proposed outlawing smoking, except in specially designated areas with their own ventilation systems, in all workplaces in the United States. In July, Canada became the first country to ban smoking on all flights operated by its own carriers.

Solar Risk Index. In June the U.S. National Weather Service began issuing an ultraviolet exposure index along with the weather forecast. The action was taken to help people avoid dangerous exposure to the Sun's ultraviolet rays, which can cause skin cancer and cataracts, as well as weakening of the body's immune system.

Issued daily for 58 cities in the United States, the index is a measure of the ultraviolet light that is forecast to hit the Earth's surface at noontime the following day. The scale ranges from 1 to 10 in most areas, and 1 to 15 in areas that get stronger solar radiation, with the lowest numbers indicating the lowest risk. The index is based on the amount of ozone in the upper atmosphere, as measured by satellite instruments. The ultraviolet exposure index is available in newspapers or by calling the National Weather Service.

Radiation Experiments. The U.S. Advisory Committee on Human Radiation Experiments, set up by President Clinton to investigate human radiation experiments in the United States and suggest whether victims should be compensated, issued an interim report in October.

The committee reported that it had officially identified about 400 such experiments carried out between 1944 and 1974 and had found data suggesting that the final total would be in the thousands. The experiments included injecting radioactive plutonium into people's bodies and releasing radiation into the environment. The committee said there was reason to believe that the government's ethical guidelines for using human volunteers were not always followed and that the subjects' consent was not always obtained.   L.H.

HONDURAS. With the inauguration of President Carlos Roberto Reina on January 27, 1994, Honduras faced the prospect of greater conflict between the government and the armed forces over power and autonomy issues. A dire economic situation also gradually worsened during the course of the year.

During his campaign as the candidate of the then-opposition Liberal Party, Reina had promised to redefine the role of the military while pursuing violations of human rights. He also announced plans to reduce the size of the Army, a statement that drew criticism from the armed forces commander, General Luis Discua. At his inauguration Reina reiterated his pledge of a moral revolution and committed his administration to investigating charges of human rights abuses contained in a December 1993 report by Honduras's Human Rights Commission.

The struggle between civil and military authorities continued throughout 1994. Discua yielded on a number of issues, including a transfer of the police force to civilian control. However, he rejected proposals for major new budget cuts and for other measures to curb traditional military autonomy. Reina's interest in far-reaching reform of police and security forces also spurred debate.

While accepting the neoliberal economic approach of the outgoing National Party administration of Rafael Leonardo Callejas, Reina called for a more humane application. Corruption and poverty were to be alleviated by a greater sensitivity to social problems.

At the same time, the fiscal deficit rose above 10 percent of gross national product as the year progressed, while the foreign debt grew to more than $3.6 billion. Some austerity measures that had been negotiated previously with the International Monetary Fund were postponed, but new taxes were levied and there was a marked slowdown in economic growth. Estimates for a higher annual inflation rate ran from 25 percent upwards, and a series of labor disputes further clouded economic prospects.

See STATISTICS OF THE WORLD.   J.D.M.

HONG KONG. *See* CHINA; STATISTICS OF THE WORLD.

HUNGARY. In May 1994, Hungarians elected a parliamentary majority consisting of ex-Communist Socialists. The tripartite, nationalist, right-of-center coalition formed in 1990 suffered a stunning defeat. Indeed, the

The left leaps in. *Gyula Horn takes the oath of office as prime minister of Hungary in July. The May election victory of Horn's Socialists (former Communists) marked a stunning defeat for the right-wing parties that had led Hungary to democracy.*

Only 43 percent of the electorate voted in December local elections for mayors and council members. In localities with fewer than 10,000 people, the majority of posts were won by independents. Elsewhere the majority shifted from liberals to Socialists.

Hungary's debt had reached $25.8 billion by May. At $2,600 per capita, it was the highest rate of debt in Eastern Europe. Foreign investment declined from $2 billion in 1993 to $600 million during the first half of 1994. Exports also declined, and the balance of trade deficit was around $3 billion. To increase exports, the forint was devalued by 8 percent in August; by year's end its value had fallen by 16.7 percent. The annual inflation rate was 20 percent. In June unemployment hovered at 11 percent of the labor force. As many as 3 million Hungarians were subsisting below the poverty line.

previously dominant Hungarian Democratic Forum won only 37 of the 386 seats. The former opposition, the Hungarian Socialist Party (HSP), and the liberal Alliance of Free Democrats took command with 209 and 70 seats, respectively.

Although they had the numbers to establish a one-party cabinet, the Socialists formed a coalition with the Free Democrats, facilitating passage even of special bills requiring a two-thirds majority of the house. No extreme right-wing or left-wing candidates were elected. The new prime minister, HSP leader Gyula Horn, had been Hungary's last foreign minister under Communism.

Efforts toward normalization of relations with Slovakia and Romania, neighbors with large Hungarian minorities, yielded little fruit. In August, Horn met with then-Slovak Premier Jozef Moravcik; the two countries were still at odds over what was once a joint plan to build a dam on the Danube. This was followed by the September visit to Budapest of Romanian Foreign Minister Teodor Melescanu, during which revival of a stalled friendship treaty was discussed; for both sides to sign, the treaty would have to include guarantees of human rights for Romania's ethnic Hungarians and of Hungary's willingness to recognize Romania's national border.

See STATISTICS OF THE WORLD.   P.P.

I

ICELAND. Iceland's July 1994 elections for mayors and municipal councils showed reduced support at the local level for the ruling government parties, the Independence Party and the Social Democratic Party. A left-center ticket gained a majority on the Reykjavik City Council, terminating the 17-year rule of the In-

dependence Party. The city's new mayor was Ingibjorg Solrun Gisladottir of the Women's Alliance.

There were angry statements, and even a few shots fired, after Icelandic trawlers began fishing in an area of the Barents Sea claimed by Norway. The Icelandic government held that the cod-rich waters were international. Briefly, there were threats to bring the case before the International Court of Justice at The Hague, but the two nations later looked set to resolve the conflict bilaterally. By year's end, however, no accord had been reached. Fishing accounts for around 80 percent of Iceland's exports.

During the summer a heated debate broke out among Icelandic officials and political parties over possible membership in the European Union (EU). Some maintained that membership was unwarranted so long as the European Economic Area (EEA) treaty—joining most non-EU European nations with the EU in one of the world's largest single markets—was in force. The debate was brought to the fore because it seemed possible that most of Iceland's non-EU partners in the EEA would, in fact, become EU members by early 1995. The Foreign Relations Committee of the Althing (Parliament) in July supported Prime Minister David Oddsson in his contention that the EEA provided all the economic advantages the EU eventually might bring.

On June 17, Iceland celebrated its 50th anniversary as an independent nation. The heads of state of the four other Nordic nations were guests at ceremonies at Thingvellir (where the new republic was founded in 1944), with about a quarter of the country's population (60,000 people) attending.

See STATISTICS OF THE WORLD. E.J.F.

IDAHO. *See* STATISTICS OF THE WORLD.

ILLINOIS. *See* STATISTICS OF THE WORLD.

INDIA. The future of the Congress Party government, economic reform, and civil strife in Kashmir continued to dominate India's domestic politics in 1994. The successful development of Agni, Akash, and Trishul rockets raised fears that India might develop the largest Asian nuclear capability outside of China. Foreign relations focused on that nuclear capability and on human rights and trade. In September an outbreak of pneumonic plague in the town of Surat led to some panic both in India and overseas, but the disease was controlled fairly readily with only some 60 deaths reported.

Political Developments. State assembly elections began in November 1994 and were expected to conclude by March 1995. The government of Prime Minister Narasimha Rao

Leaving town. Residents of Surat, India, wear protective masks as they line up for tickets for a train departing the city. Surat was the center of an epidemic of pneumonic plague that broke out in September and claimed dozens of lives in India before it was brought under control.

Assassination furor. *Rioters run from police during a general strike that took place in Bombay in August. They were protesting the killing of Ramdas Nayak, the local leader of the Bharatiya Janata Party, who had been an outspoken critic of political corruption.*

and the Congress Party hoped to extend its gains beyond the four states and Delhi Union Territory where elections were held in 1993. However, disastrous outcomes in four state elections, followed by the December resignations of three cabinet members accused of corruption, weakened Rao's hold on power. On December 24, Arjun Singh, one of Rao's leading rivals within the Congress Party, resigned as human resources minister; many believed he was trying to position himself to succeed Rao as prime minister.

The opposition parties continued to fight within and among themselves in 1994. The Bharatiya Janata Party (BJP) was split between its Hindu-fundamentalist faction and the leadership of A. B. Vajpayee and L. K. Advani, who favored a more liberal economic approach as well as the inclusion of lower-caste Hindus. The party disintegrated further as several leaders left and V. P. Singh, its chairman, had to withdraw because of poor health. Meanwhile, the Marxist parties continued rudderless as a result of the breakup of the Soviet Union. It seemed that the only thing that unified the various parties was their opposition to India's signing of the new international trade pact negotiated under the General Agreement on Tariffs and Trade (GATT).

A few successes in dealing with Muslim separatist insurgents in Kashmir bought the Rao government breathing space. In late 1993, through negotiation, the siege of the Muslim Hazratbal shrine ended without violence. In March 1994 the Rao government forced Pak-

istan to withdraw a resolution before the UN Human Rights Commission condemning India for human rights violations. The Kashmiris themselves, tired of violence, seemed ready to face up to the militants, and the Jammu and Kashmir Liberation Front (JKLF) leadership opposed integration with Pakistan even as it continued its anti-India stance. Although the insurgency in Kashmir continued despite negotiation efforts, it was at a lesser level. The JKLF stated it would not consider solutions within the existing Indian constitution, which recognizes Kashmir as an integral part of India. All parties, however, seemed to be moving toward dialogue and away from violence.

Rao's visits to Europe, the United States, and member countries of the Association of Southeast Asian Nations to attract foreign capital met with some success. Particularly heartening was a lowering of U.S. rhetoric against India's developing nuclear capabilities and the formation of a "Friends of India" lobbying group composed of 26 major corporations, including PepsiCo, Coca-Cola, and IBM.

Meanwhile, in Uttar Pradesh the ruling coalition of the Samajwadi and Bahujan Samaj parties, based on lower-caste and Muslim support, challenged entrenched upper-caste power. Clearly, the underclass was no longer willing to depend on the dominant high castes in the Congress Party or in the BJP to protect its interests.

Chief Election Commissioner T. N. Seshan continued his crusade to ensure free and fair elections. Although his rulings had originally raised consternation in many parties, eventually both Congress and the opposition felt they could be used to their own advantage. An attempted constitutional change to curb Seshan's power failed.

Charges of human rights violations continued to plague the military and police, especially in Kashmir and Punjab. A national human rights commission was established, which insisted on training for all law enforcement personnel. The courts also took on a more active role, overseeing police activities rather than relying on self-monitoring by the police.

Social Issues. In a growing reaction against the use of sex-identification testing and abortion to have sons, several states, including Punjab and Rajasthan, banned the tests during pregnancy. Muslim family law was fundamentally changed in April when the Supreme Court struck down its divorce code as unconstitutional. Indicating the growing secular trends in the community, there was virtually no negative reaction.

The Environment. The fate of India's tiger population was a major concern of wildlife conservationists. In 1989 there were more than 4,000 tigers; the total fell to around 3,000 by 1993. Poaching and population pressures were held responsible for the decline. The government promised to increase conservation measures.

Questions about the safety of India's nuclear power facilities continued to concern government and private groups alike. Unusually high incidents of illness and disfigurement were found in populations around plants such as Rawat Bata in Rajasthan, and India's Atomic Energy Commission came under attack for lax safety regulations and enforcement. Proposals to create an oversight body with new regulatory powers were under discussion.

The Economy. Progress toward economic liberalization continued slowly, primarily because of a lack of legal reform, particularly in the labor sector. The economy did, however, show a relatively healthy growth of 4 percent for the fiscal year that ended in March. Growth was expected to be around 5 percent for the rest of 1994. Agricultural production was strong as a result of an excellent monsoon season. In the first six months of fiscal year

1994-1995, exports rose more than 10 percent over the previous fiscal year and imports increased by more than 19 percent, creating a trade deficit of $1.23 billion. The government's debt fell by more than $1 billion but still caused concern since, by the spring, it represented 6.5 percent of India's gross domestic product.

According to the International Monetary Fund, India was recognized by 1994 as the world's fifth-largest economic power. The country ranked third in numbers of highly trained technical and professional people, who were increasingly in demand overseas. India's business community was well-versed in international practices, and its expanding middle class was proving to be an attractive market for foreign investments. For these reasons, firms once interested in investing in China were showing more interest in India.

These gains had their costs as well. As restrictions were lifted, tariffs cut, and outside investment encouraged, smaller firms were threatened, and layoffs were expected to occur in larger companies attempting to meet foreign competition. Pressures existed to lift land ceilings (legal restrictions on owning land, especially by foreigners) in both urban and rural areas to permit economies of scale. If effected, these changes could widen the gap between the poor and the new wealthy classes. As government scaled back spending, one of the most tragic costs was a decline in higher education investments. All state and national universities were affected, and it was doubtful whether any but the elite institutions could make up their losses through private fund-raising.

Foreign Relations. In 1994, India sought entry into the Asia-Pacific Economic Cooperation group and signed the GATT accord. During the year the government aggressively looked for trade opportunities in the United States, South Africa, and Europe. In discussions with U.S. President Bill Clinton on nuclear proliferation in June, Prime Minister Rao explored the possibility of negotiating a "non-first-use" clause as a starting point, and to demonstrate India's willingness to consider signing the Nuclear Nonproliferation Treaty.

See STATISTICS OF THE WORLD. A.N.M.

INDIANA. *See* STATISTICS OF THE WORLD.

Native American showcase. *The opening of the Smithsonian's George Gustav Heye Center of the National Museum of the American Indian (top) in October gave New York City a splendid new facility for the display of Native American art and culture. Among the works shown in the inaugural exhibitions were (left to right, above) a mask done by a Tsimshian carver in British Columbia, a Navajo Two Grey Hills rug from Arizona, and* Bird Head's Shield *by Absaroke (Crow) artist Kevin Red Star of Montana.*

INDIANS, AMERICAN. In 1994, American Indians pushed lawmakers to move from rhetoric to action in the areas of tribal sovereignty and religious freedom.

On February 11, on Alcatraz Island in San Francisco Bay, a site noted for early Indian activism, a group of Native Americans and their supporters began a 3,800-mile "walk for justice" led by Dennis Banks, cofounder of the American Indian Movement. The marchers walked across the United States to raise public awareness about matters such as the North American Free Trade Agreement, grave desecration, prisoner rights, and nuclear waste dumping and testing on native lands. In July the marchers arrived in Washington, DC, and demanded executive clemency for Leonard Peltier, an American Indian leader, who they contended was innocent of murdering two federal agents on the Pine Ridge Indian Reservation in South Dakota in 1975; Peltier was convicted of the murders in 1977.

On April 29, President Bill Clinton welcomed hundreds of elected American Indian leaders to the White House. Indians described the meeting as the first time since 1822, under President James Monroe, that the leaders of the indigenous people of the United States were invited to meet with a sitting president. During this meeting Clinton pledged to honor and respect tribal sovereignty based on the unique government-to-government relationship between the United States and its Indian nations.

In May, American Indian leaders met in Albuquerque, NM, at the National American Indian Listening Conference sponsored by Attorney General Janet Reno and Interior Secretary Bruce Babbitt. The two-day conference raised a number of significant sovereignty issues having to do with gambling, law enforcement, criminal justice, and federal responsibility for the use and management of Indian land, water, and natural resources.

A bill was introduced in the U.S. House of Representatives by Bill Richardson (D, New Mexico) extending protection to American Indians for the sacramental use of peyote in the 22 states in which it remained illegal; Senator Daniel Inouye (D, Hawaii), chairman of the Committee on Indian Affairs, had introduced similar legislation in the Senate in 1993. The bill was made necessary by a U.S. Supreme Court ruling in 1990, which said that the religious use of peyote by Indians is not protected by the First Amendment of the U.S. Constitution in *Employment Division of Oregon* v. *Smith*. The bill passed the House and the Senate by unanimous vote and was signed into law on October 7 by Clinton. Congress adjourned without completing action on another measure—the Native American Cultural Protection and Free Exercise of Religion Act of 1994, which would have protected, among other things, Native American access to and use of eagle feathers and certain plants and animals for religious purposes.

On October 30 the National Museum of the American Indian at the George Gustav Heye Center in the U.S. Custom House in New York City officially opened its inaugural exhibit to the general public. American Indians were fully involved in the planning of the museum and its extensive exhibits. B.K.M.

INDONESIA. Indonesia maintained its economic buoyancy in 1994 despite growing social tensions, financial embarrassments, and a crackdown on the press. Growth in gross domestic product continued around 6.5 percent, though inequalities in wealth and lifestyles became much more conspicuous. In November, Indonesia hosted the Asia-Pacific Economic Cooperation (APEC) conference, attended by 18 heads of state, who declared their intentions to establish a free-trade zone by 2020.

Indonesia's annexation and 18-year military rule of East Timor still attracted criticism in the global media, though local tensions had diminished. During the APEC conference, however, demonstrators staged riots in Dili, East Timor, and a sit-in at the U.S. embassy in Jakarta to draw attention to Indonesia's human rights record. The government temporarily barred foreign journalists, saying some were inciting riots, while it tried to restore order.

Workers' rights were also at issue in 1994. During the spring and summer, six East Java factory employees who had confessed to the 1993 murder of a female worker involved in a wage dispute with the factory were sentenced, but there was evidence that their confessions were extracted under torture. In April the discovery of a rubber factory employee's body days after he took part in a strike led to violence, and in the same month a woman was found drowned in a West Java textile factory where she had been organizing workers. Also in April a week of riots over low wages in Medan, Sumatra, caused major damage and alarm, with an ethnic Chinese factory owner being lynched. Growing labor militancy and a resurgence of anti-Chinese sentiments were in evidence in Java and other parts of Indonesia.

On June 21 the government closed three prominent weekly publications, *Tempo, De Tik,* and *Editor,* and the next week demonstrators opposing the closures were roughed up by the military, with 20 protesters arrested and fined. The closings were ostensibly related to criticism of an expensive deal made by Technology Minister B. J. Habibie to purchase and

Down with censorship. *Protesters are attacked by riot troops during a June demonstration in Jakarta against the banning of three magazines that had been critical of the Indonesian government.*

refurbish 39 warships from the former East Germany. The incident had a chilling effect on what had been increasingly open press coverage and public discussion of social and political issues in the country.

Publicity surrounding a series of recent financial scandals continued with the trial in the spring of businessman Eddy Tansil, who was given a 17-year sentence in August for misappropriating a $430 million State Development Bank loan arranged by influential friends, among them officials with close ties to President Suharto.

In February the finance minister reported to Parliament that state banks had a ratio of bad loans above 20 percent, totaling around $6 billion. In spite of this financial shakiness, and an external debt of $96 billion, Indonesia continued to enjoy good international credit ratings. The June aid donors' conference in Paris committed $5.5 billion (about the same as for 1993). A June incentive package allowing 100 percent initial foreign equity control and much lower ultimate divestment requirements spurred a midyear surge in foreign investment, doubling the estimate for 1994 to $20 billion (twice the previous record of 1992). Hong Kong and Taiwan were the two leading investors, with money targeted for megaprojects in telecommunications, oil refining, and cop-

per smelting and for a steel plant and a coal-fired power plant.

See STATISTICS OF THE WORLD. G.B.H.

INTERNATIONAL CONFERENCES. A highlight of 1994 was the United Nations Population Conference. Trade and the environment were among issues discussed at other international conferences.

Cairo Population Conference. About 20,000 diplomats, activists, journalists, and others attended the UN Conference on Population and Development, held September 5-13 in Cairo, Egypt. Delegates from all the more than 170 countries represented (non-attendees included Sudan and Saudi Arabia) endorsed a 113-page Program of Action, although the Vatican and some Muslim and Latin American countries indicated reservations about portions of the document dealing with abortion and contraception. The Program of Action, centered around the theme of "empowerment of women," called for efforts to stabilize global population and stressed the importance of making information available to help women play a greater role in family planning.

Group of Seven. At their 20th annual summit meeting in Naples, Italy, July 8-10, leaders of the Group of Seven major industrial nations agreed on a general seven-point plan for reducing unemployment and encouraging economic growth. The G-7 states (Canada, France, Germany, Great Britain, Italy, Japan, and the United States) promised $200 million to Ukraine to help subsidize the closing down of the Chernobyl nuclear reactor.

Summit for NATO. Leaders of the North Atlantic Treaty Organization's member states (the United States, Canada, Turkey, and 13 European countries) met January 10-11 in Brussels, Belgium. At the summit, NATO formally launched the so-called Partnership for Peace, providing for NATO military cooperation with former Soviet-bloc nations that entered the program, but stopped short of promising NATO support in the event of an attack.

Summit for the CIS. In Moscow on April 15 leaders of Russia and 11 other former Soviet republics (all except the Baltic states of Estonia, Lithuania, and Latvia) convened for a summit of the Commonwealth of Independent States. It was agreed that Russia would continue to chair the organization through 1994, overriding a 1993 decision that the chairmanship should be rotated every six months.

American Nations Confer. Delegates from members of the Organization of American States (which includes the United States, Mexico, and 30 countries of Central and South America) met March 27 in Washington, DC, and elected Colombian President César Gaviria Trujillo as OAS secretary-general over Costa Rican Foreign Minister Bernd Niehaus.

Pacific Rim Summit. The Asia-Pacific Economic Cooperation forum's summit meeting was held in Indonesia on November 15. Leaders of 18 Pacific Rim nations, including the United States, Canada, and Japan, declared in their final communiqué APEC's commitment to free trade and investment in the Asia-Pacific region by the year 2020.

Arab Maghreb Union. The Arab Maghreb Union (Algeria, Libya, Mauritania, Morocco, Tunisia), after several postponements, held its sixth summit, and its first since 1989, April 2-3 in Tunis. The members signed a series of cooperation agreements and deplored continuing UN sanctions against Libya.

Whaling Conference. At the annual conference of the International Whaling Commission, held May 23-27 in Puerto Vallarta, Mexico, members agreed to establish a whale sanctuary in Antarctic waters. The vote was 23 in favor with six abstentions. Only Japan voted no.

Endangered Species Conference. The 125 governments that have signed the Convention on International Trade in Endangered Species met in Fort Lauderdale, FL, November 7-18. A major accord to protect tigers in China, India, and other countries was reached, and new, more scientific criteria were adopted on how to decide which species should be protected in future years.

See INTERNATIONAL TRADE. W.A.M.

Moneymen. *Lewis Preston, president of the World Bank (left), and Michel Camdessus, managing director of the International Monetary Fund (center), share a joke with Kenneth Clarke, British chancellor of the exchequer, at an October meeting in Madrid prior to a joint World Bank and IMF conference commemorating the 50th anniversary of the two global financial organizations.*

Trading partners. U.S. trade representative Mickey Kantor signs the "final act" of the so-called Uruguay Round of negotiations under the General Agreement on Tariffs and Trade. As a result of the April signing of the pact by officials from more than 120 nations, GATT was replaced in 1995 by the World Trade Organization.

INTERNATIONAL TRADE. The largest free-trade agreement in history went into effect in 1995 after being signed in 1994 by more than 120 countries.

The U.S. merchandise trade deficit, according to the U.S. Census Bureau, was $151 billion in 1994, far exceeding $116 billion in 1993 and close to the 1987 record of $152 billion. Total U.S. merchandise trade in 1994 exceeded $1.17 trillion. The value of world merchandise exports was $3.645 trillion in 1993, compared with $3.651 trillion in 1992, according to United Nations data.

New GATT Pact. The historic trade accord, negotiated under the General Agreement on Tariffs and Trade, was signed in April 1994 in Morocco by more than 120 nations; it was set to take effect on the first day of 1995. Under the pact, trading nations undertook to slash tariffs by an average of about 40 percent, reduce nontariff barriers such as government price supports, free up trade in services, and install international protections for patents, trademarks, and copyrights. The agreement called for the replacement of the GATT organization, nearly half a century old, with a new World Trade Organization (WTO) to enforce the pact and resolve trade disputes.

In the United States, supporters argued that the controversial pact would greatly stimulate world trade and income, cause a net increase in American jobs (despite losses in some non-competitive industries), and help the nation maintain global economic influence now that the cold war had ended. But many of the same forces that had opposed the North American Free Trade Agreement (Nafta) the previous year lined up against GATT. They feared job losses and an adverse effect on wages; also cited were concerns that U.S. sovereignty, as well as existing labor and environmental standards, would be impaired by decision powers given to the WTO. Congress delayed voting on the GATT accord until after the November election. In the end the pact was approved easily in both houses of Congress, surprising friends and foes alike.

Nafta and Beyond. Nafta, the free-trade agreement among the United States, Canada, and Mexico, which went into effect on January 1, 1994, weathered its first year without major incident. It was one of several regional trade groupings in the western hemisphere that would be superseded under a proposed Free Trade Area of the Americas. At a Summit of the Americas, held in Miami in early December, the leaders of the hemisphere's 34 democracies agreed to negotiate and put into operation the FTAA by the year 2005. At the conclusion of the summit the United States, Canada, and Mexico announced they had agreed to admit Chile to Nafta.

U.S. Trade Disputes. Trade tensions persisted between the United States and Canada, with the former under pressure from domestic producers of poultry and dairy products to get Canada to eliminate trade barriers on these imports. Canada and the United States did reach a one-year agreement to limit Canadian exports of wheat to the United States.

The United States reached yet another accord with Japan on the latter's barriers to American products and services. The Japanese, criticized for their massive trade surplus with the United States, promised to open domestic markets for automobiles, medical devices, telecommunications equipment, and insurance. But the White House was forced to withdraw its demand for numerical targets in reducing Japan's surplus.

In a controversial decision the White House in late May renewed most-favored-nation (MFN) status for China, despite that nation's failure to meet U.S. conditions for improving its record on human rights. Subsequent renewals of MFN, the administration said, would not be tied to human rights.

Asia and the Pacific. At a summit meeting of the Asia-Pacific Economic Cooperation group, held in Bogor, Indonesia, on November 15, 18 Pacific Rim nations agreed in general to aim at "free and open trade and investment," to be achieved by the more industrialized nations by the year 2010, and by the other nations ten years later. A Pacific Rim free-trade zone, if achieved, would be larger than the currently existing American or European trading blocs.

R.J.B.

IOWA. *See* STATE GOVERNMENT REVIEW; STATISTICS OF THE WORLD.

IRAN. Iran faced internal turmoil in 1994 as terrorism and bombings increased. The deadliest bomb exploded inside the shrine of Imam Reza in Mashhad on June 20, killing about 25 pilgrims. President Ali Akbar Rafsanjani himself was the target of a failed assassination attempt, attributed to a lone gunman tied to a small Marxist group. After the Majlis (Parliament) narrowly defeated a bill that would have allowed Qazvin to become an autonomous province, indignant demonstrators rampaged through the city; at least four people were killed, according to official sources.

In March the government incarcerated Ali Akbar Saidi Sirjani, a writer and outspoken critic of the regime, charging him with drinking alcohol, possessing narcotics, gambling, homosexuality, and CIA connections. Iranian intellectuals expressed concern over his fate. He died in November; the government said the cause was a heart attack, but some critics charged he had been tortured, and the human rights group Amnesty International called for an independent investigation.

In political affairs, rivalry between powerful institutions continued. The Majlis passed Rafsanjani's second five-year development plan, while rejecting some of his reform initiatives. The clergy-dominated Guardian Council declared unconstitutional some Majlis legislation, including a bill passed in September to outlaw private ownership of a satellite dish. Meanwhile, Muhammad Hashemi, brother of the president, resigned as head of Iranian radio and television; a person favored by Islamic conservatives replaced him.

Despite inhospitable internal conditions, disappointing oil revenues, and U.S.-imposed economic sanctions, the economy grew by about 4 percent. The volume of non-oil exports increased, and dozens of new factories were built. Foreign debt remained manageable; it was officially estimated at around $20 billion, or 21 percent of gross domestic product. The most debilitating problems were rampant inflation and the chaotic foreign exchange system.

Iran's relations with neighbors in Central Asia and the Caucasus were solidified, and Iran agreed to help finance construction of a pipeline, to carry natural gas from Turkmenistan through Iran to Western Europe via Turkey. Rafsanjani paid visits to Indonesia, Malaysia, and Brunei.

A cautious rapprochement with the West continued. Germany, Iran's number one trading partner, and many other trading partners agreed to reschedule Iran's debts. However,

Déjà vu. *Showing the continuing presence of anti-American sentiment in Iran, a crowd of demonstrators in Tehran celebrates the 15th anniversary of the 1979 takeover of the U.S. embassy that precipitated a long-lasting diplomatic crisis over the holding of American hostages.*

relations with the West were inhibited by the regime's refusal to revoke the Ayatollah Khomeini's 1989 decree calling for the killing of British author Salman Rushdie for having authored a novel allegedly offensive to Islam. England accused Iran of supporting the Irish Republican Army; Iran protested the charge. U.S.-Iranian relations remained tense, as the United States, Israel, and Argentina accused Tehran in the July bombing of a Jewish center in Buenos Aires, which killed about 100 people. The Argentine Supreme Court, however, found insufficient evidence to implicate four Iranian diplomats charged in the case.

See STATISTICS OF THE WORLD.   M.M.M.

IRAQ. During 1994, Iraq's domestic and foreign policy was dominated by the effects of the UN trade embargo that was imposed after Iraq's invasion of Kuwait in 1990 and by efforts, ultimately unsuccessful, to have the embargo lifted.

Divisions at the UN. In the first part of the year Iraqi President Saddam Hussein focused

his efforts on exploiting a split in opinion among the five permanent members of the UN Security Council.

The rift became clear in March after the Security Council met for one of its regular 60-day reviews of sanctions. France and Russia, with the tacit support of China, called for a statement acknowledging Iraq's cooperation with the UN on a program to dismantle its weapons of mass destruction. The United States and the United Kingdom opposed the move, and no statement was issued.

Prime Minister Tariq Aziz led the diplomatic initiatives at the UN to press the case that Baghdad had complied with cease-fire Resolution 687, which linked disarmament with an end to the embargo. But the diplomatic initiatives showed no sign of prevailing over the clearly stated commitment by the United States to maintain the embargo, and Iraq attempted to exert pressure on the international community by massing up to 80,000 troops near the Kuwaiti border in early October. The troops began to withdraw after the United States, the United Kingdom, and France—who were among the countries that repulsed Iraq from Kuwait in 1991—responded in kind by sending land, air, and naval forces into the area. On November 10, in response to a Russian diplomatic initiative, Iraq recognized Kuwaiti sovereignty and the UN-demarcated borders—one of the key demands before sanctions could be lifted. However, the United States and the United Kingdom said the statement of recognition was only the first in a series of steps Iraq must take before sanctions could be lifted.

Economic Hardship. A collapsing currency, spiraling inflation, food shortages, and no sign of any economic respite until the end of sanctions prompted a series of drastic measures in domestic policy. In February the government dropped attempts to control the exchange rate artificially by licensing state banks and exchange houses to change money at the market rate, a fraction of the dinar's value before the invasion of Kuwait. Then, in May, Saddam sacked his prime minister and stepped in to head the cabinet himself, saying that special measures were required to combat the effects of the embargo. In his new position Saddam introduced a series of draconian punishments, including amputations for theft and for desertion from the Army. In September he slashed by half the already meager state-subsidized food rations.

Internal Conflicts. In the north of Iraq, under Kurdish self-rule since 1991, there were a series of clashes between the rival ruling factions. The heaviest fighting was in May between the Kurdish Democratic Party and the Patriotic Union of Kurdistan, which left up to 400 people dead and the region divided along party lines.

Mediation efforts by the umbrella opposition group, the Iraqi National Congress, brought an end to the conflict, and a peace agreement was signed at the end of November. In the southern marshes, a center of resistance to Baghdad since 1991, Shiite Muslim rebels faced continued attack from Iraqi ground forces. The fiercest fighting was reported in April around the town of Amara.

See STATISTICS OF THE WORLD.   E.B.

Remembering the past. *On a ten-day visit to Canada in late summer, Irish President Mary Robinson leaves a chapel after attending a religious service on Grosse-Ile in Québec. The island is the site of a memorial to the thousands of Irish immigrants who perished from disease while quarantined there in the 19th century.*

IRELAND. Peace was the dominant word in Ireland throughout 1994, following the December 1993 Downing Street Declaration signed by British Prime Minister John Major and Eire Taoiseach (Premier) Albert Reynolds. The document did not change the constitutional relationship between Britain and Ireland, but its conciliatory tone set the scene for ending hostilities in Northern Ireland.

Initially rejecting the peace declaration, the outlawed Irish Republican Army (IRA) ultimately agreed to a "complete" cessation of violence from September 1. On October 13, Protestant "loyalist" paramilitary organizations also announced a complete cease-fire. By year's end the British government had met with political representatives from both sides to negotiate terms for disposal of arms and release of prisoners. Progress was expected to be protracted and fitful, but there was real hope that Ireland's chronic political violence might finally be ending.

Meanwhile, public outrage over the acts of a priest convicted of pedophile offenses became political fury after it was revealed that the warrant for his extradition from the Republic to Northern Ireland had lain unprocessed for seven months. Reynolds was unable to satisfactorily explain this, and the ruling Fianna Fail-Labor coalition collapsed. Both Reynolds and his controversial High Court president, Harry Whelehan, resigned in November. The Reynolds debacle created in its wake a historic coalition wherein Eire's second-largest party, the right-wing, law-and-order Fine Gael, joined forces with Labor and the tiny Democratic Left. The Democratic Left had origins in the Official IRA (which split with what became the Provisional IRA in 1969). Fine Gael leader John Bruton became premier in December.

Once the door was opened for discussion of child sex abuse by priests, new allegations—and demands for disclosure—snowballed. When a priest collapsed at a gay club and was given last rites at 4 A.M. by two other club-going priests, the effect on the Irish psyche was more devastating than that from 1992 revelations about Bishop Eamonn Casey's love child.

Catholic Church authority in Ireland was hurt by these new scandals. Although he did not announce his retirement, the primate of Ireland, Cardinal Cahal Daly, 77, in December named parish priest Monsignor Sean Brady to the successor role of coadjutor-bishop.

See STATISTICS OF THE WORLD.   C.M.

IRELAND, NORTHERN. *See* GREAT BRITAIN.

ISRAEL. Dominating the news in Israel in 1994, as in past years, were events relating to its foreign policy and national security. Israel achieved a major breakthrough in October when it signed a peace treaty with Jordan. An agreement implementing the September 1993 accord between Israel and the Palestine Liberation Organization (PLO) was signed in May 1994, but acts of terrorism continued to sour the Israeli-Palestinian relationship.

Peace Treaty With Jordan. After signing an interim agreement on July 25, ending their state of belligerency, Israel and Jordan signed a full-fledged peace agreement on the desert border between the two countries on October 26. Key provisions of the treaty included the establishment of full diplomatic and consular ties; mutual cooperation against terrorism, crime, smuggling, and narcotics production and trafficking; the opening of an air corridor; the interconnecting of electric power grids in the Eilat-Aqaba region; and the joint development of the Jordan Rift Valley. Israel benefited especially from Jordan's agreement to end the economic boycott and from its willingness to bar the entry onto its territory of the military forces of a third country—thus precluding the entry of Syrian or Iraqi troops. (The Gulf Cooperation Council countries—Bahrain, Kuwait, Oman, Qatar, Saudi Arabia, and the United Arab Emirates—announced in September that they were dropping their secondary and tertiary economic boycotts of Israel.) Israel and Jordan also promised to share the limited water of the Jordan and Yarmuk rivers and to develop new water resources. Israel agreed to return a limited amount of disputed territory to Jordan in the Zofar and Naharayim regions but to lease the land back for 25 years.

Israeli-PLO Treaty. Israel's relations with the Palestinians were, at best, mixed. The negotiations for the implementation of the September 13, 1993, Declaration of Principles were supposed to take three months; instead they took almost nine. In part, the delay resulted from Israel's rising suspicion of Yasir Arafat, the PLO leader, for not condemning attacks on Israeli soldiers and civilians by Palestinian opponents of the peace process and for not convening the Palestine National Council to renounce those elements of the PLO charter calling for Israel's destruction, despite an explicit promise at the time of the 1993 agreement to do so.

Complicating the negotiations further was the terrorist act of Baruch Goldstein, a militant Israeli settler living in Qiryat Arba, a Jewish settlement on the West Bank near Hebron. Possibly reacting to terrorist attacks on Israelis, or possibly hoping to sabotage the peace talks—which threatened the future of settlements such as Qiryat Arba—Goldstein entered the Cave of the Patriarchs in Hebron, a religious site shared by Arabs and Jews, and killed 29 Arabs on February 25, 1994. Although Israeli Prime Minister Yitzhak Rabin denounced the attack and ordered the arrest of a number of anti-Arab Jewish militants, Arafat broke off the peace negotiations. After a compromise was reached allowing for the temporary stationing of international observers in Hebron, Arafat returned to the talks, and an agreement was reached on May 4.

Under the agreement, Israeli forces pulled out of Gaza and Jericho (except from positions guarding Israeli settlements in Gaza), turning over control in both regions to the newly created Palestinian National Authority, headed by Arafat. Although attacks on Israelis in the Gaza Strip continued, the next step in the peace process took place in August when Israel turned over responsibility for education in the West Bank to the Palestinian National Authority. Later in the year Israel handed over responsibility for health, tourism, welfare, and taxation.

Despite these positive steps, there was an escalation of terrorism directed against Israelis. In mid-October two Israelis (one of them an Israeli Arab) were murdered in downtown Jerusalem; an Israeli soldier was kidnapped

and later killed as Israeli forces tried to free him; and 22 Israelis were killed and 46 wounded in a bus in downtown Tel Aviv. These acts of terrorism increased the pressure on Rabin from his domestic opponents to end the peace talks until Arafat cracked down on those responsible for the terrorism—Hamas and Islamic Jihad. Rabin put strong pressure on Arafat to do so, and also sharply curtailed the entrance into Israel of Palestinian workers from Gaza and the West Bank. Ironically, in the midst of the escalation of terrorism came the announcement in mid-October that Rabin, Arafat, and Israeli Foreign Minister Shimon Peres had been awarded the Nobel Peace Prize. (*See* PRIZES AND AWARDS.)

Israeli-Syrian Developments. There was little abatement in the tension between Israel and Syria. Despite some small gestures, such as allowing Syrian Foreign Minister Farouk al-Sharaa to be interviewed by Israeli correspondent Ehud Ya'ari, Syria took few steps toward

Massacre in Hebron. Palestinians rush to a hospital a man shot during rioting that erupted in Hebron in the Israeli-occupied West Bank in late February after an Israeli settler opened fire on hundreds of Palestinians praying in a mosque.

meeting Israeli demands for security assurances in return for an Israeli pullback on the Golan Heights. Not only did Syria refuse to participate in the multilateral peace talks on water, refugees, environmental issues, regional economic development, and arms control and regional security, it also maintained its support for the guerrilla group Hezbollah, which was carrying on a guerrilla war against Israeli forces in southern Lebanon. While U.S. President Bill Clinton sought to put a positive "spin" on the progress of Israeli-Syrian peace, and there were extensive behind-the-scenes efforts during the year to expedite the peace process, most Israelis remained skeptical.

Other Foreign Relations. Relations between Israel and its most important foreign ally, the United States, remained strong in 1994. There were frequent meetings between Clinton and Rabin. Clinton promised to maintain U.S. aid to Israel at the level of $3 billion annually ($1.8 billion in military aid and $1.2 billion in economic aid), to provide Israel with two supercomputers, and to continue the U.S. share of funding for the Arrow antimissile missile, which, if perfected, would strengthen Israeli security against Scud missiles. For its part, Israel, at Clinton's request, provided police for the international effort to restore Haitian President Jean-Bertrand Aristide to power in the fall.

In other developments of note, Britain lifted its 12-year arms embargo against Israel; Turkish Prime Minister Tansu Ciller visited Israel in November, the first such visit of a Turkish prime minister (Israeli President Ezer Weizmann had visited Turkey earlier in the year); and in April, Rabin visited Moscow, where he signed several economic agreements and delivered a lecture to the general staff of the Russian Army.

Domestic Politics. Despite his successes in foreign policy, Rabin suffered a series of domestic setbacks. First, control over the Histadrut (the giant labor union) was wrested away from Rabin's Labor Party by Chaim Raimon, the minister of health. Unable to promote from within the Labor Party his plan to reform Israel's medical insurance system, Raimon decided to run on an independent ticket for the leadership of the Histadrut. His victory was seen as a major blow to Rabin. Second,

Rabin failed to convince the Shas, an ultra-Orthodox Jewish party, to return to his governing coalition, although on most votes Shas voted with the government.

Fortunately for Rabin, the main opposition party, Likud, remained divided, with Likud leader Benjamin Netanyahu unable to reach a compromise with his powerful enemies, David Levy and Ariel Sharon. In addition, the opposition Tsomet Party split over the alleged financial irregularities of its leader, Rafael Eitan, with three breakaway members forming the Yi'ud faction, which Rabin sought to win over to the governing coalition.

Economy. After several years of hovering near single digits, Israel's 12-month rate of consumer-price inflation reached 14.5 percent by December, a rise due in part to a sharp increase in housing prices. Unemployment, however, dropped by almost 4 percent in 1994 to 7.5 percent in November.

See STATISTICS OF THE WORLD. R.O.F.

ITALY. Italian news in 1994 was dominated by the rapid rise to, and subsequent fall from, political power by television tycoon Silvio Berlusconi (*see profile in* PEOPLE IN THE NEWS) at the head of an unsteady conservative government. In January, President Oscar Luigi Scalfaro dissolved Parliament and set a date for early elections to replace the country's political class discredited by the ongoing Clean Hands corruption investigation, which kept widening its scope. The elections, held on March 27 and 28 under new winner-take-all rules, radically reshaped Italy's postwar political landscape. For the first time since the dictatorship of Benito Mussolini the country shifted rightward.

However, in November, Berlusconi came under investigation for corrupt business practices, and his fragile coalition government crumbled. On December 22 he turned in his resignation.

Elections. Just three months before the 1994 vote, Berlusconi had announced that he was stepping into the political arena at the head of Forza Italia—"Go Italy." The new political movement was created, he said, to save Italy from the clutches of the former Communist Party, renamed the Democratic Party of the Left, which had dominated mayoral elections in November and December 1993. The mayoral elections are considered a bellwether of national sentiment. He won on a platform of free-market reforms and populist optimism conveyed to voters through massive amounts of political advertising on his three television stations.

During his campaign Berlusconi made ballot box alliances with the federalist Northern League in the north and the extreme right-wing National Alliance in the south. Together they formed the so-called Freedom Pole, which obtained a substantial majority of 366 seats in the 630-seat Chamber of Deputies (lower house) and a qualified majority of 155 in the 315-seat Senate (upper house). The election's big losers were the former Christian Democrats, renamed the Popular Party, who had been the cornerstone force of all previous postwar governments, as well as the Socialists, with whom they had governed during the 1980s. Other smaller, formerly governing centrist forces such as the Liberal and Social Democratic parties had disintegrated as they came under scrutiny of the two-year-old Clean Hands probe. The Democratic Party of the Left (mostly unscathed by Clean Hands), though it came in a close second to Forza Italia, failed to seize power and thus was also viewed as having suffered a stinging defeat.

New Government. After lengthy consultations with leaders of all elected forces, President Scalfaro formally designated Berlusconi as prime minister on April 28. The Chamber of Deputies on April 16 had elected Irene Pivetti, 31, a Northern League member of Parliament as its speaker. A feisty, fervent Catholic, she was the youngest to hold the country's third-most-important state post, and her popularity quickly rose in national opinion polls. Days

Top-level talks. World leaders gather at the Palazzo Reale in Naples, Italy, on the final day of the July summit meeting of the Group of Seven industrialized nations. From left to right: German Chancellor Helmut Kohl, European Union Commission President Jacques Delors, Canadian Prime Minister Jean Chrétien, Japanese Prime Minister Tomiichi Murayama, U.S. President Bill Clinton, French President François Mitterrand, Italian Prime Minister Silvio Berlusconi, Russian President Boris Yeltsin, and British Prime Minister John Major.

Physical debate. Members of the Italian Parliament come to blows in July during heated debate over a government decree curbing the use of preventive detention in a variety of crimes, including bribery and corruption. The issuance of the decree caused a furor, as many thought it deprived the authorities of a valuable weapon in Italy's ongoing corruption probe. The decree ultimately was withdrawn.

later, Carlo Scognamiglio, 49, a professor of economics and member of Forza Italia, was voted speaker of the Senate. A final vote on May 18 in the Senate cleared the way for Italy's 53rd postwar government.

From its outset it was clear that the Freedom Pole comprised forces with deeply differing agendas. The most irreconcilable goals appeared to be the Northern League's commitment to turn Italy into a Swiss-style confederation, while the National Alliance, which traced its roots back to Mussolini, professed to stand for a strong, centralized state. But more threatening to the stability of this marriage of convenience was the unfaithfulness of Northern League leader Umberto Bossi, a rabble-rouser who never ceased to be a thorn in Berlusconi's side. National Alliance leader Gianfranco Fini, Berlusconi's other ally, appeared to be more loyal.

Cool International Reception. Berlusconi's government, the first to include Mussolini's political heirs in its cabinet, was given a cool international reception. At a meeting of the European Council of Ministers on May 29, Danish and Belgian telecommunications ministers refused to shake hands with their new counterpart, Giuseppe Tatarella, a member of the National Alliance. Though they were kept out of key posts such as foreign and interior

ministries—which went, respectively, to Antonio Martino of Forza Italia and Roberto Maroni of the Northern League—the National Alliance occupied six cabinet positions in full recognition of their 13 percent electoral gain, which made them Italy's third-largest party.

Responding to international criticism, Berlusconi stressed that all his ministers were firmly committed to democracy and that Fascism had been "condemned and buried by history." Fini sought to soften his sometimes alarming tone and weed out extremists from his party to recast its image as belonging to Europe's mainstream right.

Conflict of Interest. Berlusconi also came under fire because of the blatant conflict of interest between his position as prime minister and his television, publishing, retailing, and real estate holding company Fininvest, with revenues of $7.2 billion a year. When he went into politics, he gave up operating control of his business interests and pledged to distance himself further. But a blind trust plan drafted by a committee of experts picked by Berlusconi was widely viewed with skepticism mainly because it left the choice of the trustee to Berlusconi.

The issue cast a shadow on many government decisions, such as the appointment in September of a new board of directors at state television network RAI, Fininvest's main broadcasting competitor. It also loomed in the background as Paolo Berlusconi, the prime minister's brother and business associate, and two other Fininvest executives were arrested in July for paying kickbacks to tax auditors. On December 22, Paolo was convicted of violating party funding laws and given a seven-month suspended sentence and a fine. Other graft investigations continued.

Anticorruption Investigation. Paolo Berlusconi had been previously arrested and was briefly placed in preventive custody by Milan investigative magistrates in February. Silvio Berlusconi then started waging a campaign against the Milan magistrates, whom he accused of abusing their powers for political purposes. In July the government faltered as Berlusconi tried to ram through an emergency law decree curtailing the judges' capacity to arrest corruption suspects. He was forced to withdraw it after Antonio Di Pietro, head of the Clean Hands investigative unit and a national hero, threatened his resignation. In late November, Berlusconi received notice that the magistrates were investigating his company for bribes reportedly paid to officials before he was prime minister. Di Pietro resigned in early December, saying political maneuvering was making his work impossible. However, the Berlusconi probe continued.

Collapse of the Government. Already weakened by the corruption allegations, Berlusconi's hold on power became even more tenuous when the Northern League on December 14 voted with the opposition in favor of a television oversight board, ignoring coalition unity. Rather than call for a vote of confidence, Berlusconi resigned the next week. He stayed on as caretaker premier while Scalfaro debated whether to hold new elections or appoint a new prime minister to form a new government. Berlusconi favored elections, while Bossi pushed for an appointed government.

Economy. Thanks in large part to the end of Europe's recessionary downturn and to a strongly devalued lira, which made exports very competitive, Italy enjoyed a 1.1 to 1.2 percent gross domestic product annual growth rate for 1994 (although it had an exceedingly high debt ratio), as annual inflation dropped below 4 percent by year's end. However, the uncertainty of Italy's political future caused many foreign investors to be shy.

See STATISTICS OF THE WORLD.   N.V.

IVORY COAST. *See* STATISTICS OF THE WORLD.

J

JAMAICA. *See* CARIBBEAN BASIN; STATISTICS OF THE WORLD.

JAPAN. The year 1994 witnessed a fundamental restructuring of the Japanese political scene. In the span of just 12 weeks Japan had three different prime ministers, the last of whom, Tomiichi Murayama, was Japan's first Socialist prime minister in almost half a century. His rise to power was made possible by an historical political realignment between two traditional political rivals, the Liberal Democratic Party (LDP) and the Social Democratic Party of Japan (SDPJ). He remained in office at year's end.

Political Turmoil. As the year opened the seven-party coalition government headed by Prime Minister Morihiro Hosokawa was beset by numerous troubles. Hosokawa, the first non-LDP prime minister in 38 years, found it difficult to overcome deep-rooted policy differences that divided the members of his coalition, in particular over tax reform, North Korean nuclear capability, and political reform.

The fragility of the coalition was also exposed by the determined opposition of the LDP. In March, LDP members of the Diet (the bicameral Parliament) alleged that Hosokawa had improperly used a 1982 loan to finance his election campaign for governor of Kumamoto. The LDP demanded that a special Diet committee be set up to investigate his past financial dealings. When their demand was

Japan's new leader. *Incoming Japanese Prime Minister Tomiichi Murayama poses with the members of his cabinet after their first meeting in late June. Head of a coalition government and leader of the Social Democratic Party, Murayama was the first Socialist to become prime minister of Japan since 1948.*

rejected, the LDP borrowed a tactic from the Socialists, boycotting Diet deliberations on the fiscal 1994 general account budget. With Diet proceedings at a standstill, Hosokawa on April 8 abruptly announced his decision to resign as prime minister. Insisting he had done nothing illegal, he said he was resigning to resolve the impasse in the Diet.

Tsutomu Hata, the cohead of the Japan Renewal Party and foreign minister under Hosokawa, was selected as the new prime minister on April 25. Within hours, however, his fragile coalition split apart when the SDPJ abruptly pulled out. The Socialists were already in disagreement with other coalition members over tax and foreign policy, and when they learned that Ichiro Ozawa, the Renewal Party's cohead, was attempting to fashion a new centrist party that would exclude them, it was the last straw. The SDPJ defection left the ruling coalition far short of the 256 votes it needed for a simple majority. Hata was forced to form a minority cabinet, the first since 1948. It lasted less than two months. Hata resigned on June 25, after the LDP, with SDPJ support, threatened to bring a no-confidence motion in the lower house.

After four days of intense political maneuvering, the SDPJ on June 29 sent shock waves through Japan's political world by agreeing to cooperate with its old rival, the LDP, in the crucial Diet vote to elect a new prime minister. Their combined votes were enough to give SDPJ Chairman Murayama a comfortable victory. The Socialists then changed some of their basic policy positions, in particular their long-standing opposition to the U.S.-Japan security arrangement; they also acknowledged the constitutionality of the Japanese military. Both policies had long been advocated by the LDP. Critics accused the SDPJ of sacrificing its long-standing ideological positions in an opportunistic grab for power, but supporters called the changes a long-overdue effort by the party to be more in touch with mainstream Japanese voters. The Murayama coalition also included the New Harbinger Party.

Electoral Reform. The electoral reform bill that finally won Diet approval in late November brought fundamental change to the Japanese electoral system, altering how politicians are elected to the lower house.

Under the old system Japan was divided into 130 multimember electoral districts. A party hoping to win a majority in the Diet was forced to run multiple candidates in each district. This intense competition between members of the same party was one cause of the prevalence of money in Japanese politics and also of the tendency of many politicians to rely for election on single-issue interest groups.

The new electoral system mixed 300 single-member districts with 200 members elected through a proportional representation system. Reformers hoped that the importance of money in politics would decline. The new electoral system also gave smaller parties the incentive to coalesce into larger organizations.

Opposition parties had taken a major step in this direction in September, when the main partners of the former ruling coalition, the Japan Renewal Party, the Japan New Party, and the Clean Government Party, announced they were joining with a handful of splinter parties to form a single organization. In December these parties formed a new party, the New Frontier Party. Former Prime Minister Toshiki Kaifu was chosen as its first president.

Economic Slump. Turmoil in the political world hampered efforts to end the economic recession that had beset Japan since April 1991. The economy in 1993 grew by just 0.1 percent, the worst growth record in 20 years. Figures released in September 1994 indicated that the economy in the second quarter shrank by 1.2 percent.

The Japanese government continued its efforts to expand domestic economic activity. In February the government introduced its fourth stimulus package—mostly of increased spending on public works projects—since 1992. In July it finally enacted a plan, first set in motion by Prime Minister Hosokawa, to lower personal income taxes for fiscal year 1994-1995. In September the Murayama government made clear that government efforts to increase

public works spending would continue. However, the government faced growing controversy over how to pay for these higher levels of spending. The fiscally conservative Ministry of Finance said they should be covered by an increase in the consumption tax; politicians seemed unable to reach a consensus on this unpopular move.

Trade Frictions. Japan's trade surplus with the United States surpassed $50 billion in 1993 and continued to increase through the first three-quarters of 1994. The United States, in response, intensified its pressures on the Japanese government to open the Japanese market in specific sectors. However, talks broke down in February over U.S. insistence that access to the Japanese market be measured using specific quantitative indicators. The Japanese refused to agree to this, so little progress was made on the four priority issues (insurance, automotive equipment, and government procurement of telecommunications equipment and medical equipment). The two sides appeared headed for a direct confrontation. On the eve of an October 1 deadline, with the United States threatening economic sanctions, the two sides reached a partial, last-minute compromise, which called for a "sig-

Tree's company. Japanese Emperor Akihito and Empress Michiko plant a tree at the Missouri Botanical Garden in St. Louis during a state visit to the United States in June. A potentially controversial proposed trip to Pearl Harbor, HI, the site of a 1941 Japanese air attack, was canceled before Akihito left Japan.

Plane and fancy. *The new Kansai International Airport near Osaka, Japan, which opened in September, was hailed for its stunning architecture but criticized for its costliness—both to build and, for airlines, to use.*

nificant increase in access and sales" of foreign products but explicitly rejected the use of numerical or quantitative targets. The two sides agreed on measures for increasing market access in the insurance industry and on changes in how the Japanese government procures telecommunications and medical equipment.

Foreign Affairs. Japan continued to debate whether it should seek a more active role in foreign affairs. The softening of the Socialists' foreign policy position following their ascent to power removed one of the main obstacles to a more active approach in international relations. In September the Murayama government announced it had decided to "actively" seek a permanent seat on the UN Security Council. However, Japan remained wary about taking on the sorts of global responsibilities—in particular, military obligations—this new status would imply. Nonetheless, the government made a surprisingly quick decision to send lightly armed troops to participate

in the UN Assistance Mission to Rwanda, with little of the political turmoil that surrounded the decision to let Japanese forces participate in the peacekeeping operation in Cambodia in 1992. In part this was because the strongest opponents of that decision, the Socialists, were now in the ruling coalition; it also stemmed from the relatively successful outcome of the Cambodia operation.

The new government also faced a potentially difficult crisis over North Korea. During the Hosokawa and Hata governments Japan had voiced its willingness to cooperate with the full range of U.S. efforts to prevent North Korea from developing nuclear weapons. However, the SDPJ, which had some ties to North Korea, had been uncomfortable with the idea of economic sanctions discussed by the United Nations and would have actively opposed any more drastic action. The Murayama government was thus relieved when the United States and North Korea reached an agreement in October that at least temporarily defused the situation.

See STATISTICS OF THE WORLD.   R.U.

JORDAN. On July 25, 1994, the 46-year state of war between Jordan and Israel formally came to an end when King Hussein and Israeli Prime Minister Yitzhak Rabin signed a declaration at White House ceremonies hosted by U.S. President Bill Clinton. The declaration followed June agreements between the two states covering cooperation in highway construction, aviation, counterterrorism, border demarcation, and tourism. A range of new agreements in the July declaration covered direct phone links, a joint electricity grid, an end to Jordan's support of the Arab economic boycott, establishment of a border crossing at Eilat/Aqaba, and work toward a comprehensive peace. Israel's recognition of King Hussein's "special role" in administering the Muslim shrines in Jerusalem caused tension between Jordan and the Palestine Liberation Organization. An August trip to Jordan by Rabin was the first-ever public visit by an Israeli prime minister. Around that time Israel began releasing water from the Yarmuk River to the Jordan River to help ease Jordan's severe water shortage. Security and trade agreements came later in the month. On October 26, at a desert outpost along the border, the two countries signed a formal peace treaty. In November, King Hussein paid his first public visit to Israel.

Efforts were made to improve relations with Arab Gulf states, cool since Hussein's support for Iraq in the 1990-1991 Persian Gulf War. In March the king made a pilgrimage to Mecca amid speculation that he would meet with Saudi Arabia's King Fahd. The two monarchs did not meet, but the kingdoms did increase embassy staffs in September. A Jordanian official also visited Kuwait to examine the Jordanian embassy there, closed since the war. He was met by the Kuwaiti foreign minister in what was termed a "warm reception." In late September the six-member Gulf Cooperation Council announced its support of Jordan's agreements with Israel. The following month, when Iraqi troops massed along Iraq's border with Kuwait, King Hussein condemned the buildup.

Relations with the United States were strained early in the year over Jordanian dissatisfaction with American naval inspection of ships bound for Aqaba as part of the enforcement of the United Nations economic embargo against Iraq. A compromise involving in-place inspection by Lloyds of London agents resolved the dispute. During a June official visit to Washington, Hussein obtained cancellation of Jordan's $700 million military debt and help in restructuring Jordan's $311.2 million commercial debt to American banks.

Prime Minister Abdel Salam Majali reorganized his government in June. Muslim conservatives were kept out of the cabinet.

See STATISTICS OF THE WORLD.   C.H.A.

K

KAMPUCHEA. See CAMBODIA.

KANSAS. See STATE GOVERNMENT REVIEW; STATISTICS OF THE WORLD.

KAZAKHSTAN. Elections for a full-time legislature were held in Kazakhstan on March 7, 1994, to replace the Soviet-era Supreme Soviet that had dissolved itself at the end of 1993. Foreign observers criticized voting irregularities, but there were no serious challenges to the election results.

The new Supreme Soviet contained a wide range of political groups, ranging from the Kazakh nationalist Azat movement to Lad, a group defending the interests of Kazakhstan's Russian population.

President Nursultan Nazarbayev had hoped that the elections would produce a legislature more supportive of his economic reform plans, but his hopes were frustrated. At its first meeting on May 27, the Supreme Soviet voted no confidence in Prime Minister Sergei Tereshchenko's anticrisis program. When the program showed no results by October, the president asked Tereshchenko and his cabinet to resign. The new prime minister, Akezhan Kazhegeldin, had been an architect of Nazarbayev's reform program.

The most ambitious privatization scheme in any of the Central Asian states was launched in Kazakhstan at the end of April, with 3,500 state-owned firms being slated for auction over a 15-month period. However, neither privatization nor infusions of loans and credits from foreign countries and international lending institutions stopped the post-Soviet decline in industrial and agricultural production or the high inflation. In October popular disturbances were reported in connection with a considerable increase in the price of bread.

Friction developed with Russia during the year as a result of Russian demands for a share in Kazakhstan's rich oil and gas fields. In January, Kazakhstan and Uzbekistan set up an economic union and began dismantling customs and other barriers to trade.

In November a large amount of bomb-grade uranium from a former Soviet nuclear installation in Kazakhstan was transferred to the United States. In return, Kazakhstan was to receive tens of millions of dollars in cash and specialized equipment.

See STATISTICS OF THE WORLD.   B.A.B.

KENTUCKY. *See* STATE GOVERNMENT REVIEW; STATISTICS OF THE WORLD.

KENYA. Strikes by doctors and university teaching staffs caused major dislocations in medical and educational services in Kenya in 1994. Tensions ran high between President Daniel arap Moi's ruling Kenya African National Union (KANU) party and opposition parties.

Both the doctors and teachers struck over conditions of employment—including very low salaries for highly trained medical and university professionals—and the refusal of the government to register their unions. The doctors' strike led to the virtual closure of public hospitals.

In July the country was shocked by the sudden death of Frederick Masinde, a Nairobi-based politician who was killed in a car accident just before his parliamentary by-election victory was announced. His death was blamed on suspicious circumstances arising from KANU's displeasure over a canceled political deal with the opposition candidate.

The January death of former vice president and longtime political leader Jaramogi Oginga Odinga left his party, the opposition Forum for the Restoration of Democracy (FORD Kenya), considerably weakened, as it was riven by dissension among its members. It also led to worsening relations between FORD Kenya and KANU, as Moi had had a working relationship with Odinga but did not trust the new leadership. Michael Kijana Wamalwa was named to lead FORD Kenya.

The Kenyan economy showed some signs of improvement in 1994, mainly due to liberalization policies mandated by the International Monetary Fund and the World Bank. The Kenya shilling showed increasing buoyancy and strength, but unemployment remained high, and it was clear that the rapidly growing population was increasingly outpacing the rate of economic development, leading to poverty for more citizens.

Kenya experienced pressure from donor countries, who insisted on more government accountability to the public for its actions as well as greater observance of human rights. However, compared with nearby Somalia and Rwanda, Kenya was still viewed by the international community as an area of relative stability in East Africa, and Western countries continued to use its airport and seaport facilities. Kenya strengthened economic ties with South Africa, especially after the election of Nelson Mandela to the presidency, but continued to complain about the imbalance of export trade which greatly favored South Africa. Relations with neighboring countries remained generally good, and Kenya reestablished diplomatic relations with Norway, which had been broken in 1990.

See STATISTICS OF THE WORLD.   J.G.K.

KIRIBATI. *See* STATISTICS OF THE WORLD.

KOREA. North Korea's nuclear program was the top international story for Korea in 1994. Domestically, the top story was the death of longtime North Korean President Kim Il Sung. Of special concern was the ability of Kim Il Sung's son Kim Jong Il to consolidate his power in Pyongyang.

KOREA

NORTH KOREA

On July 8, North Korean President Kim Il Sung died suddenly of a heart attack at the age of 82. Kim, who had been in power for 46 years, left the regime in the hands of his son Kim Jong Il, whom he had cultivated for over 20 years to succeed him as head of the government, party, and military. Some observers thought that Kim Jong Il could not command the kind of support his father had enjoyed, particularly in the military. The Western press painted him as a dangerous and unstable character. But most North Korea watchers advised taking Kim seriously. They noted that his years on center stage had made him a seasoned leader, and that the bureaucracy was packed with his handpicked supporters.

Kim Jong Il spent the three months following his father's death in seclusion, leaving vacant the presidency and the post of general secretary of the Korean Workers' (Communist) Party. Through the summer there were rumors about his health and a possible power struggle, but on October 16 he finally reappeared in public, apparently in effective control.

Nuclear Installations Dispute. Kim Il Sung's death concerned the international community because of the ongoing controversy over Pyongyang's suspected nuclear weapons program. The North Koreans have always claimed that their nuclear installations were for "peaceful purposes," namely electric power generation. However, the spent fuel from their Soviet-style reactors could be reprocessed to make bomb-grade plutonium. Of particular concern was a 5-megawatt reactor that was shut down briefly in 1989, during which time fuel rods containing plutonium were replaced. The waste from those rods, which could prove whether North Korea had been building nuclear bombs, was believed to be in two waste dumps that the North Koreans insisted were military sites—and therefore off-limits to inspectors from the International Atomic Energy Agency. In 1993, when the IAEA demanded access to the waste sites, North Korea responded by announcing its intention to pull out of the Nuclear Nonproliferation Treaty (NPT).

From March 1993 until October 1994 the IAEA and the United States focused their efforts on keeping North Korea in the NPT regime and maintaining surveillance of its known nuclear installations. There was more at issue than North Korea's nuclear program, however, for Pyongyang has long felt threatened by the United States. After Pyongyang threatened to renounce the NPT, the United States broke precedent and began a direct, high-level dialogue with North Korea in an attempt to work out a "package deal" involving not only the nuclear program but other political and economic issues.

In the spring of 1994 the talks broke down when the North Koreans again shut down their 5-megawatt reactor and extracted plutonium-laden spent fuel without adequate international supervision. Since these fuel rods also contained clues to the history of North Korea's nuclear program, the United Nations began discussing sanctions against Pyongyang. There was even talk of military reprisals, though most experts recognized the futility of any such action.

In June 1994, as the UN was debating sanctions, former U.S. President Jimmy Carter visited Kim Il Sung in Pyongyang. Though he was acting in a private capacity, Carter had the blessing of the Clinton administration as he tried to cut through the diplomatic tangle. After four days of meetings, Carter announced that the North Koreans had agreed to freeze their nuclear program and to negotiate with the United States and the IAEA. North Korea wanted an agreement that would replace its Chernobyl-type reactors that produce high levels of plutonium, with safer, light-water reactors that produce less plutonium. North Korea also proposed a summit meeting between the presidents of North and South Korea.

It was just at that moment that Kim Il Sung died. The summit was canceled, and many wondered if the deal brokered by Carter likewise was off. However, the North Koreans returned to the bargaining table in August, and on October 21, after much give-and-take, an agreement was signed in Geneva. It provided for freezing the North Korean nuclear program, dismantling the existing reactors and ceasing new construction, removal of spent fuel rods to a third country for storage, and international financing for a conversion to

The Great Leader is gone. *Residents of Seoul, South Korea, read about the death of North Korean leader Kim Il Sung, who passed away in July. Kim, who was known as the Great Leader, had been in power for well over 40 years.*

light-water reactor technology for two 1,000-megawatt electrical generating plants by 2003. North Korea agreed to remain in the NPT and, over time, to allow inspections by the IAEA of all its nuclear installations, including the two waste dumps.

Tensions rose again in mid-December when a U.S. Army helicopter strayed into North Korea and was shot down. One of the two pilots was killed in the crash, and the other was held captive for nearly two weeks.

Troubled Economy. North Korea continued to suffer from the loss of its partners in the former socialist bloc. Commodity shortages crippled the economy, agricultural production fell because fuel was scarce, and there were reports of food protests and illegal emigration into Manchuria by hungry people. Late in the summer there was an outbreak of cholera. Analysts expected the gross national product to decrease in 1994 for the fourth consecutive year. Despite these trends, the Supreme People's Assembly approved a budget of $18.87 billion, of which 27.4 percent was earmarked for the military.

SOUTH KOREA

In the second year of Kim Young Sam's presidency, South Korea continued in reform mode with an anticorruption campaign, a purge of top generals associated with previous military regimes, and discipline for business conglomerates. The ruling Democratic Liberal Party was riven by factions that differed mainly in their degree of support for the president. In the fall Kim tried to mend fences with former President Roh Tae Woo and his faction. Perhaps the most dramatic sign of this was the amnesty for Park Chol On, Kim's former rival within the party, who was in prison for corruption.

The opposition Democratic Party remained weakened by the retirement of its major figure, Kim Dae Jung, and by the inability of his successor, Lee Ki Taek, to rally mass support. Even the governmental refusal to amend the controversial National Security Law failed to ignite an effective opposition in the national legislature. In the streets there were demonstrations over issues like trade and reunification, but most citizens were put off by the sharp leftward tilt of Hanchongnyon, the radi-

235

cal student organization whose Jusapa faction openly drew its inspiration from the ideology of North Korean leader Kim Il Sung.

At the beginning of 1994, South Korea's gross national product stood at $328.7 billion, 3.6 percent of which went for military spending. The economy grew at a rate of 8.5 percent in the first half of 1994, continuing a strong recovery led by sharp rises in exports and investment in plants and equipment and exceeding the rise in consumer prices. The currency remained stable, energy prices dropped, and the rising yen drew business to South Korea from Japan. Electronics exports exceeded $30 billion, one-third of which in-

Threatened again. *The emir of Kuwait (right) looks on as his country's chief of staff, General Ali Momin, points to deployed Kuwaiti troops in October. The massing of tens of thousands of Iraqi troops near the border once again raised war alarms in the region.*

volved semiconductors. Unemployment fell to 2.4 percent, and there was a dramatic drop in labor conflict.

See STATISTICS OF THE WORLD. D.N.C.

KUWAIT. In mid-October 1994, Iraqi President Saddam Hussein amassed up to 80,000 troops along the UN-demarcated Kuwaiti-Iraqi border. As the United States and other countries responded by sending in massive numbers of troops, Iraq initiated a pullback of its forces. On November 10, Iraq announced that it would recognize Kuwait's independence and its current borders.

A cabinet reorganization in April resulted in a more liberal government. Two Islamists lost their posts, leaving only one Muslim conservative in the cabinet, and a liberal member of Parliament, Abdel-Mohsen al-Mudej, became oil minister. Al-Sabah family members continued to hold the defense, interior, and foreign affairs portfolios. In May a law extending citizenship rights to the sons of naturalized citizens increased the number of eligible voters from 81,000 to approximately 140,000.

The government began legal action in Britain against officials of the Kuwait Investment Office, for fraud and/or mismanagement related to KIO activities in England and Spain. The KIO announced a payments plan for creditors of its Grupo Torras in Spain, which the fraud and/or mismanagement had forced into bankruptcy in 1992. Although the Kuwaiti Parliament had repealed in January 1994 the 1990 immunity covering government officials, the Constitutional Court delayed the trial of former Oil Minister Ali al-Khalifah al-Sabah and others for the embezzlement of some $200 million from the state-run Kuwait Oil Tankers Company.

The government sought to liberalize the economy by privatizing government-owned businesses and legalizing foreign investment. The 1993-1994 fiscal year ended in June with a deficit of $4.1 billion. The deficit projected for 1994-1995 was $5.9 billion.

In May six of those accused in the 1993 plot to assassinate former U.S. President George Bush were sentenced to death by hanging. Seven others received prison sentences, and one person was acquitted.

See STATISTICS OF THE WORLD. C.H.A.

KYRGYZSTAN. Kyrgyzstan's reputation as Central Asia's most democratic country was somewhat tarnished in 1994 as a result of official assaults on freedom of information and a prolonged power struggle between President Askar Akayev and the national legislature, which the president blasted as an irresponsible Soviet-era relic for its opposition to his plans for rapid introduction of a market economy. The political atmosphere in Kyrgyzstan was heavily influenced by the worsening economic situation: By the middle of 1994 many industrial enterprises had either closed or were working at a fraction of their capacity, unemployment was spreading, and there was not an adequate social safety net to counter the impoverishment of the population. Foreign donors offered loans and other forms of assistance in tribute to Akayev's efforts to modernize and Westernize Kyrgyzstan, but these could not offset the effects of post-Soviet economic collapse.

In May journalists in Kyrgyzstan asserted that a new law on state secrets that prohibited discussion in the media of topics such as price increases, livestock deaths, and the condition of roads was tantamount to the restoration of censorship. The same charge was raised in July after Akayev told a gathering of legal officials that much of the information media in Kyrgyzstan was irresponsible in its reporting and was stirring up political and interethnic conflicts. Shortly thereafter a court in the capital city of Bishkek closed down the pro-Communist parliamentary daily. More than half of the Supreme Soviet deputies then refused to attend a final session of the legislature to set a date for a parliamentary election. The government resigned in a show of support for Akayev, on the grounds that the legislature that had appointed it had gone out of existence. The president set an election date of February 5 and warned that the political turmoil in Kyrgyzstan would only benefit the increasingly popular Kyrgyz Communist Party.

See STATISTICS OF THE WORLD.   B.A.B.

L

LABOR UNIONS. In 1994, U.S. organized labor received a boost from a court decision mandating union participation in workplace productivity groups. Less rosy was the exportation of some 20,000 jobs as the North American Free Trade Agreement (Nafta) took effect. Also of note were strikes—settled fairly quickly—that were conducted by the Teamsters and the United Auto Workers.

Legislative Issues. Organized labor's lobbying on behalf of a workplace fairness bill, intended to prevent employers from permanently replacing strikers, was blocked by a Senate filibuster for the second time (the first time was in 1992). On two tries, July 12 and July 13, 1994, the measure received 53 votes, seven short of the 60 needed to shut off debate and allow a vote on the bill.

Legal Issues. The January 21 vote of the workers at Electromation Inc. to keep Teamsters Local 364 as their bargaining representative, spurning a bid to decertify the union, was the most recent episode in a major legal dispute concerning the use of labor-management committees. In 1992 the National Labor Relations Board (NLRB) ruled that the "action committees" that Electromation management had earlier set up to blunt organizing drives were illegal "company unions." In September 1994 the U.S. Court of Appeals for the Seventh Circuit upheld the NLRB's ruling. As a result of the Electromation decisions, and a 1993 case in which the NLRB ruled that E. I. Du Pont De Nemours & Company could not exclude a union from management-led employee groups, the board sought to determine what employer actions on workplace labor-management committees to foster productivity would be acceptable under the National Labor Relations Act.

International Developments. Soon after Nafta went into effect in January, job losses or-

fected by the shift of production to Mexico or Canada. Of these, 10,345 workers were eligible for expanded benefits and training. Figures released by Secretary of Commerce Ron Brown in August showed that the U.S. trade surplus with Mexico shrank by a third in the first six months of 1994 from a year earlier, indicating a net loss of 20,000 U.S. jobs.

With the completion of the Uruguay Round of the General Agreement on Tariffs and Trade (GATT) negotiations in December 1993, the AFL-CIO urged Congress not to approve the resulting 22,000-page multilateral accord without assurances that a process would be established to ensure worker rights. In August the AFL-CIO urged Congress to reject the implementing legislation for the GATT pact, but Congress approved it following the November elections.

Membership Growth. The Federal Bureau of Labor Statistics (BLS) reported that union membership grew by 208,000 in 1993, to 16.6 million members, the first increase in 14 years. The bulk of the gain was in the public sector, where union rolls grew to 7 million in 1993 from 6.7 million in 1992. Overall, the proportion of union members remained at 15.8 percent, as wage earner employment increased by 1.4 million to 105.1 million. Some 9.6 million union members were in the private sector, constituting 11.2 percent of private sector employment, while 7 million were government employees, representing 37.7 percent of public sector employment. Union members made up 32.9 percent of employment in communications and public utilities, 28.7 percent in transportation, 20 percent in construction, and 19.2 percent in manufacturing. The BLS data also showed that the union advantage over nonunion workers in weekly earnings expanded to 35 percent in 1993 from 32 percent in 1992.

Collective Bargaining. Private sector collective bargaining settlements in the third quarter of 1994 specified wage increases averaging 0.9 percent in the first year of the agreements and 1.9 percent annually over the term of the contracts. Corresponding wage increases they replaced (which were primarily negotiated in 1991) were 2.6 percent and 2.8 percent. As of September 30, 1994, lump-sum provisions

Give us a break. *Members of United Automobile Workers Local 599 walk the picket line at GM's Buick City complex in Flint, MI, in September. They claimed that the company had dangerously stepped up the pace of production and was resisting hiring new permanent workers to lighten the load. Faced with losing sales, GM gave in within days.*

ganized labor had feared would follow were quick in coming. In Logansport, IN, 300 members of the United Paperworkers Local 7688 were notified that their jobs would be eliminated, as the White-Rodgers division of Emerson Electric Company moved its plant and jobs to Juarez, Mexico. On January 10, 136 workers of Nintendo of America in Redmond, WA, were given pink slips, as the company announced it was opening assembly operations in Mexico. The Department of Labor's Office of Trade Adjustment Assistance reported that between January 1 and September 30 it had received requests for assistance from over 20,000 workers whose jobs were adversely af-

covered 42 percent of the 5.4 million workers under major collective bargaining contracts in private industry, up from 39 percent at the end of 1993. Also as of September 30, cost-of-living provisions covered 24 percent of the 5.4 million workers under major collective bargaining contracts, the same percentage as at the end of 1993.

When the $5 billion employee buyout bid for United Airlines, negotiated in late 1993, was ratified by the Air Line Pilots Association and the International Association of Machinists in January 1994, and subsequently ratified by the United stockholders later in the spring, United became the nation's largest employee-owned company, with majority ownership by the carrier's participating 60,000 workers. Because of a drop in the price of United stock, the agreement was renegotiated in May, with the union members' equity share in the airline rising to 55 percent, from 53 percent. On July 12, United shareholders voted overwhelmingly to accept the buyout package.

Strikes. On April 6, 70,000 Teamsters, responding to a management proposal to use some lower-paid part-time workers, struck Trucking Management Inc. (TMI), the bargaining group representing 27 employers. Five major employers defected from the group, opting to continue operating and accept whatever the settlement turned out to be. After 24 days on the picket lines, the Teamsters reached agreement with TMI on a national freight contract. The agreement called for wage increases of $3.20 an hour over the four-year term, binding arbitration of deadlocked grievances, and a longer period for new hires to reach full wages. In return, the companies agreed to drop their demand for the $9-an-hour part-timers to do 24 percent of the work handled by full-time workers.

In a dispute over staff size and workloads, some 12,000 United Auto Workers members walked off their jobs at General Motors' Buick City complex in Flint, MI, on September 27. The strike almost immediately shut down production at two other GM plants and led to other shutdowns. A key issue was GM's reluctance to hire new permanent employees. When faced with lost sales, GM capitulated within days. The agreement required the company to hire 750 new workers and to implement an ergonomics program to curb repetitive trauma injuries.   G.B.Ha.

LAOS.   Although Laos remained the poorest of the Southeast Asian nations, its economic situation improved during 1994 as the country made further progress toward a market-oriented economy. Inflation was low, and the exchange rate was stable. The rate of economic growth was said to be 7 percent. Garment exports overtook electricity and timber as the

Drivers take a walk. A crowd of striking Teamsters cheers on their union president, Ron Carey, at a rally in Woburn, MA, in April. The strike, which lasted more than three weeks, was the longest ever staged by the International Brotherhood of Teamsters against the national trucking industry.

Special span. *Tens of thousands of people gather in April for the opening of the Friendship Bridge, the first road link over the Mekong River, which forms the border between Laos and Thailand.*

major earner of foreign currency. In November, in the first joint venture between the government and the private sector, Laos received a loan from the Asian Development Bank for a hydroelectric project expected to double the country's earnings from the export of electricity to Thailand. Growth effects, however, were concentrated in the towns, particularly Vientiane, increasing the economic gap between urban and rural areas.

In April the Friendship Bridge, the first land link between Laos and Thailand, was opened.

The bridge, which crosses the Mekong River, was constructed with aid from Australia. Although there was only limited traffic crossing the bridge in the succeeding months, it offered the promise of an increase in commercial interchange.

Laos remained an active observer in the Association of Southeast Asian Nations (Asean) during 1994. Although they expressed ambivalence about full membership (because of the expense involved and because of their weakness in English, Asean's language of communication), Lao authorities appeared likely to apply for full membership at the same time Vietnam did, to avoid being left behind in the regional development process.

Laos retained close links with Vietnam in 1994, though it was no longer dominated by its larger neighbor. Relations with China remained amicable. Lao-U.S. relations were cordial, with Laos cooperating in the search for remains of Americans who had crashed in remote areas of Laos during the Vietnam War, and the United States responding with humanitarian assistance.

See STATISTICS OF THE WORLD. J.J.Z.

LATVIA. After 11 months in office, the centrist government of Prime Minister Valdis Birkavs (Latvia's Way) resigned in July 1994 following the withdrawal of the Latvian Farmers' Union from the ruling coalition. After attempts by the right-wing Latvian National Independence Movement to organize a new cabinet failed, President Guntis Ulmanis turned again to Latvia's Way, and former Reforms Minister Maris Gailis finally formed a government, which showed much continuity with the Birkavs one. The Gailis government, like its predecessor, was dependent on the votes of noncoalition members. In municipal elections, which were held in May, the opposition parties captured control of Riga and other major cities.

In June the Latvian Parliament passed a long-awaited citizenship law. Public opinion was very divided on this issue and reflected a deep sense of demographic vulnerability among Latvians who had seen the forcible change of their country's ethnic composition under Soviet rule. The law included a controversial quota system for the naturalization of new citizens. Reacting to Western criticism, Ulmanis appealed to Parliament to soften the quota provisions, and largely for foreign policy reasons the legislature agreed to do so. Adopted in July, the final version of the law received the approval of the Council of Europe, although Moscow predictably continued to voice objections.

On April 30, Latvia and Russia signed agreements calling for the withdrawal of Russian troops from Latvia by August 31, establishing Russia's right to operate a radar station at Skrunda for four years, followed by dismantlement over 18 months, and providing for residence rights for more than 22,000 retired Russian military officers and their families living in Latvia. Despite opposition by conservatives, Parliament ratified the agreements in November. Latvia also pursued an active diplomacy with the West, especially seeking closer ties with the European Union and NATO.

See STATISTICS OF THE WORLD.　　　T.U.R.

LEBANON. Internal political squabbles and continued friction with Israel, along with ambitious plans to rebuild war-torn Beirut, dominated 1994's events in Lebanon.

In May, Prime Minister Rafiq al-Hariri, a Sunni Muslim, stepped down from office for a day to protest the stand taken by Maronite Christian President Elias Hrawi and Parliament Speaker Nabih Berri, a Shiite Muslim, against his proposal to reshuffle the cabinet. The crisis ended within days, with mediation by Syria's President Hafez al-Assad. In December, however, Hariri declared his resignation over a cabinet dispute. Hrawi rejected the resignation; Hariri withdrew it after Syria intervened once more.

The Lebanese Forces, the chief Christian militia in Lebanon's civil war of 1975-1990, was outlawed on March 23. Operating as a political party since militias laid down their arms in 1991 under terms ending the civil war, it was held responsible for the February bombing of a packed Maronite cathedral in which ten lives were lost. On June 13, Samir Geagea, its leader, was indicted on charges of ordering the terrorist act. To prevent the fanning of sectarian animosity, the government concurrently banned political broadcasts by radio and television stations not under government control.

Plans to rebuild the commercial district of Beirut got under way in 1994. Solidere, a $1.8 billion company created for that purpose by Parliament, announced on January 12 that, after offering shares for public purchase, it had attracted some 20,000 investors, raising $926 million rather than the targeted $650 million. Indicators for 1993 signaling strong economic recovery also sparked optimism in 1994. The gross domestic product grew by an estimated 8 percent in 1993 compared with 4 percent in 1992. Per capita GDP grew by about 4.5 percent, and inflation, measured by the consumer price index, fell dramatically: at 116 percent in 1992, it was down to 17.6 percent in 1993.

Demonstrative funeral. *In a procession in a Beirut suburb in June, angry mourners carry the coffins of guerrillas who were killed during an Israeli air raid in Lebanon's Bekaa Valley. The raid was one of Israel's heaviest in years against the Lebanon-based Hezbollah (Party of God) forces.*

Caught in the cross fire. *A Liberian refugee family crosses the Cavally River into the Ivory Coast in October. Fighting between rival militias continued to plague the Liberian populace in 1994.*

Intermittent military clashes took place throughout the year between Israel and Iranian-backed Hezbollah (Party of God), a militant Shiite Muslim group. Though concentrated in Israel's self-declared security zone along Lebanon's southern border, the clashes spilled over into southern Lebanon through Israeli air attacks and into northern Israel through Hezbollah rocket barrages. The United States called on Lebanon, Syria, and Israel to defuse the violence and prevent further damage to the stalled Middle East peace talks.

Responding in part to the July 25 termination of a state of war between Jordan and Israel, in mid-August, Foreign Minister Faris Bouez announced that a breakthrough in Lebanese peace talks with Israel might well take place within months.

For that to happen, however, Lebanon, following a policy of coordination with Syria, insisted that Israel first end its occupation in southern Lebanon or provide a timetable for withdrawal. Israel, in its turn, refused to withdraw from the area in question unless Syria pulled its 40,000 troops out of Lebanon and until the Lebanese government prevented Hezbollah and other militant groups in Lebanon from resisting the Israeli occupation.

See STATISTICS OF THE WORLD. J.A.P.

LESOTHO. *See* AFRICA; STATISTICS OF THE WORLD.

LIBERIA. High hopes for peace fostered by the 1993 Cotonou Accords dimmed in 1994 with the resumption of fighting among Liberia's warring factions and the abandonment of proposed elections for a national unity government. The pace of disarmament called for by the accords had lagged from the beginning; this was because of wrangling over the composition of the civilian Ruling Council that was to govern Liberia until the elections and because of the slow pace of efforts to reduce Nigerian domination of Ecomog, the Economic Community of West African States Monitoring Group. However, on March 7, the new five-member council, with representatives from each of the three main factions—Charles Taylor's National Patriotic Front of Liberia (NPFL), the outgoing interim government, and the United Liberation Movement for Democracy (Ulimo)—assumed executive authority. A reconstituted, more neutral Ecomog force began deployment outside Monrovia. Disarmament got under way soon thereafter.

The disarmament process was cut short when the occasional violence that had followed the 1993 cease-fire gave way to open warfare in a number of places. From mid-March through May factions within Ulimo fought each other in the western area of Liberia; further violence left some 50 people dead in two border villages in June. In the southeast a new faction, the Liberian Peace Council, composed largely of veterans of former President Samuel K. Doe's army, took control of the area around Greenville. By midsummer it was threatening Gbarnga, the NPFL stronghold. In September, after the original deadline for elections had come and gone, Ghanaian President Jerry Rawlings helped broker an agreement among the three main factions for elections by October 1995. Even while the accord was being negotiated, Gbarnga was overrun by a number of rival militias. Rawlings persuaded the various factions to resume peace talks, and on December 21 they signed a peace agreement. A ceasefire went into effect on December 28.

See STATISTICS OF THE WORLD.   G.H.L.

LIBRARIES. New technology and funding problems were two big issues confronting U.S. libraries in 1994.

Information Superhighway. The most exciting government initiative affecting libraries in the United States in 1994 was the establishment by the administration of President Bill Clinton of a 27-member National Information Infrastructure (NII) Advisory Council under the aegis of the Commerce Department. It was charged with formulating policies to guide development of the "information superhighway," a concept supported by U.S. Vice President Al Gore, among others.

The council included one library educator, Toni Carbo Bearman, and one schoolteacher, but it was dominated by representatives from government and the communications and computer industries, a fact that disquieted many librarians. Bearman voiced concern that NII enthusiasts tended to focus more on technology than on the users, and she vowed to persuade the council to consider how best to bring people and information together.

Meanwhile, libraries were exploiting the government-subsidized Internet, an ever-expanding super network with hundreds of computer databases offering information on almost any imaginable subject. The state library system in Maryland announced a plan to provide free Internet access, from either home or public library computer, to every state resident. Long strides toward this goal had already been taken by fall.

Another dramatic technological development was the North Carolina Information Highway, a statewide fiber-optic network set up and owned by a group of telephone companies, which was intended to ultimately link 3,400 sites, including hundreds of libraries. By October more than 100 sites were on-line. In July, at an international economic summit meeting, President Clinton proposed creation of a global system to link major libraries electronically, facilitating the flow of information across borders.

The Clinton administration's high valuation on technology was reflected in its fiscal 1995 budget request, which included strong funding for NII-related projects—many of which would benefit libraries. At the same time, however, the budget reduced or eliminated funding for more traditional library needs such as construction, staffing, reading materials, and literacy programs. Senator Paul Simon (D, Illi-

Searching in All the Wrong Places

It was a quiet April afternoon at the Central Library in Fort Worth, TX. Suddenly more than 500 people burst in, screaming, "Where's fiction?" The crowd tore through the books and tossed them on the floor in a wild search for—what? Had John Grisham come out with a new page-turner? Was an unpublished Charles Dickens screed stashed in the stacks?

No, the marauders were hunting for money. A radio station had placed $5 and $10 bills in books in the fiction section. KYNG-FM reps said the money totaled $100 and that a handful of people were expected to go after it (the station was encouraging use of the library, they said). But rumor made the sum $10,000—and only a librarian's announcement that the money had been found stopped the carnage.

And carnage it was. Thousands of books were damaged or ruined. Radio station executives gave $10,000 to the library and agreed to pay for the damage resulting from the melee, which gave new meaning to the term "cracking the books."

nois), a strong library supporter, warned that if public libraries, offering access to all, were not included as an integral part of the superhighway from the start, it would bypass many Americans.

Money Issues. Even as technological programs flourished, library operating budgets in many areas were stretched thin. Beset for years by budget cuts and by natural and human disasters, California libraries continued to suffer; some school libraries were virtually eliminated. Librarians in many other states also struggled with financial problems. However, a *Library Journal* survey, reported in June, disclosed that 75 percent of American referenda for public library capital improvements had passed in fiscal year 1992-1993, although less money was requested than in previous years. Governor Mario Cuomo allocated $81.3 million for New York's libraries, the largest amount for library aid in the history of that state and substantially more than its librar-

ians had anticipated. In New York City, fashion designer Bill Blass gave the public library system $10 million, one of its largest gifts ever. **American Library Association.** Elizabeth Martinez, formerly the Los Angeles Public Library director, was appointed to the executive directorship of the American Library Association. Also at ALA, a three-year demonstration project entitled Born to Read was announced. Proposed by ALA's Association for Library Service to Children, funded by a $560,000 grant from the Prudential Foundation, and graced by first lady Hillary Rodham Clinton as honorary chair, the project was to establish "five model partnerships between libraries and health care providers designed to reach out to at-risk parents-to-be to help them raise children to have healthy minds and bodies." M.G.B.

LIBYA. In 1994 rifts among Libya's leadership led to significant changes. In September, Abdul Salam Jallud, the second in command, was put under house arrest and had his pass-

Desert display. *Libyan pilgrims in Egypt brandish posters of Libyan leader Muammar al-Qaddafi in May. Their camel caravan had been organized to protest UN sanctions against Libya stemming from that country's refusal to surrender two men accused of organizing the 1988 bombing of Pan Am flight 103 over Lockerbie, Scotland.*

port removed over differences with Libyan leader Muammar al-Qaddafi. Also arrested was Major Umar al-Hariri, one of the top officers closest to Qaddafi. In February the secretary-general of the General People's Congress was replaced, as were seven other members of the Congress's secretariat. The director of national security was also replaced.

On February 3 the International Court of Justice, the judicial arm of the United Nations, rejected Libya's claims to the Aozou Strip in northern Chad. At the UN's request Libya pulled its troops out of the region at the end of May. On June 5, Libya and Chad signed a friendship and cooperation treaty.

France was unsuccessful in its continuing efforts to obtain the extradition of four Libyan suspects in the bombing of a French UTA airliner over Niger in 1989.

President Hosni Mubarak of Egypt continued to mediate between the Western powers and Libya over UN sanctions imposed over Libya's role in the 1988 bombing of Pan Am flight 103 over Lockerbie, Scotland, and over Libya's refusal to extradite suspects in the bombing. Little progress was made in the negotiations.

The UN sanctions, first imposed in 1992, were tightened in December 1993, and the new sanctions were fully implemented in 1994. Libyan assets abroad were frozen, and the supply of goods and services to the local aviation sector and of certain equipment and technology to the oil and gas industries was banned. Because of the new sanctions, there were major delays in payments to companies that sell goods to Libya.

Foreign fuel companies continued to do business in Libya in 1994. In April it was reported that a Belgium-led consortium had struck oil in an onshore field. In addition, new agreements involving oil exploration and development were signed with a number of European and Canadian companies, including an agreement late in 1993 with Italy's Agip and another in October 1994 with a group that included Spain's Repsol, Austria's OMV, and France's Total.

See STATISTICS OF THE WORLD.   M.J.D.

LIECHTENSTEIN. *See* STATISTICS OF THE WORLD.

LIFE SCIENCES. *See* BIOLOGY; HEALTH AND MEDICINE.

LITERATURE. Several notable new works by established authors appeared in 1994, but the two most eagerly anticipated American books, one by Cormac McCarthy and the other by Henry Roth, disappointed many critics. Japan's Kenzaburo Oe won the Nobel Prize. The golden age of children's picture books continued.

AMERICAN

Older writers, the pros of prose, had a good year in 1994. Grace Paley published her wry, ear-perfect short stories about New Yorkers, feminism, and radicals in *The Collected Stories;* Peter Taylor, smooth as sipping whisky, produced *In the Tennessee Country,* a novel about the disappearance of a cousin just after the Civil War. And, with hoopla and amidst cautious critical approval, Joseph Heller brought out *Closing Time,* a wistful sequel of sorts to that certified comic masterpiece, *Catch-22.*

Best Literary Works. The two best literary works of the year came from a semilegendary novelist and a dead poet: William Gaddis, author of *The Recognitions* and *JR,* published his funniest and most accessible novel, *A Frolic of His Own,* and Robert Giroux collected a fat volume of the letters of Elizabeth Bishop. Told almost entirely in dialogue, Gaddis's book takes on the law and its abuses. "Justice?— You get justice in the next world, in this world you have the law." The action focuses on the Crease family—Oscar, a professor, who is suing a movie company for stealing the idea of his play *Once at Antietam;* his father, an elderly judge, who must adjudicate a bizarre case involving a dog trapped in a piece of modern sculpture; and his shrewd, kind sister, who is married to an overworked Manhattan attorney. Around them flutter various socialites and sluts, shysters and salesmen. The result is a satirical masterpiece about the way we live now.

During her lifetime Elizabeth Bishop dwelt in the shadow of her friend the poet Robert Lowell. But no more. This "minor female Wordsworth"—her description of herself—has emerged in recent years as the most admired poet of her generation. *One Art* reveals the woman behind the poet—prey to melancholy and alcohol, long resident in Brazil with her beloved Lota Soares, in correspondence with Lowell, Marianne Moore, Randall Jarrell, James Merrill, and a host of others. Witty and gossipy, the letters also show us a woman who reads constantly, everyone from the Venerable Bede to Susan Sontag. Bishop may have called herself the loneliest person in the world, but her letters prove that she made excellent company.

New Works by Old Masters. No year is complete without critical divisiveness. The most anticipated novel of 1994 was clearly Cormac McCarthy's *The Crossing,* the second volume of *The Border Trilogy.* Its predecessor, *All the Pretty Horses,* had won major awards and been acclaimed an American masterpiece, worthy of the same shelf as *Huckleberry Finn.* So expectations ran high. One or two reviewers called the book another triumph, but most felt it reworked *Pretty Horses* territory—a boy rides south into Mexico where he must face up to life and death—in a style that could shift suddenly from the quicksilver beautiful to the long-winded and overly baroque.

But there was one book that was even

longer awaited than McCarthy's: After 60 years of literary silence, Henry Roth, author of the revered *Call It Sleep,* brought out the first volume of a multipart novel. *Mercy of a Rude Stream,* the general title, reads like fictionalized autobiography and continues the exploration of a childhood among immigrant New York Jews. Most of the notices of the book were respectful, if unenthusiastic, and several reviewers used the new novel mainly to point to the excellence of the old one.

Other Fiction. Respectful reviews also accompanied John Irving's *A Son of the Circus,* set in India and Canada. Harold Brodkey's second novel, *Profane Friendship,* about a couple of young men in Venice, explored sexuality in fine writing; it gathered more favorable notice than did his monumental *The Runaway Soul.* Tim O'Brien's *In the Lake of the Woods* continued his exploration of Vietnam and its legacy, this time in a mystery about a middle-aged man's war guilt that may have led him to murder his wife. Jayne Anne Phillips's *Shelter* uses a children's summer camp to investigate the nature of human evil. In *Brazil,* John Updike created a magical-realist version of the Tristan and Isolde story while also in-

Poets in the news. The publication of a collection of her letters provided new insights into the life of Elizabeth Bishop (right), who died in 1979. The 1994 Pulitzer Prize for poetry went to Yusef Komunyakaa (below) for his Neon Vernacular.

corporating a good deal of Brazilian history. It was, for all its beauties, a bit artificial.

There were times in 1994 when it seemed that every other book was about old New York, with two becoming critical and popular successes. E. L. Doctorow's *The Waterworks,* set in 1871, is a kind of gothicky thriller, complete with the apparently resurrected dead and a mysterious Dr. Sartorius. Doctorow, it was observed, seems to be writing a fictional history of New York City in his novels (*Ragtime, Billy Bathgate,* and so on). Perhaps even greater success attended Caleb Carr's similarly spooky *The Alienist,* also set in 19th-century Gotham, about a serial killer hunted by a journalist and an "alienist," a specialist in mental diseases.

Other historical fictions also did well in 1994. Howard Norman's *The Bird Artist,* set in a remote village in 1911 Canada, explores the consequences when a young man kills his mother's lover. Thomas Mallon's *Henry and Clara* is the tragic story, based on fact, of the couple who sat with Lincoln in his box at Ford's Theater on the night he was assassinated. It takes up "survivor trauma" and guilt and the breakdown of a marriage. In a lighter vein, Paul Auster's *Mr. Vertigo* offers a magical-realist tale about a young boy and a master magician who work the 1920s carnival circuit. It opens strikingly: "I was 12 years old when I first walked on water."

Among middle-career novelists there were several disappointments in 1994. Nicholson Baker's *The Fermata,* about a sex-obsessed nerd who can stop time, was largely dismissed as semipornographic, without the wit of his steamy *Vox* or his astonishing debut, *The Mezzanine.* John Crowley, perhaps the most highly regarded fantasy writer of his generation, brought out *Love and Sleep,* the second installment in his *Aegypt* sequence, an exploration of the strangeness of history. Most readers felt the book was somewhat diffuse, a perennial defect of midsequence novels. William T. Vollmann's *The Rifles,* the third published volume in a seven-part series about early North America, showed again this author's range and industry; critics have acclaimed Vollmann a master, but readers did not quite know what to make of this prolific young author whose contemporary novels seem unsavory in their subject matter (skinheads, prostitutes) and whose historical novels, like this one, simply seem to lumber about.

Several short-story collections published in 1994 deserved mention: John Updike's *The Afterlife,* offering his usual range and finesse; Ellen Currie's *Moses Supposes,* filled with seriocomic tales of Irish-American families; T. Coraghessan Boyle's often zany *Without a Hero;* Alison Lurie's devilishly witty *Women and Ghosts;* and *Thirteen Uncollected Stories* by John Cheever, showing this American master at the start of his remarkable career.

Poetry. In poetry, outstanding volumes included Jorie Graham's philosophical *Materialism;* Mary Jo Salter's ingratiating *Sunday Skaters;* Richard Howard's elegant elegies, *Like Most Revelations,* for his friends dead of cancer or AIDS; John Ashbery's whimsical and surreal *And the Stars Were Shining;* the amazingly fertile Kenneth Koch's funny and ingenious *One Train;* Rodney Jones's visceral *Apocalyptic Narrative;* Carolyn Forche's grim *The Angel of History;* and Charles Simic's raindrop-clear and magical *A Wedding in Hell.* James Tate's witty *The Worshipful Company of Fletchers* received the National Book Award.

Particular favorites included Philip Levine's *The Simple Truth,* poems as clean as Shaker furniture. Levine also brought out a group of autobiographical essays, several about his working-class past, *The Bread of Time.* Sadly, Amy Clampitt died shortly after her fourth book, *A Silence Opens,* reconfirmed the mastery of her first collection, *The Kingfisher,* a book that she had waited to publish until she was 63. A good overview of the year in poetry was provided by *The Best American Poetry 1994,* edited by A. R. Ammons, in consultation with the series editor David Lehman.

Awards. E. Annie Proulx won the 1994 Pulitzer Prize for best fiction for her novel *The Shipping News,* which had previously won the 1993 National Book Award. The Pulitzer for poetry went to Yusef Komunyakaa, a native of Bogalusa, LA, for *Neon Vernacular.* Komunyakaa, a Vietnam veteran, is an associate professor of English at Indiana University.

See BOOK PUBLISHING; PRIZES AND AWARDS.

M.D.

247

Northern lights. *The year saw the appearance of works by two of Canada's most distinguished fiction writers. Robertson Davies (above) scored with his novel* The Cunning Man, *which focuses on three friends' shared lives, and Alice Munro (left) published* Open Secrets, *her eighth collection of short stories.*

CANADIAN

In 1994 established Canadian authors and new writers published impressive works, many of them addressing issues of nationalism, gender, sexuality, race, and class.

Fiction. The appearance of narratives by major writers Robertson Davies, Alice Munro, and Rudy Wiebe and of striking works by newer voices distinguished the year in fiction publishing.

In his novel *The Cunning Man,* which focuses on three friends' shared lives, Davies extended his preoccupations with complex storytelling techniques and with the hidden world of saints and mystics. *Open Secrets* was Munro's eighth collection of short stories. Slices of emotional life, the stories are set mainly in Munro's mythologized small-town reality of Huron County, Ont., and enacted by independent girls and women who in their sufferings, joys, and insights seem a kind of world unto themselves. *A Discovery of Strangers* was Wiebe's eighth novel, his first in over a decade. Here, Wiebe turned away from the

massive historical stage of his fiction of the 1970s and 1980s to a more intimate tragedy of players in a drama of estranged attachments.

Other fiction by well-established Canadian writers included *Bellydancer,* a lesbian-feminist-postmodernist story collection by novelist Sky Lee; W. P. Kinsella's *Brother Frank's Gospel Hour, and Other Stories; The Rain Barrel, and Other Stories* by George Bowering; Anne Cameron's *Wedding Cakes, Rats and Rodeo Queens,* which explores the territory of "cowpunk" love; Roch Carrier's lyrical meditation on life and death *The End,* translated from French by Sheila Fischman; *Life After God* by Douglas Coupland; *Kill All the Lawyers,* the latest in William Deverell's series of novels in the legal thriller, murder mystery genre; Danny Laferrière's *Dining With the Dictator,* a novel about political anarchy in Haiti during the Duvalier regime; and Brian Fawcett's *Gender Wars: A Novel and Some Conversation About Sex and Gender,* a highly controversial parody of heterosexual sexuality and gender politics from a politically incorrect male perspective.

Several important anthologies were published, including *Her Mother's Ashes: Stories by South Asian Women in Canada and the United States,* a short-story and poetry anthology edited by Nurjehan Aziz; Ayanna Black's edition of *Fiery Spirits: Canadian Writers of African Descent;* and *Meanwhile, in Another Part of the Forest,* an anthology of gay literature edited by Alberto Manguel and Craig Stephenson.

Fiction by younger writers included *The Miss Hereford Stories* by Gail Anderson-Dargatz; *Invisible Man at the Window,* a bildungsroman by Monique Proulx, translated from French by Matt Cohen; *Casino, and Other Stories,* Bonnie Burnard's second story collection; *Bad Chemistry,* the third of Nora Kelly's Gillian Adams mysteries; *Civilization,* Paul Quarrington's comic parody of the golden age of Hollywood filmmaking; Pete McCormack's promising first novel, *Shelby;* Paul Tiyambe Zeleza's first collection of short stories, *The Joys of Exile,* set mainly in Africa; Gayla Reid's first story collection *To Be There With You; The Eagles' Brood,* the third in a series of medieval romances by Jack Whyte; Diane Schoemperlen's *In the Language of Love: A Novel in 100 Chapters;* Elizabeth Nickson's *The Monkey Puzzle Tree,* a psychological thriller; and *Funny Boy: A Novel in Six Stories,* a coming-of-age narrative set in Sri Lanka by first-time novelist Shyam Selvadurai.

Poetry. The most remarkable verse published was by seasoned poets George Woodcock, in *The Cherry Tree on Cherry Street;* P. K. Page, in *Hologram: A Book of Glosas;* Al Purdy, in *Naked With Summer in Your Mouth;* Ralph Gustafson, in *Tracks in the Snow;* Anne Hébert, in *Day Has No Equal but Light,* which was translated from French by A. Poulin; and Robin Skelton, in *Briefly Singing: A Gathering of Erotic, Satirical and Other Inscriptions, Epigrams and Lyrics From the Greek and Roman Mediterranean, 800 B.C.-A.D. 1000, Including the Complete Poems of Rufinus.*

Among collections written by younger poets, Evelyn Lau's *In the House of Slaves* was the most accomplished. Other verse of note came from Christopher Dewdney, in *Demon Pond;* Linda Rogers, in *Hard Candy;* Myles K. Blank, in *Fugue;* Anne Campbell, in *Angel Wings Over Water;* Harold Rhenisch, in *Iodine;* Barbara Carey, in *The Ground of Events;* Ethel Harris, in *A Rage of Poppies;* and Joe Rosenblatt, in *Beds & Consenting Dreamers.*

Nonfiction. The year was remarkable for several biographies and memoirs of major writers: *Reinventing Myself,* a memoir by Mavor Moore; *Earle Birney,* Elspeth Cameron's biography of Canada's greatest living poet; Carol Roberts's *Timothy Findley: A Life in Stories;* Judith Skelton Grant's *Robertson Davies: Man of Myth; On the Side of the Angels: The Second Volume of the Journals of Elizabeth Smart,* edited by Alice Van Wart; *This Year in Jerusalem,* Mordecai Richler's autobiography about growing up Jewish in Montréal, with an eye on Israel; and Carol Martin's edition of *Local Colour: Writers Discovering Canada,* a collection of travel reminiscences.

Several important political reflections by literary writers appeared. In *Selling Illusions: The Cult of Multiculturalism in Canada* novelist Neil Bissoondath investigates questions of race, culture, political correctness, and academic freedom. In *Blood and Belonging: Journeys Into the New Nationalism* novelist Michael Ignatieff explores the new nationalisms of emerging cultures and states in the former Soviet Union, in Northern Ireland, and in Québec. In *Lost in America: The Imaginary Canadian in the American Dream* playwright John Gray castigates Canadian culture, politics, and art and psychoanalyzes the subject position of chronically perplexed Canadians.

P.M.St.P.

ENGLISH

Readers of English literature had plenty of meaty material to keep them busy in 1994. Scotsman James Kelman was the controversial winner of the 1994 Booker Prize for his novel *How Late It Was, How Late.* This black comedy used strong language—one critic counted 4,000 expletives—and a heavy Glasgow accent to follow an ex-convict on a two-day drunken spree.

Fiction. A notable trend in 1994 was the preoccupation of British novelists with a wide variety of foreign settings. The Sahara was the scene of Paul Bowles's *Too Far From Home,* which portrayed the fraught relationship between an artist and his discontented sister. Lionel Davidson's *Kolymsky Heights* was a swiftly paced story of action and adventure set mainly in the Siberian Arctic. Victorian Hong Kong offered an unusual location for *The Mountain of Immoderate Desires,* by Leslie Wilson. The background of *Desperadoes* by Joseph O'Connor was 1983 Nicaragua during the civil war, and the book portrayed a couple's desperate quest for their missing son. Michael Dibdin's *Dead Lagoon* offered a disenchanted portrait of present-day Venice.

Possibly the most widely acclaimed novel of the year was *A Change of Climate* by Hilary Mantel. This ranged in time and space between South Africa in the 1950s and rural England 30 years later; the lives and moral dilemmas of the married protagonists were explored with keen but compassionate insight.

Bringing home the Booker. *The awarding of the 1994 Booker Prize to Scotsman James Kelman was both hailed and attacked. His prizewinning novel,* How Late It Was, How Late, *used both strong language and a heavy Glasgow accent in relating the comic adventures of an ex-convict.*

In a bleak yet deeply moving novel, *Felicia's Journeys,* William Trevor followed the misfortunes of a young Irish girl as she wanders through the industrial wastelands of England in vain search of the errant father of her unborn child. In David Caute's ingenious *Dr. Orwell and Mr. Blair,* a novel in which George Orwell was a central character, the author skillfully juxtaposed the opposite aspects of his subject's personality—the patrician with the down-and-out plebeian.

Other striking fiction from well-known novelists included *Mothers' Boys* by Margaret Forster and *Lost Children* by Maggie Gee. Both movingly depicted some of the painful intricacies of family relationships. The central figure in Anita Brookner's *A Private View* was a man on the verge of retirement. Brookner surveyed with sympathetic shrewdness her hero's gradual relinquishment of his soberly ordered existence to embark upon the heady delights of a dangerous unknown.

A. S. Byatt's *The Matisse Stories* illustrated the impact upon her characters of the artist's sensuous use of color. The events in *The House of Splendid Isolation* by Edna O'Brien took place in her native Ireland, whose comedies and troubles she portrayed here with characteristic vigor. In *Affliction,* Fay Weldon predictably reexplored her favorite topic, the hapless role of women in marriage, where they are foredoomed to exploitation, deceit, and final abandonment.

Biography. Lyndall Gordon's *Charlotte Brontë: A Passionate Life* offered a substantial and thought-provoking study. The book persuasively replaced the popular image of a gauche, shrinking spinster with a more robust interpretation of a rebel in her own time. In piquant contrast was the heroine of *Mother of Oscar: The Life of Jane Francesca Wilde* by Joy Melville. In her own day and way, as a self-appointed romantic and patriotic poetess, Jane Wilde was as flamboyant and eccentric as her more famous son. Her loyalty to him in his disgrace was unswerving.

Hardy, a self-styled "definitive" biography of Thomas Hardy by Martin Seymour-Smith, contained various acrimonious attacks on past fellow-biographers, and truculence abounded. But there was a generous defense of Hardy's first wife, Emma (though at the expense of his second), and a rewarding survey of his poems.

In *Kenneth Grahame: An Innocent in the Wild Wood,* Alison Prince perceptively related characters and events from *The Wind in the Willows* to various conflicts in the author's own life and personality. Prince made effective use of letters—as, for instance, that describing Grahame's enchanted discovery of the "water-world" during his Oxford school days, or the discomfiting baby talk that revealed the immaturity of his marriage.

There were two new books about Graham Greene. Norman Sherry's *The Life of Graham Greene, 1939-1955* was the second volume of his projected three-volume authorized biography. Surveying such aspects as Greene's compulsive travels, his rashly precipitate pursuit of women, and his addiction to drink and drugs, this portrait took a far more sympathetic view of its subject than did the implacable hostility of Michael Shelden in *Graham Greene: The Man Within.*

Novelist Penelope Lively in *Oleander, Jacaranda: A Childhood Perceived* recaptured with sensuous immediacy the sights, scents, and sounds of her early years. Set in Egypt before and during World War II, this memoir vividly portrayed the social life of the expatriate British community.

Drama. Many of the year's significant productions were not of new plays, but revivals and translations. Among the new dramas was David Edgar's *Citizen Locke,* about the personality and trials of the 17th-century philosopher John Locke as he returned from political exile to pursue his pioneering radical activities at home. Another historical play, *Hated Nightfall* by Howard Barker, was a complex reenactment of the circumstances surrounding the murder of the Romanov royal family in 1918. The play's chief protagonist was Dancer, the family tutor, a volatile, enigmatic character who may have been the family's executioner. The basis for Barker's conjecture was the discovery of two unidentified bodies in the communal grave.

Another chilling but arrestingly original play was *The Skriker* by Caryl Churchill (who recently made a vigorous translation of Seneca's *Thyestes*). The Skriker of her title was a malign embodiment of evil—an ancient crone who could change shape at will in order to wreak mischief upon her unwary victims and lure them to doom in the underworld, with the help of her attendant ghosts, hags, and black dogs. The mythological idea in this cleverly inventive and imaginative play effectively framed the modern urban characters and their setting.

The achievements of three eminent men of the theater—actors John Gielgud and Alec Guiness and playwright Harold Pinter—were celebrated during 1994 in composite tributes from their friends and admirers. The tributes were entitled *Notes From the Gods* and *Sir John: The Many Faces of Gielgud; Alec: A Birthday Present for Alec Guiness;* and *Conversations With Pinter.*   M.W.

WORLD

Collections and anthologies of short stories by international authors introduced a great number of younger writers to English-speaking audiences in 1994. *The Pinch Runner Memorandum,* a novel by the Japanese writer Kenzaburo Oe, was published in English in 1994; Oe received the 1994 Nobel Prize for literature (see PRIZES AND AWARDS). As usual, however, most translations into English came from the works of Spanish and Latin American authors. On the whole, fewer translations of literary works were published in 1994 than was the case in 1993.

Spanish. Reinaldo Arenas's novel *The Assault,* translated by Andrew Hurley, paints a harrowing picture of dehumanization in Fidel Castro's Cuba. Similarly, the main character of Gioconda Belli's *The Inhabited Woman,* translated by Kathleen March, joins an underground movement to fight the injustices of a dictatorship.

The drama of a sexually liberated woman's obsession with an outlaw lover is played out in Sergio Galindo's novel *Otilia's Body,* translated by Carolyn and John Brushwood. Social injustices and political horrors drive the characters in Liliana Heker's collection of six short stories, *The Stolen Party,* translated by Alberto Manguel. Grotesque male and female characters of all ages populate Rima de Vallbona's short-story collection *Flowering Inferno: Tales of Sinking Hearts,* translated by Lillian Lorca de Tagle. Enrique Jaramillo Levi introduces the reader to the irrational side of human existence in his *Duplications and Other Stories,* translated by Leland H. Chambers.

In *Empire of Dreams,* translated by Tess O'Dwyer, the Puerto Rican writer Giannina Braschi speaks of her love affair with New York City. The poetic scene in Mexico comes to life in *Light From a Nearby Window: Contemporary Mexican Poetry,* in which the editor, Juvenal Acosta, presents works of 21 contemporary poets.

Chinese. A new tone in contemporary Chinese writing emerges in Feng Jicai's novel *The Three-inch Golden Lotus,* translated by David Wakefield and portraying the ugly contradiction of foot binding, still practiced in the 20th century. In his novel *Remote Country of Women,* translated by Qingyun Wu and Thomas O. Beebee, Bai Hua challenges conventional evaluations regarding the barbarous versus the civilized in Chinese culture.

Two collections of poems introduced the reader to the maximlike thinking of a great deal of Chinese poetry: Bei Dao's *Forms of Distance,* translated by David Hinton, and Su Tung-Po's *Selected Poems,* translated by Burton Watson.

French. One of the most important publications of 1994 was the comprehensive *Darkness Moves: An Henri Michaux Anthology: 1927-1984,* translated by David Ball. Another highly important 1994 collection, *The Writings of Christine de Pizan,* edited by Charity Cannon Willard, includes nearly all of de Pizan's more than 20 works.

The translator Edouard Roditi published *God's Torment,* a new volume of poetry by Alain Bosquet, a giant of contemporary French literature. The young French novelist Marie Redonnet made her entrance into the English-speaking world with three novels: *Hôtel Splendid, Forever Valley,* and *Rose Mellie Rose.* Cyril Collard meanwhile presented a shocking portrait of reckless youth in the age of AIDS in his novel *Savage Nights,* translated by William Rodarmor; it was also made into an extremely successful movie.

German. Two young writers made their debut in English with a pair of dark novels of contemporary life. Gert Jonke, in *Geometric Regional Novel* (translated by Johannes W.

Vazulik), develops an innovative satire of officialdom's insidious pervasion of society. And in a translation by Peter Tegel, Uwe Timm's novel *Headhunter* portrays a commodities trader who steals millions from clients and then gets caught.

The insightful autobiographical sketches and essays of one of the most prominent 20th-century women writers in German, Else Lasker-Schüler, are collected in *Concert,* translated by Jean M. Snook. The fablelike stories of Johannes Bobrowski (1917-1965) relating the dreary existence of East German life in the 1950s and 1960s were published as *Darkness and a Little Light,* translated by Leila Vennewitz. And the refined and highly imaginative poems of Olly Komenda-Soentgerath were finally introduced to an English-speaking audience in her collection *Under My Eyelids,* translated by Tom Beck.

The Father of a Murderer, written by Alfred Andersch and translated by Leila Vennewitz, was first published posthumously in German in 1980. Portraying a high school instructor who wants to teach a political lesson to German youths and through them settle some accounts with their fathers, this novel was generally considered Andersch's masterpiece.

Italian. Many important women writers who published their stories in newspapers during the 1920s and 1930s are revived in *Unspeakable Women: Selected Short Stories,* translated by Robin Pickering-Iazzi. In these 16 stories, the women react to the self-sacrificing ideal of the "New Woman" of fascism. Included in the collection is Grazia Deledda, who won the Nobel Prize for literature in 1926.

Meanwhile, Umberto Saba, one of Italy's most important poets, finally made his way into English with *The Dark of the Sun: Selected Poems of Umberto Saba.* Translated by Christopher Millis, these works create a vision of the world that moves between suffering and celebration and between sensuality and defeat. The anthology *Italian Landscape Poems,* which was translated by Alistair Elliot, focuses on the concept of *paese,* a term Italians use to mean "my town, my village, the countryside I come from."

Japanese. *The Pinch Runner Memorandum* by Nobel laureate Kenzaburo Oe was trans-

Laureate from Japan. *Novelist Kenzaburo Oe, hailed internationally as one of the most penetrating analysts of postwar Japanese society, was awarded the 1994 Nobel Prize in literature.*

lated into English by Michiko N. Wilson and Michael K. Wilson. The work explores the private and public ramifications of life with Mori, Oe's retarded son.

Another Japanese work, *The Name of the Flower: Stories by Kuniko Mukoda* (translated by Tomone Matsumoto), charts the ordinary life of Japanese families and includes vivid portraits of secret unhappiness and betrayal.

R.S.

BOOKS FOR CHILDREN

In 1994 children's and young adult books continued to flow from publishers in a steady stream, with many excellent new books by established authors, a spate of well-produced reissues of classic works, and an outpouring of fine picture books and nonfiction, especially biography.

Picture Books. The golden age of picture books was in fine form in 1994. Among famous picture book authors, William Steig returned to his magic object theme (exemplified in his works *Sylvester and the Magic Pebble* and *The Amazing Bone)* in *Zeke Pippin.* Zeke, a cheerful young pig, finds and learns to play a harmonica which, unbeknownst to him, puts people to sleep. Deeply offended by his family's sleepy reception to an exhibition of his new skill, he runs away from home and learns that his harmonica is more useful than he thought, and, indeed, it saves his life.

Bernard Waber returned to a favorite hero, Lyle the crocodile, in *Lyle at the Office,* where Lyle spreads more of his usual good cheer and friendliness. The well-known New Zealand author Margaret Mahy joined with illustrator Steven Kellogg in an effervescent story, *The Rattlebang Picnic,* about a large, poor but lively family that drives a rattlebang car and picnics widely, even on a volcano.

Among newer talents, Robert Sabuda produced *The Christmas Alphabet,* a pop-up book extraordinaire, with an elegantly engineered foldout for each letter. *Good Night, Gorilla* by Peggy Rathmann is the gentle story of a kindly zookeeper whose affectionate charges follow him home and attempt to keep him company as he sleeps. And *Don't Fidget a Feather!* by Erica Silverman, illustrated by S. D. Schindler, tells the story of a silly competition between a duck and a gander over which of them is the champion that almost terminates in disaster when a fox comes on the scene.

Fiction. Outstanding new novels for young and intermediate readers were few in 1994. Perhaps most unusual was *Flour Babies* by Anne Fine, in which the hero, Simon, takes part in a class exercise in which he must tend a bag of flour as if it were a baby for several weeks. *The Barn* by Avi is a stark and gritty picture of pioneer life and family solidarity. Three motherless children try to care for their paralyzed father, tend to their farm, and build a barn because the youngest child believes that a barn will give their father the will to live. The outcome is bittersweet and unforgettable.

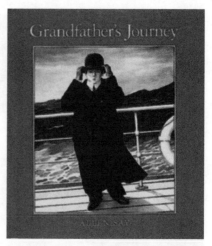

Bicultural heritage. Grandfather's Journey, written and illustrated by Allen Say, won the 1994 Caldecott Medal. The book recounts how the author's grandfather traveled from Japan to the United States and tells of the grandfather's (and the author's) love for both countries.

Among the many excellent retellings and reissues in 1994 was James Thurber's *The Great Quillow,* with the inspired selection of Steven Kellogg as illustrator. The story of a town besieged by a giant who is outwitted by a clever toymaker, *The Great Quillow* displays Thurber's legendary whimsical charm. Another splendid reissue was Dickens's *Oliver Twist,* with newly discovered illustrations by the late Don Freeman.

Fiction for Young Adults. Young adult fiction took on some interesting twists and explored some new contemporary themes. Chris Lynch, a new young adult author clearly of the genre of Robert Cormier, explored young lives lived seemingly without hope or redemption. His powerful novel *Iceman* tells of Eric, whose only way of expressing his feelings is in violent confrontations while playing ice hockey. *Am I Blue?: Coming Out From the Silence,* edited by Marion Dane Bauer, is an outstanding collection of original stories by well-known authors about young people becoming aware of and declaring their homosexuality.

Peter Dickinson embarked on a new subject in *Shadow of a Hero,* a political novel about the attempted restoration of a small, imaginary Balkan state swallowed up by the convulsions of the 20th century. In alternating chapters of myth and realism, Dickinson convinces the reader of the existence of the country of Varina and of its ongoing struggle. The historical novel took a new and realistic direction in *Catherine, Called Birdy* by Karen Cushman. Set in the 13th century, the book pulls no punches in describing the squalor of medieval life and the thoughtful, rebellious 14-year-old heroine who has no illusions as to what the future holds for her.

Nonfiction. Biography was the bright star of children's literature in 1994. Russell Freedman introduced, in a polished text and outstanding photographs, an unknown hero and a subject of interest to children in his *Kids at Work: Lewis Hine and the Crusade Against Child Labor.* Jean Fritz created in *Harriet Beecher Stowe and the Beecher Preachers* a lively picture of the struggle of an intelligent, determined, and ultimately very famous author and her social and political milieu. For younger readers, Diane Stanley's and Peter Vennema's *Cleopatra* presented a glamorous yet realistic short biography of the celebrated queen. The illustrations, drawn from such architectural and artistic details of the period as mosaics, enhanced the feeling for the place and time. The splendid *Unconditional Surrender: U. S. Grant and the Civil War* by Albert Marrin seamlessly combined biography and history.

Other trends in nonfiction included several excellent series of books on art, including Little, Brown's *Portraits of Women Artists for Children* and Abrams' *First Impressions*. Joanna Cole continued her Magic School Bus series by offering another wild adventure of science teacher Ms. Frizzle in *The Magic School Bus in the Time of the Dinosaurs,* illustrated by Bruce Degen.

A number of well-known books for children appeared in Spanish, such as Elizabeth Borton de Treviño's *Yo, Juan de Pareja,* translated from her award-winning *I, Juan de Pareja.* Dual-language books in Spanish and English also appeared; a fine example was *The Piñata Maker/El Piñatero* by George Ancona about a popular subject and with exceptional photographs.

In poetry, the reissue of Langston Hughes's 1932 book *The Dream Keeper and Other Poems* has strong, contemporary illustrations by Brian Pinkney.

Awards. The 1994 Newbery Medal was presented to Lois Lowry for *The Giver.* The 1994 Caldecott Medal, another major award, was given to Allen Say for *Grandfather's Journey.*

A.A.F.

LITHUANIA. In 1994, President Algirdas Brazauskas's Democratic Labor Party, the successor to the Lithuanian Communist Party of the Soviet era, continued to dominate both the executive and legislative branches of the government.

The major domestic issue was the economy, where performance lagged behind the levels achieved in Estonia and Latvia, Lithuania's two Baltic neighbors. The average monthly wage in August was half that in the other two Baltic states. Lithuania was unable to attract much foreign investment, and it was plagued by energy problems related to the uncertain supply of oil from Russia and the questionable status of the Chernobyl-type nuclear power plant at Ignalina.

Historically, Lithuania had had a special, but troubled relationship with Poland. In April the presidents of the two countries signed a long-awaited friendship treaty that was ratified by both Parliaments in October. Although the two sides could not agree on an assessment of the past, they did recognize each other's territorial integrity and the inviolability of current borders. Moreover, they guaranteed cultural rights to the Polish and Lithuanian minorities

No place to rest. *Lithuanian police transport a body to be cremated in the town of Shilute in March. Flooding of the Nemunas River was so extensive that cemetery burials had become impossible.*

residing in the other country, especially the right to a native-language education.

Despite the departure of ex-Soviet troops from Lithuania in August 1993, relations with Russia did not show significant improvement during 1994. The main bone of contention was the issue of Russian land access through Lithuania to Moscow's heavily militarized exclave of Kaliningrad. Russia also put pressure on Lithuania by applying heavy tariffs on Lithuanian goods. Like the other Baltic states, Lithuania sought to balance the imposing Russian presence by forming closer ties with major Western international organizations. In January, Lithuania became the first Baltic state to apply for full membership in NATO.

See STATISTICS OF THE WORLD.   T.U.R.

LOUISIANA. *See* STATISTICS OF THE WORLD.

LUXEMBOURG. The most noteworthy event in Luxembourg in 1994 was the unexpected nomination of Prime Minister Jacques Santer to the presidency of the European Commission. His selection by the 12 heads of government of the European Union was approved in the European Parliament on July 21 by 260 to 238 votes, with 23 abstentions. Santer was expected to remain at the head of Luxembourg's coalition government (Christian Democrats and Socialists) until assuming the European Commission presidency in January 1995.

National elections on June 12 coincided with elections to the European Parliament. In the national elections both the Christian De-

mocrats and the Socialists lost one seat each, giving them 21 and 17 seats in the legislature, respectively. The Liberal Party gained one seat, for a total of 12, and the Greens also gained one, for a total of five. Smaller parties won five seats altogether. There were no changes in the country's representation in the European Parliament, where the Christian Democrats and the Socialists continued to hold two seats each, the Liberals and Greens one seat each.

In mid-August, German neo-Nazis staged a demonstration commemorating the death of Rudolf Hess; they were then expelled back into Germany. On September 9-10 the capital celebrated the 50th anniversary of its liberation from German troops during World War II. Allied troops and veterans participated in the celebrations.

Luxembourg remained the only European Union member to fulfill all preconditions—including strict limitations on the inflation rate and on currency devaluations—for eventual conversion to a European monetary union. The gross domestic product for 1994 was projected to grow at a rate of about 2 percent. Inflation moderated, after reaching a high of 3.6 percent in 1993. Industrial output for 1994, including steel, the mainstay of Luxembourg's industry, was expected to increase by a mere 1 percent. Unemployment hovered around 3 percent.

See STATISTICS OF THE WORLD.   F.G.E.

M

MACEDONIA. In an attempt to get concessions from the former Yugoslav Republic of Macedonia in the dispute over the republic's name and national symbols, Greece imposed in February 1994 an embargo on all goods going into Macedonia except food and medicine. (Greece claimed that the republic's name and symbols implied aspirations to Greece's northern province of Macedonia.) Since 70 percent of Macedonia's imports and exports were shipped through the Greek port of Thessaloniki, hundreds of millions of dollars were

added to the estimated $3 billion Macedonia had already lost because of international sanctions against Serbia and Montenegro.

At midyear ten ethnic Albanians were found guilty of treason and conspiracy against the government and sentenced to prison terms of up to eight years. The convicted included members of Macedonia's foremost ethnic Albanian political party, the Party of Democratic Prosperity (PDP). A short boycott of Parliament by ethnic Albanian deputies followed, adding to ethnic tensions in Macedonia.

The tensions peaked during a statewide census in July. Ethnic Albanians and other minorities claimed they were being undercounted, contesting results even before they were announced. The census triggered street fights, one of which, in Tetovo, led to the murder of a Macedonian youth by an Albanian. It was one of a series of extremist incidents that threatened the fragile peace in the republic. Reports of the establishment of parallel institutions of education and government by ethnic Albanians in western Macedonia were considered likely to spark a Macedonian nationalist backlash.

Presidential and parliamentary elections were held in October. Incumbent President Kiro Gligorov won easily, as did the ruling coalition of Gligorov's Alliance for Macedonia (three leftist parties) and the PDP. However, the nationalist parties had boycotted the second round of voting, charging fraud in the first round. Without their participation, the government would find it much more difficult to compromise with Greece. Furthermore, infighting in the PDP had fragmented the ethnic Albanian vote in the parliamentary elections, and in the face of the Alliance's overwhelming success (it won 95 seats out of 120, to 10 for the PDP) the PDP was essentially marginalized as a coalition partner. Some observers feared the party might either withdraw from the government or play obstructionist politics.

See STATISTICS OF THE WORLD.　　　　O.K.

MADAGASCAR. *See* STATISTICS OF THE WORLD.

MAGAZINES AND NEWSPAPERS. In 1994 the U.S. newspaper industry and a number of U.S. magazines celebrated the long-awaited return of advertising dollars after several years of reductions in the numbers of advertising pages. Many publications reported double-digit revenue growth and robust earnings. There was also some bad news: readership declined for all of the ten largest U.S. metropolitan dailies and the vast majority of the top 100.

New Hands and New Faces. Media mogul Rupert Murdoch, who initially made his name in newspapers, took another step away from print in February when he sold the tabloid *Boston Herald* to its publisher, Patrick J. Purcell. The sale of the struggling *Herald,* which

had long run a distant second in circulation to the *Boston Globe,* offered further proof that Murdoch saw a greater portion of the media of the future linked to television.

In March, Canadian Conrad Black, who already owned scores of small U.S. newspapers in 29 states, made his first big purchase in the United States when he bought the *Chicago Sun-Times,* the nation's 11th-largest newspaper and ninth-largest metropolitan daily, for $180 million. The purchase—by American Publishing Company, a subsidiary of Black's Vancouver-based Hollinger, Inc.—also included about 60 smaller Chicago-area newspapers. Among Black's other holdings are the *Daily Telegraph* in London and the *Jerusalem Post.* In July, Morris Communications of Augusta, GA, agreed to buy the Stauffer Group, a Kansas-based collection of newspapers and

Artistic license? Considerable controversy broke out when, in its coverage of the O. J. Simpson murder case, Time *magazine dramatically darkened Simpson's police "mug shot" in its June 27 cover story. (*Newsweek's *issue of the same week did not alter the mug shot.)* Time *defended its cover picture as a "photo-illustration," but many critics assailed it as irresponsible journalism, charging that the darkening of the mug shot made Simpson seem guilty and reflected a racist attitude.*

Rupert Murdoch

Rupert Murdoch has long wielded a mighty sword in the newspaper world. In 1994 the communications mogul strengthened yet another arm of his international media empire when he persuaded the New World Communications Group to align a dozen of its local television stations with his Fox TV network. The move was a significant blow to a major competitor: eight of the stations, in such key cities as Detroit and Dallas, had been CBS affiliates.

Born in Australia in 1931, Keith Rupert Murdoch began building his media empire after inheriting a newspaper from his father in the 1950s. The risk-taking entrepreneur crashed the British market, where he became known as king of the tabloids. Today, Murdoch's U.S. holdings alone include Fox Television, Fox Video, 20th Century-Fox Film Corporation, the HarperCollins publishing company, *TV Guide,* the *New York Post,* and Delphi Internet Services. Murdoch's debt burden almost sank him in 1990—but his investments now seem to be paying off.

G.H.

television and radio stations, for approximately $280 million. The deal was subject to approval by the Federal Communications Commission.

Her New York, a weekly newspaper for women started by financier Steven Hoffenberg in 1993, ceased publication in February, the same month Hoffenberg was arrested in connection with an ongoing government investigation of his business dealings. Among *Her New York* creditors were dozens of freelance writers who were denied their pay on the ground that their articles had been commissioned by "rogue editors." In November, Hoffenberg agreed to pay $60 million in restitution for what officials described as a vast Ponzi scheme; his investors collectively lost more than $450 million.

The *New York Times* broke from tradition in April and went outside its ranks to appoint a new managing editor, Eugene Roberts, Jr., former executive editor of the *Philadelphia Inquirer.* (Roberts had worked for the *Times* from 1965 to 1972.) Roberts, whose staff at the *Inquirer* earned 17 Pulitzer Prizes during his 18 years at the paper, was part of an executive remodeling at the *Times* that saw managing editor Joseph Lelyveld promoted to executive editor. Lelyveld succeeded Max Frankel, who became a columnist for the Sunday *Times Magazine.*

New Reality. If the year's promising news that *USA Today,* the colorful, innovative, and financially draining brainchild of Gannett Corporation, had finally turned a profit suggested that better days were ahead for newspapers, a series of hikes in the cost of newsprint brought expectations in line with reality. Newsprint manufacturers had taken big losses during the early 1990s, and the improved economy and an increased demand for paper presented them with the opportunity to increase prices.

Generally flat or depressed circulation figures offered no indication that readers were rushing back to newspapers. The price increases and the lackluster readership numbers contributed to a widespread malaise among the major newspaper stocks and seemed to underscore long-term concerns about the newspaper industry's ability to attract and hold a new generation of readers.

The Times Mirror Company launched online versions of the *Los Angeles Times* and *Newsday,* which joined more than 30 other newspapers in the United States offering online service.

Magazine Comings and Goings. The year brought some revenue improvements, but for many magazines the advertising drought lingered. Meanwhile, the explosion in niche publications continued. Among 1994's more notable launches were *Urban Fitness,* a Seattle-based health magazine targeting gay and lesbian readers, and *Family PC,* a computer magazine that was a joint effort of Ziff-Davis and the Walt Disney Company. The Library of Congress was associated with a new magazine called *Civilization,* offering in-depth reviews and essays. Contributors to the bimonthly, whose first issue appeared in the fall, included prominent writers and intellectuals.

There were changes at the top of several major magazines. Condé Nast Publications led the shuffle by naming in January a new company president, Steven T. Florio, formerly president and chief executive of the *New Yorker.* In the wake of that appointment, new publishers were designated at several Condé Nast publications. Florio's brother, Thomas T. Florio, became publisher at the *New Yorker;* Gina Sanders at *Details;* Michael Perlis, formerly of Playboy Enterprises, at *GQ;* and Mitchell Fox at *Vanity Fair.* At *National Geographic* magazine, William H. Allen was appointed editor in July, replacing William Graves, who retired. Gilbert Grosvenor, president and chairman of the National Geographic Society, announced he would step down in 1996 at age 65.   T.J.

MAINE. *See* STATISTICS OF THE WORLD.

MALAWI. *See* AFRICA; STATISTICS OF THE WORLD.

MALAYSIA. A political shake-up in the eastern Malaysian state of Sabah led to the loss of an opposition party foothold in 1994. The chief minister, Joseph Pairin Kitingan, resigned in March following a corruption conviction for awarding contracts to relatives. The charges had been brought shortly after his party, the Christian-dominated United Sabah Party (PBS), went into opposition in 1990. The PBS won a slim victory in state elections in February 1994 over the national ruling coalition, the National Front, led by the United Malays National Organization (UMNO), the party of Prime Minister Mahathir Mohamed. But successful PBS candidates were persuaded to join the National Front, giving it a majority. Sabah

UMNO leader Sakaran Dandai became the new chief minister.

The chief minister of the state of Melaka and president of UNMO Youth, Abdul Rahim Thamby Chik, resigned from all government and party posts in September following allegations of involvement with a 15-year-old schoolgirl. In November he was charged with corruption while in office.

In August the government banned the Islamic group Al-Arqam after Malaysia's highest Islamic body cited it for deviant teachings. The government accused it of threatening national security and training a death squad in Thailand, where its leader, Ashaari Muhammad, had been living. Ashaari was arrested when he returned to Malaysia in September. In October he renounced his teachings.

Forecasts for Malaysia's economy continued rosy, with annual growth of more than 8 percent expected through 1995. In February, ar-

Pointed gesture. Malaysia's new King Tuanku Jaafar prepares to kiss a traditional Malay sword during his ceremonial installation in Kuala Lumpur. Under the country's system of government, monarchs are chosen by the heads of Malaysia's nine hereditary states and rule for five years.

ticles in the *Sunday Times* of London provoked a government ban on awarding contracts to British firms. The paper wrote that in 1985 a British company gave a middleman $50,000 to pay off Malaysian officials to approve an aluminum smelter, and alleged Malaysia received $156 million in aid for the Pergau Dam in return for an $870 million arms purchase. Negotiations got the ban lifted in September.

The government finalized a deal in June to purchase 18 high-performance MIG-29 fighter planes worth nearly $600 million from Russia. At the same time, Russia agreed to buy $150 million in palm oil and other products from Malaysia.

See STATISTICS OF THE WORLD.   K.M.

MALDIVES. See STATISTICS OF THE WORLD.

MALI. See STATISTICS OF THE WORLD.

MALTA. See STATISTICS OF THE WORLD.

MANITOBA. See STATISTICS OF THE WORLD.

MARSHALL ISLANDS. See STATISTICS OF THE WORLD.

MARYLAND. See STATISTICS OF THE WORLD.

MASSACHUSETTS. See STATE GOVERNMENT REVIEW; STATISTICS OF THE WORLD.

MAURITANIA. See STATISTICS OF THE WORLD.

MAURITIUS. See STATISTICS OF THE WORLD.

MEXICO. Ernesto Zedillo Ponce de León, 43, took office as president of Mexico on December 1, 1994. He became the Institutional Revolutionary Party's (PRI) candidate following the March 23 assassination of Luis Donaldo Colosio Murrieta. The killing was one of two political murders that, combined with peasant uprisings, kidnappings, and financial scandals, stunned Mexico during what turned out to be a difficult year. By the end of 1994 the country had plunged into a full-blown economic crisis.

Politics. By winning 50.18 percent of the votes in the most hotly contested election in 50 years, Zedillo, a former education minister, virtually guaranteed that the PRI—which had governed Mexico since 1929 and in 1994 was the longest-ruling political party in the world—would continue in power until the end of the century. At the same time, however, Zedillo pledged to continue political reforms aimed at making the country more democratic and less authoritarian.

Although his predecessor, Carlos Salinas de

Gortari, was criticized for not doing more to foster democracy, under Salinas's administration an opposition party won in statewide elections for the first time in six decades and threatened to win the presidency as well.

Following the election, the PRI controlled only 55 percent of the lower house of Congress and for the first time faced serious oppo-

Ernesto Zedillo Ponce de León

In the wake of the March assassination of its presidential candidate, Mexico's ruling Institutional Revolutionary Party searched for a replacement who could help build the nation's economy. It picked a quiet economist by the name of Ernesto Zedillo Ponce de León—the murdered candidate's campaign manager. Zedillo won just over half the vote, coming in more than 20 percentage points ahead of his nearest rival.

Born in 1951 in Mexico City, Zedillo sold newspapers and shined shoes as a teenager to help finance his studies at the National Polytechnic Institute. He earned a doctorate in economics at Yale University and went on to serve as minister of planning and budget and minister of education. Zedillo is married and has five children.

Zedillo's mettle was tested soon after his inauguration, as Mexico was thrown into an economic crisis with potentially significant international repercussions. He appointed a new finance minister just before the year closed.   J.B.

sition in the Senate. Similarly, 200 of the 500 seats in the Chamber of Deputies were set aside for the opposition under a system of proportional representation. With nine parties participating in the August 21 election, a record 78 percent of the registered voters cast ballots. New procedures were instituted to prevent fraud, and a reported 90,000 observers from Mexico and abroad certified the election. Still, numerous irregularities were reported. In a few cases results were overturned by the recently constituted Federal Election Tribunal. In Monterrey, Mexico's third-largest city, the mayoralty that was originally awarded to the PRI eventually went to the opposition National Action Party.

Rebellion and Crime. Although apparently unrelated, the January insurgency, the murder of Colosio, and the assassination six months later of José Francisco Ruíz Massieu (the PRI secretary-general who had been scheduled to become the next majority leader in the Chamber of Deputies) were all linked to the cause of political reform.

On New Year's Day some 2,000 Maya peasants calling themselves the Zapatista National Liberation Army seized and briefly held a few towns in Chiapas State before being driven into the hills. Nearly 100 combatants died in about two weeks of fighting before a cease-fire was declared, but insurgents still held control of remote, isolated territory near the Guatemala border. Grinding poverty apparently sparked the uprising, but the primary rebel demand was for Salinas to resign and for a democratic provisional government to replace him. The insurgents refused to sign a peace agreement until these conditions were met. In December a commission was established to resolve the conflict, but shortly afterward, violence erupted again as peasants in Chiapas blocked highways and took over a town hall. Government troops were sent in, and the rebels disappeared.

Colosio was regarded as a reformer who, like Salinas, favored change. The PRI has been a party without ideology, committed only to maintaining power, often overlooking corruption. PRI reformers were seen as a threat to traditionalists, whom reformers, in turn, dismissed as "dinosaurs." Moments after Colosio

Who Was Zapata?

When the Zapatistas seized several towns in southern Mexico early in 1994, even some Mexicans didn't recognize the origin of the guerrillas' name (although movie buffs recalled the 1952 film *Viva Zapata!* starring Marlon Brando).

But in parts of Mexico, Emiliano Zapata's name and spirit never died.

Zapata was born in 1883 in southern Mexico to peasants of mixed blood. As a teenager he was arrested for protesting a hacienda's takeover of land formerly farmed by the people of his village. He spent most of the rest of his life fighting to restore land to its rightful owners. His guerrillas often seized land by force, sometimes burning haciendas and killing landowners.

Zapata's forces helped oust dictator Porfirio Díaz and install Francisco Madero in 1911 but found the new president a disappointment. In 1919, Zapata was killed in an ambush apparently ordered by then President Venustiano Carranza.   I.S.

was shot, his killer, Mario Aburto Martínez, 23, was seized. The evidence suggested that Aburto was a deranged loner, but there was widespread belief, according to a poll published by the Mexico City newspaper *Reforma,* that Colosio was a victim of a plot hatched by "dinosaurs" in the PRI.

The conspiracy theory was bolstered by the shooting of Ruíz Massieu. His assassin implicated nearly two dozen "Old Guard" PRI politicians, several of them from Tamaulipas, a state bordering Texas and noted as home of widespread cocaine trafficking into the United States. In mid-November, Ruíz Massieu's brother, Mario, deputy attorney general in charge of enforcing Mexico's narcotics laws, resigned, accusing the PRI of impeding the investigation into the assassination. Party leaders responded by accusing Mario Ruíz Massieu of conducting a witch hunt. The deputy attorney general believed that narcotics traffickers and the PRI's "dinosaurs" were allied, the traffickers favoring politicians willing to be bribed. Many Mexicans feared their country would become a "narco-republic."

Career cut short. *Mexican politics received an un-expected jolt in March when Luis Donaldo Colosio Murrieta (above), the clear front-runner in the presidential race, was cut down by an assassin's bullet while campaigning in Tijuana. At right, two women holding campaign posters are among the mourners gathering to pay their respects at the Mexico City funeral home holding Colosio's remains.*

During 1994 more than 1,000 kidnappings were reported, and experts suspect that easily twice as many went unreported for fear of reprisals. In one instance, $30 million may have been paid to ransom an obviously wealthy banker.

Several businessmen went into hiding when it was disclosed that they were involved in major scandals. Executives of the Havre Group, which controlled an insurance company and a stock brokerage, became fugitives when they were accused of funneling $200 million in loans from government development funds into nonexistent companies. Also in hiding was Carlos Cabal Peniche, who borrowed a reported $700 million in unsecured loans from banks he controlled to purchase Del Monte Fresh Produce. And Gerardo de Prévoisin, the ousted chairman of Aeroméxico and Mexicana, the country's two largest airlines, was presumed to have fled the country after creditors accused him of criminal mismanagement.

Economy. These white-collar crimes struck hard at Salinas's privatization policies. During his administration 159 federally controlled businesses were sold to private investors. Among these were the two airlines and the banks controlled by Cabal Peniche. During Salinas's six years in office his administration reduced public debt by 24 percent, to $75 billion, and trimmed interest payments from 44 percent of the gross national product to 12 percent. The federal budget was balanced and the inflation rate reduced from 52 percent in 1988 to about 7 percent in 1994. Per capita income nearly doubled, hitting an estimated $4,324 in 1994, although distribution was uneven. Although private investment was up 60 percent (an estimated $10 billion came in from abroad during 1994, a 27 percent increase over 1993), the economy expanded by only an estimated 2.4 percent, held back by anti-inflation policies and high interest rates. The country's largest labor federation claimed that many

Mexicans had seen their buying power shrink by as much as 50 percent since 1980, while more than 20 Mexicans, according to *Forbes* magazine, had become billionaires.

The country's economic uncertainties came to a head at year's end as the government abandoned its efforts to defend the peso, causing it to plunge nearly 30 percent in a week, alarming foreign investors, threatening inflation, and presenting a major crisis of confidence in the new administration. The United States said it would offer billions in debt and currency aid to help the Zedillo government weather the crisis.

Foreign Relations. Many analysts considered Salinas's greatest triumph to be bringing Mexico into the North American Free Trade Agreement. They noted that in the first half of 1994 exports to the United States increased by 20.5 percent while sales to Canada leaped 36.1 percent. However, U.S. efforts to stem illegal Mexican immigration placed a strain on bilateral relations. Merchants in U.S. border cities criticized Mexico's reducing from $300 to $50 the value of goods citizens could import duty-free by land. Salinas's meeting with Fidel Castro in mid-1994 also caused distress, as did Mexico's investment of $200 million in a Cuban oil refinery and purchase of 49 percent of the Cuban telephone company.

See STATISTICS OF THE WORLD.   J.B.

MICHIGAN. *See* STATE GOVERNMENT REVIEW; STATISTICS OF THE WORLD.

MICRONESIA. *See* STATISTICS OF THE WORLD.

MIDDLE EAST. *See* PALESTINE LIBERATION ORGANIZATION; PERSIAN GULF STATES; *articles on individual countries.*

MILITARY AND NAVAL AFFAIRS. As regional conflicts multiplied in the wake of a reduction in superpower tensions, the U.S. military during 1994 found itself stretched. While the United States continued a dramatic overall force reduction in Europe, many troops were assigned to peacekeeping and humanitarian operations in such areas as Bosnia-Hercegovina, Somalia, and Rwanda. In the fall there were new U.S. troop deployments to the Persian Gulf region and to Haiti.

Persian Gulf. After several thousand Iraqi troops suddenly massed near the Kuwaiti border, raising fears that Iraq might invade Kuwait, as it had in 1990, President Bill Clinton on October 6 ordered a massive buildup of U.S. forces in the region, involving more than 30,000 Army and Marine troops, an aircraft carrier, and several hundred combat aircraft. When the Iraqis pulled back later in October, recognizing Kuwait's sovereignty, the U.S. presence was reduced to approximately 12,000 troops, in addition to the 12,000 permanently stationed in the region.

On April 14 two American F-15s shot down two U.S. Army helicopters over northern Iraq, killing all 26 persons aboard. The more senior of the two Air Force pilots involved, Lieutenant Colonel Randy W. May, was charged with negligent homicide and dereliction of duty; the charges were later dismissed because of insufficient evidence, but May still faced the possibility of disciplinary action. Five crew members of an Air Force Awacs radar plane who had failed to warn that friendly helicopters were in the area were initially accused of dereliction of duty; one of them, Captain Jim Wang, who was in charge of the controllers aboard the radar plane, was recommended for a court-martial. The two helicopters had been engaged in a United Nations humanitarian mission in a "no-fly" zone imposed after the 1991 Persian Gulf War to protect Kurds in the region from Iraqi government repression. The helicopters were visually misidentified by the pilots as Iraqi.

Haiti Crisis. On September 19 a last-minute diplomatic effort spearheaded by former President Jimmy Carter produced a new political settlement between the United States and Haiti; it provided for the departure of the military regime and the reinstatement of the elected civilian president, Jean-Bertrand Aristide, who had been ousted in a 1991 coup. U.S. forces, prepared for a full-scale military invasion, instead entered the country peacefully as part of Operation Restore Democracy. More than 20,000 Army and Marine troops arrived within a week to restore order and help rebuild the nation; their stay was expected to last more than a year.

Asian Developments. After extensive negotiations, the United States and North Korea reached an accord in October, as part of a plan to end the North Koreans' nuclear

Early retirement. *U.S. Navy Admiral Frank Kelso holds a press conference in February to say that he would be resigning two months earlier than originally planned. The announcement came after a Navy judge had criticized Admiral Kelso for his handling of the Tailhook sexual harassment scandal.*

weapons development program. The deal included provisions for shipment of heavy oil to North Korea, as well as for talks on opening diplomatic offices.

Improved relations with North Korea were threatened in mid-December when a U.S. Army helicopter flew, reportedly by accident, into North Korean territory and was shot down. One of the two pilots, Chief Warrant Officer David Hilemon, was killed; the other, Chief Warrant Officer Bobby Hall, was captured and accused of espionage. He was freed at the end of the month, however.

On February 3, 19 years after the end of the Vietnam War, President Clinton rescinded the U.S. trade embargo against Vietnam. Clinton said the action offered the best chance of resolving the fate of more than 2,200 American servicemen listed as missing in action in Southeast Asia. His decision was opposed by many veterans' groups, but it was endorsed by retired General William C. Westmoreland, the most prominent commander of U.S. forces during the Vietnam War.

Exit From Somalia. A final contingent of U.S. troops left Somalia in March, ending an ill-fated deployment in which a total of 44 Americans died and 175 were wounded. More than 25,000 troops had been stationed in Somalia under UN auspices since December 1992 to help distribute food and supplies to starving Somalis. But the humanitarian emphasis of the mission shifted as U.S. and other troops suffered casualties under fire, and unsuccessful efforts were made to capture Somali faction leader Muhammad Farrah Aideed. After an October 1993 firefight with Somali factional militiamen left 18 American soldiers dead, the United States announced a plan, ultimately implemented, for withdrawal of all its forces by March 31, 1994. In a major incident in January, prior to the pullout, U.S. marines, allegedly shot at by snipers, opened fire in a Mogadishu street, killing at least eight people.

Retrenchment. As a result of the end of the cold war and the 1992 breakup of the Soviet Union, the military was under pressure to reduce its size and scope. By the end of the year U.S. troop strength in Europe (which in 1990 stood at 340,000) had been slashed to 140,000.

The magnitude of the pullback was apparent in the Pentagon budget for the 1995 fiscal year (beginning October 1, 1994), which emphasized funds for readiness and training rather than for new weapons systems. Continuing cuts in the defense budget even had some impact on training activities. In September the Navy canceled training programs for about 20,000 reservists after running out of money.

Some defense experts claimed that U.S. combat readiness was beginning to suffer.

Continued easing of nuclear tensions with the former Soviet Union prompted the Pentagon to discard its Doomsday Project, an effort begun in 1983 to allow the United States to withstand a hypothetical six-month nuclear war with the Soviet Union. The Air Force removed the last of 150 Minuteman II missiles from a silo in South Dakota and began a three-year program to destroy the silos, where missiles had been on nuclear alert for 32 years. In a September summit meeting in Washington, DC, Clinton and Russian President Boris Yeltsin agreed to make new, deeper cuts in their nuclear arsenals as soon as both countries ratified the 1993 Strategic Arms Reduction Treaty (Start II). Meanwhile, the older Start I treaty, which was already being implemented, officially went into effect and acquired legal status in December; this step had been delayed until Ukraine agreed to ratify the accord and the Nuclear Nonproliferation Treaty.

Defense Budget. The Clinton administration's proposed U.S. defense budget for the 1995 fiscal year, released in February 1994, requested spending authority of $263.7 billion, a $2.8 billion increase from the previous year's projected spending. Adjusted for inflation, this level of spending amounted to a decline for the tenth consecutive year and was 35 percent below levels of a decade before. The new budget sharply curtailed weapons spending and increased funding for peacekeeping operations, base closings, defense conversion activities, and programs to keep "defense-unique" industries like nuclear shipbuilding alive. The largest weapons request was $3.3 billion, for a variety of ballistic missile defense programs.

In September, Congress approved a defense authorization for fiscal year 1995 amounting to $243.8 billion, slightly more than the president had requested. In December, Clinton said he wanted to increase budgeted military spending by about $25 billion over six years,

Rwanda mission. U.S. soldiers disembark from their plane at the airport in Kigali, Rwanda, at the end of July. Their mission was to help open the airport of the beleaguered city, which had been nearly depopulated by Rwanda's civil conflict. Troops from the United States and other nations also provided humanitarian aid to displaced persons in Rwanda and refugees who had fled to neighboring countries.

China talk. U.S. Defense Secretary William Perry (center) talks with a Chinese military officer in Beijing in October. At right is U.S. Senator Sam Nunn, chairman of the Senate Armed Services Committee. The occasion marked the first visit to China by top-level U.S. defense officials in five years.

in what was said to be an effort to improve readiness and the quality of life of U.S. soldiers. This proposal, which would eventually reverse the decline in military spending, but not before fiscal year 1998, was criticized by Republicans as inadequate.

Weapons Systems and Mergers. Development continued on a handful of new weapons systems. The largest such program was the Air Force's F-22 jet fighter, which was expected to cost $72 billion, despite a cut in procurement from 750 to 442 aircraft.

The Army chose a new air-defense missile system in February, the Extended Range Interceptor (later renamed the Patriot Advanced Capability), rejecting a revised version of the old Patriot missile, whose performance during the Persian Gulf War had been sharply criticized by defense officials. The Navy commissioned a new Trident ballistic missile submarine, two fast-attack nuclear submarines, a guided missile cruiser, and two missile destroyers.

Mergers and consolidations swept through the defense industry. Lockheed and Martin Marietta announced a $10 billion merger on August 30; the new company, called Lockheed Martin Corporation, became the largest U.S. military contractor. In April, Northrop outbid

Martin Marietta and acquired Grumman in a $2.1 billion hostile takeover.

Women. In February a Navy judge dismissed three legal cases in the Tailhook sexual harassment scandal because of insufficient evidence. A fourth, and last, case was dismissed by the Marine Corps in June. Although 140 officers were implicated in misconduct during that 1991 convention of naval aviators, none were court-martialed. About 50 Navy and Marine officers received administrative punishment. Pentagon investigators concluded that 83 women had been assaulted or molested during the convention. Lieutenant Paula Coughlin, who ignited the controversy by alleging that she had been sexually assaulted, resigned from the Navy in February.

The chief of naval operations, Admiral Frank B. Kelso II, retired at four-star rank on April 30, two months ahead of schedule, after being accused of misconduct in the Tailhook affair. A Navy judge charged he lied in claiming not to have observed sexual harassment at the convention; Kelso denied the charge. The Senate narrowly approved Kelso's retirement at four-star rank; all seven women senators had wanted his rank—and his pension—reduced.

Equal-opportunity barriers in the military loosened considerably after the Pentagon in

January ordered all the services to open more assignments to women. The aircraft carrier U.S.S. *Eisenhower* became the first Navy warship to receive women crew members, beginning in March. By year's end women were serving as combat pilots in all three military branches. Lieutenant Kara Hultgreen, the first woman to qualify as a Navy combat pilot, died in a training accident on October 25.

The Army opened more combat support positions to women but retained the prohibition against women being directly involved in ground combat.

A highly decorated Army nurse who had been discharged because she was an avowed lesbian was reinstated by a federal appeals court in July. A lower court had ruled that Colonel Margarethe Cammermeyer's ouster from the Washington State National Guard was unconstitutional.

Cheating Scandal. Twenty-four midshipmen were expelled from the U.S. Naval Academy on April 28 in the worst cheating scandal in the history of the institution.

The scandal arose in late 1992, when students gained access in advance to a pirated copy of an electrical engineering examination. Of 106 midshipmen examined in hearings before an officers' panel, more than 30 were exonerated; others faced punishments that were less severe than expulsion. A congressional investigation and a Navy inspector general's report criticized academy officials for laxity in the investigation.

Command Change. In February, William J. Perry was confirmed by the Senate as defense secretary, replacing Les Aspin. Retired Admiral Bobby Ray Inman had originally been nominated for the post, but he abruptly withdrew his name in January, claiming in a rambling speech that critics had conspired to damage his reputation. T.D.

MINNESOTA. See STATE GOVERNMENT REVIEW; STATISTICS OF THE WORLD.

MINORITIES IN THE UNITED STATES. In 1994 the National Association for the Advancement of Colored People (NAACP), long the largest and most influential civil rights group in the United States, staggered through a year of crises. Also in the news were challenges to affirmative action and racially tai-

lored voting districts, belated justice in the murder of a civil rights hero, and compensation of $54 million made by a company accused of racism.

Turmoil in the NAACP. In August the NAACP's board voted overwhelmingly to remove the Reverend Benjamin F. Chavis, Jr., from the post of executive director, which he had held for little over a year. His ouster followed revelations that he had secretly pledged several hundred thousand dollars of NAACP funds to a female former aide to settle a complaint against him and the NAACP for sexual discrimination and harassment. Chavis's brief tenure was further marred by charges of financial mismanagement that had turned a budget surplus into a deficit of over $3.5 million, leading the Ford Foundation to freeze $250,000 in aid and prompting several NAACP chapters to suspend dues payments; by November the depletion of cash reserves impelled board members to furlough without pay most of its 100 national staff workers. Chavis had also occasioned controversy when, in June, he welcomed the black separatist leader Louis Farrakhan of the Nation of Islam to the NAACP's three-day National African American Leadership Summit in Baltimore.

Race-conscious Remedies. The creation of voting districts expressly to help elect black or other minority candidates—a practice encouraged by federal courts for more than a decade—increasingly came under judicial challenge following a 1993 Supreme Court ruling that disallowed "bizarre"-looking districts solely for racial reasons. In July a three-judge federal panel struck down a black majority district created in Louisiana in April expressly to meet earlier judicial objections to "racial gerrymandering." The following month a three-judge panel struck down three oddly shaped congressional districts in Dallas and Houston, two of them with a black majority and the third with a Latino majority; the Texas Legislature was required to redraw the boundaries early in 1995. In September judges in Georgia similarly ordered black-majority districts redrawn. The Supreme Court stayed both the Louisiana and Georgia rulings until it could convene after the November elections to consider the appeals. An exception to the weakening of racial redistricting plans was a federal court's two-to-one ruling in July that upheld two black-majority congressional districts in North Carolina as necessary to ensure the "fair and effective representation of all citizens."

Officials also sent conflicting messages concerning the legality of affirmative action programs in employment and higher education. In August a federal district judge in Austin, TX, ruled that use of separate admissions committees for whites and minorities by the University of Texas Law School (a policy since discontinued) was unconstitutional; nonetheless, the judge did not require the school to admit four white plaintiffs who claimed that reverse racism had led to rejection of their applications. In September, Sharon Taxman, a white teacher discharged by a school board in New Jersey so a black teacher of equal seniority and

merit could be retained, won her suit charging racial discrimination and received a $144,000 judgment in federal court for back pay and damages. A month later, however, the U.S. assistant attorney general for civil rights, Deval Patrick, backed the school district's appeal, reversing the Justice Department's support for Taxman during the Bush administration.

Race and Education. The cause of integrated education appeared to be losing ground for black and Hispanic pupils, according to a study by the National School Boards Association issued on May 11, nearly 40 years after the Supreme Court ruled that segregation in public education was unconstitutional. Although a survey released the same day showed that most Americans (87 percent) approved of integrated education, only the South, the region originally targeted by the desegregation

Chavis chastised. Benjamin Chavis, Jr., executive director of the National Association for the Advancement of Colored People, speaks to the National African American Leadership Summit in June. Standing to Chavis's immediate left is William F. Gibson, chairman of the board of the NAACP; at the far right is Louis Farrakhan, leader of the Nation of Islam. Chavis was ousted by the NAACP's board two months later. His efforts to forge an alliance with the black separatist Farrakhan had provoked controversy, and he had been charged with using NAACP funds to head off a sex discrimination suit.

Overdue recognition. *Civil War uniforms are worn by some of the participants in the September groundbreaking ceremony for a memorial honoring black soldiers who served in the Union forces during the U.S. Civil War. The African-American Civil War Memorial is being built in one of the oldest black neighborhoods in Washington, DC.*

ruling, had made clear progress, with nearly three-quarters of black students going to mostly white schools. The Northeast, with its largely segregated residential patterns, had the country's most segregated schools: half of black students and 46 percent of Hispanic students attended schools where 90 percent or more of students were minorities.

That integration could trigger new racial tensions was underscored when Hulond Humphries, a white high-school principal in the small Alabama town of Lake Wedowee, threatened in February to cancel the school prom to prevent interracial dating and allegedly told a mixed-race student, Revonda Bowen, that her birth had been a mistake. Bowen sued and won a $25,000 settlement from the school district in June, but the conflict triggered bomb threats, school boycotts, and the torching of the high school in August by an unknown arsonist. The school board, under pressure from the Justice Department, then reassigned Humphries away from the school.

Verdict in Medgar Evers Case. In February a Mississippi jury of eight blacks and four whites unanimously convicted a white supremacist, Byron De la Beckwith, 73, of killing a black leader, Medgar Evers, 30 years earlier. New testimony by former companions sealed the case against Beckwith, who had twice escaped conviction in 1964 when all-white juries deadlocked. He was immediately sentenced to life imprisonment.

Restitution by Denny's. In May, Flagstar, the parent company of Denny's national fast-food chain, agreed to pay $54 million to settle lawsuits by blacks that charged racial discrimination, including refusal of service in various outlets. In November a black-owned company in Atlanta, NDI Inc., arranged with the Denny's chain to buy or build and operate up to 47 franchises in New York and New Jersey. The deal, coming when just two of the more than 1,500 Denny's franchises were owned by blacks, went far toward honoring the chain's "Fair Share" agreement with the NAACP in 1993 to create substantial minority ownership, management, and employment.

Race and Living Standards. Census data showed that vast disparities in wealth, health,

269

and perceptions of opportunity in American society persisted among different racial and ethnic groups. While the overall net worth of U.S. households stood at $36,623, white households averaged $44,408, nearly ten times more than black households ($4,604) and nearly nine times more than Hispanic households of all races ($5,345). Health and mortality statistics indicated similar patterns of white privilege and black risk. The data showed that black women were ten times more likely than white women to die from AIDS, black men were seven times more likely than white men to be murdered, and infant mortality rates for blacks were twice the rates for whites.

Explanations for these gaps in quality of life similarly varied by race and ethnicity. In March a survey commissioned by the National Conference of Christians and Jews showed that while a majority of whites believed the nation's minorities enjoyed equal opportunity in society, most African-Americans, Latinos, and Asian-Americans disagreed. In *The Bell Curve,* a book published in the fall, two white social scientists, Charles Murray and Richard J. Herrnstein, further polarized opinion by asserting some genetic connection between race and level of intelligence.

The chasm in social perceptions between whites and blacks was underscored by reactions to the arrest and prosecution of O. J. Simpson (*see profile in* PEOPLE IN THE NEWS), an immensely popular former professional football star who was charged with murdering his ex-wife and her friend. In a survey by *Newsweek* released on July 9, over three-quarters of whites but only about one-third of blacks thought Simpson should stand trial. A *USA Today*-CNN-Gallup poll the previous week showed that three-fifths of black respondents thought Simpson innocent, but fully two-thirds of whites believed him guilty. Further emphasizing these differences, more than half the white respondents (57 percent) claimed that whites and blacks fared about equally well in the country's criminal justice system, but nearly three-quarters of blacks (74 percent) said blacks suffered harsher treatment.

Differences in the priorities of whites and blacks surfaced during months of congressional maneuvering over President Bill Clinton's $32 billion anticrime bill. The 38-member Congressional Black Caucus, though concerned with violent crime in the inner cities, tied passage of the bill to an amendment to let death row inmates challenge their sentences based on statistical evidence of racial bias. But in August the Congress passed the bill minus the "racial justice" provision, after the president had agreed to strike this item because of strong opposition on the part of conservative Republicans.

Gay Culture Affirmed. In June three independently organized events in New York City affirmed gay culture and encouraged gay pride. From June 18 through 25, male and female homosexual athletes from 44 countries competed in the fourth quadrennial Gay Games. On June 26 over 100,000 men and women marched in two parades through Manhattan to celebrate the 25th anniversary of a protest against a police raid on a gay bar, the Stonewall Inn, which had sparked the gay rights movement. The absence of arrests at these events (in contrast to the police brutality at Stonewall in 1969), President Clinton's ten-day waiver of visa requirements for foreign visitors with the AIDS virus, and an appearance by New York Mayor Rudolph Giuliani at the massive "Stonewall 25" parade suggested homosexuals were making progress toward mainstream acceptance.

A New Miss America. In September, Heather Whitestone, a 21-year-old, severely hearing-impaired collegian from Alabama, became the first contestant with a major disability to win the Miss America crown in the pageant's 74-year history. Whitestone's first-place finish in the talent competition, with a dance performance that she synchronized to the music by memorizing the beats, reinforced her message to the disabled that "anything is possible."

See CRIME AND LAW ENFORCEMENT; INDIANS, AMERICAN; WOMEN.   R.W.

MISSISSIPPI. *See* STATISTICS OF THE WORLD.

MISSOURI. *See* STATISTICS OF THE WORLD.

MOLDOVA. In February 1994, Moldova held its first post-Communist elections, with a resounding victory for politicians favoring independence over unification with Romania or closer ties with Russia. President Mircea Snegur's Agrarian Party swept a majority of seats in Parliament. Although he and his close colleagues were former Communists, they had records of strong support for political pluralism and market economic reform. Indeed, Moldova was widely praised during 1994 for its economic and political reforms by the International Monetary Fund, NATO, the European Union, the Council of Europe, and the United States. Moldova joined the Commonwealth of Independent States in April, but Snegur stressed that cooperation in the Russian-dominated organization had only economic, not military or political, implications, a claim reinforced by his earlier accession to NATO's Partnership for Peace.

A new constitution was adopted in July 1994 with autonomy for Transdniestria, a thin swatch of land on the east bank of the Dniester River, bordered by Ukraine, with a population 25.5 percent Russian, 28 percent Ukrainian, and 40 percent Moldovan. In early 1992 the Russian Fourteenth Army had supported a secessionist movement in the region, but after a few months the vicious civil war subsided into an uneasy stalemate. In April 1994, Snegur initiated talks with the aid of mediators from Russia and the Conference on Security and Cooperation in Europe, and in October, Russia and Moldova agreed to a phased withdrawal over three years despite the vehement objections of the Fourteenth Army commander, Aleksandr Lebed, and local Russians.

After a prolonged drought during the summer months Moldova was devastated by rainstorms at the end of August. These catastrophes blackened a rosy economic picture and posed a serious threat to financial stability by the end of the year.

See STATISTICS OF THE WORLD.   M.E.F.

MONACO. *See* STATISTICS OF THE WORLD.

MONGOLIA. In 1994, Mongolia's National Democratic (MNDP) and Social Democratic (MSDP) parties held spring demonstrations to pressure the ruling Mongolian People's Revo-

New experience. *Protesters demanding the ouster of Mongolia's government gather in front of the Parliament building in Ulan Bator in April. The action was part of a series of protests in the spring that represented the first substantial demonstrations seen in the country since the fall of Communism.*

271

lutionary Party (MPRP) for a more representative role in the country's political life. Encouraged by the electorate's broad support (58 percent) for President Punsalmaagiyn Ochirbat, their candidate in the 1993 elections, the MNDP and MSDP protested MPRP corruption and government monopoly of the media. As a result, anticorruption laws and measures to free the media were drafted.

Meanwhile, former Premier Dashiyn Byambasuren resigned his membership in the MPRP to form the Mongolian Democratic Renewal Party. The party's platform accused the MPRP of pursuing neo-Communist policies.

Gross industrial production rose 2.8 percent in the first six months of 1994, and consumer price rises were down to 3.7 percent, while inflation was on course for the International Monetary Fund's target of 51.5 percent for 1994. However, unemployment climbed, and more than one-fourth of Mongolians were living below the official subsistence level ($7-8 a month per capita). The government's property privatization scheme was undermined by failed new businesses, and there was little interest in new joint ventures, except for those involving gold mining.

Money to cover the budget deficit and fuel economic aid projects poured in from Japan and the United States and from international banks. Total aid pledged in 1993 amounted to $238.9 million in grants and $532.7 million in credits for medium-term projects in food industry development, power station improvements, and railway modernization.

Imports and exports in 1993 had been roughly equal but were more than 10 percent down from 1992; this trend continued in 1994. Reduced and irregular supplies of oil and gasoline from Russia forced temporary closures of coal mines and of some rail and air services.

See STATISTICS OF THE WORLD.   A.J.K.S.

MONTANA. See STATISTICS OF THE WORLD.

MONTENEGRO. See YUGOSLAVIA.

MOROCCO. Concrete progress was achieved in 1994 toward a settlement of the dispute over the status of the Western Sahara that had troubled Morocco for 19 years. During the spring and summer the Identification Commission of the UN Mission for the Organization of a Referendum in the Western Sa-

hara received voter application forms from both parties to the conflict: Morocco, which claimed the former Spanish territory, and the Polisario Front, the national liberation movement, which wanted an independent Saharan state. In late November, UN Secretary-General Boutros Boutros-Ghali visited the area for consultations with the two parties to ensure the holding of a referendum in 1995.

On May 25, King Hassan II appointed Foreign Minister Abdellatif Filali as prime minister, replacing Muhammad Karim Lamrani, who had headed a nonparty government of technocrats since November 1993. The political opposition welcomed the change and considered it a step toward a more substantive dialogue with the government on the issue of political liberalization.

In a rare incident of political terrorism, armed men killed two Spanish tourists in August in a Marrakech hotel. Police subsequently arrested four individuals in other parts of Morocco and found weapons caches in the Rif region in the north. Shortly thereafter, Morocco required resident and transit visas for all Algerians. In response, Algeria closed its border with Morocco and required visas for Moroccans transiting Algeria. In September the Moroccan interior minister announced that the individuals arrested had been aided by members of the Algerian security services.

Morocco hosted two important international economic conferences in 1994. The 125 member states of the General Agreement on Tariffs and Trade (GATT) met at a ministerial conference in Marrakech in April to complete the Uruguay Round of GATT negotiations.

Business people and government officials from 65 countries met in Casablanca in late October at the first Middle East/North Africa Economic Summit. Arab, Israeli, and Western leaders agreed to establish a regional development bank, a tourism board, a chamber of commerce, and a business council in order to promote regional trade and economic development and interdependence.

See STATISTICS OF THE WORLD.   J.D.

MOTION PICTURES. Amid the cynicism rampant in the United States in 1994, as evidenced by the political anger reported in public opinion polls, a film heralding human goodness turned out to be one of the favorites at U.S. box offices. *Forrest Gump,* with total earnings of $298.5 million, was second only to Disney's animated *The Lion King,* at $300.4 million. (The figures include two days of 1995 grosses.)

Directed by Robert Zemeckis, *Forrest Gump* was another powerful showcase for Tom Hanks, portraying a backward but thoroughly decent man who conquers life through a set of accidental situations. Audiences immediately took to the story, and dialogue from the film was often quoted. The role of Gump appeared to put Hanks in line for yet another Oscar nomination. The film also gained from the outstanding performances of Sally Field, Gary Sinise, and Robin Wright.

Another film that tapped into the public's sense of morality was Robert Redford's *Quiz Show.* This exposé of the dishonesty involved in a television quiz program scandal that made headlines in the 1950s focused on an honest government investigator's relentless pursuit of the truth.

Abundant Talent. Each year the excitement of filmmaking is renewed by special talent, and 1994 had its favorites. Two directors, Quentin Tarantino and John Dahl, received accolades. Tarantino made the biggest splash with *Pulp Fiction,* which won the Palme d'Or at the Cannes Film Festival and was the opening night selection at the New York Festival. His film approached the world of crime with a comic-strip élan, and many lauded his gift for dialogue and film technique. Since his previous film, *Reservoir Dogs,* dealt with a similar milieu, as did his violent script for Oliver Stone's satire on the nation's preoccupation with violence, *Natural Born Killers,* it remained to be seen whether Tarantino could expand his horizon.

Critics also increased their admiration for John Dahl as a master of contemporary film noir, a genre of dark, tough, often intricately plotted crime dramas popular in the 1940s and 1950s. His previous *Red Rock West* was regarded as a sleeper, and when he followed up with *The Last Seduction,* his abilities were even more apparent. This time the story featured a delightfully wicked woman as the protagonist who outwits every man in executing a

Tom Hanks

Everyone knows nice guys finish last and don't often win Oscars. That is, unless they're Tom Hanks. Hanks won the best actor award in 1994 for his performance as a gay lawyer dying of AIDS in *Philadelphia*—a change of pace from the comedy-oriented roles the genial star was usually seen in.

Hanks, who plausibly claims to do the dishes at home, was born in 1956 and attended at least five different grammar schools as his father changed jobs and marriages. Hanks's own first marriage, to Samantha Lewes, ended in divorce (the couple had two children). He and second wife Rita Wilson have a son.

Seeing Eugene O'Neill's *The Iceman Cometh* in college drew Hanks to the stage. He later won a role as a young man who falls for a mermaid in the movie *Splash* (1984). He then played a bemused regular guy in such hit films as *Big* (1988), which won him an Oscar nomination, and *Sleepless in Seattle* (1993).

In 1994, Hanks starred in *Forrest Gump,* another box-office success, as a simple-minded Alabama lad who bumps shoulders with great names in recent history. Somehow, being Tom Hanks, he survives it all with his likability intact.   W.A.M.

What Might Have Been

Humphrey Bogart and Ingrid Bergman were so perfect in the movie *Casablanca* that it's nearly impossible to imagine anyone taking their place. Yet Warner Brothers first planned to cast George Raft and Ann Sheridan in that 1943 classic. In their recent book *Hollywood's First Choices,* Jeff Burkhart and Bruce Stuart name many other memorable films featuring actors or actresses in parts originally slated for someone else. Each star below was not the first choice for the role listed. Can you guess who was?

1. Richard Burton and Elizabeth Taylor as George and Martha in *Who's Afraid of Virginia Woolf?* (1966): (*a*) Cliff Robertson and Glenda Jackson, (*b*) Burt Lancaster and Joanne Woodward, (*c*) Cary Grant and Ingrid Bergman, (*d*) David Niven and Anne Bancroft

2. Peter O'Toole as *Lawrence of Arabia* (1962): (*a*) Marlon Brando, (*b*) Terence Stamp, (*c*) Sean Connery, (*d*) Michael Caine

3. Gloria Swanson as Norma Desmond in *Sunset Boulevard* (1950): (*a*) Helen Hayes, (*b*) Mae West, (*c*) Bette Davis, (*d*) Tallulah Bankhead

4. Rex Harrison as Professor Henry Higgins in *My Fair Lady* (1964): (*a*) David Niven, (*b*) Laurence Harvey, (*c*) Peter O'Toole, (*d*) Christopher Plummer

5. Clint Eastwood as *Dirty Harry* (1971): (*a*) Steve McQueen, (*b*) John Wayne, (*c*) Gene Hackman, (*d*) Robert Mitchum

6. Marlon Brando as Don Corleone in *The Godfather* (1972): (*a*) Rod Steiger, (*b*) George C. Scott, (*c*) Peter Falk, (*d*) Sir Laurence Olivier

7. Dustin Hoffman as Benjamin Braddock in *The Graduate* (1967): (*a*) Jon Voight, (*b*) Richard Dreyfuss, (*c*) James Caan, (*d*) Warren Beatty

8. Harrison Ford as Indiana Jones: (*a*) Robert Redford, (*b*) Nick Nolte, (*c*) Tom Selleck, (*d*) Martin Sheen

Answers:

(1) *c,* (2) *a,* (3) *b,* (4) *c,* (5) *b,* (6) *d,* (7) *d,* (8) *c.*

criminal game plan. The superbly played role was likely to enhance the career of actress Linda Fiorentino.

Three filmmakers, Steve James, Frederick Marx, and Peter Gilbert, scored a success by teaming up on the unusual *Hoop Dreams,* a documentary that was featured in the First Cinema section of the Toronto International Film Festival and packed the power of a dramatic feature. For five years they followed the fortunes of two young African-American students who wanted to become basketball players, and the revelations about their lives, their hopes, and the sport itself were spellbinding.

Kevin Smith and Scott Mosier, young novice filmmakers from New Jersey, raised $27,000 for their first venture, *Clerks,* showcased at the Sundance Film Festival and then in the New Directors/New Films series in New York City. Their ribald, outrageous comedy about a day in the life of two convenience store workers brought them Hollywood offers as well as controversy. The barrage of profanity in the dialogue resulted in a stringent NC-17 rating (no one under 17 allowed), but Miramax, the distributor, won a rare victory on appeal to the ratings board of the Motion Picture Association of America, and an R was assigned instead.

Among the many individual performers who merited special attention were Jim Carrey, who exhibited his comic talent in three hits, including *The Mask;* Rosie Perez, who, in addition to winning an Oscar nomination and a Berlin International Film Festival Special Mention award for her performance in *Fearless,* was a standout in the comedy *It Could Happen to You;* Meryl Streep, who broke out of the mold by rafting in *The River Wild;* Terence Stamp, who portrayed a transsexual in Australia's offbeat *The Adventures of Priscilla, Queen of the Desert;* Crissy Rock, who won the Berlin festival's best actress award for her searing portrayal of a mother whose children are taken away in Ken Loach's *Ladybird Ladybird;* Tim Robbins and Morgan Freeman for their performances as convicts in *The Shawshank Redemption;* Martin Landau for his hilarious portrait of horror star Bela Lugosi in *Ed Wood;* Dianne Wiest, who played an egocentric actress in Woody Allen's *Bullets Over Broadway;* Chaz Palminteri for his role as a play-writing

Disney roars. *Disney continued its string of successful animated features with* The Lion King, *which took in over $300 million during the year.*

gangster in the same film; Paul Newman for his memorable performance in *Nobody's Fool;* and Nigel Hawthorne as Britain's troubled ruler in *The Madness of King George.*

Horror Revisited. With *Mary Shelley's Frankenstein,* Britain's extremely talented Kenneth Branagh went back to Shelley's 1818 novel to retrieve the social comment inherent in the work but lost in Hollywood's highly entertaining but simplistic 1931 classic and its offshoots. Branagh, who played Dr. Frankenstein and directed the film, stressed the scientific experiment angle and made his creature, sympathetically played by Robert De Niro covered with surgical stitching, a pitiful, lost soul unjustly scorned by society. The film was a tour de force and anything but a typical horror flick.

Another excursion into the genre was *Interview With the Vampire,* based on the Anne Rice novel and replete with homosexual implications, with Tom Cruise in a role unusual for the Hollywood heartthrob. Director Wes Craven further parlayed his incredibly successful *Nightmare on Elm Street* series with *Wes Craven's New Nightmare,* which premiered at the Toronto International Film Festival and satirized the very making of horror films. In a twist on the horror category, Tim Burton's *Ed Wood* was a comic tribute to the late director, who was known for making terrible horror flicks, such as *Plan 9 From Outer Space.*

Big Guns. The marketplace was glutted with films given big send-offs by major studios and distributors. Among the high-profile group were *True Lies,* with Arnold Schwarzenegger as a James Bond type; the fanciful, often very funny *Junior,* with Schwarzenegger as the first pregnant man; *Nell,* starring Jodie Foster as a Tennessee woman who lives in isolation; and a remake of *Little Women* starring Winona Ryder, Trini Alvarado, Claire Danes, Susan Sarandon, and Gabriel Byrne.

Also receiving big promotions were *Clear and Present Danger,* starring Harrison Ford; *Speed,* one of the year's best action films, directed by Jan de Bont; *Crooklyn,* Spike Lee's intimate drama about a Brooklyn family; *Disclosure,* a timely, riveting drama based on Michael Crichton's novel dealing with sexual harassment; *Cobb,* with Tommy Lee Jones as the legendary baseball player Ty Cobb; *Ready to Wear (Prêt-à-porter),* the film about the fashion world that director Robert Altman had been planning for years; *The Hudsucker Proxy,* a Joel and Ethan Coen film finding laughs in clichéd films about the American dream; a remake of *Miracle on 34th Street,* with Richard Attenborough in the Kris Kringle role; and *Love Affair,* a bland remake of *An Affair to Remember,* this time with Warren Beatty and Annette Bening playing the lovers.

In addition, there were *Wolf,* starring Jack Nicholson as a man who turns into a creature

Crime pays. *Director Quentin Tarantino's* Pulp Fiction, *a tongue-in-cheek crime thriller, made one of
the biggest splashes of the year, winning the Palme
d'Or at the Cannes Film Festival and opening the
New York Film Festival. Among its stars was Uma
Thurman.*

of the night; *When a Man Loves a Woman,*
with Meg Ryan emoting as an alcoholic; *Only
You,* a romantic fable with Marisa Tomei and
Robert Downey, Jr.; *Wyatt Earp,* a slow-paced,
heavy-handed film with Kevin Costner in the
title role; and the lively *Maverick,* with James
Garner, Jodie Foster, and Mel Gibson.

Independent Voices. Some of the greatest
pleasures were afforded audiences who chose
offbeat films from the United States and
abroad. Intense, interesting conversation highlighted *Barcelona,* Whit Stillman's film about
Americans in Spain. An acerbic look at legendary writer and wit Dorothy Parker dominated Alan Rudolph's somber *Mrs. Parker and
the Vicious Circle.* Louis Malle made an en-
grossing film from André Gregory's staging of
Chekhov's *Uncle Vanya,* under the title *Vanya
on 42d Street.* The conflicting feelings many
women harbor about having children provided
Henry Jaglom with the basis for his thought-
provoking *Babyfever.*

A brutal murder of a woman in New
Zealand by two teenage girls, one of them her
daughter, was the factual basis for *Heavenly
Creatures.* The turbulent lives of T. S. Eliot and

his wife provided fodder for *Tom and Viv,* with
Miranda Richardson and Willem Dafoe.
Death and the Maiden, an adaptation of Ariel
Dorfman's play about revenge for political torture, was directed by Roman Polanski and
starred Sigourney Weaver and Ben Kingsley.
Marcel Ophuls created a powerful documentary, *The Troubles We've Seen,* about the work
and ethics of war correspondents.

Among the outstanding foreign language imports were *Eat Drink Man Woman,* about a
Taiwanese chef and his spirited daughters; the
French *Le Colonel Chabert,* with Gérard De-
pardieu as a war hero presumed to have been
killed and Fanny Ardant as a supposed widow;
two superior Italian films, *Caro Diario,* Nanni
Moretti's take on life in Italy, and *Ciao, Profes-
sore,* Lina Wertmuller's wise film about the
plight of education in southern Italy; the intensely political *To Live,* Zhang Yimou's saga
of individuals struggling to survive in China;
and from Argentina, *I Don't Want to Talk
About It,* directed by Maria Luisa Bemberg and
dealing sensitively with love between a young
female dwarf and an understanding older man.

Colorful trio. *With the release of both* White *and*
Red *(following his earlier* Blue*), Polish filmmaker
Krzysztof Kieslowski completed his highly praised*
Three Colors *trilogy, based on the colors of the
French flag and the motto of the French Revolution
(Liberty, Equality, and Fraternity). One of the stars of*
Red *was Irène Jacob.*

Polish filmmaker Krzysztof Kieslowski completed his *Three Colors* trilogy, with the release of both *White* and *Red,* which followed his earlier *Blue.*

Business. The film community reacted with astonishment when three powerful men in the industry—Steven Spielberg (*see profile in* PEOPLE IN THE NEWS), Jeffrey Katzenberg, and David Geffen—announced that they would be forming a new studio. Although Spielberg had his own film company, he had also worked through Universal, where he got his start. Katzenberg was a major creative force at Disney until he resigned after not being promoted. Geffen, affiliated with Universal, earned his riches in the record business.

Some skeptics wondered whether the studio would actually materialize, but there was agreement that if it did, it would constitute a major new force in Hollywood. There was speculation that Universal, part of MCA Inc., might be bought back from the Matsushita Electrical Industrial Company, or that MCA's top executives, Lew Wasserman and Sidney Sheinberg, might leave the company because of unhappy relations with the Japanese owners. Such developments could affect the future of the Spielberg-Katzenberg-Geffen project because of Spielberg's close relationship with Sheinberg.

The Sony Corporation announced in November that it was taking a $2.7 billion write-off on Columbia and TriStar, the two Hollywood studios that it had acquired for $5 billion in 1989. The write-off was necessitated by a series of box-office flops and costly executive buyouts.

Attention was also focused in Hollywood on the growing potential for technological advances that would have an impact on how the public saw movies. Influential agent Michael Ovitz, broadening his scope at his Creative Artists Agency, was engaged by Bell Atlantic, Nynex, and Pacific Telesis to establish a project linking movies and phone systems.

The Oscars. Steven Spielberg finally won an Oscar for best direction, the recognition coming for *Schindler's List,* which also won for best picture, adapted screenplay, art direction, original score, cinematography, and editing. Tom Hanks took the best actor Oscar for

Face facts. *One of the year's most notable performances was given by actor Jim Carrey in* The Mask, *the story of an average guy who acquires new abilities and conquers new worlds when he dons a peculiar mask.*

Philadelphia. Holly Hunter (*see profile in* PEOPLE IN THE NEWS) won as best actress for *The Piano;* Anna Paquin was named best supporting actress for her work in that film, which also earned Jane Campion the Oscar for best original screenplay. Tommy Lee Jones was best supporting actor for *The Fugitive.* The Oscar for best foreign-language film went to Spain's *Belle Epoque.*   W.W.

MOZAMBIQUE. Peaceful elections in Mozambique on October 27-29, 1994, culminated the UN-aided peace process that began with the Rome peace treaty two years before. Despite delays in the demobilization of troops, the formation of a new national Army, and election preparations, the elections went without major incident. Nearly 90 percent of registered voters went to the polls despite the last-minute threat of a boycott by Afonso Dhlakama, leader of the rebel group Renamo (Mozambican National Resistance).

Election results gave 53.3 percent of the presidential vote to incumbent Mozambican Liberation Front (Frelimo) candidate Joaquim Chissano, with 33.7 percent going to Dhlakama and the remainder split among ten other candidates.

Frelimo won the legislative race as well, though by a somewhat smaller margin. International observers judged the process substantially free and fair, although Renamo charged fraud and threatened briefly not to accept the results. President Chissano's new cabinet was generally praised as including more competent technocrats but did not include significant opposition or nonpartisan figures.

The peace process and election preparations were facilitated by the presence of as many as 7,000 UN military and civilian peacekeeping personnel. For the elections, foreign contributions amounted to more than $60 million, and $19 million was specially allocated to Renamo to facilitate its transformation from a military group into a political party. More than 75,000 soldiers, 19,000 from Renamo and 56,000 from Frelimo, were demobilized during 1994. Although the new national Army was to include 15,000 from each side, the total of those recruited and trained came to only roughly 10,000 by year's end.

By mid-1994 more than 1 million of an estimated 1.5 million refugees had returned to Mozambique, and nearly all were expected to return by year's end. Of the approximately 3.5 million people left internally displaced when the war ended, about 75 percent had been resettled.

Total grain production in the 1993-1994 growing season increased some 7 percent, but with drought in some areas and a cyclone in northern Nampula Province some 1.1 million were still estimated to be in need of food assistance.

See STATISTICS OF THE WORLD.   W.M.

MUSIC. The music industry prospered in 1994, as composers produced new works, popular singers and bands took to the road for the first time in decades, and the Rolling

Stones proved that 50-year-olds can still play rock and roll. A compact disk (CD) of Gregorian chant developed an unexpected crossover audience and sold 4 million copies.

POPULAR MUSIC

In 1994, music fans found their way back to the garden a quarter of a century after the original Woodstock. The garden now had a corporate sponsor, an album, a home video, and a pay-per-view telecast attached to it, but music—and mud—still defined Woodstock '94 as 350,000 people gathered for three days in August in Saugerties, NY.

Michael Jackson, who spent much of 1993 battling child molestation charges and an addiction to prescription drugs, bounced back in 1994. In January the case was settled out of court, with Jackson allegedly paying his accuser an estimated $20 million. In May, Jackson stunned the world by marrying Elvis's little girl, Lisa Marie Presley, in a secret civil service in the Dominican Republic.

One of the saddest stories of 1994 was the April 5 suicide of Nirvana leader Kurt Cobain (*see* OBITUARIES). Whether his suicide symbolized the futility felt by Generation X'ers, as many observers suggested, or whether it was simply the desperate act of an unhappy individual, Cobain's death effectively silenced one of the great bands to come into prominence in the 1990s.

Success Stories. Disney produced a lion that roared its way all the way up the charts. The sound track to *The Lion King*, penned by Elton John and Tim Rice, was one of 1994's best-selling albums, tying for first place late in the year with *The Sign* by the new Swedish pop act Ace of Bass. By year's end *The Lion King* had sold more than 6 million copies in the United States.

But the real music news in 1994 was the astonishing number of new acts that broke through the clutter. Besides Ace of Bass, major label debuts by Dylan devotees Counting Crows and pop punksters Green Day surpassed the 3 million sales mark. Another act breaking through the floodgates was All-4-One, with its remakes—R & B/pop harmony laden—of *So Much in Love* and *I Swear*. Others were hard rockers Candlebox, folk rocker Sheryl Crow, punkers Offspring, winsome

Day breaks through. *One of the most notable bands to come to the fore during the year was Green Day, whose major-label debut album, entitled* Dookie, *passed the 3 million sales mark. The punk rock trio is comprised of drummer Tré Cool (foreground), singer-guitarist Billie Joe (top left), and bassist Mike Dirnt (top right).*

New York discovery Lisa Loeb, and Southern rockers Collective Soul.

More familiar names were also proving their staying power. Boyz II Men dominated the charts with its second album, aptly titled *II*, and its single *I'll Make Love to You*, which threatened to break Whitney Houston's record for the most weeks at No. 1 on Billboard's Hot 100 Singles chart. But Houston had no reason for tears, as she won several awards at both the American Music Awards and the Grammy Awards in 1994. Additionally, her 1992 sound track to *The Bodyguard* notched 11 million in

domestic sales in 1994, passing Garth Brooks's 1990 release *No Fence* for the best-selling album of the 1990s.

For every success there was an equally impressive failure. New releases by ZZ Top, Hammer, Vanilla Ice, and Traffic, among others, fell very short of sales expectations.

R & B and Rap. Rappers continued to experience great success in 1994, with several new hip-hop artists like Coolio and Warren G, as well as Da Brat, scoring major hits with their album debuts. However, rap yielded a portion of its hold on the chart to smooth-styled vocalists coming back in vogue. After a long absence Anita Baker returned with a graceful collection of songs, and Luther Vandross released a collection of cover tunes that seemed to strike a chord with audiences.

Artists who landed somewhere in between rap and R & B also found success. Smooth R & B/hip-hopper R. Kelly made his mark in virtually every aspect of music. As an artist, he saw his album *12 Play* stay on top of the R & B charts for a record-breaking nine weeks, while the single *Bump n' Grind* set a record for consecutive weeks at No. 1 on the Hot R & B Singles chart.

Kelly also scored as a producer with new sensation Aaliyah (whom Kelly married, or so rumor had it, sometime during the year) and as a songwriter for the new hit female duo Changing Faces. Several other female R & B-based acts also broke through during 1994, among them Zhane, Xscape, Brandy, and Sudden Change.

But the news was not all positive for the R & B/rap community in 1994. Concern over the negative impact that some gangsta rap lyrics may have on listeners was the subject of both House and Senate hearings in early 1994. At year's end no action had resulted from the hearings.

Country. The illegitimate son of baseball player Tug McGraw had a few hits of his own in 1994. Tim McGraw's second album, *Not a Moment Too Soon*, spent a staggering 26 weeks on top of Billboard's Top Country Albums chart and sold more than 3 million copies. A number of other artists broke through in 1994, including Faith Hill and Martina McBride.

Reba McEntire

In Reba McEntire's songs, fickle lovers abound. But in 1994, McEntire was doing anything but nurse a broken heart over that most fickle of lovers, fame. The country music star's career was in full flower; she released her 23rd album (*Read My Mind*), a video (*Why Haven't I Heard From You?*), and an autobiography (*Reba: My Story*).

The daughter of a champion steer roper, McEntire was born in Oklahoma in 1955 and sang at local rodeos before being discovered at 19. Her career took off when she changed recording companies in 1984, moving from Mercury to MCA.

Unlike the sometimes passive women in her songs, McEntire has toughed her way through painful losses. In 1991, seven band members and McEntire's road manager died in a plane crash. McEntire, who was not aboard, returned to the stage within weeks.

In 1987, McEntire divorced rodeo rider Charlie Battles, her husband since 1976, and in 1989 she married band manager Narvel Blackstock. They have one son.

I.S.

Vince Gill continued to collect awards, capturing the male vocalist award for a record-breaking fourth time and entertainer of the year award for the second time at October's Country Music Association Awards.

While he released no records in the United States (other than a special promotional charity album available only through McDonald's), Garth Brooks focused on the international market. He set both Europe and Australia ablaze, drawing 72,000 people in Dublin over eight nights, making him the biggest draw since the pope's tour in 1979.

In 1993 country showed its connection with 1970s pop via *Common Thread,* a collection of Eagles songs recorded by today's country stars. Similarly, in 1994 it displayed its relationship to great Memphis soul classics through *Rhythm, Country & Blues,* a duets album that paired country acts with R & B greats.

Trends. The biggest musical trend in 1994 was tribute albums. No fewer than 20 recordings of various acts performing songs by artists who had influenced them hit the streets. Among the artists paid homage to were Merle Haggard, the Carpenters, Black Sabbath, Lynyrd Skynyrd, Keith Whitley, Van Morrison, Curtis Mayfield, Arthur Alexander, Kiss, and Richard Thompson.

In what was perhaps the ultimate version of a tribute album, Atlantic announced its plans to release a tribute to Carole King, with different artists performing their favorite song from her best-selling album *Tapestry.*

On the Road. Acts who had spent years, some even decades, off the road returned to performing, creating a banner year for the concert industry. Both Pink Floyd, which scored a major hit with its new album, *The Division Bell,* and the Rolling Stones set milestones by earning more than $100 million in ticket sales on their tours. But the performances everyone was talking about took place on Barbra Streisand's five-city tour, her first in 27 years. Tickets were priced as high as $350, with scalpers getting many times that from fans desperate to see their favorite diva up close. Also hitting the road after a prolonged absence were the re-formed Eagles, whose first tour in 14 years was cut short by Glenn Frey's intestinal problems. Although the tour was not to start until 1995, Led Zeppelin leaders Robert Plant and Jimmy Page announced their intention to play again together, ending a long separation, and released a recording of the band's *Unledded* MTV acoustic concert, called *No Quarter.*

Legal Decisions. Pop musicians found themselves in the courts almost as frequently as in the studio in 1994. One of the most watched cases was George Michael's suit against Sony Records, in which the British superstar sued his label for restraint of trade in an attempt to be let out of his contract. The case, which was heard in England's High Court, was adjudicated in Sony's favor.

Michael Bolton also lost during his day in court when a U.S. federal jury ruled that his 1991 hit *Love Is a Wonderful Thing* borrowed significant elements from the Isley Brothers' 1966 song of the same name. Bolton's attorney filed a motion to appeal.

Another copyright case made it all the way to the Supreme Court in March, when the highest court in the United States decided that 2 Live Crew's rap parody of Roy Orbison's *Oh Pretty Woman* was entitled to fair-use exemption under U.S. copyright law. While the Court upheld the principle of parody, it stopped short of saying that all parodies fall under the fair-use umbrella.

During the summer, top rock group Pearl Jam (*see profile in* PEOPLE IN THE NEWS) filed an antitrust complaint with the U.S. Justice Department against Ticketmaster, a nationwide ticket service. The complaint led to two hearings, in June and September, by separate committees of the U.S. House of Representatives. After the June hearing Representative Gary Condit (D, California), who had chaired the hearing, sent a letter to the Justice Department asking it to reconsider its 1991 decision that Ticketmaster's purchase of competitor Ticketron did not give Ticketmaster a monopoly on ticket distribution. At the September hearing a panel of the House Energy and Commerce Committee considered a bill requiring ticket agencies to print individual surcharge prices on tickets, but the bill died with the end of the congressional term.

Technology. Much of the hardware that was supposed to have ingratiated itself with the American public by now, such as minidisk players and compact digital disk players, had yet to make more than a blip on the collective consciousness by year's end.

Instead, the format that appealed to artists and consumers alike was CD-ROM. David Bowie, Peter Gabriel, and Prince were among those who released in 1994 CD-ROMs that allowed hackers to interact with the music and images created by their favorite musicians. Todd Rundgren formed an interactive record label that, in addition to producing new music, would focus on releasing classic rock albums in several formats including CD-ROM, Philips's interactive CD-I, and the 3DO videogame technology.

Music also created a traffic jam on the information superhighway. On-line networks and services such as CompuServe provided a way to keep up-to-date on a band's activities, and it was not uncommon for music, or at least snippets of it, to be available to on-line service subscribers before it arrived in stores. Songs, complete or in snippets, by such acts as Aerosmith, Neil Young, and Madonna, were all on-line before the recordings came out.

Grammy Awards. The Grammys for best single and best female pop vocalist went to Whitney Houston for *I Will Always Love You;* Houston's *The Bodyguard,* featuring music from the 1992 film of the same name, won the top album Grammy. The best song award went to *A Whole New World (Aladdin's Theme)* from the film *Aladdin* (1992). Sting was named best male pop vocalist for *If I Ever Lose My Faith in You,* and Dwight Yoakam won the Grammy for top male country vocalist for *Ain't That Lonely Yet.* The best female country vocalist was Mary Chapin Carpenter, for *Passionate Kisses.* Aerosmith won the Grammy for best rock duo or group (*Livin' on the Edge*), and Sade for best rhythm and blues duo or group (*No Ordinary Love*). The best new artist was Toni Braxton.   M.A.N.

CLASSICAL MUSIC

One of the two big events in classical music in 1994 was the Three Tenors reunion concert by Luciano Pavarotti, Placido Domingo, and José Carreras at Los Angeles's Dodger Stadium in July. The other was *Chant,* a recording of unadorned Gregorian chant by the Benedictine

Three for the show. *One of the biggest musical events of 1994 was the reunion in the summer of the "three tenors"—(left to right) Placido Domingo, José Carreras, and Luciano Pavarotti—who reprised their 1990 joint concert with an appearance in Los Angeles. The recording of the event sold over 2.5 million copies.*

monks of Santo Domingo de Silos that astounded industry observers by becoming the year's classical best-seller.

The two typified the increasing polarization of classical music: While the tenor event—whose recording sold some 2.5 million units for Atlantic before year's end—was performance based, *Chant*—which sold 4 million units for EMI—was entirely a recording phenomenon. The tenors drew a loyal old guard that turns out for brand-name events, while *Chant* seemed to tap into a mostly young, more elusive group of rock and jazz refugees ranging in age from 16 to 50. *Chant* had no strong associations with any other cultural or demographic group and melded well with a number of recordings by popular, spiritually oriented contemporary composers such as John Tavener, whose *Akathist of Thanksgiving* (Sony) used Byzantine chant, Henryk Gorecki's *Miserere* (Nonesuch), which was associated with Catholic liturgy, and Gavin Bryars's meditative *Vita Nova* (ECM). Particularly successful was the ancient music group Anonymous 4, whose Harmonia Mundi recording of works from the 13th-century Montpellier manuscript sold 55,000 copies in its first three weeks of release.

More Than Minimal. The trance-inducing repetitiveness of minimalist composers may have laid the groundwork for the popularity of

music such as *Chant*. And minimalists too enjoyed a very good year, even though most had moved on to less minimal styles. British composer Michael Nyman enjoyed acclaim for his score to the film *The Piano*, although many critics were not as excited about his recasting of the music into his Piano Concerto (Argo). John Adams unveiled his splendid new Violin Concerto in Minneapolis in January, a work that continued the more harmonically sophisticated, polytonal adventures begun in his 1992 Chamber Symphony. Dutch minimalist Louis Andriessen received increased American recognition, not only in residence at the annual Festival of Contemporary Music at Tanglewood, MA, but also with the release of his *De Stijl* (Nonesuch). Philip Glass's Symphony No. 2 was not well received in its October premiere with the Brooklyn Philharmonic Orchestra, though his operatic reworking of the Jean Cocteau film *La belle et la bête*, which toured Europe throughout the summer months, drew some favorable notice.

The most remarkable feat of new-music programming came from cellist Yo-Yo Ma, who premiered four different cello concertos in as many cities, all of them winners: Christopher Rouse's work in Los Angeles in January, John Harbison's gamelan-influenced composition in Boston in April, film composer John Williams's surprisingly assured endeavor at

Tanglewood in July, and Richard Danielpour's fearlessly introspective concerto in San Francisco in September. Ma recorded Rouse's and Danielpour's works with the Philadelphia Orchestra late in the year and issued Stephen Albert's brooding masterpiece in the genre on *The New York Album* on Sony. Albert, who was killed in a 1992 car accident, left a somewhat unfinished Symphony No. 2, which was premiered by the New York Philharmonic in November.

Opera. New operas did not fare as well. Dominick Argento's *The Dream of Valentino* was respectfully panned at the Washington (DC) Opera in January, though reviews ranged from ecstatic to disappointed for Conrad Susa's *Dangerous Liaisons,* which opened in September at the San Francisco Opera with a charismatic cast including Thomas Hampson, Frederica von Stade, and Renée Fleming. Opera Theater of St. Louis gave a rare revival of Susa's more substantial *Black River* in June, as well as the successful U.S. premiere in May of Leonard Bernstein's final version of his Broadway operetta *Candide.* At Lyric Opera of Chicago, Samuel Ramey scored a major suc-

Heavenly Hits From a Monastery

Over the years, as the Benedictine monks of Santo Domingo de Silos in Spain recorded the centuries-old Gregorian chants they sang in worship, making a name as a pop music sensation was surely far from their minds. But *Chant,* a selection from those recordings first released in Spain in 1993, became a worldwide hit and the fastest-selling classical album ever. In the United States, *Chant* zoomed to No. 1 on the classical charts in 1994—and reached No. 3 on the pop charts as well.

Perhaps it was the music's otherworldly purity. Perhaps it was a slogan—"Prepare for the Millennium"—and a surrealistic cover showing hooded monks among the clouds. Whatever the reason, *Chant* rang up tens of millions of dollars in sales.

The monks gave most of their unexpectedly high royalties to charity, and, under a barrage of media and tourist attention, closed the monastery doors.

But before the year was over, they had another hit on their hands as *Chant Noel,* also made up of chants they had recorded years before, joined *Chant* in the top ten of the classical music charts.

MUSIC

cess singing the title role in *Boris Godunov* for the first time in the United States. The Metropolitan Opera broke out of its standard-repertoire conservatism with Verdi's early, rarely heard *I Lombardi*, broadcast nationwide on PBS in March, though its semisurreal production was not universally loved. On disk, conductor James Levine led the Met in a well-received recording of Verdi's *Il Trovatore* (Sony). Levine's recording of Wagner's *Parsifal* on Deutsche Grammophon (DG), however, was damned for its slow tempos. Clearly, the best dramas were backstage: The reputedly temperamental Kathleen Battle was fired from a production of *Daughter of the Regiment* in February, and the young soprano Harolyn Blackwell did well in her place.

News From the Podium. The great orchestral relationships continued to be Kurt Masur and the New York Philharmonic, which produced some excellent CDs of Shostakovich and Kurt Weill, and Pierre Boulez in his unofficial guest-conducting relationship with the Chicago Symphony Orchestra. Both David Zinman (Baltimore Symphony Orchestra) and Esa-Pekka Salonen (Los Angeles Philharmonic) were responsible for some of the year's most innovative programming, the latter recording Witold Lutoslawski's Symphony No. 4 (Sony), which became something of a memorial after the composer's death on February 7. Leonard Slatkin announced he would leave the St. Louis Symphony Orchestra for the National Symphony Orchestra in Washington, DC, beginning in 1996, and Herbert Blomstedt wrapped up his final season with the San Francisco Symphony, making way for Michael Tilson Thomas.

Recordings. Competition from reissues and cheap Eastern European recordings dampened the market for new orchestral recordings of standard repertoire. Though Newport Classics issued the most expensive CD to date (a super-high-fidelity recording of Strauss's *Also Sprach Zarathustra* priced at $49.95), CDs generally became less expensive, particularly with large music-store chains selling them below cost and driving retail profit margins down to near-crisis point.

However limited the market, excellent new recordings of standard repertoire came out. A clutch of young violinists—Maxim Vengerov, Gil Shaham, Anne Akiko Meyers, and others—made impressive showings both in concert and on disk. Though conductor Myung-Whun Chung was abruptly fired from the Paris Opera Bastille in August, he left great recordings of Verdi's *Otello*, with Placido Domingo and Cheryl Studer, and one of Olivier Messiaen's last orchestral works, *Illuminations of the Beyond* (both DG). Berlioz's four-hour *Les Troyens* was recorded with fiery briskness by the Montréal Symphony Orchestra under Charles Dutoit (London).

Claudio Abbado led the most convincing recording yet of Mussorgsky's *Boris Godunov* in its original orchestration (Sony). Jessye Norman lent her considerable vocal riches to the title role of Strauss's *Salome* (Philips). London's Entartete Musik series—works suppressed by Nazi Germany—was represented by Viktor Ullmann's chilling, acerbic satire of the Third Reich, *The Emperor of Atlantis*, written in 1943 shortly before his death in Auschwitz, and Bertholt Goldschmidt's highly original *Der Gewaltige Hahnrei*, which brought belated recognition to the composer, who is in his 90s and living in London.

John Eliot Gardiner led the recording premiere of Berlioz's early, recently discovered *Messe Solennelle* (Philips), which proved to be full of ideas the composer recycled into later pieces. Another important rediscovery was a set of Samuel Barber songs (including some early, unpublished gems) by Studer, Hampson, and pianist John Browning (DG). The biggest orchestral surprise, though, was a complete recording of Charles Koechlin's orchestrally extravagant *The Jungle Book*, conducted by Zinman (RCA). Welsh bass-baritone Bryn Terfel made an acclaimed Met debut in October in *The Marriage of Figaro* in tandem with the release of his excellent recording of the title role (DG). Krystian Zimerman's recording of Debussy's preludes (DG) would have been the best piano recording of the year were it not for the imposing *Richter: The Authorized Recordings* (Philips), a 21-CD set of recent recordings, ranging from Bach to Prokofiev, by the visionary Russian pianist Sviatoslav Richter. It was the recording event of the year.   D.P.S.

MYANMAR.   *See* BURMA.

N

NAMIBIA. *See* Africa; Statistics of the World.

NAURU. *See* Statistics of the World.

NEBRASKA. *See* Statistics of the World.

NEPAL. *See* Statistics of the World.

NETHERLANDS, THE. In August 1994, following protracted interparty negotiations, a new coalition government headed by Wim Kok of the Labor Party took power in the Netherlands, replacing a coalition of Labor and the Christian Democrats, both of which had suffered severe losses in the elections of May 3. The Christian Democrats had lost 20 of 54 seats, while Labor had lost 12 of 49. Labor's partners in the new coalition, the two liberal parties, were the big winners in the elections: the right-of-center People's Party for Freedom and Democracy (VVD) with 31 seats and the left-of-center Dem-ocrats 66 (D'66) with 24 seats. For the first time since the early 1970s, the Christian Democrats found themselves excluded from the government.

In June elections to the European Parliament, however, the Christian Democrats remained the strongest Dutch party, with ten seats, followed by the Labor Party (eight), the VVD (six), D'66 (four), and the Greens (one).

In an effort to counteract unemployment and trim the budget deficit, the incoming Kok government proposed cuts in social security, state pensions, higher education, and health care. As the country looked set to benefit from a mild recession recovery, a windfall in revenues allowed the new government to downscale the 1994 budget deficit forecast from 3.3 percent of gross domestic product to 3 percent. GDP growth for 1994 was estimated at about 2 percent, backed by improved industrial production. The trade balance showed a surplus of exports over imports for the second consecutive year. Investment in Eastern Europe, having grown steadily in recent years, exceeded $1.3 billion in 1994. Among the negative features of the resurgent economy were a slight increase in inflation (after a 1993 decline) and worsening unemployment, which hovered near 8 percent for much of the year.

Meanwhile, on June 29 the Belgian and Dutch defense ministers signed an agreement to combine their respective navies into an integrated command structure. The combined fleet would be under a Dutch admiral and based at the Dutch Den Helder naval base, but each fleet retained the right to act independently. The planned integration would reduce operational costs and available tonnage. A similar cooperation agreement was signed in mid-August between the heads of the Dutch and Belgian air forces. Proposed cuts in the Dutch defense budget caused the resignation of the chief of staff.

See Statistics of the World.   F.G.E.

NEVADA. *See* Statistics of the World.

NEW BRUNSWICK. *See* Statistics of the World.

NEWFOUNDLAND. *See* Statistics of the World.

NEW HAMPSHIRE. *See* Statistics of the World.

NEW JERSEY. *See* State Government Review; Statistics of the World.

NEW MEXICO. *See* Statistics of the World.

NEW YORK. *See* State Government Review; Statistics of the World.

NEW ZEALAND. New Zealand Prime Minister Jim Bolger's National Party continued in power in 1994, weathering a difficult August by-election. Bolger reshuffled his cabinet in late 1993, dismissing Finance Minister Ruth Richardson. Her departure left only one woman in the Bolger government, a political embarrassment for the prime minister. Bolger was able to consolidate his one-seat majority in Parliament somewhat by securing the election of an opposition member, Labor's Peter Tapsell, as speaker; Tapsell was the first Maori to hold the position.

However, the government's tenure was jeopardized when Richardson resigned her parliamentary seat in July 1994, forcing a by-election the following month. The National Party narrowly prevailed over the rival left-wing Alliance in the balloting, with the Labor Party finishing a distant third.

Princely greeting. *Great Britain's Prince Charles (left) receives a "hongi," a traditional Maori greeting, while visiting Waitangi, New Zealand, in February. During the year revelations about indecorous behavior by members of the British royal family stimulated debate on whether New Zealand should retain the British monarch as its official head of state.*

In November, Alliance leader Jim Anderton, who topped opinion polls as preferred prime minister, resigned from the party leadership for personal reasons, jeopardizing his party's future prospects.

Intraparty divisions became more noticeable during the year as incumbent members of Parliament competed for renomination, the result of a reduction in the number of constituencies required under the new electoral system approved in a 1993 referendum. In April, Bolger announced that he would be willing to cooperate with members resigning from the National Party to form new political parties, considering them to be potential coalition partners. As a result, however, the National Party lost its overall majority.

The new electoral system inspired formation of several Green parties. Three Maori organizations challenged aspects of a voter registration campaign for Maori voters. Even so, the number of parliamentary seats reserved for Maori rose from four to five.

Revelations about the British royal family brought the question of its role in New Zealand society and government to the fore. Bolger called for debate on the question, suggesting the year 2000 as "an appropriate symbolic moment" for a change in the country's head of state.

New Zealand forces joined the United Nations peacekeeping mission in Bosnia-Hercegovina in September, the country's biggest commitment of military personnel to a combat zone since the Vietnam War. New Zealand also took part in an airlift of food to Rwandan refugees in Goma, Zaire, in August. A New Zealand platoon attached to the UN returned in June from Somalia.

Although inflation rose slightly, to around 3 percent, New Zealand's growth rate in 1994 exceeded 6 percent for the first time in a decade. The government enjoyed its first surplus in 17 years. The value of the New Zealand dollar also rose steadily, and unemployment dropped to around 8.4 percent from 11 percent in 1992.

See STATISTICS OF THE WORLD.   S.L.

NICARAGUA. In January 1994, Nicaragua's National Assembly agreed to reform the constitution, approved in 1987 during the previous Sandinista administration. More than 100 amendments and 20 new articles were proposed. In November the Assembly passed an amendment preventing sitting presidents or their relatives from serving consecutive terms.

Following heavy losses in battles against the Army in January, the last major armed contra group, the Northern Front 3-80, agreed in April to demobilize. Many of its members began training in the National Police Academy.

Although 650 rebels had demobilized by April, small armed groups were still present in the north. On several occasions during 1994 former Sandinista Army soldiers occupied foreign embassies in Managua to exert pressure on the Nicaraguan government to pay them compensation. In July the Assembly approved a new military code intended to bolster civilian control of the Army. The code included a special article arranging for the head of the Army, General Humberto Ortega (brother of former President Daniel Ortega), to resign in February 1995.

In January the U.S. government released $40 million in aid that had been held back since June 1993 in a dispute over compensation for or return of land taken during the agrarian reform by the Sandinista government.

In April, Nicaragua signed an austerity agreement with the International Monetary Fund in which the government promised to cut spending and control inflation. The IMF in June approved a $173 million low-interest loan to be disbursed during the next three years. The accord was expected to clear the way for increased foreign aid and to help Nicaragua achieve gross domestic product growth of 2 percent in 1994. Nicaragua's foreign debt rose to $11.1 billion, one of the highest per capita in the world. Unemployment estimates ranged as high as 60 percent, and more than half of the population was said to be living in poverty.

In January police seized a large shipment of Colombian cocaine on the southern coast. In September the Second Regional Conference on Drug Control met in Nicaragua; the conference's primary purpose was to set a drug-fighting agenda. Both drug use and trafficking had begun to increase in Nicaragua a few years before the conference was held.

In October, at a Central American summit conference in Managua, an agreement to begin a process of ecological, social, and economic change was signed by Nicaragua along with Belize, Costa Rica, El Salvador, Guatemala, Honduras, and Panama.

See STATISTICS OF THE WORLD.   J.F.A.

NIGER. *See* STATISTICS OF THE WORLD.

NIGERIA. Nigeria was buffeted by political instability and economic decline during much of 1994 as the regime of General Sani Abacha faced down challenges from prodemocracy

Giving peace a chance. *Nicaraguan Interior Minister Alfredo Mendieta (right) accepts the rifle of guerrilla commander José Angel Talavera, nicknamed the Jackal, in April. With the agreement to end hostilities by Talavera, who led the last significant group of one-time U.S.-backed contra rebels, Nicaragua's long era of guerrilla warfare appeared to have come to an end.*

Pile of trouble. *In August, Nigerian women carry trash to a huge dump in Lagos that had not been emptied for two months. The city had been brought nearly to a standstill by a series of paralyzing strikes touched off by oil workers' unions. The oil workers were demanding that the reigning hard-line government recognize the results of the 1993 national election, which had been annulled.*

activists and curtailed a long-standing economic reform program.

Political Turmoil. Following his seizure of power from a civilian caretaker government in November 1993, Abacha proceeded to consolidate his regime while offering vague assurances of an eventual return to civilian democracy. The regime slated a Constitutional Conference, comprised of appointees and elected members, to discuss a new framework for democratic rule. Originally scheduled for March 1994, the conference ultimately convened in June. Lacking significant participation from leading civilian political groups or democratic organizations, it was viewed with skepticism by a weary public.

The contention over democratic rule sharpened in late June, when Moshood K. O. Abiola, widely recognized as the victor in 1993's abortive presidential election, declared himself president and challenged the military leadership to step aside. Shortly thereafter, Abiola was arrested and charged with treason. Although an appeals court granted Abiola bail in November, he was still being detained at year's end. His imprisonment incited bitter resentment among his main constituency, the Yoruba of the southwest, and galvanized a broader array of democratic activists.

In early July the national petroleum workers' union went on strike to demand Abiola's release and an immediate transition to democratic rule.

The union protests, which lasted for over two months, badly undermined Nigeria's petroleum-based economy. At the peak of the strikes, oil exports (which provide nearly all Nigeria's foreign exchange) were down by at least a third. Even more important was the strangulation of domestic fuel supplies, causing weeks of nationwide paralysis.

The oil workers' actions were accompanied by strikes in the banks and universities, as well as by a brief sympathy action from the national labor confederation. Street protests in major southwestern cities resulted in at least 100 deaths, mainly from police shootings.

Abacha took a hard line toward the protests, refusing to negotiate with the unions, detaining leading prodemocracy activists, and stationing troops in oil refineries. In September the regime broke the strikes by taking over the petroleum unions and arresting their leaders. These actions were accompanied by a set of draconian decrees placing the military outside the jurisdiction of the courts and closing the country's leading independent media outlets.

In December, in an unexpected show of independence, the Constitutional Convention recommended that the military government step down within a year. However, there were signs later of a retreat from this timetable.

Economic Malaise. The Abacha regime adopted a new economic stance along with its sharpened authoritarian tilt. The program of economic liberalization launched in 1986 by

President Ibrahim Babangida was abruptly rescinded in the January 1994 budget. A new system of restricted trade, administered exchange rates, and foreign currency rationing was imposed. The turn toward renewed state intervention had a chilling effect on the economy as manufacturers, farmers, and investors were discouraged by the cutoff of foreign exchange. Growing corruption and political uncertainty compounded the economic malaise, as businesses and capital markets were idled for much of the year. Levels of fiscal insolvency and malfeasance had been growing in recent years, and in October the Okigbo panel investigating the operations of the Central Bank revealed that $12.2 billion had been diverted to off-budget accounts between 1988 and mid-1994.

Foreign Affairs. Nigeria faced two major international challenges in 1994. The dispute with Cameroon over the Bakassi Peninsula erupted into armed skirmishes and diplomatic quarrels throughout much of the year. Regional mediation attempts were inconclusive. Nigeria continued its ill-fated involvement in the Liberian peacekeeping force, Ecomog, although a December truce offered hope it could soon withdraw from this costly and frustrating imbroglio.

See STATISTICS OF THE WORLD.   P.M.L.

NORTH CAROLINA. See STATE GOVERNMENT REVIEW; STATISTICS OF THE WORLD.

NORTH DAKOTA. See STATISTICS OF THE WORLD.

NORTHERN MARIANA ISLANDS. See STATISTICS OF THE WORLD.

NORTHWEST TERRITORIES. See STATISTICS OF THE WORLD.

NORWAY. In a referendum on November 28, 1994, a majority of Norwegians turned down membership in the European Union, with 52 percent against and 48 percent in favor; voter participation was nearly 90 percent. While EU membership found favor in the south and in urban areas, it was largely rejected in agricultural and fishing communities, particularly in the north. Norwegians went to the polls only weeks after similar referenda in Finland and Sweden, in which voters gave approval to joining the EU.

Prime Minister Gro Harlem Brundtland's La-bor Party government had strongly supported EU membership, as had the opposition Conservative Party, traditionally Norway's second-strongest party. The rural anti-EU Center Party, however, had actively campaigned against membership. The referendum came 22 years after Norwegian voters turned down a similar invitation to join the European Community (the precursor of the EU) by 53 percent to 47 percent of the vote.

In February, Lillehammer hosted the Winter Olympic Games amid glorious sunshine and in cold temperatures that may have shocked guests from warmer climes. Norwegian athletes delighted the home crowds by beating all comers in the medal count, excelling particularly in speed skating and the men's ski events. The spectators won the hearts of the international audience by cheering such athletes as U.S. skater Dan Jansen, who won a gold medal in the last race of his final Olympics.

The economy continued to recover from the longest slump since the Great Depression. Unemployment, which had approached 10 percent of the labor force, declined by about one-third by late 1994. Steadily rising oil and gas production and firm prices contributed to a large current account surplus, while the inflation rate remained among the lowest in Europe. In October, Finance Minister Sigbjorn Johnsen presented a budget with a projected deficit only half as large as the one contained in the budget two years earlier.

In October the Norwegian Nobel Committee awarded the peace prize jointly to Israeli Prime Minister Yitzhak Rabin, Israeli Foreign Minister Shimon Peres, and PLO leader Yasir Arafat. Nobel Committee member Kare Kristiansen resigned in protest at the inclusion of Arafat. Norwegian negotiators, including the late Foreign Minister Johan Jorgen Holst, had played key roles in the Israel-PLO talks that led to the signing of the 1993 accord on Palestinian self-rule. Norway also took the lead in pledging financial support for Palestinian home rule in Jericho and Gaza.

See SPORTS: Winter Olympics; STATISTICS OF THE WORLD.   K.S.

NOVA SCOTIA. See STATISTICS OF THE WORLD.

NUCLEAR POWER. See POWER AND ENERGY.

O

OBITUARIES. The following people are among the notable personalities whose death was reported in 1994.

Anderson, Lindsay, 71, British film director who won an Oscar for his 1954 documentary *Thursday's Children;* he revitalized the British cinema with such films as *This Sporting Life* (1963), starring Richard Harris as an inarticulate rugby player, and *If . . .* (1968), about students in a British public school. He also directed *The Whales of August* (1987). August 30 in the Dordogne region of France.

Anderson, Paul, 61, dubbed the world's strongest man. Anderson won an Olympic gold medal in 1956 for a clean and jerk of 413.5 pounds, a feat he accomplished despite having a 103°F fever. In 1957, Anderson lifted 6,270 pounds by climbing under a table

PAUL ANDERSON

loaded with calibrated weights—a world record that still stood at the time of his death. August 15 in Vidalia, GA.

Araki, Ali Muhammad. A grand ayatollah, Araki was the supreme spiritual leader, or *marja taqlid* ("source of emulation"), of the Shiite Muslims, a position he had held for a year. He was reportedly 103 years of age by the Islamic lunar calendar but was possibly as old as 106. November 29 near Tehran, Iran.

Ball, George W., 84, undersecretary of state in the Kennedy and Johnson administrations. Throughout his career in government, Ball's voice was usually that of the loyal opposition. He wrote many books, among them *Error and Betrayal in Lebanon* (1984). May 26 in New York City.

Beckwith, Charles Alvin, 65, U.S. Army colonel and covert warrior who commanded Delta Force, a unit he organized to carry out top-secret missions. He was best known for leading the abortive 1980 mission to rescue 52 Americans being held hostage in Tehran, Iran. June 13 in Austin, TX.

Belluschi, Pietro, 94, Italian-born modernist architect and educator. He won great acclaim in 1947 with the 12-story Equitable (later Commonwealth) Building in Portland, OR, the first curtain-wall structure of glass in the United States. His subsequent works included midtown Manhattan's Pan Am (later MetLife) Building (1962) and San Francisco's Bank of America Building (1970). February 14 in Portland, OR.

Benson, Ezra Taft, 94, 13th head of the Mormon church and onetime U.S. secretary of agriculture. He was named to the 12-member ruling council of the Church of Jesus Christ of Latter Day Saints (Mormons) in 1943, taking a leave of absence to serve as President Dwight D. Eisenhower's agriculture secretary from 1953 to 1961. Benson publicly opposed the civil rights movement and feminism, and he kept the church on a firmly ultraconservative path as its president from 1985 until his death; during that time, membership increased almost by half. May 30 in Salt Lake City.

Bich, Baron Marcel, 79, Italian-born inventor of the Bic pen whose company also produced other disposable items such as razors and lighters. Bich, a onetime fountain pen salesman, launched the cheap plastic pen that made his fortune in the early 1950s; by 1993 his company's revenues had topped $1 billion. May 30 in Paris.

Birdwhistell, Ray, 76, anthropologist whose research centered on the meaning of body language, or kinesics. Birdwhistell's *Introduction to Kinesics* (1952), one of his many writings, marked the inception of research into the topic. October 19 in Brigantine, NJ.

Blaustein, Albert, 72, framer of constitutions. A lawyer and professor at Rutgers University School of Law, Blaustein helped write constitutions for more than 40 nations, including those in use in 1994 in Liberia, Fiji, Peru, and elsewhere. August 21 in Durham, NC.

Bloch, Robert, 77, mystery writer whose novel *Psycho* was the basis for the classic 1960 Alfred Hitchcock film of the same name. September 23 in Los Angeles.

Bonica, John J., 77, anesthesiologist and pain researcher. His experiences tending the wounded during World War II led him to study the alleviation of pain, and he was instrumental in the development of epidural anesthesia after his wife almost died under ether anesthesia during childbirth. Bonica's two-volume book *The Management of Pain* (1953) was rewritten and republished in 1990 and had been translated into six languages at the time of his death. August 15 in Rochester, MN.

Boulle, Pierre, 81, French novelist and author of *The Bridge Over the River Kwai* (1954) and *Planet of the Apes* (1963), both of which were made into films within a few years of their publication. January 30 in Paris.

Bukowski, Charles, 73, American poet, novelist, and subject of the 1987 film *Barfly*. His life and writings were full of carnality, grit, booze, and hard times, all seen with an eye for the absurd. Among his works were *Flower, Fist, and Bestial Wail* (1959), *Notes of a Dirty Old Man* (1969), and *Ham on Rye* (1982). March 9 in Los Angeles.

Calloway, Cab (Cabell), 86, jazz band leader and singer. Calloway's trademark, devised during a live radio broadcast in 1931, was a scat lyric he inserted into the song *Minnie the Moocher* when he forgot the words. The nonsense syllables "hi-de-hi-de-hi-de-ho" were echoed back, with great enthusiasm, by that audience and countless others for decades afterward. Calloway was the inspiration for the character Sportin' Life in the musical *Porgy and Bess,* a role Calloway himself played on stage for more than three years. November 18 in Hockesin, DE.

Candy, John Franklin, 43, hefty Toronto-born comic actor who won two Emmys for comedy writing and later starred in such Hollywood comedies as *Splash* (1984), *Uncle Buck* (1989), and *Cool Runnings* (1993). At 300 pounds, he was an unmistakable presence, but he was known as much for his geniality as his girth. March 4 in Chupaderos, Mexico.

Canetti, Elias, 89, Bulgarian-born novelist and playwright and winner of the 1981 Nobel Prize for literature for his body of work. He wrote in German. One of Canetti's earliest themes, the effect of social forces on individuals, was the topic of *Mass und Macht* (1960; *Crowds and Power,* 1962); he returned to the subject in later years with a four-volume autobiography. August 13 in Zürich, Switzerland.

Carter, Kevin, 33, photojournalist who won a 1994 Pulitzer Prize for his heartrending and horrifying photo of a starving Sudanese child being stalked by a vulture. He committed suicide on July 27 in a suburb of Johannesburg, South Africa.

Cartier, Rudolph, 90, television producer responsible for 120 dramas during 23 years at the BBC. Cartier is well remembered for a 1954 adaptation of George Orwell's *1984* that drew public ire for a scene in which the hero is threatened with torture using live rats. Cartier's later works included pioneering operas and a version of *Anna Karenina* (1961) starring the soon-to-be-famous Sean Connery. June 7 in London.

Childress, Alice, 73, actress and author. Her best-known work, the young-adult novel *A Hero Ain't Nothin' but a Sandwich* (1973), about the recovery of a 13-year-old black heroin user, was banned in some schools. August 14 in New York City.

Clavell, James, 69, best-selling novelist. Clavell wrote his first novel, *King Rat* (1962), after a writers' strike interrupted his screen-writing career in 1960. Based on his experiences during World War II, the book was made into a film in 1965. Clavell went on to write seven more best-sellers, including two—*Shogun* (1975) and *Noble House* (1981)—that were made into television miniseries in the 1980s. September 6 in Vevey, Switzerland.

Cobain, Kurt, 27, singer-songwriter and symbol of Seattle's "grunge rock" musical style. The songs he wrote and recorded with his band, Nirvana, were often abrasive and furious. Many of Cobain's fans saw the alienation and torment in his words and voice as emblematic of their own. Although the band presented itself as being in opposition to mass-appeal pop music, the unanticipated wildfire sales of its 1991 album *Nevermind* launched Cobain into the international spotlight. He committed suicide on April 5 in Seattle.

Cotten, Joseph, 88, actor who made his screen debut in *Citizen Kane* (1941). A tall, trim man who often played sad or quiet characters, he first won acclaim for his Broadway appearance in *The Philadelphia Story* (1939-1940). His

KURT COBAIN

best-known performances were in movies of the 1940s, including *The Magnificent Ambersons* (1942), *Gaslight* (1944), and *The Third Man* (1949). February 6 in Los Angeles.

Curry, John, 44, innovative British figure skater and winner of the 1976 Olympic gold medal at Innsbruck, Austria. He changed the course of figure skating, leading it into the realm of art as well as sport, by bringing to it the influence of ballet. His show *IceDancing* ran on Broadway in 1977-1978. April 15 in Binton, England.

Cushing, Peter, 81, actor known for his roles in such horror films as *The Curse of Frankenstein* (1957); more recently, he played the evil Grand Moff Tarkin in *Star Wars* (1977). August 11 in Canterbury, England.

Delvaux, Paul, 96, surrealist painter. By the mid-1940s, Delvaux was one of Belgium's most celebrated painters, reknowned for his dreamlike erotic paintings of nudes. July 20 in Veurne, Belgium.

Doisneau, Robert, 81, French photographer. His elegant black-and-white images included news photos of the 1944 liberation of Paris, portraits of famous artists, and the 1950 image, reproduced on countless postcards and posters, entitled *Kiss by the Hôtel de Ville, Paris.* April 1 in Paris.

Ellison, Ralph (Waldo), 80, renowned African-American author. His novel *Invisible Man* (1952), the story of an unnamed black man's awakening to racial prejudice in the United States, is considered one of the most important works of 20th-century fiction. The book received massive popular and critical acclaim. April 16 in New York City.

Erikson, Erik, 91, German-born psychoanalyst who coined the term "identity crisis." In contrast to Sigmund Freud, Erikson believed that an individual's personality develops throughout life and is influenced by society. He identified eight life stages from infancy to old age, each marked by a conflict to be resolved. One of Erikson's books, a "psychobiography" of Mohandas K. Gandhi called *Gandhi's Truth* (1969), won the Pulitzer Prize in 1970. May 12 in Harwich, MA.

Ewell, Tom (Yewell Tompkins), 85, character actor best known for his role opposite Marilyn Monroe in the film *The Seven Year Itch* (1955).

RALPH ELLISON

He also starred in his own television sitcom, *The Tom Ewell Show* (1960). September 12 in Woodland Hills, CA.

Faubus, Orval, 84, former governor of Arkansas. As governor in 1957, he refused to comply with a federal order to allow nine African-Americans to enroll at Central High School in Little Rock, until then attended solely by white students. (The order came in response to the Supreme Court's 1954 landmark civil rights ruling in *Brown* v. *Board of Education*.) Then-President Dwight D. Eisenhower was forced to nationalize the Arkansas National Guard and send in 1,200 U.S. paratroopers to enforce the desegregation order. Faubus went on to serve four more terms as governor. December 14 in Conway, AR.

Firkusny, Rudolph, 82, Czech-born pianist and composer; he was a student of Leos Janacek. The elegant Firkusny was an unpretentious crowd pleaser who in 1990, at the age of 78, appeared in concert dress on a basketball court for an athletic shoe commercial with the explanation, "Music needs all kinds of encouragement." July 19 in Staatsburg, NY.

Fisher, Avery, 87, American philanthropist and founder of the Fisher high-fidelity electronics equipment company. After selling the company in 1969 for over $30 million, he turned to philanthropy, especially music-related; New York City's Lincoln Center renamed Philharmonic Hall for him in 1973. February 26 in New Milford, CT.

Flood, Daniel, 90, U.S. representative from Pennsylvania for 32 years. The wax-mustachioed Democrat controlled large amounts of money as head of the House Appropriations Committee's subcommittee on labor and health, education, and welfare. He resigned in 1980 after being accused of taking bribes and later pleaded guilty to one count of conspiracy. May 28 in Wilkes-Barre, PA.

Furness, Betty (Elizabeth Mary Furness), 78, television reporter and consumer advocate. Having become a celebrity in the 1950s through her live television advertisements for Westinghouse refrigerators and vacuum cleaners, she developed an interest in consumer advocacy that led to her 1967 appointment by U.S. President Lyndon Johnson as his special assistant for consumer affairs. She pioneered

BETTY FURNESS

television consumer journalism as a reporter and investigator on NBC's *Today* show from 1976 to 1992, broadcasting the names of faulty products and confronting store proprietors on camera. April 2 in New York City.

George, Zelma, 90, African-American singer. George broke Broadway's color barrier in 1950 as the title character in the folk opera *The Medium.* She later earned a Ph.D. in sociology at New York University. July 3 in Cleveland.

Gerulaitis, Vitas, 40, tennis star who at one time ranked third in the world; he ranked in the top ten from 1977 to 1982. Fond of the nightclub scene, "Broadway Vitas" was known as much for his party-going as for his tennis skills. September 18 in Southampton, NY.

Greenberg, Clement, 85, art critic who championed abstract expressionism. Greenberg's contention that the proper study of art was art itself became known as "Greenberg formalism." His persistent praise helped establish the career of painter Jackson Pollock. May 7 in New York City.

Grès, Alix, 89, French clothing designer whose death in a nursing home was kept secret by her daughter for more than a year. In September 1994 the Costume Institute of New York's Metropolitan Museum of Art held a retrospective of Grès's work. November 24, 1993, in St.-Paul-de-Vence, France.

Grizzard, Lewis, 47, humor writer and syndicated columnist. Grizzard drew on his Southern roots in his writings, which included such titles as *Elvis Is Dead, and I Don't Feel So Good Myself* and *Chili Dawgs Always Bark at Night.* March 20 in Atlanta.

Hawkins, Erick, 85, modern dance choreographer. A charter member of George Balanchine's Ballet Caravan—forerunner of the New York City Ballet—he became the first male permanent dancer in Martha Graham's troupe in 1936; he and Graham were briefly married. Hawkins later formed his own dance company, performing into his 60s. He was awarded the National Medal of Arts in 1994. November 23 in New York City.

Henry, William, III, 44, journalist and critic. Henry won two Pulitzer Prizes, one in 1975 as part of a team reporting on racial conflict in Boston and the other in 1980 for television

criticism; his TV documentary *Bob Fosse: Steam Heat* won a 1990 Emmy Award. He also wrote several books, among them a biography of Jackie Gleason. June 28 in Maidenhead, England.

Herrnstein, Richard, 64, controversial psychologist who argued that intelligence was inherited. Herrnstein expressed his views in magazine articles and in his books *I.Q. in the Meritocracy* (1973); *Crime and Human Nature* (1983), coauthored with James Q. Wilson; and *The Bell Curve* (1994), coauthored with Charles Murray. Herrnstein declared that he was consistently misrepresented as racist. September 13 in Belmont, MA.

Hodgkin, Dorothy, 84, winner of the 1964 Nobel Prize in chemistry. Hodgkin's studies of penicillin made her a pioneer in the use of X-

EUGENE IONESCO

ray techniques for developing antibiotics; she also carried out ground-breaking studies on vitamin B_{12} and insulin. She was also a dedicated peace activist. July 29 in Shipston-on-Stour, England.

Honecker, Erich, 81, pragmatic Marxist politician who led East Germany for 18 years. Under Honecker, East Germany became the Soviet bloc's industrial powerhouse, but by the time a popular uprising toppled his government in 1989 the country's infrastructure was crumbling and environmental pollution was rampant. He was charged with manslaughter in the newly united Germany for ordering guards to shoot on sight anyone attempting to escape to West Germany, but his failing health saved him from being tried. May 29 in Santiago, Chile.

Horton, Mildred McAfee, 94, director during World War II of the U.S. Navy's Women Accepted for Volunteer Emergency Service, known as WAVES. She was also a former president of Wellesley College. September 9 in Randolph, NH.

Houser, Allan, 80, well-known Chiricahua Apache sculptor to whom President George Bush awarded the National Medal of Arts in 1992. Houser's stone, wood, and bronze sculptures contained such recurring images as mother and child and Apache fire dancers. August 22 in Santa Fe, NM.

Ionesco, Eugène, 81, Romanian-born French surrealist playwright. Beginning with *The Bald Soprano* (1950), his works—part of a movement that came to be called the theater of the absurd—often addressed serious and troubling subjects. March 28 in Paris.

Jobim, Antonio Carlos, 67, Brazilian composer whose eminently hummable tunes, notably *Girl From Ipanema*, sparked a worldwide bossa nova craze in the 1960s. December 8 in New York City.

Judd, Donald Clarence, 65, sculptor, designer, and art critic whose sleek, nonrepresentational sculptures were highly influential in the post-World War II minimalist movement. February 12 in New York City.

Julia, Raul, 54, Puerto Rican-born actor who performed leading roles regularly in New York City's Shakespeare Festival and on Broadway before becoming known to millions as Gomez

RAUL JULIA

in the films *The Addams Family* (1991) and its sequel, *Addams Family Values* (1993). He was also lauded for his role in the movie *Kiss of the Spider Woman* (1985). October 24 in Manhassett, NY.

Kabibble, Ish (Merwyn Bogue), 86, musician. As a cornetist with Kay Kyser's Big Band orchestra in the 1930s and 1940s, Kabibble was appreciated for his playing but loved for his comedy routines. Among his comic poems: "I sneezed a sneeze into the air/it fell to earth I know not where/But you should see the looks on those/in whose vicinity I snooze." June 5 in Palm Springs, CA.

Kelley, Virginia Clinton, 70, retired nurse-anesthetist and mother of U.S. President Bill Clinton. Known for her resilience and vivaciousness, she endured the deaths of three husbands, one of whom was abusive, as well as family drug and alcohol problems. She was an enthusiastic presence in her son's 1992 presidential campaign. January 6 in Hot Springs, AR.

Kildall, Gary, 52, computer scientist who developed CP/M, a seminal operating system (the set of instructions that runs a computer's "brain"). Kildall's software firm enjoyed almost explosive earnings until 1981, when it began losing ground in head-to-head sales competition with Microsoft's similar but far cheaper MS-DOS. July 11 in Monterey, CA.

Kim Il Sung, 82, president of North Korea and the longest-ruling Communist leader. Born to peasant parents in 1912, Kim became premier of North Korea in 1948 under the wing of the Soviet Union. In 1950 he attempted to unite the Korean Peninsula by invading South Korea, thus initiating what came to be known as the Korean War; the fighting continued until 1953. A despot at home, Kim had increased his diplomatic weight abroad in recent years by threatening to develop atomic weapons. July 8 in North Korea.

Kirby, Jack (Jacob Kurtzberg), 76, influential cartoonist who created numerous comic book heroes and illustrated their adventures in a dramatic, vigorous style. Among Kirby's early superheroes was Captain America, whom he developed with collaborator Joe Simon in 1940. Later, at Marvel Comics and DC Comics, he invented the Incredible Hulk, the Fantastic Four, X-Men, and others. February 6 in Thousand Oaks, CA.

Kirk, Russell, 75, author who lent momentum to the conservative movement in the United States. His widely respected book *The Conservative Mind: From Burke to Santayana* (1953) established him as a spokesman for conservatism, a position he maintained through hundreds of essays, reviews, syndicated columns, and speeches. April 29 in Mecosta, MI.

Knoll, Erwin, 63, editor for 21 years of *The Progressive,* a liberal magazine based in Madison, WI. In 1979 a federal court ordered the magazine not to print a story revealing how easy it would be to make an atomic bomb—information, Knoll said, that came entirely from the public domain. When another periodical printed similar information, the *Progressive* story ran without changes. Knoll was a regular commentator on the television program *The McNeil/Lehrer News Hour.* November 2 in Madison, WI.

Lancaster, Burt, 80, actor and film producer who won an Academy Award for best actor for his role as a con-artist preacher in the 1960 film *Elmer Gantry.* Lancaster became an actor after a hand injury put an end to his early career as a circus acrobat. He appeared in a number of successful movies, including *From Here to Eternity* (1953), *Sweet Smell of Success* (1957), and *Birdman of Alcatraz* (1961). His performance in the 1981 film *Atlantic City* was said to be among his finest. October 20 in Century City, CA.

Lebow, Fred (Fischl Lebowitz), 62, founder of the New York City Marathon in 1970. His enthusiasm for running helped fuel the popularity of what became an international pastime—during his tenure as president of the New York City Road Runners Club, the organization grew to 30,000 members. He helped start several marathons in the United States and Europe. October 9 in New York City.

Leckenby, Derek, 51, lead guitarist and cofounder of the British rock group Herman's Hermits. The group's first hit, in 1964, was *I'm Into Something Good,* followed by *Mrs. Brown You've Got a Lovely Daughter, No Milk Today,* and others. The band performed into the 1990s. June 4 in Manchester, England.

Lerman, Leo, 80, trend-spotting author and editor for such Condé Nast magazines as *Vogue* and *Mademoiselle* and editor in chief at *Vanity Fair* during 1983, one of its most turbulent

KIM IL SUNG

BURT LANCASTER, in *Elmer Gantry*

work in film and television and 20 Grammys for his recordings. His work appeared in almost 250 films, but he was best known for the songs *Moon River,* composed for *Breakfast at Tiffany's* (1961), and *Days of Wine and Roses,* used in the 1962 movie of the same name. June 14 in Los Angeles.

Masina, Giulietta, 73, Italian actress and widow of film director Federico Fellini. Masina's role as the waif Gelsomina in *La Strada,* Fellini's 1954 classic, earned her lasting fame. She played other acclaimed roles in Fellini's films, among them the female leads in *Juliet of the Spirits* (1965) and *Ginger and Fred* (1986). March 23 in Rome.

May, Rollo, 85, psychologist who helped found the humanistic psychology movement, which concerns itself with personal growth. May's books included *The Meaning of Anxiety* (1950) and *Love and Will* (1969). October 22 in Tiburon, CA.

McRae, Carmen, 74, contralto jazz singer whose genius for bringing lyrics to life helped make her one of the top vocalists of the big-band era. November 10 in Beverly Hills, CA.

HENRY MANCINI

years. He was later named editorial adviser of Condé Nast. August 22 in New York City.

Lutoslawski, Witold, 81, Polish composer whose orchestral and chamber works reflected traditional ideas of musical beauty while also using such avant-garde techniques as atonality and orchestral improvisation. His works included *Concerto for Orchestra* (1954) and *Chain 2* (1985). February 7 in Warsaw.

Lwoff, André, 92, French biologist who shared the 1965 Nobel Prize in physiology or medicine. Lwoff's work at the Pasteur Institute played a key role in the development of modern molecular biology. He was also an active part of the resistance against Germany's occupation of France during World War II. September 30 in Paris.

Mancini, Henry, 70, popular composer. Mancini won four Academy Awards for his

MELINA MERCOURI

Mercouri, Melina, 68, Greek actress and politician. Her best-known screen role was as a flamboyant prostitute in *Never on Sunday* (1960). Exiled in 1967 because of her outspoken opposition to the junta then in power, she returned to Greece in 1974 and in 1977 was elected to Parliament as a Socialist. After becoming minister of culture in 1981, she fought for the return of the Elgin Marbles, statues taken from the Acropolis and sold in the 1800s and housed in the British Museum. March 6 in New York City.

Morgan, William, 88, astronomer who discovered the spiral structure of the band of stars known as the Milky Way. He was also codeveloper of the Morgan-Keenan system for determining the distance of stars from Earth by measuring their apparent brightness, a system he used to reach his eye-opening scientific discoveries. June 21 in Williams Bay, WI.

Nelson, Harriet, 85, actress who was the on-screen and off-screen wife of actor and bandleader Ozzie Nelson. The couple played suburban parents rearing two children—played by the Nelsons' real-life children—in the quintessential 1950s-era television show *The Adventures of Ozzie and Harriet.* The show stayed

on the air for 14 years, until 1966. October 2 in Laguna Beach, CA.

Nixon, Richard (Milhous), 81, 37th president of the United States and the first to resign from office. A bootstrap Republican, he was a complex, pragmatic man with conservative instincts who had a singular ability to polarize the electorate. Supporters admired his pugnacious tenacity; to his enemies he was the Machiavellian "Tricky Dick."

Nixon was elected to Congress in 1946 and gained fame as an anti-Communist crusader on the House Un-American Activities Committee. After winning a Senate seat in 1950, he was elected vice president in 1952 and again in 1956 as Dwight Eisenhower's running mate. Defeated in his own 1960 attempt to win the presidency and in a subsequent bid for the governorship of California, Nixon came back to win election as president in 1968 and again in 1972.

During Nixon's administration, U.S. economic woes led him to freeze wages and prices and devalue the dollar on world currency markets. Controversy over his hawkish Vietnam policy roiled the nation, yet Nixon pushed for détente in the cold war, becoming in 1972 the first U.S. president to visit the capitals of both China and the Soviet Union.

In June 1972, burglars connected with the Republican campaign effort were caught breaking into Democratic Party offices at the Watergate complex in Washington. The ensuing scandal snowballed, and lengthy investigations led to guilty pleas or convictions for more than 30 Nixon officials. Implicated in a cover-up, Nixon chose to avoid impeachment by resigning, in August 1974.

In his later years Nixon published several books on politics and foreign policy. April 22 in New York City.

Odinga, Jaramogi Oginga, 82, Kenyan political leader. After helping guide Kenya to independence in 1963, Odinga served for three years as vice president under Jomo Kenyatta before resigning and forming the Kenyan People's Union, an opposition party on the left. Odinga was instrumental in restoring multiparty elections to Kenya in 1992. January 20 in Kisumu, Kenya.

Onassis, Jacqueline (Bouvier) Kennedy, 64, widow of President John F. Kennedy and of Greek shipping magnate Aristotle Onassis. As the president's wife, she so captivated the world with her charisma and elegance that after the couple's 1961 visit to France, President Kennedy jokingly identified himself as "the man who accompanied Jacqueline Kennedy to Paris." After redecorating the White House—a move that inspired some controversy—she endeared herself to the American public by offering a televised tour. Her grace and composure after her husband's assassination in 1963 secured her place as one of the great first ladies of the United States. She married Onassis in 1968; he died in 1975. In the following years she worked as a book editor. May 19 in New York City.

O'Neill, Thomas P. ("Tip"), Jr., 81, Massachusetts Democrat and speaker of the House for ten years. An enormously popular congressman, he was a self-described "old liberal" who fought proudly for social programs to help workers, the poor, the sick, and the needy; he was also a leading advocate of congressional reform. January 5 in Boston.

Osborne, John, 65, British playwright known for his vitriolic dramas. Osborne's 1956 play *Look Back in Anger* made his reputation. He also wrote screenplays, such as that for *The Entertainer* (1960), based on his eponymous 1958 play; he won an Oscar for his screenplay for *Tom Jones* (1963). His books included *A Better Class of Person* (1991) and *Damn You, England* (1994). December 24 in Shropshire, England.

Pauling, Linus, 93, winner of the 1954 Nobel Prize for chemistry and the 1963 Nobel Peace Prize. Pauling's research on the chemistry of molecular bonds led to the discovery (by others) of the structure of DNA; the Peace Prize arose from his campaign against nuclear testing. Pauling stirred controversy in the 1970s by advocating large doses of vitamin C as a safeguard against and treatment for illnesses ranging from colds to cancer. August 19 in Big Sur, CA.

Peppard, George, 65, actor who appeared in more than 25 films, including *Breakfast at Tiffany's* (1961) opposite Audrey Hepburn. He played leading roles in several television series, notably *The A-Team* (1983 to 1987). May 8 in Los Angeles.

Plunkett, Roy, 83, inventor of Teflon, the non-stick substance that revolutionized the plastics industry and the way Americans cook. Teflon

LINUS PAULING

makes it possible to cook with little or no oil. In 1994 three-fourths of the pots and pans sold in the United States were lined with Teflon or a Teflon-like substance. May 12 in Corpus Christi, TX.

Potter, Dennis, 59, British television script-writer whose brooding dramas were influenced by his sufferings from a crippling skin and joint disease called psoriatic arthropathy. Several of his pieces were banned for linking sex and religion, among them *Brimstone and Treacle* (1977), in which a disabled girl is cured by being raped by a demon. Potter's works included *Pennies From Heaven* (1978) and the film *Gorky Park* (1984). June 7 in Ross-on-Wye, England.

Puller, Lewis B., Jr., 48, author of the Pulitzer Prize-winning autobiography *Fortunate Son* (1991). The son of the most decorated marine in U.S. history, Puller lost both legs and parts of both hands in the Vietnam War; his book tells of his wartime experiences and subsequent struggles. He committed suicide on May 11 in Alexandria, VA.

Ray, Dixy Lee, 79, chairwoman of the U.S. Atomic Energy Commission from 1973 to 1975 and governor of the state of Washington for one term, beginning in 1977. January 2 in Fox Island, WA.

Raye, Martha, 78, comedian and singer who served as a wartime entertainer in stage shows during three wars. She appeared in a number of films, including Charlie Chaplin's *Monsieur Verdoux* (1947). She married at least seven times. October 19 in Los Angeles.

Reynolds, R. J., III, 60, tobacco industry executive and grandson of the founder of R. J. Reynolds Tobacco Company. His doctor said cigarettes caused his death; in lieu of flowers, mourners were asked to donate money to Citizens for a Smoke-free America. June 28 in Pinehurst, NC.

Roebling, Mary, 89, pioneering woman banker. Roebling was the first woman president of a major U.S. bank and governor of the American Stock Exchange. Roebling took the helm of Trenton Trust during the Depression and was able to quadruple its assets; in 1984, when she retired, the bank—by then called the National State Bank—had assets of $1.2 billion. October 25 in Trenton, NJ.

MENACHEM M. SCHNEERSON

Roland, Gilbert (Luis Antonio Damaso de Alonso), 88, dashing film and television actor who played the Cisco Kid in 11 films. Roland appeared opposite Mae West in *She Done Him Wrong* (1933) and alongside Errol Flynn in *The Sea Hawk* (1940). May 15 in Beverly Hills, CA.

Romero, Cesar, 86, actor and grandson of Cuban revolutionary patriot José Martí. Romero started out in motion pictures playing a gigolo in the 1934 comedy *The Thin Man;* in the 1960s he played the Joker in the camp television series *Batman,* and in the 1980s he appeared as Jane Wyman's husband on the nighttime TV soap *Falcon Crest.* January 1 in Santa Monica, CA.

Rubin, Jerry, 56, 1960s radical who was a member of the "Chicago Seven," defendants tried in 1969 on charges of conspiring to disrupt the 1968 Democratic National Convention in Chicago. Rubin helped found the Youth International Party, or Yippies. November 28 in Los Angeles.

Rudolph, Wilma, 54, the first American woman to win three gold medals in track and field at one Olympics, in Rome in 1960. The feat was even more remarkable as she had had scarlet fever, double pneumonia, and polio as a child and was told she would not be able to walk. November 12 in Nashville, TN.

Rusk, Dean, 85, secretary of state for Presidents John F. Kennedy and Lyndon B. Johnson. During his eight years in the post, Rusk became a lightning rod for popular protest against U.S. involvement in the Vietnam War—a policy he defended staunchly. December 20 in Athens, GA.

Savalas, Telly (Aristotle Savalas), 70, bald, lollipop-sucking actor whose trademark greeting, "Who loves ya, baby?" became an American catchphrase. He was known above all else for his title role in the television series *Kojak* (1973 to 1978), where he played a charismatic, street-smart, New York City detective. However, he had character roles in a long list of movies before his television breakthrough at age 51. January 22 in Universal City, CA.

Scarry, Richard, 74, author and illustrator of children's books. Scarry's detailed, whimsical drawings captivated children; at his death more than 250 of his books were in print in 30 languages, among them *Richard Scarry's Best Word Book Ever* (1963) and *Richard Scarry's What Do People Do All Day?* (1968). April 30 in Gstaad, Switzerland.

Schneerson, Menachem M., 92, Russian-born grand rabbi, or rebbe, of the Lubavich sect of Hasidic Jews and arguably the most influential Jewish religious leader of his time. Schneerson so inspired his ultraconservative followers—members of a sect that originated in Eastern Europe in the 18th century—that they launched a fervent campaign to encourage lapsed and nonconservative Jews to reexamine their faith. The seventh in a line of hereditary grand rabbis, Schneerson left no heir, and many Lubavichers believed that he was the Messiah. June 12 in New York City.

Schwinger, Julian, 76, theoretical physicist who won the Nobel Prize in 1965 and the National (U.S.) Medal of Science in 1964. Schwinger shared the Nobel with Richard Feynman and Shinichiro Tomonaga; the three, who had worked independently, were honored for advancing the field of quantum electrodynamics. July 16 in Los Angeles.

Senna da Silva, Ayrton, 34, Brazilian race car driver. Considered the world's best driver, the three-time Formula One world champion was a national hero in Brazil. One million people turned out to view his funeral cortege. His car was going almost 200 miles per hour when it veered off the track and struck a concrete wall. May 1 in Bologna, Italy.

Shilts, Randy, 42, author and journalist whose *San Francisco Chronicle* articles on AIDS were, in the early 1980s, among the first to appear on the subject. Two books, *And the Band Played On* (1987), a history of the AIDS epidemic, and *Conduct Unbecoming* (1993), about homosexuals in the U.S. military, were best-sellers. He learned that he was HIV-positive in 1987. February 17 in Guerneville, CA.

Shore, Dinah (Frances Rose Shore), 76, upbeat singer and television host. She began recording hits in the 1940s (among them *Buttons and Bows* and *I'll Walk Alone*), then went on to host the enormously popular *Dinah Shore Chevy Show,* a weekly variety program that aired on television from 1956 to 1963. In the 1970s she hosted television talk shows and

AYRTON SENNA DA SILVA

JESSICA TANDY

paved the way for the countless programs in that format that followed. For more than 20 years she sponsored a golf tournament in California. February 24 in Beverly Hills, CA.

Smith, Hazel Brannon, 80, courageous Mississippi newspaper owner and editor who spoke out for civil rights in the 1950s and 1960s. In 1954, Smith wrote a front-page editorial for the *Lexington* (MS) *Advertiser* that criticized a local sheriff for shooting an African-American in the back. The piece so angered local whites that they boycotted the newspaper for ten years and finally forced it to close. Ironically, the boycott ended the year Smith became the first woman ever to win a Pulitzer Prize for editorial writing. May 14 in Cleveland, TN.

Smith, Willie Mae Ford, 89, gospel singer. A pioneer of the blues-influenced gospel singing style created by Thomas A. Dorsey, she toured frequently as a soloist in the 1930s and 1940s, recording her first album in 1950. A 1972 ap-

pearance at the Newport Jazz Festival led to increased national recognition. February 2 in St. Louis.

Spivak, Lawrence, 93, television interviewer. For more than a quarter of a century, on his much-imitated NBC news discussion program *Meet the Press,* he put challenging questions to national and international leaders. March 9 in Washington, DC.

Styne, Jule, 88, composer whose melodies brought to life the lyrics of such popular tunes as *Three Coins in the Fountain* (1954), *Everything's Coming Up Roses* (1959), and *People* (1960). He wrote the music to such classic Broadway musicals as *Gypsy, Gentlemen Prefer Blondes,* and *Funny Girl.* The songmeister estimated in 1987 that he had published 1,500 songs, including 200 hits. September 21 in New York City.

Synge, Richard Laurence Millington, 79, British biochemist who shared the 1952 Nobel Prize in chemistry for developing a technique for separating amino acids called paper chromatography. He was in later years a peace activist and member of the Pugwash Movement. August 18 in Norwich, England.

Tandy, Jessica, 85, leading lady of stage and screen. Among her many theater roles, Tandy originated the character of Blanche Dubois in Tennessee Williams's *A Streetcar Named Desire* in 1947, playing opposite Marlon Brando and Kim Hunter in a legendary production directed by Elia Kazan. She also appeared in numerous films, including *The Birds* (1963), *Driving Miss Daisy* (1989), for which she won an Academy Award for best actress, and *Fried Green Tomatoes* (1991), for which she received an Oscar nomination. In 1994 she was awarded the first Tony ever given for lifetime achievement—her fourth Tony—which she shared with her husband, Hume Cronyn. September 11 in Easton, CT.

Taylor, Peter, 77, fiction writer. Taylor's métier was tightly wrought tales of Southern society's Old Guard. He was an acknowledged master of the short story, but it was his novel, *A Summons to Memphis,* that earned him the Pulitzer Prize in 1987. November 2 in Charlottesville, VA.

Temin, Howard M., 59, scientist. An opponent of tobacco use, he won the 1975 Nobel

Prize for medicine for genetics discoveries that helped in the identification of the AIDS virus. February 9 in Madison, WI.

Throneberry, Marvin ("Marvelous Marv"), 60, baseball player famous for his genial but hapless performance in 1962, the New York Mets' first year, when the team racked up a losing season (40-120) that still stood as a record in 1994. Years later he appeared in ads for Miller Lite beer saying, "I still don't know why they asked me to do this commercial." June 23 in Fisherville, TN.

Tinbergen, Jan, 91, Dutch economist who shared the first Nobel Prize for economics in 1969. Tinbergen was known for creating mathematical models for economic processes; the model of the U.S. economy that Tinbergen completed for the League of Nations in 1938 was the precursor for the computer models now used widely in economic forecasting. June 9 in Amsterdam.

Vines, Ellsworth, 82, tennis star of the 1930s. His shots' accuracy and speed were legendary: In one tournament, an opponent's racket was knocked out of his hand. March 17 in La Quinta, CA.

Warren, Earle, 79, lead saxophonist for the Count Basie Orchestra from 1937 to 1951, except for a break from 1945 to 1947, during which he led his own band. Warren's embouchure and genial demeanor earned him the nickname Smiley. He later played for the vocal group the Platters and performed in Europe. June 4 in Springfield, OH.

Washington, Fredi (Fredricka), 90, actress. A founder of the Negro Actors Guild, she was best known for her role as an anguished young African-American who "passes" for white in the movie *Imitation of Life* (1934). June 28 in Stamford, CT.

Wörner, Manfred, 59, secretary-general of the North Atlantic Treaty Organization (NATO) from 1988 until his death. The first German in the post, Wörner steered NATO through the fall of the Berlin Wall in 1989. August 13 in Brussels. B.D. & S.H.P.

OHIO. See STATE GOVERNMENT REVIEW; STATISTICS OF THE WORLD.

OKLAHOMA. See STATISTICS OF THE WORLD.

OMAN. See PERSIAN GULF STATES; STATISTICS OF THE WORLD.

ONTARIO. See STATISTICS OF THE WORLD.

OREGON. See STATE GOVERNMENT REVIEW; STATISTICS OF THE WORLD.

ORGANIZATION OF PETROLEUM EXPORTING COUNTRIES. See POWER AND ENERGY.

P

PACIFIC ISLANDS. The South Pacific Forum, a regional organization whose member states include Pacific island countries as well as Australia and New Zealand, was granted observer status at the United Nations General Assembly in 1994. The Forum's 25th annual heads-of-government meeting emphasized environmental issues, including the preservation of coral reef ecosystems and the establishment of a code of conduct governing logging of indigenous forests. Pacific island states widened diplomatic and cultural contacts with leaders from Indian Ocean and Caribbean islands by taking part in the Alliance of Small Island States and in the Global Conference on Sustainable Development of Small Island States.

Cook Islands. The government of Prime Minister Geoffrey Henry won an overwhelming election victory in March, taking 20 of 25 seats in Parliament. Proposals to change the country's name, flag, and national anthem were all rejected by voters.

Fiji. Prime Minister Sitiveni Rabuka was reelected in a snap election called as a result of divisions within the ruling party. Former Prime Minister Ratu (Chief) Kamisese Mara was selected by the Great Council of Chiefs as Fiji's president following the death of Ratu Penaia Ganilau.

Kiribati. Kiribati was governed for several months by a three-person Council of State when the government was defeated in Parliament following allegations about misuse of public funds by a cabinet minister. Most members of the governing National Progressive Party lost their seats in July elections. A new president, Teburoro Tito, was elected in October.

Marshall Islands. The possibility of a nuclear-waste storage dump to be situated on atolls in the Marshall Islands aroused controversy within the Pacific region, with leaders of other island states indicating their disapproval of the project.

Niue. Niue's efforts to gain greater acceptance as a self-governing state were enhanced when it was admitted to two UN agencies, Unesco and the World Health Organization.

Palau (Belau). The last UN trust territory, Palau became independent on October 1, the day that its compact of free association with the United States came into effect. Palau was admitted to UN membership in December.

Papua New Guinea. Prime Minister Paias Wingti's attempt to extend his government's term of office was unanimously ruled null and void by the country's Supreme Court. Within days Deputy Prime Minister Julius Chan, who was prime minister from 1980 to 1982, regained the position, winning election after Wingti withdrew his candidacy. The new government negotiated a fragile cease-fire with secessionist rebels on the island of Bougainville, but peace talks fell apart in October.

In September a volcano erupted through two cones near Rabaul, virtually destroying the city (*see* EARTH SCIENCES: Geology).

Tonga. Five members of the Tongan Parliament formed the country's first political party, the Tonga Democratic Party, committed to introducing constitutional changes to restrict the powers of the king.

Tuvalu. The governor-general, Toomu Sione, appointed by the previous government, was forced to resign by Prime Minister Kamuta Laatasi only seven months into a four-year term. Sione was replaced by Tulaga Manuella.

Vanuatu. Government candidate Jean-Marie Leye was elected Vanuatu's president in March; he was the first Roman Catholic and the first French-speaking person to serve as its head of state.

See STATISTICS OF THE WORLD.   S.L.

PAKISTAN. The quality of life in Pakistan did not improve significantly during 1994. Damage from floods was moderate, but the summer was unusually hot, made worse by frequent power shutdowns and shortages of drinking water. Ethnic and sectarian violence continued to bring ruin to Karachi, the country's largest city.

The economy moved sluggishly in fiscal year 1993-1994. Agriculture grew by 2.6 percent, manufacturing by 0.5 percent, and the foreign trade deficit decreased by about $1 billion. The energy supply increased by 7 percent, but demand went up by 12 percent. The population grew at a rate of over 3 percent. Government spokespersons placed inflation at 10.6 percent, but other observers claimed it was as high as 15 percent.

The government's budget for fiscal 1994-1995 anticipated $10.95 billion in revenue and $12.42 billion in expenditures, with a deficit of $1.47 billion. The predicted revenue included $2.66 billion in foreign aid and $9.03 million in new taxes. The budget set aside $2.90 billion for government-sponsored development programs, but in the operating budget

A Pain in the Neck

Inhabitants of chilly northern climes have long fantasized about the balmy islands of the South Pacific, where the coconuts fall into your lap, the fish leap into your boat, and a few yards of cloth are enough for all the clothes you need.

Alas, score one for encroaching civilization. President Amata Kabua of the Marshall Islands—two chains of coral atolls some 2,300 miles southwest of Hawaii—decreed that any man entering the new government center in Majuro, the capital, must wear a necktie. Enforcement was seen to by the center's guards, who denied entry to every tieless gentleman.

Predictably, the rule had many men tied up in knots. As a local newspaper editor put it, "They're always complaining about people not paying taxes, and now you have to wear a tie to pay taxes." Not everyone was griping, though. The country's three stores that sold neckties reported that business was brisk.

Worthy women. *Benazir Bhutto (left), prime minister of Pakistan, inspects an honor guard in January as she opens a police station staffed entirely by women. She called the new facility "the first step toward equal access to justice."*

defense and service charges on the debt would, together, consume most of the net revenue receipts.

Politics in Pakistan remained unruly and, one might say, unprincipled. In February the Pakistan People's Party (PPP), headed by Prime Minister Benazir Bhutto, engineered defections from a coalition of the Nawaz Sharif-led faction of the Pakistan Muslim League (PML) and the Awami National Party (ANP), which had been ruling in the North-West Frontier Province. As a result, this coalition lost power and another coalition, led by the PPP, replaced it. In retaliation, the PML and the ANP embarked upon a program of destabilizing the national government. They alleged that Bhutto and her colleagues were corrupt and incompetent, that their policies were calculated to destroy the national economy, that they were subservient to India and the United States, and that they were traitors to the country inasmuch as they had, under American pressure, agreed to reduce Pakistan's nuclear program.

In August the PML, ANP, and a few other opposition groups initiated a mass movement to force Bhutto out of power. They organized "whistle stop" train rides, rallies, protest marches, and general strikes to bring the government to a halt. Their efforts received much public support but not enough to unsettle the regime. Assured of the Army's neutrality, Bhutto took these challenges in stride.

No new initiatives were discernible in Pakistan's foreign policy. Relations with India remained tense, and differences with the United States over the country's nuclear program were not resolved. Washington continued to withhold the delivery of some 30 F-16 fighters toward the cost of which Pakistan had already paid more than $600 million. But there was improvement on other fronts. In September, U.S. Energy Secretary Hazel O'Leary led a delegation of American business executives to explore possibilities of investment in Pakistan's energy sector.

See STATISTICS OF THE WORLD.   A.S.

PALAU. *See* PACIFIC ISLANDS; STATISTICS OF THE WORLD.

Self-rule achieved. *Palestine Liberation Organization Chairman Yasir Arafat signs the accord giving
Palestinians control of the West Bank enclave of Jericho and the Gaza Strip. Assisting him at the May
ceremony in Cairo is Rami Shaath, son of Nabil
Shaath, the PLO's chief negotiator. Behind them is a
statue of the ancient Egyptian fertility goddess, Isis,
holding a dove of peace.*

PALESTINE LIBERATION ORGANIZATION.

It was not until May 4, 1994, that the PLO and
Israel worked out the specifics of their 1993
agreement on establishing a degree of Palestinian self-rule in the West Bank and Gaza
Strip. Days later, contingents of the Palestinian
police force crossed into Gaza and Jericho,
and the Israel Defense Forces (IDF) turned over
the civil administration of Gaza to the Palestinians.

PLO Chairman Yasir Arafat appointed a 19-
member Palestinian National Authority,
headed by him, to run Palestinian affairs in the
self-rule areas on an interim basis, and in July
he took up permanent residence in Gaza.

By August, Israel had released hundreds of
Palestinian political prisoners and agreed to
transfer responsibility for health, education,
and other civil duties to the Palestinians.

Extremists on both sides attempted to derail
the peace process. In February a right-wing
Jewish settler killed 29 Muslim worshipers in
the Hebron Ibrahimi Mosque/Cave of Mach-
pela (Cave of the Patriarchs); many other
Palestinians were killed by the IDF in the riots
that followed. Hamas, a militant Islamic fundamentalist group, kidnapped and took
hostage an Israeli soldier, who was killed
along with the kidnappers when the IDF tried
to rescue him. In October a member of Hamas
detonated a bomb on a Tel Aviv bus, killing 22
Israelis. In November, Palestinian police loyal
to Arafat opened fire on militant Islamic
demonstrators; 14 protesters and one police
officer were killed. Such violent acts embittered people on both sides but did not push the
peace process off track.

Yet the violence, together with the slow
progress of the peace process, dampened
Palestinian support for the PLO and Arafat.
Many were disappointed by the delays in implementation, continued Israeli human rights
violations, and the meager flow of the
promised $2.4 billion in international aid. It
was not until late autumn that a major infusion
of aid—some $200 million in emergency fi-
nancial relief—was agreed on.

Most of the dissatisfaction was directed at
Arafat for apparently agreeing to major concessions with the Israelis and for seeming to
take orders from Israeli Prime Minister Yitzhak
Rabin. Arafat was also criticized for appointing his cronies, for refusing to comply with international demands for financial accountability, and for his autocratic behavior. As a result
of the pessimism among Palestinians, support
for the peace process dropped from 69 percent
in late September 1993 to just 54 percent a
year later.

Despite his increasing unpopularity, Arafat
took some solace in being awarded the Nobel
Peace Prize, together with Rabin and Israeli
Foreign Minister Shimon Peres, in late Octo-

ber. But only improvements in the quality of life for Palestinians in the West Bank and Gaza, progress toward full implementation of the 1993 accord, and gradual Palestinian control over the rest of the West Bank and Arab Jerusalem would rescue his credibility and that of the PLO. P.M.

PANAMA. Presidential and legislative elections held in May 1994 appeared to create the preconditions necessary for establishment of a more stable democratic order in Panama, after some 25 years of military rule and elections marred by fraud.

The winning presidential candidate, Ernesto Pérez Balladares, represented the Revolutionary Democratic Party, which was founded by strongman General Omar Torrijos in 1978 as a vehicle for the consolidation of the military's civilian power base. Following the elections, the country gained readmission to the Rio Group, a prestigious regional organization from which Panama had been expelled during the late 1980s when former dictator General Manuel Antonio Noriega held power.

The new president assumed office on September 1 and immediately began to work toward establishing a new government of national consensus and unity. He advocated that the country seek membership in the North American Free Trade Agreement as a means of revitalizing and diversifying Panama's economy. In October a new economic plan for the nation was unveiled that stressed reduction in the size of the public sector and changes in the labor code.

Panama continued its long tradition of welcoming refugee groups and exiled leaders. In August, Pérez Balladares agreed to accept up to 10,000 Cuban refugees if the United States paid all expenses and administered the refugee camps. Tensions erupted into riots at a camp in December, as the refugees hung in diplomatic limbo, uncertain of their future. Two exiled Haitian generals, Raoul Cédras and Philippe Biamby, and their families were also granted asylum in October.

In July, Panama was the site of an airplane bombing in which all 21 people aboard (12 of whom were Jewish businessmen) were killed. Although the disaster was widely thought to be the work of an Islamic extremist group, Pana-

manian officials did not rule out possible connections to drug trafficking.

See STATISTICS OF THE WORLD. S.C.R.

PAPUA NEW GUINEA. See PACIFIC ISLANDS; STATISTICS OF THE WORLD.

PARAGUAY. Social unrest and political turmoil marked 1994 as Paraguay continued to deal with the challenge of democratization. The year saw the breakdown of a 1993 compromise agreement referred to as the governability pact. The pact stipulated that all important political initiatives be submitted to the leaders of Paraguay's political parties prior to any congressional or presidential action. It had nearly collapsed in mid-December 1993, when President Juan Carlos Wasmosy's ruling Colorado Party (Asociación Nacional Republicana) challenged a congressional plan for reorganizing the judicial system and three of the country's leading opposition parties objected to Colorado's stance. A negotiated settlement was quickly reached, however, whereby the government and opposition parties would collectively work toward the appointment of "consensus" candidates to the judicial bench.

A more serious government crisis occurred in June 1994. After the National Congress overrode Wasmosy's veto of a law barring military and police officials from being members of political parties, Colorado leaders asked the Paraguayan Supreme Court to rule on the law's constitutionality. This led opposition leaders to announce their parties' withdrawal from the governability pact. The law was ruled unconstitutional in October.

Concerns over land and economic policies sparked rural protests in 1994. Squatter evictions and protests over the government's minimum price for cotton and other products led to disturbances in rural districts during February and March. Industrial unions staged a protest march in Asunción on February 26. Social tensions increased in the wake of the country's first general strike in decades on May 2. The government mandated a 10 percent wage increase for all workers in July, but union demands for a minimum 25 percent wage hike promised continued conflict.

See STATISTICS OF THE WORLD. D.Le.

PENNSYLVANIA. See STATE GOVERNMENT REVIEW; STATISTICS OF THE WORLD.

People in the News

Murder charges against ex-football great O. J. Simpson provoked more tabloid ink—and TV time—in 1994 than any other single news story, although continuing reports of unseemly behavior by members of the British royal family also stirred up a tidal wave of media madness. The White House found itself on the defensive for much of the year, and the Republicans dominated the November elections.

Was it just us, or did 1994 seem more than a little *odd*? Hanky-panky in the house of Windsor, O. J.'s fugitive Ford Bronco, an ice princess with a battered knee, a peripatetic cat, the Jackson-Presley wedding, and no World Series—if the year were a canvas, you'd want **Salvador Dalí** to paint it, or maybe even **Hieronymus Bosch**.

In Britain, royal foibles and follies continued to dominate the media. In a television interview **Prince Charles**, heir to the throne, admitted he had been unfaithful to his estranged wife, **Princess Diana**. A tabloid reported that

Di's guy. British newspapers labeled former Army Major James Hewitt a rat and a stinker for reportedly telling the author of a biography of Princess Diana that he had had an affair with the lonely lady.

Diana herself had made hundreds of crank calls to a London art dealer; the princess denied the story, saying "sinister forces" were out to destroy her. Meanwhile, Anna Pasternak's *Princess in Love* recounted in overripe detail an alleged adulterous romance between Di and **James Hewitt**, the riding instructor who called her Squidgy, and new books by Jonathan Dimbleby and Andrew Morton aired more of the Windsors' dirty linen. Dimbleby's authorized biography brought a rare public rebuke from Charles's father, **Prince Philip**, portrayed unflatteringly in the book. "I've never discussed private matters," said Philip, "and I don't think the queen has either."

For U.S. President **Bill Clinton** and first lady **Hillary Rodham Clinton**, 1994 was a nightmare. Less than a week into the new year **Virginia Kelley**, the president's mother, died of cancer. Much of the rest of the year was equally bleak. Congress was balky, and health care reform went down the tubes. An aggressive new Whitewater independent prosecutor, **Kenneth Starr**, set up shop in Little Rock. A former Arkansas state employee, **Paula Jones**, filed a civil suit against the president, charging him with sexual harassment when he was governor (a federal judge, however, ruled the case could not come to trial while Clinton remained in the presidency). **Webster Hubbell**, who resigned his Justice Department post and pleaded guilty to charges in connection with overbilling legal clients, was one of a number of friends and associates to be implicated in scandal. And the November elections were a debacle for the Democrats, who lost control of both houses of Congress.

Among the Clintons' few bright public mo-

Clothes call. *When Hillary Rodham Clinton accompanied hubby Bill to Europe in June, some journals there raked her over the coals for her fashion sense—or, rather, lack thereof.*

ments, the president's half brother, **Roger Clinton**, married **Molly Martin**, and in the first White House nuptials in 23 years the first lady's younger brother, **Tony Rodham**, wed **Nicole Boxer**, daughter of U.S. Senator **Barbara Boxer**.

Hugh Rodham, older brother of the first lady, had a less happy fate; swept up in the huge anti-Clinton tide on Election Day, he came nowhere near winning a U.S. Senate seat from Florida. Among the many Republicans carried into office was former **Cher** husband and rock star **Sonny Bono**, now a U.S. representative from Palm Springs, CA. Two sons of former President **George Bush** also ran in November, both for governorships: **George W.** triumphed in the Texas gubernatorial race, defeating incumbent **Ann Richards**, although **Jeb** fell short in his effort to dethrone Florida Governor **Lawton Chiles**.

Former President **Jimmy Carter**, freelance world peacemaker, negotiated a nuclear agreement with North Korea, smoothed the way for the return of President **Jean-Bertrand Aristide** to Haiti, and in December took a stab at the knotty Bosnian problem. Late in the year former Vice President **Dan Quayle** was

Nixon's passing. *The funeral of former U.S. President Richard Nixon in April was attended by President Bill Clinton and no fewer than four ex-presidents, all with their first ladies. Left to right: Bill and Hillary Clinton, George and Barbara Bush, Ronald and Nancy Reagan, Jimmy and Rosalynn Carter, and Gerald and Betty Ford.*

hospitalized for blood clots in his lungs, and former President **Ronald Reagan** acknowledged in a letter that he had incipient Alzheimer's disease.

All five living U.S. presidents—Clinton, Reagan, Carter, Bush, and Ford—and their wives attended the April funeral of former President **Richard M. Nixon**; the misdeeds that led to Nixon's resignation seemed almost forgotten for a time, as the media stressed his foreign policy triumphs. A month later, Americans mourned the death of one of history's most popular and elegant first ladies, **Jacqueline Kennedy Onassis**.

Kim Il Sung, "Great Leader" of North Korea since the 1940s, died in July, apparently passing the mantle on to his son **Kim Jong Il**. **Nelson Mandela** became the first black president in modern South African history; he also published his autobiography, *Long Walk to Free-*

Doubles. U.S. Open tennis champion Andre Agassi and actress Brooke Shields formed a new power couple on the celebrity scene.

dom. Palestine Liberation Organization Chairman **Yasir Arafat**, winner (with Israeli Prime Minister **Yitzhak Rabin** and Foreign Minister **Shimon Peres**) of the 1994 Nobel Peace Prize, announced that he and his wife, **Suha Tawil**, were expecting their first child.

Former Australian Prime Minister **Bob Hawke** and his wife, **Hazel**, called it quits after 38 years of marriage, and **Susana Higuchi** served divorce papers on her husband, Peruvian President **Alberto Fujimori**. In Canada separatist leader **Lucien Bouchard**, one of Québec's most popular politicians, had his left leg amputated after it was infected by flesh-eating bacteria. French President **François Mitterrand** and his wife, **Danielle**, went under the knife, he for complications from prostate cancer, she for a cardiopulmonary problem. The Socialist leader acknowledged that, as a right-winger during World War II, he had a role in the collaborationist Vichy regime.

Named *Time* magazine's Man of the Year, **Pope John Paul II** spent much of 1994 recovering from surgery to replace a right thighbone broken in a bathroom fall at the Vatican in April; meanwhile, his *Crossing the Threshold of Hope,* reflections in response to a journalist's questions, became a global best-seller. After the death of **Ezra Taft Benson**, the Church of Jesus Christ of Latter-Day Saints chose **Howard W. Hunter**, an 86-year-old former corporate lawyer, as president of the world's 8.7 million Mormons. Hasidic Jews mourned the death at 92 of **Menachem Mendel Schneerson**, the Lubavitcher rebbe.

With major league baseball on strike and the fall ice-hockey season a washout, much of the year's sports-related news came from the police blotter. The biggest story emerged when actor and former football great **O. J. Simpson** was accused of having brutally murdered his former wife, **Nicole Brown Simpson**, and her friend **Ronald Goldman**. Simpson surrendered to police after a long, low-speed car chase watched by millions on television; court proceedings, which began in the fall under a media spotlight, made celebrities of a cast of subsidiary characters, starting with the judge in the case, **Lance Ito**.

While Winter Olympics stars like **Dan Jansen** and **Oksana Baiul** made headlines, the

Duet. *One of the most unexpected marriages in many a honeymoon united Lisa Marie Presley, daughter of Elvis, with pop star Michael Jackson. Here, the couple, accompanied by a Hungarian midget, visit a Budapest children's hospital in August.*

biggest Olympic names in the news were those of skater **Nancy Kerrigan**, who was whacked on the knee beforehand at a Detroit arena, and rival **Tonya Harding**, whose ex-husband admitted to having helped plan the attack. (Both women competed in the Olympics; Harding finished well out of medal range, but Kerrigan placed second, after Baiul.) Harding struck a plea bargain in the ensuing court case, admitting to having conspired to hinder the prosecution in the attack; she was fined, sentenced to community service, and required to resign from the U.S. Figure Skating Association.

In other sports news, pro golfer **Kim Williams** was injured in a parking lot when she took a stray bullet in the neck. Teenage tennis pro **Jennifer Capriati** was arrested in Florida for possession of marijuana (she later entered a rehab center), and outfielder **Darryl Strawberry**, also treated for drug abuse, was later indicted for tax evasion. Pitcher **Dwight Gooden** and soccer star **Diego Maradona** were suspended from competition after flunking drug tests. In Colombia, soccer player **Andres Escobar** was murdered outside a restaurant, apparently because he had kicked a goal into his own net in a World Cup match against the United States. Austrian skier **Ulrike Maier** died after breaking her neck in a downhill race in Germany, and Brazilian Formula One driver **Ayrton Senna** was killed in a crash at an Italian grand prix race.

Basketball superstar **Michael Jordan**, embracing a new challenge, became a mediocre minor league baseball player. Two tennis greats said farewell, as **Martina Navratilova** and **Ivan Lendl** called it quits. Meanwhile, **Andre Agassi**, linked romantically to actress **Brooke Shields**, scored a comeback victory at the U.S. Open. One of the year's most authentic and surprising sports heroes was **George Foreman**, who—at the age of 45—struck a blow for middle-aged spread by reclaiming boxing's heavyweight crown.

Among high-profile court cases, "death doctor" **Jack Kevorkian** was acquitted of having violated a Michigan law banning assisted suicide, and white supremacist **Byron De la Beckwith** was convicted in the murder of civil rights leader **Medgar Evers** over 30 years earlier. Abortion foe **Paul J. Hill** was sentenced to death for murdering a doctor and his bodyguard outside a Pensacola, FL, abortion clinic. Former CIA officer **Aldrich Ames** received a life term after pleading guilty to having spied on a massive scale for the KGB; his wife, **Rosario**, also pleaded guilty and was sentenced to 63 months.

The trial of the **Menendez** brothers, **Lyle** and **Erik**, for the murder of their parents in their Beverly Hills, CA, mansion, ended in a hung jury in January. Serial killer **John Wayne Gacy** was executed by lethal injection, while the

Rewedded bliss. Model Christie Brinkley came out of a scary skiing-trip helicopter crash in April with a few bruises and a new husband. One of her fellow survivors was Los Angeles real estate developer Ricky Taubman, whom she married eight months later after divorcing rocker Billy Joel.

Tying the knot. *Comedian-actress Whoopi Goldberg and union organizer Lyle Trachtenberg got married in October.*

even more notorious killer-cannibal **Jeffrey Dahmer** was murdered in a Wisconsin prison, apparently by a fellow inmate.

Lorena Bobbitt, who had severed the penis of her abusive husband, **John**, with a kitchen knife in 1993, was found not guilty by reason of temporary insanity; both Bobbitts spent much of 1994 cashing in on their very temporary celebrity. In a criminal case with international repercussions, **Michael Fay**, a 19-year-old American living in Singapore, was flogged with a cane for vandalizing cars. **Susan Smith**, a 23-year-old South Carolina mother, shocked her neighbors and the nation, first by claiming her two children had been abducted by a carjacker, then by admitting she had drowned them herself.

For **Tupac Shakur**, a big name in "gangsta rap," both life and art grew ever more violent; shot five times and robbed in early December, he was convicted only two days later on a sex abuse charge lodged against him in 1993. The rock scene reeled at the suicide in April of **Nirvana**'s **Kurt Cobain**. The silver anniversary in August of the 1960s cultural get-together known as Woodstock was mainly 1990s (featuring such performers as **Green Day**, **Spin Doctors**, and **Nine Inch Nails**), but the mud was as mucky as it was in 1969.

Madonna released a new album, *Bedtime Stories*, and had a much-publicized spat on camera with talk-show host **David Letterman**, whose program dominated late-night TV. Other comic talents included **Jim Carrey**, rubber-faced star of *The Mask*, and **Tim Allen**, who scored a rare triple with a top-rated TV sitcom (*Home Improvement*), movie (*The Santa Clause*), and book (*Don't Stand Too Close to a Naked Man*). *Forrest Gump*, starring **Tom Hanks**, was the runaway hit of the summer film season, but **Quentin Tarantino**'s controversial *Pulp Fiction*, a grand prize winner at Cannes, was the buzz movie of the year.

Accused of sexually molesting a teenage boy, superstar **Michael Jackson** settled out of court for undisclosed millions, in exchange for the boy's promise not to testify against him.

The Jackson story took a new twist when it was announced in midsummer that the "king of pop" had married **Lisa Marie Presley**—yes, the daughter of **Elvis**, king of rock 'n' roll. Also tying the knot were Oscar nominee **Liam Neeson** and actress **Natasha Richardson**; comedian **Whoopi Goldberg** and movie-union organizer **Lyle Trachtenberg**; outgoing Senate Majority Leader **George Mitchell** and marketing consultant **Heather MacLachlan**; jazz singer-pianist **Harry Connick, Jr.**, and lingerie model **Jill Goodacre**; Canadian singer **Celine Dion** and her manager, **Rene Angelil** (the 500 wedding guests included former Prime Minister **Brian Mulroney**); and **Christopher Dean** (half of Britain's sizzling ice duo **Torvill and Dean**) and U.S. figure skating champion **Jill Trenary**. Computer billionaire **Bill Gates**, said to be the world's richest bachelor, lost his claim to that title when he married marketing executive **Melinda French** on a secluded Hawaiian island; he also kept in the news by coming up with the winning $30.8 million bid for a **Leonardo Da Vinci** notebook auctioned off at Christie's.

After spending $30,000 for a full-page ad in

Splitting up. Roseanne and Tom Arnold were all smiles in March as Roseanne signed her new book, My Lives, at a California store, but later in the year their marriage crashed.

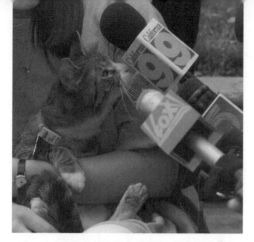

The fur flew. Three-year-old tabby cat Tabitha responds to reporters' questions after logging 32,000 miles in the fuselage of a jumbo jet in July. Tabitha had somehow got loose from her carrier and spent 12 days in the plane's belly before the airline, feeling the heat from animal rights activists, permitted her owner to search the premises.

ran away from home, moved in with the Twiggs, accused **Robert Mays** (the man who had raised her) of sexual abuse, and then admitted the accusation was untrue. **Rodney King**, whose 1991 beating by Los Angeles police officers was captured on videotape, was awarded well over $3 million in compensatory damages. In October the U.S. government quietly dropped its long legal effort to discharge an openly gay sailor, Petty Officer **Keith Meinhold**.

Last but not least, **Heather Whitestone**, a 21-year-old Alabaman who lost nearly all her hearing at the age of 18 months, became the first woman with an acknowledged disability to be crowned Miss America.   G.H.

Miss America. Heather Whitestone is crowned Miss America of 1994 by the 1993 title holder, Kimberly Aiken (left). Whitestone, a 21-year-old Alabamian who lost nearly all her hearing at the age of 18 months, was the first woman with an acknowledged disability to win the crown.

the *Times* of London to reaffirm their commitment to each other, supermodel **Cindy Crawford** and actor **Richard Gere** announced that their marriage was, in fact, kaput. Also splitting up were singer **Billy Joel** and model **Christie Brinkley**; singer-dancer **Paula Abdul** and *Mighty Ducks* star **Emilio Estevez**; action hero **Steven Seagal** and actress **Kelly Le Brock**; actor-director-producer **Kevin Costner** and his long-ago college sweetheart and wife of 16 years, **Cindy Silva**; not-always-lovable comics **Roseanne Barr** and **Tom Arnold**; and, after 45 years of comic-strip camaraderie, **Tess Trueheart** and **Dick Tracy**. The on-again, off-again marriage of on-again, off-again movie stars **Don Johnson** and **Melanie Griffith** was on again at the end of 1994.

The midyear saga of **Tabitha** the cat, who logged 32,000 miles aboard a 747 jet, had a happy ending. Aided by a psychic, anxious owner **Carol Ann Timmel** finally found her missing pet in the cargo hold, where she had escaped from her cat carrier on a New York–Los Angeles flight 12 days earlier. Tabitha was in fairly good shape—but slightly underweight and suffering from jet lag.

Kimberly Mays, the "switched at birth" teenager who made headlines in 1993 by persuading a court to let her cut all ties with her biological parents, **Regina** and **Ernest Twigg**,

SILVIO BERLUSCONI

SILVIO BERLUSCONI

There is perhaps no better example of the volatility of Italian politics than the dizzying career of Silvio Berlusconi, who in less than a year went from hero to failure.

Before becoming Italy's prime minister in May 1994, Silvio Berlusconi was known as a self-made man who had created Italian private television. The son of a Milanese bank clerk, Berlusconi was born in 1936. After working his way through the University of Milan, he started out in real estate, putting together a series of property deals during the 1960s that culminated in the construction of Milano Due, a huge residential complex. Then, inspired by a cable television channel he had installed at Milano Due, he proceeded to buy up local stations. To circumvent a law giving state television RAI a broadcasting monopoly, Berlusconi in 1980 created a de facto network by airing the same programs simultaneously on all his stations.

Thanks to his close ties with then-Socialist Prime Minister Bettino Craxi, the legal loophole remained open, and by 1984, Berlusconi's Canale 5, Italia 1, and Rete 4, which brought American game shows and soap operas into Italian households, were watched by approximately half the country's television audience. He expanded his holding company, Fininvest, into an empire grossing $7.2 billion a year. It included his hometown soccer team, A. C. Milan; Italy's largest advertiser, Publitalia; the country's largest supermarket chain, Standa; Mondadori publishers; and Mediolanum insurance. The expansion caused Fininvest to accumulate a $2.3 billion debt.

In January 1994, as the Democratic Party of the Left (former Communist Party) seemed poised to replace centrist forces swept away by corruption scandals, Berlusconi announced he wanted to save Italy from both corruption and Communists. Heading a rightist, reformist new party, Forza Italia (Go, Italy), he dominated the March elections through a blitz of television ads that promised jobs and tax cuts.

Soon after taking office, however, he made a serious misstep by trying to curb the power of Italy's anticorruption magistrates. By November he was being investigated for possible antitrust and other violations in relation to his business empire. The following month it became clear that Berlusconi would not survive a no-confidence vote in Parliament, and he opted to resign. N.V.

STEPHEN G. BREYER

On August 3, 1994, Stephen Gerald Breyer was sworn in as the U.S. Supreme Court's 108th justice. He replaced Harry A. Blackmun, who retired after 24 years on the Court.

STEPHEN G. BREYER

Breyer, who had been a federal appeals court judge in Boston, won Senate confirmation by a vote of 87-9. The ease of his confirmation practically duplicated the warm reception given Ruth Bader Ginsburg a year earlier. The two newest justices seemed to demonstrate President Bill Clinton's ability to select, after some initial uncertainty, moderate judges with impeccable legal backgrounds to fill vacancies on the Court.

Breyer's nomination enjoyed broad bipartisan support, including that of Republicans who had worked with him when he served as counsel to the Senate Judiciary Committee before his 1980 appointment to the federal bench. The strongest opposition arose over Breyer's questionable investment in the Lloyd's of London insurance syndicate, which posed conflict-of-interest concerns. Some critics said Breyer might be forced to disqualify himself from decisions involving toxic waste and asbestos because they could mean additional liability for the insurance investors.

During three days of testimony before the Senate Judiciary Committee in July, Breyer expressed general support for affirmative action, separation of church and state, and abortion rights. But he also indicated backing for capital punishment and stiff sentencing of convicted criminals, and some liberals said Breyer's background demonstrated too much of a pro-business leaning.

Breyer was born in 1938 in San Francisco and graduated from Stanford University with highest honors. At Oxford University, where he was a Marshall scholar, he earned first-class

honors in philosophy, politics, and economics. He graduated with high honors from Harvard Law School, then served as law clerk for Supreme Court Justice Arthur Goldberg before going to work for the Justice Department's antitrust division in 1965.

Breyer joined the faculty at Harvard Law School in 1967 and became chief counsel to the Senate Judiciary Committee in 1979. He was chief judge of the First U.S. Circuit Court of Appeals in Boston when Clinton tapped him for the Supreme Court. He married Joanna Hare in 1967; they have three children.   J.R.

BILL CLINTON

See UNITED STATES OF AMERICA: The Presidency.

PRINCESS DIANA

The year 1994 produced new convulsions for the British monarchy. Amid new allegations about Princess Diana's love life and new revelations by Prince Charles (from whom Di had separated in 1992), the royal couple seemed headed for divorce.

The portrait of a marriage gone awry already had been painted in a 1992 book, *Diana: Her True Story,* by journalist Andrew Morton; Morton depicted Diana as an unloved, unhappy princess who suffered from the eating disorder bulimia nervosa and made repeated, halfhearted suicide attempts that were unheeded cries for help.

Another piece was added to the picture in July 1994 when, in a television documentary produced by journalist Jonathan Dimbleby, Charles admitted that he had been unfaithful to Diana after their marriage "had irretrievably broken down." And in August the tabloid *News of the World* alleged that a presumably unhinged Diana had made some 300 hang-up calls from Kensington Palace to Oliver Hoare, a former mediator between the prince and princess. (Diana denied the story, citing a diary showing she had been elsewhere when some of the calls were supposedly made.)

And the books kept on coming, with ever-more-intimate "revelations." Anna Pasternak's *Princess in Love* hit the bookstores in October; based on an interview with former Major James Hewitt, it tells the story of an alleged five-year affair between the princess and her unchivalrous riding instructor. Then Dimbleby's *Prince of Wales* appeared, a book on which the prince cooperated. British tabloids interpreted the book as saying that Charles had been pressured by his father into marrying a woman he did not love and whom he found obsessively jealous and given to bouts of depression. After excerpts appeared in London's *Sunday Times* in October, Diana fled briefly to the United States to escape the media attention in Britain. Another book by Morton, *Diana: Her New Life,* which highlighted her side of the story, came out in November; in this volume she was cast as a POW ("Prisoner of Wales"), unable either to be Charles's fairy-tale princess or to have a new life of her own.

The final chapters of this very public saga have yet to be written. Also unknown is its impact on the couple's two sons—and on the future of the British monarchy. W.A.M.

PRINCESS DIANA

HOLLY HUNTER

HOLLY HUNTER

In 1994, Holly Hunter won an Oscar (and a Cannes Film Festival award) for best actress for a role she almost didn't get: Ada in Jane Campion's *The Piano* (1993).

At first glance, Hunter would seem an unlikely choice for the part. Campion says she imagined Ada, a mute (but not deaf) 19th-century Scotswoman, as "tall and statuesque." Hunter is a slim 5'2". A self-described type A personality, Hunter talks with a twang as thick as yesterday's grits.

About the only obvious thing Ada and Hunter have in common is an ability to communicate passion through the piano. Hunter, who took lessons throughout her teens, performed all the musical sequences in the movie. In fact, it was her musical ability that persuaded Campion that she could indeed be Ada—that and her intelligence, likability, and dark, penetrating eyes.

The youngest of seven children, Holly Hunter was born in Atlanta in 1958. Her parents, who ran a cattle and hay farm in nearby Conyers, never expected her to stay a farm girl. They sent Holly to dancing school, encour-

MIGUEL INDURAIN

earned her first Oscar nomination as a perfectionist producer in *Broadcast News* (1987), and won an Emmy and a Cable Ace Award for her over-the-top performance in *The Positively True Adventures of the Alleged Texas Cheerleader-murdering Mom* (1993). She scored a rare Academy Award double in 1994 when, in addition to winning an Oscar for *The Piano,* she was nominated for her supporting role as a gum-chewing secretary in *The Firm* (1993).

G.H.

MIGUEL INDURAIN

In 1994, Spanish cyclist Miguel Indurain unarguably secured his spot as one of the greatest bicycle racers ever. "Big Mig," as he is known by the other riders, won his fourth consecutive Tour de France, becoming only the third rider to accomplish the feat. Frenchman Jacques Anquetil won his first in 1957, then put together a four-year string from 1961 to 1964. Belgian Eddy Merckx, considered by many to be the greatest cyclist of all, won from 1969 to 1972 and added a fifth title in 1974.

In addition, Indurain capped the 1994 season by breaking the world hour record, one of the most torturous tests in cycling. Riding a specially made Pinarello bicycle on a velodrome in Bordeaux, France, Indurain rode 53.040 kilometers in 60 minutes (an average speed of 32.96 miles per hour).

Among cycling insiders and knowledgeable fans, however, Indurain earned the most respect in 1994 for the way he rode. In previous years Indurain had been criticized as a "bland" and "boring" champion. Because he is a big man—6'2" and 176 pounds—he would ride only hard enough in the mountains to stay close to his main rivals, then demolish them in time trials on flat terrain, where his size is an asset. This strategy produced decisive, but unexciting, victories. In 1994, however, Indurain rode aggressively in the Tour's uphill stages and won the 21-stage race by his greatest margin, 5 minutes and 39 seconds.

Indurain, who has ridden for the Spanish Banesto team since 1990, also receives acclaim for his physical attributes. His resting heart rate of 28 beats per minute is 37 bpm lower than an average athlete's. His lung capacity has measured as high as 7.8 liters, which is higher than even Merckx's. And al-

aged her musical studies, and gave her their full support when she made it clear that she wanted to become a professional actress.

After graduating from Carnegie Mellon University, where she studied theater, Hunter went to New York City. Almost immediately she snagged a bit part in a very forgettable horror flick, *The Burning* (1981). Her big break came less than two years later, when she took over for Mary Beth Hurt in *Crimes of the Heart,* a Pulitzer Prize-winning play by a fellow Southerner, Beth Henley. Starring roles in other Henley dramas followed.

On screen, Hunter has done all kinds of comedy—deadpan, screwball, romantic—and earned a solid reputation for portraying quirky, often troubled characters. She played the eccentric Officer "Ed" in *Raising Arizona* (1987),

though Indurain can produce an astonishing amount of power—550 watts, which is about twice the figure for the average amateur racer—his recovery is perhaps the quickest in professional cycling. Thirty seconds after a peak effort his heart rate drops from 150 beats per minute to 60 beats per minute.

Although famous throughout Europe, Indurain is a low-key champion. Born in 1964 in Villava, a farm village just south of the Pyrenees, he continues to live a quiet rural life there, feeding his chickens himself in the off-season. He describes himself as "a simple country man" and "reserved." B.S.

JOHN MAJOR

It was another year to endure for John Major, the Conservative prime minister of Britain. As he sought out the middle ground in 1994 in an attempt to counter the appeal of the opposition parties, he added to the bitterness of the small group of right-wing Conservative members of Parliament who still clung to the legacy of his predecessor, Margaret Thatcher. In November he drove eight of them out of the parliamentary party after they objected to increases in the British contribution to the European Union

JOHN MAJOR

budget. Since the Conservatives held a majority of only 14 in the House of Commons, the fact that the eight now felt free to vote with the opposition removed his parliamentary majority. The rebels took advantage by helping the opposition kill a controversial tax proposal. The prime minister's authority over his party was seriously eroded.

Nor could Major look to the polls for any comfort. In an August poll his party trailed a Labor Party rejuvenated by its new leader, Tony Blair, by 34.5 percentage points.

Major did, however, have one major triumph in 1994. The Downing Street Declaration of December 1993 finally led to a ceasefire by the Irish Republican Army and the Protestant paramilitaries in Northern Ireland and to the prospect of a permanent peace after 25 years of violence. Moreover, Major's government brought Britain out of the 1991-1992 recession and into high growth and low inflation, although he and his chancellor of the exchequer, Kenneth Clarke, were given little credit for this achievement. A debt-ridden public seemed untouched by the "feel-good factor" on which recent Conservative election victories had been based.

On the plus side, Major's economic strategy left room for preelection tax cuts in 1995. But could the bitterly divided Conservatives hold together under his leadership until then? And could his great strengths, his dogged determination and appearance of decency, compete with the charisma of Labor's Blair and the Liberal Democrats' Paddy Ashdown?

At the Conservative Party's conference in October, Major presented himself as a man who, although not an inspiring orator, gets things done. A British public still suffering from the effects of the flamboyant Thatcher era may well be prepared to vote once more for Major's "steady as she goes" government—if the Thatcherites allow him to survive to fight in the next election. S.W.

NELSON MANDELA

In February, early in the presidential campaign leading up to South Africa's first free elections, Nelson Mandela paid a visit to Robben Island, where he spent 18 of the 27 years he was imprisoned for opposing the apartheid system. The sentimental visit was ideal for generating

NELSON MANDELA

good publicity, but it also epitomized the reasons why he was seen as not just another candidate but the president-in-waiting: his personal sacrifice, lack of bitterness, and serene consciousness of his role in history.

Few doubted that Mandela's African National Congress (ANC), generally recognized as the principal organization dedicated to South Africa's freedom from oppressive rule by a white minority, would win the election on April 26-28. Mandela's stature was even higher than that of his movement. The stately leader, who turned 76 on July 18, had become a worldwide symbol not only of revolutionary dedication but also of pragmatism and reconciliation. No one had been surprised when Mandela was awarded the Nobel Peace Prize in 1993, although many of his followers resented that he had to share it with outgoing South African President F. W. de Klerk.

Mandela, born to a chiefly family in the rural eastern Cape Province, studied at Fort Hare University, where he was suspended for participating in a student protest. He later gained a law degree by correspondence, organized the ANC Youth League in 1944, led a campaign of nonviolent resistance in the 1950s, and was imprisoned in 1962, charged with plotting sabotage. Released from prison in 1990, he emerged to live up to the myth of greatness inspired by his imprisonment. Far from being a figurehead, he managed the complex negotiations leading to agreement on nonracial elections in 1994.

Taking office on May 10, he brought into his cabinet opposition leaders such as de Klerk and even Chief Mangosuthu Gatsha Buthelezi, whose violent rivalry and threats of boycott had almost derailed the election process. Mandela's efforts to transform economic conditions for blacks proved to be a difficult undertaking. However, in August his support among urban South Africans reached 9.2 on a ten-point scale, with ratings of 6.9 and 7, respectively, among Indians and people of mixed race. His rating among whites rose from 3.8 in early 1994 to 6, just short of de Klerk's 7.   W.M.

MARK MESSIER

By acquiring Mark Messier in a trade with the Edmonton Oilers just before the 1991-1992 season, the New York Rangers sent a clear message to their long-suffering fans. The franchise was more serious than ever about winning a Stanley Cup. Messier had been part of five National Hockey League (NHL) championship seasons in Edmonton, Alberta, his hometown. On four of those teams he was overshadowed by Wayne Gretzky, arguably the greatest hockey player ever to take the ice. But after Gretzky was dealt to the Los Angeles Kings, Messier became the leader of the Oilers' surprise success in 1989-1990. He was a hardworking, intimidating player who once broke a rival player's jaw with one punch.

So it was with considerable fanfare that the much-decorated veteran center arrived in New York, where the Rangers had not won a Cup since 1940. Messier heard all about the supposed "curse" of the Rangers and tried to dismiss it, but not until June 14, 1994, did the long dry spell end for the team. On that evening in Madison Square Garden the Rangers beat the Vancouver Canucks, 3-2, in the seventh and deciding game of the Stanley

MARK MESSIER

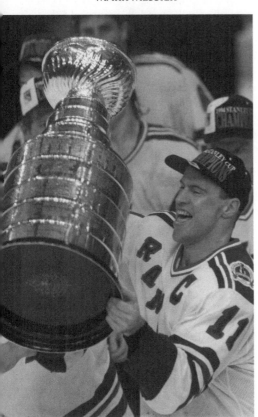

Cup finals. "I don't know quite how to describe this," said Messier, who thus became the first player ever to serve as captain of two different NHL champions. "I don't know if there are proper words."

Messier had asserted himself in the previous round against the feisty New Jersey Devils. The Rangers were down in the best-of-seven Eastern Conference final, three games to two, and they had to play in the Meadowlands, the Devils' home arena. Before the do-or-die sixth game, Messier "guaranteed" a Ranger victory. "We will win," he said. Messier's prediction did not look good after the Devils jumped to a 2-0 lead. But then he took over, assisting once and scoring three times in the third period to propel the Rangers to a stirring 4-2 triumph. The Rangers went on to win the series.

Messier wound up with 12 goals and 18 assists in 23 playoff games for the Rangers, but there was no way to measure his leadership. He said the Rangers would win, and he would not let them lose.

Messier, who was born in 1961, has never been married but has a six-year-old son, Lyon, who lives in Virginia with his mother, Lesley Young, a former model.   B.V.

HAKEEM OLAJUWON

Hakeem Abdul Olajuwon's life has been a storybook adventure that has taken him from a vacant-lot soccer field in Nigeria to big-time sports arenas in the United States.

In 1994, Olajuwon led his team, the Houston Rockets, to its first-ever National Basketball Association (NBA) championship. He was named Most Valuable Player for the regular season and the championship round, and he took Best Defensive Player honors for the second season in a row. As the first center since 1983 to win regular-season MVP honors, Olajuwon was third in scoring (27.3), fourth in rebounding (11.9), and second in blocked shots (3.71). His 23-game playoff statistics were even more overwhelming—he led all scorers (28.9) and averaged 11.0 rebounds and 4.0 blocked shots a game.

What singles out Olajuwon is his versatility. He plays like a guard or a small forward, coiling along the baseline to get his shot and then flying back across the court to block a shot. More multifaceted than other centers, Olajuwon has both a perimeter and a power game and is blessed with soft hands and grace. But then, Olajuwon started out as an all-around athlete, concentrating on soccer and team handball at Muslim Teachers College. That was where Oliver Johnson, an American who managed the Nigerian national team, saw the young man and insisted that anybody who was that tall (almost 7 feet) should be playing basketball. Olajuwon went on to dominate the boards in All Africa tournaments, leading both junior national and national teams to third-place finishes.

In October 1980, Olajuwon, then a skinny, polite 17-year-old with size 17 feet, arrived in New York with a college shopping list. His first stop was to have been St. John's University, but it was so cold outside that he flew on to the warmest spot on the list—the University of Houston, where he enrolled. After sitting out the 1980-1981 season, Olajuwon helped lead the Cougars to three straight National Collegiate Athletic Association Final Four berths before opting for the NBA draft in 1984. The Houston Rockets, with the first pick, chose Olajuwon. He has played for the Rockets ever since, signing a four-year contract extension, reportedly worth $25 million, in March 1992. In April 1993, Olajuwon—born in 1963 in Lagos, Nigeria—became a U.S. citizen.   S.G.

PEARL JAM

Maybe 1994's most important arena concert tour was the one that didn't happen. Mindful that many of their fans are as broke as the band members themselves were just a few years ago, Pearl Jam—now one of the hottest acts in rock 'n' roll—wanted to charge only $18 per ticket and limit the service fee to 10 percent. According to the band, this proposal ticked off Ticketmaster, the billion-dollar booking agency that has exclusive rights to outside sales for nearly two-thirds of the seats in U.S. concert venues.

Lawyers for Pearl Jam alleged that Ticketmaster urged leading concert promoters not to deal with the group as long as the service charge was limited to $1.80 a head. (Ticketmaster denied any wrongdoing.) Forced to change its summer plans, Pearl Jam took its case all the way to the U.S. Congress, where hearings were held in the House of Representatives in June and September, and filed a complaint with the Antitrust Division of the Justice Department, which, at year's end, was still looking into the matter.

Two founders of Pearl Jam, guitarist Stone Gossard and bassist Jeff Ament, played together in the bands Green River and Mother Love Bone in the 1980s before recruiting guitarist Mike McCready and lead singer Eddie Vedder in 1991. (Pearl Jam's original drummer, Dave Krusen, was replaced by Dave Abbruzzese, who left the band in the summer of 1994.) Boosted by the hype surrounding Nirvana, another Seattle band, Pearl Jam's first studio album, *Ten* (1991), was an immediate smash.

HAKEEM OLAJUWON

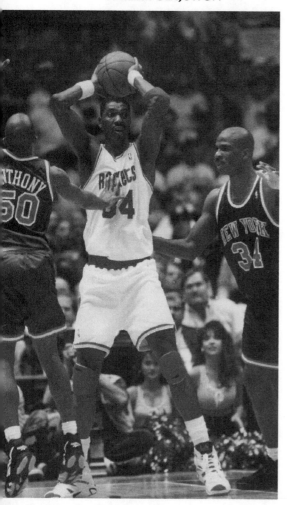

PEARL JAM

Vedder's potent vocals, a passionate performance on *MTV Unplugged,* and an award-winning video for the haunting single *Jeremy* all won new friends for the group.

Another chart-topping album, *Vs.,* followed in 1993. By the end of 1994—when their third studio album, *Vitalogy,* appeared—*Ten* and *Vs.* (for which the band made no videos) had each sold about 6 million copies. Ill at ease with their pop-star fame and fortune, troubled by the suicide in April of Nirvana's Kurt Cobain, Vedder and his bandmates continued to make music that critics called angry and anguished, sometimes confused, but always memorable and emotionally honest.   G.H.

SUSAN POWTER

"Stop the insanity!" Susan Powter likes to yell. The "insanity," according to this spike-haired health and fitness guru who came to fame as an infomercial hostess, is the diet industry, whose programs she criticizes for seldom leading to lasting weight loss, and the exercise industry, which she says caters to the already healthy. Powter is out to teach obese Americans—especially women—how to lose weight and get in shape without starving or suffering humiliation in aerobics classes designed for people who are already fit.

Powter says she once weighed 260 pounds and had little self-esteem. She tried dieting and exercise, but to no avail. However, Powter found her own way to enduring slimness: a very-low-fat, high-carbohydrate diet and regular exercise that was suited to her level of fitness. Her formula is simple: "Eat, move, and breathe." She admits that her message is nothing new, but somehow women are responding to it.

Powter was born in Sydney, Australia, in 1957; her family moved to the United States when she was ten. She already had weight problems before her first marriage in 1982, and having two children in two years only made things worse. Then her husband began an affair with a slimmer woman, the couple divorced, and Powter turned to food for solace. While she admits she began her weight-loss efforts because she felt inferior to her ex-husband's girlfriend, she now counsels women to take charge of their physical and psychological health for themselves, not to win a man's love. Powter, who now checks in at around 120

SUSAN POWTER

nothing is *everything. Seinfeld* thrives on the quandaries and taboos of ordinary life—finding your car in a parking garage, deciding what to bring to a dinner party, low-fat yogurt, nose picking, masturbation. Around such pointedly pointless themes each half-hour program weaves an elaborate comic counterpoint involving the neighbors and friends of a standup comic played by—surprise!—Jerry Seinfeld, a standup comic. Seinfeld's loopy (whiny, if you don't like him) routines open and close every episode.

Born in Brooklyn, NY, in 1954, Jerry Seinfeld grew up on Long Island in the town of Massapequa ("It's an old Indian name that means 'by the mall,'" he jokes). After graduating from Queens College in 1976, he began refining his craft at open-mike nights in New York City's comedy clubs. Four years later he was out in Los Angeles, where he was "discovered" at a comedy club and hired for a disastrously brief fling at sitcom gag writing.

JERRY SEINFELD

pounds (she's 5'6"), resides in Los Angeles with her second husband, Lincoln Apeland, and her two sons.

Powter has written books, such as the bestselling *Stop the Insanity,* and has made several exercise videos. She began hosting her own nationally syndicated TV talk show in fall 1994, writes a syndicated newspaper column, hosts a radio show, and gives inspirational talks. Late in 1994 she was involved in legal wrangling when the president of her company filed suit against her for breach of contract. She countered by filing for bankruptcy, a claim which the opposition disputed. Whatever the outcome, it remains the case that while some find her strident and her diet advice unreasonable, clearly many Americans hunger for what Susan Powter is dishing out.   I.S.

JERRY SEINFELD

"Nothing comes of nothing," said the Greek philosopher Epicurus, but don't try to tell that to the folks behind *Seinfeld,* NBC's hip primetime series, winner of the 1994 Golden Globe Award for best television comedy. For them,

Seinfeld continued honing his standup routine until a 1981 guest shot on Johnny Carson's *Tonight Show* started him on a rocket ride to stardom: 300 dates a year on the club and campus circuit, his own HBO special, an American Comedy Award in 1988 as funniest male standup comic. Then NBC said yea to a pilot for a sitcom that Seinfeld and his comedian pal Larry David had dreamed up one evening.

Almost from the outset *Seinfeld* was a cult hit and a critical favorite, winning a loyal following among the free-spending viewers in the 18-34 age group that advertisers love. But the show didn't become a ratings smash until NBC positioned it after the long-running *Cheers* on Thursday nights. When the *Cheers* gang closed up the bar in 1993, *Seinfeld* became the anchor for NBC's Thursday night lineup. That year *Seinfeld* won three Emmys, including for best comedy series.

Seinfeld also launched the 1993 book *SeinLanguage,* a collection of Jerry's comic musings that sold so well that it was still listed on the *New York Times* best-seller list in 1994, totting up a total of 33 weeks.   G.H.

O. J. SIMPSON

Just minutes after midnight on June 13, 1994, O. J. Simpson's ex-wife Nicole Brown Simpson and her friend Ronald Goldman were found knifed to death in a pool of blood outside Nicole's posh Brentwood, CA, town house. Within days O. J. himself became the prime suspect, and he was charged with the murders on June 17. When Simpson pleaded not guilty, millions wanted to believe him.

For countless Americans the name O. J. ("The Juice") Simpson conjured up an image of a tall, handsome man with an irresistible smile dashing through an airport, briefcase in hand, in his role as TV spokesman for Hertz—a man they felt they knew personally and whom it seemed impossible to dislike. Others remembered the grace and athleticism of his days as a football superstar. It was difficult to reconcile either image with the somber-faced, sad-eyed man who sat in court surrounded by famous lawyers, listening while the evidence was presented.

There was, however, a less attractive side to O. J. He was divorced from his first wife, Mar-

O. J. SIMPSON

guerite Whitney, with whom he had three children, in 1979 amid rumors of womanizing. He married Nicole Brown in 1985. They had two children together, but it was a stormy relationship. Police were often called to their home during violent disputes; in 1989, O. J. pleaded no contest to a wife-beating charge.

Orenthal James Simpson was born in a black ghetto of San Francisco in 1947. A few years later his father left the family, which by then included four children. O. J. sometimes got in trouble with the law, but his athletic talent took him to the University of Southern California, where, as a running back, he led the team to two Rose Bowls and won the Heisman Trophy. In 1969 he began an 11-year career in the National Football League (most of it with the Buffalo Bills) and in 1973 broke the all-time rushing record for a single season. He was inducted into the Pro Football Hall of Fame in 1985.

When he retired, Simpson built his charm and personable appeal into a lucrative career as a sportscaster, occasional actor, and endorser of products—a career that might very well be over no matter what the outcome of his trial.   W.A.M.

STEVEN SPIELBERG

When, on the evening of March 21, 1994, Steven Spielberg accepted the Academy Award for best picture for *Schindler's List,* his treatment of the Holocaust that devastated European Jewry in the 1940s, the director completed what was surely the most astounding double triumph in the history of motion pictures. Spielberg's previous film, the 1993 dinosaur epic *Jurassic Park,* had by that time become the most popular movie of all time.

Spielberg was born in Cincinnati in 1947. His family moved often, and Steven ended up,

STEVEN SPIELBERG

ultimately, in California. He got a degree in English from California State College at Long Beach in 1970, and his 22-minute film *Amblin',* made while he was still in school, impressed executives at Universal Studios, who signed him to a seven-year contract.

Spielberg quickly showed his stuff, coming up with such megahits as *Jaws* (1975), Hollywood's biggest box-office moneymaker up to that point, and *E.T.* (1982), which surpassed *Jaws.* Spielberg married actress Amy Irving in 1985; the marriage ended in divorce in 1989, and Spielberg married actress Kate Capshaw two years later.

For Spielberg, making a film out of Australian writer Thomas Keneally's fact-based 1982 novel *Schindler's List*—the story of Oskar Schindler, a German industrialist who set up a factory in Nazi-occupied Poland and saved over 1,000 Jews from the death camps—meant coming to terms with his own past. In high school he suffered anti-Semitic taunts and was eager to assimilate into the gentile world. Yet his parents told him about the Nazi genocide (relatives died in Poland and Ukraine), and he learned his numbers from an Auschwitz survivor who showed him the Nazi identification numbers tattooed on his arm.

The horrific subject matter of *Schindler's List* was not an obvious box-office winner, but Spielberg's track record and enormous clout enabled him to get it made. As he put it, "I wanted to take the power I have in Hollywood and not squander it to make more money. I would love the studio to recoup its investment, but I really don't care if it does. I wanted to do this for my own children."   J.G.

BORIS YELTSIN

Russian President Boris Yeltsin's popularity among his people was on the wane in 1994, but for most of the year he continued to command respect abroad—until he sent troops into the separatist region of Chechnya.

The new constitution approved in December 1993 had been widely regarded as tailor-made for Yeltsin, and it was assumed he would continue to play a vigorous leadership role. But by mid-1994 a majority of Russians appeared to have lost confidence in their president. In a July poll only 29 percent of respondents wanted him to run for a second term.

BORIS YELTSIN

Yeltsin seemed no longer to have a clear sense of what he wanted for Russia. He increasingly attempted to assert Russian power abroad while focusing on law and order at home. He vowed to make the war on crime, rather than economic reform, his top priority. Crime had become a major threat, with more than 5,000 gangs said to be in operation in Russia, dealing in drugs and money laundering and preying on the new young capitalists to extort protection money from them.

A brush in the summer with Lieutenant General Aleksandr Lebed showed that Yeltsin was well aware of the shallowness of his popular support. When the Russian Defense Ministry ordered Lebed to resign his command of the Fourteenth Army, then stationed in Moldova, Lebed said that he would rather leave the Army than obey such an order. He bragged of his troops' support for him and dismissed Yeltsin as a "minus."

But Yeltsin went out of his way to support Lebed, whose dismissal was rescinded. Clearly, the president felt that such a popular officer had to be placated even at the cost of ignoring the principle of civilian control of the military.

Supporters argued that Yeltsin now saw his role not as a hands-on leader but as a statesman striving to consolidate his accomplishment of founding Russia's first post-Communist political system. His lack of vigor may also have been due to health problems and (as many claimed) overindulgence in alcohol.

Yeltsin met often with other heads of state, gave a major address at the United Nations in September, and at the Conference on Security and Cooperation in Europe, warned of a "cold peace" if NATO were expanded to include countries in Eastern Europe.

In December he finally lost patience with the secessionist government of Chechnya and dispatched troops—an act that drew criticism from a broad range of political camps at home and was questioned in many quarters abroad. Some outsiders wondered if he had capitulated to hard-liners and even if he still remained in control. L.T.L.

327

PERSIAN GULF STATES. A number of regional and foreign agreements were concluded in 1994 by the small Persian Gulf nations of the Arabian Peninsula. Renewed Iraqi threats to Kuwait were a cause of concern.

Persian Gulf Turmoil. Bahrain, Oman, Qatar, and the United Arab Emirates (UAE) joined the widespread condemnation of Iraqi President Saddam Hussein's October deployment of his forces on Iraq's border with Kuwait and supported the immediate armed response to the threat by the United States. A U.S. proposal to maintain a military presence in a buffer zone between Iraq and Kuwait caused misgivings, however. Many Gulf nations liked neither the idea of a long-term U.S. military presence nor the prospect of sharing its costs.

BCCI Scandal. A January agreement between the United States and Abu Dhabi in the Bank of Credit and Commerce International fraud case resulted in the extradition to the United States, in May, of former BCCI director Swaleh Naqvi. A U.S. judge later sentenced him to eight years in prison and ordered him to pay $255.4 million in restitution. In June an Abu Dhabi court found 12 former BCCI officials guilty on a number of charges. Bank founder and president Aga Hassan Abedi was sentenced, in absentia, to eight years, Naqvi to 14 years. The 12 defendants were also ordered to pay around $9 billion in damages to BCCI owners. In October, BCCI creditors accepted an Abu Dhabi offer of $1.8 billion in compensation.

Domestic Politics. Oman's sultan appointed two women to the Omani Consultative Council in November; they were the first women to serve on a Gulf state's council. Islamic fundamentalist leaders in Oman were sentenced to long prison terms.

Regional and Foreign Affairs. Oman and Israel conferred on regional water problems, and Qatar and Israel conferred on arms control, regional security in Qatar, and the importation of natural gas. In September the six-member Gulf Cooperation Council (GCC) announced its support of the Jordan-Israel peace agreements and its decision to partially lift a longtime boycott of companies trading with Israel.

Implementation of the Damascus Declaration, under which Egypt and Syria were to join with the Gulf states in a multilateral peacekeeping force, petered out during 1994 to economic and political cooperation. Qatar signed a bilateral defense agreement with France.

Between March and October there were several shooting incidents on the Qatar-Saudi Arabia border.

Iran rejected a GCC plea that it accept international arbitration in its quarrel with the UAE over ownership of the Abu Musa and Tunb islands.

In July, Gulf Air, the national carrier of Bahrain, Oman, Qatar, and the UAE, began the first direct flights between the Gulf region and the United States. The plague epidemic in India late in the summer led to greatly restricted travel between the Gulf area and the Indian subcontinent.

Economic Affairs. Low oil prices and overproduction slowed Gulf economies. Quotas set by the Organization of Petroleum Exporting Countries remained in place throughout the year as all producers, led by non-OPEC member Oman, worked for greater cooperation in order to boost oil prices. With national incomes down, the UAE and Oman sought to limit the inflow of expatriate workers.

In two major natural gas deals concluded during the year, Oman and India agreed to construct an underwater pipeline between the two countries, and Qatar concluded a similar pact with Pakistan.

See STATISTICS OF THE WORLD.   C.H.A.

PERU. The Peruvian economy showed signs of recovery in 1994. The administration of President Alberto Fujimori pressed ahead with its program to privatize most of Peru's state-owned firms, including the national oil, steel, and fishing companies. Government economists reported significant increases in private investment and productivity and predicted that inflation (7,500 percent when Fujimori took office in 1990) would be about 20 percent in 1994. Little progress was made, however, against Peru's massive unemployment.

The government seemed close to victory by year's end in its struggle against an insurgency that had claimed some 30,000 lives since it began in 1980. In late 1993, Abimael Guzmán Reynoso, the imprisoned founder of

First-family feud. The 1995 re-election chances of Peruvian President Alberto Fujimori (left) were called into question by his much-publicized rift with his wife, Susana Higuchi (right). After she criticized his policies and charged his family and administration with corruption, he relieved her of her duties as first lady.

the Shining Path guerrillas, called for a truce with the government. Some 6,000 insurgents had taken advantage of Peru's 1992 "repentance law" before it expired on November 1, 1994. The law promised pardons or greatly reduced prison terms for rebels who surrendered. But Shining Path militant Oscar Ramirez Durand (alias Comrade Feliciano) and his Red Path faction waged a sporadic terrorism campaign in metropolitan Lima. In April the Peruvian armed forces launched Operation Aries, an ambitious offensive against the only other significant concentration of Shining Path cadres, in the Huallaga Valley—the high jungle region where guerrillas have often cooperated with cocaine lords in a common struggle against Peruvian and U.S. antidrug agencies.

Public interest in the campaign for the April 1995 presidential election was heightened by a rupture between President Fujimori and his wife, civil engineer Susana Higuchi, who openly criticized her husband's economic program as unjustly burdensome for the nation's poor. Suggestions that Higuchi might run for Congress led Fujimori to secure a law barring members of the president's family from public office. On August 23, Fujimori announced that he had "removed" his wife from her duties as first lady because she was emotionally unstable. While Fujimori sought to evict Higuchi from the national palace, she formally charged her husband with "psychological and moral violence" under Peru's domestic abuse law.

In October, Higuchi filed a petition to become a presidential candidate running against her husband, who had announced he would seek a second term. The National Electoral Board later ruled that many of the signatures on her party's petition were invalid, leaving Higuchi short of the 100,000 signatures required for candidacy.

In December, Higuchi said that she would seek a civil divorce and a Roman Catholic annulment of her marriage. She also announced she would run for Congress. Meanwhile, several other women had filed to become presidential candidates. Opinion polls ranked Fujimori the strongest candidate, however, with over 40 percent supporting his reelection, followed by former United Nations Secretary-General Javier Pérez de Cuéllar with just under 24 percent.

See STATISTICS OF THE WORLD. D.P.W.

Top cat. *The Best Cat of 1994, as chosen by the Cat Fanciers' Association, was Grand Champion National Winner Pajean's Trinket Love.*

PETROLEUM. *See* POWER AND ENERGY.

PETS. There were 53 million dogs and 64 million cats in the United States at the beginning of 1994. Dog-owning households numbered 36.4 million, accounting for 37.7 percent of the U.S. population. There were 31.7 million households with cats, 32.9 percent of the population. Households owning both dogs and cats numbered 14.7 million, 15.3 percent of the U.S. population.

Popular Breeds. The number of purebred dogs registered with the American Kennel Club in 1993 was down from the previous year. Only 1,422,559 individual dogs were registered in 1993, down 105,833. The Labrador retriever was the most popular breed for the third year in a row, with 124,899 dogs registered, while the rottweiler ranked second for the second year in a row, with 104,160 dogs registered—an increase of 8,715 from 1992. German shepherd dogs were in third place in 1993, up from fourth place the year before, with a total of 79,936 individual registrations. The cocker spaniel, which had ranked third in 1992, showed a marked decline of 17.5 percent in registrations for 1993.

The Cat Fanciers' Association once again ranked the Persian as the most popular breed

of cat in the country, with 48,010 registered in 1993. This figure was down 2,124 from 1992. The Maine coon cat was a distant second, with only 3,549 registered. Third-place ranking went to the Siamese, with 2,979 individual cats registered. The Siamese ranked third for the second year in a row.

Shows. The 118th Westminster Kennel Club Dog Show, held in New York City in February, was won by Champion Chidley Willum the Conqueror, a Norwich terrier. The Cat Fanciers' Association's Best Cat of the Year for 1994 was the tabby Persian Grand Champion National Winner Pajean's Trinket Love.

Legislation. Legislation was passed in California in August that banned the tripping of horses for entertainment or sport. Prompted by media reports on the Mexican-style rodeo tradition of manganas, a horse tripping event, Bill 49X was the first of several such bills expected to be introduced in states where Mexican-style rodeos are held.

Legislation restricting ownership of wolf hybrids was passed in Georgia, Massachusetts, and New Hampshire. The laws prohibit residents from possessing dog-wolf crossbreeds, which have been implicated in a number of attacks on humans in recent years. On the federal level, the National Senior Citizens Pet Ownership Act, which would allow senior citizens in federally funded housing to own pets, was introduced in Congress; it was expected to come to a vote in 1995. A.P.

PHILIPPINES. In 1994 the Philippines enjoyed economic growth and relative political stability.

Economic Achievements. The vast improvement in the Philippine economy in 1994 could be explained by one main factor: the end of the energy crisis. With the construction of more power lines, what had become daily power outages ended in November 1993, and the added electricity supply led to increased productivity in 1994. Gross domestic product growth in 1994 was just short of the 5 percent President Fidel Ramos had projected in his 1993 plan for economic development.

Ramos launched bold economic initiatives in 1994, including completing the breakup of such oligarchies as the family-owned Philippine Long Distance Telephone Company and opening up the commercial banking system to foreign participation. Amid much controversy and public protest, he also pushed through an expanded value-added tax measure and asked Congress for extraordinary powers to reform the bureaucracy in such areas as tax collection. Critics worried that Ramos was "scattering his resources and biting off more than he can chew."

Although the United States remained the Philippines's largest trading partner, major investments came in from Japan, South Korea, and Taiwan, as the Philippines began to join the regional boom. It was unclear by year's end, however, whether this boom had improved the dire economic situation in the countryside, where the people were poorest.

As usual, the country was visited by typhoons and heavy rains, which triggered mudflows from Mount Pinatubo, causing loss of lives and property damage.

Political Situation. In 1994 the Ramos administration continued to negotiate with right-wing, left-wing, and Muslim rebel groups, with varying success. Only the military right-wing group took up the government's offer of amnesty. Full negotiations could not be carried out with the left, whose leadership was partly in exile in the Netherlands and near collapse. A cease-fire with the Moro National Liberation Front, the main Muslim insurgent group, appeared to be holding, and by the end of the year talks concerning greater Muslim autonomy on the southern island of Mindanao were making headway. However, the radical Muslim group Abu Sayyaf carried out a string of kidnappings and anti-Christian bombings on Mindanao in 1994, and another splinter group, the Moro Islamic Liberation Front, was blamed for several kidnappings in the fall. In early December, Ramos approved a unilateral cease-fire between the government and all rebel groups from December 16 to January 8, 1995. By year's end it appeared to be holding, although one guerrilla attack in mid-December claimed the lives of at least four soldiers.

A diplomatic row erupted in June over holding a conference in Manila on the Indonesian occupation of East Timor. Indonesia vigorously protested the conference. The issue was resolved in favor of Indonesia when Ramos banned foreign delegates from entering the Philippines, including France's first lady, Danielle Mitterrand, who was supposed to keynote the conference. Ten foreign delegates attended the meeting in spite of the ban, but they were allowed to leave the country peacefully after the conference.

Church-State Relations. Ramos launched a family-planning program in 1994, putting him on a collision course with the Roman Catholic Church, which counted 85 percent of Filipinos as adherents. Health Secretary Juan Flavier continued to aggressively promote the use of condoms to reduce the country's 2.3 percent birthrate, one of the highest in Southeast Asia. Cardinal Jaime Sin, the top prelate in the Philippines, accused the government of promoting abortion.

In August, Cardinal Sin rallied the country to oppose sending a Philippine delegation to the Cairo population conference in September. After a massive demonstration the government altered its conference delegation by removing two leading women's-rights advocates and signed a position paper that strongly rejected abortion.

See STATISTICS OF THE WORLD.   B.A.A.

PHOTOGRAPHY. Many of 1994's photography exhibitions spotlighted the work of often-forgotten 19th-century masters. In the photography market 19th-century pictures tended to fetch higher prices than did modern ones.

Exhibition Highlights. The Richard Avedon retrospective at the Whitney Museum of American Art in New York City was controversial even before it opened. A major fashion photographer of the second half of the 20th century, Avedon sought to be considered a fine-art photographer, too. In this endeavor he attracted both admiration and opprobrium. His portraits of celebrities, taken with a large-format camera against a white background, tend to denigrate the subject. His similarly realized pictures of working people in the American West often have a startling visual punch. Certainly his greatest achievements are his portraits of his father in the older man's last years. Here Avedon's emotions come to the fore and his ego recedes. Yet his overblown, mural-sized pictures of people at the Berlin Wall are surely among the most pretentious works

Celebrating a life in pictures. *The long and distinguished career of the Swiss-born American photographer Robert Frank was surveyed in a major restrospective at the National Gallery of Art in Washington, DC.*

imaginable. The catalog was more successful than the exhibition in tracking Avedon's fashion and fine-art career in parallel.

"Pictorial Effect/Naturalistic Vision" contrasted the work and theories of Henry Peach Robinson and Peter Henry Emerson. Organized by Ellen Handy of the Chrysler Museum, Norfolk, VA, and opening at the Art Museum at Princeton University, this exhibition was a model of modern historical scholarship and presented the rarely seen original work of two important 19th-century image makers. The most famous British photographer of his time, Robinson championed academic models of picture making, arranging his scenes and making combination prints from several negatives. His approach was challenged by Emerson, whose photographs of the landscape and people of the British marshes mirrored his ideas about the importance of truth to nature. Handy's argument that Robinson was as much an ancestor of postmodernism as Emerson was of modernism was well supported.

The National Gallery in Washington, DC, hosted a major retrospective of the work of the reclusive Robert Frank, best known for his book *The Americans.* With grainy, not always sharp images and tilted frames, Frank captured a country of loneliness and alienation. This exhibition also included many of Frank's more personal later works, which confronted loss, aging, and death.

New York's Metropolitan Museum of Art staged the first major exhibition of the 19th-century French photographer Edouard Baldus. Baldus's pictures of the ancient monuments and new buildings and railroads of France, photographed in the 1850s and 1860s, are extraordinary. Using paper negatives and a large camera, Baldus achieved a remarkable degree of sharpness and subtlety of tone. The exhibition was accompanied by a fine catalog.

The Smithsonian's African American Museum Project mounted "Imagining Families," which included a racially diverse group of photographers who addressed issues of family and racism. Particularly effective were Lonnie Graham's re-creation of his aunt and uncle's living room, Pat Ward Williams's wall-sized mural incorporating family snapshots, and Lorie Novack's moving slide installation.

Other exhibitions of note included "André Kertész: A Centennial Tribute," at the J. Paul Getty Museum (Malibu, CA); retrospectives of the work of Frederick Sommer (also at the Getty) and Wright Morris, at the Museum of Fine Arts, Boston; recent work by Carl Chiarenza, at the Mead Art Museum, Amherst College, and Moneeta Sleet, Jr., at the High Museum of Art (Atlanta); "Photography and the Photographic" at the California Museum of Photography (Riverside); the daguerreotypes of T. M. Easterly at the Missouri Historical Society (St. Louis); "American Politicians," a trenchant look at the subject with pictures from Mathew Brady to Garry Winogrand, at the Museum of Modern Art (New York); and a ten-year retrospective of the work of Andres Serrano, a favorite target of Senator Jesse Helms and the religious right, at Philadelphia's Institute of Contemporary Art.

Events of Interest. Auction results were disappointing as buy-in rates were high and many top lots did not sell. Still, record prices were set for Robert Frank, Bill Brandt, and Karl Struss. Prices remained high for Alfred Stieglitz and Edward Weston. In all, 19th-century work fared better than 20th-century. The Thurman "Jack" F. Naylor Collection, the world's premier private collection of images, cameras, and other photography-related material, was sold for between $7 million and $10 million to the Japanese government. The collection was to be housed in a museum in Yokohama.

Kudos. Robert Adams, best known for his photographs of the contemporary western United States, was named a MacArthur Foundation Fellow. Henri Cartier-Bresson received the Master of Photography Award from the International Center of Photography, while Willis Hartshorn was appointed to succeed Cornell Capa as ICP director.   S.P.

PHYSICS. Physicists in 1994 found increasing evidence for the long-predicted top quark, and new studies of protons raised questions regarding proton spin.

Top Quark. A huge experimental team working at the Fermi National Accelerator Laboratory near Chicago obtained strong (but not conclusive) evidence for the existence of the long-sought top quark. If confirmed in follow-up experiments, the sighting would fill one of the two remaining empty slots for particles predicted to exist by the Standard Model, a collection of quantum theories that represents physicists' current understanding of elementary particles.

According to the Standard Model, all of matter is ultimately composed of particles called quarks, leptons, and gauge bosons. For reasons not yet understood, quarks appear to come in pairs. Ordinary nuclei are made of up and down quarks, and it is possible in high-energy particle accelerators to create members of a second pair, strange and charm quarks. When physicists discovered a fifth, bottom quark in the 1970s, they immediately assumed that there would be a mate, tentatively labeled the top quark.

The Tevatron accelerator at Fermilab was the first with enough energy to create the top quark, which has nearly the mass of an entire atom of gold, whose constituent parts include 79 protons and 118 neutrons. The high mass of the top quark places severe constraints on elaborations of the Standard Model that attempt to unify the separate quantum theories into one.

Large Hadron Collider. When Congress canceled the Superconducting Super Collider in the fall of 1993, American physicists immediately began seeking alternatives to that mammoth $11 billion accelerator that was to have been built in Texas.

As it happened, European physicists were working on plans for a more modest but still capable machine called the Large Hadron Collider (LHC), to be located at the European Laboratory for Particle Physics (also known as CERN), which straddles the border between Switzerland and France near Geneva. Even at the current cost estimate of $3 billion, the LHC stretches the research budgets of the CERN member nations in Europe, so the laboratory is seeking participation from elsewhere.

A U.S. Department of Energy (DOE) advisory panel recommended that the United

States declare its intention to join other nations constructing the LHC and to initiate negotiations toward that goal. DOE and congressional response to the report was favorable, but U.S. action awaited further developments, not the least of which was formal agreement by the CERN member nations to proceed; in a mid-December vote the 19 CERN members gave the go-ahead for the LHC.

Proton Spin. Quantum chromodynamics is the quantum theory that describes how gluons bind quarks together to form protons, neutrons, the various mesons, and other members of the class of particles called hadrons. The simplest model of the proton consists of two up quarks and one down quark, with gluons constantly being exchanged between the quarks. The basic properties of the proton are then obtained simply by summing over these constituent particles. Unfortunately, this straightforward approach does not invariably work, and there is increasing evidence that the proton is actually a much more complex entity than this model suggests.

A case in point is the quantum mechanical spin of the proton, a kind of angular momentum that has a value of ½. During 1994 both U.S. and European physicists confirmed earlier measurements of that part of the proton spin due to the constituent quarks. The average of these measurements indicates that only about one-third of the proton spin is due to the constituent quarks, a finding that raises the question of where the proton spin comes from. A further troublesome finding is that part of the spin is due to strange quarks, not normally part of the proton at all.

The evidence from the proton spin experiments, as well as new results of other experiments in the field, leads to the conclusion that the gluons and other phenomena play a much more important and complex role in the proton than the simple constituent quark model suggests.

Fusion Research. Physicists would like to make miniature versions of the Sun in so-called inertial confinement fusion reactors that would serve as sources of energy, replacing our dependence on fossil fuels and other nonrenewable sources, but that would also be useful in nuclear weapons simulations, thereby possibly providing a way to "test" weapons designs after a comprehensive test ban treaty is signed. The most highly developed method of achieving this is called laser fusion, in which multiple, high-power laser beams compress and heat a tiny target containing deuterium and tritium (isotopes of hydrogen comprising a proton and a neutron and a proton and two neutrons, respectively).

In October the DOE announced its decision to move ahead with initial planning for a proposed National Ignition Facility, to be located at the Lawrence Livermore National Laboratory in California. When completed in 2002, the $1.1 billion facility would aim 192 laser beams at a cylindrical target a centimeter (two-fifths of an inch) or so in diameter. The DOE decision was based in part on successful experiments at Livermore's current Nova laser facility, many details of which did not become declassified until 1994. These experiments demonstrated the required ability to uniformly irradiate and compress the targets. Because of its weapons connections, however, the project is highly controversial, and the decision to begin studies is only an early step before seeking final approval.

An alternative to laser fusion for energy (but not for weapons simulation) is magnetic fusion, which uses strong magnetic fields to confine a deuterium-tritium plasma. (A plasma is a gas in which all the electrons have been stripped from the atoms.) The plasma is then heated by one or more means, including electric currents induced in it by the fields, injection of energetic particles, and beams of microwaves. The leading candidate for a magnetic fusion reactor is called a tokamak, originally a Russian concept. In November 1994 scientists at Princeton University's Plasma Physics Laboratory reported they had set a new record for power output from a tokamak, generating 10.7 million watts from their Tokamak Fusion Test Reactor, enough power for several thousand homes. The energy output, however, was about four times less than that injected into the plasma, leaving the experimenters still short of the break-even point at which the energy produced matches that required to initiate the reaction.

See PRIZES AND AWARDS.　　A.L.R.

POLAND. The victory of the political left in fall 1993 ushered in a year of relative political stability in Poland. Dire predictions that the government of Prime Minister Waldemar Pawlak of the Polish Peasant Party and his coalition partners of the Democratic Left Alliance would bring economic reform to a halt were not fulfilled in 1994.

President Versus Government. Pawlak's government and President Lech Walesa engaged in a continuing political battle that peaked in October when the lower house of Parliament voted 305 to 18 (with 22 abstentions) to call upon the president to stop pursuing policies that destabilized the political system. At the heart of the struggle lay deep ideological differences and Walesa's desire for greater political authority. The issues dividing president and government ranged from disagreements over key governmental appointments to policy matters concerning abortion, church-state relations, and the speed of the economic privatization process.

Despite the power struggle between the president and the government, Pawlak's government was able to pursue consistent lines of policy. The greatest attention was given to Finance Minister Grzegorz Kolodko's economic reform package, which pushed for the development of a predominantly market economy in Poland. In October, after some delay because of concerns that it would allow too high a level of foreign control, Pawlak approved the last group of state firms to be included in the mass privatization program.

Economic Recovery. Poland continued to experience the highest growth rates of any country in Europe—4 percent growth in gross domestic product in 1993, with a slightly higher increase expected for 1994. Industrial production through September had increased about 8 percent, compared with the same period in 1993, and the trade deficit for 1994 was expected to drop to less than $1 billion (down from $2.3 billion in 1993).

Inflation, however, threatened to top 30 percent by the end of the year, and unemployment stood at 16 percent by late summer. Moreover, the number of Poles living below the poverty line had increased dramatically since the late 1980s.

Church and State. The return to power of the political left resulted in growing conflict between the Roman Catholic Church and the government. The church successfully opposed abortion (through a veto by Walesa) and continued to call for enshrining moral values in the new constitution being prepared by legislators. In August, however, the government postponed ratification of the Concordat—an agreement between Poland and the Vatican regulating legal relations between church and state—until after the new constitution had been approved.

Foreign Policy. Poland applied for membership in the European Union and continued to agitate for entrance into NATO. At the same time Poland attempted to improve its relations with Russia, especially in the economic field; Polish exports to Russia grew by over 50 percent in 1994.

Poland also continued to look to the United States for economic and political support; as of May 1994, U.S. investments in Poland totaled $1 billion, 40 percent of all foreign investment in the country. In October, as part of the effort

Bridge to the East. *A U.S. soldier (left) and a Czech colleague discuss weaponry during a joint military exercise near Poznan, Poland, in September. The exercise was the first ever held by NATO troops in a nation that was once a member of the Warsaw Pact.*

to maintain good relations with the United States, Poland sent 50 troops to Haiti to assist in retraining the Haitian police.

See STATISTICS OF THE WORLD.   R.E.K.

PORTUGAL. In 1994, Portugal celebrated the 20th anniversary of the Revolution of the Carnations, which overthrew more than four decades of dictatorship and ushered in democracy. In voting for the European Parliament, a consultative body elected by the people of the member countries of the European Union (EU), the left-of-center Socialist Party outpolled the right-of-center Social Democrats, but by a smaller margin than expected. The economy improved slightly over 1993.

In the June elections for the European Parliament the opposition Socialist Party edged out the governing Social Democrats by 34.8 percent to 34.4 percent. Pollsters had predicted that the left-of-center Socialists would lead by five points. Nevertheless, the victory gave the Socialists ten parliamentary seats and marked a solid increase from the 28.5 percent share of the vote that they received in the previous European Parliament election, held in 1989. The Social Democrats held steady at nine seats, while the right-wing Social Democratic Center/Popular Party maintained its three. The orthodox Portuguese Communist Party dropped from four seats to three; observers believed its lost votes went to the Socialists. Voter turnout was phenomenally low—only about one-third of the electorate bothered to vote.

The increase in voter support gained the Socialist Party some momentum for the October 1995 national legislative elections (there was speculation regarding a Socialist-Communist alliance), while the Social Democrats hoped they might still score a third consecutive absolute majority.

While Portugal was emerging out of recession more slowly than many of its EU partners, the economic picture became increasingly brighter as 1994 progressed. The inflation rate was expected to be approximately 5 percent, exports were up, and the gross domestic product was expected to be about 1 percent, the first increase in several years.

The news was not all rosy, however. Fishermen staged demonstrations to protest EU di-

rectives that allowed, for example, cheap Spanish frozen fish into Portuguese markets. Traffic on the April 25 Bridge, which crosses the Tejo (Tagus) River at Lisbon, was paralyzed several times as commuters and truck drivers protested toll increases introduced to fund the building of another bridge. Bad weather and competition from EU imports hurt productivity in the agrarian sector; especially hard hit was the wine industry, which saw imports increase 15-fold from 1993, when 52,000 hectoliters (more than 137,000 gallons) were brought in, to a projected 800,000 hectoliters (more than 2 million gallons) for 1994.

While public spending on infrastructure declined in comparison to previous years, major projects included adding rail traffic to the April 25 Bridge, building a third bridge over the Tejo River, extending the Lisbon subway system, and general infrastructure improvements in preparation for Expo-98.

Portugal continued its push for a diplomatic solution to Indonesia's brutal dominance of the former Portuguese colony of East Timor, but a resolution remained evasive. The nation was also supportive of the first free elections in Mozambique, held in the fall.

See STATISTICS OF THE WORLD.   C.A.C.

POWER AND ENERGY. Oil prices in 1994 recovered somewhat from their five-year low of December 1993. At mid-1994, for the first time in history, imports accounted for more than half of the U.S. petroleum supply.

Overall, a recent study estimated that during the next two decades more than 45 percent of the growth in the worldwide demand for energy would occur in the developing countries of Asia.

World Overview. *Petroleum.* Although the overall quota of 24.52 million barrels per day (b/d) adopted in 1993 by the Organization of Petroleum Exporting Countries was intended to last only through the first quarter of 1994, it remained in place throughout 1994. Given the recovery of economies in the United States and Europe, and continuing growth in much of Asia, prices in 1994 were up from the five-year low of $10.38 per barrel in December 1993. At a November 1994 meeting in Bali, Indonesia, OPEC ministers extended the quota for another full year. One reason the quota had become so stable was that it was high enough to discourage cheating by some OPEC members.

In the first half of 1994, OPEC accounted for 43 percent of world production. Although this was an increase from the 35 percent share that OPEC had in 1988, it was considerably short of the 55 percent share of world production that OPEC commanded in 1973. Furthermore, the approximately 5 million b/d increase in OPEC output between 1988 and 1994 essentially just offset the plunge in production in the former Soviet Union.

Because of rapidly escalating demands for oil and gas in China, where the economy was booming, the Chinese government was trying to increase oil and gas production. Chinese oil production in the first half of 1994 increased almost 10 percent over 1993 production.

Nuclear Power. Nuclear electric power generation in the world (excluding Eastern Europe) increased 3.8 percent, to 1,922.7 billion kilowatt-hours (kW-hr.) in 1993. Because of the turmoil in Eastern Europe, reliable data for that region are not available. The largest producers of nuclear electric power in 1993 were the United States with 642.0 billion kW-hr., France with 366.7 billion kW-hr., Japan with 243.5 billion kW-hr., and Germany with 153.3 billion kW-hr. These figures represent gross generation, which includes electricity consumed by the generating plant and is ordinarily about 5 percent higher than net generation.

Natural Gas. In Europe the desire to reduce sulfur dioxide emissions is driving the demand for natural gas faster than European producers can supply the fuel. Western European natural gas demand is expected to increase from about 10.7 trillion cubic feet (cu. ft.) per year in 1992 to about 17 trillion cu. ft. in 2010. In 1980 gas provided 14.5 percent of primary energy demand in Western Europe. It furnished 17.6 percent in 1992 and is expected to increase to 23 percent by the year 2010. European gas production is expected to rise as a result of greater production from North Sea fields, but the rate of growth will lag behind the growth in demand. Consequently, Western Europe will become more dependent on imports. The former Soviet Union will remain Western Europe's most important source of gas imports if economic and political problems do not curtail exports from that area. In 1992, Western Europe produced 7.5 trillion cu. ft. of gas and imported 3.2 trillion cu. ft. Algeria, Iran, Qatar, and other Middle East countries, in addition to the former Soviet Union, all have substantial quantities of gas available, but not at 1994 European market prices, which were about $2.75 per million British thermal units (Btu). More than 30 percent of world gas reserves are in the Middle East. Much of this gas can be produced at low cost, but transportation costs would require an increase in European gas prices to justify the large capital costs for pipeline development.

U.S. Production Developments. *Oil.* Although the relatively low oil prices were welcomed by consumers, the longer-term effects

A plant dies. *The last shipment of uranium fuel leaves the Shoreham nuclear power plant on Long Island, NY, in June. The controversial facility, built in the 1970s and 1980s, never went into commercial operation, because of concerns that the area could not be safely evacuated in the event of a reactor accident.*

may not be so beneficial. The number of oil wells completed dropped another 7 percent in 1993, to 8,070, the lowest figure since compilation of these data began in 1949. Domestic crude oil production fell 4.5 percent in 1993, to 6.847 million b/d. Domestic crude production had peaked in 1970 at 9.637 million b/d. Average daily production in 1993 was the lowest since 1958. Since new oil discoveries lagged behind production, proved crude oil reserves declined 3.3 percent in 1993, to 22.957 billion barrels; 1993 was the sixth consecutive year in which proved reserves of crude oil had declined.

Domestic petroleum consumption rose 1.2 percent in 1993, to an average 17.237 million b/d. As a result of the rise in consumption and drop in domestic crude oil production, net oil imports surged 9.8 percent in 1993, to an average 7.618 million b/d.

These trends continued in 1994. As a result of the continuing economic expansion in the United States, domestic petroleum consumption rose during the first half of 1994 to an average 17.6 million b/d, an increase of about 4 percent above consumption in the first half of 1993. During the same time period domestic crude production fell 3 percent, to an average 6.7 million b/d. Net imports surged. In July 1994 net imports accounted for more than 50 percent of the U.S. petroleum supply for the first time in history. Strengthening economies in the United States and Europe, combined with production restraint by OPEC, resulted in rising crude oil prices during the second quarter of 1994. Average U.S. wellhead prices increased from $10.51 per barrel in January to $14.95 per barrel in June, with moderately higher prices seen later in the year.

Natural Gas. Production of dry natural gas rose 2.9 percent in 1993, to 18,351 billion cu. ft., the highest production level since 1981. Imports rose to a record 2,350 billion cu. ft. in 1993, primarily because of greater imports from Canada. Net imports accounted for a record 11.6 percent of U.S. gas consumption. Natural gas consumption increased 3.8 percent in 1993, to 20,296 billion cu. ft., the highest level since 1974.

Natural gas prices seemed weaker in 1994. Spot prices fell from about $2 per thousand cu.

ft. in January to $1.30 per thousand cu. ft. in October. This weakness was not expected to persist, however. Indeed, as it turned out, slightly higher prices occurred later in the year.

Two factors were pushing up natural gas demand. The first was the increasing use of compressed natural gas (CNG) as a transportation fuel to meet Clean Air Act requirements. By September over 900 CNG refueling stations were in operation in the United States, and new stations were being installed at a rate of three or four per week. California had the most stations with 109, followed by Texas with 75, Utah with 48, and Oklahoma with 42.

The other important factor driving U.S. natural gas demand in the United States was cogeneration of electric power. The Public Utility Regulatory Policies Act, passed by Congress in 1978, requires electric utilities to connect their transmission grids to nonutility generators and purchase the excess power generated by any qualified facility. The theory behind this legislation was that by purchasing power from nonutility generators, investor-owned utilities could postpone construction of costly baseload generating capacity. Natural gas is widely used in cogeneration plants, partly because it is a clean-burning fuel that can be used in urban areas.

Coal. Although coal production declined slightly in 1993 to 945.424 million tons, consumption increased to a record 925.944 million tons, of which 87.9 percent, or 813.508 million tons, was used by the nation's electrical utilities for power generation.

Electrical Energy. Electrical energy generation grew 3.0 percent, to a record 2,882.525 billion kW-hr. in 1993, partly because of the expanding U.S. economy. The combustion of coal provided 56.9 percent of this electric energy. Hydroelectric power generation fluctuates from year to year because of water conditions, principally in the western states. The fluctuations should not be interpreted to mean that hydroelectric generating capacity has been added or deleted.

Nuclear power provided 21.2 percent of the nation's electrical energy generation in 1993. Electrical energy generation by nuclear reactors dipped 1.4 percent in 1993, partly because of a lower plant capacity factor. On

September 1, 1994, there were 109 operable nuclear units in the United States.

Total Energy Consumption. As a result of the economic expansion, U.S. energy consumption rose 2.21 percent in 1993, to 83.957 quadrillion Btu. One measure of energy efficiency is the amount of energy consumed per dollar of gross domestic product produced. In terms of 1987 dollars, energy consumption per dollar GDP dropped sharply between 1970 and 1986, falling from 23,100 Btu to 16,900 Btu. Following the sharp drop in oil prices in 1986, energy consumption per dollar of GDP continued to decline, but at a very much slower rate: the energy efficiency figure for 1993 was 16,400 Btu.

These trends continued in 1994. U.S. energy consumption in the first half of 1994 totaled 43.418 quadrillion Btu, compared to 41.996 quadrillion Btu during the same period of 1993, an increase of 3.4 percent.

Reformulated Gasoline. Federal regulations mandated the use of a new reformulated gasoline (RFG) beginning January 1, 1995, in nine U.S. cities and portions of 14 states, mostly in the Northeast. The 1990 Clean Air Act amendments required development of RFG for sale in regions that do not meet federal air-quality criteria. The legislation specified that the RFG must contain at least 2 percent oxygen by weight. In implementing the legislation the U.S. Environmental Protection Agency (EPA) issued a rule requiring that U.S. renewable fuels, mainly ethanol, provide 15 percent of the oxygenate content by January 1, 1995, and 30 percent of the oxygenate content by January 1, 1996. In September 1994 a federal appeals court in Washington, DC, issued an order blocking the ethanol mandate. The National Petroleum Refiners Association and the American Petroleum Institute had filed an appeal against the EPA mandate. The court order did not affect EPA's requirement that RFG be used in air quality nonattainment areas beginning January 1, 1995. Supplies of RFG were expected to be adequate but tight in the future.

D.F.A.

PRESIDENT OF THE UNITED STATES. *See* UNITED STATES OF AMERICA: The Presidency.

PRINCE EDWARD ISLAND. *See* STATISTICS OF THE WORLD.

PRIZES AND AWARDS. The following is an annotated listing of selected prizes awarded during 1994. Some awards in specific fields are covered in separate articles such as BROADCASTING; MOTION PICTURES; AND MUSIC.

NOBEL PRIZES

Valued at about $930,000 for each category, the Nobel Prizes were presented, as usual, on December 10, the anniversary of Alfred Nobel's death.

Peace. Israeli Prime Minister Yitzhak Rabin, Israeli Foreign Minister Shimon Perez, and Palestine Liberation Organization leader Yasir Arafat shared the 1994 Nobel Peace Prize for their efforts to create peace in the Middle East. The awarding of the prize was prompted by a historic 1993 accord between Israel and the PLO that was designed to pave the way for Palestinian self-rule in the Israeli-occupied Gaza Strip and Jericho region of the West Bank. The peace prize announcement generated widespread expressions of anger, and one Nobel jurist resigned in protest at the inclusion of Arafat, who had been at one time an open advocate of terrorism in the conflict between Palestinians and Israel.

Literature. The works of Kenzaburo Oe of Japan, the Nobel laureate for literature, deal with such subjects as his struggle to come to terms with the atomic bombing of Hiroshima during World War II and his difficulties as the father of a brain-damaged son. His books include *A Personal Matter* (1969) and *Teach Us to Outgrow Our Madness* (1977).

Economics. For their work in game theory, which originated in the analysis of strategic games such as poker and tries to predict what will happen when competitors meet in the marketplace, the Nobel Memorial Prize in Economic Science went to John F. Nash, a researcher on the campus of Princeton University; John C. Harsanyi of the Haas School of Business at the University of California at Berkeley; and Reinhard Selten of the University of Bonn.

Physiology or Medicine. The Nobel for physiology or medicine was awarded to two scientists for their work on G proteins, which regulate how cells respond to their environment. The two were Alfred G. Gilman of the University of Texas Southwestern Medical

Nobel laureates. *Martin Rodbell (at left with wife Barbara) shared a Nobel Prize with Clifford G. Shull (above) for research on proteins that enable cells to respond to hormones made by the body in reaction to environmental stimuli.*

Center and Martin Rodbell, who had just retired from the National Institute of Environmental Health Sciences. Rodbell had shown that G proteins exist; Gilman had been the first to isolate one. Their work contributed to medical knowledge of diseases as disparate as cancer, diabetes, and alcoholism.

Physics. Clifford G. Shull, retired from the Massachusetts Institute of Technology, and Bertram N. Brockhouse of McMaster University in Ontario shared the physics Nobel for work done in the 1940s and 1950s on the development of neutron-scattering techniques that are now routinely used in laboratories around the world.

Chemistry. The Nobel in chemistry went to George A. Olah of the University of Southern California. Olah was a researcher at Dow Chemical Company in 1962 when he found that powerful acids could slow the reaction time of short-lived hydrocarbon molecules called carbocations—which normally exist for less than a millionth of a second. His work contributed to the development of many environmentally friendly fuels and plastics.

PULITZER PRIZES

The Pulitzer Prizes, worth $3,000 each, were awarded in April by Columbia University.

David Remnick's *Lenin's Tomb: The Last Days of the Soviet Empire,* written in the words of Soviet leaders and the victims of their power, won the general nonfiction prize. *W. E. B. Du Bois: Biography of a Race, 1868-1919,* describing the first half of Du Bois's life, won author David Levering Lewis the prize for biography.

E. Annie Proulx took the fiction prize for *The Shipping News,* her novel about an aging reporter in a small Newfoundland town. The prize for drama went to Edward Albee for *Three Tall Women,* a play chronicling the life of his mother. *Neon Vernacular,* a collection of poems, won Yusef Komunyakaa the year's prize for poetry. The prize for music went to Gunther Schuller for "Of Reminiscences and Reflections," a 22-minute orchestral piece written in memory of his late wife.

In journalism, Eileen Welsome of the *Albuquerque* (NM) *Tribune* won the prize for national reporting for her stories, based on an investigation that lasted more than six years, about 18 hospital patients who were injected with plutonium between 1945 and 1947 in top-secret medical research carried out by the U.S. government. Freelancer Kevin Carter won the feature photography prize for his photo of a Sudanese toddler who had collapsed from hunger in the presence of a stalking vulture. Carter committed suicide later in the year.

Other Pulitzers awarded in journalism were as follows:

Reporting, Beat. Eric Freedman and Jim Mitzelfeld, *Detroit News.*

Reporting, International. Staff, *Dallas Morning News.*

Reporting, Investigative. Staff, *Providence* (RI) *Journal-Bulletin.*

Reporting, Spot News. Staff, *New York Times.*

Explanatory Journalism. Ronald Kotulak, *Chicago Tribune.*

Feature Writing. Isabel Wilkerson, *New York Times.*

Public Service. *Akron* (OH) *Beacon Journal.*

Commentary. William Raspberry, *Washington Post.*

Criticism. Lloyd Schwartz, *Boston Phoenix.*

Editorial Writing. R. Bruce Dold, *Chicago Tribune.*

Editorial Cartooning. Michael P. Ramirez, *Commercial Appeal* (Memphis).

Spot News Photography. Paul Watson, *Toronto Star.*

OTHER PRIZES AND AWARDS

Among many other significant awards in 1994 were the following:

Academy of American Poets. Tanning Prize ($100,000) to W. S. Merwin.

American Academy of Arts and Letters. Gold medals to Walter Jackson Bate (biography) and Hugo Weisgall (music). Award for Distinguished Service to the Arts to Arthur Mitchell. Award of Merit for Painting to Alfred Leslie. Arnold W. Brunner Memorial Prize in Architecture to Renzo Piano. Academy Awards in Architecture to Craig Hodgetts and Hsin-Ming Fung. Jimmy Ernst Award in Art to Tom Doyle. Louise Nevelson Award in Art to Carol Wax. Richard and Hinda Rosenthal Foundation Award in Art to Brett Bigbee. Academy Awards in Art to Stephen Brown, Susanna Coffey, John Dobbs, Janet Fish, and Ursula von Rydingsvard. Richard and Hinda Rosenthal Foundation Award for Literature to Janet Peery for *Alligator Dance.* E. M. Forster Award to Janice Galloway. Sue Kaufman Prize for First Fiction to Emile Capouya for *In the Sparrow Hills.* Jean Stein Award for Fiction to Chris Offutt. Harold D. Vursell Memorial Award in Literature to Darryl Pinckney. Academy Awards in Literature to Jon Robin Baitz, Marvin Bell, Stuart Dybek, Adrienne Kennedy, Tony Kushner, Mary Lee Settle, Chase Twichell, and Geoffrey Wolff. Rome Fellowship in Literature to Karl Kirchwey. Academy Awards in Music to David Chaitkin, Katherine Hoover, Michael Kurek, and John H. Thow. Wladimir and Rhoda Lakond Prize in Music to Ray Shattenkirk. Charles Ives Fellowship in Music to Augusta Read Thomas.

Bristol-Myers Squibb Research Awards. Awards, worth $50,000 for each category, went to Arnold J. Levine (cancer); Robert M.

Three of the best. *Shown here are three of the entertainment figures awarded Kennedy Center Honors in 1994: (left to right) composer Martin Gould, actor Kirk Douglas, and singer Aretha Franklin. Also honored were theater producer-director Harold Prince and folk singer Pete Seeger.*

Chanock (infectious disease); Désiré Collen, Aaron J. Marcus, and Marc Verstraete (cardiovascular research); Stanley B. Prusiner (neuroscience); Doris Howes Calloway (nutrition); William F. Enneking (orthopedic research); and Allan I. Basbaum (pain).

General Motors Cancer Research Foundation. One of three $100,000 awards was shared by Mario R. Capecchi of the Howard Hughes Medical Institute in Salt Lake City and Oliver Smithies of the University of North Carolina at Chapel Hill; a second went to Laurent Degos of the Saint Louis Hospital in Paris and Wang Zhen-Yi of Shanghai Second Medical University, China; the third went to Tony Hunter of the Salk Institute in La Jolla, CA.

Grawemeyer Awards. Prizes of $150,000 each to nurture creative thought were awarded to John Bruer for *Schools for Thought* (education), Stephen Carter for *The Culture of Disbelief* (religion), and Toru Takemitsu for *Fantasma/Cantos* (music).

Kennedy Center Honors. Honored were actor Kirk Douglas, singer Aretha Franklin, composer Morton Gould, theater producer/director Harold Prince, and folk singer Pete Seeger.

MacArthur Foundation. Five-year awards of $235,000 to $375,000, intended to free "exceptionally gifted individuals" from economic constraints so they can develop their potential,

Honored poet. Adrienne Rich was one of the recipients of a so-called genius award, a fellowship from the MacArthur Foundation.

were made to photographer Robert Adams; dance company director Jeraldyne Blunden; saxophonist Anthony Braxton; sociologist and political historian Rogers Brubaker; jazz musician Ornette Coleman; mathematician and biologist Israel Moiseevich Gelfand; anthropologist Faye D. Ginsburg; economist Heidi Hartmann, cofounder of the Institute for Women's Policy Research; dance company cofounder Bill T. Jones; entomologist Peter E. Kenmore; Boys Club director Joseph E. Marshall; artisans' association director Carolyn McKecuen; environmental writer and professor Donella Meadows; dance company founder and director Arthur Mitchell; Hugo Morales, cofounder and director of Radio Bilingue; college president Janine Pease-Windy Boy; Willie Reale, artistic director of the 52nd Street Project; poet Adrienne Rich; musician, scholar and administrator Sam-Ang Sam; and physicist Jack Wisdom.

National Book Critics Circle Awards. Recipients were Ernest J. Gaines for fiction (*A Lesson Before Dying*), Alan Lomax for general nonfiction (*The Land Where the Blues Began*), Mark Doty for poetry (*My Alexandria*), Edmund White for biography (*Genet*), and John Dizikes for criticism (*Opera in America: A Cultural History*). The Nona Balakian Citation for Excellence in Reviewing went to Brigitte Frase.

National Medal of Arts. Honorees were actor and singer Harry Belafonte, jazz musician Dave Brubeck, singer Celia Cruz, violinist Dorothy DeLay, actress Julie Harris, choreographer Erick Hawkins, actor and dancer Gene Kelly, folk singer Pete Seeger, arts patron Catherine Filene Shouse, painter Wayne Thiebaud, poet Richard Wilbur, and the nonprofit arts organization Young Audiences.

Philadelphia Liberty Medal. An award of $100,000 was presented to Vaclav Havel, president of the Czech Republic.

Robert F. Kennedy Human Rights Award. A prize of $30,000 was shared by the imprisoned Chinese dissidents Ren Wanding and Wei Jingsheng.

Samuel H. Scripps American Dance Festival Award. An award worth $25,000 went to choreographer Trisha Brown.

Templeton Prize for Progress in Religion. Awarded to Michael Novak, Roman Catholic theologian whose writings focus on democratic capitalism, was a prize of about $1 million.

Wolf Foundation Prizes. One award of $100,000 was given to physicists Yoichiro Nambu and Vitaly Ginzburg; another $100,000 award went to mathematician Jurgen Moser.

World Food Prize. A prize of $200,000 went to Bangladeshi banker Muhammad Yunus, whose Grameen Bank makes small loans, most worth about $100, to help impoverished small-business owners.   S.H.P.

PUBLISHING. *See* BOOK PUBLISHING; LITERATURE; MAGAZINES AND NEWSPAPERS.

PUERTO RICO. Washington, DC, became a focal point of Puerto Rican politics in 1994 in the wake of a November 1993 plebiscite in which Puerto Ricans narrowly voted to retain the island's commonwealth status. Voters did, however, call for the island's relationship with the United States to be defined in a bilateral pact between Washington and San Juan; other proposed changes involved tariffs and federal program funding.

The response from Washington on the plebiscite was ultimately inconclusive. In March the Clinton administration formed an Interagency Working Group on Puerto Rico to study the island's status and economic needs. In May, Representative Don Young (R, Alaska) included Puerto Rico in legislation intended, he said, to provide a clear path for U.S. territories to obtain "full citizenship rights." Young was ranking GOP member of the House Committee on Natural Resources, which oversees the House Subcommittee for Insular and International Affairs, a key committee for legislation affecting Puerto Rico. The proposed bill angered some Puerto Ricans, who argued that Puerto Rico's inclusion showed a disregard of the plebiscite results. Late in the year Young and Senator Paul Simon (D, Illinois) introduced a bipartisan resolution denouncing the proposed changes in the commonwealth relationship as neither politically nor economically viable.

After U.S. elections in November, Young was selected to head the House insular affairs subcommittee when the 104th Congress convened in January. He replaced the longtime chairman, Delegate Ron De Lugo (D) of the Virgin Islands, who retired. Senator Frank Murkowski, another Republican from Alaska, was selected to become the head of the Senate's panel on insular affairs.

Economic growth in 1994 was expected to fall short of the projected 2.9 percent, largely because of Washington's reduction of tax incentives for investment and an extended drought that cut agricultural productivity.

The government stepped up its efforts to promote tourism, and in the spring Governor Pedro Rosselló traveled to Mexico in order to pave the way for increased trade under the North American Free Trade Agreement.

See STATISTICS OF THE WORLD.   M.J.C.

Q

QATAR. *See* PERSIAN GULF STATES; STATISTICS OF THE WORLD.

QUEBEC. *See* CANADA; STATISTICS OF THE WORLD.

R

RACIAL ISSUES. *See* MINORITIES IN THE UNITED STATES.

RAILROADS. *See* ACCIDENTS AND DISASTERS; TRANSPORTATION.

Religion

Gender and sexuality-related issues continued to foster controversy in 1994; a UN-sponsored population conference drew opposition from some religious leaders. The Vatican observed Holocaust Remembrance Day for the first time, and Pope John Paul II's health provoked concern.

The pontiff was also in the news for publishing a book that turned into a best-seller. The Talmud was published in a Russian-language edition for the first time. Several Muslims received key posts in the new South African government.

PROTESTANT AND ORTHODOX CHURCHES

Charges of paganism and goddess worship swept through American Protestantism in 1994, the fallout from a highly controversial feminist conference. A continuing focus of controversy was the prominence of the religious right, which was credited with having a significant impact on the congressional elections that took place in the United States in November.

Feminist Conference. A "Re-Imagining" conference held in November 1993 in Minneapolis led to major clashes within the Protestant churches in 1994.

About 2,000 people, most from mainline denominations such as the Presbyterian Church (U.S.A.) and the United Methodist Church, had

Change in the church. In a historic ceremony in Bristol Cathedral in March, Bishop Barry Rogerson (seated) ordained 32 women as the first female priests in the history of the Church of England. The previous month the church's governing body had voted to allow women to be priests—a decision that caused considerable controversy and led to a number of defections from the church.

attended the conference, which promoted alternatives to traditional male-dominated images of God. Conference critics objected to the use of "Sophia" (a Greek word for wisdom) as a feminine personification for God and, in general, to what was said to be a strong lesbian presence at the gathering. Within the Presbyterian Church (U.S.A.), the conservative Presbyterian Lay Committee called for the firing or disciplining of staffers who had helped organize the conference, and 12 individual Presbyterian congregations issued similar demands. Presbyterian authorities rejected these calls, however. Supporters of the conference portrayed it as essentially a tool for promoting empowerment of women in the face of widespread abuse.

The Church and Sexuality. The National Council of Churches is accustomed to being on the giving end of societal critiques. But the ecumenical agency, representing 32 Protestant and Orthodox churches, was on the receiving end in June, when some 200 church activists encircled NCC headquarters in Manhattan to demonstrate against church treatment of homosexuals. Demonstrators wrapped the building, known popularly as the God Box, with a protest ribbon, after lesbian and gay clergy from several denominations read off a litany of grievances—including bans by nearly all denominations against the ordination of practicing homosexuals.

Sexuality, homosexuality in particular, was a major topic in two prominent mainline denominations in 1994—the Episcopal Church and the Evangelical Lutheran Church in America. In September the Episcopal Church's House of Bishops, bowing to protests from critics, downgraded a controversial, liberal-minded pastoral statement on sexuality from a "teaching" document to a "study" document. Critics of the document had argued that it diluted the notion of marriage and opened the way for ordination of noncelibate gays and lesbians by suggesting that homosexual, as well as heterosexual, relationships can be "chaste, faithful, and committed." Meanwhile, in November, the Evangelical Lutheran Church in America released a cautiously worded revised draft on human sexuality. The original 1993 version had sent shock waves through the de-

---

naDev tlhIngan Hol jatlhlu'!*

The Bible has been translated into hundreds of languages spoken on Earth—but not into a language purportedly spoken elsewhere. Not, that is, until the Klingon Bible.

Klingons are a familiar presence on the *Star Trek* TV and movie series. Their language was invented in 1984 for the movie *Star Trek III: The Search for Spock*. Klingon's tiny vocabulary, however, has led to a doctrinal dispute—and two separate Klingon Bibles. Literalists believe in using Klingon equivalents to biblical terms, while paraphrasers say that with Klingon's mere 2,000 words a literal rendering is impossible. The gospel passage "We have five loaves and two fishes" shows the problem. Literalists use "grain food" and "water animal," while paraphrasers came up with "We have only five blood pies and two serpent worms."

No one knows which version the Klingons prefer—nor, for that matter, who will take on the assignment as missionary.

*Klingon spoken here.

---

nomination because of its permissive views on masturbation and homosexuality. The new version steered away from any clear-cut opinion on the question of sexual relations between persons of the same sex and avoided any reference at all to masturbation. It called for continued deliberation about the morality of homosexual relationships, while supporting maintenance of current policies that barred the ordination of noncelibate homosexuals and the blessing of same-sex unions.

Ecumenism. The year saw significant rapprochements between various religious groups. In March, leaders of evangelical Protestants and Roman Catholics (groups that historically have not worked together) signed a joint mission statement that called for evangelism against "resurgent spiritualities and religions that are explicitly hostile to the claims of Christ." A month later, social service activists from the more liberal Protestant churches, along with some Catholic activists, put the finishing touches on a document they had

Orthodox address. *Varthol-omeos I, ecumenical patriarch of Constantinople, speaks before the European Parliament in Strasbourg, France, in April 1994. The religious leader said that the Orthodox Church had long sought European unification but cautioned that the European Union had an obligation to protect the rights of minorities.*

worked on since 1987, laying out the theological underpinnings of joint ventures in the social service arena.

Also in April, the Evangelical Lutheran Church in America issued a declaration distancing itself from 16th-century reformer Martin Luther's anti-Semitic writings, such as his tract "Against the Jews and Their Lies." And in June members of the second Anglican/Roman Catholic International Commission issued a statement saying that "painful and perplexing" disagreements on such topics as abortion, contraception, and remarriage after divorce are "not on the level of fundamental moral values" but involve "their implementation in practical judgments."

Religion and the Workplace. After months of controversy, the federal Equal Employment Opportunity Commission voted in September to scrap proposed guidelines on workplace harassment, including harassment based on religion. With near unanimity, religious groups had argued that the guidelines on religion were vague and that they might be interpreted in ways that could interfere with freedom of religious expression.

The Religious Right. President Bill Clinton and the religious right locked horns on a number of occasions during the year. Perhaps the most bitter confrontation came in the spring, when conservative evangelist Jerry Falwell began marketing a video containing highly extreme, undocumented charges against the president. Clinton fired back in comments on a St. Louis radio talk show, calling the tape "scurrilous."

A major Jewish rights organization, the Anti-Defamation League, issued a lengthy report in June accusing the religious right of trying to improperly fuse church and state, partly through efforts to Christianize public school curricula in the United States. Within the ranks of evangelical Christianity itself, a group known as Evangelicals for Social Action accused Pat Robertson's conservative Christian Coalition of ignoring the biblical mandate to love one's neighbor. The accusation came after a Christian Coalition official criticized the Clinton health care proposal for including coverage for substance abuse treatment and mental health care.

At a convention in September in Washington, DC, the Christian Coalition appeared to moderate some of its rhetoric, while uniting with conservative Jews and Catholics and, in effect, seeking to promote political candidates with congenial views on both social and economic issues. The coalition was credited with having exerted a strong influence on the November congressional elections, in which Republicans gained control of both houses and many conservatives were brought into office. Following the elections, House Republican leaders indicated they would seek a constitutional amendment to allow prayer in the schools. While the suggestion drew criticism from some religious leaders, as well as from civil liberties groups, President Clinton, in an apparent reversal of past positions, said there was "room for compromise" on the issue.

Financial Woes.   Financial problems continued to bedevil church institutions in 1994. The Episcopal Church, viewed historically as the seat of power and wealth in Protestantism, approved $4 million in budget cuts in February, including the elimination of 43 jobs on the church's national staff.   That represented 17 percent of the headquarters staff, which had been cut by one-fifth just three years earlier.

The National Council of Churches was rocked in the spring by revelations that it may have lost $8 million through investments in high-yield bank notes issued by the Banka Bohemia in Prague. Throughout the year officials of the council—which operates on an annual budget of about $50 million—scrambled to recover the funds

Overseas Hot Spots.   There was strong support from many Protestant leaders for action to restore democratically elected President Jean-Bertrand Aristide to power in Haiti; he had been ousted in September 1991 after less than a year in power. In March, leaders of six black Protestant churches called for President Clinton to remove leaders of the military junta; in July, NCC General Secretary Joan Campbell issued a cautious endorsement of the use of force in Haiti. After U.S. troops landed there in September, under the umbrella of a new last-minute diplomatic agreement providing for Aristide's return, a coalition of mainstream Protestant, African-American, and Jewish leaders praised the move.

Civil warfare in Rwanda, rooted largely in ethnic divisions, took the lives of hundreds of thousands of civilians, including a number of church leaders.   An investigator for the Geneva-based World Council of Churches concluded that Protestant and Catholic churches alike in Rwanda had taken positions along tribal lines and were "tainted, not only by passive indifference, but by errors of commission as well."

In war-torn Bosnia-Hercegovina, Serbian Orthodox church leaders opposed Pope John Paul II's planned "pilgrimage of peace" visit to the besieged city of Sarajevo—which was ultimately canceled—because of what they considered the Catholic Church's failure to condemn atrocities committed by Catholics against Serbs during World War II.

Concern for Christians in Iran heightened when the bodies of the Reverend Mehdi Dibaj, an Assemblies of God pastor, and the Reverend Tateos Michaelian, of the Tehran Presbyterian Church, were discovered in July. The deaths, which followed the murder earlier in the year of the Reverend Haik Hovsepian-Mehr, superintendent of the Assemblies of God in Iran, led to fears that a new round of persecution against Christians was under way in this predominantly Muslim nation.

In October the world was shocked by the grisly discovery of 53 bodies—48 in two compounds in Switzerland and five in Québec—of persons who were associated with a sect known as the Order of the Solar Temple. Police found evidence that many of the dead, including children, were probably murdered before the premises were blown up. The sect's leader, a Canadian named Luc Jouret, was found to be among the dead.   G.D.S.

ROMAN CATHOLIC CHURCH

Concern over the health of Pope John Paul II was a focus of attention in the Roman Catholic Church in 1994, along with women's issues and tension over the United Nations Conference on World Population and Development.

Pope's Health.   On April 28, shortly before turning 74, John Paul II fell and broke his right thighbone, requiring surgery from which he appeared to recover slowly.   The pontiff's health had been a source of some concern ever since he underwent tumor surgery in

1992. In 1993 he fractured his shoulder in a fall; in 1994 he was showing signs of frailty and had a noticeable tremor in his left hand.

John Paul's surgery and convalescence required him to cut back on his travel itinerary; among other things, a planned October visit to the United Nations and cities in the eastern United States had to be canceled. He did, however, make brief visits to Croatia and to Sicily, and it was announced late in the year that he would make a planned trip to Southeast Asia and Australia in early 1995.

Women and the Church. The Vatican appeared to be anxious to meet increasing demands for a greater role for women in the church but at the same time remained wary of feminist demands. In March the Congregation for Divine Worship and the Sacraments granted permission to bishops' conferences worldwide to allow females to act as altar servers. The Vatican department emphasized, however, that this step should not be interpreted as a move toward relaxing the ban on the ordination of women.

The pope explicitly excluded the possibility of female ordination in an apostolic letter issued in May. And the topic was totally excluded from the agenda of the October Synod of Bishops in Rome, which discussed the role of priests, nuns, and religious brothers in the church. The synod made the cautious recommendation that "consecrated women" participate more in consultations and decision making "as situations require." At their November meeting in Washington, DC, American bishops pledged a commitment to "enhancing the participation of women in every aspect of church life" but refrained from discussing female ordination.

The English-language edition of the new universal *Catechism of the Catholic Church*—delayed more than 18 months because of objections to an earlier version with gender-inclusive language—was published in May, with traditionalist, male-oriented language restored. Objections to the change were strong in many feminist quarters.

In June the pope articulated some of his thoughts on the feminist movement, saying it should be based on the concept of dignity of the human person, both male and female.

Women should be "equal but different," he stated. A chapter on women in the pope's new mass-market book, *Crossing the Threshold of Hope,* reflected a similar view. The book, which went on sale in October in 35 countries, answered questions posed by a journalist on topics relevant to religion and the church; it became a best-seller.

Cairo Conference. The Vatican conducted a yearlong campaign of opposition to documents for September's UN population conference in Cairo, charging that, if adopted as drafted, they would promote abortion on demand and undercut family values. The pope voiced his anxieties to U.S. President Bill Clinton at a June meeting in Rome. And in August papal spokesman Joaquin Navarro-Valls specifically criticized Vice President Al Gore, purportedly for misrepresenting the conference's intentions.

At the Cairo conference the Vatican delegation succeeded in diluting the language on abortion, then gave partial assent to the conference's conclusions. However, the delegation stressed that the Holy See had not changed its moral position.

Papal Travel. John Paul's itinerary outside Italy was limited to a single 24-hour trip in September to Zagreb, Croatia. The pope, who had canceled a planned visit to Lebanon for fear of "serious and unforeseeable incidents" and had dropped other travel plans for reasons of health, had hoped to make a wider tour of the former Yugoslavia. But a stop in Sarajevo, Bosnia-Hercegovina, was eliminated for security reasons, and a planned visit to Belgrade, Serbia, was canceled after opposition was expressed by the Serbian Orthodox Church.

Sexual Abuse. The problem of sexual molestation by clergy continued to vex the church. The archdiocese of Santa Fe, NM, faced with the possibility of bankruptcy, placed 12 properties on the market to help pay for costs stemming from more than 100 sex abuse cases. In several instances, sexual abuse cases came to trial; in Massachusetts a priest of the Boston archdiocese, Reverend John R. Hanlon, 65, received three concurrent life sentences for raping and sexually assaulting an altar boy 14 years earlier. In Canada, 28 men filed claims against the Toronto Christian

Difficult mission. Croatian President Franjo Tudjman (right) shakes hands with Pope John Paul II after the pontiff delivered a speech in Zagreb in September. The occasion marked the first visit by John Paul to the former Yugoslavia, but he was forced to cancel a visit to Sarajevo, the capital of war-torn Bosnia-Hercegovina.

Brothers, alleging they had been physically and sexually abused as children at St. John's Training School for Boys.

A case involving Chicago's Cardinal Joseph Bernardin had a happier ending for church authorities when, in February, a federal judge dismissed sexual abuse charges lodged against the prelate in 1993. Bernardin's accuser had withdrawn his original charges; these were based on "repressed memories" revived by hypnosis, which he subsequently believed to be untrustworthy. Bernardin had denied any wrongdoing.

Turmoil in Africa. A monthlong convocation of Africa's bishops concluded May 6 in Rome with a plea to the United Nations to help establish peace on that "burning and bleeding" continent and to Western nations to halt arms shipments. Civil warfare in Rwanda resulted in the murders in June of Archbishop Vincent Nsengiyumva of Kigali, two other bishops, and ten priests.

Diplomatic Front. In September the pope declared that China's estimated 3 million Catholics were obliged to recognize their link to Rome, as distinct from the "official" church approved by the Communist government. That same month, diplomatic ties with Israel

were finalized when the pope received Shmuel Hadas, Israel's first ambassador to the Vatican. In October the Vatican established official ties with the Palestine Liberation Organization, though these fell short of full diplomatic relations.

New Cardinals. In October, 30 appointments were made to the College of Cardinals by Pope John Paul. The new cardinals included two Americans (Archbishop William H. Keeler of Baltimore, president of the National Council of Catholic Bishops, and Archbishop Adam J. Maida of Detroit), a Cuban, a Vietnamese, and a prelate from Bosnia, Archbishop Vinko Puljic—who, at 49 was the youngest of the group. One of the new cardinals, from Belarus, had spent ten years in a Soviet labor camp. The additions meant that about 100 of 120 cardinals eligible by age to vote in a conclave electing a new pope had been appointed by John Paul.

Deaths. Death claimed Cardinal Joseph Cordeiro, 76, retired archbishop of Karachi, Pakistan, on February 11; Cardinal François Marty, 89, former archbishop of Paris, on February 16; and Cardinal Owen McCann, 86, retired archbishop of Cape Town, South Africa, on March 26. Cardinal Antonious Butros

Khreish, 87, Lebanon's highest-ranking Maronite Catholic prelate, died August 1; Cardinal Albert Decourtray, 71, the archbishop of Lyon, France, died September 16; and Cardinal Vicente Enrique y Tarancon, 87, former archbishop of Madrid, died November 28. John L. May, the ecumenical-minded archbishop of St. Louis, passed away on March 24 at the age of 71.   J.G.D.

JUDAISM

In 1994, terrorist acts were directed against Jewish targets in London, Buenos Aires, and New York City. A Vatican concert commemorated victims of the Nazi Holocaust. There was controversy over apparent instances of anti-Semitism among blacks.

Former Soviet Republics. The rebuilding of Jewish life in the states of the former Soviet

Guilty as charged. Paul Touvier, former intelligence chief of the Vichy militia in Lyon, sits in a court in Versailles in March. Accused of executing seven Jewish prisoners in 1944, he became the first Frenchman ever to be convicted by a French court of crimes against humanity.

Union continued, while emigration stayed at about the same level as in previous years. At year's end preliminary figures showed that approximately 100,000 Jews had emigrated, with two-thirds of them going to Israel; the figure for the whole of 1993 was 105,000. A strong showing by Communist and ultranationalist parties in Russia's December 1993 parliamentary elections fueled worries over the future of the Jewish community there and contributed to continuing emigration. Israeli Prime Minister Yitzhak Rabin discussed his concern over Russian anti-Semitism when he made his first official visit to Moscow, in April 1994, and met there with his Russian counterpart, Prime Minister Viktor Chernomyrdin.

In May the first-ever Russian-language edition of the Talmud was published; the project was cosponsored by the American Jewish Joint Distribution Committee and the Russian Academy of Sciences.

Terrorist Bombings. In mid-July a huge car bomb leveled the building housing the central Jewish organization in Buenos Aires, killing about 100 people and injuring about 150; a Lebanese-based Islamic radical group later claimed responsibility. Argentine President Carlos Saúl Menem sealed the country's borders and ordered the recall of Argentina's ambassador to Iran. Also in July, two bombs went off in London, one near the Israeli embassy, the other at the offices of the Joint Israel Appeal, a fund-raising organization. Neither resulted in fatalities.

European Jewry. Two former Communist states in Eastern Europe agreed to pay restitution to Jews for property seized between 1939 and 1945. In April the government of Hungary signed an agreement with the World Jewish Restitution Organization, pledging that it would either return the property or pay compensation. Slovakia had already signed a similar agreement in November 1993. In May the Parliament of the Czech Republic passed legislation authorizing the return of property seized during World War II, but only to individual citizens of the republic.

That same month, the lower house of the German Parliament passed a bill toughening penalties for violence by right-wing extremists. A memorial to the Jews of France deported to

Nazi death camps during the Vichy regime was dedicated in July by French President François Mitterrand.

In April the 50th anniversary of the deportation of 600,000 Hungarian Jews by the Nazis was commemorated both by the Hungarian government and by Jewish communities in the United States and Israel. During the same month the Vatican officially observed Holocaust Remembrance Day for the first time, by hosting a special memorial concert—an event carried live on European television.

Nazi War Criminals. In April, Paul Touvier, former intelligence chief of the Vichy militia in Lyon, became the first Frenchman to be convicted by a French court of crimes against humanity. He received a life sentence, which was unsuccessfully appealed.

The U.S. Justice Department ordered the deportation of several accused Nazi war criminals, after stripping them of their citizenship for having lied about their past. The case against an alleged war criminal living in Massachusetts, 87-year-old Aleksandras Lileikis, was considered particularly significant because, as Lithuanian Gestapo chief between 1941 and 1944, he stood accused of responsibility in the deaths of thousands of Lithuanian Jews. The Lithuanian government supplied documentation from its archives to U.S. federal prosecutors. The United States said it would seek to deport him, and Lithuanian Prime Minister Adolfas Slezevicius indicated he would seek extradition of Lileikis (this would expedite Lileikis's removal to Lithuania, since the U.S. deportation process is slow and subject to appeals).

American Jewry. Bill Clinton became the first U.S. president to participate in Rosh Hashanah (New Year), by attending services while on vacation at Martha's Vineyard, MA, in September.

A speech delivered in November 1993 at Kean College in New Jersey by Khalid Abdul Muhammad, an official of the black nationalist Nation of Islam, fueled a controversy over alleged black anti-Semitism. Muhammad's speech referred to Jews as "bloodsuckers of the black nation" who control the government and the media. In February 1994, after the speech was attacked by the Anti-Defamation League of B'nai B'rith, a Jewish rights group, Nation of Islam leader Louis Farrakhan called Muhammad's remarks "vile and repugnant in manner" and suspended him from his post. But he added that Muhammad's words were, in substance, "true." The Reverend Jesse Jackson and other black leaders joined Jewish organizations in condemning both Muhammad's speech and Farrakhan's response. Similar issues were raised by reports of anti-Semitic speeches by Leonard Jeffries, chairman of black studies at New York's City College. An effort by the college to remove him as department chairman was rebuffed in the courts, but the U.S. Supreme Court, in November 1994, ordered that the case be reconsidered.

In March a van carrying Lubavitch Hasidic youngsters was sprayed with gunfire as it crossed New York's Brooklyn Bridge, returning the group from a visit to the ailing Lubavitch leader, Grand Rebbe Menachem Schneerson; one student was killed, and three others were wounded. The accused gunman, Lebanese-born Rashid Baz, was tried and convicted of murder and attempted murder. The grand rebbe himself died in June at age 92, after a long illness.

After 13 years of planning and fund-raising, ground was broken in October for a museum and memorial to Jewish victims of the Nazi Holocaust, located at the tip of Manhattan.

L.G.

ISLAM

In 1994, Muslim minority communities continued to bear the brunt of renewed nationalism in Europe. Turkish immigrants in Germany suffered attacks by neo-Nazi groups. North African immigrants in France were insulted by the declaration of a ban on the wearing of traditional Islamic head scarves by girls in schools. Most serious of all, Bosnian Muslims continued to be a target of Serb efforts at "ethnic cleansing" in the civil war between Muslims, Serbs, and Croats in Bosnia-Hercegovina.

In Algeria negotiations were held during September between Islamist leaders and the military government that had seized power in January 1992, after halting free elections that the Islamic Salvation Front was poised to win. However, the talks, aimed at bringing about fresh elections, broke down in late October.

Shining shrine. *The completion of the renovation of the seventh-century Dome of the Rock shrine in Jerusalem was marked by a ceremony in April. The mosque, which received a gold-leaf roof as part of the restoration, is located on the third-holiest site in Islam, the place from which Muhammad is said to have ascended into heaven.*

The government then launched a major offensive against Islamic militants. In January 1995, representatives of the militants and other opposition groups reported being near a ceasefire proposal. Developments in Algeria were being closely monitored in such countries as Egypt, Jordan, and Tunisia, where Islamists have been opposing the government.

In South Africa, meanwhile, Muslims reaped the benefits of their participation in the struggle to end apartheid. Although representing less than 5 percent of the population, Muslims were elected to several regional offices in postapartheid elections, and President Nelson Mandela appointed several Muslims to key offices in his federal government, including Dullah Omar, said to be the first Muslim ever named minister of justice in a non-Muslim country. A female Islamic scholar, Amina Wadud, addressed worshipers at one gathering in a Cape Town mosque, in what many wel-

comed as a significant symbolic step toward women's participation in Islamic society.

Another challenge to traditional patriarchal dominance in Islam was a controversy over the feminist Bangladeshi physician Taslima Nasreen (*see* BANGLADESH) and her novel *Lajja (Shame),* which traces the fate of a Hindu family in Bangladesh during riots sparked by the demolition of a mosque in India by Hindu fundamentalists. The novel was banned in Bangladesh in 1993, but pirated copies were used by Hindu fundamentalists in India to inflame anti-Muslim sentiments, prompting some Islamic clerics to call for Nasreen's assassination. When a public statement she made about the Koran was interpreted as defaming Islam, the Bangledeshi government issued a warrant for her arrest. Nasreen, who eventually went into voluntary exile in Sweden, remained convinced that her views on such matters as women's empowerment were the real issues involved, rather than alleged impiety.

Tensions over women's rights and other liberal values emerged at the United Nations Conference on Population and Development, held in Cairo in September. Despite differences in the past, Muslims formed a conservative "holy alliance" with the Vatican in condemning aspects of the conference's agenda and seeking changes in the wording of documents so as to reflect traditional family values. Muslims were especially concerned over language that might seem to condone homosexuality, promiscuity, or prostitution, and they were able to secure some changes to avoid such implications. T.S.

FAR EASTERN FAITHS

Despite reports citing increased political repression in Tibet and the routine torture of Tibetan Buddhists, U.S. President Bill Clinton in June 1994 renewed China's most-favored-nation trading status, a decision that was criticized by human rights groups.

Controversy continued within the Tibetan Buddhist Karma Kagyu suborder over which of two boys was the reincarnation of a lama and the proper claimant to one of the sect's highest offices. The Dalai Lama, exiled leader of the Tibetan people, early in 1994 reaffirmed the identification made in 1992 of Ogyen Trinley as the 17th Gyalwa Karmapa—and as such one of the three most important and revered leaders of the Tibetan people. The identification was made on the basis of clues supposedly written by the 16th Gyalwa Karmapa and discovered years after his 1981 death. The new Gyalwa Karmapa was installed in 1992 at the Tsurphu Monastery in Tibet, but some Buddhists continued to denounce the clues as a forgery and put forth the claims of a rival.

In another controversy, reformist monks in April accused Suh Eui Hyun of corruption and protested his reelection as administrative head of the Chogye group, South Korea's largest Buddhist sect. There were clashes between Suh supporters and riot police at the Chogye temple complex in Seoul; 38 monks were injured, and about 140 were arrested. The incident provoked Suh's resignation.

Violence flared in western Cambodia in April, when the Khmer Rouge fired rocket grenades into a group of peace marchers; a Buddhist monk and a Buddhist nun were killed, and several others were injured.

In Japan, Buddhist monk Wakyo Goda, after reportedly being demeaned, punched in the head, and fired by superiors, joined with six of the Kokubunji Temple's other monks in Osaka to form the Kokubunji Seven, possibly the world's first religious labor union.

Director Bernardo Bertolucci's film *Little Buddha* was released throughout the United States in May. Interweaving the story of the historical Buddha with that of a modern-day American boy recognized as the reincarnation of a lama, the film presented Buddhist teachings and ceremonies to a wide audience.

In India, Hindu spiritual leader Chandrashekhara Saraswathi, 99, died in his sleep, January 8 in Kanchipuram. Many considered Saraswathi one of the greatest Hindu sages of contemporary times. He was revered by Hindus and Muslims alike for his emphasis on religious tolerance.

The New Delhi city legislature passed a law in March banning the slaughter of cows, considered holy by Hindus. The Hindu fundamentalist Bharatiya Janata Party, which controlled the legislature, had promised to enact the measure.

During September as many as 60 people died as a result of an epidemic of pneumonic plague centered in the western Indian city of Surat. The outbreak was attributed to poor sanitary conditions, which fostered a huge rat population. Local officials said the rat infestation was never controlled because of the animal's association with the popular Hindu god Ganesha.

In December some 400 Muslims gathered in New Delhi at India's largest mosque. They called for the reconstruction of a mosque in Ayodhya destroyed two years earlier by Hindu militants who claimed it was the site of the birthplace of the Hindu deity Rama.

A 4-foot-high stone that unexpectedly came to serve as a shrine for worship of the Hindu god Shiva was removed in January from Golden Gate Park in San Francisco. Officials contended that once the stone became an object of worship to devout Hindus, its presence there violated the constitutional separation between church and state.   K.M.S.

REPUBLICAN PARTY. See ELECTIONS IN THE UNITED STATES; UNITED STATES OF AMERICA: Congress.

RHODE ISLAND. See STATISTICS OF THE WORLD.

RHODESIA. See ZIMBABWE.

ROMANIA. Political stalemate continued during 1994 in post-Communist Romania, where President Ion Iliescu's Party of Social Democracy in Romania had governed with a minority of parliamentary seats since the September 1992 elections. Informally supported by five small extremist parties (nationalists and former Communists), the government had survived several motions of no confidence in 1993. The divided opposition introduced another no-confidence motion in July 1994 and also tried to impeach Iliescu. Both the government and the president survived the attacks, but at the price of giving several ministerial portfolios to the extreme nationalists, thus further weakening the opposition groups that had started the fray. During October, King Michael, exiled since the Communists had forced his abdication in 1947, tried to visit the country but was turned back at the Bucharest airport. Although opinion polls have always shown little support for a restoration of the monarchy, the weak government was taking no chances.

The economy featured slow progress toward privatization and market reforms. An austerity budget was adopted in late May at the insistence of the International Monetary Fund, which then approved a new loan of $500 million to bring Romania's total foreign debt to about $4 billion. On several occasions the streets of Bucharest were filled with thousands of strikers and demonstrators protesting inflation, unemployment, and declining living standards, but no major violence occurred.

U.S.-Romanian relations improved as Romania in January became the first former Soviet ally to join NATO's Partnership for Peace. In addition, a U.S.-Romanian agreement on military cooperation was signed in June, and Iliescu met with U.S. President Bill Clinton in New York in September. Russia granted Romania preferential trade status (customs duties on Romanian goods were reduced by 50 percent), but Romania finalized no bilateral treaties of friendship with Russia, Ukraine, or Moldova, because of Romanian territorial claims stemming from World War II. Despite a new and friendlier government in Budapest, treaty negotiations with Hungary also dragged on without result, largely because of conflicts inside Romania between the Hungarian minority and Romanian nationalists over a new education law and excavations in Cluj, where attempts to uncover Roman sites threatened Hungarian monuments.

See STATISTICS OF THE WORLD.   M.E.F.

RUSSIA. For most of 1994, Russia seemed to be experiencing a relatively calm period, compared to the dramatic events and bruising conflicts of preceding years. Some observers said this fragile stability showed that political and economic reforms were beginning to take hold and to achieve results; others were more pessimistic and pointed to evidence of growing disillusionment. The year ended in crisis, as the central government applied military force against the secessionist region of Chechnya.

New Constitution. In order to justify the bloodshed of October 1993, when he ordered the shelling of the Russian Parliament, President Boris Yeltsin (*see profile in* PEOPLE IN THE NEWS) had to produce a workable constitution with solid legitimacy. The voters approved that constitution in December 1993 by a slim

majority, but the turnout barely reached 50 percent of eligible voters, the minimum necessary for the constitution to take effect. Furthermore, an investigative commission later claimed this result was obtained by government manipulation of electoral statistics; however, the constitution remained in force.

The framework set up by the constitution is closest to the French mixed parliamentary-presidential system. The president and the Parliament (called the Federal Assembly) are directly elected. The Federal Assembly is divided into two houses: the lower house (representing population) is called the Duma, and the upper house (representing local regions and republics) is known as the Council of the Federation. Since the cabinet actually runs the government, its head is considered to be the prime minister. The prime minister and other top officials are appointed by the president; the legislature can express its disapproval of his choices, but in most cases cannot veto them.

Election Aftermath. Elections to the new Duma were held at the same time as the plebiscite on the constitution. The strong showing of nationalist demagogue Vladimir Zhirinovsky, head of the misnamed Liberal Democratic Party, which won a plurality of votes, came as an embarrassing surprise to Yeltsin, who had clearly underestimated popular dissatisfaction. Zhirinovsky's success was upsetting to many, both within Russia and abroad, because of the violence of his rhetoric and his open advocacy of expansionism. Although it seemed unlikely that the votes for Zhirinovsky implied support for the more bizarre aspects of his program (for example, annexation of Finland), the right-wing leader showed an alarming potential for political extremism.

Yeltsin supporters were thus still in a minority in the new Duma, but as the year began, all parties seemed weary of the confrontational politics of the recent past. Partly in response to the shaky legitimacy of the new constitution, Yeltsin engineered a "civic peace accord," which was signed in April 1994. The aim of the accord was to lay out rules of the political game that would keep conflict within bounds and promote some measure of predictability. An unexpectedly wide range of political lead-

Ruble trouble. *As the value of the ruble plummeted in October, Russians flocked to currency exchanges, such as this one in Moscow. The acting finance minister was fired and the chairman of the central bank forced to resign while the government took measures to prop up the currency.*

ers lent their signatures to the document. The leader of the Communist Party of the Russian Federation, Gennady Ziuganov, did not sign but did attend the signing ceremony. Surprisingly, Zhirinovsky signed, although he withdrew in a fit of temper in October.

Parties in Flux. Russian political parties remained weak and underdeveloped; for the most part they were little more than support organizations for prominent individuals. Because of this weakness and because of the powers given to the president by the constitution, political conflict became focused on the presidential election scheduled for 1996. Since it seemed less and less likely that Yeltsin himself would run, other candidates began positioning themselves for the race.

At one end of the spectrum were radical reformers such as Yegor T. Gaidar, who founded a new party, Democratic Choice of Russia, in June. (Gaidar was the main architect of the intensely unpopular "shock therapy" economic reforms of 1992.) Reformers who hoped for a less disruptive transition to a market economy found their most prominent spokesman in economist Grigory A. Yavlinsky.

At the center were leaders who relied more on their own experience and elite contacts than on any grand vision of reform. Among them was Prime Minister Viktor Chernomyrdin, who appeared to be in the best position to succeed Yeltsin as president, if he were fortunate enough to avoid any major crises before 1996. Many other ambitious politicians among the regional economic and political elite (for example, Yuri Luzhkov, the mayor of Moscow) were also ready to step in, especially if Chernomyrdin were to be somehow discredited.

At the other end of the spectrum from the radical reformers were those who rejected the legitimacy of the regime. Their enemies called these antireformers the red-brown alliance (red for Communism, brown for Fascism), but their own name for themselves was "patriots." Among them, the Communist Party of the Russian Federation had the most effective network of local organizations—an inheritance from the past—but it had trouble defining itself convincingly.

One of the most charismatic leaders was Aleksandr V. Rutskoi, Yeltsin's former vice president who later became his deadly foe. In July, Rutskoi founded his own party, *Derzhava*

(Great Power), which aimed at re-creating a state with the same borders as the old Soviet Union—although on a purely voluntary basis. Meanwhile, Zhirinovsky's party was suffering from its leader's erratic behavior and beginning to come apart.

Doubts About Democracy. As the political elites fought among themselves, there was a growing sense of doubt in the country over whether Russia was really on the path to democracy. One antidemocratic proposal came from a prominent Yeltsin supporter, Vladimir Shumeiko, who suggested that the elections for president and legislature scheduled for 1996 be postponed. Shumeiko reasoned that politicians would make tough decisions more effectively if they did not have to fear the wrath of the electorate. And Yeltsin's minister of information, Boris Mironov, openly called for nationalization of the press. Yeltsin, however, refrained from endorsing Shumeiko's position and dismissed Mironov.

Another symptom of disillusionment was the changed official attitude toward the attempted coup of August 1991, in which many top leaders of the Soviet government had declared a state of emergency and tried to depose then-President Mikhail Gorbachev. Yeltsin's role in aborting the coup gave him the power to break up the old Soviet Union later that year; since then, the coup's leaders had sat in prison awaiting trial. In February 1994, however, the new Duma insisted on granting amnesty to the coup leaders as well as to the leaders of the parliamentary resistance in October 1993. Among those released from prison was Rutskoi, a leader of the anti-Yeltsin forces who occupied the Parliament building.

Also among the imprisoned was General Valentin Varennikov, who refused to accept the amnesty because he wanted to defend his actions in an open trial. Varennikov argued that it was not the leaders of the coup but Gorbachev who deserved most of the blame for what happened. In August the court acquitted the general on the ground that his motives had been honorable. Rutskoi applauded the verdict, even though he had allied himself with Yeltsin in 1991 in opposing the coup.

Solzhenitsyn Comes Home. The famous novelist Aleksandr Solzhenitsyn returned to Russia after 20 years in the United States. (Solzhenitsyn had been exiled by the Soviet government for his grim portrayal of the Soviet prison-camp system.) Back in his homeland, he sounded a note of discouragement: "I have become convinced since my arrival, as I have journeyed, that Russia today is in the midst of a great, grievous, and multifaceted calamity." Many Russians agreed with him: according to a midyear poll by the *Moscow News,* only 19 percent of the population felt that Russia was ruled by democrats.

Economic and Social Reform. The economic strategy of Prime Minister Chernomyrdin was to steer a middle course between bringing down inflation and avoiding a collapse of production and thus mass unemployment. During the summer inflation was held at a record low of 4-5 percent a month, although the rate went up again in the fall. The fragility of the economy was underscored when, in a delirious day in October, the ruble plunged in value from just over 3,000 to the dollar to just under 4,000. The free fall was, however, largely due to central bank mismanagement, and while the ruble soon recovered, the longtime head of the Central Bank, Viktor Gerashchenko, was forced to resign.

The grotesque side of Russia's new capitalism was exposed by the MMM scandal. Most observers described the MMM company (no one seemed to know what the Ms stood for) as a classic pyramid scheme, that is, the promised rise in stock value came entirely from getting ever more people to buy, thus enriching the original buyers. When the inevitable crash came in early August, many stockholders turned their anger not against MMM but against the government for its investigation and arrest of Sergei Mavrodi, the founder of the company. The collapse of MMM threatened to become a major political scandal when stockholders organized a petition campaign asking for a vote of no confidence in Yeltsin. But the vote never took place; in October, Mavrodi was released from prison after he was elected to fill a seat in Parliament left vacant when a Moscow legislator was killed by a gang. (As a deputy he was immune from prosecution.)

Many Russians felt that Russia was headed

not toward a Western-style capitalist welfare state but a new kind of system in which the economy was controlled by the old elite (the so-called *nomenklatura*) and a new economic elite arising out of marketing and finance rather than production. The system was accompanied by a frightening growth of crime and extortion, a dearth of public services, and economic penetration by foreigners.

Corruption began to seem the norm rather than an exception. In October, Dmitri Kholodov, a 27-year-old reporter who had been investigating corruption in the military, was killed by a letter bomb in the offices of *Moskovski Komsomolets,* the newspaper with the largest circulation in Russia.

Conflict in Chechnya. A long-standing ethnic/political conflict erupted into a major confrontation late in the year when Yeltsin dispatched troops to Chechnya. The tiny, oil-rich, mostly Muslim republic in the northern Caucasus Mountains had declared its independence in November 1991, just before the collapse of the Soviet Union. Significant fighting between Chechen government forces and Russian-supported rebels opposed to the separatist regime of President Dzhokhar M. Dudayev broke out in September 1994. Yeltsin's decision in December to apply military force drew protests from representatives of a broad range of political opinion, including a number of liberals and reformers. Dudayev's supporters vowed to fight to the end for their freedom as Russian forces surrounded the Chechen capital, Grozny, and conducted air strikes. As the year ended, Russian troops were attempting to capture Grozny despite stiff Chechen resistance.

Foreign Affairs. During 1994, Russia tried to move beyond the subservience to the West and confusion that had marked its foreign policy in the first years after the collapse of Communism. Although Foreign Minister Andrei Kozyrev remained at his post as a sign of continuity, his rhetoric now emphasized Russia's need to assert itself overseas and to protect its national interests. The new attitude in foreign affairs also reflected the shrinking influence of the reformers in Russian domestic politics. In relation to the "near abroad" (the former republics of the Soviet Union), the new foreign affairs outlook meant encouragement of greater political and economic coordination, insistence on Russia's role as a protector of Russian-speaking minorities, and a claim that Russia had a special responsibility for peacekeeping in the region.

Russia strove with partial success to make its presence felt within such international organizations as the European Union and the Group

Caucasian hot spot. Chechen government troops keep their eye on Russian-supported opposition forces near the city of Grozny, the capital of separatist Chechnya, in September. Much heavier fighting developed in December as Chechen loyalists fiercely resisted direct attacks by the Russian military.

357

of Seven advanced industrial nations. The Russian government objected strongly to any expansion of NATO to Eastern Europe that would exclude Russia and thus seemingly be aimed against it. In order to meet these objectives, NATO proposed an intermediate status called Partnership for Peace. With great reluctance Russia agreed to join this new organization in June. Russia also went to bat diplomatically for traditional allies such as the Iraqis and the Serbs.

See STATISTICS OF THE WORLD. L.T.L.

RWANDA. Civil war erupted anew in Rwanda in 1994 following the death of President Juvénal Habyarimana when his plane crashed in April, reportedly shot down. Habyarimana, a member of the majority Hutu tribe, had ruled Rwanda for 21 years. Within weeks of his death the Tutsi-led Rwandan Patriotic Front (FPR) took control of most of the country, and some 2 million Hutu fled over the borders, most of them to Zaire, some to Burundi and Tanzania. In July the Patriotic Front

declared victory and formed a new government. But despite offers of reconciliation by the FPR, the majority of refugees were too fearful to return home.

Prelude to Terror. The core of the FPR comprised members of Rwanda's Tutsi minority, in exile since the Hutu rebelled in 1959 and took control of the government. The conflict between the Tutsi—some of them family members of Rwanda's ruling elite—and the Hutu had continued sporadically since then. In 1990, FPR guerrillas invaded Rwanda from neighboring Uganda. Unable to crush the invasion and under internal pressure for reform, President Habyarimana signed a power-sharing agreement with the FPR in Arusha, Tanzania, in August 1993. Under the terms of the Arusha agreement, a transitional government would be formed, to rule until multiparty elections could take place. Habyarimana's National Republican Movement for Democracy and Development (MRNDD) would retain the presidency, but the FPR and the four other

Prelude to war. Rwandan rebel soldiers inspect wreckage from the April plane crash that killed Rwandan President Juvénal Habyarimana and Burundian President Cyprien Ntaryamira at Kigali, Rwanda's capital. The plane was reportedly shot down, and bloody civil conflict ensued in the ethnically divided nation.

main opposition parties would control the ministerial council and the legislature.

Implementation of the agreement was held up, however, and by the spring of 1994 the transitional government had not yet been sworn in. The lack of progress was caused by delays in deployment of a United Nations observer force, divisions within various political parties, and probably also by stalling on the part of the regime. (Many members of Habyarimana's government were hard-line Hutu, opposed to compromise not only with the FPR but also with the Hutu-led internal opposition.)

President Killed. On April 6 a plane carrying President Habyarimana and Burundian President Cyprien Ntaryamira crashed in Rwanda's capital, Kigali, killing all aboard. Habyarimana was returning from Tanzania, where he and FPR leaders had agreed on modalities for implementing the Arusha agreement. The plane was reportedly shot down and the president assassinated as part of a coup attempt by Hutu extremists in the Presidential Guard, who opposed the peace accord. Within hours of the crash the Guard and Hutu militias arrested or assassinated ministers, other officials, and civilians; among those slain was Premier Agathe Uwingiliyamana. By April 9 a new militant Hutu government had been formed. An estimated 500,000 people—most of them Tutsi, but Hutu dissidents, priests and nuns, and human rights monitors among them as well—were killed by the extremists in the weeks that followed, while the world looked on in apparent indifference.

FPR Advances, France Intervenes. The FPR, meanwhile, refused to accept the legitimacy of the new government and announced it was taking up arms again to stop the killings and to restore peace to Rwanda. By June, FPR forces had gained control of much of the country. As the FPR tightened its grip on Kigali, violence against civilians spread, and Hutu fearing FPR retaliation fled the country in droves, France attempted to interest other governments in joining what it called a military-humanitarian intervention. (Critics noted that the French had intervened in Rwanda in November 1990, supposedly to protect the Europeans of Kigali, who were threatened by the 1990 FPR offensive. The French then stayed on, and under

Safe haven. *Refugees fleeing the slaughter in Rwanda found protection in a zone established at midyear in the southwestern part of the country by French troops.*

their tutelage the mostly Hutu Rwandan Army grew from 5,000 to 40,000 men.) Failing to get support for military action, the French government obtained United Nations approval for Operation Turquoise, a two-month operation under which France would send 2,500 troops to Rwanda to protect civilians. When the militant Hutu government that took power in April collapsed just two weeks after the beginning of Operation Turquoise, France established a safe haven in southwestern Rwanda to shelter refugees fleeing the FPR. The last of the French forces withdrew from the safe zone in late August and were replaced by UN peacekeepers.

FPR Victorious. On July 18 the Rwandan Patriotic Front proclaimed victory, declared a cease-fire, and proceeded to form a new government. Under the Arusha agreement, Habyarimana's MRNDD party was to receive the presidency (which was, however, reduced to a ceremonial position) and five ministerial posts. The FPR named as president Pasteur Bizimungu, a Hutu who came from the same area as Habyarimana. Bizimungu had headed the power utility Electrogaz before fleeing in August 1990 to Uganda, where he joined the FPR. The FPR created a new post of vice president, which was assumed by Major-General Paul Kagame, a Tutsi raised in Uganda and a leader of the military offensive that overthrew the government. Kagame also became the new defense minister. The FPR kept for itself three of the five ministerial posts that had been set aside at Arusha for the MRNDD, as well as the five posts it had been allocated.

Faustin Twagiramungu, a Hutu from the opposition Democratic Republican Movement (MDR) who had been designated premier at Arusha, was confirmed in that position. The MDR also received three other ministerial posts, including that of foreign affairs. Of the 21 ministerial posts, 12 went to Hutu and nine to Tutsi, even though four-fifths of Rwandans are Hutu.

The Refugees. The new government offered reconciliation to its former enemies and urged the more than 2 million Hutu refugees—possibly a quarter of the population—to come home. The refugees had been living in unspeakably squalid conditions in camps at Goma, Zaire, and elsewhere, and countless thousands had died from disease, including dysentery and cholera, or starvation.

Nevertheless, very few were willing to return. Many appeared to have been intimidated by Hutu extremists from the Rwandan Army and its associated militias, who in effect controlled most of the camps. A UN war crimes commission investigating the Rwanda massacres reported in December that there was overwhelming evidence of systematic genocide against the Tutsi by Hutu extremists and that many of those accused of atrocities were living in the refugee camps.

See STATISTICS OF THE WORLD.   T.E.T.

S

SAHARA, WESTERN. See MOROCCO.

ST. LUCIA. See CARIBBEAN BASIN; STATISTICS OF THE WORLD.

ST. VINCENT AND THE GRENADINES. See CARIBBEAN BASIN; STATISTICS OF THE WORLD.

SAMOA, AMERICAN. See STATISTICS OF THE WORLD.

SAMOA, WESTERN. See STATISTICS OF THE WORLD.

SAN MARINO. See STATISTICS OF THE WORLD.

SÃO TOMÉ AND PRINCIPÉ. See STATISTICS OF THE WORLD.

SASKATCHEWAN. See STATISTICS OF THE WORLD.

SAUDI ARABIA. The Saudi regime continued to take action against its Muslim critics in 1994, prompting criticism from the United States about human rights abuses. In April, Muhammad al-Masaari, a founder of the Committee for the Defense of Legitimate Rights, the principal Islamist opposition group, fled to London after government warnings to limit his activities. Also in April the government stripped Usama bin Laden, a member of a wealthy business family, of his Saudi citizenship for his financial support of Islamist groups both outside and within the kingdom.

In September the government arrested 110 pro-Islamist dissidents, including Islamist preacher Sheikh Salman bin Fahd al-Audah. After an additional wave of arrests, a group calling itself the Battalions of Faith threatened to carry out terrorist attacks on foreigners and members of the royal family if Audah was not released within five days, but the deadline passed without incident.

In October, in an effort to deflect conservative opposition, King Fahd appointed a Supreme Council of Islamic Affairs.

Political reforms initiated in 1993 were completed when in January 1994 the appointed members of both the national and regional Consultative Councils (advisory councils on domestic matters) began deliberations. The reforms have been one of the main causes of Islamist opposition.

Low oil prices and the residual financial effect of the 1990-1991 Persian Gulf War continued to put pressure on Saudi finances. The 1994 budget, announced in January, set spending at $42.7 billion, 20 percent lower than 1993 spending. The budget deficit was expected to be significantly lower than 1993's $7.4 billion. The kingdom's overall debt was estimated at $61 billion.

In the face of declining revenues the kingdom restructured some $10 billion in payments and delayed implementation of several construction projects in its massive military development program. Despite the financial problems, the kingdom announced in February that it would rebuild its commercial airline fleet with the purchase of some 50 new planes, valued at $6 billion, from Boeing and McDonnell Douglas. In May, AT&T won a $4 billion contract to install a digital communication system throughout the kingdom. Both deals had the strong backing of the U.S. government, and foreign competitors accused the Americans of unfair dealings.

In November the Saudi government refused a U.S. request to keep planes, tanks, and other military equipment in the kingdom.

See STATISTICS OF THE WORLD. C.H.A.

SENEGAL. *See* STATISTICS OF THE WORLD.

SERBIA. *See* YUGOSLAVIA.

SEYCHELLES. *See* STATISTICS OF THE WORLD.

SIERRA LEONE. *See* STATISTICS OF THE WORLD.

SINGAPORE. Four foreign students accused of vandalism in September 1993 became the focus of world media attention in 1994 when one of the students, Michael Fay, an American, was fined and sentenced by a Singaporean court to four months in jail and six strokes by rattan cane.

Fay's parents sought media attention and political intervention. U.S. President Bill Clinton publicly asked for leniency and called the sentence a mistake, but Singaporean leaders rejected his pleas, saying the United States exemplified the laxity of laws and public morals in the West. In response, the United States sought to block an offer by Singapore to host the inaugural meeting of the World Trade Organization.

On appeal, the president of Singapore, Ong Teng Cheong, reduced Fay's caning to four strokes. Another of the students, Hong Kong national Shiu Chi Ho, was sentenced to twelve strokes and eight months in prison; the sen-

Raising cane. *Singapore's practice of flogging some criminals with a rattan cane received wide international attention as a result of the case of American Michael Fay, seen here being released from prison in June. Despite protests by human rights organizations and the U.S. government, Fay received four strokes of a cane following his conviction on a vandalism charge.*

tence was reduced by the president to six strokes and six months, but he was released after four months. The other two students were fined. While Singapore's practice of caning attracted most attention, its mandatory death sentences for drug trafficking led to the hanging of a Dutch businessman in September and a Ghanaian in October.

On April 1 a 3 percent goods and services tax was implemented with income tax reductions and rebates. Despite the consumption tax, economic growth throughout the year remained robust, estimated at nearly 10 percent.

In what was regarded as a test case for press freedom, five prominent Singaporeans—an official at the Monetary Authority, two members of a securities firm, and two journalists with the *Business Times*—were found guilty and fined in March for violating the Official Secrets Act. The charges arose from the mid-1993 publication of government economic estimates before they were officially released.

See STATISTICS OF THE WORLD. K.M.

SLOVAKIA. In 1994, the second year since the dissolution of the nation of Czechoslovakia, Slovakia experienced two abrupt shifts in the balance of political power. In March, after almost two years of sparring between Prime Minister Vladimir Meciar and his parliamentary rivals, Meciar's ruling coalition fell to a vote of no confidence. Six months later, after an interim government introduced economic and social reforms, Meciar was restored to power in the fall general elections.

Meciar's government was voted out of power after it was perceived to have delayed and manipulated the privatization of Slovakia's ailing military-industrial sector, raising doubts in the international community about Slovakia's commitment to democracy and the free market. In the government's last days Meciar hurried through a series of below-market-value privatizations that were later challenged as political cronyism; many were later voided.

Between the no-confidence vote and the election, a coalition government headed by Prime Minister Jozef Moravcik began to refurbish Slovakia's international image by renewing the push for privatization and by making concessions—such as passing laws on language rights—to the ethnic Hungarians who make up more than a tenth of Slovakia's population. Double-digit unemployment and inflation stabilized, the gross domestic product rose, and interest in Slovakia picked up among foreign investors.

By the time elections were held on September 30 and October 1, however, the nationalistic Meciar had recouped his popularity by attacking the interim government for catering to Hungarian and other foreign interests. Voters granted his party, the Movement for a Democratic Slovakia, and its electoral coalition partners a plurality. After a ten-week crisis over the composition of the government, the new left-wing Slovak Workers' Association agreed to join Meciar's party and the right-wing Slovak National Party in a coalition announced December 11. Meanwhile, in November, Meciar and his allies gathered enough votes to cancel the privatization projects approved by Moravcik's government.

The government's continued enthusiasm for regional cooperation and full membership in the European Union was likely to meet with European skepticism in the absence of greater internal stability and commitment to reform.

See STATISTICS OF THE WORLD.   C.S.L.

SLOVENIA. In 1994, Slovenia found itself in the midst of crises similar to those of the other former Yugoslav republics and became entangled in border and national disputes with Croatia and Italy.

Although Slovenia managed to maintain modest economic growth in 1994, it failed to stem growing unemployment (at 14 percent) or to counter the effects of the loss of the united market that had existed in the former Yugoslavia. Signaling that Slovenia was ready to put aside political grudges against other Yugoslav republics in favor of economic interests, the Slovene Adria Airlines announced its resumption of flights between Ljubljana, the capital, and the Yugoslav capital of Belgrade shortly after the United Nations Security Council authorized the opening of Belgrade's airport in October.

After a series of scandals had rocked the government, President Milan Kucan sacked controversial Defense Minister Janez Jansa in March. The illegal selling of weapons to the government of Bosnia-Hercegovina, in which millions of dollars were never accounted for, was only the most visible manifestation of Jansa's abuse of power.

With Jansa's removal, Slovenia's fragile ruling coalition began to unravel. In October the fissures between the Liberal Democratic Party and the Christian Democrats widened when Foreign Minister Lojze Peterle unexpectedly resigned.

Also in October, Parliament enacted a new electoral boundaries law that included four Croatian villages, reigniting the festering Slovene-Croat border dispute. At the same time Slovenia found itself in a dispute with Italy over claims for restitution or compensation for property in Slovenia owned by Italians before World War II. Slovenia's ability to settle these disputes in a timely manner could determine its success in its bid for European Union membership. Failure could lead to a nationalist backlash that might undermine its economic and international standing.

See STATISTICS OF THE WORLD.   O.K.

SOLOMON ISLANDS. *See* Statistics of the World.

SOMALIA. The year 1994 marked the third anniversary of the Somali civil war.

Grassroots Developments. The year began with renewed hope for peace, as grassroots organizations mushroomed throughout the country. Traditional leaders were given monetary incentives to use their good offices to mediate among the warring groups. For example, the imam of the Hirab subclans (including the Abgal and the Habar Gedir) got involved in January in the formation of the Hirab Reconciliation Committee. The administration of the United Nations Operation in Somalia (Unosom) funded the imam's initiative, believing that a solution to the problems in Mogadishu might lead to an overall settlement of the Somali predicament. The initiative led to the Nairobi Declaration of March 24, signed by General Muhammad Farrah Aideed of the Somali National Alliance (SNA) and Ali Mahdi Muhammad of the Somali Salvation Alliance. The declaration called for a national reconciliation conference to be held in Mogadishu in May, leading to the formation of a new government, but the conference was postponed.

In September the UN secretary-general gave the Security Council three reasons for this postponement. First, the factions agreed to accommodate the Somali Salvation Democratic Front's congress in the northeast; delegates at the congress were entrusted with the difficult task of electing a new leadership. Second, a reconciliation conference in the Lower Jubba region coincided with the May 15 deadline for the national conference. Finally, the postponement of the meeting was meant to give enough time for consultations on the possible inclusion of the Somali National Movement in the reconciliation process.

This third point attested to the tension that was building up between the UN and the authorities in the breakaway Somaliland Republic, where the government of President Muhammad Ibrahim Egal ordered the expulsion of Unosom representatives from the territory in August.

Out of Africa. *American soldiers load a helicopter on a transport plane in Mogadishu, Somalia, in February as U.S. forces prepare to leave the country. The following month saw the official conclusion of the 15-month U.S. mission in the embattled African nation.*

Somaliland. In October war broke out in Hargeysa, the capital of Somaliland. Egal's forces launched an attack on the positions of the opposition militia controlling Hargeysa's airport. Egal's forces captured the airport, but the opposition militia simply regrouped outside the capital. The fighting in Hargeysa shattered the relative peace that the region had enjoyed since the overthrow of former dictator Siad Barre's government in January 1991. In the meantime, the authorities in Somaliland introduced a new currency. The new Somaliland shilling was used in tandem with the Somali shilling for three months, after which the old currency was phased out.

Unosom to Pull Out. In central Somalia, Unosom's inability to ward off attacks on the town of Belet Huen, where Zimbabwean forces were overrun by SNA militia, precipitated similar attacks on UN forces in a number of other places in the south. The attacks constituted great danger for the Unosom forces as the deadline for their pullout—which the UN in November set for March 31, 1995—approached.

By 1994's end Unosom humanitarian operations had been cut to half their midyear size. In December, Unosom radio broadcasts were terminated, and the last issue of Unosom's newspaper, *Maanta*, came out.

As the year concluded, there was no end in sight to the Somali civil war. Two parallel conferences on national reconciliation were held in Mogadishu, one in the north and another in the south of the city. Participants shied away from forming two parallel governments; such an action would have constituted a true recipe for disaster. Otherwise, the factions continued to jockey for control of Mogadishu's port and airport in anticipation of the post-Unosom era.

See STATISTICS OF THE WORLD.   A.J.A.

SOUTH AFRICA. In 1994, for the first time ever, South Africans of all races went to the polls together to elect a new government. The election victory of former political prisoner Nelson Mandela (*see profile in* PEOPLE IN THE NEWS) and the peaceful installation of a new government of national unity won praise around the world. But the new South African government faced an enormous legacy of social and economic inequality under difficult economic conditions.

Transition Process. The transition process, agreed upon after more than three years of negotiations, was headed by the Transitional Executive Council (TEC), a multiparty oversight body dominated by the African National Congress (ANC) and the incumbent National Party (NP). The TEC, which began functioning in December 1993, had the responsibility of overcoming obstacles to the election, which was set for April 26-28. The election process itself was overseen by a separately constituted Independent Electoral Commission.

The major obstacle, besides continuing political violence, was opposition to the interim constitution from a Freedom Alliance coalition of white and black right-wing groups. The nominally independent homeland of Bophuthatswana, under President Lucas Mangope, refused to allow campaigning, but Mangope was ousted from power after popular protest in March. Although white right-wing commandos came to his regime's defense, the South African Army proved loyal to the TEC and took charge of the homeland. One of the leaders of the Freedom Alliance, General Constand Viljoen, withdrew his opposition to the vote and decided to contest the election under the banner of the new Freedom Front. He said he would continue to campaign for a white Afrikaner-run autonomous state, or *volkstaat.*

Also in March the Goldstone Commission investigating political violence issued a report that implicated top police generals in the instigation of conflict between the ANC and other groups, in particular the Inkatha Freedom Party, headed by Chief Mangosuthu Gatsha Buthelezi. Buthelezi, demanding greater autonomy for his KwaZulu homeland, threatened to boycott the election until a week before the vote. He gained constitutional protection for the Zulu monarchy, but his last-minute reversal was also attributed to a lack of support from the South African military and the international community.

Election. Under the interim constitution, 200 members of a National Assembly were chosen in proportion to the national vote and 200 in proportion to the votes within nine provinces. The National Assembly chose the president.

Police action. Police clash with Inkatha Freedom Party protesters in one of several incidents of violence that marred South Africa's transition to democracy. An Inkatha protest march in Johannesburg in late March led to street battles with police and members of the African National Congress that left dozens of people dead. Earlier in the same month an investigative commission issued a report implicating top police generals in the instigation of conflict between the African National Congress and other groups, particularly Inkatha.

Each province elected a provincial assembly, which then chose ten national senators. The resulting Parliament (National Assembly plus Senate), with a five-year term, was to draw up a permanent constitution.

Despite administrative difficulties, the election ran relatively smoothly in most parts of the country. The ANC won 252 of the 400 seats in the National Assembly, with 62.7 percent of the 19.5 million votes. The NP won 82 seats with 20.4 percent of the vote, and the Inkatha Freedom Party won 43 seats with 10.5 percent of the vote. Smaller parties gaining seats in the National Assembly were the Freedom Front (nine), the Democratic Party (seven), the Pan-Africanist Congress (five), and the African Christian Democratic Party (two).

The ANC also carried seven of the nine provinces. But the NP won a majority in the Western Cape, where many "Coloured" (mixed-race) voters responded to fears of the ANC's black constituency. In a negotiated deal after charges of massive fraud in Inkatha-controlled areas, the ANC conceded victory in KwaZulu/Natal to Inkatha.

President Mandela chose the ANC's Thabo Mbeki as first vice president. Former President F. W. de Klerk was chosen by the National Party as second vice president. The 30-member cabinet, chosen after intense bargaining among parties, included NP incumbents Derek Keys at finance and Kraai van Niekerk at agriculture. Buthelezi was given the Home Affairs Ministry; defense went to Joe Modise and police to Sydney Mufamadi, both ANC stalwarts.

Meeting Expectations. The new South African government faced huge challenges. South African whites had a per capita income level 9.5 times that of blacks. The United Nations Development Program's *Human Development Report for 1994* ranked South Africa 93rd out of 173 countries on its Human Development Index. White South Africa alone would rank 24th, just after Spain, while black South Africa alone would rank 123rd, just above Congo.

The ANC campaigned on an ambitious Reconstruction and Development Program (RDP), intended to meet basic needs, develop human resources, and democratize the society while also stimulating economic growth. The program, developed with much input from the ANC-allied trade union movement and civic groups, rested on an active state role in such concerns as land redistribution, health, education, and housing. Yet with incumbent civil servants guaranteed tenure by the transition agreement, and the need to assure both South African and foreign investors of a stable business climate, the ANC also recognized that implementation would be slow.

Business people were reassured by the reap-

365

Redrawing the map. Under its new constitution, South Africa was restructured into nine provinces (PWV stands for Pretoria-Witwatersrand-Vereeniging). Each has its own legislature and sends ten representatives to the Senate. The so-called black homelands were abolished.

pointment of Keys as finance minister. The budget Keys presented in June was a conservative one, aimed at lowering the budget deficit while still freeing up some funds for RDP programs. The higher-than-expected cost of the election transition was covered by a one-time tax on high-income companies and individuals. Keys resigned for personal reasons in July and was replaced by Afrikaner banker Chris Liebenberg.

Another issue that threatened relations between the ANC and its coalition partners was the terms of a Truth Commission, being set up to bring out into the open political crimes in the apartheid period. While Justice Minister Dullah Omar and others were insisting on full disclosure as a condition for amnesty, National Party officials and the security establishment were resisting.

In general, however, the new government enjoyed a honeymoon period. According to a poll released in August, 75 percent of Indians, 70 percent of blacks, 63 percent of Coloureds, and 58 percent of whites thought the government was doing well.

Political Conflict in KwaZulu/Natal. Although Inkatha gained control of the provincial government and political violence declined significantly, controversy continued over investigations into hit squads associated

with the KwaZulu police. New political battles erupted, moreover, as Zulu King Goodwill Zwelithini, his budget secured by the national government, broke with his adviser Chief Buthelezi and moved closer to ANC-aligned and other non-Inkatha members of the royal family. Many ANC supporters in the province remained bitter at the decision not to challenge fraud in the provincial results.

Economic Developments. The growth rate in South Africa's gross domestic product, which had recovered to a modest 1.2 percent in 1993 after a 2.2 percent drop in 1992, was predicted to reach about 2.7 percent for 1994. New trade, investment, and aid packages from Japan, the United States, and Europe were all initiated during the year, but their impact on the nation's economy was not expected to take effect for some time.

Strikes were up substantially over 1993, with 1.2 million workdays lost in the first six months compared with 700,000 in 1993. The upsurge followed three years of recession and no real wage increases. Although the Congress of South African Trade Unions (Cosatu) was a major component of the ANC's electoral base, the government took a relatively hard line against strikes, pleasing business opinion at the risk of offending union allies. Although Mandela was received warmly at the Cosatu conference in September, analysts anticipated rising tensions between workers and the government.

Business ties between the United States and South Africa, partially interrupted by anti-apartheid sanctions imposed in 1986 and lifted in 1991, continued to climb, if slowly. The number of U.S. companies with direct investment presence passed 150, up from the 1991 low of 104 but short of the 267 that were there before the sanctions. Consumer firms, such as PepsiCo, Coca Cola, and Heinz, were prominent in expanding their direct investments, but many potential investors held back. South Africa's debt rating was upgraded to investment grade by Moody's, a Wall Street bond-rating firm.

See STATISTICS OF THE WORLD. W.M.

SOUTH CAROLINA. See STATISTICS OF THE WORLD.

SOUTH DAKOTA. See STATISTICS OF THE WORLD.

SOUTH WEST AFRICA. See STATISTICS OF THE WORLD: Namibia

SOVIET UNION. See RUSSIA; *other former Soviet republics.*

SPACE EXPLORATION. The United States flew seven space shuttle missions in 1994, while Russia maintained a crew on its *Mir* space station as the two nations began melding their manned programs, working toward building a new, international space station. Japan launched its first domestically designed and built large rocket. A lunar probe mapped the Moon's surface in unprecedented detail but was unable to complete the second phase of its mission.

U.S.-Russian Cooperation. Sergei Krikalev, one of Russia's most experienced cosmonauts, became the first to fly on a U.S. shuttle, launching on *Discovery* in February with five Americans. Two U.S. National Aeronautics and Space Administration (NASA) astronauts, physician Norman Thagard and microgravity researcher Bonnie Dunbar, took up residence at the Yuri Gagarin Cosmonaut Training Center in Star City outside Moscow. They began training to fly on board a Soyuz capsule to Russia's *Mir* space station. Thagard was to fly first, spending three months on *Mir* in 1995 and returning with the crew of the first U.S. shuttle to dock to the Russian station.

Radar mapper. A mission flown by the space shuttle Endeavour in the early fall featured use of advanced radars for mapping and for studying how the Earth's global environment is changing. Seen here is the shuttle's open cargo bay containing the Space Radar Laboratory (marked JPL). In resting position to the right of the SRL is the shuttle's Canadian-made remote manipulator arm.

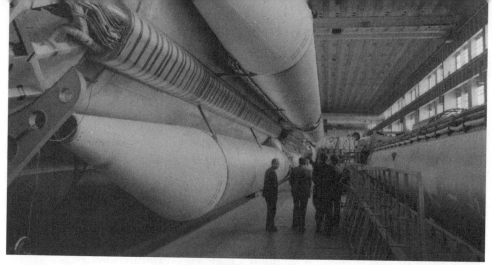

Russian success story. *Despite its economic difficulties, Russia has found that some of its products are in demand in the West. One of them is rocketry, with Western companies and governments placing orders in the last several years that add up to more than $1 billion. Here, a Proton rocket undergoes inspection in a factory near Moscow.*

On the industrial side, U.S. aerospace companies began forming alliances with what had been the state-owned design bureaus and production organizations of the Soviet Union. Notably, a joint venture of Lockheed, Khrunichev Space Center, and NPO Energia began marketing satellite launching services in the West using Russia's reliable Proton rockets.

Astronomical Research. *Clementine,* the first U.S. lunar spacecraft since Apollo 17 (1972), was launched in January and orbited the Moon for 71 days. It was a small spacecraft developed by the military to test new lightweight sensors for possible use in defending against ballistic missiles. In 350 orbits it mapped the Moon extensively for the first time and gathered data about lunar geology and chemistry, including strong hints that water ice exists in small amounts at the poles. The little spacecraft was to fly on to an encounter with a near-Earth asteroid, 1620 Geographos, but a malfunction exhausted the propellant used by *Clementine*'s jets to keep it properly pointed and it was left spinning.

The *Hubble Space Telescope,* which shuttle astronauts had repaired and refurbished in December 1993 in a record five days of back-to-back space walks, was tested early in 1994. Scientists were delighted to find that the *Hub-ble*'s flawed optics not only had been fixed, but the correction worked so well that the instrument now exceeded the original specifications and could perform near the physical limit for a telescope of its size.

Later, scientists used the telescope to find what they said was "seemingly conclusive proof" of the existence of black holes, objects so dense their gravity will not allow matter or energy to escape. Another group found evidence suggesting that the universe is much younger than previously thought: 8-12 billion years old, not the 15 billion or even 20 billion some had supposed. That conclusion was based on observations that led to a calculation of the expansion rate of the universe, called the Hubble constant. This type of research was one of the prime reasons the telescope had been built. In another effort for which scientists had long wanted an observatory beyond Earth's obscuring atmosphere, two independent research groups concluded that the simplest explanation for so-called dark matter could not be true. The movement of stars and galaxies had long suggested that "missing mass" is pulling on objects that can be seen. The conservative explanation held that there are vast numbers of faint red dwarf stars that cannot be seen with ground-based telescopes.

The spacecraft *Ulysses,* operated by the European Space Agency and NASA, went into solar orbit and began exploring the Sun's south pole in 1994. *Ulysses* had been launched on the shuttle in 1990 and sent past Jupiter so that the massive planet's gravity could sling the spacecraft out of the orbital plane of the planets and into a polar orbit around the Sun. Although that orbit is twice as distant as Earth's from the Sun, the unique vantage point immediately began providing an extraordinary flow of data that is expected to continue at least through 2000, when *Ulysses* is to be again over the south solar pole.

Launch Vehicles. Japan, Europe, and the United States took important steps in 1994 concerning new launch vehicles. Japan launched the first big rocket it developed on its own, the H-2, on its first two missions. The European Space Agency neared completion of its heavy-lift Ariane 5 rocket. And the United States, after flying a vehicle designed to test a single-stage-to-orbit concept, said it would develop a reusable launcher to lower the cost of flying into space.

See also the feature article COMETS: MYSTERIOUS VISITORS FROM OUTER SPACE; ASTRONOMY.

J.R.A.

SPAIN. In 1994, Spanish Prime Minister Felipe González Márquez successfully resisted challenges from the right and left calling for his resignation. He refused to call early general elections and continued to preside over a corruption-marred government as the economy began to emerge from a two-year recession; but he was in a precarious political position at year's end.

Political Alliance. In June the conservative Popular Party swept European parliamentary elections and took away the majority of the Spanish Socialist Workers' Party (PSOE) in the Andalusian regional government, the party's strongest regional base. The PSOE government then relied almost exclusively on parliamentary support from the Catalan nationalist party, Convergence and Union (CiU), to avoid a crippling vote of no confidence and to pass important legislation, including liberalized labor laws and a 1995 austerity budget.

Corruption Scandals. A major problem for Spain was that the country's young democracy was forced to withstand a third straight year of high-level political and economic corruption scandals. The country's fourth-largest bank, Banesto, was discovered to have been involved in illegal business practices costing over $3 billion. Mario Conde, a symbol of the "get rich quick" ethos of the 1980s, was removed as head of Banesto after the near-collapse of the financial institution in late December 1993.

In February the Spanish Parliament opened an investigation of Luis Roldán, former director of Spain's Civil Guard police, who was accused of bid-rigging, taking kickbacks, and illegal use of secret government discretionary accounts. Roldán fled the country in April.

Also in April the government opened an investigation into alleged tax evasion, insider trading, and illegal use of public accounts by the former governor of the Bank of Spain, Mariano Rubio. Rubio faced possible jail time.

After some recuperation of his political fortune over the summer, González was further racked by scandal both inside and outside his government. In October the arrest of Catalan financier Javier De la Rosa on fraud charges related to allegations that he had illegally fi-

Right on! *Happy supporters of Spain's conservative Popular Party celebrate their party's victory in the European Parliament elections in June. The conservatives' triumph was considered a serious setback to Spain's ruling Socialist government.*

Spanish Alphabet Downsized

The Spanish alphabet once boasted 29 letters. It now has just 27. After centuries of faithful service two letters were voted out of existence in 1994.

The outcast letters—*ch* and *ll*—had their own names—*che* and *elle*—and their own dictionary headings. *Cha* (tea), for instance, has traditionally been alphabetized after *comida* (food). Under the new system, however, *cha* belongs under *c*, so that it now precedes the meal.

The change was designed mainly to increase the language's computer compatibility with English. The European Union had urged its 12 member nations, including Spain, to take steps to ease translation and computer standardization. Of 18 votes cast among the members of the Association of Spanish Language Academies, 17 were *sí*. Only Ecuador was against it.

But the world's 300 million Spanish speakers still have one more letter than English speakers. The ñ lives on!

nanced the CiU party threatened to undermine the CiU-PSOE alliance. Then, in November, González was further stung by allegations against his brother-in-law involving influence peddling, and in December by new revelations from paroled national policemen directly linking the PSOE government to antiterrorist paramilitary death squads responsible for 23 deaths of alleged Basque separatist supporters in southwestern France from 1983 to 1987.

Economic Revival. Economic growth resumed in Spain in 1994. The gross domestic product (GDP) increased 1.7 percent during the year, after falling about 1 percent in 1993, and was projected to reach 2.8 percent in 1995. Inflation remained steady at around 4 percent. The second quarter showed the first small signs since the recession began in mid-1992 of an increase in domestic consumption and investment, as well as significant improvement in Spain's balance of trade. The orderly takeover of Banesto by Banco Santander along with falling interest rates and relative currency stability revived confidence in the economy's

ability to sustain growth well into 1995. The government was still far behind schedule in meeting the economic and financial targets set by the 1992 Maastricht Treaty, however. The deficit was at 6.7 percent of GDP, well above the 1995 Maastricht target of 5.9 percent. The unemployment rate remained consistently near 25 percent in 1994, more than double the European Union's average.

Labor Relations. The failure of a January 27 general strike to force changes in government labor policies revealed the declining strength of unionism in Spain, and the gradual movement of politics toward the right. It was clear that organized labor would be unable to turn back government attempts to liberalize the labor market.

Regionalism. In September the presidents of all 17 major autonomous regions except the Basque Country took part in the first parliamentary debate on the model set forth in the 1978 constitution for central government relations with Spain's autonomous regions. The leaders forged a fragile consensus recognizing differences among regions within Spain, including the role each region would play in the European Union, and set forth a project of integration of national and ethnic diversity. The leaders pledged loyalty to the constitution but agreed to support an amendment making the Senate a territorial chamber.

Foreign Affairs. In 1994 much of Spain's attention abroad was focused on Bosnia-Hercegovina, where over 1,200 Spanish peacekeepers were stationed. Spain opposed the U.S. decision to end the arms embargo to Bosnia in November. Spain repeatedly called for a conference on security and cooperation in the Mediterranean and worked to protect its interests in Algeria, where Islamic fundamentalists threatened to cut off strategic energy supplies to the Iberian Peninsula. In September, in an effort to promote a peaceful transition to democracy in Cuba, Spain sponsored talks in Madrid between the Castro government and prominent Cuban exile leaders.

Society and Culture. In a blow to lovers of the fine arts everywhere, the historic Liceo opera house in Barcelona burned to the ground on January 31.

See STATISTICS OF THE WORLD.　　　　R.R.

Sports

Big winners in 1994 included the Houston Rockets, who took the National Basketball Association championship, and the New York Rangers, who captured the National Hockey League's Stanley Cup for the first time in over half a century. Boxer George Foreman, himself not much less than half a century old, won a world heavyweight title. The major league baseball season was cut short by a labor dispute, making 1994 only the second year in the sport's history that the World Series was canceled.

The Winter Olympics took place in early 1994, and soccer's World Cup during the summer (*see the feature article* WORLD CUP '94: SOCCER'S BIG SHOW COMES TO THE UNITED STATES). Spanish cyclist Miguel Indurain (*see profile in* PEOPLE IN THE NEWS) won his fourth consecutive Tour de France. Back in the United States, the National Football League's 1994 season culminated with a Super Bowl in early 1995 won in crushing fashion by the San Francisco 49ers.

AUTOMOBILE RACING

The year 1994 saw the 78th Indianapolis 500-mile race. Exploiting a loophole in the rules, Roger Penske, Ilmor Engineering, and automaker Mercedes-Benz built a special engine—a 209-cubic-inch pushrod V8 that could produce considerably more horsepower than conventional IndyCar engines. Powered by that new engine, Penske's three-car entry of Al Unser, Jr., Emerson Fittipaldi, and Paul Tracy appeared to be all but unbeatable in the race. Fittipaldi dominated most of the day, but less than 40 miles from the finish he crashed into the wall. Unser subsequently cruised to his second Indy 500 victory.

The Penske organization used its standard 2.65-liter Ilmor V8 to dominate the rest of the PPG IndyCar World Series season as no other team in history ever had. Unser won eight of the 16 races and the season championship, Fittipaldi won one, and Tracy won three.

The Indianapolis Motor Speedway also was the site of the inaugural Brickyard 400-mile stock car race, which was won by Jeff Gordon, a former resident of Pittsboro, IN, who was driving a Chevrolet Lumina for car owner Rick Hendrick. The Daytona 500 was won by Chevy driver Sterling Marlin. Dale Earnhardt equaled Richard Petty's record by winning a seventh Winston Cup season championship. Penske's stock car team and driver Rusty Wal-

Inaugural Brickyard. The first-ever Brickyard 400-mile stock car race at the Indianapolis Motor Speedway was won, fittingly, by Jeff Gordon, who grew up in Pittsboro, IN, just a few miles down the road from Indianapolis.

lace won the most races (eight) but could do no better than third in the point standings to Earnhardt. Drivers Neil Bonnett and Rodney Orr both died after crashes during preliminary events at Daytona.

In the spring Ayrton Senna of Brazil, considered by many the best driver of all time, died in a crash at Imola, Italy. Michael Schumacher of the Benetton team narrowly edged Damon Hill of the Williams team for the world driving championship.

The International Motor Sports Association, based in Tampa, FL, not only launched its new World Sports Car category but was sold to a new owner. Despite the new WSC category for sports/racing cars, IMSA's two major races, the 24 Hours of Daytona and 12 Hours of Sebring, were won by production-based Nissan 300ZX coupes. Steve Millen was in the winning car in both races. The new WSC championship was won by Wayne Taylor in a Mazda-powered Kudzu chassis. Scott Pruett

Oklahoma's OK. Tim Walton celebrates by jumping on his teammates' backs after the University of Oklahoma beat Georgia Tech, 13-5, to win the College World Series in June. The Sooners, who were unranked in the major college baseball polls at the beginning of the season, set a record for most runs scored in the collegiate championship series.

won the other major American sports car series, the SCCA Trans-Am, in a Chevrolet Camaro owned by Buz McCall.

The 62nd 24 Hours of Le Mans endurance classic competition was won by a Dauer Porsche 962LM driven by American Hurley Haywood, Yannick Dalmas of France, and Mauro Baldi of Italy.   L.E.

BASEBALL

In 1994, for the first time in recent memory, baseball failed to hold a World Series. The reason was a labor dispute that ended the season on August 12, the day on which the players, having failed to reach an agreement with the owners over salary structures and cost containment, staged a walkout. After weeks of fruitless negotiations, Acting Commissioner Bud Selig canceled the remainder of the schedule on September 14.

Not only was the World Series shelved, but the leagues' championship series and the newly instituted wild-card playoff rounds were short-circuited as well. The only previous cancellation of the World Series occurred in 1904, when the New York Giants of the National League refused to play the Boston Pilgrims of the American League because the Giants' manager, John McGraw, was feuding with Ban Johnson, who was president of the new American League.

The strike represented the eighth work stoppage in 23 seasons, and it was the lengthiest disruption ever. The previous record was a 50-day strike in 1981, but that mark was surpassed by the 1994 walkout, which automatically extended to 52 days when the owners canceled the remainder of the season.

Short but Exciting Season. The two sides' inability to reach an agreement eclipsed one of the most interesting seasons in recent memory. Ken Griffey, Jr., of the Seattle Mariners and Matt Williams of the San Francisco Giants were both in earnest pursuit of Roger Maris's single-season home run record of 61, set in 1961. At the time of the strike, Williams had slugged 43 home runs with 47 games to go, and Griffey had hit 40 homers with 50 games left. Frank Thomas of the White Sox had 38 home runs, along with a .353 average and 101 runs batted in (RBIs), making him a strong candidate to win the Triple Crown. The Giants'

The old brawl game. *In October the White House tapped William Usery, Jr., to mediate between baseball team owners and players. At Usery's first press conference were, left to right, Donald Fehr of the Major League Baseball Players Association, Usery, Labor Secretary Robert Reich, and Acting Baseball Commissioner Bud Selig.*

Barry Bonds had 37 home runs. At the very least, it appeared baseball would have three or more hitters reaching 50 home runs, which had never occurred before. Similarly, Tony Gwynn of the San Diego Padres was on the verge of becoming the first player to hit .400 since Ted Williams batted .406 in 1941. Gwynn was batting .394 at the time play was suspended.

The presidents of both leagues decided that because the season was abridged, there would be no official pennant winners. That meant that the Toronto Blue Jays and the Philadelphia Phillies, the respective American League and National League victors in 1993, would reign as champions for one more season (or however long it might take for the players' strike to be settled).

At the time play stopped, the New York Yankees were leading the American League Eastern Division. The Chicago White Sox were atop the league's Central Division, and the Texas Rangers claimed the Western Division. The Cleveland Indians, who posted the league's next-best record after the division leaders, would have qualified as the wild-card team in the opening round of the American League playoffs.

In the National League, the Montréal Expos were leading the Eastern Division. The Cincinnati Reds were in first place in the Central Division, and the Los Angeles Dodgers were leading in the Western Division. The Atlanta Braves would have qualified as the league's wild-card team.

Labor Dispute. The primary issue of the dispute was the owners' desire for a salary cap that split industry revenues 50-50 with the players. Under a proposal hatched during the previous off-season, the teams would set an "average" payroll—which would be half the earnings of the clubs divided by 28. After four years, payrolls would have to fall within a range of 84 percent of the average as a minimum, or 110 percent as a maximum. The owners offered to reduce the length of service required for a player to claim free agency from six years to four if the players would agree to a complete elimination of salary arbitration and if the current club would have the right of first refusal for any free agent (that is, it would have the right to meet his salary demand before being required to let him go).

The players wanted to return salary arbitration eligibility from three years to two years. They further sought to increase the minimum salary from $109,000 to somewhere between $175,000 and $200,000. The players also were demanding payment of $7.8 million to their pension fund, which the owners were withholding and, in addition, greater income for playoff and World Series pools.

The road to the strike actually began on December 31, 1993, when the previous collective bargaining agreement expired. On January 18, 1994, the owners agreed to the revenue-sharing formula, and on June 14 they formally proposed the plan to the players. The players rejected it four days later, and on July 28, fearing that the owners would exploit their antitrust exemption and simply impose the new economic plan, they set August 12 as a strike date.

The strike indeed began on August 12, and although talks were held for nearly a month, no progress was made. On September 14 the owners voted, 26-2, to cancel the remainder of the season. In October, President Bill Clinton sent veteran labor mediator William Usery, Jr., to urge the warring sides to negotiate an agreement. His efforts accomplished little, and in late December, with the talks at an impasse, the owners unilaterally imposed a salary cap under which the players would receive 50 percent of revenues. The players were expected to fight the cap and challenge baseball's antitrust exemption in court.

All Star Game. The 65th All Star Game was held on July 12 at Pittsburgh's Three Rivers Stadium. The National League defeated the American League for the first time in seven years, 8-7, in ten innings. With the score tied, 7-7, Tony Gwynn, leading off the tenth inning, singled off Jason Bere and then scored on Moises Alou's game-winning double. The National League was paced by home runs by Marquis Grissom and Fred McGriff, whose blast tied the game in the ninth inning.

Hall of Fame. Pitcher Steve Carlton was elected to the Hall of Fame in his first year of eligibility. The left-hander's career spanned 24 years with the Cardinals, Phillies, Giants, White Sox, Indians, and Twins. Carlton was 329-244 with an earned-run average (ERA) of 3.22 and finished with 4,136 strikeouts, the most ever by a left-hander. He won the first of his four Cy Young Awards in 1972 with the Phillies, when he was 27-10 with a 1.98 ERA.

Managers Hired and Fired. There were no managerial changes during the abbreviated season, but soon after its cancellation Butch Hobson of the Boston Red Sox, Hal McRae of the Kansas City Royals, Johnny Oates of the Baltimore Orioles, Tom Trebelhorn of the Chicago Cubs, and Kevin Kennedy of the Texas Rangers were dismissed. McRae was replaced by Bob Boone, and Oates by Phil Regan. Kennedy got the post in Boston, and Oates took Kennedy's old job. Jim Riggleman left the San Diego Padres to become the manager of the Cubs; he was replaced by third-base coach Bruce Bochy.

New League. In September a group of promoters announced plans to form a new baseball league. Called the United Baseball League, it would be launched in 1996 with teams in ten cities, including one in Mexico.

B.K.

MAJOR LEAGUE BASEBALL FINAL STANDINGS, 1994

American League

Eastern Division	W	L	Pct.	GB
New York Yankees	70	43	.619	—
Baltimore Orioles	63	49	.563	6½
Toronto Blue Jays	55	60	.478	16
Boston Red Sox	54	61	.470	17
Detroit Tigers	53	62	.461	18

Central Division	W	L	Pct.	GB
Chicago White Sox	67	46	.593	—
Cleveland Indians	66	47	.584	1
Kansas City Royals	64	51	.557	4
Minnesota Twins	53	60	.469	14
Milwaukee Brewers	53	62	.461	15

Western Division	W	L	Pct.	GB
Texas Rangers	52	62	.456	—
Oakland Athletics	51	63	.447	1
Seattle Mariners	49	63	.438	2
California Angels	47	68	.409	5½

National League

Eastern Division	W	L	Pct.	GB
Montréal Expos	74	40	.649	—
Atlanta Braves	68	46	.596	6
New York Mets	55	58	.487	18½
Philadelphia Phillies	54	61	.470	20½
Florida Marlins	51	64	.443	23½

Central Division	W	L	Pct.	GB
Cincinnati Reds	66	48	.579	—
Houston Astros	66	49	.574	½
Pittsburgh Pirates	53	61	.465	13
St. Louis Cardinals	53	61	.465	13
Chicago Cubs	49	64	.434	16½

Western Division	W	L	Pct.	GB
Los Angeles Dodgers	58	56	.509	—
San Francisco Giants	55	60	.478	3½
Colorado Rockies	53	64	.453	6½
San Diego Padres	47	70	.402	12½

BASKETBALL

In 1994, Arkansas won the National Collegiate Athletic Association (NCAA) championship, and the Houston Rockets ended the Chicago Bulls' three-year reign as the National Basketball Association (NBA) champion by defeating the New York Knickerbockers.

College. *NCAA Men's Season.* March madness came to a frenzied end on April 4 at the Charlotte (NC) Coliseum with Arkansas defeating Duke, 76-72. In completing a 31-3 season with their chief fan, President Bill Clinton, cheering them on, the Razorbacks kept Duke (28-6) from winning a third championship in four years. Arkansas had advanced to the finals by defeating Arizona, 91-82, while Duke eliminated Florida, 70-65.

The championship was decided in the final minute when sophomore Scotty Thurman's three-point basket with 50.7 seconds remaining broke a 70-70 tie. Thurman's shot, with Antonio Lang, Duke's 6'8" forward, lunging toward him with arms outstretched, came with one second left on the 35-second shooting clock and put the Razorbacks ahead to stay.

Previously, Grant Hill, the Duke star who shot four for 11 from the field and had nine of his team's 23 turnovers, had deadlocked the game with a dramatic three-pointer with 1:30 remaining. Arkansas coach Nolan Richardson, the Coach of the Year, then called a time-out. His plan was to get the ball to Corliss Williamson, the Final Four's Most Outstanding Player, but point guard Corey Beck could not get the ball to Williamson and had to pass to Dwight Stewart at the top of the key. Stewart then passed to Thurman, who took the three-point shot. The Razorbacks scored inside and outside and from three-point range, but it was their full-court pressure defense, half-court traps, and a thick zone that troubled the Duke players, Hill in particular.

Arkansas's first national championship in 53 years of basketball was the perfect ending to a tumultuous season. With the shot clock reduced from 45 to 35 seconds, the most talented teams were expected to dominate. Instead, increased use of the three-point shot created upset after upset. That was illustrated in a record season in which six different teams held the No. 1 spot in the national polls.

Hog Heaven. *Led by the stellar play at both ends of the court of forward Corliss Williamson (right), the Arkansas Razorbacks defeated Duke on April 4 to win the National Collegiate Athletic Association men's basketball crown. Williamson was named Most Outstanding Player in the championship tournament's Final Four.*

A new NCAA rule stipulated that a student opting to be eligible for the NBA draft before the senior year can back out if dissatisfied with the outcome. Such a change of mind is allowed for 30 days after the draft, and a player may exercise the option only once during a college career. Purdue's Glenn Robinson, the College Player of the Year and the year's top scorer, was selected by the Milwaukee Bucks as the first player in the 1994 NBA draft.

North Carolina Women. Charlotte Smith, better known as a rebounder than a scorer, hit a three-pointer at the buzzer to give North Carolina an improbable 60-59 victory over Louisiana Tech and its first title in the 13-year history of the NCAA women's tournament. With seven-tenths of a second remaining and the Lady Techsters ahead, 59-57, the Tar Heels

Shot heard round the world. *With a mere seventenths of a second remaining in the game, Charlotte Smith of North Carolina shoots the three-point basket that gave her team a 60-59 victory over Louisiana Tech in the final game of the women's National Collegiate Athletic Association tournament.*

had the ball under the Louisiana Tech basket. Stephanie Lawrence then snapped a pass to Smith, a 6-foot junior, who unleashed a 20-footer that swished through the basket. Smith, who set a championship game record with 23 rebounds, was named the Final Four's Most Outstanding Player.

Other Championships. In beating Southern Indiana, 92-86, California State-Bakersfield became the first team to defend its NCAA men's Division II title since Kentucky Wesleyan in 1968 and 1969. In Division III, New York University was beaten by Lebanon Valley, PA, 66-59, in overtime. In women's play, North Dakota State defeated California State-San Bernadino, 89-56, for Division II honors; Capital of Columbus, OH, won the Division III

title by defeating Washington University of St. Louis, 82-63.

In championships on other levels, Oklahoma City won the National Association of Intercollegiate Athletics title by defeating Life College of Georgia, 99-81. Hutchinson Community College (KS) edged Three Rivers (MO), 78-74, for National Junior College honors. Villanova won the National Invitation Tournament by outscoring Vanderbilt, 80-73.

Professional. *Houston's Dream Season.* Hakeem ("The Dream") Olajuwon (*see profile in* PEOPLE IN THE NEWS) lived up to his nickname by taking the Houston Rockets along for one of the dreamiest rides in NBA history. En route to his selection as the first player to win the league's Most Valuable Player award, Defensive Player of the Year honors, and selection as the finals MVP in the same season, the 31-year-old center carried his teammates from a record-tying 15 straight victories at the season's start all the way to the championship.

It was the lowest-scoring series in 40 years. Not since the introduction of the 24-second shooting clock for the 1954-1955 season had there been a seven-game series in which each team failed to score 100 points at least once. Houston scored the fewest points in any seven-game playoff series in NBA history—603, an average of 86.1 points. The Knicks scored the second fewest, 608, or 86.9. But scoring was off for the whole season, which saw an average drop of nearly five points a team, or ten points a game.

As if to deny the scoring drought, David Robinson of the San Antonio Spurs scored 71 points in the final game of the regular season to edge Shaquille O'Neal of the Orlando Magic for the scoring title. Robinson, the first center to win the scoring championship since Bob McAdoo of the Buffalo Braves in 1976, finished with 2,383 points in 80 games, an average of 29.787 to O'Neal's 29.346.

Playoffs. The Denver Nuggets, seeded No. 8 in the Western Conference after a 42-40 finish, turned the playoffs into a free-for-all in the opening round by upsetting the top-ranked Seattle SuperSonics (63-19) in a five-game series. It was the first time since 1984 (when the NBA adopted its current playoff format) that a last seed defeated a No. 1.

The finals matched two of the game's finest centers, Olajuwon and Patrick Ewing. The series began in Houston on June 8 with an 85-78 Rocket victory in which Olajuwon had 28 points. Two nights later the Knicks, playing the style that earned them honors as the league's best defensive team, tied the series with a 91-83 triumph. The series then moved to New York for three games. Houston scored the final seven points of Game Three, including a three-pointer by rookie Sam Cassell with 32.6 seconds remaining, for a 93-89 victory on June 12. Three nights later, 21 late points—in-

Star of stars. *The Indiana Pacers' irrepressible Reggie Miller was hitting on all cylinders as he led the U.S. squad ("Dream Team II") to an easy victory in the World Championship of Basketball tournament in Toronto. Miller hit 30 three-pointers as the Dream Teamers won their eight games by an average of 37.8 points.*

NATIONAL BASKETBALL ASSOCIATION, 1993-1994

REGULAR SEASON

Eastern Conference

Atlantic Division	W	L	Pct.	GB
New York Knicks	57	25	.695	—
Orlando Magic	50	32	.610	7
New Jersey Nets	45	37	.549	12
Miami Heat	42	40	.512	15
Boston Celtics	32	50	.390	25
Philadelphia 76ers	25	57	.305	32
Washington Bullets	24	58	.293	33

Central Divison	W	L	Pct.	GB
Atlanta Hawks	57	25	.695	—
Chicago Bulls	55	27	.671	2
Cleveland Cavaliers	47	35	.573	10
Indiana Pacers	47	35	.573	10
Charlotte Hornets	41	41	.500	16
Detroit Pistons	20	62	.244	37
Milwaukee Bucks	20	62	.244	37

Western Conference

Midwest Division	W	L	Pct.	GB
Houston Rockets	58	24	.707	—
San Antonio Spurs	55	27	.671	3
Utah Jazz	53	29	.646	5
Denver Nuggets	42	40	.512	16
Minnesota Timberwolves	20	62	.244	38
Dallas Mavericks	13	69	.159	45

Pacific Division	W	L	Pct.	GB
Seattle SuperSonics	63	19	.768	—
Phoenix Suns	56	26	.683	7
Golden State Warriors	50	32	.610	13
Portland Trail Blazers	47	35	.573	16
Los Angeles Lakers	33	49	.402	30
Sacramento Kings	28	54	.341	35
Los Angeles Clippers	27	55	.329	36

PLAYOFFS

First Round
Atlanta defeated Miami, 3 games to 2
New York defeated New Jersey, 3 games to 1
Chicago defeated Cleveland, 3 games to 0
Indiana defeated Orlando, 3 games to 0
Denver defeated Seattle, 3 games to 2
Houston defeated Portland, 3 games to 1
Phoenix defeated Golden State, 3 games to 0
Utah defeated San Antonio, 3 games to 1

Second Round
New York defeated Chicago, 4 games to 3
Indiana defeated Atlanta, 4 games to 2
Houston defeated Phoenix, 4 games to 3
Utah defeated Denver, 4 games to 3

Conference Finals
New York defeated Indiana, 4 games to 3
Houston defeated Utah, 4 games to 1

Championship Finals
Houston defeated New York, 4 games to 3

cluding five three-pointers by Derek Harper—enabled the Knicks to tie the series with a 91-82 win. On June 17 the Knicks took a 3-2 advantage by outscoring the Rockets, 13-4, during the final three minutes for a 91-84 victory. The series returned to Houston for the final games. In Game Six on June 19, Houston preserved an 86-84 victory when Olajuwon blocked John Starks's potential game-winning three-pointer with two seconds left. In the final game on June 22, Olajuwon's 25 points sparked Houston to a 90-84 victory and the long-awaited championship.

Odds and Ends.   After a 13-year playing career with the Detroit Pistons, 12 as an All Star guard, Isiah Thomas began a new career as part owner and vice president of the Toronto Raptors, which, along with the Vancouver Grizzlies, were slated to join the NBA as an expansion franchise for the 1995-1996 season.

Months after coaching the University of Wisconsin to its first NCAA tournament berth in 47 years, Stu Jackson was named Vancouver's vice president and general manager.

Earvin ("Magic") Johnson, who had long wanted to be an NBA owner, finally achieved his goal by purchasing an undisclosed percentage of the Lakers from Jerry Buss, the majority owner.

The unbeaten United States (Dream Team II) overwhelmed Russia, 137-91, to win the world championship of basketball in Toronto.

Among several rule changes adopted by the NBA in October, the three-point line was brought in to a uniform 22 feet from the basket, and three foul shots were to be awarded to a player fouled while shooting a three-pointer.

S.G.

BOXING

When 1994 began, Evander Holyfield of Atlanta and Lennox Lewis of Great Britain held the world heavyweight championships. When it ended, the champions were 45-year-old George Foreman of Houston, the oldest ever to hold the title, and Oliver McCall of Chicago. And McCall was preparing for his first defense against Larry Holmes of Easton, PA, like Foreman a 45-year-old former champion.

Holyfield lost the World Boxing Association (WBA) and International Boxing Federation (IBF) versions of the title on April 22 in Las Vegas on a majority decision to Michael Moorer of Monessen, PA. Moorer became the first left-handed heavyweight champion in the history of boxing.

Then Moorer, in his first defense, fought Foreman on November 5 in Las Vegas. Foreman, a 3-to-1 underdog, was losing and his left eye was almost punched shut when he landed a straight right to the jaw in the tenth round.

George Foreman

On November 5, 45-year-old boxer George Foreman regained his long-lost world heavyweight title. Knocking Michael Moorer, 26, to the canvas with a right-hand punch, Foreman became the oldest champion ever. He had been saving that "hambone to the chin" ever since he lost the title to Muhammad Ali in 1974.

The Texas-born Foreman had a troubled childhood and dropped out of junior high school. He joined the Job Corps and learned discipline from the boxing instructor at an industrial training center. After winning a gold medal in the 1968 Olympics, he turned pro, upsetting Joe Frazier for the heavyweight crown in 1973. Four years later, Foreman quit boxing to become a storefront preacher in Houston. He also "started enjoyin' life. Started eatin'!"

Foreman returned to boxing in 1987—partly to make money for his parish—and the Moorer victory raised his record since then to 28-2. The amiable preacher-fighter, whose five sons are all named George, is a familiar figure on television, where he has hawked fast food and mufflers and starred in a 1993 sitcom, *George.*   W.A.M.

Moorer went down and was counted out, and Foreman, who had lost the title 20 years before to Muhammad Ali, became a champion again. Later, at age 23, Moorer retired.

Lewis said McCall did not "command respect," but on September 25 in London, McCall stopped the heavily favored Lewis in the second round and took his World Boxing Council (WBC) title. McCall then announced plans to meet Holmes early in 1995.

McCall, who was once a $2,000-a-week sparring partner for Mike Tyson, said he wanted to fight Tyson in 1995 after Tyson's scheduled release from an Indiana prison, where he was serving a six-year sentence for rape. It was a frustrating year for Tyson. The U.S. Supreme Court declined to hear his appeal, rejecting his claim that he had been denied a fair trial. An Indiana judge refused to reduce Tyson's sentence to time already served. And Tyson failed a high-school equivalency exam. Had he passed, he would have had six months trimmed from his sentence.

Foreman and Holmes were not the only active former champions. Roberto Duran of Panama was still fighting at age 43, and Alexis Arguello of Nicaragua, retired for eight years, returned to the ring at age 42.

The world champion with the greatest longevity, 35-year-old Azumah Nelson of Ghana, was defeated by Jesse James Leija, losing the WBC superfeatherweight title he had held since 1988. Pernell Whitaker of Norfolk, VA, perhaps the sport's best fighter, outpointed Santos Cardona of Puerto Rico and Buddy McGirt of New York in defense of his WBC welterweight title.

Julio César Chávez of Mexico lost his WBC superlightweight title to Frankie Randall of Morristown, TN, then regained it in a rematch when the fight was stopped because a head butt by Randall had opened a cut over Chávez's eye.   F.L.

FOOTBALL

The collegiate bowl games following the 1994 season saw the Nebraska Cornhuskers finally win the national title that had been eluding them for so many years. The National Football League's season was crowned by Super Bowl XXIX in early 1995, with the San Francisco 49ers demolishing the San Diego Chargers.

College. Once again the two top college teams did not meet in a postseason bowl game, and the national championship was determined by the polls. Number two Penn State, as Big Ten champion, was committed to go to the Rose Bowl, while number one Nebraska went to the Orange Bowl.

The Nebraska Cornhuskers ended years of frustration on New Year's night with a 24-17 victory over Miami in the Orange Bowl that gave Coach Tom Osborne the first national championship of his illustrious career. The victory came a year after Nebraska lost a chance at a national title with an 18-16 loss to Florida State in the Orange Bowl. Against Miami, Nebraska rallied from a 17-7 deficit behind two touchdown runs by fullback Cory Schlesinger in the fourth quarter. The victory

Rocky Mountain high. Colorado's tailback Rashaan Salaam was the easy winner of the Heisman Trophy as the best player in college football. He led the nation in rushing, scoring, and all-purpose yards.

ended Nebraska's seven-game losing streak in bowls; it gave the Cornhuskers a 13-0 record and earned them first place in both the Associated Press and *USA Today*/CNN polls.

Penn State, which also finished undefeated—beating surprising Oregon, 38-20, in the Rose Bowl—was second in both polls. The Nittany Lions scored at least 31 points in every game and set 11 school records on offense during the season. In a rare bowl rematch, Florida State extended its nation-best bowl-winning streak to ten games with a 23-17 victory over Florida in the Sugar Bowl. The teams had played to a 31-31 tie late in the regular season. In the Fiesta Bowl, Colorado easily defeated Notre Dame, 41-24. The loss put the finishing touches on a disappointing season for the Irish, who finished with a 6-5-1 mark. In the most lopsided bowl matchup, Southern Cal set Cotton Bowl records for points and total yards in a 55-14 demolition of Texas Tech. Texas Tech finished in a five-way tie for the Southwest Conference title but was awarded the Cotton Bowl bid because, of the five contenders, it had the longest span since its last appearance in the game.

Colorado's Rashaan Salaam, who became only the fourth running back in Division I-A history to gain 2,000 yards in a season and also led the country in touchdowns, was the recipient of the Heisman Trophy, given annually to the top player in the country. Salaam easily outdistanced Penn State running back Ki-Jana Carter and Alcorn State quarterback Steve McNair in the voting. McNair attracted more attention than any Division I-AA player in recent history after setting several passing records and becoming college football's all-time leader in total offense. In addition to being a Heisman finalist (a major accomplishment for a defensive player), Miami defensive tackle Warren Sapp won the Lombardi Award as the nation's top lineman. The Outland Trophy, given to the best interior lineman, went to Nebraska offensive tackle Zach Wiegert, while Illinois linebacker Dana Howard won the Butkus Award.

As always, there were plenty of coaching changes and perhaps none was bigger than Bill Walsh, who led San Francisco to three Super Bowl titles, resigning from his post at Stanford.

Walsh left the Cardinals after posting a 16-17-1 record in three years in his second stint at the school. The most surprising coaching move came when Colorado's Bill McCartney announced after the Buffaloes completed a 10-1 regular season that he was resigning.

The 1994 season, however, may well be remembered for a game that featured one of the most fantastic finishes in college football history. Colorado was trailing Michigan, 26-21, in a battle of undefeated teams at Michigan Stadium on September 24 when quarterback Kordell Stewart unleashed a "Hail Mary" pass that traveled over 70 yards through the air, was tipped near the goal line, and came down in the hands of wide receiver Michael Westbrook to bring about a miraculous, improbable Colorado victory.   A.C.

Professional. Many changes marked the 1994 season of the National Football League (NFL)—new rules that helped the offense, a new coach for the Dallas Cowboys (the coach who led them to the two previous Super Bowl championships lost a battle of egos with club owner Jerry Jones), and new quarterbacks for many teams, largely because of unrestricted free agency and the demands of the salary cap. There was something old, too: the best teams once again were the Cowboys and the San Francisco 49ers.

More Offense. The club owners approved rules that put more excitement into the game. The new rules created more kickoff returns by moving kickoffs back by 5 yards to the 30-yard line and also by reducing the 3-inch kicking tee to 1 inch. They discouraged long field-goal attempts by giving the ball, after a miss, to the other team at the point where the ball was spotted rather than at the line of scrimmage. The club owners helped pass receivers by ordering stricter enforcement of the rule that barred defensive contact with potential receivers more than 5 yards downfield. Pass blocking was aided by allowing some offensive linemen to line up a little behind the line of scrimmage. In a boost to trailing teams, the option to run or pass for two points after a touchdown was introduced.

The changes produced the desired results. Scoring rose from 37.4 points per game in 1993 to 40.5, the highest in the 1990s. There were more touchdowns (1,020 against 906 in 1993), fewer field goals (640 against 673 in 1993), and record passing yards (an average of 427 per game).

All that was achieved despite quarterback shuffles that found 20 veterans with new teams. Salary cap or not, bidding was often spirited for free-agent quarterbacks. Jim Harbaugh, Chris Miller, and Erik Kramer signed with new teams as free agents, and Warren Moon, Jim Everett, and Jeff George were traded. The richest contract went to Scott Mitchell, who moved from the Miami Dolphins to the Detroit Lions for $11 million over three years (and proved a disappointment).

Regular Season and Playoffs. The 49ers (13-3) thrived on the quarterbacking of Steve Young, the receiving of Jerry Rice, and the defensive and kick-returning skills of their newly signed cornerback, Deion Sanders. The Cowboys (12-4) remained solid behind quarterback Troy Aikman, running back Emmitt Smith, and Barry Switzer, who had replaced Jimmy Johnson as coach.

In the National Conference wild-card playoff round, Chicago upset Minnesota, 35-18, behind Steve Walsh's passing, and Green Bay eliminated Detroit, 16-12, holding Barry Sanders, the NFL's best runner, to minus 1 yard on 13 carries. The following weekend San Francisco scored on six of its first seven possessions and routed Chicago, 44-15, and Dallas whipped Green Bay, 35-9, as Troy Aikman passed for 337 yards and two touchdowns. In the conference championship game San Francisco beat Dallas, 38-28, as the Cowboys never recovered from committing three turnovers in the first eight minutes, giving the 49ers 21 quick points.

The American Conference playoffs started with Miami defeating Kansas City, 27-17, as Dan Marino outpassed Joe Montana, and Cleveland getting by New England, 20-13, on Vinny Testaverde's control passing. A week later Pittsburgh overran Cleveland, 29-9, with 238 yards rushing, and San Diego beat Miami, 22-21, when Miami's Pete Stoyanovich missed a 48-yard field goal with one second left. Then San Diego surprised everyone by shutting down Pittsburgh's powerful running game, stopping the Steelers on fourth and goal from

the 3-yard line with 68 seconds left and winning the conference title, 17-13.

That sent San Diego up against San Francisco on January 29, 1995, in the first all-California Super Bowl. The 49ers routed the

---

NATIONAL FOOTBALL LEAGUE, 1994

REGULAR SEASON
American Conference

Eastern Division	W	L	T	Pct.
Miami Dolphins[1]	10	6	0	.625
New England Patriots[2]	10	6	0	.625
Indianapolis Colts	8	8	0	.500
Buffalo Bills	7	9	0	.438
New York Jets	6	10	0	.375

Central Division	W	L	T	Pct.
Pittsburgh Steelers[1]	12	4	0	.750
Cleveland Browns[2]	11	5	0	.688
Cincinnati Bengals	3	13	0	.188
Houston Oilers	2	14	0	.125

Western Division	W	L	T	Pct.
San Diego Chargers[1]	11	5	0	.688
Kansas City Chiefs[2]	9	7	0	.563
Los Angeles Raiders	9	7	0	.563
Denver Broncos	7	9	0	.438
Seattle Seahawks	6	10	0	.375

National Conference

Eastern Division	W	L	T	Pct.
Dallas Cowboys[1]	12	4	0	.750
New York Giants	9	7	0	.563
Arizona Cardinals	8	8	0	.500
Philadelphia Eagles	7	9	0	.438
Washington Redskins	3	13	0	.188

Central Division	W	L	T	Pct.
Minnesota Vikings[1]	10	6	0	.625
Green Bay Packers[2]	9	7	0	.563
Detroit Lions[2]	9	7	0	.563
Chicago Bears[2]	9	7	0	.563
Tampa Bay Buccaneers	6	10	0	.373

Western Division	W	L	T	Pct.
San Francisco 49ers[1]	13	3	0	.813
New Orleans Saints	7	9	0	.438
Atlanta Falcons	7	9	0	.438
Los Angeles Rams	4	12	0	.250

[1]Division title, automatic playoff berth
[2]Wild-card playoff berth

PLAYOFFS
Wild-card Games
Green Bay defeated Detroit, 16-12
Chicago defeated Minnesota, 35-18
Miami defeated Kansas City, 27-17
Cleveland defeated New England, 20-13

Divisional Games
San Francisco defeated Chicago, 44-15
Dallas defeated Green Bay, 35-9
Pittsburgh defeated Cleveland, 29-9
San Diego defeated Miami, 22-21

Conference Finals
San Francisco defeated Dallas, 38-28
San Diego defeated Pittsburgh, 17-13

Super Bowl XXIX
San Francisco defeated San Diego, 49-26

Chargers, 49-26, and became the first team to win five Super Bowls. They jumped out to a 14-0 lead with less than five minutes gone in the game and never looked back, as Steve Young set a Super Bowl record by tossing six touchdown passes, three of them to Jerry Rice. Young, who completed 24 of 36 passes for 325 yards, was named the game's Most Valuable Player. It was the 11th time in a row that the National Conference champion had won the Super Bowl.

Other Leagues. The British Columbia Lions won the Canadian Football League's Grey Cup championship game with a last-play field goal that beat the new Baltimore team, 26-23. The Arizona Rattlers won the indoor Arena League title by downing the Orlando Predators, 36-31, on a last-minute touchdown.   F.L.

GOLF

Players from outside the United States swept all four majors on the Professional Golfers' Association (PGA) tour, and two South Africans (Ernie Els and Simon Hobday) captured the U.S. Open and the U.S. Senior Open. If not for team victories in the inaugural Presidents Cup and the women's Solheim Cup—and Mark McCumber winning for a third time in the season-ending Tour Championship—U.S. pride would have suffered a worse blow.

Zimbabwe's Nick Price dominated, breaking his own tour money-winning record with $1,499,927 in earnings and winning seven times—two majors (British Open and PGA Championship), four tour events (Western and Canadian opens, Colonial, and Honda Classic), and one tournament in South Africa. His 50-foot eagle putt at the British Open's 71st hole was perhaps the most memorable stroke of the year, enabling him to overtake surprising leader Jesper Parnevik of Sweden. And Price's performance at Southern Hills in Tulsa, OK, turned the PGA into a runaway and made him the leading candidate for Player of the 1990s.

The other majors were won by players considered tomorrow's superstars. Spain's José-María Olazábal used his scrambling mastery to win his first major, the Masters. The key hole was the 15th, where he sank an eagle putt and then watched his main pursuer, American Tom Lehman, narrowly miss his own eagle try. Olazábal also won the World Series of Golf

and several events in Europe. South Africa's Ernie Els realized his promise by taking big titles on three continents, including the U.S. Open. Els made a clutch 4-foot putt on the 72nd green at Oakmont to get into an 18-hole playoff with Loren Roberts and Scotland's Colin Montgomerie. Els and Roberts were still tied after an extra 18; then Els won with a par on the second sudden-death hole.

Australia's Greg Norman had another good year. He won the Vardon Trophy (for lowest scoring average) for a third time even though his only win in 1994 was a record-setting 24-under effort at the Players Championship.

Among U.S. players, Fred Couples hurt his back at the Doral in March and never got back to the top level. Paul Azinger sat out most of the year battling lymphoma in his shoulder. Payne Stewart changed equipment but struggled all year. Long-hitting John Daly won the BellSouth Classic in Atlanta in May but finished the year on a "voluntary suspension" following an altercation with an elderly observer at the World Series of Golf.

England's Laura Davies established herself as the clear-cut top player on the Ladies Professional Golf Association Tour, winning three times, twice in Europe and once in Asia. Other leading players included Sweden's Liselotte Neumann, who totaled five wins on both sides of the Atlantic; Patty Sheehan, who won her second U.S. Open and her fifth major; 38-year-old Beth Daniel, whose startling comeback after two winless years featured four victories; and rising star Donna Andrews, whose three wins included the Dinah Shore.

On the Senior PGA Tour, Lee Trevino was again dominant, winning six times. Raymond Floyd won one senior tour major, the Tradition, but lost another, the PGA Seniors Championship, to Trevino; Floyd hit two balls in the water at the 15th hole on the last day and lost a four-shot lead.

The player who most dominated his peers was probably amateur Eldrick ("Tiger") Woods. In August he won the Western Amateur and became the youngest player and the first black golfer to win the U.S. Amateur. He also led the U.S. team to victory in the World Amateur Team Championship (Eisenhower Trophy) near Paris.

Tiger, tiger, burning bright. *At age 18, Eldrick ("Tiger") Woods helped lead the U.S. team to victory in the World Amateur Team Championship in France in October and thus solidified his place as one of the most exciting young golfers to come along in years.*

Stanford won its first National Collegiate Athletic Association championship since 1953. Wendy Ward of San Antonio helped her Arizona State team earn its second straight NCAA title and led the U.S. win in the Women's World Amateur Team Championship (Espirito Santo Trophy). G.V.S.

HARNESS AND HORSE RACING

Despite his withdrawal from the Triple Crown series following an uncharacteristically dull effort in the Kentucky Derby and his absence from the season-ending Breeders' Cup, Holy Bull was the dominant equine figure throughout the 1994 season. Tabasco Cat won the final two-thirds of the Triple Crown, but neither he nor Kentucky Derby winner Go For Gin was capable of defeating Holy Bull when they met later in the year. Paradise Creek dominated turf racing from January until November, when he was defeated in the Breeders' Cup.

Three-year-olds. With the early favorite, Dehere, out of training after having been injured two months prior to the Kentucky Derby, Go For Gin staged an upset victory at Churchill Downs. The Derby winner lost the winning touch, however, and finished runner-up to Tabasco Cat in the Preakness in Baltimore and the Belmont Stakes in New York.

After his never-explained failure in the Derby, Holy Bull went on to dominate. His owner and trainer, Warren ("Jimmy") Croll, restructured the gray colt's campaign after the Derby, and Holy Bull performed brilliantly through the remainder of the season, defeating top-class older horses in the prestigious Metropolitan Handicap in New York and dominating other three-year-olds in the Haskell Invitational in New Jersey and the Travers Stakes at Saratoga Springs, NY, where he defeated both Tabasco Cat and Concern, the eventual Breeders' Cup Classic winner. Ineligible for the Breeders' Cup because of Croll's failure to nominate him as a yearling, Holy Bull concluded his campaign in the Woodward Stakes at Belmont Park, NY, where he easily defeated a field that included Go For Gin, as well as the season's leading older horses.

Older Horses. Paradise Creek, who raced exclusively on grass courses, was at age five the leading figure among older Thoroughbreds. Although he failed to win the Breeders' Cup Turf in his final race in the United States, Paradise Creek sustained a January-to-November campaign during which he won eight stakes races, including the Arlington Million and the Washington, DC, International over the best available American and European competition.

Female Horses. Both Sky Beauty, the season's dominant older female, and Heavenly Prize, the most accomplished of the female three-year-olds, were defeated in the Breeders' Cup Distaff, which went to long shot One Dreamer. Nevertheless, Sky Beauty won five important races prior to the Breeders' Cup. Heavenly Prize, ill during the early portion of the season, emerged in midsummer and won three important races, the Alabama Stakes, Gazelle Handicap, and Beldame Stakes, all run in New York.

Milestones. Jockey Mike Smith broke his own single-season record for number of stakes winners ridden with 64 when he rode Cherokee Run and Tikkanen to victories in Breeders' Cup races. Smith also became the first rider whose mounts earned purses in excess of $15

Unbeata-bull. With jockey Mike Smith aboard, Holy Bull thunders down the stretch at Belmont Park, NY, in September to win the Woodward Stakes by five lengths. It was an impressive win over a star-studded field. The victory made the gray colt a shoo-in for Horse of the Year.

million in a single season. Inductees to the Hall of Fame were former jockey Steve Cauthen; trainer Jimmy Croll; and horses Arts and Letters, Ta Wee, Eight Thirty, and Flatterer.

Harness Racing. The three-year-old pacer Cam's Card Shark won only one of the Triple Crown races in his division but was, nevertheless, harness racing's dominant figure for most of the season. Cam's Card Shark won the Messenger Stakes, North America Cup, and Meadowlands Pace.

Magical Mike won the Little Brown Jug at Delaware, OH, in September. Victory Dream won the Hambletonian in August at the Meadowlands in New Jersey and interrupted a bid by Bullville Victory for the Trotting Triple Crown. Bullville Victory won the series's first leg, the Yonkers Trot, and the last, the Kentucky Futurity.   P.Mo.

ICE HOCKEY

The 1993-1994 National Hockey League (NHL) season saw the New York Rangers win their first Stanley Cup in 54 years. The 1994-1995 season was postponed, however, because of the inability of the owners and the players to sign a new collective bargaining agreement.

Stanley Cup. The Rangers, featuring a roster with a strong balance of experience and youth, defeated the Vancouver Canucks, 3-2, in Game Seven of the Stanley Cup finals on June 14, 1994, in New York City's Madison Square Garden. The triumph rewarded a lengthy effort by the Rangers under their new coach, Mike Keenan, and ended the "curse" that loyal Ranger fans had endured since the Rangers had last earned the NHL title, in 1940. (Keenan left the Rangers after the end of the season to become the coach of the St. Louis Blues. He was replaced in New York by Colin Campbell.)

The Rangers had built up a seemingly insurmountable 3-1 lead in games during the best-of-seven set. They lost the opener at home on May 31 but then ran off three straight victories—winning 3-1 at home on June 2, 5-1 at Vancouver's Pacific Coliseum on June 4, and 4-2 at Vancouver on June 7. However, the Canucks spoiled the victory party at New York on June 9 with a 6-3 conquest, then squared the series at 3-3 with a 4-1 triumph on home ice on June 11.

NHL Playoffs. The Rangers had a grueling path to their first Stanley Cup final since 1979.

NATIONAL HOCKEY LEAGUE, 1993-1994

REGULAR SEASON
Eastern Conference

Atlantic Division	W	L	T	P
New York Rangers	52	24	8	112
New Jersey Devils	47	25	12	106
Washington Capitals	39	35	10	88
New York Islanders	36	36	12	84
Florida Panthers	33	34	17	83
Philadelphia Flyers	35	39	10	80
Tampa Bay Lightning	30	43	11	71

Northeast Division	W	L	T	P
Pittsburgh Penguins	44	27	13	101
Boston Bruins	42	29	13	97
Montréal Canadiens	41	29	14	96
Buffalo Sabres	43	32	9	95
Québec Nordiques	34	42	8	76
Hartford Whalers	27	48	9	63
Ottawa Senators	14	61	9	37

Western Conference

Central Division	W	L	T	P
Detroit Red Wings	46	30	8	100
Toronto Maple Leafs	43	29	12	98
Dallas Stars	42	29	13	97
St. Louis Blues	40	33	11	91
Chicago Blackhawks	39	36	9	87
Winnipeg Jets	24	51	9	57

Pacific Division	W	L	T	P
Calgary Flames	42	29	13	97
Vancouver Canucks	41	40	3	85
San Jose Sharks	33	35	16	82
Anaheim Mighty Ducks	33	46	5	71
Los Angeles Kings	27	45	12	66
Edmonton Oilers	25	45	14	64

PLAYOFFS
Conference Quarterfinals
NY Rangers defeated NY Islanders, 4 games to 0
New Jersey defeated Buffalo, 4 games to 3
Washington defeated Pittsburgh, 4 games to 2
Boston defeated Montréal, 4 games to 3
San Jose defeated Detroit, 4 games to 3
Toronto defeated Chicago, 4 games to 2
Vancouver defeated Calgary, 4 games to 3
Dallas defeated St. Louis, 4 games to 0

Conference Semifinals
NY Rangers defeated Washington, 4 games to 1
New Jersey defeated Boston, 4 games to 2
Toronto defeated San Jose, 4 games to 3
Vancouver defeated Dallas, 4 games to 1

Conference Finals
NY Rangers defeated New Jersey, 4 games to 3
Vancouver defeated Toronto, 4 games to 1

Stanley Cup Finals
NY Rangers defeated Vancouver, 4 games to 3

Though they swept the New York Islanders and rolled over the Washington Capitals in the first two rounds, the Eastern Conference final was another story. The New Jersey Devils assumed a 3-2 lead in games, then mounted a 2-0 lead after one period in Game Six on home ice. However, New York's Mark Messier (*see profile in* PEOPLE IN THE NEWS) scored three times in the third period to bring the Rangers a 4-2 victory. In Game Seven at New York, Stephane Matteau scored at 4:24 of the second overtime to provide the Rangers with a clinching 2-1 triumph.

The Canucks, meanwhile, were on the brink of elimination in the first round when they fell behind, 3-1, in games to the Calgary Flames. But the Canucks rallied to win the Western Conference quarterfinals. They then beat the Dallas Stars and Toronto Maple Leafs to advance to the finals.

The Flames, who had finished atop the Pacific Division during the regular season, were not the only first-place team to be upset. The Detroit Red Wings, who won the Central Division, were spilled by the San Jose Sharks, decided underdogs, and the Pittsburgh Penguins, who finished first in the Northeast Division, were knocked out by Washington, also in the opening round.

Regular Season. With Gary Bettman serving his first full season as commissioner, the NHL enjoyed a boom in two new areas. The expansion Anaheim Mighty Ducks proved to be a solid organization. Their regalia were wildly popular on the marketing front, and the team finished ahead of the rival Los Angeles Kings, an established franchise. The Florida Panthers, playing in Miami, fared even better, as they missed qualifying for the playoffs by a single point. The Kings' Wayne Gretzky rebounded from a serious injury the previous season to amass 38 goals and 92 assists for 130 points and his tenth scoring title. Sergei Fedorov of Detroit finished second with 56 goals and 64 assists for 120 points.

Labor Woes. The 1994-1995 NHL season did not begin on October 1 as scheduled because the team owners and the players' association could not come to terms on a range of issues, including a tax plan that would penalize teams whose payrolls exceeded a set limit. The players charged that this amounted to a salary cap that would limit players' salaries. Negotiations dragged on fruitlessly through autumn, and in mid-December, Bettman announced that if no agreement had been reached by January 16, 1995, the season would be canceled entirely.

World Championships. Canada defeated Finland to win the World Ice Hockey Championships at Milan, Italy. The title was the first for Canada since 1961.

See SPORTS: Winter Olympics. B.V.

SKIING

The eyes of the competitive skiing world were firmly fixed on the Olympics in Lillehammer, Norway, during the 1994 season (*see* SPORTS: Winter Olympics), but those games were merely one stop for the sport's elite.

In the men's Alpine World Cup final standings, Norway's Kjetil-Andre Aamodt toppled defending champion Marc Girardelli of Luxembourg with a total of 1,392 points. Girardelli was second, and Italy's flamboyant Alberto Tomba edged Austria's Guenther Mader by a single point for third. Aamodt won the combined, Girardelli the downhill, Tomba the slalom, Austria's Christian Mayer the giant slalom, and Norway's Jan Einar Thorsen the Super G.

Switzerland's Vreni Schneider conquered the women's Alpine World Cup field, taking first place with 1,656 points. Sweden's Pernilla Wiberg came in second, and Germany's Katja Seizinger was third. Seizinger won both the downhill and the Super G, while Schneider was first in the slalom, Austria's Anita Wachter took the giant slalom, and Wiberg won the combined.

Austria defended its Nations Cup crown scoring 8,852 points overall, including the men's title, but Germany won the women's title with 3,786. Switzerland again placed second overall with 6,314, and Italy placed third with 6,054.

Patrick Staub of Switzerland won the slalom en route to taking the Europa Cup title with 145 points. His countryman Urs Kaelin was second. In the women's competition, Canada's Melanie Turgeon was first with 138, followed by Norway's Anne Berge.

In the Nordic World Cup, Kazakhstan's Vladimir Smirnov returned to his championship form of 1991, winning the men's cross-country title with 830 points. Defending champion Bjorn Dahlie of Norway was second. Another champion fell in the women's field as Italy's Manuela Di Centa amassed 790 points, edging Russia's Lyubov Yegorova by 50.

The United States won its ninth consecutive crown in freestyle skiing. Russia's Sergei Shu-

pletsov won the World Cup men's title, and Canada's David Belhumeur was second. American Kristean Porter won the women's overall with 156 points, shading Russian Natalia Orekhova by a mere 1.5.

Austrian Bernhard Knauss was the top money winner on the U.S. Professional Tour, earning $241,671, but he finished fourth in the overall standings. Sebastian Vitzthum finished first in the standings, as Austrians swept the top five places. Sweden's Camilla Lundback finished first in the women's standings and was first on the women's money list with earnings of $97,337. D.L.

SOCCER

The World Cup inevitably dominated the 1994 soccer scene (*see the feature article* WORLD CUP '94: SOCCER'S BIG SHOW COMES TO THE UNITED STATES), but there was plenty of life beyond the tournament. Early in the year the African Nations championship was won by Nigeria, while in December the Toyota Cup, for the world's top club team, was captured by Velez Sarsfield of Argentina.

FIFA (Fédération Internationale de Football Association), the world governing body of soccer, expanded its membership to 191 nations, largely by incorporating the new countries formed as a result of the breakup of the Soviet Union. The World Cup itself, which FIFA organizes, was also enlarged. Starting with the 1998 competition, to be staged in France, the final rounds of the tournament will feature 32 teams—up from the 24 that played in the United States in 1994. The second Women's World Cup was scheduled to be staged in Sweden in 1995. (The first, played in China in 1991, was won by the United States.)

João Havelange, the formidable 78-year-old Brazilian who had been president of FIFA since 1974, was reelected in 1994 for another four-year term. An incipient opposition movement, led by those who felt Havelange was too old, was ruthlessly quashed.

In the United States the highly successful staging of the 1994 World Cup produced contradictory results. The good news was the $40 million in profits that went into the coffers of the United States Soccer Foundation to be used for promoting the sport of soccer within the United States. Yet the man largely responsible for this windfall—Alan Rothenberg, the World Cup's chairman and chief executive officer—barely scraped home when, soon after the end of the tournament, he stood for reelection as president of the United States Soccer Federation.

There was widespread disquiet among the soccer community—made up almost entirely of volunteers—at the size of Rothenberg's personal gain from World Cup '94: a salary of $4 million, plus a $3 million bonus. The criticism of Rothenberg's compensation increased when, in November, he finally admitted—after many delays and assertions that everything was on course—that the much-awaited professional major league would not begin operations in 1995. When FIFA, in 1988, had granted the United States the rights to stage the 1994 World Cup tournament, it had expressed the strong desire that a major national professional league (lacking since the demise of the

North American Soccer League in 1984) should be formed. But lining up investors in the league proved to be much more difficult than expected.

The league—Major League Soccer (MLS)—was postponed until 1996. The benefits of what Rothenberg himself had termed "catching the wave"—the timely exploitation of the enthusiasm generated by the 1994 World Cup—were now lost.

The delay also opened up the possibility of a 1996 confrontation with the struggling American Professional Soccer League, which was the beneficiary of an unopposed year in which to strengthen itself. Originally envisaged as a 12-team league, the proposed 1996 version of the MLS included only ten sites. Eight of these were named in November 1994: Chicago; Columbus, OH; Boston; Los Angeles; New Jersey/New York; San Jose, CA; Tampa, FL; and Washington, DC.   P.G.

SWIMMING

Over a three-week period in August and September 1994, Kieren Perkins, a 20-year-old Australian distance freestyler, won four gold medals and broke two world records in the Commonwealth Games and then won two gold medals and broke one world record in the world championships.

In most years his achievements would have been the most important in the sport. But in 1994 they were overshadowed by the feats of the Chinese women, who won 12 of their 16 finals in the world championships, held September 5-11 in Rome, while setting five world records. Although the Chinese had won four women's gold medals in the 1991 world championships and four more in the 1992 Olympics, their overwhelming success in these championships led to charges by coaches, officials, and other swimmers that the Chinese had used banned bodybuilding drugs. Chinese officials denied the allegations, but at the Asian Games in October, 11 Chinese athletes—seven of them swimmers—tested positive for performance-enhancing drugs. All seven swimmers, including Lu Bin, who won three gold medals in Rome and four at the Asian Games, were subsequently banned for two years.

In the world championships the United

Flying feet. *Eddie Newton of Chelsea (right) tries to get the ball away from Manchester United's Paul Ince as their teams square off in London's Wembley Stadium in May in the English Football Association Cup final, a game won by Manchester United, 4-0. United had taken the English Premier League crown two weeks earlier and thus became only the fourth team in the 20th century to win both titles.*

Record triumph. *Freestyler Kieren Perkins of Australia broke two world records in one race at the Commonwealth Games in August.*

States won four gold medals, ten silver, and seven bronze, and its total of 21 led all nations. China was next with 19, all by its women. The only U.S. individual winners, however, were Janet Evans, the defender, in the women's 800-meter freestyle (8 minutes 29.85 seconds) and Tom Dolan in the men's 400-meter individual medley (4:12.30, a world record).

The three world records set by Perkins were 3:43.80 for 400 meters, 7:46.00 for 800 meters, and 14:41.66 in the 1,500 meters, the last two records coming in the same race. Aleksandr Popov of Russia lowered the men's 100-meter freestyle record to 48.21 seconds, and Le Jingyi of China set women's freestyle records of 24.51 seconds for 50 meters and 54.01 seconds for 100 meters.

In the Goodwill Games, held July 22 to August 7 in St. Petersburg, Russia, a breakdown in the filtration system led to discolored water and forced all races to be swum on one day. Of the 20 events, the United States won six, Russia won six, and China won five. In the

Commonwealth Games, held August 19-24 in Victoria, British Columbia, Australia won 24 of the 32 events.

Evans won seven U.S. titles, and her career total of 42 left her six short of Tracy Caulkins's all-time U.S. career record.   F.L.

TENNIS

Pete Sampras and Aranxta Sánchez Vicario dominated tennis in 1994, each capturing two Grand Slam titles. But the hottest topic all year was the waning popularity of the sport. A May cover story in *Sports Illustrated* entitled "Is Tennis Dying?" brought the crisis to a head. While the media debated the reasons, the men's Association of Tennis Professionals (ATP) implemented rule changes to make tennis more enjoyable for spectators, and the Women's Tennis Association (WTA) planned to do the same in 1995. A men's tournament in New Haven, CT, went as far as playing rock music during player introductions and changeovers, an experiment that met with mixed reviews from players and fans.

The tennis world paid tribute to Martina Navratilova, who retired at age 38 in November. Her 167 singles career titles made her the winningest tennis player of all time. Also retiring was Ivan Lendl, 34, who announced in December that chronic back problems were forcing him to call it quits. In the 1980s Lendl was the No. 1 player for a record 270 weeks; he won a record $20.5 million in his career. In contrast, Jennifer Capriati, 18, was arrested in Miami in May for possession of marijuana and did not play a tournament until October. Capriati's early burnout was a major reason why the WTA raised the age limit at which girls are allowed to play an unlimited amount of pro tournaments from 14 to 18.

Vitas Gerulaitis, 40, winner of the 1977 Australian Open, died of accidental carbon monoxide poisoning on September 18.

Writer Bud Collins and player Hana Mandlikova were inducted into the International Tennis Hall of Fame.

Men's Tour. Pete Sampras dominated the first half of the year, winning the Australian Open and Wimbledon. After defending his Wimbledon title, however, Sampras developed tendinitis in his left ankle and was never the same. He lost at the U.S. Open to Peruvian

Jaime Yzaga. Two weeks later he defaulted a match because of a hamstring injury in the U.S. Davis Cup semifinal tie against Sweden, contributing greatly to a 3-2 U.S. defeat. Sampras still managed to finish the year ranked No. 1. He also won the year-end ATP Tour world championship.

Spain's Sergi Bruguera, the best clay-court player in men's tennis, defended his French Open title, beating a countryman, the unheralded Alberto Berasategui, in the final. The charismatic Andre Agassi, with his girlfriend, actress/model Brooke Shields, at every match, gave tennis a bolt of excitement by winning the U.S. Open.

Russian Yevgeny Kafelnikov was the year's brightest newcomer, rocketing from No. 104 to No. 11 in the rankings by year's end. The doubles team of brothers Luke and Murphy Jensen, who did not win a tournament all year, surprised the tennis world with their enormous popularity, due entirely to their colorful outfits and personalities.

Women's Tour. Steffi Graf won the Australian Open in January and by April was the proud owner of a 36-match winning streak. At the Citizen Cup, however, in a sign of things to come, she lost to Aranxta Sánchez Vicario. Despite finishing the year at No. 1, Graf stumbled repeatedly throughout 1994. She lost to Mary Pierce in the semifinals of the French Open, to Lori McNeil in the first round at Wimbledon, and to Sánchez Vicario in the final of the U.S. Open. Meanwhile, Sánchez Vicario captured the French and U.S. opens.

Conchita Martínez took the title at Wimbledon for her first Grand Slam victory, and Gabriela Sabatini won the year-end Virginia Slims championships. For the second straight year the doubles team of Natalia Zvereva and Gigi Fernandez won the first three majors but failed to win a doubles Grand Slam, as they lost at the U.S. Open. Former No. 1 Monica Seles, who was stabbed in the back by a crazed fan in April of 1993, did not return to the tour during the year.   B.C.

Czech-ing out. *Two tennis greats, both born in Czechoslovakia and both of whom became U.S. citizens, retired late in 1994. Ivan Lendl (below left), citing a bad back, once held the world's No. 1 ranking for a record 270 weeks. Martina Navratilova, seen below right saying farewell after bowing out in the opening round of the Virginia Slims Championships in November, amassed a record 167 singles titles.*

TRACK AND FIELD

A highlight of track and field in 1994 was Sonia O'Sullivan, a 24-year-old Villanova University graduate from Ireland who was the year's most successful female runner, after having learned a lesson in 1993.

When Chinese women won three distance titles in the 1993 world championships with unheard-of performances, many opposing runners and coaches accused them of using banned performance-enhancing drugs. O'Sullivan said only that the Chinese inspired her to train even harder, and her diligence paid off. She set 1994's only women's world record for a running or field event, a time of 5 minutes 25.36 seconds for 2,000 meters, July 8 in Edinburgh. She also led the world at 1,500 meters (3:59.10), one mile (4:17.25), and 3,000 meters (8:21.64) and won the European title at 3,000 meters (8:31.84).

O'Sullivan never raced in 1994 against Wang Junxia and Qu Yunxia, the record-breaking Chinese women, because they avoided international competition until the Asian Games in October in Hiroshima, Japan. They won their races there, but in times slower than their best.

The men's world records in the three longest track races—3,000, 5,000, and 10,000 meters—fell to Africans. They were Noureddine Morceli of Algeria (7:25.11 for 3,000 meters, August 3 in Monte Carlo); 5'3", 119-pound Haile Gebresilasie of Ethiopia (12:56.96 for 5,000 meters, June 4 in Hengelo, the Netherlands); and William Sigei of Kenya (26:52.23 for 10,000 meters, July 22 in Oslo).

Sergei Bubka of Ukraine and Leroy Burrell of the United States broke world records. Bubka's pole vault of 20 feet 1¾ inches (6.14 meters) on July 31 in Sestriere, Italy, was his 17th world record outdoors—to go with his 18 indoor records. Burrell, who took the 100-meter record from his training partner Carl Lewis in 1991, did it again when he ran 9.85 seconds on July 6 in Lausanne, Switzerland.

Despite his world record, Burrell was not the year's dominant 100-meter sprinter. Linford Christie of Great Britain won his third consecutive European 100-meter title and also won in the Commonwealth Games and the World Cup. Colin Jackson, also of Great Britain, was undefeated in the men's 110-meter hurdles and in addition won European titles both outdoors and indoors.

Javier Sotomayor of Cuba was the year's highest high jumper outdoors (7 feet 11¼ inches, or 2.42 meters) and indoors (7 feet 10½ inches, or 2.40 meters). He lost only once all year. On the Grand Prix summerlong circuit, Wilson Kipketer of Kenya won the 800-meter run eight times, and Mike Conley of the United States the triple jump six times.

Fastest man alive. *Runner Leroy Burrell of the United States raises his arms in triumph as he crosses the finish line of the 100-meter sprint at a July meet in Lausanne, Switzerland. Burrell ran the distance in 9.85 seconds and set a new world record.*

Michael Johnson of the United States ran the year's fastest times for 200 and 400 meters (19.94 seconds and 43.90 seconds). Dan O'Brien of the United States became the first decathlete to score 8,700 points three times in one year.

Morceli won the Grand Prix men's overall title, and Jackie Joyner-Kersee of the United States the women's. During the year Joyner-Kersee twice jumped 24 feet 7 inches (7.49 meters), the second-longest women's long jumps in history.

Among the women, Sally Gunnell of Great Britain won 12 of 13 finals in the 400-meter hurdles, with titles in the European championships, European Cup, World Cup, and Commonwealth Games. Maria Mutola of Mozambique was unbeaten at 800 meters, and her time of 1:55.19 was the fastest in five years. Inna Lasovskaya of Russia broke the world indoor record in the triple jump three times in one month, raising it to 48 feet 10¾ inches (14.90 meters).   F.L.

Great skates. *To many observers the Olympic Games' most impressive athlete was Norwegian speed skater Johann Olav Koss ("The Boss"), who won three gold medals, setting three world records.*

WINTER OLYMPICS

"The best Olympic Games ever." So said Juan Antonio Samaranch, the president of the International Olympic Committee, at the closing ceremonies of the XVII Olympic Winter Games, which were held in February 1994 in and around Lillehammer, Norway. Norway's King Harald V was among the thousands in attendance, and millions of television viewers worldwide, who were watching the ceremonies that day, but Samaranch was not just being polite.

The overwhelming consensus among those who went to Lillehammer was that he was right. Norwegians had spent more than $1 billion on facilities and infrastructure to stage the games. For 16 days the competitions were hard fought and exciting, the weather was cold but sunny, the setting—with snow-covered trails winding around rugged peaks, through piney forests and postcard villages—was magnificent, and the Norwegians proved to be the perfect hosts.

The closing ceremonies reinforced the point. As the frozen breath of 40,000 fans sparkled under the lights, nearly 2,000 happy Olympians paraded into the Lysgardsbakkene Ski Jumping Arena to say good-bye to the throngs who had welcomed them so warmly. It was a happy and heartfelt farewell. The fireworks display that followed, although spectacular, seemed anticlimactic.

Joyful and Vibrant. Norway, with only about 4 million people, won more medals in the games than any other nation, and yet that was not the country's greatest achievement. The games staged there seemed to excite a new belief in the ideals of sportsmanship and peaceful cooperation that originally inspired the Olympics. By raising money for a Sarajevo relief fund, the organizers reminded the world of the terrible fate of the war-ravaged Bosnian capital that just a decade earlier had hosted the 1984 Winter Games.

At the same time, the hosts, the athletes, and two weeks of sunny days and starry nights created an atmosphere so joyful that even the most cynical observers could tune out the event's rampant commercialism. (In the quaint Norwegian towns, advertising for official Olympic sponsors such as Visa, Kodak, and Xerox seemed to be plastered on every object that didn't move—and some that did; for example, every single bus in Lillehammer bore an IBM logo.)

The upbeat feeling was enhanced by the scenic backdrop of the games, the Gudbrandsdalen Valley. An extraordinarily heavy snowfall had coated Lillehammer and the other host communities beside frozen Lake Mjosa, north of Oslo, with a frosting of pure white, and the constant subfreezing temperatures kept the fairy-tale-like scene from melting or turning to slush. Far from gray and somber, Norway revealed itself to be colorful and vibrant. The opening ceremonies at Lysgardsbakkene on February 12 introduced the world to enchanting characters out of Norse folklore who emerged from beneath the snow. In a moment of high drama the Olympic torch was delivered into the stadium by a skier flying off the 120-meter ramp. The crowd, seemingly indifferent to the frigid temperatures, roared with

Gold at last. *After winning the 1,000 meters, U.S. speed skater Dan Jansen, who was competing in his third Winter Olympics, skated a victory lap carrying his baby daughter.*

approval. Hardiness, clearly, is a Norwegian national attribute.

Even the Olympic facilities were notable. Several of the hockey games were played in the Cavern Hall in Gjovik, an arena built inside a hollowed-out mountain on the west shore of Lake Mjosa. Shavings from the mined granite were incorporated into the gold, silver, and bronze medals awarded to the athletes. Up the road in Hunderfossen, designers minimized the environmental impact of the luge and bobsled tracks by building the runs into the lay of the land. And in Hamar, Olympic Hall, as striking inside as out, came to be known as the Viking Ship because of its design, which caused it to resemble the overturned hull of an ancient Norse craft.

Planning Makes Perfect. This was Norway's second Olympics—Oslo had staged the 1952 Winter Games. Armed with that experience, the organizers developed a plan for nearly every eventuality and stuck to it. More than 20,000 enthusiastic volunteers worked 12-hour shifts at the competition sites and on the roads, directing traffic and answering visitors' questions. Although traffic could be slow (what is normally a 40-minute trip from Lillehammer to Hamar, site of the skating competitions, routinely took two hours), their efforts helped keep the games on schedule and eliminated snafus. Volunteers also ran concession stands, sold tickets, acted as ushers, and guarded doors. Security was tight but unobtrusive.

The most obvious threat to the smooth running of events came as a result of something no one could have foreseen—the Nancy Kerrigan-Tonya Harding fiasco. On January 6, U.S. figure skater Nancy Kerrigan had been struck on the knee by a club-wielding assailant as she was leaving a practice session in Detroit, where she had gone to compete in the U.S. Figure Skating Association Championships. A week later three men were arrested in connection with the attack, all of them associated with Kerrigan rival Tonya Harding. Kerrigan recovered and was able to compete in the Olympics; Harding, who also made the U.S. team, disclaimed any foreknowledge of the plot. (In March she pleaded guilty to hindering the criminal investigation and was forced

Nancy Kerrigan

U.S. figure skater Nancy Kerrigan arrived at the 1994 Winter Olympic Games in Norway in a blinding glare of publicity. On January 6 she had been the victim of a bizarre crime: As she left the ice at a Detroit rink, an attacker hit her on the knee with a metal bar. Four men, one the ex-husband of rival skater Tonya Harding, later pleaded guilty to charges connected with the assault; Harding pleaded guilty to hindering the investigation of the attack.

Kerrigan went to the Olympics amid doubts that she could recover physically and emotionally before the February games. Yet she took the top score in the short program and completed a long program with five triple jumps, ultimately finishing second only because of a dazzling performance by Ukraine's Oksana Baiul.

Born in 1969 in Massachusetts, Kerrigan was a skating prodigy by age six. Her father, a welder, took extra jobs, borrowed money, and remortgaged his home to pay for training that eventually cost $50,000 a year. But the lessons paid off: after the Olympics, silver medalist Kerrigan's endorsement deals were worth an estimated $20 million. J.G.

to resign from the U.S. Figure Skating Association, a move that made her ineligible for the world championships later that month. In late June the USFA stripped her of her 1994 national championship title and banned her for life, which meant she could never again compete in any USFA-sanctioned amateur or professional event.) The bizarre episode was the subject of a feeding frenzy among reporters, and the media's pursuit of the rival American figure skaters strained security and the limited seating capacity and press facilities at the Olympic Amphitheater in Hamar.

Stars New and Old. Despite the media attention given in the United States to Harding and Kerrigan, fans at the games seemed more interested in what athletes did in competition. Marking the start of a new Olympic schedule (with summer and winter events held in different years), the Lillehammer games were only two years removed from the last Winter Olympics—in Albertville, France. Thus, the 1994 games featured many familiar stars, such as ski jumper Jens Weissflog of Germany, Italy's man-about-skiing Alberto Tomba, and American speed skater Bonnie Blair.

The Norwegians themselves celebrated the feats of homegrown talent such as the dashing cross-country skier Bjorn Dahlie and the acrobatic Stine Lise Hattestad, who captured the women's freestyle moguls gold medal. But the Norwegians were also won over by the gritty performances that produced double gold medals for both Italy's Manuela Di Centa in cross-country skiing and Canada's Myriam Bédard in the biathlon. And they cheered just as lustily for American speed skater Dan Jansen as they did for their own superhero, Johann Olav Koss. "We love you, Dan Jansen," gushed a local television reporter interviewing the American skater after his world-record, gold-medal performance in the men's 1,000-meter race. Then, to the astonishment of Jansen, she gave him a big kiss.

Although acknowledged as the best in the world at the shorter distances, Jansen had been plagued in his Olympic career by a series of mishaps. In the Calgary, Alberta, games in 1988 he had had to compete just after learning of the death of his sister from leukemia, and he fell on the ice. Two races at Albertville in

OLYMPIC MEDAL WINNERS
Medalists are listed in order of gold, silver, and bronze.

BIATHLON

MEN

10 kilometers
Sergei Chepikov, Russia
Ricco Gross, Germany
Sergei Tarasov, Russia

20 kilometers
Sergei Tarasov, Russia
Frank Luck, Germany
Sven Fischer, Germany

4 x 7.5-km Relay
Germany
Russia
France

WOMEN

7.5 kilometers
Myriam Bédard, Canada
Svetlana Paramygina,
 Belarus
Valentyna Tserbe, Ukraine

15 kilometers
Myriam Bédard, Canada
Anne Briand, France
Ursula Disl, Germany

4 x 7.5-km Relay
Russia
Germany
France

BOBSLEDDING

Two-man
Gustav Weder and Donat
 Acklin, Switzerland
Reto Goetschi and Guido
 Acklin, Switzerland
Gunther Huber and Stefano
 Ticci, Italy

Four-man
Germany II
Switzerland I
Germany I

ICE HOCKEY
Sweden
Canada
Finland

LUGE

MEN

Singles
Georg Hackl, Germany
Markus Prock, Austria
Armin Zoggeler, Italy

Doubles
Kurt Brugger and Wilfried
 Huber, Italy
Hansjorg Raffl and Norbert
 Huber, Italy
Stefan Krausse and Jan
 Behrendt, Germany

WOMEN

Singles
Gerda Weisensteiner, Italy
Susi Erdmann, Germany
Andrea Tagwerker, Austria

SKATING, FIGURE

MEN
Aleksei Urmanov, Russia
Elvis Stojko, Canada
Philippe Candeloro, France

WOMEN
Oksana Baiul, Ukraine
Nancy Kerrigan, U.S.A.
Chen Lu, China

PAIRS
Yekaterina Gordeyeva and
 Sergei Grinkov, Russia

Natalya Mishkutyonok and
 Artur Dmitriev, Russia
Isabelle Brasseur and Lloyd
 Eisler, Canada

ICE DANCING
Oksana Grishchuk and
 Yevgeni Platov, Russia
Maya Usova and Aleksandr
 Zhulin, Russia
Jayne Torvill and Christo-
 pher Dean, Great Britain

SKATING, SPEED
(LONG TRACK)

MEN

500 meters
Aleksandr Golubev, Russia
Sergei Klevchenya, Russia
Manabu Horii, Japan

1,000 meters
Dan Jansen, U.S.A.
Igor Zhelezovsky, Belarus
Sergei Klevchenya, Russia

1,500 meters
Johann Olav Koss, Norway
Rintje Ritsma, Netherlands
Falko Zandstra, Netherlands

5,000 meters
Johann Olav Koss, Norway
Kjell Storelid, Norway
Rintje Ritsma, Netherlands

10,000 meters
Johann Olav Koss, Norway
Kjell Storelid, Norway
Bart Veldkamp, Netherlands

WOMEN

500 meters
Bonnie Blair, U.S.A.
Susan Auch, Canada
Franziska Schenk, Germany

1,000 meters
Bonnie Blair, U.S.A.
Anke Baier, Germany
Ye Qiaobo, China

1,500 meters
Emese Hunyady, Austria
Svetlana Fedotkina, Russia
Gunda Niemann, Germany

3,000 meters
Svetlana Bazhanova, Russia
Emese Hunyady, Austria
Claudia Pechstein, Germany

5,000 meters
Claudia Pechstein, Germany
Gunda Niemann, Germany
Hiromi Yamamoto, Japan

SKATING, SPEED
(SHORT TRACK)

MEN

500 meters
Chae Ji Hoon, South Korea
Mirko Vuillermin, Italy
Nicholas Gooch, Great
 Britain

1,000 meters
Kim Ki Hoon, South Korea
Chae Ji Hoon, South Korea
Marc Gagnon, Canada

5,000-m Relay
Italy
U.S.A.
Australia

WOMEN

500 meters
Cathy Turner, U.S.A.

Zhang Yanmei, China
Amy Peterson, U.S.A.

1,000 meters
Chun Lee Kyung, South
 Korea
Nathalie Lambert, Canada
Kim So Hee, South Korea

3,000-m Relay
South Korea
Canada
U.S.A.

SKIING, ALPINE

MEN

Combined
Lasse Kjus, Norway
Kjetil Andre Aamodt, Norway
Harald Strand Nilsen,
 Norway

Downhill
Tommy Moe, U.S.A.
Kjetil Andre Aamodt, Norway
Ed Podivinsky, Canada

Slalom
Thomas Stangassinger,
 Austria
Alberto Tomba, Italy
Jure Kosir, Slovenia

Giant Slalom
Markus Wasmeier, Germany
Urs Kaelin, Switzerland
Christian Mayer, Austria

Super Giant Slalom
Markus Wasmeier, Germany
Tommy Moe, U.S.A.
Kjetil Andre Aamodt, Norway

WOMEN

Combined
Pernilla Wiberg, Sweden
Vreni Schneider, Switzerland
Alenka Dovzan, Slovenia

Downhill
Katja Seizinger, Germany
Picabo Street, U.S.A.
Isolde Kostner, Italy

Slalom
Vreni Schneider, Switzerland
Elfriede Eder, Austria
Katja Koren, Slovenia

Giant Slalom
Deborah Compagnoni, Italy
Martina Ertl, Germany
Vreni Schneider, Switzerland

Super Giant Slalom
Diann Roffe-Steinrotter,
 U.S.A.
Svetlana Gladischeva,
 Russia
Isolde Kostner, Italy

SKIING, FREESTYLE

MEN

Aerials
Andreas Schoenbaechler,
 Switzerland
Philippe Laroche, Canada
Lloyd Langlois, Canada

Moguls
Jean-Luc Brassard, Canada
Sergei Shupletsov, Russia
Edgar Grospiron, France

WOMEN

Aerials
Lina Cherjazova, Uzbekistan
Marie Lindgren, Sweden
Hilde Synnove Lid, Norway

Moguls
Stine Lise Hattestad,
 Norway

Liz McIntyre, U.S.A.
Yelizaveta Kozhevnikova,
 Russia

SKIING, NORDIC

MEN

**Combined
Individual**
Fred Borre Lundberg,
 Norway
Takanori Kono, Japan
Bjarte Engen Vik, Norway

Team
Japan
Norway
Switzerland

**Cross-country
10 kilometers**
Bjorn Dahlie, Norway
Vladimir Smirnov,
 Kazakhstan
Marco Albarello, Italy

30 kilometers
Thomas Alsgaard, Norway
Bjorn Dahlie, Norway
Mika Myllyla, Finland

50 kilometers
Vladimir Smirnov,
 Kazakhstan
Mika Myllyla, Finland
Sture Sivertsen, Norway

40-km Relay
Italy
Norway
Finland

Pursuit Method (15 km)
Bjorn Dahlie, Norway
Vladimir Smirnov,
 Kazakhstan
Silvio Fauner, Italy

**Ski Jumping
90 meters**
Espen Bredesen, Norway
Lasse Ottesen, Norway
Dieter Thoma, Germany

120 meters
Jens Weissflog, Germany
Espen Bredesen, Norway
Andreas Goldberger, Austria

120-m Team
Germany
Japan
Austria

WOMEN

**Cross-country
5 kilometers**
Lyubov Yegorova, Russia
Manuela Di Centa, Italy
Marja-Liisa Kirvesniemi,
 Finland

15 kilometers
Manuela Di Centa, Italy
Lyubov Yegorova, Russia
Nina Gavriluk, Russia

30 kilometers
Manuela Di Centa, Italy
Marit Wold, Norway
Marja-Liisa Kirvesniemi,
 Finland

20-km Relay
Russia
Norway
Italy

Pursuit Method (10 km)
Lyubov Yegorova, Russia
Manuela Di Centa, Italy
Stefania Belmondo, Italy

Sharpshooter. *Canada's Myriam Bédard took home the gold in the women's 7.5-kilometer and 15-kilometer biathlons.*

1992 produced two more failures. And in his first race at Lillehammer, the 500 meters (his specialty), he finished eighth after slipping on a turn. It was a poignant moment, indeed, when after his 1,000-meter triumph Jansen skated a victory lap before a cheering crowd, carrying an infant daughter named after his late sister, Jane.

Cross-country skiing and speed skating are to Norway what baseball and football are to the United States, so they drew the most intense interest. Despite the bitter cold, fans camped out in tents at the farthest points of the cross-country track, miles from town, so that they could maintain choice viewing positions. They weren't disappointed. Dahlie, next to Koss the country's brightest star, won two gold medals and one silver. And the Olympic Hall speed skating oval in Hamar was filled to capacity hours before long-track events. Or-

ange-clad Dutch supporters clashed in color with the red-clad locals, but they were all united in appreciation of the sport.

There was no shortage of support for the other sports. Upset victories by two American Alpine skiers, Tommy Moe in the men's downhill and Diann Roffe-Steinrotter in the women's super giant slalom, were accompanied by a cacophonous roar of cowbells and whistles all the way down both courses. The roar grew even louder in the men's combined event, in which Norwegian skiers swept all three medals. At Lysgardsbakkene Arena, where veteran Weissflog captured the 120-meter title, Norway's ski jumpers delighted their fans by winning three out of a possible six individual medals—including a gold in the 90-meter event for high-flying Espen Bredesen (ski jumps are measured from the end of the ramp to what is known as the K point, a spot where the hill begins to flatten out). The hosts didn't win a single medal in the biathlon, bobsled, or luge, but fans packed those events anyway.

Ironically, the one sport that did not excite Norwegians was figure skating. The designated venue, the Olympic Amphitheater, had a seating capacity of only 6,500. That total would have been strained even without the Harding-Kerrigan fuss. Still, for those who were lucky enough to be there, the Amfi, as it was called, was a wonderfully intimate stage for what may have been the greatest figure skating competition ever held. This was the first Winter Olympics in which former Olympic stars who had turned professional were permitted to reenter the games, and thus the lineup of competitors included a stunning array of talent.

The high standard was established right at the start, by the pairs competition. Returning professionals Yekaterina Gordeyeva and Sergei Grinkov of Russia, the Olympic champions from 1988, were brilliant, but their margin of victory was narrow over fellow Russians Natalya Mishkutyonok and Artur Dmitriev, gold medalists in 1992, and Isabelle Brasseur and Lloyd Eisler of Canada, the reigning world champions.

The lineup in the men's competition was unprecedented in star power, as it included American Brian Boitano, Ukrainian Victor Petrenko, and Canadian Kurt Browning, athletes who together had won seven world championships and two Olympic gold medals. Surprisingly, however, they all skated poor short programs, leaving an opening for Russia's Aleksei Urmanov, who outdueled Canada's Elvis Stojko for the gold medal.

In the dance competition, Jayne Torvill and Christopher Dean of Great Britain won the hearts of the fans but not of the judges, who placed them third. Some observers believed that the judges saw their routine, which consisted of ballroom dancing to Irving Berlin music, as outdated; in any case, they gave the gold to Oksana Grishchuk and Yevgeni Platov of Russia, who boogied to 1950s rock and roll.

Finally, it was the women's turn. The field was a strong one. Kerrigan, Oksana Baiul of Ukraine, Chen Lu of China, Josée Chouinard of Canada, Yuka Sato of Japan, and Surya Bonaly of France all had legitimate chances at medals. (Harding, for all her notoriety, did not.) Kerrigan skated a flawless short program and narrowly led Baiul and Bonaly going into the free skate. But Baiul, a precocious teenager with a flair for the dramatic, prevailed in the end, leaving Kerrigan with the silver and Chen Lu with the bronze.

Although much attention was paid to the Kerrigan-Harding brouhaha, Baiul's story was compelling in its own right. Her struggle to the top came in the face of formidable odds; her

Super giant upset. *Diann Roffe-Steinrotter of the United States was an unexpected gold medal winner in the women's super giant slalom.*

mother died in 1991, leaving her without parents, and the breakup of the once-formidable Soviet sports machine had left her with little funding, coaching, or practice opportunities.

Class Acts. Many athletes distinguished themselves by their character as much as by their performances. Italy's Deborah Compagnoni, who won the women's giant slalom gold medal, tearfully dedicated her victory to her friend Ulrike Maier, an Austrian giant slalom specialist who was killed in a World Cup event in Germany only weeks before the games. Figure skater Katarina Witt, a two-time Olympic gold medalist from Germany, performed her long program to the song *Where Have All the Flowers Gone,* in tribute to the embattled people of Sarajevo, where she had first won Olympic gold. And Bosnia itself was represented at the games by, among other competitors, a four-man bobsled team. The Bosnian sledders did not challenge the mighty Germans for gold, but they did offer a symbolic ray of hope for the shattered country—the team was composed of a Muslim, a Croat, and two Serbs.

If the spirit of the Lillehammer games had a face, it fittingly belonged to a Norwegian—Johann Olav Koss. The strapping 25-year-old medical student from Oslo ruled the speed skating oval. That was as it should be: A religious fervor grips Norwegians during speed skating races, and Koss was the local deity. For each race he would stand at the starting line looking like something out of science fiction, his red, skintight uniform barely containing his enormous thighs, the chiseled features of his handsome face hardened with determination. Speed skating is a sport that is determined by thousandths of a second; Koss won the 10,000 meters by more than 18 seconds. In all, he entered three races and won three gold medals, making three world-record performances.

But Koss was a modest hero compared to the prima donnas of professional sport. He celebrated his successes in the Speedskater Bar on the pedestrian mall in Hamar. After the 5,000-meter race he pledged his gold medal bonus—the equivalent of $30,000—to the Sarajevo Relief Fund that had been set up by the Lillehammer organizing committee. And

It's a winner! Peter Forsberg of Sweden flips the puck past the Canadian goalie in the gripping overtime shoot-out of the Olympics' gold-medal hockey game. Forsberg's score gave his team the victory.

his call to all Norwegians to pledge 10 krone (about $1.40) to the fund resulted in a landslide of donations.

Drawing to a Close. The last day of the games was bittersweet. Fittingly, the final competition—the gold-medal hockey game between favored Sweden and underdog Canada—was edge-of-the-seat exciting and went to overtime and finally a shoot-out before Sweden won, 3-2. In the dying moments of the contest, before the teams lined up for the shootout, the public address system played a traditional tune that hearkened back to the old days when Norwegians danced to keep themselves warm. The song had been played countless times at every Olympic venue for weeks. Anywhere else, the melody, endlessly repeated, would have exasperated the audience. But at Lillehammer the simple tune had the power to get people up and dancing one last time. Fans from all over waved their flags to the beat. Ushers and volunteers danced together in the corridors and took pictures to record the moment. Even the usually dour denizens of the press box joined in. It was like something out of a long-ago, simpler time.

That was the beauty of the Lillehammer Olympics.   J.De.

SRI LANKA. The climate of pessimism about the prospects for an end to Sri Lanka's ten-year civil war turned toward optimism in 1994 with the election of a new government. The elec-

tion of Chandrika Kumaratunga first as prime minister and subsequently as president spread hope that she would succeed in her pledge to end the war.

Kumaratunga led her leftist People's Alliance to a narrow victory in August parliamentary elections, forming a coalition with Tamil and Muslim parties to create a majority. It was the first change in governing party in 17 years. The previous United National Party (UNP) government had refused to negotiate with the separatist Liberation Tigers of Tamil Eelam (LTTE) until they gave up the war, which had continued in the northern and eastern areas of the country with neither side gaining an advantage.

In mid-October, Kumaratunga sent representatives to meet with LTTE leaders in the rebel stronghold in the northern province of Jaffna. Talks were suspended, however, after the UNP presidential candidate, Gamini Dissanayake, and more than 50 others were killed by a suicide bomber at a Colombo election rally on October 23. Most analysts believed that the LTTE was responsible for the bomb. The UNP replaced Dissanayake with his wife, Srima, and the election was held as scheduled on November 9. Kumaratunga won more than 62 percent of the presidential vote. She named her mother, Sirimavo Bandaranaike, to replace her as prime minister.

Kumaratunga's overwhelming victory was viewed by many as a vote for peace. The LTTE announced a cease-fire after her elevation to the presidency was officially announced. However, the Sri Lankan Army refused to abide by the cease-fire; Kumaratunga attempted to reshuffle the security force leadership to force it to obey her orders. In a renewed effort toward ending the war, the government in mid-December announced plans to resume negotiations with the LTTE.

Political events overshadowed a very strong economy during 1994. The reduced violence from the civil war led to a surge in tourism, while adequate rains fostered rice production. However, the war, along with uncertainty about the policies of a postelection government, restrained foreign investment in Sri Lanka. Kumaratunga allayed many of the fears that her leftist coalition would restrict private investment by surrounding herself with advisers known to be sympathetic to the international investor community.

Kumaratunga loosened government restrictions on the media, promising an unbiased government media and allowing private radio and television stations to broadcast news reports, adding to the new atmosphere of hope for peace.

See STATISTICS OF THE WORLD. R.C.O.

STAMPS AND STAMP COLLECTING. A blunder by the U.S. Postal Service kept stamps in the news throughout 1994. A pane of stamps commemorating "Legends of the West" purported to include African-American cowboy and rodeo star Bill Pickett, but it actually depicted one of his brothers or cousins. At the urging of Pickett's descendants, Postmaster General Marvin Runyon decided to correct the mistake and to destroy the stamps that contained the mistake. The date of issue was postponed from March to October.

Before the error stamps could be destroyed, post offices in different parts of the United States had sold more than 100 sheets of them. Meanwhile, Runyon came under pressure from Congress not to waste the money that the reprinting would cost. As a compromise, he decided to place 150,000 of the error panes on sale by mail order on a first-come, first-served basis, on October 1.

Two major stamp dealers sued in federal court, asking that the Postal Service be required to sell unlimited quantities of the error. A group of collectors who had purchased panes before the problem was recognized sued to prevent any further distribution. Both suits were dismissed, and the error panes were distributed as planned.

The fourth annual World War II miniature sheet commemorated events of 1944. Educator Allison Davis appeared on the annual Black Heritage stamp. Souvenir sheets and companion stamps commemorated the 25th anniversary of the first man on the Moon, the World Cup soccer tournament, and artist Norman Rockwell. Single commemorative stamps honored Buffalo Soldiers (all-black Army regiments that helped tame the American West after the Civil War), Edward R. Murrow, George Meany, James Thurber, and Virginia Apgar.

Sets of stamps saluted silent screen stars and popular, blues, and jazz singers. Topical issues pictured locomotives, winter Olympic sports, summer garden flowers, sea creatures, and Christmas motifs.

Engraved $1 and $5 stamps reproduced unused designs of the 1869 pictorial issue on the 125th anniversary of that set, and a souvenir sheet observed the Bureau of Engraving and Printing's postage stamp centennial by reproducing the $2 stamp of 1894. Postal cards pictured Abraham Lincoln's Illinois home, Myers Hall at Wittenberg University in Ohio, and Canyon de Chelly National Monument in Arizona. A stamped envelope pictured a football.

Several new stamp products were introduced as the Postal Service announced a goal of $1 billion in annual philatelic sales. Keith A. Wagner retired as the executive director of the American Philatelic Society, the largest stamp hobby organization. He was succeeded by Robert E. Lamb, a former U.S. ambassador to Cyprus.

The Palestinian National Authority became a new stamp-issuing entity in 1994. An Israeli stamp commemorated the Palestinian peace accord. China and the United States issued

Some notable stamps of 1994. A U.S. pane honoring "Legends of the West" was delayed for months because the initial printing showed the wrong man as rodeo star Bill Pickett; at top left, two stamps from the final issue, with the real Pickett and sharpshooter Annie Oakley. To their right is a French stamp celebrating the new English Channel tunnel connecting France and Britain. A joint issue by China and the United States focused on two protected cranes—China's black-necked crane (shown here in the second row) and the U.S. whooping crane. The woolly mammoth next to the cranes is from a Canadian block of four featuring extinct mammals. Canines were a frequent subject in 1994, the year of the dog in the Chinese lunar calendar, and the two stamps below the mammoth are from a miniature sheet issued by St. Vincent and the Grenadines. Peace with the Palestinians is the subject of the stamp from Israel, below the crane on the left. To the right of the peace stamp are Sweden's tribute to the 25th anniversary of the first Moon landing and the Marshall Islands' nod to the 50th anniversary of the end of the German siege of Leningrad. At bottom left are two stamps from Canada's most popular issue of 1994, a miniature sheet commemorating the International Year of the Family; at bottom right: a Latvian souvenir sheet for the Winter Olympic Games.

matching stamps featuring species of cranes. The opening of the Channel Tunnel was celebrated on a joint stamp issue of France and Great Britain. More than 600,000 collectors attended an international stamp exhibition in Seoul, South Korea, in August. No legendary classic stamps appeared on the auction market in 1994, but stamp prices continued to advance modestly.   K.L.

STATE GOVERNMENT REVIEW. States saw good financial times return in 1994. Officials running for reelection in November (*see* ELECTIONS IN THE UNITED STATES) vied to be toughest on crime and welfare fraud.

Tax and Finance. For the first time in years nearly every state finished the fiscal year ending June 30 in the black. As the national economy improved, the number of people working increased, which meant states collected more income taxes. More people working also translated into more spending, so states collected more in sales taxes, too. As a result, few states were forced to increase taxes and some even cut them. The biggest tax cut was in New Jersey, where first-year Republican Governor Christine Todd Whitman and the Republican-controlled state Legislature laid out in June a plan to reduce income taxes by 10 percent starting January 1995 and by 30 percent over Whitman's term.

The other major tax action was in Michigan, where voters in March approved a plan to implement a two-cent increase in the sales tax in order to lower property taxes for funding schools. In 1993, Michigan lawmakers had voted to do away with property taxes for schools entirely, but when they met in 1994 they decided that was too drastic. Still, state spending on education in Michigan was expected to shoot up by 72 percent. In Oregon a property tax cut approved by voters in 1990 resulted in the state's taking on a bigger share of school spending in 1994.

A survey conducted by the National Conference of State Legislatures and released in August found that the largest share of state general fund budgets continued to go to K-12 school spending. Next in line was spending on Medicaid, the federal-state health care program for the poor, followed by higher education and corrections spending.

Pete Wilson

Politicians often seem to win elections by exploiting controversies that draw their supporters to the polls. For California Governor Pete Wilson (R), the hot-button issue in 1994 was Proposition 187, an initiative that was designed to deny many government services to undocumented immigrants.

In centering his reelection bid on illegal immigration, Wilson regained the popularity he lost because of a tax hike and the state's prolonged recession. Wilson took 55 percent of the vote; Prop 187 received 59 percent (although a federal judge blocked, at least temporarily, most of its provisions from taking effect). At the same time, Wilson set out a key issue for Republicans in 1996—and became a plausible aspirant for vice president or even president.

Born in 1933 in a Chicago suburb, Peter Barton Wilson grew up in affluence during the Great Depression. Educated at Yale, he fulfilled an ROTC obligation as a Marine rifle-platoon leader, then earned a law degree from the University of California at Berkeley before entering politics. He lives in Sacramento with his second wife, Gayle, and two stepsons.   G.H.

The bad financial news was limited to less than a handful of states, including California and Texas, both of which struggled to avoid deficits. At least California received good news from the U.S. Supreme Court in June, when the Court upheld the method the state had formerly used to tax the California income of foreign-based multinational businesses. If the ruling had gone the other way, California could have faced a $4 billion liability for tax refunds.

California was in the news again in December, as wealthy Orange County filed for bankruptcy. Treasurer Robert Citron had lost $2 billion of county funds by investing heavily in risky fixed-income securities, whose value declined precipitously throughout 1994 as interest rates went up. And later in the same month Proposition 187, meant to ease illegal aliens' burden on the state treasury, suffered a serious setback. Passed by California voters in November, Proposition 187 would deny most government services, including public education and nonemergency medical care, to illegal aliens. But a federal district judge issued a preliminary injunction barring the state from carrying out most of Proposition 187's provisions until after a lawsuit filed against it by civil rights and immigrant advocacy groups had been tried.

Health. While Congress failed to act on President Bill Clinton's health care reform package, some states moved ahead on their own. Minnesota approved a plan for universal health care by 1997. Florida, which had already approved the idea of universal coverage, got federal approval for a managed care system in Medicaid. The September 14 waiver of federal rules allowed the state to subsidize insurance premiums for working, uninsured, low-income Floridians currently ineligible for Medicaid. Kentucky passed health care reforms guaranteeing people coverage and the right to take their insurance from job to job. Pennsylvania expanded its health insurance coverage to more uninsured low-income children ages six to 13. Tennessee pronounced its TennCare program, passed in 1993, a success, crediting savings from Medicaid with funding a 1994 tax cut and teacher and state worker pay raises. Tennessee officials said that in

1994 the plan insured 245,000 people who were previously uninsured. Oregon postponed until 1998 its requirement for employers to offer health insurance.

Welfare. States took a more punitive stance toward welfare assistance—adopting carrots and sticks to cut down the number of those on public aid. Carrots included giving some benefits, including health care and child care, to former welfare recipients who take jobs or receive job training. Sticks included work requirements and demonstration programs, usually with federal waivers, requiring recipients to keep children in school or get their children health services. The most controversial stick was the family cap, which denies increased payments for children conceived by a mother on welfare. Caps on payments for more children were approved by Arkansas, California, Georgia, Massachusetts, Nebraska, Virginia, and Wisconsin. Time limits on welfare also gained favor. States that vowed to let people stay on welfare for a maximum of two years included Florida, Iowa, Vermont, Virginia, and

Orange crush. Orange County Treasurer Robert Citron took much of the heat when the California county was forced to declare bankruptcy in December; it had lost some $2 billion from the failure of risky investments. Citron resigned the same month.

Wisconsin. In an attempt to reduce welfare fraud, fingerprinting of welfare recipients was adopted in California and Pennsylvania and expanded in New York. To make these and other major changes in federally funded welfare aid, however, states had to obtain waivers from the federal Department of Health and Human Services.

Education. The question of how to fund schools equitably despite differences in local property-tax wealth continued to plague states. Courts ruled school funding systems unconstitutional in Arizona, New Jersey, Ohio, and Alabama. At issue in every state was reliance on

Bitter reminder. In a display organized by antiviolence groups, 681 pairs of shoes—one pair for every gun-related death in Wayne County, MI, in 1993— are arrayed in front of the Detroit City Council building. The shoes were sent on to Washington, where in September they were exhibited along with some 40,000 other empty pairs as part of a "silent march" to promote stronger gun control.

local property taxes that produced aid disparities among local districts. The Montgomery County Circuit Court gave Alabama until March 15, 1995, to come up with a new school-financing system. The New Jersey Supreme Court gave that state until 1997-1998 to equalize per pupil spending among districts. Ohio appealed the lower court ruling, which held its system invalid.

The concept of allowing parents or teachers to start their own public schools gained ground, with Arizona and Kansas bringing the total number of states allowing charter schools to 11. Minnesota, California, and Colorado all had charter schools operating in 1994; Michigan and Massachusetts approved charters for schools to open in 1995.

Crime and Punishment. Governors and legislatures rushed to be seen as tough on crime in the 1994 election year. Following the 1993 approval by Washington State voters of a law mandating life without parole for three-time serious offenders, at least ten states enacted versions of three-strikes laws. Among those mandating longer sentences for three-time violent criminals were California, Connecticut, Georgia, Indiana, Kansas, Maryland, New Mexico, North Carolina, Virginia, and Wisconsin. Other states moved to require violent criminals to serve more of their sentences, including Florida, Michigan, and Missouri.

Many states turned their attention to juvenile crime. Typical were measures to allow violent juvenile criminals to be tried in adult court and to keep guns out of the hands of youngsters. In 1994 possession of a gun by a child was made a crime in Kansas, Kentucky, South Dakota, and Tennessee, for example. Penalties were increased for selling or giving a weapon to a child in Arizona, California, Delaware, North Carolina, and Utah. Virginia abolished parole for all offenders and lowered to 14 the age at which a juvenile would be tried as an adult for a serious crime. Colorado followed up its 1993 special session on juvenile justice with new programs funded in 1994 to pay for community crime prevention programs for at-risk youth. Iowa, Minnesota, North Carolina, and Washington also funded early intervention programs to head off juvenile crime.

In North Carolina, Tennessee, and Washington, violence-prevention programs funded in 1994 included community service programs for very young children and families. In an attempt to crack down on family violence, New York required police to make arrests in domestic violence cases, even if no one was willing to press charges.

Tough new drunk driving laws were passed in New York and Virginia. California became the first state in the nation to require unlicensed drivers, including those with suspended or revoked licenses, to permanently forfeit their cars when caught driving on California's roads.   E.S.

STOCK MARKETS. See BANKING AND FINANCE: Stock Markets.

SUDAN. In 1994, Sudan witnessed more misery and hardship, as the continuing civil war caused many casualties and displaced millions. In February northern Islamic government forces scored several victories against the rebel Sudan People's Liberation Army, which was seeking political self-rule in the largely Christian and animist South. Continuing infighting within the SPLA over leadership and ideology also weakened its cause.

After Nigerian-sponsored peace negotiations failed in 1993, talks resumed in March in Nairobi, Kenya, under the sponsorship of the Intergovernmental Authority for Drought and Development (IGADD). In July a cease-fire was agreed on, but it had no discernible effect on the fighting at the front. In September the SPLA seemed willing to agree to an IGADD initiative calling for a nonreligious, democratic political system, but the government rejected it. The government's top priority remained a military defeat of the SPLA.

Intense fighting resumed in November, as the government aimed to cut the rebels' supply lines from Uganda. An estimated 50,000 Sudanese were said to be heading for Uganda, home to the majority of the 400,000 Sudanese who had become refugees in neighboring countries since the 11-year war began.

The government was at odds with a United Nations special envoy's report on human rights. The report cited specific instances of torture and abuse in Sudan and reported that many of Sudan's Islamic laws violated human rights. The government accused the report of being blasphemous to Islam. The UN report, along with the 1993 U.S. designation of Sudan as a sponsor of terrorism, made it difficult for the country to obtain nonhumanitarian foreign aid and loans.

In August the Sudanese government handed over to France one of the most notorious international terrorists, known as Carlos the Jackal (Ilich Ramírez Sánchez). He was believed to have been living in Sudan for the previous three years. As part of the deal, France helped set up Sudanese government bases in the Central African Republic and Zaire and also provided the government with aerial satellite photos of SPLA positions.

The government's main source of income continued to be taxes on income, goods, and services; it was not nearly enough to support its efforts against the SPLA. In the fall the International Monetary Fund praised Sudan's efforts to stabilize its economy and delayed until 1995 consideration of the expulsion of Sudan from the IMF because of its failure to pay arrears on a $1.7 billion debt.

The people of Sudan faced increasing daily hardships because of the war and worsening economy. More than 1 million Sudanese had died since the fighting began, most of starvation. Both sides had used food as a weapon. Relief groups estimated that 4.7 million were in need of immediate food aid, at least another 500,000 were in imminent danger of dying in southern Sudan, and as many as 280,000 could die of starvation in 1994.

See STATISTICS OF THE WORLD.   M.B.

SUPREME COURT OF THE UNITED STATES. See UNITED STATES OF AMERICA: Supreme Court.

SURINAME. See STATISTICS OF THE WORLD.

SWAZILAND. See STATISTICS OF THE WORLD.

SWEDEN. In March 1994, Swedish negotiators reached agreement with the European Union on the official terms under which Sweden would enter the EU. The Swedish government, led by conservative Carl Bildt, opted to schedule a popular referendum on EU membership after general elections slated for September 18. The referendum was held on November 13, and Swedes voted 52.2 percent to 46.9 percent to enter the EU. It was the highest turnout ever for a referendum—82 percent. While the major political parties supported membership, disagreement reigned within the parties. For example, only 55 percent of Social Democrats favored membership. Support was concentrated in urban areas, southern Sweden, and among male voters. In December, Parliament finalized approval of Sweden's entry into the EU.

Meanwhile, the September elections had resulted in the return of the Social Democrats to power. This came as little surprise, since widespread discontent had been produced by Sweden's sluggish economy and mounting unemployment (9 to 14 percent, depending on whether those covered by government-subsidized work schemes were included) and by the nonsocialist Bildt government's austerity policies for dealing with a budget deficit of about 13 percent of gross domestic product and a total public debt nearing 90 percent of GDP. Opinion polls since early 1993 had shown the Social Democrats gaining popularity. When the Social Democrats on August 19 announced their plan for dealing with government finances, including higher taxes and spending cutbacks, this helped to stabilize interest rates, which had jumped in anticipation of a Social Democratic victory.

The Social Democrats received 45.3 percent of the vote (an increase of 7.6 percentage points over 1991), their second-best showing in 24 years. The Left Party and the Green Party also gained, partly due to their opposition to EU membership, with the Greens returning to Parliament after a three-year hiatus. Bildt's conservative party (Moderates) maintained its previous share of seats, but its coalition partners—the Center Party, the Liberals, and the Christian Democrats—all lost ground. The radical-right New Democracy party failed to overcome the 4 percent threshold for representation. The elections resulted in a world record for female parliamentary representation: over 40 percent of the 349 members.

The new government, headed by former Prime Minister Ingvar Carlsson, was sworn in on October 7. Carlsson said he would give priority to dealing with the budget deficit and reducing unemployment while safeguarding the welfare state and increasing Sweden's commitment to international cooperation.

See STATISTICS OF THE WORLD. L.C.E.

SWITZERLAND. A development in Switzerland in 1994 that made headlines around the world was the mass suicide/murder of members of a religious cult, the so-called Order of the Solar Temple. A total of 48 bodies were found in October in two Swiss villages; another five turned up in Québec, Canada. The bodies had been incinerated in explosions, but police found evidence that some of the victims had been murdered. Authorities eventually concluded that one of the corpses was that of cult leader Luc Jouret. In December, French police arrested 42 people linked to the cult; 20 were released immediately.

Torrential rain caused flooding in several northern cantons in May. In addition, a series of accidents disrupted Switzerland's railway system: in mid-March a derailment in Zürich caused a major gasoline spill and fire; later that month eight passengers were killed in a construction mishap in Solothurn Canton; and July saw a chemical spill in Lausanne station.

In politics, the government officially supported Swiss entry into the European Union, but opposition parties were divided over the issue. The Liberal Party, the Independent Alliance, and the Protestant People's Party supported government policy, while the Action for an Independent and Neutral Switzerland, the Auto (Freedom) Party, the Green Party, and the League of Ticino rejected it—as did Finance Minister Otto Stich, who served as president of the Swiss Confederation in 1994. Opponents sought a referendum on the issue that could put an end to any government negotiations aimed at Swiss membership.

In a referendum on February 20, voters approved an initiative to ban transit of foreign trucks through Switzerland, as of the year 2004. In a June 12 referendum voters rejected propositions that would have eased citizenship requirements for children of immigrants, provided military personnel for United Nations peacekeeping missions, and subsidized cultural and artistic endeavors.

A referendum on December 4 saw voters overwhelmingly approve a law aimed at fighting drug dealing. The referendum authorized broad new search, arrest, and detention powers for authorities to use in dealing with asylum seekers and illegal aliens.

Cult deaths. *In October, in what appeared to be a case of mass suicide or murder, the bodies of 19 members of the Order of the Solar Temple were found in this room in a Swiss farmhouse. Inset, Luc Jouret, leader of the sect.*

Several Swiss firms acquired U.S. companies: Roche bought Syntex, Sandoz acquired Gerber baby foods, Ciba took over the eye-care division of Johnson & Johnson, and Nestle absorbed Alpo pet foods.

See STATISTICS OF THE WORLD. C.F.S.

SYRIA. In 1994, Syria remained fundamentally intransigent in its ongoing negotiations with Israel. President Hafez al-Assad traveled to Geneva early in the year to confer with U.S. President Bill Clinton. At the end of the six-hour January 16 summit, Assad stated that Syria envisaged "a new era of security and stability in which there are normal peaceful relations among all."

This pronouncement heartened U.S. officials but elicited little enthusiasm from Israel. At the end of April (and again in September) the Israeli leadership offered to carry out a gradual withdrawal from the Golan Heights. Damascus replied that it would accept nothing less than a complete and unconditional evacuation of the territory, which Israel had captured in the 1967 Arab-Israeli War.

Two rounds of shuttle diplomacy on the part of U.S. Secretary of State Warren Christopher, one in early May and the other in mid-July, failed to break the impasse. Christopher visited Syria again in October and again returned empty-handed. He was followed to the Syrian capital by Clinton, whose one-day stopover on

his way to Israel for the signing of the Israeli-Jordanian peace agreement improved the atmosphere of U.S.-Syrian relations but left prospects for an agreement with Israel no brighter than before.

In November the European Union lifted its eight-year arms embargo on Syria. Israel criticized the move. Nonetheless, high-level talks between Israel and Syria continued through December.

Earlier in the year, when Jordan had signaled its intention to conclude a formal agreement with Israel, Syrian newspapers castigated King Hussein for pursuing "a separate peace" that would jeopardize Arab interests. The July 25 ceremony in Washington, DC, announcing the proposed Israeli-Jordanian accord prompted a second wave of criticism in the Syrian press, although the signing was shown on Syrian television and Assad refrained from explicitly denouncing the pact.

Throughout 1994 the Syrian regime took further steps to encourage private enterprise. Long-standing restrictions on the importation of agricultural machinery were lifted in April, following an exceptionally bountiful cereals harvest. At the same time, the government reduced some subsidies, including those on bread and fuel, cushioning the resulting price rises by granting public sector workers a 30 percent raise in salary. As of September, government-run companies were allowed to sign contracts without consulting the appropriate ministry.

On January 21, Assad's eldest son, Basil, died in an automobile crash on the Damascus airport road. Basil, who was 31 years old and commanded the presidential guard corps, had been considered a possible successor to the presidency. Speculation concerning Assad's successor heightened again in August when the president unexpectedly dismissed more than a dozen key military commanders, in-

cluding Ali Haidar, head of the Special Forces, and Shafiq Fayyad, commander of the Third Army. The influential chiefs of general intelligence and of political security were replaced at the end of October.

Parliamentary elections in late August gave Assad's Baath Party and its partners in the National Progressive Front coalition 167 of 250 seats in the People's Assembly. Independents, most of them members of the country's urban bourgeoisie, captured the rest.

See STATISTICS OF THE WORLD.   F.H.L.

T

TAIWAN. Constitutional amendments were passed in 1994 that altered the structure of Taiwan's government. In April the Central Committee of the ruling Nationalist Party (Kuomintang) passed amendments whereby, starting in 1996, the president and vice president will be directly elected, a further step in Taiwan's rapid democratization. Another amendment ended the premier's power to countersign presidential appointments and dismissals, making the country's polity more clearly a presidential one.

In December 3 elections the opposition Democratic Progressive Party won the mayoralty of Taipei. The Nationalists won the governorship of the island—the first time a governor had been elected—and the mayoralty of Kaohsiung, Taiwan's second-largest city.

Taiwan's relations with China, which had improved in recent years, deteriorated after 24 Taiwanese tourists were robbed and murdered in China and the Beijing government attempted to cover up what became known as the Quindao Lakes affair. This, plus worry that Taiwan was investing too heavily in China, prompted the government to announce an economic "southern strategy" to give Southeast Asian countries, including Communist Vietnam, a higher priority in capital investments and trade.

Although 12 UN member-nations asked that Taipei be given a voice in the organization, the

effort failed, as expected. President Lee Tenghui made an official trip abroad to Nicaragua, Costa Rica, South Africa, and Swaziland—the first for a Taiwanese head of state in 17 years.

Taiwan's economy grew at a rate of over 6 percent, with exports and foreign investments increasing markedly. Nonetheless, the legislature cut the central government's budget for the first time in recent history, by 1.2 percent for 1993-1994, to control tax increases and rein in a $49 billion debt. Every major line item was reduced, except social welfare, which grew with the passage of a national health insurance bill. The legislature approved funds for Taiwan's fourth nuclear power plant.

See STATISTICS OF THE WORLD.   J.F.C.

TAJIKISTAN. Throughout 1994 armed groups of sympathizers with the banned Tajik Islamic opposition carried out almost daily attacks on Russian and Tajik border troops guarding the Tajikistan-Afghanistan frontier. Most of the Tajik opposition to Tajikistan's neo-Communist government was based in Afghanistan, where it enjoyed the support of Afghan fundamentalist groups and, in the latter half of 1994, volunteers from Arab states.

In late summer a group of armed oppositionists inside Tajikistan succeeded in seizing control of an important highway east of the capital city of Dushanbe for several days. Russian forces were heavily engaged in protecting the border with Afghanistan (viewed by

Russia as the most important line of resistance against a threatening tide of Muslim fundamentalism), but Russian military units stationed in Tajikistan refused to become involved in fighting between Tajik government and internal opposition troops. Under pressure from Russia and UN officials, the Tajik leadership agreed to peace talks with the opposition-in-exile. Two rounds of talks, in Moscow in April and in Tehran in June, ended inconclusively. In September a temporary cease-fire agreement was finally negotiated, and in late October the cease-fire was extended for three months. In a November 6 vote that was boycotted by the opposition, acting head of state Imomali Rahmonov, an ex-Communist, was elected president.

Tajikistan's government remained dependent on Russia not only to hold the border against the constant military threat but also to support the country's economy, weakened by warfare. In January, Tajikistan adopted the new Russian ruble as the first step toward complete integration of the Tajik economy with that of Russia. Russian financial officials were less enthusiastic about the proposed monetary union than was the Tajik government.

See STATISTICS OF THE WORLD. B.A.B.

TANZANIA. Progress toward democratization continued in Tanzania in 1994. The government party, Chama Cha Mapinduzi, easily won three by-elections held in the first half of 1994. However, the results of one were annulled by the High Court in August because of CCM campaign irregularities. In mid-August the government refused opposition demands to hold a constitutional convention or to amend existing laws that gave the government extensive powers and CCM campaign advantages. Radio Tanzania reported that local elections, which were held in October, resulted in a landslide victory for CCM candidates.

In a party referendum, 61 percent of 1.3 million CCM members voted to keep the current, two-government arrangement, consisting of a national government and a regional government for Zanzibar. Consequently, in late August, Parliament revoked a 1993 motion for a separate Tanganyika regional government, which could have led to the breakup of the union of Zanzibar and the mainland.

In December the president reshuffled his cabinet, appointing a new prime minister and secretary-general of CCM.

Burundian refugees continued to flee into northwestern Tanzania in early 1994, following the abortive Army coup d'état the previous November. A much larger group of refugees entered the same area to escape the Rwandan civil war. By November the refugees had grown to almost 600,000, turning the village of Benako into Tanzania's second-largest "city." Despite the genocide inflicted by Rwandan government forces, the Tanzanian government continued to support the power-sharing agreement negotiated in August 1993 at Arusha, Tanzania, between the Rwandan government and the Tutsi-led Rwandan Patriotic Front, until the rebel victory in July.

Gross domestic product rose 4.1 percent in the fiscal year ending in July 1994, but poor harvests resulting from the late 1993 drought indicated lower GDP growth in 1994-1995. Tanzania was unable to take advantage of the rise in world coffee and cotton prices, owing to low stocks. At the beginning of June, 600,000 Tanzanians, as well as the Burundian and Rwandan refugees, needed emergency food aid. In its budget announced in June, the government counted on external assistance for more than 40 percent of its planned expenditures of $990 million. Civil service salaries were increased and the minimum wage was doubled, but neither provided a sufficient income for a family, resulting in continuing corruption and employee absenteeism.

See STATISTICS OF THE WORLD. N.K.

TECHNOLOGY. *See* COMPUTERS; ELECTRONICS; HEALTH AND MEDICINE; SPACE EXPLORATION.

TELEVISION. *See* BROADCASTING.

TENNESSEE. *See* STATE GOVERNMENT REVIEW; STATISTICS OF THE WORLD.

TEXAS. *See* STATISTICS OF THE WORLD.

THAILAND. Political uncertainty intensified in Thailand in 1994, as Prime Minister Chuan Leekpai sought to hold together his fractious five-party coalition while facing a contentious opposition. The government suffered a blow in March when opposition members and Senate allies banded together to defeat eight proposed constitutional amendments; the changes would have more than halved the Senate membership. The government refused to dissolve Parliament over this setback. In May, Chalad Vorachat, whose publicly staged 1992 hunger strike eventually led to the collapse of the government, resumed his fast, this time demanding a more democratic constitution. His action provoked large demonstrations urging the government to reform the appointed Senate, select only elected parliamentarians as cabinet ministers, and require elections for provincial governors and mayors.

The Thai military maintained a generally low profile in 1994. The chief of the Army, General Wimol Wongwanisch, continued a campaign to professionalize and depoliticize the Army. Ongoing violence by Muslim separatists in the south, however, caused many Thais to demand a stronger military response. The military was criticized internationally for allegedly supporting the Khmer Rouge in Cambodia, and for assisting the military regime in Burma (Myanmar) by closing the border to ethnic minority refugees and pressuring resident refugee communities to return to Burma.

Rapid economic growth continued, with the gross domestic product rising more than 8 percent, inflation at around 5 percent, and foreign trade expanding 15 percent. Strong foreign investment continued, especially from Japan, and domestic credit expanded by 23 percent. In a move toward broader regional cooperation, Thailand in September hosted a meeting at which Burma, Cambodia, China, Laos, and Vietnam joined it in signing a multibillion-dollar Mekong Delta agreement to build a network of cross-border roads, bridges, and gas pipelines and hydroelectric and irrigation projects in the region.

Bangkok's hotel and tourism sector suffered a setback after widespread reports of the high incidence of AIDS in its notorious commercial sex trade; in response, the government enacted tougher laws against prostitution and child exploitation.

See STATISTICS OF THE WORLD.   G.B.H.

THEATER. To appreciate the 1993-1994 New York theater season, one needed to look no further than 1945. That was the year the Rodgers and Hammerstein musical *Carousel* and the J. B. Priestley play *An Inspector Calls* received their first major productions. A half

Regal performance. *Diana Rigg won a Tony Award in June for her portrayal of the tormented queen Medea in a revival of Euripides's classic tragedy.*

century later these two shows revved up a rickety Broadway engine faster than you could say London's Royal National Theater, which dusted them both off and exported them to the colonies in exhilarating new stagings.

Where the original *Carousel* and *An Inspector Calls* showcased the talents of John Raitt and Ralph Richardson, respectively, the stars to emerge from these visually resplendent revivals were two brilliant director/designer teams. Nicholas Hytner's dramatically taut *Carousel* highlighted the musical's darker textures, while a huge factory clock and shimmering full moon courtesy of designer Bob Crowley offered haunting suggestions of people ensnared in an eternal human comedy. A pounding rainstorm and Ian MacNeil's giant, collapsible dollhouse provided memorable apocalyptic images for *An Inspector Calls*. Stephen Daldry's dazzlingly visceral deconstruction helped make a didactic staple of England's regional theaters one of the few nonmusical successes of the Broadway year.

The generous critical and commercial reception for these two 1940s chestnuts served to underscore a theater season so dependent on the achievements of yesteryear that the Tony Award committee felt compelled to split its sole revival category. (*Carousel* won best musical revival, *An Inspector Calls* best dramatic revival.) Beginning with a ramshackle touring production of *Camelot* (with former Lancelot, Robert Goulet, ascending the throne of King Arthur), the ensuing season proved crazy for yore.

Glitz was the name of the game in the Tommy Tune-produced *Grease* and a Cecil B. DeMille-redolent British makeover of *Joseph and the Amazing Technicolor Dreamcoat,* replete with a children's chorus of 50. Audiences flocked to see Richard Chamberlain resuscitate the ghost of Rex Harrison as Henry Higgins in *My Fair Lady* and Diana Rigg re-create her explosive performance in *Medea* from London's maverick Almeida Theater.

The American class acts in the revival field came from San Diego's Old Globe Theatre and New York's Roundabout. The Globe's mint-fresh version of *Damn Yankees* received a shot of 1990s adrenaline from director Jack O'Brien, while George Abbott, the show's 106-year-old director and coauthor, basked in glory at the revival's Broadway opening. Over at the Roundabout, Scott Ellis proved equally adept at galvanizing musical and dramatic ensembles with a captivating re-treat of the 1963 Bock/Harnick/Masteroff tuner *She Loves Me* and a crisply performed staging of William Inge's *Picnic.*

The year's retro mode governed many of the new offerings, musicals in particular. Walt Disney's lavish expansion of its animated film *Beauty and the Beast,* along with such misbegotten sequels as a leering *Best Little Whorehouse Goes Public* and a downscaled *Annie Warbucks,* recycled traditional musical-comedy values so determinedly that they felt like revivals of old shows. The hydraulics-heavy *Cyrano* from the Netherlands was a mediocre attempt at reworking the epic pop-opera formula patented by the authors of *Les Misérables* and *Miss Saigon.*

Love and libido fueled the more striking new musicals. Ettore Scola's film *Passione d'Amore* provided the raw material for Stephen Sondheim's and James Lapine's *Passion.* A dreary tale of romantic obsession in 19th-century Italy, this chamber musical stirred to occasional life via a second-tier Sondheim score

and an emotionally naked performance by Donna Murphy as the sickly Fosca. *Hello Again,* a time-tripping rethink of Austrian playwright Arthur Schnitzler's *La Ronde* at Lincoln Center Theater, boasted the eclectic talents of an impish composer/lyricist named Michael John LaChiusa (whose sassy *First Lady Suite* enjoyed a brief December run at the Joseph Papp Public Theater). Sublimated libidinous energy informed the wonderfully kinetic *Stomp,* a percussive dance romp from England that featured an octet of working-class revelers banging energetically on everything including the kitchen sink.

The predominance of revivals could not obscure a very respectable parade of new plays, off and on Broadway, from established writers and up-and-comers alike. Leading the old guard was Edward Albee, whose remarkable *Three Tall Women* marked the playwright's

A woman obsessed. Donna Murphy (seen here with costar Jere Shea) took home the Tony Award for best actress in a musical for her portrayal of a lovesick Italian woman in Stephen Sondheim's Passion, *which also won the award for best musical.*

Tony Kushner

In 1994, for the second year in a row, playwright Tony Kushner won a Tony for best play. The award honored *Perestroika,* the second half of his two-part drama *Angels in America.* (The first half, *Millennium Approaches,* received both the Tony and a Pulitzer in 1993.)

With *Angels in America,* subtitled *A Gay Fantasia on National Themes,* Kushner had clearly tapped into the national zeitgeist. The two contiguous plays portray a nation on the brink of transition as AIDS and conservatism jolt a radical rethinking of values.

Kushner was born in 1956 to musician parents and raised in Lake Charles, LA. After earning an undergraduate degree from Columbia University, he pursued theater directing at New York University. Kushner's 1994 projects included an adaptation of *The Dybbuk;* his play *Slavs* opened in New York in December. He was also working on a screenplay for *Angels in America,* to be filmed by Robert Altman.   J.St.

the venerable Arthur Miller (*Broken Glass*), Neil Simon (*Laughter on the 23rd Floor*), Brian Friel (*Wonderful Tennessee*), and Frank D. Gilroy (*Any Given Day*).

Easily the most exciting of the newer blood was Tony Kushner, whose *Perestroika* provided a bracing conclusion to *Angels in America,* his sprawling two-part panoply of gay men, bewildered Mormons, and Roy Cohn. Kushner's dynamic synthesis of Socratic debate and straight-from-the-hip humor was a rare instance in which Broadway audiences embraced overtly political theater. Another epic American canvas, which failed to connect in New York, was Robert Schenkkan's Pulitzer Prize-winning *Kentucky Cycle,* an honorable attempt at a historical family chronicle that had the calculated air of a middle-brow television miniseries adapted for the stage.

The spectre of AIDS hovering over *Angels in America* also inhabited *Pterodactyls,* Nicky Silver's breathlessly fast satire of family denial in Philadelphia. Silver's brainy and unsentimental brand of absurdism descended from the same line as such razor-tipped writers as Christopher Durang and the late Harry Kondoleon. Representing an even darker side of urban malaise was Howard Korder's *The Lights,* a chilly, poetic elegy to alienation in the big city and Korder's most fulfilled work to date. Equally austere and theatrically potent was Elizabeth Egloff's *The Swan,* a broodingly expressionistic fantasy of a woman's sexual longings in rural America.

Reflecting an economically stressed time for theater, the season seemed to have more than the usual share of one-person shows, including three works by veteran solo performers. Anna Deavere Smith followed her landmark *Fires in the Mirror* with an even more ambitious piece of docu-theater, *Twilight: Los Angeles, 1992,* in which she impersonated dozens of observers to the Los Angeles riots touched off by the Rodney King beating. Just when it seemed Eric Bogosian had played out his gallery of goons, cretins, and fast-talkers, he advanced his technique by implicating himself in *Pounding Nails in the Floor With My Forehead.* Spalding Gray brought his microphone, wooden table, and peerless storytelling craft to *Gray's Anatomy,* a dryly hilarious ode to

first unmitigated triumph in over two decades. With this prismatic portrait of a coddled dowager as she looks back over her life, Albee brandished his trademark steel edge and a heretofore unseen residue of heart.

Later Life, A. R. Gurney's bittersweet September song, and *A Perfect Ganesh,* Terrence McNally's impassioned study of two Connecticut matrons in India, showed each playwright working at full steam. Lesser efforts came from midlife health panic. A welcome newcomer to the solo field was Claudia Shear, whose charismatic and touching account of odd employments, *Blown Sideways Through Life,* became a surprise downtown hit.

The backward glancing of the 1993-1994 season promised to extend into the next, as Harold Prince's massive rendering of *Showboat* chugged onto the scene in October, and *Sunset Boulevard,* Andrew Lloyd Webber's soft-focus stage version of the 1950 film classic opened in November, monopolizing media coverage of the theater.   J.St.

TOGO. See STATISTICS OF THE WORLD.

TONGA. See PACIFIC ISLANDS; STATISTICS OF THE WORLD.

TRANSPORTATION. A nationwide Teamsters' strike, further trucking deregulation, proposed railway mergers, and an impasse on maritime reform were highlights in U.S. transportation in 1994. The outstanding event on the international scene was the opening of the "Chunnel," an enormous rail tunnel beneath the English Channel.

Trucking. April saw a 23-day strike by the International Brotherhood of Teamsters against 22 of the largest U.S. less-than-truckload motor carriers. Churchill Truck Lines of Missouri closed down permanently as a result of the strike. The union and the major carriers eventually agreed to raise a full-time Teamster's base pay from $17.20 to $18.55 an hour by 1998. The new contract gave casual part-time workers $14.45 an hour (the carriers had wanted to pay only $9.00 an hour). However, the union agreed to lower the minimum number of hours for casuals from six to four. The union made one major concession, allowing the truck companies to increase the amount of freight that could be moved by rail in trailer-on-flatcar piggyback operations up to a maximum of 28 percent.

As 1994 drew to a close, trucking in the United States became virtually economically unregulated. The Trucking Industry Regulatory Reform Act of 1994 eliminated the requirement for truckers to file single line rates with the Interstate Commerce Commission. The law also stated that only a finding of "safety fitness" would be required in the future for entry into the industry. In addition, amendments to the Aviation Act allowed, effective January 1, 1995, federal preemption of individual states' intrastate economic regulation of trucking.

In trucking safety matters, the use of radar detectors on larger trucks became illegal on January 19, 1994.

Railroads. In July of 1994 the Burlington Northern made an offer to acquire the Santa Fe Pacific Corporation, parent of the Atchison, Topeka & Santa Fe Railroad. This merger would create the largest rail carrier in the United States. The BN offer was bettered by the Union Pacific Corporation. In October, BN matched UP's approximately $3.2 billion bid; no deal was concluded in 1994. A proposed purchase of the Kansas City Southern by the Illinois Central collapsed after months of negotiations. Looking north, the Canadian Pacific made an offer for the eastern Canadian Lines of the Canadian National.

The only major rail strike was against the Soo Line. However, on November 1 the rail industry served notice on the United Transportation Union that they would be bargaining over crew consists (the number of crewmen required on a train) and basic pay issues. High-speed passenger rail in the United States remained alive as President Bill Clinton signed the Swift Rail Development Act—named after U.S. Representative Al Swift (D) of Washington State—which authorized $184 million over three years for high-speed passenger rail planning and development. Separately, the state of Florida promised a $70 million per year operating subsidy if a high-speed rail system were to be built in the state.

The Express Industry. United Parcel Service (UPS) announced in September that it would guarantee next-morning delivery in major cities by 8:30 A.M., but at a premium price of $40 for letters and $45 for packages. This compared to about $13 for Federal Express delivery by 10:30 A.M. Federal Express Corporation officially changed its brand name and company logo to "FedEx." FedEx Chairman Fred Smith said that in order to improve efficiency the company would be opening new air hubs and would begin moving more freight by truck, easier henceforth thanks to recent deregulatory legislation.

411

Ocean Shipping. Maritime reform or, more correctly, the issue of subsidies for American flag merchant ships continued to be a political football in the U.S. Congress. The year ended with no new legislation and two American firms, Sea-Land Services and American President Lines, threatening to operate their new large container ships under foreign flags. On the U.S. maritime labor front, longshoremen in Philadelphia and some Gulf ports agreed to concessions in order to combat job losses to nonunion operators. Ocean freight rates and complaints about the "conferences" that set them were a matter of contention among shippers, carriers, and governments throughout the year. In late October the European Commission ruled that the Trans-Atlantic Agreement had been operating illegally since 1992 and shippers could sue for a refund of the resulting overcharges. A new agreement, the Trans Atlantic Conference Agreement, was scheduled to take effect at the beginning of 1995.

International Developments. May 6, 1994, marked the official opening of the English Channel "Chunnel," the rail tunnel connecting England and France and, arguably, the most significant transportation project of the century. The opening was more symbolic than substantive since full services were not scheduled to begin until 1995. However, at the end of October, company officials announced that the "Le Shuttle" freight service, in which trucks are moved on trains through the tunnel, was already carrying 12 percent of the trucks moving between England and France. Passenger cars are also carried on trains. Regular "luxury" passenger train service began on November 14, 1994. On this service high-speed trains cruise at up to 300 kilometers (nearly 200 miles) per hour, connecting London with both Paris and Brussels.

A serious future problem for European freight transport arose in February when Swiss voters decided to ban through international trucks on Swiss highways by 2004.   J.P.R.

TRINIDAD AND TOBAGO. *See* STATISTICS OF THE WORLD.

TUNISIA. Tunisia in 1994 saw opposition party members enter Parliament for the first time since independence in 1956—a development heralded by top government officials as a serious step on the path to realizing genuine political pluralism and democracy in the nation. President Zine al-Abidine Ben Ali, running uncontested, won a second five-year term in the March 20 elections. Ben Ali's party, the Constitutional Democratic Rally (RCD), won 97.7 percent of the vote and claimed 144 seats, while six legal opposition parties divided up the remaining 19. Ben Ali's and the RCD's widespread popular support derived from Ben Ali's ability to steer Tunisia down a relatively stable, secular course of political and economic liberalization by banning the radical Islamic al-Nahda (Renaissance) Party. Had Nahda been able to compete in the elections, it undoubtedly would have won a significant percentage of the vote.

During the election campaign period Tunisian officials barred numerous foreign reporters on grounds that they were penning unjustifiably harsh criticisms of Tunisia's human rights record and the electoral process. The government's hard line toward domestic and foreign critics continued even after its electoral success.

Ben Ali ended his one-year term as president of the Arab Maghreb Union; domestic instability in Algeria and Libya's international ostracism frustrated efforts to further the union's interests. Ben Ali assumed the presidency of the Organization of African Unity on June 13, succeeding President Hosni Mubarak of Egypt. Relations with South Africa were restored, and relations with Kuwait and Israel improved.

A new 1994 census revealed that Tunisia had 8.7 million inhabitants. Despite a poor agricultural harvest, the country grew economically by a respectable 5 percent; the government delivered on promises to privatize public sector companies.

See STATISTICS OF THE WORLD.   K.J.B.

TURKEY. During 1994, Turkey experienced economic crises, turbulent domestic politics, and continuing civil war with the Kurds.

Political Developments. In municipal elections held in March the coalition government of the right-of-center True Path Party and the Social Democratic Party faced its first major electoral test since assuming office in June 1993. The pro-Islamist Welfare Party scored the biggest gains by winning mayorships in 30

Show of strength. *Muslim fundamentalists wave their party colors after a rally in Istanbul in March, two days before local elections were to be held in Turkey. The fundamentalist party captured nearly one-fifth of the vote—a strong sign that the influence of pro-Islamist groups in the country was growing.*

of Turkey's 76 provinces, including Istanbul. Polls taken in October predicted that the Welfare Party would also be a big winner in the parliamentary by-election scheduled for December. Of the 22 vacant parliamentary seats, 13 were a result of the government's banning of the nationalist Kurdish Democratic Party and its deputies earlier in the year.

In mid-November, however, Prime Minister Tansu Ciller canceled December elections after a court ruled that electoral lists must include Kurdish immigrants who moved to the cities to escape the fighting in the southeast.

Civil War. The war against the Kurdish Workers Party (PKK), the main Kurdish guerrilla organization, continued full throttle in 1994. The government mobilized an estimated 300,000 troops, massive air power, as well as a phalanx of commandos and secret agents to destroy by any means, including assassinations, the Kurdish nationalist movement and its estimated 10,000 armed guerrillas. Several hundred villages were razed, and their residents removed or killed, in order to establish a security belt along the border with Iraq.

The PKK responded to these massive attacks by committing terrorist acts in Istanbul and other larger cities on the Aegean and Mediterranean coasts in an attempt to cripple Turkey's tourist industry, a major source of the country's hard currency.

Economy. The deterioration of the economy continued throughout 1994. The major factors contributing to the crisis were careless government spending, a soaring trade deficit, and high foreign debt. Some opposition figures contended that the cost of the war against the Kurds was the biggest economic drain on the country. An austerity package to cut the budget deficit, combat inflation, and placate international creditors was implemented in the spring. But by October these measures appeared to have had little effect. Inflation and interest rates hit 100 percent late in the year, and the gross domestic product, which saw 7 percent growth in 1993, was expected to shrink in 1994.

Foreign Affairs. Economic restraints impeded foreign policy initiatives in support of the Bosnian Muslims and compelled acquies-

413

We're with you. Turkish Prime Minister Tansu Ciller (right) was joined by Pakistani Prime Minister Benazir Bhutto (left) in a February visit to Sarajevo, Bosnia-Hercegovina, that was intended to show support for the population of the besieged city. Despite Turkey's sympathies for the Bosnian Muslims, economic restraints hampered efforts to aid them.

cence to Russian power in the Caucasus, especially in Azerbaijan, and in the Turkic republics of Central Asia. Relations with Iraq, Syria, and Iran improved. However, Turkey maintained a hard line with Greece regarding the divided island of Cyprus and the delimitation of territorial waters, airspace, and resources of the Aegean Sea. Tensions between the two countries escalated late in the year after Greece threatened to extend its control of the Aegean under a new international law that took effect in November.

See STATISTICS OF THE WORLD.   R.O.

TURKMENISTAN. Despite Turkmenistan's attractiveness to foreign investors, particularly oil and gas firms, its economy in 1994 suffered from the post-Soviet slump in industrial output experienced throughout the Commonwealth of Independent States (CIS). The instability of the manat, whose value against the U.S. dollar declined rapidly during 1994, was another problem. In May, President Saparmuryad Niyazov issued decrees launching privatization, but it moved very slowly, for a lack both of monetary resources and of a strong commitment on the part of the government.

Turkmenistan proved a problematic member of the CIS, turning off the gas supply to several CIS states to force them to pay their debts for earlier gas shipments. Niyazov incurred the wrath of Western countries through his courtship of Iran, which promised financial support for a project to ship Turkmen natural gas across Iran to Turkey and Western Europe; however, outside observers questioned whether Iran had the necessary funds.

Despite increasingly close relations with Iran, Turkmenistan also sought to maintain its ties to the West: In May, Turkmenistan became the first Central Asian state to join the NATO-sponsored Partnership for Peace, which extends cooperation with—but not membership in—NATO to the countries of the former Soviet bloc.

President Niyazov's personality cult continued to flourish; in January, 99.9 percent of the country's voters approved a parliamentary proposal to extend his term in office until 2002, without his having to run for reelection in 1997, so that he could oversee completion of a ten-year prosperity plan. Niyazov continued to persecute his few political opponents inside Turkmenistan, and in October the state prosecutor asked the Russian Federation to extradite Turkmen dissidents in exile in Moscow.

See STATISTICS OF THE WORLD.   B.A.B.

TUVALU. See PACIFIC ISLANDS; STATISTICS OF THE WORLD.

U

UGANDA. In March 1994, Uganda held nationwide elections to choose delegates to the assembly charged with creating a new constitution. There were no restrictions placed on the nomination of candidates, but opposition parties were not allowed to campaign.

The elections were marked by exceptionally high registration and turnout, even in regions that opposed the government. With local exceptions, the conduct of the campaigns and counting of ballots was considered to be open and fair.

By November the most significant issues that the Constituent Assembly had debated were the restoration of multiparty competition versus the continuation of a nonpartisan "movement" government, and unitary government versus federalism. In November there was a major cabinet reshuffle which included the first woman to be appointed the country's vice president. In December, Parliament granted the assembly a six-month extension to complete its work, which will lengthen the interim period before Uganda returns to civilian rule.

Government policies to maintain economic growth and monetary stability were highly successful for the second year. The economy grew 4 percent in the year ending in June 1994, held back by lower agricultural output due to drought. Tripling of world coffee prices led to an estimated doubling in national export earnings. Through August yearly inflation remained impressively low at 12 percent. In June 1994, Uganda's total debt was $2.6 billion. Since 72 percent of this debt was owed to multilateral creditors who would not reschedule loan obligations, it was likely that Uganda would pay back more than it received over the next several years.

The Lord's Resistance Army, a rebel group in the north, broke off peace negotiations with the government in late February and engaged in a stream of attacks through August. In early September an Army official said 96 rebels had been killed in a six-week offensive. The government claimed the rebels were receiving training and arms from the Sudanese government, and in early October it canceled its military monitoring agreement with Sudan.

Severe food shortages led to famine in two districts in the east, causing some 300 deaths by August.

See STATISTICS OF THE WORLD.   N.K.

UKRAINE. In 1994, Ukraine's parliamentary and presidential elections revealed deep cleavages between easterners and westerners. With its economy verging on collapse, Ukraine was promised international support late in the year as it moved toward fundamental economic reforms and agreed to become a nuclear-free nation.

Elections. In democratic elections on July 10, Leonid Kuchma, onetime director of the former Soviet Union's largest missile factory, narrowly defeated incumbent Leonid Kravchuk, the first president of independent Ukraine. Kuchma, Ukraine's former prime minister, gained considerable support from the more Russified and industrial eastern Ukraine. Kravchuk, a former Communist ideologue, elicited his support from the more agrarian and nationalist western Ukraine.

Shaping the future. A woman presents her identification card at the registration desk during the March elections for Uganda's Constituent Assembly. The assembly was to create a new constitution for the country, debating such issues as the restoration of multiparty competition and centralized government versus federalism.

In Ukraine's first free parliamentary elections the multitude of candidates and a cumbersome electoral law requiring a 50 percent turnout and at least a 50 percent majority of the vote to win necessitated runoffs and by-elections in certain districts; by late November, 403 of 450 seats were filled. A left-wing coalition of Communists, Agrarians, and Socialists emerged as the most powerful voting bloc, electing the speaker and first deputy speaker. These groups opposed privatization, favoring the current command economy, integration into the Commonwealth of Independent States (CIS), and close cooperation with Russia. Right-wing groups tended to be pronationalist and pro-Western and to support socioeconomic reform. The more centrist groups also tended to favor economic reform.

Economic Decline. Ukraine's economy declined for the third consecutive year, with industrial production expected to fall more than 30 percent in 1994. Deficit spending spurred hyperinflation, and industry was hurt by chronic supply shortages. The value of the currency, the karbovanets, depreciated from 30,000 to the U.S. dollar to more than 100,000 by the end of the year. Ukraine's immense trade deficit, primarily a result of oil and gas purchases from Russia, was only partly offset by vigorous activity in the unofficial economy.

In October, President Kuchma announced comprehensive economic reforms, including reduced subsidies, lifting of price controls, lower taxes, privatization of industry and agriculture, and reforms in currency regulation and banking. Parliament approved the plan's main points. The International Monetary Fund promised a $360 million loan to initiate reforms, and Ukraine hoped to obtain over $5 billion in loans and grants over the next few years to support fundamental restructuring.

Foreign Relations. Although Ukraine had previously transferred its tactical nuclear warheads to Russia, it stalled on the transfer of long-range missiles. The resulting diplomatic isolation of Ukraine was broken by a trilateral agreement, signed by Presidents Bill Clinton, Boris Yeltsin, and Kravchuk on January 14. The agreement included explicit recognition of Ukraine's borders. In November the Ukrainian Parliament, having unconditionally ratified the Strategic Arms Reduction Treaty earlier in the year, ratified the Nuclear Nonproliferation Treaty, a pledge to rid itself of all nuclear weapons. By November nearly half of the country's 1,800 warheads had been transferred to Russia. Ukraine was to receive technical and financial assistance in dismantling the missiles as well as compensation for the country's enriched uranium.

Russo-Ukrainian relations were strained because of pressure put on Ukraine by Russia to integrate into the CIS, Ukraine's nonpayment of debt, and Russian claims to Crimea, where a pro-Russian president was elected in January. Numerous meetings to divide the Black Sea fleet of the former Soviet Navy failed because of Russia's insistence on taking most of the fleet and obtaining extensive basing rights, including Sevastopol harbor. Although the climate between the two countries improved after the election of Kuchma, major issues remained unresolved at year's end.

See STATISTICS OF THE WORLD. Z.E.K.

UNION OF SOVIET SOCIALIST REPUBLICS. *See* RUSSIA; *other former Soviet republics.*

UNITED ARAB EMIRATES. *See* PERSIAN GULF STATES; STATISTICS OF THE WORLD.

UNITED NATIONS. In 1994 the United Nations continued to focus on peacekeeping operations and responses to numerous global crises. Despite the increased demand for UN involvement, the organization was underfunded as many member states fell behind in their payments.

The Budget Shortfall. As of November 30 the combined regular and peacekeeping budgets faced a $2 billion shortfall; the United States alone owed $666 million. The budget shortfalls had an especially serious impact on social and economic development programs and on humanitarian programs in 1994. In May the secretary-general submitted his Agenda for Development, describing the past and present conflicts shaping the current struggle for economic and social development. The report recognized that "development is in crisis" and that "the poorest nations fall further behind." But many in the UN and among member states viewed the agenda as short on concrete proposals, and it never received the high-level attention that greeted the 1993 Agenda for Peace. In the report the secretary-general admitted that some countries cut their support for UN development activities because of increased peacekeeping costs. Industrialized countries' contributions to overseas development aid dropped to an average of only 0.29 percent of their gross national product; 0.7 percent was the agreed target.

Even the Office of the High Commissioner for Refugees, charged with the care of more than 49 million displaced people and refugees worldwide and one of the best-funded UN agencies, faced a $300 million shortfall from its $1.3 billion budget.

Peacekeeping. The UN's peacekeeping function was stretched almost beyond capacity in 1994, with 20 peacekeeping operations staffed by about 77,000 UN troops and 2,600 international civilian peacekeepers. In March the UN initiated plans for a standby force, to which member states would commit specific numbers of troops, supplies, or equipment; members could refuse specific missions, however. (When the sudden need for peacekeeping troops in Rwanda came up in the spring, all of the 28 countries that had agreed in principle to commit standby forces refused to participate in that emergency deployment.)

By the summer Security Council decisions had shifted away from direct UN involvement toward grants of UN authority to specific member states to intervene in conflict areas alone or in "coalitions" led by a powerful state. In June the Council authorized France to deploy "Operation Turquoise" in Rwanda; in July it authorized Russia to keep troops in Georgia, facing the Abkhazian separatist movement, and it authorized the United States unilaterally to send troops to Haiti.

War in the Balkans. The UN Protection Force (Unprofor) remained the UN's largest peacekeeping operation, fielding 38,000 military personnel and costing $5 million per day. The UN was also responsible for maintaining the arms embargo against all of the former Yugoslavia and for humanitarian aid to besieged cities and towns in Bosnia. Peace talks sponsored by the UN and the European Union on a plan that would have divided Bosnia into eth-

Rights watchdog. *José Ayala Lasso, formerly Ecuadoran ambassador to the United Nations, holds a press briefing in Geneva in March. He was appointed the previous month to the newly created post of UN high commissioner for human rights.*

nic ministates broke down early in 1994. In July the so-called contact group (the United States, Britain, France, Germany, and Russia) proposed a settlement that would allocate 51 percent of the land to the Muslim-Croat federation within Bosnia (set up in March) and 49 percent to the Bosnian Serbs. The Serbs, already in possession of 70 percent of the land, rejected the proposal. In return for the lifting of some UN sanctions, the Yugoslav government took measures to limit its cross-border military and economic support of Serbian-held territories in Bosnia, but the Bosnian Serbs continued their assault.

The UN had some success in Sarajevo, still a focus of fierce attack in early 1994. Unprofor and NATO negotiated a cease-fire from Serb military assaults on the city following the shelling of a crowded market in February that left many dead. However, some shelling and sniper attacks resumed in July and continued until Christmas. The "safe areas" defined by the Security Council remained largely unprotected. Late in the year Bosnian Serbs (helped by Serbs from Croatia) were poised to overrun one such area, Bihac, after repulsing an initially successful offensive by the Army of the Muslim-led Bosnian government. After turning down UN pleas for a cease-fire, the Serbs

UN refugee chief. *Sadako Ogata, UN high comissioner for refugees, visits the besieged city of Sarajevo in March. Bosnia-Hercegovina was just one of the many troubled regions of the globe that complicated the UN's role in aiding refugees worldwide. At right is British Lieutenant General Michael Rose, head of the UN peacekeeping forces in Bosnia.*

made the UN's role in Bosnia virtually impossible, harassing UN forces and refusing to allow passage of either Unprofor or aid convoys. Talk of a UN withdrawal rose and fell, and there was some feeling that the UN mission in Bosnia had lost its credibility and its direction. As the year ended, however, UN mediators succeeded in extending a seven-day cease-fire, negotiated by former U.S. President Jimmy Carter between the Bosnian government and Bosnian Serbs, into a four-month cessation of hostilities.

Throughout 1994 tensions between the UN and NATO had complicated the situation in Bosnia. While NATO's political leadership claimed it wanted to respond more aggressively to continued Serb attacks (air strikes were authorized under certain conditions), the Unprofor command, representing the same powers as NATO, voiced opposition for fear of retaliation against UN troops, and the air strike option was virtually eliminated. There were also disagreements between the United States and its European allies over lifting the arms embargo against Bosnia. On November 4 the UN General Assembly recommended lifting the embargo, but the Security Council refused. The United States ended its participation in enforcing the embargo in mid-November, but the results of this action were minimal.

A UN commission determined in May that grave violations of international humanitarian law had been committed in the former Yugoslavia. In July the Security Council appointed Richard J. Goldstone, a respected South African judge, as chief prosecutor for the international war crimes tribunal that had been established in 1992.

Somalia. In February the UN initiated new contacts with various factions in still-riven Somalia. But tensions remained high; seven Indian UN peacekeepers were killed in August. Progress toward peace remained stalled, and in November the UN voted to withdraw the last 17,000 UN troops by March 31, 1995. The operation had cost $1 billion.

Rwanda. Following the death of the Rwandan president in a suspicious plane crash in April, the fragile transition period agreed to in 1993 by the government and the rebel Rwandan Patriotic Front was shattered by all-out violence. Most members of the UN Assistance Mission to Rwanda (Unamir), a small UN contingent stationed in Rwanda to oversee the transition, were withdrawn. In May the UN reversed itself and authorized 5,500 more peacekeepers but was unable to get troop commitments.

Also in May, the UN sent a special envoy to Rwanda to investigate accounts of genocide by the Army against the minority Tutsi tribe. His report in June moved the Security Council to establish a commission whose work later led to the setting up of a war crimes tribunal. Meanwhile, on June 22 the Council gave France a two-month military mandate for a humanitarian mission, which was called Operation Turquoise.

Following the killing of hundreds of thousands of people, the Army was routed by the Rwandan Patriotic Front in July. An unprecedented humanitarian crisis ensued, with almost 2 million refugees fleeing the country, most of them into Zaire and Tanzania. The UN coordinated a massive relief operation. By late 1994 the overthrown government's Army was escalating attacks on refugees and theft of relief supplies and threatening UN and other relief workers in the camps.

Iraq. Iraq remained subject to strict economic sanctions imposed by the UN after the 1990 Iraqi invasion of Kuwait. Just before the October release of a report by the UN's special commissioner stating that Iraq had in fact complied with weapons-monitoring arrangements that the UN required be put in place before the oil embargo could be lifted, Iraq, in an apparent attempt to exert pressure on the international community, moved troops toward Kuwait. The United States responded by massing troops near the border, and the efforts by some Security Council members, especially France and Russia, to set a timetable for lifting sanctions were derailed. Iraq later agreed, however, to recognize Kuwait's sovereignty and borders.

Haiti. In May, UN sanctions against the military junta ruling Haiti were strengthened. On July 11 the UN's human rights monitors were expelled from Haiti. The Security Council then authorized the United States to send troops against the military government and restore to power President Jean-Bertrand Aristide, who had lived in exile since the military's takeover in late 1991. UN troops would then monitor Haiti's return to democracy. In September, after former U.S. President Jimmy Carter, retired U.S. General Colin Powell, and U.S. Senator Sam Nunn (D, Georgia) negotiated with the junta leaders to step down, U.S. troops landed without having to use military force. Aristide was returned to power in October. Despite continuing attacks on civilians and human rights violations by the Haitian military, the United States announced its intention to leave Haiti by early 1995; it was unclear when UN peacekeepers would be sent.

UN Reform. Member states and a special General Assembly committee continued to look at the need for major reforms in UN structure and function. For some countries, notably the major powers, the focus was on fiscal and management practices and the need to secure permanent Security Council seats for Germany and Japan. For many other countries reform needs were broader. These countries wanted more openness in debate and decision making, and they wanted to change the serious imbalance among permanent Security Council members between the wealthy industrialized North and the poor and developing countries of the South. Proposals ranged from expanding the Council and ensuring the South's permanent representation on it to eliminating the veto power of the Council's permanent members. There was minimal progress on the openness issue in November, when the Council decided to institutionalize participation in its peacekeeping decisions by countries that were not on the Council but were nonetheless providers or potential providers of UN peacekeepers. All other work on reform, however, was deferred until 1995.

Special Development Activities. The General Assembly had designated 1994 the International Year of the Family, and related activities were held throughout the world. The International Conference on Population and Development was held in Cairo in September. The conference was widely viewed as a major advance in linking issues of population growth with uneven development and questions of women's empowerment in areas of development, health, and reproduction. However, opposition to part of the Program of Action, led by the Vatican, meant that the program finally agreed on was far less specific than organizers had hoped.

In May the first Global Conference on Sustainable Development of Small Island States was held in Barbados, part of the follow-up to the UN's 1992 Rio Conference on Development and Environment (the so-called Earth Summit). Also in May, Japan hosted the World Conference on Natural Disaster Reduction, resulting in a plan for integrating disaster preparedness with development efforts.

New Member. The Pacific island nation of Palau became the UN's 185th member in December 1994.   P.B.

United States of America

For President Bill Clinton, 1994 was a better year in foreign policy than on the domestic front. Despite high hopes as the year opened, the Democratic-dominated Congress accomplished relatively little, and the November elections gave the Republicans control of both House and Senate.

The Whitewater scandal continued to dog Clinton. Although Congress approved a crime bill supported by the president, his bid for health care reform failed. A new justice joined the Supreme Court. Deposed Haitian President Jean-Bertrand Aristide was restored to power under the protection of U.S. troops.

THE PRESIDENCY

Early in 1994, outlining his ambitious legislative agenda for the coming year, President Bill Clinton focused primarily on domestic issues such as health care reform and passage of a comprehensive crime bill; he set himself no specific foreign policy goals. But 1994 brought few conspicuous domestic successes for Clinton. Although the cold war was over, he still found himself confronted by numerous foreign policy crises, and it was, ironically, in certain areas of foreign policy that he was most visibly effective. Unfortunately for the president, neither foreign policy successes nor an improving economy (which, polls showed, many people did not notice) was enough to win public approval. He was accused of lacking basic political principles he was willing to stick to, or of being a "tax and spend" Democrat disguised as a centrist. And the Whitewater scandal remained alive, raising continued character issues. The first family even had to endure a few physical assaults on the executive mansion; these incidents, beginning in September with the crash of a small plane into the White House below the presidential living quarters, did not come close to harming family members (who were not even home at the time of the plane crash) but raised some security issues nonetheless. In the November elections voters expressed their dissatisfaction with the president and his agenda by electing Republican majorities in both houses of Congress, radically shifting the balance of power in Washington.

Failed Health Care Reform. One of the biggest defeats suffered by Clinton during the year was the collapse of his health care reform initiative, which he had originally submitted to Congress in October 1993 after lengthy preparations by a task force chaired by first lady Hillary Rodham Clinton. The president had given this issue top priority, and in his State of the Union address in January 1994 he expressed a determination to "guarantee every American private health insurance that can never be taken away." But the tide was already turning against his sweeping, complex reform package. Most Americans never clearly understood the plan, several powerful interest groups strongly opposed features of it, Republicans effectively portrayed it as bureaucratic, and alternative health care reform programs were floated in Congress by members of both parties. Neither these programs nor Clinton's was able to attract broad support, and no proposal came to a floor vote.

Welfare Reform. In June the White House sent its long-awaited welfare reform proposal to Capitol Hill. Projected to cost $9.3 billion over five years, the plan set a two-year time limit for adult recipients to get off the welfare rolls. After that, they would be enrolled in a government-paid community service job. It also allowed states to cap benefits for dependent children. Democrats kept their distance from the bill, which Clinton himself regarded as less pressing than health care reform, and in the end it went nowhere.

Crime Bill Passes. Clinton did score a success with his crime program. After a prolonged and divisive political process, a $30 billion anticrime bill passed both houses of Congress in August. The bill that emerged from 14 days of votes and debate had most of the features the president wanted, including a "three strikes and you're out" provision for repeated criminal offenders, an assault weapons ban, billions of dollars for prison construction and for more police on the streets, and spending programs targeted at crime prevention (although these were opposed by many Republicans as a waste of money). To gain passage of the measure, Clinton had to obtain some GOP support by inviting Republicans into the negotiating process; he did so successfully.

European Journey. In early January, Clinton embarked on an eight-day European trip intended to put his stamp on the historic changes sweeping the continent in the wake of the cold war. It was the first of four foreign journeys for the president in 1994, and the most eventful. In Brussels for a NATO conference, he obtained approval for an arrangement called the Partnership for Peace, which would loosely affiliate Eastern European countries with NATO without giving them the full security guarantee provided by NATO membership. Clinton also announced an agreement between the United States, Ukraine, and Russia to remove all nuclear weapons from Ukraine—the world's third-largest nuclear arsenal. In Moscow, Clinton and Yeltsin agreed to no longer target each other's country with nuclear weapons. The U.S. president put his signature on the Moscow summit by appearing at an electronic "town hall" meeting to answer questions from viewers and promote Yeltsin's reform program.

Foreign Policy Bonuses. Later in the year, with his legislative agenda floundering, Clinton enjoyed some unexpected foreign policy successes. The first involved North Korea,

which had reportedly been developing nuclear bombs and had resisted inspection of its nuclear facilities. In June, as tensions with North Korea heightened, Clinton allowed former President Jimmy Carter to meet with North Ko-

Leon Panetta

As a presidential candidate, Bill Clinton called himself a Washington outsider. But in June 1994, with the White House in political trouble, Clinton chose Leon Panetta—decidedly a Washington insider—as his chief of staff.

Leon Edward Panetta, born in 1938 in California, once directed the Office of Civil Rights as a Republican under President Richard Nixon. Fired for being too zealous about school desegregation, Panetta was elected to Congress in 1976 as a Democrat. During 16 years in the House, Panetta became chairman of the Budget Committee; in 1992, Clinton tapped him to head the Office of Management and Budget.

As chief of staff, Panetta was charged with setting more orderly procedures for the president's staff, and the president himself, while acting as a key administration spokesman and congressional lobbyist. Faced with a balky Congress, Panetta hammered out a compromise on a federal crime bill but could not save the president's health reform package. The November 1994 election, which put Republicans in the majority in the House and Senate, left Panetta with greater challenges still.   W.A.M.

The Clinton Team

Vice President Albert Gore, Jr.

Secretary of State Warren M. Christopher
Secretary of the Treasury Lloyd M. Bentsen[1]
Secretary of Defense William J. Perry
Attorney General Janet Reno
Secretary of the Interior Bruce E. Babbitt
Secretary of Agriculture Mike Espy[2]
Secretary of Commerce Ronald H. Brown
Secretary of Labor Robert B. Reich
Secretary of Health and Human Services Donna E. Shalala
Secretary of Housing and Urban Development Henry G. Cisneros
Secretary of Transportation Federico F. Peña
Secretary of Energy Hazel R. O'Leary
Secretary of Education Richard W. Riley
Secretary of Veterans Affairs Jesse Brown
Administrator, Environmental Protection Agency Carol M. Browner
Director, Office of Management and Budget Alice M. Rivlin[3]
Chair, Council of Economic Advisers Laura D. Tyson
U.S. Representative to the United Nations Madeleine K. Albright
U.S. Trade Representative Michael (Mickey) Kantor
Director, Office of National Drug Control Policy Lee P. Brown
White House Chief of Staff Leon E. Panetta[4]
Administrator, Small Business Administration Philip Lader[5]
National Security Adviser Anthony Lake
Director, Central Intelligence Agency R. James Woolsey[6]
Surgeon General M. Joycelyn Elders[6]
Chairman of the Joint Chiefs of Staff General John M. Shalikashvili

[1]Resigned in December; Robert E. Rubin named as replacement.
[2]Resigned effective December 31.
[3]Replaced Leon E. Panetta in midyear.
[4]Replaced Thomas F. McLarty III in midyear.
[5]Replaced Erskine B. Bowles in October.
[6]Resigned in December.

rean leaders. The North then agreed to negotiations in Geneva and, ultimately, to an accord under which it pledged to freeze its nuclear program. However, an incident in December, when a U.S. military helicopter reportedly strayed into North Korea and was apparently shot down and a pilot was held hostage for two weeks, illustrated that the potential for sharp tensions between the United States and North Korea remained high.

The Clinton administration also achieved apparent success in Haiti. On September 15, seeking to generate public support for a U.S. invasion to restore Haiti's exiled, democratically elected president to power, Clinton gave an Oval Office address in which he invoked graphic images of brutality by the current military leaders and warned that they must return ousted President Jean-Bertrand Aristide to power or be removed by U.S. military force. When this ultimatum failed, he authorized an invasion.

As U.S. warships steamed toward the Caribbean, Clinton also played a diplomatic card: he sent to Haiti's capital former President Carter, along with Senator Sam Nunn (D, Georgia) and retired General Colin Powell, former chairman of the Joint Chiefs of Staff. A last-minute deal was struck, under which the Haitian junta would step down by October 15. Arriving in Haiti, the American forces met with welcome rather than resistance; and on October 15, Aristide, with the backing of a U.S. military presence, entered the country to reassume office.

Also in October, Clinton met head-on a threatening buildup of Iraqi troops on the border of Kuwait—the nation whose invasion by Iraq had been repulsed by U.S. and allied forces in 1991. He ordered a rapid deployment of ships, troops, and high-performance aircraft to the region; in response, Iraqi President Saddam Hussein pulled back his forces.

Clinton then made a swing through the Middle East; there he witnessed signing of a peace treaty between Israel and Jordan and reviewed U.S. troops in Kuwait. He also visited Syria to try to advance peace talks between that Arab nation and Israel.

Presidential Scandals. The so-called Whitewater controversy did not go away in 1994. This scandal centered on the tangled affairs of the Whitewater Development Corporation, a failed Arkansas real estate venture in which the Clintons had formerly invested, and Madison Guaranty, a failed savings and loan association, owned by James McDougal, a partner of the Clintons in the Whitewater venture. Among other things, there were allegations that Madison Guaranty had improperly channeled money into Whitewater and into Clinton campaign funds.

During 1994 the affair came under investigation by two independent counsels. The first, former U.S. Attorney Robert Fiske, was appointed in January by Attorney General Janet Reno, after Clinton, under pressure from members of Congress, requested an investigation. In the summer, after legislation covering independent counsels had been revived by Congress, a panel of federal judges replaced Fiske with Kenneth Starr, a Washington lawyer with strong Republican ties—considered by some to be too partisan for the post. Also during the summer, both the Senate and the House of Representatives held hearings on limited aspects of the Whitewater affair.

The scandal had heated up in early March, when the administration acknowledged that Treasury Department regulators had met with White House officials to give them advance notice of criminal referrals made by the Resolution Trust Corporation (the agency handling the savings and loan cleanup for the Treasury Department) relating to questionable conduct by Madison Guaranty. The dreaded word "cover-up" began to be heard once again in Washington, and top administration officials who had attended the briefings—including White House counsel Bernard Nussbaum and Deputy Treasury Secretary Roger Altman—eventually resigned over this incident. Meanwhile, at a news conference in late March the president vigorously defended his own conduct and that of his wife—who, as a partner in the Rose law firm, had represented Madison

Guaranty before Arkansas banking regulators appointed by Bill Clinton, then governor of Arkansas.

Among other disclosures that complicated matters, records released by the Clintons in late March showed that losses they had sustained on their Whitewater investment were substantially less than they had previously claimed. The White House also released records indicating that Hillary Rodham Clinton had turned an investment of $1,000 in high-risk commodities into nearly $100,000 in less than ten months during 1978 and 1979.

In May a former Arkansas state employee named Paula Jones filed a lawsuit alleging that Bill Clinton had made an unwanted sexual advance toward her three years earlier. The president denied the allegation, which was unsubstantiated, and the Clintons subsequently established a legal defense fund to help cover their expenses in connection with this suit and the Whitewater probe. In December a federal judge ruled that although the president could be questioned, the sexual harassment suit could not go to trial until after he left office.

Changes of Office. In June, Thomas ("Mack") McLarty, a close Clinton friend and Washington outsider, was replaced as White House chief of staff by Leon Panetta, director of the Office of Management and Budget. A man with a reputation for getting things done, Panetta took steps to tighten up management

Whitewater woes. The year saw new allegations, and stepped-up federal investigative efforts, into the Whitewater affair—focusing primarily on the financial dealings of Bill and Hillary Clinton during the two decades before he took office as president. It sometimes seemed as if no one in the White House might be above suspicion, not even the Clintons' cat.

of the White House staff and the president's time, in an effort to increase Clinton's political effectiveness. He was replaced as budget chief by his deputy, Alice Rivlin.

The first person to leave the Clinton cabinet was Defense Secretary Les Aspin, who resigned under pressure in December 1993. Admiral Bobby Ray Inman, who had accepted Clinton's invitation to replace him, suddenly withdrew his name in January, in a rambling speech that blamed others for attacking him; Deputy Defense Secretary William J. Perry assumed the post instead. Mike Espy announced he would resign as agriculture secretary, effective the end of 1994. Espy was the object of a probe by an independent counsel into allegations he had accepted improper gifts from an Arkansas chicken producer; named to replace him was U.S. Representative Dan Glickman (D, Kansas), who was defeated for reelection in November. Surgeon General Joycelyn Elders, chronically in trouble for outspoken views that many found offensive, was ultimately forced to depart in December, after a remark that appeared to endorse teaching masturbation to schoolchildren. Also resigning in December was CIA Director R. James Woolsey, who was under fire for his handling of the investigation into double agent Aldrich Ames.

Treasury Secretary Lloyd Bentsen, one of Clinton's most valued aides, left his post near the end of 1994 to rejoin the private sector; as his replacement, Clinton named economic adviser Robert Rubin. Press Secretary Dee Dee Myers also resigned in December; named as her replacement was State Department spokesman Mike McCurry.

Webster Hubbell, a close associate of the Clintons and onetime legal partner in the Rose law firm, resigned in March as number three official in the Justice Department. Nine months later he pleaded guilty to tax evasion and mail fraud, in connection with having fraudulently billed his law firm and legal clients for a total of some $400,000.

On a brighter note, the president had a new opportunity to make a Supreme Court appointment when Justice Harry Blackmun retired at the end of June. After lengthy deliberation, Clinton named federal appeals court Judge Stephen G. Breyer (see profile in PEOPLE IN THE NEWS), a moderate whom he had considered for the previous Court vacancy. Breyer's nomination was easily approved in the Senate, and he took his seat at the start of the Court's fall term in October.

Republicans Sweep Congress. On November 8, in a victory that stunned the White House, the Republicans gained control of both the Senate and the House (see ELECTIONS IN THE UNITED STATES). Republicans elected to the House had endorsed a ten-point platform known as the Contract With America; its goals included a balanced budget amendment, term limits, and tax relief. Many GOP candidates ran against the president personally; some "morphed" the face of their Democratic opponent in television ads so it merged into that of Bill Clinton. Clinton campaigned hard against the Republican contract (which he dubbed a contract on America), but to no avail.

After the Elections. While his foreign policy activities apparently did not help him on Election Day, Clinton went ahead after the elections with a long-planned ten-day trip centered around a visit to Indonesia, which was hosting a summit meeting of the Asia-Pacific Economic Cooperation group of nations. He used the occasion to press for expanded U.S. trade in the region.

The lame-duck 103rd Congress was called back to vote on a new GATT (General Agreement on Tariffs and Trade) world trade accord, due to take effect January 1, 1995. Despite strong opposition from some quarters, the measure passed with bipartisan support, leaving Clinton with a record on free trade any commerce-minded Republican would envy.

Clinton's long-awaited reaction to the election came in a televised address on December 15. Most of his speech was devoted to proposals for cutting middle-class taxes—as he had originally promised during his presidential campaign (but later had shelved in favor of efforts to cut the federal deficit).

Late in the year, polls by Gallup and Times Mirror showed Clinton losing to a generic Republican in a hypothetical 1996 matchup. He had the lowest approval rating after two years of any modern president—except one. That president, however, was Ronald Reagan.

C.M.C.

Newt Gingrich

When Newt Gingrich (R, Georgia) was a freshman in Congress, he said he had two goals: to make an impact on national politics and to become speaker of the House. By January 1995 he had accomplished both of them.

When Newton Leroy McPherson was born in Pennsylvania in 1943, his parents' marriage had already broken up. He got the name Gingrich when his mother's second husband adopted him. At 19, Gingrich married his former high-school math teacher. He later studied history at Tulane, earning a Ph.D. in 1971; student deferments kept him out of the Vietnam War. At Tulane, Gingrich was considered a liberal, but he took a turn to the right after two failed bids for a congressional seat and won election to the House in 1978. During the next two years the marriage foundered, and Gingrich divorced his wife as she was being treated for uterine cancer—leading opponents to deem hypocritical his commitment to "family values." (He remarried in 1981.)

Gingrich's pugnacious style in the House helped young Republicans gain visibility and power, and he was elected minority whip in 1989. On conservative issues, Speaker Gingrich promised to push the White House hard; on matters of common economic interest, he expressed a willingness to work with the opposition.

G.H.

CONGRESS

The 103rd Congress, dominated by Democrats in both chambers, started out in January 1993 with high hopes of a long and successful production, directed by the first Democratic president in 12 years. By the time the curtain closed in October 1994, however, Republicans had stolen the show, and Congress was being booed offstage by angry voters (see ELECTIONS IN THE UNITED STATES) who, at least in the Congress's second year, saw little accomplished other than partisan bickering and political infighting. A special session late in the year that brought congressional approval of a new world trade pact did not alter the overall picture.

As members rushed home to campaign for the November 8 elections, much of what President Bill Clinton and the Democrats had hoped would be the legacy of the 103rd Congress lay in shambles—shattered by successful Republican opposition that was aided by presidential missteps and division among Democrats themselves. A major health care reform program, campaign-finance and lobbying reforms, and most of the environmental initiatives were among the casualties, despite earlier promises that a Democratic-controlled Congress working with a Democratic president would mean an end to legislative gridlock. There were concrete accomplishments in 1993, but there were embarrassing defeats as well. And the record for 1994 was slim. Even many of the victories—a $30 billion anticrime bill, several education bills, a measure to protect California deserts, and legislation making it a federal crime to block access to abortion clinics—barely made it through Congress.

In the November elections voters made it clear what they thought of Congress's performance. Republicans won a majority in the House for the first time in 40 years and returned to power in the Senate after an eight-year hiatus. Among Democratic casualties were some powerful politicians, including House Speaker Tom Foley (D, Washington); Dan Rostenkowski (D, Illinois), who had stepped down as House Ways and Means Committee chairman earlier in the year, after being indicted on corruption charges; and Senate Budget Committee Chairman Jim Sasser (D,

Tennessee). No Republican incumbent was defeated.

As a result of the midterm elections, Republicans picked up a total of 52 seats in the House and eight in the Senate. A day after the election Senator Richard Shelby of Alabama— a Democrat who frequently voted with Republicans—officially switched parties, bringing the GOP gain in the Senate to nine.

What Congress Did. In an effort to combat violence at abortion clinics, Congress passed legislation in May making it a federal crime to use or threaten force to intimidate anyone seeking or performing an abortion. Violators of the law could face criminal penalties, as well as civil damages and restraining orders.

Responding to voters' concern over crime, Congress in August passed a $30.2 billion anticrime bill that, among other things, banned the manufacture, sale, and possession of 19 types of assault weapons, provided $8.8 billion in funds for hiring of new police officers, extended the death penalty to more than 50 federal crimes, and allotted $6.9 billion for programs aimed at crime prevention. Each house had passed its own version of an anticrime bill the previous year, and in July 1994, House and Senate negotiators had crafted a compromise between the two versions. The new bill included an assault weapons ban but dropped a provision that would have allowed use of sentencing statistics to challenge death sentences as racially discriminatory. Anti-gun-control Democrats joined Republicans in an unsuccessful effort to block the revised bill in the House; in the Senate, supporters mustered the necessary votes to cut off debate after a few days and get the measure passed there as well, by late August.

Congress also approved legislation that would eliminate barriers to interstate banking. The nation's largest banks had for years been lobbying to create nationwide branch networks. Supporters of the legislation said the change would streamline the banking system and make it more profitable. Opponents, led by consumer groups and smaller banks, said the move would result in the concentration of the banking industry in too few hands.

In its last act before preelection adjournment Congress passed a bill to protect millions of acres of California desert. The action, the most comprehensive U.S. land conservation measure since 1980, marked the end of an eight-year battle. Under the bill, whose passage was spearheaded by Senator Dianne Feinstein (D, California), land from the Sierra Nevada to the U.S.-Mexico border was to be protected as wilderness, and national monument areas in Death Valley and at Joshua Tree were to become national parks. The Mojave area was designated as a national preserve—a step below national park status—as a concession to hunters. A filibuster on the bill was cut short, partly because of the bipartisan appeal of protecting the large area from developers and partly because of lawmakers' desire to return to their home states to campaign.

In education, Congress passed several initiatives, including renewal of a $12.4 billion elementary and secondary aid program to help the nation's poorest children, curb school violence, and bring more technology to classrooms. Other measures funded a job skills program to help students not planning to attend college become more employable, set national education goals for all students and schools, expanded the Head Start program to disadvantaged preschoolers under the age of three, and overhauled the college student loan program.

Members of Congress were focusing on the Whitewater investigation—a look into allegations of financial wrongdoing related to an Arkansas resort development in which the Clintons had invested—when the legislators reinstated the independent counsel law, some 18 months after the 1978 statute had expired. The law provides for the appointment of prosecutors outside the Justice Department to investigate alleged misconduct of high-ranking officials. Shortly after President Clinton signed the bill in late June, an independent prosecutor was appointed to investigate Whitewater allegations and another to examine charges against Agriculture Secretary Mike Espy involving gifts from a poultry business regulated by the Agriculture Department. As a result of the probe into his affairs, Espy, saying he had broken no laws or ethics rules, announced he would resign as of December 31.

Congress put the Federal Bureau of Investi-

MEMBERSHIP OF THE 103rd CONGRESS IN 1994

Senators   **Term Expires**

ALABAMA
Howell Heflin (D) 1997
Richard C. Shelby (D) 1999
ALASKA
Ted Stevens (R) 1997
Frank H. Murkowski (R) 1999
ARIZONA
Dennis DeConcini (D) 1995
John S. McCain (R) 1999
ARKANSAS
Dale Bumpers (D) 1999
David Pryor (D) 1997
CALIFORNIA
Dianne Feinstein (D) 2001
Barbara Boxer (D) 1999
COLORADO
Hank Brown (R)...........................1997
Ben Nighthorse Campbell (D) 1999
CONNECTICUT
Christopher J. Dodd (D) 1999
Joseph I. Lieberman (D) 2001
DELAWARE
William V. Roth, Jr. (R) 2001
Joseph R. Biden, Jr. (D)..............1997
FLORIDA
Bob Graham (D)...........................1999
Connie Mack (R) 2001
GEORGIA
Sam Nunn (D) 1997
Paul Coverdell (R) 1999
HAWAII
Daniel K. Inouye (D)....................1999
Daniel K. Akaka (D) 2001
IDAHO
Larry Craig (R) 1997
Dirk Kempthorne (R) 1999
ILLINOIS
Paul Simon (D).............................1997
Carol Moseley-Braun (D) 1999
INDIANA
Richard G. Lugar (R)....................2001
Dan Coats (R) 1999
IOWA
Charles E. Grassley (R) 1999
Tom Harkin (D)..............................1997
KANSAS
Bob Dole (R) 1999
Nancy Landon Kassebaum (R)...1997
KENTUCKY
Wendell H. Ford (D) 1999
Mitch McConnell (R).....................1997
LOUISIANA
J. Bennett Johnston (D) 1997
John B. Breaux (D) 1999
MAINE
William S. Cohen (R) 1997
George J. Mitchell (D) 1995
MARYLAND
Paul S. Sarbanes (D) 2001
Barbara A. Mikulski (D) 1999
MASSACHUSETTS
Edward M. Kennedy (D)...............2001
John F. Kerry (D) 1997
MICHIGAN
Donald W. Riegle, Jr. (D) 1995
Carl Levin (D)...............................1997
MINNESOTA
Dave Durenberger (R)..................1995
Paul D. Wellstone (D) 1997
MISSISSIPPI
Thad Cochran (R) 1997
Trent Lott (R)................................2001

MISSOURI
John C. Danforth (R)...................1995
Christopher S. Bond (R).............1999
MONTANA
Max Baucus (D) 1997
Conrad R. Burns (R) 2001
NEBRASKA
J. James Exon (D) 1997
J. Robert Kerrey (D) 2001
NEVADA
Harry Reid (D) 1999
Richard H. Bryan (D)...................2001
NEW HAMPSHIRE
Bob Smith (R)..............................1997
Judd Gregg (R) 1999
NEW JERSEY
Bill Bradley (D) 1997
Frank R. Lautenberg (D) 2001
NEW MEXICO
Pete V. Domenici (R) 1997
Jeff Bingaman (D) 2001
NEW YORK
Daniel Patrick Moynihan (D) 2001
Alfonse M. D'Amato (R) 1999
NORTH CAROLINA
Jesse Helms (R)..........................1997
Lauch Faircloth (R).......................1999
NORTH DAKOTA
Kent Conrad (D) 2001
Byron L. Dorgan (D) 1999
OHIO
John Glenn (D).............................1999
Howard M. Metzenbaum (D).......1995
OKLAHOMA
David L. Boren (D)[1] 1994
Don Nickles (R) 1999
OREGON
Mark O. Hatfield (R) 1997
Bob Packwood (R) 1999
PENNSYLVANIA
Arlen Specter (R) 1999
Harris Wofford (D) 1995
RHODE ISLAND
Claiborne Pell (D)........................1997
John H. Chafee (R) 2001
SOUTH CAROLINA
Strom Thurmond (R) 1997
Ernest F. Hollings (D)..................1999
SOUTH DAKOTA
Larry Pressler (R).........................1997
Thomas A. Daschle (D)...............1999
TENNESSEE
Jim Sasser (D) 1995
Harlan Mathews (D)[2] 1994
TEXAS
Phil Gramm (R) 1997
Kay Bailey Hutchison (R) 2001
UTAH
Orrin G. Hatch (R) 2001
Robert F. Bennett (R)..................1999
VERMONT
Patrick J. Leahy (D) 1999
James M. Jeffords (R).................2001
VIRGINIA
John W. Warner (R) 1997
Charles S. Robb (D)....................2001
WASHINGTON
Slade Gorton (R) 2001
Patty Murray (D)...........................1999
WEST VIRGINIA
Robert C. Byrd (D) 2001
John D. Rockefeller IV (D) 1997

WISCONSIN
Herb Kohl (D) 2001
Russell D. Feingold (D)...............1999
WYOMING
Malcolm Wallop (R)......................1995
Alan K. Simpson (R) 1997

Representatives
ALABAMA
1. Sonny Callahan (R)
2. Terry Everett (R)
3. Glen Browder (D)
4. Tom Bevill (D)
5. Robert E. ("Bud") Cramer, Jr. (D)
6. Spencer Bachus (R)
7. Earl F. Hilliard (D)
ALASKA
(at large)
Don Young (R)
ARIZONA
1. Sam Coppersmith (D)
2. Ed Pastor (D)
3. Bob Stump (R)
4. Jon Kyl (R)
5. Jim Kolbe (R)
6. Karan English (D)
ARKANSAS
1. Blanche M. Lambert (D)
2. Ray Thornton (D)
3. Y. Tim Hutchinson (R)
4. Jay Dickey (R)
CALIFORNIA
1. Dan Hamburg (D)
2. Wally Herger (R)
3. Vic Fazio (D)
4. John T. Doolittle (R)
5. Robert T. Matsui (D)
6. Lynn C. Woolsey (D)
7. George Miller (D)
8. Nancy Pelosi (D)
9. Ronald V. Dellums (D)
10. Bill Baker (R)
11. Richard W. Pombo (R)
12. Tom Lantos (D)
13. Fortney ("Pete") Stark (D)
14. Anna G. Eshoo (D)
15. Norman Y. Mineta (D)
16. Don Edwards (D)
17. Sam Farr (D)
18. Gary A. Condit (D)
19. Richard H. Lehman (D)
20. Calvin M. Dooley (D)
21. William M. Thomas (R)
22. Michael Huffington (R)
23. Elton Gallegly (R)
24. Anthony C. Beilenson (D)
25. Howard P. ("Buck") McKeon (R)
26. Howard L. Berman (D)
27. Carlos J. Moorhead (R)
28. David Dreier (R)
29. Henry A. Waxman (D)
30. Xavier Becerra (D)
31. Matthew G. Martinez (D)
32. Julian C. Dixon (D)
33. Lucille Roybal-Allard (D)
34. Esteban Edward Torres (D)
35. Maxine Waters (D)
36. Jane Harman (D)
37. Walter R. Tucker III (D)
38. Stephen Horn (R)
39. Edward R. Royce (R)

40. Jerry Lewis (R)
41. Jay Kim (R)
42. George E. Brown, Jr. (D)
43. Ken Calvert (R)
44. Alfred A. (Al) McCandless (R)
45. Dana Rohrabacher (R)
46. Robert K. Dornan (R)
47. Christopher Cox (R)
48. Ron Packard (R)
49. Lynn Schenk (D)
50. Bob Filner (D)
51. Randy ("Duke") Cunningham (R)
52. Duncan Hunter (R)

COLORADO
1. Patricia Schroeder (D)
2. David E. Skaggs (D)
3. Scott McInnis (R)
4. Wayne Allard (R)
5. Joel Hefley (R)
6. Dan Schaefer (R)

CONNECTICUT
1. Barbara B. Kennelly (D)
2. Sam Gejdenson (D)
3. Rosa L. DeLauro (D)
4. Christopher Shays (R)
5. Gary A. Franks (R)
6. Nancy L. Johnson (R)

DELAWARE
1. Michael N. Castle (R)

FLORIDA
1. Earl Hutto (D)
2. Douglas ("Pete") Peterson (D)
3. Corrine Brown (D)
4. Tillie K. Fowler R
5. Karen L. Thurman (D)
6. Cliff Stearns (R)
7. John L. Mica (R)
8. Bill McCollum (R)
9. Michael Bilirakis (R)
10. C. W. Bill Young (R)
11. Sam Gibbons (D)
12. Charles T. Canady (R)
13. Dan Miller (R)
14. Porter J. Goss (R)
15. Jim Bacchus (D)
16. Tom Lewis (R)
17. Carrie P. Meek (D)
18. Ileana Ros-Lehtinen (R)
19. Harry Johnston (D)
20. Peter Deutsch (D)
21. Lincoln Diaz-Balart (R)
22. E. Clay Shaw, Jr. (R)
23. Alcee L. Hastings (D)

GEORGIA
1. Jack Kingston (R)
2. Sanford D. Bishop, Jr. (D)
3. Mac Collins (R)
4. John Linder (R)
5. John Lewis (D)
6. Newt Gingrich (R)
7. George ("Buddy") Darden (D)
8. J. Roy Rowland (D)
9. Nathan Deal (D)
10. Don Johnson (D)
11. Cynthia A. McKinney (D)

HAWAII
1. Neil Abercrombie (D)
2. Patsy T. Mink (D)

IDAHO
1. Larry LaRocco (D)
2. Michael D. Crapo (R)

ILLINOIS
1. Bobby L. Rush (D)
2. Mel Reynolds (D)
3. William O. Lipinski (D)
4. Luis V. Gutierrez (D)
5. Dan Rostenkowski (D)
6. Henry J. Hyde (R)
7. Cardiss Collins (D)

8. Philip M. Crane (R)
9. Sidney R. Yates (D)
10. John Edward Porter (R)
11. George E. Sangmeister (D)
12. Jerry F. Costello (D)
13. Harris W. Fawell (R)
14. J. Dennis Hastert (R)
15. Thomas W. Ewing (R)
16. Donald A. Manzullo (R)
17. Lane Evans (D)
18. Robert H. Michel (R)
19. Glenn Poshard (D)
20. Richard J. Durbin (D)

INDIANA
1. Peter J. Visclosky (D)
2. Philip R. Sharp (D)
3. Tim Roemer (D)
4. Jill L. Long (D)
5. Stephen E. Buyer (R)
6. Dan Burton (R)
7. John T. Myers (R)
8. Frank McCloskey (D)
9. Lee H. Hamilton (D)
10. Andrew Jacobs, Jr. (D)

IOWA
1. James A. Leach (R)
2. Jim Nussle (R)
3. Jim Lightfoot (R)
4. Neal Smith (D)
5. Fred Grandy (R)

KANSAS
1. Pat Roberts (R)
2. Jim Slattery (D)
3. Jan Meyers (R)
4. Dan Glickman (D)

KENTUCKY
1. Thomas J. Barlow III (D)
2. Ron Lewis (R)[3]
3. Romano L. Mazzoli (D)
4. Jim Bunning (R)
5. Harold Rogers (R)
6. Scotty Baesler (D)

LOUISIANA
1. Bob Livingston (R)
2. William J. Jefferson (D)
3. W. J. ("Billy") Tauzin (D)
4. Cleo Fields (D)
5. Jim McCrery (R)
6. Richard H. Baker (R)
7. James A. Hayes (D)

MAINE
1. Thomas H. Andrews (D)
2. Olympia J. Snowe (R)

MARYLAND
1. Wayne T. Gilchrest (R)
2. Helen Delich Bentley (R)
3. Benjamin L. Cardin (D)
4. Albert Russell Wynn (D)
5. Steny H. Hoyer (D)
6. Roscoe G. Bartlett (R)
7. Kweisi Mfume (D)
8. Constance A. Morella (R)

MASSACHUSETTS
1. John W. Olver (D)
2. Richard E. Neal (D)
3. Peter Blute (R)
4. Barney Frank (D)
5. Martin T. Meehan (D)
6. Peter G. Torkildsen (R)
7. Edward J. Markey (D)
8. Joseph P. Kennedy II (D)
9. John Joseph Moakley (D)
10. Gerry E. Studds (D)

MICHIGAN
1. Bart Stupak (D)
2. Peter Hoekstra (R)
3. Vernon J. Ehlers (R)[4]
4. Dave Camp (R)
5. James A. Barcia (D)

6. Fred Upton (R)
7. Nick Smith (R)
8. Bob Carr (D)
9. Dale E. Kildee (D)
10. David E. Bonior (D)
11. Joe Knollenberg (R)
12. Sander M. Levin (D)
13. William D. Ford (D)
14. John Conyers, Jr. (D)
15. Barbara-Rose Collins (D)
16. John D. Dingell (D)

MINNESOTA
1. Timothy J. Penny (D)
2. David Minge (D)
3. Jim Ramstad (R)
4. Bruce F. Vento (D)
5. Martin Olav Sabo (D)
6. Rod Grams (R)
7. Collin C. Peterson (D)
8. James L. Oberstar (D)

MISSISSIPPI
1. Jamie L. Whitten (D)
2. Bennie G. Thompson (D)
3. G. V. ("Sonny") Montgomery (D)
4. Mike Parker (D)
5. Gene Taylor (D)

MISSOURI
1. William (Bill) Clay (D)
2. James M. Talent (R)
3. Richard A. Gephardt (D)
4. Ike Skelton (D)
5. Alan Wheat (D)
6. Pat Danner (D)
7. Mel Hancock (R)
8. Bill Emerson (R)
9. Harold L. Volkmer (D)

MONTANA
(at large)
Pat Williams (D)

NEBRASKA
1. Doug Bereuter (R)
2. Peter Hoagland (D)
3. Bill Barrett (R)

NEVADA
1. James H. Bilbray (D)
2. Barbara F. Vucanovich (R)

NEW HAMPSHIRE
1. William H. Zeliff, Jr. (R)
2. Dick Swett (D)

NEW JERSEY
1. Robert E. Andrews (D)
2. William J. Hughes (D)
3. Jim Saxton (R)
4. Christopher H. Smith (R)
5. Marge Roukema (R)
6. Frank Pallone, Jr. (D)
7. Bob Franks (R)
8. Herb Klein (D)
9. Robert G. Torricelli (D)
10. Donald M. Payne (D)
11. Dean A. Gallo (R)[5]
12. Dick Zimmer (R)
13. Robert Menendez (D)

NEW MEXICO
1. Steven H. Schiff (R)
2. Joe Skeen (R)
3. Bill Richardson (D)

NEW YORK
1. George J. Hochbrueckner (D)
2. Rick Lazio (R)
3. Peter T. King (R)
4. David A. Levy (R)
5. Gary L. Ackerman (D)
6. Floyd H. Flake (D)
7. Thomas J. Manton (D)
8. Jerrold Nadler (D)
9. Charles E. Schumer (D)
10. Edolphus Towns (D)
11. Major R. Owens (D)

12. Nydia M. Velázquez (D)
13. Susan Molinari (R)
14. Carolyn B. Maloney (D)
15. Charles B. Rangel (D)
16. José E. Serrano (D)
17. Eliot L. Engel (D)
18. Nita M. Lowey (D)
19. Hamilton Fish, Jr. (R)
20. Benjamin A. Gilman (R)
21. Michael R. McNulty (D)
22. Gerald B. H. Solomon (R)
23. Sherwood L. Boehlert (R)
24. John M. McHugh (R)
25. James T. Walsh (R)
26. Maurice D. Hinchey (D)
27. Bill Paxon (R)
28. Louise McIntosh Slaughter (D)
29. John J. LaFalce (D)
30. Jack Quinn (R)
31. Amo Houghton (R)

NORTH CAROLINA
1. Eva M. Clayton (D)
2. Tim Valentine (D)
3. H. Martin Lancaster (D)
4. David E. Price (D)
5. Stephen L. Neal (D)
6. Howard Coble (R)
7. Charlie Rose (D)
8. W. G. ("Bill") Hefner (D)
9. J. Alex McMillan (R)
10. Cass Ballenger (R)
11. Charles H. Taylor (R)
12. Melvin L. Watt (D)

NORTH DAKOTA
(at large)
Earl Pomeroy (D)

OHIO
1. David Mann (D)
2. Rob Portman (R)
3. Tony P. Hall (D)
4. Michael G. Oxley (R)
5. Paul E. Gillmor (R)
6. Ted Strickland (D)
7. David L. Hobson (R)
8. John A. Boehner (R)
9. Marcy Kaptur (D)
10. Martin R. Hoke (R)
11. Louis Stokes (D)
12. John R. Kasich (R)
13. Sherrod Brown (D)
14. Thomas C. Sawyer (D)
15. Deborah Pryce (R)
16. Ralph S. Regula (R)
17. James A. Traficant, Jr. (D)
18. Douglas Applegate (D)
19. Eric Fingerhut (D)

OKLAHOMA
1. James M. Inhofe (R)[6]
2. Mike Synar (D)
3. Bill K. Brewster (D)
4. Dave McCurdy (D)
5. Ernest J. Istook, Jr. (R)
6. Frank D. Lucas (R)[7]

OREGON
1. Elizabeth Furse (D)
2. Robert F. (Bob) Smith (R)
3. Ron Wyden (D)
4. Peter A. DeFazio (D)
5. Michael J. Kopetski (D)

PENNSYLVANIA
1. Thomas M. Foglietta (D)
2. Lucien E. Blackwell (D)
3. Robert A. Borski (D)
4. Ron Klink (D)
5. William F. Clinger, Jr. (R)
6. Tim Holden (D)
7. Curt Weldon (R)
8. James C. Greenwood (R)
9. Bud Shuster (R)
10. Joseph M. McDade (R)
11. Paul E. Kanjorski (D)
12. John P. Murtha (D)
13. Marjorie Margolies-Mezvinsky (D)
14. William J. Coyne (D)
15. Paul McHale (D)
16. Robert S. Walker (R)
17. George W. Gekas (R)
18. Rick Santorum (R)
19. William F. Goodling (R)
20. Austin J. Murphy (D)
21. Thomas J. Ridge (R)

RHODE ISLAND
1. Ronald K. Machtley (R)
2. Jack Reed (D)

SOUTH CAROLINA
1. Arthur Ravenel, Jr. (R)
2. Floyd Spence (R)
3. Butler Derrick (D)
4. Bob Inglis (R)
5. John M. Spratt, Jr. (D)
6. James E. Clyburn (D)

SOUTH DAKOTA
(at large)
Tim Johnson (D)

TENNESSEE
1. James H. (Jimmy) Quillen (R)
2. John James Duncan, Jr. (R)
3. Marilyn Lloyd (D)
4. Jim Cooper (D)
5. Bob Clement (D)
6. Bart Gordon (D)
7. Don Sundquist (R)
8. John S. Tanner (D)
9. Harold E. Ford (D)

TEXAS
1. Jim Chapman (D)
2. Charles Wilson (D)
3. Sam Johnson (R)
4. Ralph M. Hall (D)
5. John Bryant (D)
6. Joe Barton (R)
7. Bill Archer (R)
8. Jack Fields (R)
9. Jack Brooks (D)
10. J. J. Pickle (D)
11. Chet Edwards (D)
12. Pete Geren (D)
13. Bill Sarpalius (D)
14. Greg Laughlin (D)
15. E. de la Garza (D)
16. Ronald D. Coleman (D)
17. Charles W. Stenholm (D)
18. Craig A. Washington (D)
19. Larry Combest (R)
20. Henry B. Gonzalez (D)
21. Lamar S. Smith (R)
22. Tom DeLay (R)

23. Henry Bonilla (R)
24. Martin Frost (D)
25. Michael A. Andrews (D)
26. Richard K. Armey (R)
27. Solomon P. Ortiz (D)
28. Frank Tejeda (D)
29. Gene Green (D)
30. Eddie Bernice Johnson (D)

UTAH
1. James V. Hansen (R)
2. Karen Shepherd (D)
3. Bill Orton (D)

VERMONT
(at large)
Bernard Sanders, Ind.

VIRGINIA
1. Herbert H. Bateman (R)
2. Owen B. Pickett (D)
3. Robert C. Scott (D)
4. Norman Sisisky (D)
5. L. F. Payne, Jr. (D)
6. Bob Goodlatte (R)
7. Thomas J. Bliley, Jr. (R)
8. James P. Moran (D)
9. Rick Boucher (D)
10. Frank R. Wolf (R)
11. Leslie L. Byrne (D)

WASHINGTON
1. Maria Cantwell (D)
2. Al Swift (D)
3. Jolene Unsoeld (D)
4. Jay Inslee (D)
5. Thomas S. Foley (D)
6. Norman D. Dicks (D)
7. Jim McDermott (D)
8. Jennifer Dunn (R)
9. Mike Kreidler (D)

WEST VIRGINIA
1. Alan B. Mollohan (D)
2. Robert E. Wise, Jr. (D)
3. Nick J. Rahall II (D)

WISCONSIN
1. Peter W. Barca (D)
2. Scott L. Klug (R)
3. Steve Gunderson (R)
4. Gerald D. Kleczka (D)
5. Thomas M. Barrett (D)
6. Thomas E. Petri (R)
7. David R. Obey (D)
8. Toby Roth (R)
9. F. James Sensenbrenner, Jr. (R)

WYOMING
(at large)
Craig Thomas (R)

PUERTO RICO
(resident commissioner)
Carlos A. Romero-Barceló (D)

AMERICAN SAMOA
(delegate)
Eni F. H. Faleomavaega (D)

GUAM
(delegate)
Robert A. Underwood (D)

VIRGIN ISLANDS
(delegate)
Ron de Lugo (D)

WASHINGTON, DC
(delegate)
Eleanor Holmes Norton (D)

---

[1]Retired November 15; James Inhofe (R) was elected to serve out Boren's term (which expires January 3, 1997) and was sworn in November 17.

[2]Appointed to the Senate seat vacated by Vice President Gore, Mathews resigned December 1; Fred Thompson (R) was elected to serve out that term (which expires January 3, 1997) and was sworn in December 9.

[3]Elected May 24, 1994, to fill vacancy due to the death of William Natcher (D) March 3.

[4]Elected December 7, 1993, to fill vacancy due to the death of Paul B. Henry (R) July 31, 1993.

[5]Died November 6, 1994.

[6]Resigned November 15, 1994, to be sworn in to Senate seat left vacant by the resignation of David L. Boren (D); election winner Steve Largen (R) sworn in to Inhofe's old seat November 29.

[7]Elected May 10, 1994, to fill vacancy due to the resignation of Glenn English (D) January 7.

429

gation in charge of counterintelligence and authorized a broad review of intelligence agencies in the new era following the end of the cold war. The move came in the aftermath of the case of Aldrich H. Ames, a longtime Central Intelligence Agency officer who spied for the Soviet Union and Russia from 1985 until his arrest and conviction earlier in 1994. The FBI had complained that the CIA was slow to inform the bureau that Ames was suspected of espionage.

In an accomplishment unusual in recent decades, the appropriations bills for the new fiscal year were passed by Congress, and signed by the president, before the new fiscal year began on October 1.

Congress returned from election adjournment to a special lame-duck session in order to approve the international trade agreement reached in the so-called Uruguay Round of the General Agreement on Tariffs and Trade. The GATT treaty lowered tariffs worldwide and covered for the first time such areas as intellectual property rights and agricultural commodities. It won congressional support across party lines, clearing the House of Representatives by a vote of 288-146 and the Senate by a 76-24 vote.

What Congress Did Not Do. President Clinton's sweeping plan for restructuring the nation's health care system died in September, after Congress had spent a year considering it, along with a number of less complicated alternatives. The 1,342-page bill, a key element in the president's legislative program, had been formally presented to Congress in October 1993, following months of deliberation, often behind closed doors, by a task force headed by his wife, Hillary Rodham Clinton. The plan, criticized by some as too bureaucratic, called for basic benefits to be made available to all, paid partly by business and partly by the consumer (with government subsidies to help individuals and small companies pay). Premiums were to be collected by regional "health alliances" that negotiate with networks of health care providers and offer a choice among them; a panel appointed by the president was to oversee the system, establish standards, and monitor quality of services. The Republicans and the health insurance industry strongly opposed the plan, while Democrats never settled differences among themselves. A bipartisan proposal to make incremental changes came too late in the game, and the measure was abandoned before any legislation reached the House or the Senate floor.

The Senate defeated a proposed constitutional amendment requiring the federal government to balance the budget each year unless three-fifths of both chambers approved lifting the requirement. The measure, which had also been defeated in 1992 and failed to get to the floor in 1993, faced better prospects in 1995, however, with Republicans dominating both chambers. In fact, House Republicans made it one of the top ten legislative priorities outlined in their Contract With America, a set of proposals they promised to introduce, or reintroduce, in Congress in 1995. (If the proposed constitutional amendment should pass Congress, it would then have to gain approval from three-fourths of the 50 state legislatures in order to go into effect.)

An attempt to change the way congressional campaigns are financed failed in the face of Republican opposition to public financing and Democratic differences over whether to limit contributions from political action committees. The bill—which would have set voluntary spending limits on congressional races, with public matching funds for those candidates who comply—died in the Senate in September, when Democrats failed to stop a Republican-led filibuster. Democrats may have contributed to the measure's downfall by waiting until the last minute to propose a compromise. This was the fourth consecutive Congress to witness the demise of a Democratic campaign finance bill.

Congress also failed to pass a bill that would have tightened financial disclosure requirements for lobbyists and barred them from providing meals, entertainment, and travel to members of Congress and their staffs. The measure died when the Senate could not get the votes to quell a Republican-led filibuster near the end of the session. Both the House and the Senate had originally passed lobbying disclosure and gift ban provisions by wide margins.

A comprehensive bill to reauthorize the nation's most important water pollution law never made it to the floor of either chamber of Congress; the measure had cleared a Senate committee but ran into trouble in the House Public Works and Transportation Committee. Controversy over federal restrictions on wetlands development continued to be the major stumbling block.

A bill that would have revised the nation's drinking water laws died when House and Senate negotiators failed to work out differences over several issues, including the health risks posed by certain contaminants in drinking water. One key proposal would have created a revolving loan fund to help state and local governments build and improve drinking water treatment plants.

Another environmental bill, to overhaul the nation's hazardous waste program, died in the final weeks of the congressional session, a victim of partisan politics and differences over issues such as insurance, taxes, and fair wages.

Senate Republicans, threatening a filibuster, stopped a bill that would have made it illegal for employers to permanently replace workers striking over wages and benefits.

An attempt to rewrite the country's telecommunication laws and permit competition between telephone and cable television companies got disconnected in September, as a result of insurmountable differences among rival industry groups and between Democrats and Republicans.

The 104th Congress. In the weeks following the elections, members of each party in each chamber met to select leaders for the new Congress, which was to convene in early January 1995. Robert H. Michel, the Republican leader in the House in the 103rd Congress, was retiring; for speaker in the new GOP-controlled House, Republicans chose the fiery Newt Gingrich of Georgia, who had previously been the minority whip. Texans Dick Armey and Tom DeLay were selected as, respectively, House majority leader and majority whip, and John Boehner of Ohio became chair of the Republican caucus. House Democrats elected Richard Gephardt of Missouri as minority leader (he had served as majority leader under Speaker Foley). The two other top Democratic leadership positions went to David

Bonior of Michigan (minority whip) and Vic Fazio of California (chair of the Democratic caucus).

In the upper chamber, Senator Robert Dole of Kansas, minority leader in the 103rd Congress, was chosen as majority leader; for the post of his deputy, or majority whip, Republicans elected Trent Lott, a conservative from Mississippi. Democrats selected Thomas Daschle of South Dakota as Senate minority leader; chosen as his deputy was Wendell Ford of Kentucky, who had been majority whip under the Democratic leader in the 103rd Congress, Senator George Mitchell of Maine. Mitchell himself retired in 1994.

The November election results meant that committees in both houses would have Republican majorities and new Republican chairs. House Republicans also announced plans to make sweeping changes—among other things, eliminating several committees and two dozen subcommittees, cutting hundreds of employees from the House payroll, limiting the tenure of committee chairs, eliminating funding for caucuses (interest groups for representatives, such as the Congressional Black Caucus), and banning most closed-door hearings. These changes, some of which many Democrats also supported, required approval by the full House in order to go into effect.

K.L.S.

SUPREME COURT

The Supreme Court's 1993-1994 term was marked by a dwindling number of signed opinions, though there were many high-profile cases. The High Court handed down signed decisions in 84 cases, the lowest total since 1955-1956.

Justice Harry A. Blackmun completed his 24-year career on the Court by retiring at the end of the 1993-1994 term, on June 30. He concluded a remarkable ideological journey. Appointed by then-President Richard Nixon, he had been expected to be a dependable conservative, but Blackmun, author of the Court's 1973 ruling legalizing abortion, was instead the most consistently liberal member of the Court by the time he retired.

Stephen G. Breyer (see profile in PEOPLE IN THE NEWS), a federal judge from Boston, was named by President Bill Clinton to succeed

Saying good-bye. *Justice Harry A. Blackmun announces in April that he is retiring from the U.S. Supreme Court. Blackmun, who joined the Court in 1970, was replaced by Stephen G. Breyer.*

Blackmun. Confirmed by the Senate, 87-9, after placid, uneventful hearings, he took his seat when the Court reconvened in October.

Overall Trends. In case after case the Court's centrists held the balance of power. Justice Anthony Kennedy, who dissented in only five of the cases decided by written opinions during the 1993-1994 term, appeared to be in the middle of the moderately conservative Court. The others whose votes often were crucial for producing a majority were Justices Ruth Bader Ginsburg, David H. Souter, and Sandra Day O'Connor. Chief Justice William H. Rehnquist occupied the conservative wing along with Justices Antonin Scalia and Clarence Thomas. Justice John Paul Stevens most often was allied with Justice Blackmun on the left.

Abortion Access. At the end of the 1993-1994 term, the Court ruled, 6-3, that abortion protesters may be barred from demonstrating too close to abortion clinics. The justices upheld a 36-foot buffer zone, the core of an injunction issued by a Florida court to keep protesters at a distance. The opinion, in *Madsen* v. *Women's Health Center,* written by Chief Justice Rehnquist, said the buffer zone was necessary to protect such important interests as

free access to the clinic and did not infringe excessively on rights of free expression.

In another case involving antiabortion protests—*National Organization for Women* v. *Scheidler*—the justices unanimously ruled that abortion clinics could use the federal Racketeer Influenced and Corrupt Organizations Act to sue violent antiabortion protesters for damages.

Crime and Punishment. Voting 5-4, the justices said in *Montana* v. *Kurth Ranch* that states may not follow up a narcotics conviction by imposing a special tax on the illegal drugs. The ruling overturned a Montana law, similar to statutes in many states, on grounds that such penalties amount to unconstitutional double jeopardy or multiple prosecutions.

In a capital punishment case, *Simmons* v. *South Carolina,* the Court said that if the state seeks the death penalty because it believes the defendant may be dangerous in the future, jurors must be told whether a life sentence would allow for parole. The 7-2 ruling threw out a death sentence imposed under a state law that had barred jurors from being told there was no such possibility.

The Court unanimously ruled that prison officials can be held to account for failing to protect an inmate from violence. In *Farmer* v. *Brennan* the Court said there can be liability if the officials fail to take steps to head off a substantial risk of serious harm. The case involved the rape of a transsexual prisoner who had been placed in the general population of a federal prison.

Church and State. In *Board of Education of Kiryas Joel* v. *Grumet* the Court ruled, 6-3, that New York State had violated constitutionally required separation of church and state when it created a school district to help disabled Hasidic Jewish schoolchildren.

Discrimination. New rules aimed at eliminating the taint of discrimination in jury selection were extended to gender. The Court, in *J.E.B.* v. *T.B.*, ruled that the Constitution's guarantee of equal protection bars excluding potential jurors on the basis of their sex. The 6-3 decision extended the scope of previous rulings barring jury selection based on race.

The Court relieved the judicial system of a potential major burden when it ruled that the Civil Rights Act of 1991 did not cover thousands of cases still pending when the law was passed. (The law restored and expanded remedies for job discrimination after the Supreme Court issued rulings in 1989 limiting earlier civil rights statutes.) The Court handed down a pair of 8-1 decisions on retroactivity, in *Landgraf* v. *USI Film Products* and *Rivers* v. *Roadway Express.*

In *Johnson* v. *DeGrandy* justices found, 7-2, that the federal Voting Rights Act does not require a state to have as many districts as possible in which minority-group voters make up a majority of the electorate. The Court held merely that minorities must be adequately represented.

Free Speech. A unanimous ruling in *City of Ladue* v. *Gilleo* ruled that cities may not bar residents from posting signs on their own property. The decision struck down an ordinance in a St. Louis suburb that had barred an antiwar sign.

Property Rights and Copyright. The Court in *Dolan* v. *City of Tigard* placed new limits on how far governments can go to require portions of private land to be set aside for environmental or other public purposes. The 5-4

ruling said regulators must show proportionality between such required set-asides and the potential harm of new development.

The Court unanimously ruled in *Campbell* v. *Acuff-Rose* that parody can be exempt from copyright law, giving parody writers greater scope to exploit original songs. The case involved a raunchy version, recorded by the rap group 2 Live Crew, of the rock classic *Oh, Pretty Woman.*

Military Bases. In *Dalton* v. *Spencer* the justices unanimously held that federal courts lack authority to overrule the government's choices of which military bases to shut down. The ruling barred a challenge by officials trying to save the Philadelphia Naval Shipyard from closure.

Autumn 1994. The Supreme Court opened its 1994-1995 term by disposing of new appeals that had accumulated over the summer recess. In an unusual move the justices failed to grant review in any of the more than 1,600 new cases. The Court's docket still included two cases important for the constitutional law of search and seizure. In *Vernonia School District* v. *Acton* the Court agreed to address the issue of whether public schools can subject students to random drug tests. And in *Wilson* v. *Arkansas* the question posed was whether in executing a search warrant police officers must first announce their presence and give the occupant time to open the door before forcing their way inside.

The Court issued a decision in November in a child pornography case, *United States* v. *X-Citement Video.* Taking a broad interpretation of the relevant law, the justices ruled, 7-2, that the government must prove the defendant, in this case a video retailer, was aware that performers in sexually explicit photographs or films were under the age of 18.

Another early ruling, announced in December, involved a Texas veteran who was disabled after back surgery at a Veterans Administration hospital. The Court in *Brown* v. *Gardner* ruled unanimously that he could collect damages without having to prove negligence on the part of the hospital. The VA estimated that this ruling, applied to all similar cases, would cost the federal government $1 billion over five years.   J.R.

UNITED STATES OF AMERICA

FOREIGN AFFAIRS

President Bill Clinton discovered in 1994 that he could no longer give foreign policy a low priority, second to domestic affairs. During the year he traveled to Europe, Asia, and the Middle East to meet foreign leaders, and he was instrumental in returning President Jean-Bertrand Aristide to power in Haiti. However, the November 8 elections, which gave the Republican Party a majority in both houses of Congress, introduced uncertainty about the future course of U.S. foreign policy.

Showdown in Haiti. The biggest foreign policy story of the year took place close to American shores—in Haiti. With the help of U.S. forces and U.S. diplomacy, democratic rule was finally restored. For almost three years the combined efforts of the United States and the United Nations had failed to dislodge the brutal, illegal regime of General Raoul Cédras, in power since the overthrow of President Aristide in a 1991 coup. The Cédras regime had terrorized much of the Haitian population, with thousands of people taking to sea in fragile boats in hope of reaching the United States. Many refugees perished, but most were picked up by U.S. Coast Guard vessels and placed in camps at the U.S. naval base at Guantánamo Bay in Cuba.

Throughout the summer the United States assembled military forces and threatened to invade Haiti unless Cédras stepped down—this despite the fact that Clinton had little public or congressional support for sending U.S. troops to fight and die in order to restore Aristide. On September 17, with the invasion only hours away, former President Jimmy Carter, accompanied by the former chairman of the Joint Chiefs of Staff, General Colin Powell, and Senator Sam Nunn (D, Georgia), the chairman of

Top-level trio. *Arriving in Haiti in September are (bottom to top) former President Jimmy Carter, retired General Colin Powell, and Senator Sam Nunn. The American delegation negotiated the return of deposed Haitian President Jean-Bertrand Aristide.*

the Senate Armed Services Committee, went to Haiti to try to negotiate a settlement. After several tense meetings with Cédras, Carter persuaded the Haitian leader to step down and to allow U.S. forces to occupy his country. The agreement included a face-saving departure for Cédras. Two days later, U.S. troops landed peacefully on Haiti's shores to an enthusiastic welcome from its people. Cédras departed for Panama on October 15; Aristide returned to Haiti the same day and set about organizing a new government.

Cuban Exodus. The Haitian question was complicated by the decision of Fidel Castro to permit Cubans to leave for the United States. During the summer thousands departed on flimsy rafts—often no more than an inner tube and a few boards—soon to be picked up by U.S. Coast Guard and naval vessels and taken to Guantánamo. Some were later transferred to camps in Panama. In early September, in return for a U.S. promise to grant at least 20,000 entry visas a year to Cubans, Castro agreed to prevent the further flight of refugees.

Middle East Peace Efforts. The year 1994 saw progress toward peace in the Middle East, where, in spite of sporadic violence by extremist groups, the 1993 accord between Israel and the Palestinians continued to be implemented. In October 1994, Israel signed a peace treaty with Jordan; Clinton attended the ceremony, which took place on the Israeli-Jordanian border. On the same trip Clinton visited President Hafez al-Assad in Damascus in order to push for a settlement between Israel and Syria. The combination of constructive U.S. encouragement, economic aid, and shuttle diplomacy throughout the year by Secretary of State Warren Christopher contributed to these achievements.

Saddam Backs Down. Meanwhile, Iraqi President Saddam Hussein, who remained in power despite Iraq's economic deterioration (caused largely by a UN embargo on trade), continued to repress minorities and refused to acknowledge the independence of Kuwait. In October, in a seeming replay of the aggression that sparked the 1991 Persian Gulf War, Saddam moved troops toward the Kuwaiti borders. The United States responded immediately with air and ground reinforcements for the region. Iraq got the message, pulled back the threatening forces, and said it recognized Kuwait's sovereignty. UN sanctions remained in place pending Iraqi compliance with other 1991 cease-fire conditions.

Bosnian War. Year's end brought faint signs of possible change in the seemingly intractable problem of the civil war in Bosnia, where Bosnian Serbs, perceived by the United States as aggressors, were fighting with Bosnian Muslims and Bosnian Croatians. During the year the United States had stepped up efforts to assert international leadership in order to end the fighting on a basis short of complete victory for the Serbs, but to no immediate avail. In June the United States, along with Britain, France, Germany, and Russia, endorsed a division of Bosnia in which 51 percent of the territory would go to Bosnian Muslims and Croats and 49 percent would go to the Serbs. But the Serbs, who now occupied about 70 percent of the country, turned down the plan, and numerous cease-fires were routinely violated.

In November the United States ceased adhering to the embargo against supplying arms to the Muslims but could not persuade the major European powers to do the same. Fighting continued in northwest Bosnia and resumed sporadically in the much-battered city of Sarajevo. In December the United States said it stood ready to provide up to 25,000 troops to NATO as protective cover should the UN decide to withdraw its beleaguered peacekeepers. Jimmy Carter later that month flew to Bosnia on a peace mission; a resulting week-long cease-fire between the Bosnian Serbs and the Muslim-dominated Bosnian government gave way at the end of the year to agreement on a four-month cessation of hostilities.

Korean Threat Defused. Potentially the most dangerous foreign policy problem of 1994 was North Korea's nuclear weapons program. U.S. intelligence estimated that North Korea could well have developed one or two nuclear bombs already and was without a doubt accelerating its program in violation of its signature of the Nuclear Nonproliferation Treaty. Early in the year Washington declared that the possession of nuclear weapons was a threat to the peace of Asia and the world. But its efforts to win full cooperation from China and Japan for drastic economic sanctions against North Korea failed.

In June, at the peak of the crisis, Jimmy Carter gained Clinton's permission to visit North Korean leader Kim Il Sung in Pyongyang, the capital. Carter conferred with the aged leader, but a few days later Kim Il Sung died. Shortly thereafter U.S. and North Korean diplomats began to negotiate in Geneva. In October they reached a compromise under which North Korea agreed to suspend the development of nuclear weapons while the United States promised to finance a nuclear power generating program of a type that did not produce weapons-grade by-products. In addition, North Korea was allowed to keep certain facilities off-limits to inspectors for a period of five years. Observers were divided over whether the accord was a contribution to lasting peace or appeasement of an untrustworthy adversary.

In a mid-December incident that threatened to derail the agreement, a U.S. Army helicopter strayed into North Korea and was shot down; one of the two pilots was killed in the crash, and the other was held captive and accused of espionage. U.S. officials went to North Korea to discuss the issue, and the pilot was released at the end of the month.

World Trade. Late in the year, Congress, after a bitter debate, approved a sweeping new world trade treaty, negotiated under the General Agreement on Tariffs and Trade. The pact called for drastic reductions in trade barriers under the administrative supervision of a World Trade Organization. Supporters claimed the treaty would open many new markets to U.S. goods; critics charged that it lacked adequate environmental protections, would cost American factory workers jobs, and above all would subject the United States to the tyranny of a supranational bureaucracy.

In mid-December the United States hosted a Summit of the Americas in Miami, where the leaders of the western hemisphere's 34 democracies agreed to work toward a hemisphere-wide free-trade area.

Trade continued to be a contentious issue with Japan, with lots of talk but with little new opening of that country to American imports. In May, President Clinton renewed most-favored-nation status for China, thereby siding with advisers who said that the best way to get China to improve its human rights record was to have the greatest possible trade and not to use restrictions on trade as punishment.

Former Soviet Republics. U.S. relations with Russia were generally good for much of the year. President Clinton and President Boris Yeltsin met twice—in Europe and in Washington. The United States provided technical assistance in the difficult task of dismantling Russian nuclear weapons and welcomed Russia's indications in June that it would loosely affiliate with NATO through a vague concept called the Partnership for Peace. There were, however, disagreements between the two powers over policy toward the war in Bosnia and Russia's later dismissal of the Partnership for Peace concept. In December the United States watched from the sidelines as Russia used military force in an effort to block the Caucasian region of Chechnya's bid for independence.

After secret negotiations with Kazakhstan, the United States transferred some 1,300 pounds of bomb-grade uranium from the former Soviet republic to a specialized containment site in Tennessee. The move was designed to prevent sabotage or illegal sale of the material.   G.S.

UPPER VOLTA. *See* STATISTICS OF THE WORLD: Burkina Faso.

URUGUAY. In November 1994, in what was called Uruguay's closest election ever, former President Julio Sanguinetti (he served from 1985 to 1990) of the centrist Colorado Party defeated candidates from the conservative ruling National Party and the leftist Progressive Encounter. Sanguinetti was expected to pursue many of the economic reforms begun by the previous administration of Luis Alberto Lacalle Herrera but to do so at a slower pace. He also called for a strong state presence in key economic sectors.

Lacalle, who was prohibited by the constitution from running for reelection, had introduced free-market reforms, increased foreign investment, cut the foreign debt, and reduced inflation from 129 percent in 1990 to 42 percent in 1994. But he faced strong parliamentary criticism of his economic policy, with concerns centered around sharp falls in industrial production and an increased trade deficit. The unemployment rate ran near 10 percent in 1994, and a drop in real wages resulted in several major labor strikes. Gross domestic product, which had grown by more than 7 percent in 1992, was expected to increase by less than 2 percent in 1994.

In a plebiscite held on August 28, voters unexpectedly rejected two constitutional reforms in what political observers felt represented a widespread vote of no confidence for the Uruguayan political system. Four days before the plebiscite a demonstration protesting the extradition to Spain of three alleged Basque terrorists resulted in a confrontation with law enforcement in which two protesters were killed and a number of civilians and police were injured.

In August the parties to the Mercosur Treaty (a pact established in 1991 to create a free-trade zone among Argentina, Brazil, Paraguay, and Uruguay) concluded negotiations on common external tariffs that were to take effect on January 1, 1995. Uruguay's trade with members of Mercosur during the first half of 1994 increased by more than 20 percent, to $980.9 million; however, the balance of trade was still strongly negative.

See STATISTICS OF THE WORLD.   J.A.K.

UTAH. *See* STATISTICS OF THE WORLD.

UZBEKISTAN. In January the leaders of the Central Asian states met in the Uzbek town of Nukus to set up a five-year program to improve the environmental situation in the Aral Sea basin. Foreign experts were concerned that Uzbekistan's leadership was interested only in limiting the ecological damage result-

ing from the shrinking of the sea, rather than in restoring it—Uzbekistan needs water from the Aral feeder rivers to grow cotton, and the restoration of the sea would require a drastic reduction in irrigation.

In late January, President Islam Karimov launched privatization in Uzbekistan with a decree authorizing auctions of small shops and service enterprises. Major price increases for basic goods and energy were announced in the spring and summer, with wage and pension increases announced at the same time in order to avoid the disturbances that accompanied the first postindependence price rises in 1992. In July the country's new currency, the sum, went into circulation, replacing the sum coupons issued in late 1993.

Repression of Uzbek opposition groups by the government continued throughout 1994. In May a number of opposition leaders were arrested inside the country, and in May and June opposition members were reported to have been seized in neighboring Kazakhstan by Uzbek law enforcement officials. In the fall a number of activists from the Erk (Freedom, or Will) Party went on trial in Uzbekistan on charges of antigovernment activity. All genuine opposition groups were excluded from the parliamentary election, the first round of which took place in December.

In regional affairs, Uzbekistan continued its support of the neo-Communist regime in Tajikistan. Afghan government officials accused Uzbekistan of interfering in Afghanistan's internal affairs through active support of Afghan faction leader Abdul Rashid Doestam, an ethnic Uzbek.

See STATISTICS OF THE WORLD.   B.A.B.

V

VANUATU. *See* PACIFIC ISLANDS; STATISTICS OF THE WORLD.

VENEZUELA. In 1994, Venezuela continued to suffer from economic woes, which were compounded by political infighting, capital flight, and a major crisis in the banking sector.

Crime and overcrowded jails continued to be major problems as well.

President Rafael Caldera took office in February for the second time (he was president from 1969 to 1974). He replaced the interim government that had been in place since President Carlos Andrés Pérez was forced to resign in 1993 on charges of corruption. Caldera used his popularity with the people to establish strong executive control of policy. He also held the military and the ever-present threat of a coup in check throughout the year.

Frequently bypassing the fragmented, opposition-dominated Congress, Caldera tackled the problems of the economy through a series of presidential decrees. The emergency measures emphasized a reduction of the budget deficit, control of inflation, spending cuts, and a revision of the tax system. In late June, Caldera imposed rigorous price and exchange controls and suspended certain constitutional rights; the government, for example, was given the power to detain people without charge, restrict free movement, and seize private property. Caldera's stated purpose was to halt the deepening economic crisis by reversing the free-market reforms of the past five years.

In July, Congress attempted to annul a number of the president's far-reaching executive orders. Caldera responded by threatening to hold a national plebiscite that would, he felt, bring about constitutional reforms and that would give him power to dissolve Congress until a new constitution was drafted.

In September, Caldera moved away from his populist measures in an effort to placate angry business leaders. The government began to lift controls selectively as the interest rate was reduced and other austerity measures were imposed. This shift in policy counted on increased domestic petroleum prices and faster privatization, neither of which could be considered a sure thing. The unemployment rate was estimated to be at least 13 percent late in the year, with half the population living at a subsistence level.

Government policies were seriously undercut by a banking crisis of unprecedented magnitude. The collapse of Banco Latino, the country's second-largest bank, due to fraud and mismanagement was eventually followed by the official takeover of another 14 financial institutions. The government had spent more than $6 billion by year's end in its rescue efforts, which pushed inflation to 65 percent. Foreign investors viewed the situation warily.

See Statistics of the World.   J.D.M.

VERMONT.   See Statistics of the World.

VIETNAM. Although full diplomatic relations were not established between Vietnam and the United States in 1994, the 19-year U.S. trade embargo against Vietnam was lifted by U.S. President Bill Clinton in February, and total U.S. investment during the year jumped from some $3 million in March to $190 million by the end of October.

Vietnam's program of economic and legislative reform continued, but bureaucratic obstacles, a lack of laws governing commerce, a primitive banking system, reluctance among state-owned enterprises to undergo privatization, and political caution hampered the transition to a fully open market economy.

Meanwhile, foreign trade was booming. Vietnam continued to export crude oil and coal and remained the world's third-largest rice exporter. There were many new lines of manufactured exports as well. Imports grew faster than exports, however, and they included cars, bicycles, beer, and a variety of other consumer goods that were smuggled from China.

Gross domestic product growth was expected to reach nearly 9 percent in 1994 (up from 8 percent in 1993), although GDP per capita remained one of the lowest in Asia at about $250. Unemployment remained high; foreign investment created about 100,000 new jobs in 1994, but not enough to absorb the 1.5 million young people entering the workforce, many of them formerly in the Army or working for state-owned firms.

A major public investment program began that was designed to repair and upgrade Vietnam's dilapidated transportation network and other infrastructure. A $500 million power line was completed connecting the Hoa Binh hydroelectric plant near Hanoi to Ho Chi Minh City. Vietnam planned to invest an additional $4 billion in power development by the turn of the century.

Tax reform increased government revenue by 50 percent in 1994, but salary increases and infrastructure investment pushed the budget deficit toward $1 billion. The exchange rate with the U.S. dollar depreciated slightly to just over 11,000 dong. The trade and budget deficits, along with the rapid economic

Window on the West. *Vietnam's slow transition to a fully open and competitive market economy got a boost in February when the United States ended its 19-year trade embargo. The first commercial American trade fair after the lifting of the embargo was the Vietnamerica Expo, held in Hanoi in April.*

growth, pushed inflation to around 10 percent (up from 5 percent in 1993).

In November foreign aid of $2 billion (slightly more than in 1993) was pledged at the donor conference sponsored by the World Bank in Paris.

It was announced in October that Vietnam would be admitted to the Association of Southeast Asian Nations as a full member in 1995, and in November, Vietnam signed several eco-nomic cooperation agreements with China. Border disputes continued, however, with Cambodia, Laos, and China, as did disputes with Taiwan, the Philippines, Malaysia, and Brunei over the Paracel and Spratly islands.

See STATISTICS OF THE WORLD.   G.B.H.

VIRGINIA. *See* STATE GOVERNMENT REVIEW; STATISTICS OF THE WORLD.

VIRGIN ISLANDS. *See* STATISTICS OF THE WORLD.

WASHINGTON. *See* HEALTH AND MEDICINE; STATE GOVERNMENT REVIEW; STATISTICS OF THE WORLD.

WESTERN SAHARA. *See* MOROCCO.

WESTERN SAMOA. *See* STATISTICS OF THE WORLD.

WEST VIRGINIA. *See* STATISTICS OF THE WORLD.

WISCONSIN. *See* STATE GOVERNMENT REVIEW; STATISTICS OF THE WORLD.

WOMEN. In U.S. politics, 1994 was dubbed by some the Year of the Man, although women lost few seats overall at the state and federal levels. On Capitol Hill lawmakers protected women's interests by approving a series of bills aimed at cracking down on criminal violence against women and strengthening funding to promote gender equity in schools.

Women in Politics. At the federal level, women obtained an additional seat in the Sen-

439

Big win. *Rena Weeks celebrates winning a record verdict in a sexual harassment case against her former employer in early September. The jury determined that the law firm Baker & McKenzie and one of the firm's partners should pay Weeks $7.1 million, believed to be the largest sum ever awarded in such a case. A judge later reduced the award, but it remained a record, and the law firm appealed. Here, Weeks is flanked by her lawyers, Alan Exelrod (left) and Philip Kay.*

ate, for a total of eight, and held even in the House at 47. In keeping with the Republican Party's winning back control of both the House and the Senate, GOP women made gains. The number of Republican women in the House increased from 12 to 17, while the number of Democratic women dropped from 35 to 30. One new Republican woman was elected to the Senate—Olympia Snowe of Maine—while California Democratic Senator Dianne Feinstein beat back a high-dollar challenge from Representative Michael Huffington.

Republican women also fared well in state legislative races. Overall, the number of women who would be serving in state legislatures in 1995 was down by 12 from the number before the November 1994 election—a drop from 1,547 to 1,535 (this represents about a fifth of all legislators).

The losers were mostly Democrats, though, and party ratios changed noticeably. As a result of the November election, some 44 percent of women state legislators who took office in January 1995 were Republicans and 55 percent were Democrats. (The remainder were independents.) That compared with a split of 38 percent Republicans to 62 percent Democrats before the 1994 election.

The number of women holding statewide office, from governor to auditor, increased for both parties, from a total of 73 before the 1994 election to 84 taking office in 1995. The number of women governors fell from four to one, with two Democratic governors, Joan Finney of Kansas and Barbara Roberts of Oregon, re-

tiring in 1994 and a third Democrat, Ann Richards of Texas, losing to Republican challenger George W. Bush, son of former President George Bush. The remaining female governor, Republican Christine Todd Whitman of New Jersey, was not up for reelection.

Abortion. The Supreme Court ruled unanimously on January 24 that abortion providers may use federal racketeering laws to sue antiabortion groups that cause damage to clinics. In its decision in *National Organization for Women* v. *Scheidler* the Court overturned a lower court ruling that the federal Racketeer Influenced and Corrupt Organizations Act applied only to organizations motivated by economic gain. The Court's ruling had the effect of reinstating a lawsuit in which NOW accused Operation Rescue and other antiabortion groups of a conspiracy to close clinics through a pattern of violence and intimidation.

Clinic violence in the form of bombings, arson, and vandalism continued in 1994, although some numbers were down. The National Abortion Federation, an organization representing abortion providers, reported 141 incidents of violence as of December 31, compared with 434 in all of 1993. Perhaps not coincidentally, in May 1994, President Bill Clinton signed into law the Freedom of Access to Clinic Entrances Act, which established criminal penalties for clinic blockades, vandalism, and threats and violence aimed at abortion providers.

There were four abortion-related murders in 1994. On July 29 physician John Britton and his security escort, retired Air Force Lieutenant Colonel James Barrett, were shot and killed at the Ladies Center abortion clinic in Pensacola, FL. Paul Hill, an antiabortion activist and former preacher who admitted to the murders, was sentenced to die in the electric chair by a Florida state court.

On December 30 a gunman killed two receptionists and wounded five other people at two abortion clinics in Brookline, MA. John Salvi, a 22-year-old New Hampshire man, was arrested the following day after allegedly firing at a Norfolk, VA, abortion clinic and was charged with the shootings.

The French abortion pill RU-486 began to be tested in the United States in 1994. The Population Council, a New York City-based contraceptive research group, launched a series of tests after Roussel Uclaf, the French developer of the drug, transferred to it all patent rights for free.

Sexual Harassment. On September 1 a San Francisco jury awarded Rena Weeks, a former secretary at Baker & McKenzie, said to be the largest law firm in the world, a record $7.1 million in punitive damages for sexual harassment that occurred on the job.

Of that total, $6.9 million was to come from Baker & McKenzie and $225,000 from Martin R. Greenstein, a former partner at the firm. A judge later cut the judgment against the firm to $3.5 million (still a record in such a case) because Baker & McKenzie did not deliberately violate the employee's rights. The punitive damages against Greenstein were upheld, since he had, the judge said, shown "seriously abusive" conduct toward women and had "denied or minimized his actions." Baker & McKenzie appealed the judgment.

In the aftermath of the 1991 Tailhook scandal, which led to harassment charges against 140 naval aviators, ex-Navy Lieutenant Paula Coughlin won $1.7 million in damages on October 28 from the Las Vegas Hilton, where the Tailhook convention of Navy fliers was held. Coughlin, who had resigned from the Navy earlier in the year, was one of more than 80 women who alleged that they had been assaulted or molested by aviators at the convention. The damage award, handed down by a U.S. district court jury, was the first verdict to

result in the scandal. The jury said the hotel had failed to provide adequate security. In another case involving the military, the Navy announced late in the year that it would court-martial four male instructors for pressuring female students to have sex. The trial was not expected to begin before 1995.

Discrimination Suit. On December 7 the Central Intelligence Agency agreed to pay $410,000 to a senior female case officer to settle a sex discrimination suit. A former station chief in Jamaica, the woman alleged that CIA officials had accused her of alcoholism and promiscuity after she reported a subordinate male officer for spousal abuse. The CIA settled rather than face a class action suit involving more than 100 other female case officers.

Women's Equity. In January outgoing Defense Secretary Les Aspin announced a revised policy opening more combat roles to women. Put into operation on October 1, the ruling opened an additional 80,000 military service

Penn pal. The cause of women in higher education took a step forward with the appointment of Judith Rodin, formerly provost of Yale University, to the presidency of the University of Pennsylvania. Rodin became the first female permanent president of an Ivy League school.

441

provisions to women and rescinded the so-called risk rule that barred women from units that would be in danger during ground combat. Women were still barred from high-risk infantry, armored tank, and field artillery posts. The Navy also gave notice that it would assign its first women to combat ships.

On Capitol Hill lawmakers passed measures requiring schools to report on their treatment of women athletes, to promote female students' participation in math and science programs, and to pursue dropout prevention strategies for teen parents. Also passed was the Omnibus Crime Control and Safe Streets Act, which boosted federal funding for programs that are designed to curb violence against women.   E.N.C.

WYOMING. *See* STATISTICS OF THE WORLD.

YEMEN. The unrest that had marked the four-year-old union between North and South Yemen escalated in 1994 into a full-scale civil war that ended in victory by the north.

Yemen slid into chaos early in the year. There were riots over inflation, estimates of which ranged from 100 to 300 percent. Along with kidnappings of foreign oil workers, a se-

The war is over. A tank belonging to forces loyal to Yemeni President Ali Abdullah Saleh proceeds down a street in Aden after the city was captured in July. The fall of Aden marked the end of a nine-week civil war in which the southern section of Yemen unsuccessfully tried to secede from the country, which had been united only since 1990.

ries of terrorist assassinations of South Yemeni politicians took place.

Vice President Ali Salim al-Baidh, the former president of South Yemen, which is comparatively richer in oil, wanted to loosen the ties between North and South Yemen; he resisted the authority of President Ali Abdullah Saleh, who was supported by the north. War began on May 4 when Saleh launched a military attack to subdue Baidh. On May 21, Baidh announced the formal secession of the south.

Although the early weeks of the war saw Scud missile attacks on Sana, most of the military activity focused on North Yemen's advance and assault on Aden, South Yemen's former capital. Southern planes managed to destroy an important power plant near Al Mukha, but by the end of June northern forces had surrounded Aden. The city fell on July 7, and Baidh fled to Oman.

In the aftermath of the fighting Yemen was beset by food and water shortages, and an outbreak of cholera in Aden killed some 40 people. The conflict, which cost an estimated $7.5 billion, also caused a government financial crisis.

In September, Saleh and the Parliament abolished the five-seat Presidential Council, which Saleh had chaired, in favor of a single president. On October 1 the Parliament elected Saleh to a five-year term. In the government formed by new Prime Minister Abdul Aziz Abdul Ghani, Saleh's General People's Congress held 16 of the 27 cabinet posts; the al-Islah Party, a pro-Saudi coalition, held nine; and independents held two.

In March, Abdullah al-Salal died. Salal led the 1962 military coup that overthrew Yemen's monarchy but was himself ousted from power in 1967.

See STATISTICS OF THE WORLD.   C.H.A.

YUGOSLAVIA. Despite a dramatic stabilization of the economy in 1994, Yugoslavia (Serbia and Montenegro) was still beset by political upheaval, economic uncertainty, and partial isolation as a result of its role in the war in Bosnia-Hercegovina. The easing of international sanctions in October provided a psychological boost to beleaguered Yugoslavs, but it came at a high price—the imposition of an economic and political blockade against Bosnian Serbs—which divided Serbs and increased political tensions.

Economic Stabilization. On January 24 a new economic austerity program was announced. Designed by a team of economists and financial experts, the plan tightly controlled government expenditures, restricted the printing of currency, and pegged the new "super dinar" to the German mark at an exchange rate of one to one. Within a few months inflation decreased dramatically (from 320 percent in December 1993 to single and double digits in 1994), while wages increased and production picked up. However, the gains made under the plan were fragile. Their continued success was contingent on Yugoslavia's ability to attract desperately needed foreign capital, impossible while UN sanctions, imposed because of Yugoslavia's support for the Bosnian Serbs, remained in place.

Political Volatility. The need to have the UN sanctions lifted and the desire to avoid a threatened tightening of those sanctions were major factors in the August 4 decision of Serbian President Slobodan Milosevic, the dominant political figure in Yugoslavia, to impose his own set of sanctions on the Bosnian Serbs. He did so to try to pressure the Bosnian Serbs into accepting the peace plan proposed for Bosnia-Hercegovina by the so-called contact group (Britain, France, Germany, Russia, and the United States). Milosevic's action produced severe internal political strains. Most opposition parties, with the exception of the Coalition of Democratic Opposition of Serbia, condemned Milosevic's "betrayal" of the Serbs in Bosnia and pledged support to the Bosnian Serb political leadership headed by Radovan Karadzic.

Knowing that his decision to abandon the nationalist platform put him in an extremely vulnerable position, Milosevic undertook several measures to secure his power. The Yugoslav government was shaken up and new ministers were appointed in mid-September. Milosevic increased his hold on television and other media by firing several key individuals; by doing so he eliminated overnight any mention of the Bosnian Serbs and the Serbs in the Krajina region of Croatia. In October several officers of the Yugoslav Army were forced to

War talk. *UN special representative Yasushi Akashi (left) meets in Belgrade with Serbian President Slobodan Milosevic (center) and Bosnian Serb leader Radovan Karadzic (right) in April to discuss an ongoing offensive by Serb Bosnian forces against the Bosnian Muslim enclave of Gorazde. Members of NATO, which had already bombed Bosnian Serb positions, threatened further air strikes if the Serbs did not withdraw; the Serbs eventually pulled back.*

resign and financial pressure was applied to the military in order to control any threat that it might pose to Milosevic and his Socialist Party of Serbia (SPS).

Vojislav Seselj, the leader of the nationalist Serbian Radical Party, was stripped of his parliamentary immunity in September and sentenced to a month in jail for a physical assault on SPS leader Radovan Bozovic.

In October, Seselj was sentenced to serve an additional three months for a previous assault on Bozovic for which he had originally received a suspended sentence. Seselj's imprisonment and the attempt to strip the parliamentary immunity of Democratic Party leader Zoran Djindjic led observers to conclude that Milosevic was trying to silence his most visible opponents.

Split in the SPS. The Bosnia question also triggered the development of factionalism within the SPS. In October the party's leading ideologue, Mihailo Markovic, came under public criticism from Milosevic's wife and leader of the Yugoslav Union of Leftists, Mirjana Markovic. Mirjana Markovic's attack on Mihailo Markovic and his response, communicated through the news media, represented the most open display of political infighting within Belgrade's elite.

Between War and Peace. Milosevic's decision to apply pressure to the Bosnian Serbs to extract their support for the contact group's peace plan gave him an opportunity to crack down on his internal opponents and to undermine any challenge that Bosnian Serb leader Karadzic might pose to his base of power. On the economic side, however, it failed to win significant concessions from the international community beyond the symbolic opening of Belgrade's airport and the easing of sanctions on culture and sport in October. The UN indicated that trade sanctions would continue at least until Serbia recognized Croatia's and Bosnia-Hercegovina's internationally accepted borders. Offering such recognition, however, might lead Milosevic's nationalist opponents to take to the streets. The four-month cessation of hostilities that began in Bosnia-Hercegovina on January 1, 1995, seemed to put the issue on hold.

See BOSNIA-HERCEGOVINA; CROATIA; MACEDONIA; SLOVENIA; STATISTICS OF THE WORLD.   O.K.

YUKON TERRITORY. *See* STATISTICS OF THE WORLD.

Z

ZAIRE. Zaire continued to be plagued by governmental chaos and an out-of-control economy in 1994. The state-owned mining company Gécamines was near collapse, and the country was ravaged by AIDS. The arrival of more than a million Rwandan refugees resulted in clashes between violent refugees and the Zairean Army.

Early in the year the prime minister of one of Zaire's two competing Parliaments, Faustin Birindwa, resigned. Members of the Parliament that Birindwa had headed, which backed longtime Zairean leader Mobutu Sese Seko, were absorbed by the High Council of the Republic, the nation's transitional Parliament. In June the High Council elected Léon Kengo wa Dondo as Birindwa's replacement.

Meanwhile, popular leader Etienne Tshisekedi, a member of the Kasai Luba ethnic group, continued to meet with his government. (In 1992, Tshisekedi had been prime minister of the Parliament that preceded the High Council, but his government had been pushed aside after Mobutu organized a rival Parliament.) However, Tshisekedi was increasingly irrelevant; three of his ministers joined Kengo's cabinet, and the public had apparently tired of his calls for resistance.

Kengo, who had been prime minister twice in the 1980s, was considered an advocate of fiscal austerity as promoted by the International Monetary Fund. His candidacy was put forward by his party—the Union of Independent Democrats—and other moderate groups of the Sacred Union of the Opposition, a coalition of parties opposing Mobutu. The radical wing of the Sacred Union called Kengo's election illegal and said Tshisekedi was the legitimate prime minister.

Kengo reserved three minor cabinet posts for Tshisekedi's party and made it clear he was willing to offer more important posts once it joined his government. Tshisekedi declined the offer. Zaire's principal political and economic partners—Belgium, France, and the United States—failed to persuade Tshisekedi to negotiate; all three then issued carefully worded statements implicitly recognizing the Kengo government.

The question was whether Kengo could succeed where Tshisekedi had failed by reaching a working arrangement with Mobutu. Kengo had promised to establish central bank autonomy, halt public sector corruption, end the security forces' reign of terror, and rebuild the transportation, education, and health sectors. But by year's end he had failed to gain control over the Bank of Zaire, the central bank. A "new zaire" currency had been introduced late in 1993 with an official rate of about three to the dollar. By late 1994 the new currency was valued at more than 3,000 to the dollar.

See STATISTICS OF THE WORLD.   T.E.T.

Dangerous place. A Zairean soldier stands guard in Goma, Zaire, amid rocks thrown by angry demonstrators. Thousands of protesters, including refugees from Rwanda, took to the streets in August after a Zairean soldier killed a black-market money changer. Violence in the refugee camps created in eastern Zaire in the wake of the civil war in neighboring Rwanda was an ongoing problem for the Zairean authorities and for international relief officials in 1994.

ZAMBIA. Charges of high-level corruption and drug trafficking dogged the Zambian government during 1994. At a December 1993 World Bank meeting in Paris, donor governments reduced Zambia's aid by $100 million and demanded that President Frederick Chiluba fight corruption. The Zambia Congress of Trade Unions called on the president to dissolve the cabinet and appoint ministers untainted by scandal.

Chiluba angrily brushed aside the corruption allegations (which had been repeated for years) and demanded their substantiation. Nevertheless, two implicated cabinet members and another top official resigned in early January, and four cabinet members were dismissed. As a result, Chiluba's Movement for Multiparty Democracy lost four by-election seats to the National Party, and several MMD members of Parliament defected to the NP in February.

In July the legal affairs minister, Ludwig Sondashi, claimed to have evidence that Chiluba was getting rich through the drug trade. He was immediately dismissed and charged with defaming the president. Vice President Levy Mwanawasa, the leader of the National Assembly, resigned in protest. Chiluba named Godfrey Miyanda, formerly a minister without portfolio, as the new vice president. In October two more cabinet ministers were sacked.

Amid this disorder the five-year structural adjustment program launched in 1993 under the sponsorship of the International Monetary Fund and the World Bank stalled. In June it was announced that only 11 of the 150 parastatal, or government-linked, corporations had been privatized. Nevertheless, in September the World Bank's International Development Association and some European donor countries provided funds to enable Zambia to reduce its commercial debt by one-tenth. Zambia's $6.9 billion debt was one of the world's highest per capita. In 1994 international agencies and donor countries rescheduled or forgave 80 percent of Zambia's official debt.

See STATISTICS OF THE WORLD.　　　K.W.G.

ZIMBABWE. Zimbabwe faced a mixed economic picture in 1994. As of midyear, the average wages for the nation's workers were at a 20-year low, and real per capita income had fallen to its lowest level in more than a decade, At the same time, unemployment figures continued to grow.

Meanwhile, annual inflation was above 25 percent, but that figure was an improvement from the record 50 percent in 1993. Zimbabwe's agriculture-based economy, boosted during the year by good rains, was forecast to grow by 4 to 7 percent in 1994, up from 2 percent growth in 1993 and minus 12 percent in 1992, a drought year.

President Robert Mugabe devoted his opening speech to Parliament in late June to the economy. He pledged to cut spending on the armed forces, reducing troop strength from 70,000 to 35,000 in two years; to halve the country's budget deficit (running at an estimated 10 percent of gross domestic product); and to speed up the forcible purchase of white-owned farms in order to resettle thousands of landless peasants.

The land policy, legitimated in the Land Acquisition Act of 1992, was a cause of embarrassment to the Mugabe government. The process was going slowly, and in April it was disclosed that senior officials (cabinet ministers, civil servants, military officers, and police chiefs among them) had won choice leases and were renting 98 state-owned farms that had been previously allocated for division among small-scale farmers. The outcry from the opposition parties, the independent press, and the public eventually forced members of the ruling party, the Zimbabwe African National Union-Patriotic Front, to join the criticism. Eventually, in June, Mugabe backed down from the policy, but not from his commitment to redistribute land.

These contentious economic and ethical issues provided the background for general elections slated for early 1995. Although the opposition received new life from the land scandal, it remained splintered and ineffective. In January, Bishop Abel Muzorewa of the United African National Council and Edgar Tekere, leader of the Zimbabwe Unity Movement, agreed to merge their respective organizations under the ZUM name. An attempt in October to reorganize the merged group as the United Party quickly collapsed.

See STATISTICS OF THE WORLD.　　　K.W.G.

CHRONOLOGY FOR 1994

January

1•The North American Free Trade Agreement, which phases out tariffs between Canada, Mexico, and the United States, goes into effect.

•"Zapatista" rebels seize four towns in the Mexican state of Chiapas. Clashes with government troops in the following days leave nearly 100 people dead before negotiations with the government begin.

6•U.S. Olympic figure skating hopeful Nancy Kerrigan is attacked after a practice session at a Detroit rink and suffers an injured knee.

14•Russia, Ukraine, and the United States sign an agreement for the dismantling of Ukraine's nuclear arsenal.

17•A strong earthquake shakes Los Angeles, leaving more than 50 people dead and thousands homeless; aftershocks continue for weeks.

20•A special prosecutor is chosen to head a federal inquiry into the role—and possible illegal financial dealings—of President Bill Clinton and of his wife, Hillary, in the Whitewater land development venture.

24•The U.S. Supreme Court rules that abortion rights groups may use an antiracketeering law to sue antiabortion demonstrators who organize violent and criminal acts against abortion clinics.

29•Japan's Parliament approves a political reform package designed to reduce corruption and reorganize the electoral system.

February

3•President Clinton lifts a 19-year ban on U.S. trade with Vietnam, in response to Vietnamese cooperation in the search for the remains of American soldiers listed as missing in action in the Vietnam War.

4•The continuing civil war in Sudan sees the Islamic military government launch a massive ground and air attack on the rebel Sudanese People's Liberation Army, setting off a surge of refugees to Uganda.

5•A mortar shell explodes in a marketplace in Sarajevo, killing 68 people—the highest death toll in a single incident during a 22-month siege of the city by Bosnian Serbs.

8•Three of four cases in the Tailhook scandal—involving alleged assaults on women at a 1991 naval aviators' convention—are dismissed by a U.S. Navy judge, who also says Admiral Frank Kelso II, the chief of naval operations, misrepresented his knowledge of what occurred. The Marine Corps later dismisses the fourth case.

•Canada slashes its cigarette tax to fight widespread tobacco smuggling from the United States.

12•The XVII Winter Olympic Games open in Lillehammer, Norway. By the games' February 27 conclusion, Norway has earned the most medals, 26, followed by Germany with 24 and Russia with 23.

22•Former CIA official Aldrich Ames and his wife, Rosario, are charged with spying for the Soviet Union and Russia. The couple plead guilty in April, with Ames receiving a life sentence.

25•Israeli settler Baruch Goldstein opens fire on Muslim worshipers in a West Bank mosque, killing 29 Palestinians, and is himself killed in the ensuing melee.

March

4•A federal jury finds four defendants guilty of all charges against them in the bombing of New York City's World Trade Center in February 1993.

12•The Church of England ordains 32 women, who become the first female priests in its 460-year history.

16•U.S. Olympic ice skater Tonya Harding pleads guilty to hindering the prosecution in the January attack on fellow skater Nancy Kerrigan; the U.S. Figure Skating Association later strips Harding of her 1994 national title and bans her from the organization for life.

21•*Schindler's List,* Steven Spielberg's Holocaust drama about a real-life industrialist who saved Jewish workers from World War II death camps, wins seven Oscars, including best picture; Spielberg takes best director honors.

23•Luis Donaldo Colosio Murrieta, the presidential candidate of Mexico's governing party, is assassinated while campaigning in Tijuana. Within days Ernesto Zedillo Ponce de León, Colosio's campaign manager and a former government minister, is named as his replacement.

25•A day after two key Somali clan leaders sign a peace accord paving the way for elections, U.S. troops officially end a humanitarian relief and peacekeeping mission in Somalia that had begun in 1992.

28•A right-wing political alliance led by media tycoon Silvio Berlusconi claims victory in Italy's two-day parliamentary elections.

•French Prime Minister Edouard Balladur abandons a government decision to lower the minimum wage for young people, after nearly a month of demonstrations disrupted major cities.

April

6•The presidents of Rwanda and Burundi are killed when their plane is reportedly shot down in Kigali, Rwanda's capital. The incident touches off weeks of civil war in Rwanda that leave some 500,000 dead.

11•In Bosnia, U.S. jets under NATO command bomb Serbian positions near the predominantly Muslim town of Gorazde for the second day in a row, in response to Serb forces' disregard of UN demands to pull back their weapons.

14•In a case of mistaken identity, two U.S. Army helicopters are downed by American fighter planes enforcing a no-fly zone over northern Iraq; all 26 people on board are killed.

19•Paul Touvier, former intelligence chief of a pro-Nazi militia in Lyon charged with killing seven Jews in 1944, becomes the first Frenchman to be convicted of crimes against humanity for collaboration with Nazi German occupiers.

26•Sweeping aside 300 years of white minority rule, South Africa begins its first fully democratic, nonracial elections. Voters turn out in huge numbers for the three-day balloting despite more than a dozen pre-election bomb explosions.

May

4•Israel and the Palestine Liberation Organization sign an agreement formally beginning Israel's withdrawal from the Gaza Strip and Jericho and implementing Palestinian self-rule in those areas.

6•The Channel Tunnel, linking Britain and France by rail, is inaugurated by Queen Elizabeth II and President François Mitterrand months before the start of regular train service.

10•Nelson Mandela is sworn in as South Africa's president.

16•Under pressure from the Clinton administration, the French manufacturer of the abortion pill RU-486 agrees to donate U.S. patent rights and related technology to a nonprofit research organization.

17•The U.S. Federal Reserve raises two short-term interest rates by half a percentage point, their sharpest increase in more than five years, to avert possible inflationary pressure.

25•Astronomers say that the *Hubble Space Telescope* has provided conclusive evidence for the existence of a black hole.

26•President Clinton renews China's most-favored-nation trade status.

27•After nearly 20 years' exile, spent mainly in the United States, Nobel Prize-winning Russian writer Aleksandr Solzhenitsyn returns to his homeland.

31•Influential U.S. Representative Dan Rostenkowski (D, Illinois) is indicted on 17 felony counts, including embezzlement, fraud, and obstruction of justice.

June

1•Saudi Prince Al-Waleed bin Talal rescues the ailing Euro Disney by buying a 24.5 percent stake in the theme park, located east of Paris.

17•Former professional football star O. J. Simpson is arrested and charged with killing his ex-wife, Nicole Brown Simpson, and a friend of hers, Ronald Goldman.

27•President Clinton shuffles his senior aides, replacing White House Chief of Staff Mack McLarty with Leon Panetta, head of the Office of Management and Budget.

July

1•PLO leader Yasir Arafat visits Gaza, setting foot on Palestinian soil for the first time in nearly three decades.

8•Kim Il Sung, North Korea's leader for nearly half a century, dies; his son, Kim Jong Il, assumes power.

14•The flow of Rwandan refugees into Zaire reportedly reaches more than 500,000, in an exodus spurred on by Tutsi-led rebels' July 4 capture of major government installations in the Rwandan capital and their subsequent advance westward.

16•Pieces of Comet Shoemaker-Levy 9 begin to hit Jupiter, producing enormous fireballs—at least one larger than Earth—to the delight of astronomers.

17•Brazil's soccer team wins its fourth World Cup, beating Italy in a goal-less final ultimately decided, 3-2, by penalty kicks.

21•The European Parliament endorses the appointment of Luxembourg's premier, Jacques Santer, to a five-year term as president of the European Commission.

25•In Washington, DC, Israeli Prime Minister Yitzhak Rabin and King Hussein of Jordan agree to end the nearly five-decade-long state of war between their countries and to cooperate in development projects.

29•A doctor who performed abortions and his bodyguard are shot to death by an antiabortion protester in Pensacola, FL—the second such shooting outside a Pensacola clinic in 17 months.

•U.S. Supreme Court nominee Stephen G. Breyer is confirmed by the Senate. Breyer replaces Justice Harry A. Blackmun, who is retiring.

August

12•American major league baseball players go on strike.

14•Notorious international terrorist Carlos the Jackal (Ilich Ramírez Sánchez) is arrested in Sudan and extradited to France.

449

14•The weekend-long Woodstock '94 concert, drawing more than 300,000 people despite rain, comes to an end; it marks the 25th anniversary of the era-defining 1969 Woodstock concert.

17•Robert Altman, U.S. deputy treasury secretary and a top Clinton adviser, resigns, followed, on August 18, by Treasury Department General Counsel Jean Hanson; congressional lawmakers accused Altman of giving misleading testimony concerning the Whitewater affair.

19•With growing numbers of Cubans fleeing to the United States by boat or raft, President Clinton reverses U.S. policy allowing easy entry for Cuban refugees, saying that refugees picked up at sea would be held in custody at the U.S. naval base at Guantánamo Bay in Cuba.

21•Ernesto Zedillo Ponce de León is elected president of Mexico, taking slightly over 50 percent of the vote.

25•The U.S. Senate completes legislative action on a Clinton-supported anticrime bill, four days after the House passed it. The bill includes $6.9 billion for crime prevention programs and bans assault weapons.

31•The Irish Republican Army declares a cease-fire in its 25-year fight to get the British out of Northern Ireland.

September

5•A UN conference on population and development begins in Cairo. Disputes over abortion rights, sex education, and cultural differences mark its opening days, but at its conclusion delegates formally agree that the education and empowerment of women are key to limiting world population growth.

9•The United States government agrees to accept a minimum of 20,000 legal Cuban immigrants per year in exchange for Cuba's promise to deter its citizens from fleeing to U.S. shores.

12•In Québec the separatist Parti Québécois, led by Jacques Parizeau, narrowly wins a parliamentary election.

18•Haiti's military-led government agrees to step down. The following day more than 3,000 American troops land in Haiti as part of a military operation to oversee the reinstatement of exiled President Jean-Bertrand Aristide.

26•Health care reform legislation, a key goal of President Clinton, is effectively declared dead in Congress as Senate Majority Leader George Mitchell says he will not try to bring a reform bill to the Senate floor in the current session.

29•The Pan American Health Organization says polio is eradicated in North America, Latin America, and the Caribbean; the last known case reportedly occurred in 1991.

October

5•In what appears to be a collective suicide or mass murder, 48 members of the Order of the Solar Temple religious sect are found dead in two Swiss villages, and five others linked to the sect are found dead in Québec.

8•The United States begins sending troops to the Persian Gulf region in response to a buildup of Iraqi forces near the Kuwaiti border. By October 11, Iraq had begun to withdraw.

14•PLO leader Yasir Arafat, Israeli Foreign Minister Shimon Peres, and Israeli Prime Minister Yitzhak Rabin are jointly awarded the Nobel Peace Prize.

15•Aristide returns to power after 1,111 days in exile, two days after Haiti's deposed military leader, Raoul Cédras, and his top deputy arrive in Panama City.

November

8 • U.S. elections leave Republicans with control of the House and Senate, as well as with a majority of state governorships.

15 • At the Asia-Pacific Economic Cooperation summit meeting in Indonesia, leaders of Pacific Rim nations agree to move toward free trade in the region by 2020.

17 • Albert Reynolds resigns as Ireland's prime minister in the wake of a split in his coalition government. Fine Gael leader John Bruton becomes the country's prime minister in December.

20 • The Angolan government and Unita rebels sign a peace treaty to end a 19-year civil war that had intensified following 1992 elections.

21 • NATO warplanes bomb a Serb air base in Croatia, in a response to attacks by Serb planes in the UN "safe area" around Bihac, Bosnia. Serb forces subsequently react to the raid and to a second bombing on November 23 by taking hundreds of UN peacekeeping forces hostage.

23 • The United States completes a secret operation to move more than 1,300 pounds of poorly protected weapons-grade uranium from Kazakhstan to a U.S. storage facility.

28 • Convicted serial killer Jeffrey Dahmer—who admitted to the murders of 17 young men and boys—is bludgeoned to death by a fellow inmate in a Wisconsin prison.

• Norway begins a two-day referendum that sees voters reject joining the European Union; earlier in the year voters in Austria, Finland, and Sweden approved EU entry.

December

1 • The U.S. Senate approves a bill implementing the sweeping world trade treaty negotiated under the General Agreement on Tariffs and Trade (GATT), two days after the House of Representatives passed it.

6 • Orange County, CA, files for bankruptcy; with the county's losses eventually estimated to exceed $2 billion, the case is the largest bankruptcy to involve a unit of American government.

9 • U.S. Surgeon General Joycelyn Elders is forced to resign by the White House over her controversial remarks about sex education and drug legalization.

11 • Russian armed forces enter the secessionist Muslim republic of Chechnya with orders to quash its bid for independence.

• Leaders from 34 western hemisphere nations agree to establish a free-trade pact, as the so-called Summit of the Americas concludes in Miami.

17 • A U.S. Army helicopter strays into North Korean airspace and is forced down; one of the two pilots aboard is killed. North Korea, saying the helicopter was on a hostile surveillance mission, holds the other pilot captive until December 30.

18 • Jimmy Carter arrives in Sarajevo hoping to mediate between Bosnian Serbs and the Muslim-led Bosnian government; the two sides later agree to a short-term cease-fire.

22 • Weakened by corruption allegations and loss of parliamentary allies, Italian Prime Minister Silvio Berlusconi resigns.

26 • French commandos storm a hijacked airliner in Marseille, freeing some 170 hostages and killing four Islamic fundamentalist terrorists who had seized the plane in Algiers two days before.

29 • After weeks of economic crisis in Mexico, marked by a plummeting peso, President Zedillo announces the resignation of his finance minister and outlines an emergency stabilization plan to slash the country's foreign trade debt.

STATISTICS OF THE
WORLD: COUNTRIES

Nation Capital	Population[1]	Area of Country sq mi (sq km)	Type of Government	Heads of State and Government	Currency: Value of U.S. Dollar[2]
AFGHANISTAN Kabul	17,800,000 2,000,000	251,826 (652,225)	Transitional	Interim pres., Burhanuddin Rabbani Prime min., Gulbuddin Hekmatyar	afghani 2,600[8]
ALBANIA Tirana	3,400,000 251,000	11,100 (28,748)	Nascent democracy	Pres., Sali Berisha Prime min., Aleksander Meksi	lek 100
ALGERIA Algiers	27,900,000 1,507,000	919,595 (2,381,740)	Republic	Pres., Lamine Zeroual Prime min., Mokdad Sifi	dinar 31.44
ANDORRA Andorra la Vella	59,000 19,000	175 (453)	Parliamentary democracy	Prem., Oscar Ribas Reig	Spanish peseta/ French franc 131.88/5.54
ANGOLA Luanda	11,200,000 1,200,000	481,350 (1,246,700)	Transitional	Pres., José Eduardo dos Santos Prime min., Marcolino José Carlos Moco	new kwanza 96,965
ANTIGUA AND BARBUDA St. John's	66,000 36,000	171 (443)	Parliamentary state (C)	Gov.-gen., James Carlisle Prime min., Lester Bird	EC dollar[20] 2.70
ARGENTINA Buenos Aires	33,900,000 12,538,000[21]	1,073,400 (2,780,092)	Federal republic	Pres., Carlos Saúl Menem	peso 0.9974
ARMENIA Yerevan	3,700,000 1,202,000	11,510 (29,800)	Republic	Pres., Levon Ter-Petrosyan Vice pres., Gagik Arutyunyan	dram n.a.
AUSTRALIA Canberra	17,800,000 324,600[21]	2,966,155 (7,682,300)	Federal parliamentary state (C)	Gov.-gen., William George Hayden Prime min., Paul Keating	dollar 1.37
AUSTRIA Vienna	8,000,000 1,539,800	32,377 (83,855)	Federal republic	Pres., Thomas Klestil Chancellor, Franz Vranitzky	schilling 11.19
AZERBAIJAN Baku	7,400,000 1,080,500	33,440 (86,600)	Republic	Pres., Haidar Aliyev Prime min., Surat Huseynov	manat n.a.
BAHAMAS Nassau	264,000 171,500	5,380 (13,935)	Parliamentary state (C)	Gov.-gen., Clifford Darling Prime min., Hubert Ingraham	dollar 1.00
BAHRAIN Manama	538,000 151,500	267 (691)	Monarchy	Emir, Isa bin Sulman al-Khalifa Prime min., Khalifa bin Sulman al-Khalifa	dinar 0.377
BANGLADESH Dhaka	116,600,000 3,397,200	55,598 (143,998)	Republic (C)	Pres., Abdur Rahman Biswas Prime min., Khaleda Ziaur Rahman	taka 40.38
BARBADOS Bridgetown	259,000 6,700	166 (430)	Parliamentary state (C)	Gov.-gen., Nita Barrow Prime min., Owen Arthur	dollar 2.0113
BELARUS Minsk	10,300,000 1,633,600	80,155 (207,600)	Republic	Pres., Alyaksandr Lukashenka Prime min., Mikhail Chigir	ruble 1,971
BELGIUM Brussels	10,100,000 950,300[21]	11,783 (30,518)	Constitutional monarchy	Head of state, King Albert II Prime min., Jean-Luc Dehaene	franc 32.76

This section on countries presents the latest information available. All monetary figures are expressed in United States dollars. The symbol (C) signifies that the country belongs to the Commonwealth of Nations; n.a. means that the data were not available; and the symbol * indicates that the category does not apply to the country under discussion. GDP stands for gross domestic product. Footnotes and source notes are located at the end of the section.

Revenue Expenditure in millions[3]	GDP in billions[4] GDP Per Capita	Imports Exports in millions[5]	Elementary Schools: Teachers Students	Secondary Schools: Teachers Students	Colleges and Universities: Teachers Students
n.a.	$3	$616	n.a.	n.a.	1,342
n.a.	$700	$188	n.a.	n.a.	24,333
$1,100	$2.7[7]	$524	28,798	9,708	1,680
$1,400	$1,100	$70	551,294	205,774	22,835
$14,400	$47	$7,770	161,802	135,730	20,336
$14,600	$5,800	$10,230	4,436,363	2,305,198	298,117
$138	$0.760[7]	n.a.	n.a.	n.a.	n.a.
$177	$14,000[2]	$30	n.a.	n.a.	n.a.
$928	$3.4	$1,600	31,062	n.a.	439
$2,500	$1,200	$3,000	990,155	186,499	6,534
$105	$0.368	$215	n.a.	400	n.a.
$161	$5,800	$32	9.298	5,845	n.a.
$33,100	$110.3	$16,784	275,162	283,583	89,609
$35,800	$6,200	$13,118	4,874,306	2,160,410	1,077,212
n.a.	$1.9	$87[19]	n.a.	n.a.	n.a.
n.a.	$2,300	$31[19]	592,000[10]	—[10]	66,100
$71,900	$310.2	$45,577	97,955	104,110	27,442
$83,100	$17,600[2]	$42,723	1,623,012	1,294,596	559,365
$52,200	$189.4	$48,578	33,507	80,980	16,188
$60,300	$18,800	$40,174	382,663	768,176	221,389
n.a.	$4.4	$240[19]	n.a.	n.a.	10,743
n.a.	$2,400	$355[19]	267,946	891,839	100,985
$628.5	$3.7	$1,801	n.a.	n.a.	n.a.
$574.0	$11,100	$1,517	31,601	29,863	n.a.
$1,200	$4.4	$3,825	3,312[28]	3,132	582
$1,600	$8,000	$3,689	68,898	51,413	7,763
$2,500	$24.5	$3,987	189,508	130,949	22,447
$3,700	$1,250	$2,272	11,939,949	3,592,995	
$547	$2.2[7]	$574	1,553	n.a.	n.a.
$620	$8,700	$179	26,662	n.a.	6,888
n.a.	$16.0	$743	117,500	n.a.	17,200
n.a.	$6,300	$710	635,100	970,300	187,700
$97,800	$221.5	$125,047[22]	72,589	110,599	28,058
$109,300	$18,400[2]	$123,132[22]	711,521	765,672	276,248

Nation Capital	Population[1]	Area of Country sq mi (sq km)	Type of Government	Heads of State and Government	Currency: Value of U.S. Dollar[2]
BELIZE.....................................230,000		8,866	.......Parliamentary	........Gov.-gen., Colville Young ....dollar	
Belmopan	3,700	(22,963)	state (C)	Prime min., Manuel Esquivel	2.00
BENIN..............................5,300,000		43,475	.......Republic	...............Pres., Nicéphore Soglo..CFA	
Porto-Novo	208,300	(112,600)			franc[23]
					554.465
BHUTAN 600,000		17,954	.......Monarchy	...............King, Jigme Singye Wangchuk.................................ngultrum	
Thimbu	30,000	(46,500)			31.37
BOLIVIA 8,200,000		424,165	.......Republic	...............Pres., Gonzalo Sánchez de Lozada.........................boliviano	
Sucre (legal cap.)	105,800	(1,098,581)		Vice pres., Víctor Hugo Cárdenas	4.66[18]
La Paz (admin. cap.)	669,400				
BOSNIA- 4,600,000		19,741	.......Emerging	...............Pres., Alija Izetbegovic ....none	
HERCEGOVINA		(51,129)	democracy	Prem., Haris Silajdzic	n.a.
Sarajevo	415,600				
BOTSWANA.......................1,400,000		224,700	.......Republic (C)	........Pres., Quett K. J. Masire.......................................pula	
Gaborone	138,500	(582,000)		Vice pres., Festus Mogae	2.77
BRAZIL 155,300,000		3,286,488	.......Federal	.......Pres., Itamar Franco ....real	
Brasília	1,596,300	(8,511,965)	republic		2,499.14[8]
BRUNEI................................268,000		2,226	.......Constitutional	........Head of state and prime min.,................................dollar	
Bandar Seri Begawan	45,900	(5,765)	monarchy (C)	Sultan Muda Hassanal Bolkiah	1.5268
BULGARIA........................8,400,000		42,855	.......Emerging	.............Pres., Zheliu Zhelev ....lev	
Sofia	1,141,000	(110,994)	democracy	Prime min., Lyuben Berov	53.84
BURKINA FASO 10,100,000		105,870	.......Republic	...............Pres., Blaise Compaoré..CFA	
Ouagadougou	442,200	(274,200)		Prime min., Youssouf Ouedraogo	franc[23]
					554.465
BURMA (MYANMAR) 45,400,000		261,288	.......Military	.................Head of state and prem., Than Shwe ....kyat	
Rangoon (Yangon)	2,513,000	(676,577)	regime		5.9147
BURUNDI..........................6,000,000		10,745	.......Republic	...............Pres., Sylvestre Ntibantunganya ....franc	
Bujumbura	215,200	(27,830)		Prem., Anatole Kanyenkino	252.78
CAMBODIA....................10,300,000		69,898	.......Constitutional	........Head of state, King Norodom Sihanouk ....riel	
Phnom Penh	800,000	(181,035)	monarchy	Copremiers, Prince Norodom and	3,500.00
				Ranariddh Hun Sen	
CAMEROON 13,100,000		183,569	.......Republic	...............Pres., Paul Biya..CFA	
Yaoundé	750,000	(475,442)		Prime min., Simon Achidi Achu	franc[23]
					554.465
CANADA 29,100,000		3,849,670	.......Federal	...............Gov.-gen., Ramon Hnatyshyn.......................................dollar	
Ottawa	314,000	(9,970,610)	parliamentary state (C)	Prime min., Jean Chrétien	1.39
CAPE VERDE 350,000		1,557	.......Republic	...............Pres., Antonio Mascarenhas ....escudo	
Praia	61,700	(4,033)		Prime min., Carlos Veiga	84.42
CENTRAL AFRICAN.......3,100,000		240,535	.......Republic	...............Pres., Ange Patasse...CFA	
REPUBLIC		(622,984)		Prime min., Jean-Luc Mandaba	franc[23]
Bangui	452,000				554.465
CHAD................................6,500,000		495,800	.......Republic	...............Pres., Idriss Déby ....CFA	
N'Djamena	530,000	(1,284,000)		Prime min., Delwa Koumakoye	franc[23]
					554.465
CHILE..............................14,000,000		292,135	.......Republic	...............Pres., Eduardo Frei Ruíz-Tagle ....peso	
Santiago	4,628,000	(756,626)			422.01[18]
CHINA.......................1,192,000,000		3,691,500	.......Communist	..........Pres., Jiang Zemin ....yuan	
Beijing	7,050,000	(9,560,940)	state	Prem., Li Peng	8.65
COLOMBIA...................35,600,000		440,831	.......Republic	...............Pres., Ernesto Samper Pizano...................................peso	
Bogotá	5,026,000	(1,141,748)			826.9[18]

Revenue Expenditure in millions[3]	GDP in billions[4] GDP Per Capita	Imports Exports in millions[5]	Elementary Schools: Teachers Students	Secondary Schools: Teachers Students	Colleges and Universities: Teachers Students
$126.8	$0.497	$281	1,776	622	n.a.
$123.1	$2,400	$115	46,874	8,901	n.a.
$218	$2.1	$207	13,180[28]	n.a.	956
$355	$1,700	$97	457,140[28]	n.a.	10,873
$100	$0.5[7]	$102	1,859	n.a.	197
$112	$700	$72	56,773	5,500	1,524
$3.19	$6.6	$1,206	51,763	12,434	n.a.
$3.19	$2,300	$728	1,278,775	219,232	145,000
n.a.	$1.8	n.a.	n.a.	n.a.	n.a.
n.a.	$4,500	n.a.	543,500	173,100	37,500
$1,700	$3.9	$1,776	10,409	4,467	682
$1,990	$5,200	$1,725	301,482	81,316	6,409
$113,000	$441	$27,740	1,253,029	248,705	133,135
$109,000	$5,700	$38,597	28,742,471	3,558,946	1,565,056
$1,300	$5.0	$2,000	2,561	2,248	340
$1,500	$6,600	$2,300	39,782	26,836	1,756
$14,000	$20.6[7]	$2,800	61,148	30,005	21,976
$17,400	$5,000[2]	$3,500	877,189	374,514	195,447
$483	$3.3	$533	9,165	n.a.	205
$548	$850	$106	530,013	115,753	5,675
$8,100	$13	$814	147,578	67,000	5,600
$11,600	$810	$583	5,384,539	1,295,000	154,000
$318	$1	$204	10,400	2,562	556
$326	$600	$68	651,086	55,713	4,256
$350	$2.4	$360	n.a.	n.a.	n.a.
$350	$520	$70	n.a.	n.a.	n.a.
$1,700	$10.4	$1,175	38,430	n.a.	1,086
$2,400	$2,210	$1,815	1,964,146	500,272	33,177
$136,230	$710.7	$139.035	145,425	153,883	67,122
$175,527	$20,500	$145,178	2,438,436	2,392,064	1,942,814
$104	$0.376	$145	2,028	n.a.	n.a.
$133	$1,800	$6	67,761	n.a.	n.a.
$175	$1.3	$165	3,581	n.a.	n.a.
$312	$1,100	$124	323,661	n.a.	4,000
$115	$1.4	$297	9,238	n.a.	n.a.
$412	$750	$194	591,417	n.a.	n.a.
$10,900	$44.1	$11,125	81,742	49,082	n.a.
$10,900	$8,700	$9,202	2,033,982	699,455	286,962
n.a.	$507.5	$103.088	5,526,500	3,624,200	387,585
n.a.	$2,200	$90.970	122,012,800	53,544,000	2,270,772
$11,000	$46.7	$6,516	162,445	130,514	54,164
$12,000	$6,200	$6,917	4,525,959	2,686,515	510,649

Nation Capital	Population[1]	Area of Country sq mi (sq km)	Type of Government	Heads of State and Government	Currency: Value of U.S. Dollar[2]
COMOROS Moroni	497,000 22,000	838 (2,171)	Islamic republic	Pres., Said Muhammad Djohar Prime min., Muhammad Abdou Madi	franc 415.85
CONGO Brazzaville	2,400,000 938,000	132,000 (342,000)	Republic	Pres., Pascal Lissouba Prime min., Jacques-Joachim Yhombi-Opango	CFA franc[23] 554.465
COSTA RICA San José	3,200,000 296,600	19,730 (51,100)	Republic	Pres., José María Figueres Olsen	colón 156
CROATIA Zagreb	4,800,000 726,800	21,829 (56,537)	Parliamentary state	Pres., Franjo Tudjman Prime min., Nikica Valentic	kuna 5.97
CUBA Havana	11,100,000 2,096,100	42,804 (110,861)	Communist state	Pres., Fidel Castro Ruíz	peso 1.3203
CYPRUS, Greek sector Nicosia	549,000 166,500	2,277 (5,896)	Republic (C)	Pres., Glafcos Clerides	pound 2.0678
CYPRUS, Turkish sector Levkosía	176,000 39,500	1,295 (3,355)	Republic	Pres., Rauf Denktash	Turkish lira 32,118
CZECH REPUBLIC Prague	10,300,000 1,215,100	30,450 (78,864)	Republic	Pres., Vaclav Havel Prime min., Vaclav Klaus	Czech koruna 28.41
DENMARK Copenhagen	5,200,000 619,000	16,638 (43,093)	Constitutional monarchy	Head of state, Queen Margrethe II Prime min., Poul Nyrup Rasmussen	krone 6.25
DJIBOUTI Djibouti	542,000 317,000	8,960 (23,200)	Republic	Pres., Hassan Gouled Aptidon Prem., Barkat Gourad Hamadou	franc 177.72
DOMINICA Roseau	109,000 20,800	290 (750)	Republic (C)	Pres., Crispin Sorhaindo Prime min., Mary Eugenia Charles	EC dollar[20] 2.70
DOMINICAN REPUBLIC Santo Domingo	7,800,000 2,700,000	18,704 (48,442)	Republic	Pres., Joaquín Balaguer Vice pres., Carlos A. Morales Troncoso	peso 13.20[9]
ECUADOR Quito	10,600,000 1,100,800	109,484 (283,561)	Republic	Pres., Sixto Durán Vice pres., Alberto Dahik	sucre 2,310[9]
EGYPT Cairo	58,900,000 6,452,000	386,661 (1,001,450)	Republic	Pres., Hosni Mubarak Prime min., Atef Sidqi	pound 3.3545
EL SALVADOR San Salvador	5,200,000 422,600	8,248 (21,361)	Republic	Pres., Armando Calderón Sol Vice pres., Enrique Borgo	colón 8.75[9]
EQUATORIAL GUINEA Malabo	417,000 10,000	10,831 (28,051)	Transition to democracy	Pres., Teodoro Obiang Nguema Mbasogo Prime min., Silvestre Siale Bileka	CFA franc[23] 554.465
ERITREA Asmara	3,500,000 367,000	45,783 (118,577)	In transition	Pres., Isaias Afewerki	burr n.a.
ESTONIA Tallinn	1,500,000 502,400	17,410 (45,100)	Republic	Pres., Lennart Meri Prime min., Mart Laar	kroon 12.85
ETHIOPIA Addis Ababa	55,200,000 1,700,000	437,340 (1,132,705)	In transition	Pres., Meles Zenawi Prime min., Tamirat Layne	birr 5.58[18]
FIJI Suva	758,000 71,600	7,078 (18,333)	Republic	Pres., Kamisese Mara Prime min., Sitiveni Rabuka	dollar 1.4596
FINLAND Helsinki	5,100,000 501,500	130,559 (338,145)	Republic	Pres., Martti Ahtisaari Prime min., Esko Aho	markka 5.301

Revenue Expenditure in millions[3]	GDP in billions[4] GDP Per Capita	Imports Exports in millions[5]	Elementary Schools: Teachers Students	Secondary Schools: Teachers Students	Colleges and Universities: Teachers Students
$96	$0.36[7]	$70	1,894[28]	n.a.	n.a.
$88	$700	$24	75,577	15,878	223
$765	$2.9	$472	7,626	6,851	1,159
$952	$2,850	$1,029	502,918	183,023	12,045
$1,100	$7.1	$2,907	15,107	8,263	n.a.
$1,340	$6,100	$2,085	484,958	160,343	80,442
n.a.	$10.7	$4,700	23,077	12,278	6,550
n.a.	$4,300	$3,900	436,755	190,926	77,689
$12,460	$11.37	$1,700	76,161	92,813	25,264
$14,450	$1,100	$1,500	942,431	819,712	198,474
$1,700	$6.9[7]	$2,590	3,410[12]	4,217[12]	479[12]
$2,200	$9,600[2,9]	$867	64,313[12]	51,641[12]	7,757[12]
$273	$0.55[7]	n.a.	n.a.	n.a.	n.a.
$360	n.a.	n.a.	n.a.	n.a.	n.a.
$11,900	$26.0	$13,487	65,186	62,102	14,798
$11,900	$7,400	$12,929	1,160,510	549,266	116,560
$48,000	$145.5	$29,521	28,501	n.a.	n.a.
$55,700	$19,100	$35,914	327,024	455,639	150,159
$170	$0.466	$219	787	347	n.a.
$203	$1,100	$16	33,005	9,740	1,074
$70	$0.185[7]	$111	608	n.a.	40
$84	2,100[2]	$56	12,795	6,179	658
$1,400	$8.3	$2,443	21,850[28]	n.a.	n.a.
$1,800	$3,400	$555	1,032,055[28]	n.a.	n.a.
$1,900	$13.2	$2,562	62,451	n.a.	12,856
$1,900	$4,600	$3,904	1,827,920	n.a.	206,541
$16,800	$43.3	$8,184	273,005	283,170	n.a.
$19,400	$4,050	$2,244	6,541,725	5,284,174	708,417
$846	$6.4	$1,912	23,339	n.a.	4.216
$890	$2,400	$732	1,028,877	105,093	78,211
$32.5	$0.175	$92	n.a.	n.a.	58
$35.9	$700	$41	n.a.	n.a.	578
n.a.	n.a.	n.a.	n.a.	n.a.	n.a.
n.a.	$500	n.a.	n.a.	n.a.	n.a.
$223	$1.7	865	4,695	11,868	n.a.
$142	$6,300	765	119,409	121,798	24,768
n.a.	$3.4	$258	69,743	22,572	1,697
$1,200	$410	$199	1,855,894	720,779	26,218
$455	$1.6	$634	4,644	3,631	277
$546	$4,800	$405	145,630	66,890	7,908
$26,800	$106.2	$18,000	n.a.	n.a.	n.a.
$40,600	$16,000	$23,400	392,754	463,121	186,182

Nation Capital	Population[1]	Area of Country sq mi (sq km)	Type of Government	Heads of State and Government	Currency: Value of U.S. Dollar[2]
FRANCE	58,000,000	211,208	Republic	Pres., François Mitterrand	franc
Paris	2,175,100	(547,026)		Prime min., Edouard Balladur	5.5447
GABON	1,100,000	103,347	Republic	Pres., Omar Bongo	CFA
Libreville	352,000	(267,667)		Prime min., Casimir Oye-Mba	franc[23]
					554.465
GAMBIA, THE	1,100,000	4,361	Republic (C)	Head of state, Yahya Jammeh	dalasi
Banjui	44,200	(11,295)			9.83
GEORGIA	5,500,000	26,910	Republic	Head of state and speaker of the	coupon
Tbilisi	1,283,000	(69,700)		Parliament, Eduard A. Shevardnadze	n.a.
GERMANY	81,200,000	137,858	Federal	Pres., Roman Herzog	mark
Berlin	3,437,900	(357,050)	republic	Chancellor, Helmut Kohl	1.5935
Bonn (seat of govt.)	294,300				
GHANA	16,900,000	92,098	Republic (C)	Pres., Jerry John Rawlings	cedi
Accra	867,500	(238,533)			935
GREAT BRITAIN	58,400,000	94,216	Constitutional	Head of state, Queen Elizabeth II	pound
London	6,679,700[21]	(244,019)	monarchy (C)	Prime min., John Major	1.5493
GREECE	10,400,000	50,944	Republic	Pres., Constantine Karamanlis	drachma
Athens	3,096,800[21]	(131,944)		Prem., Andreas Papandreou	240.6
GRENADA	95,000	133	Parliamentary	Gov.-gen., Reginald Palmer	EC dollar[20]
St. George	35,700	(344)	state (C)	Prime min., Nicholas Braithwaite	2.70
GUATEMALA	10,300,000	42,042	Republic	Pres., Ramiro de León Carpio	quetzal
Guatemala City	1,132,700	(108,889)			5.7381
GUINEA	6,400,000	94,926	Republic	Pres., Lansana Conté	franc
Conakry	705,300	(245,857)			976.69
GUINEA-BISSAU	1,100,000	13,948	Republic	Pres., João Bernardo Vieira	peso
Bissau	125,000	(36,125)			12,369
GUYANA	990,000	83,000	Republic (C)	Pres., Cheddi Jagan	dollar
Georgetown	188,000[21]	(215,000)		Prime min., Samuel Hinds	134.2
HAITI	7,000,000	10,714	Republic	Pres., Jean-Bertrand Aristide	gourde
Port-au-Prince	1,402,000	(27,750)		Prime min., Smarck Michel	12.00
HONDURAS	5,300,000	43,277	Republic	Pres., Carlos Reina	lempira
Tegucigalpa	608,100	(112,088)			8.085[9]
HONG KONG	5,800,000	414	Republic	Gov., Christopher Patten	dollar
		(1,072)			7.729
HUNGARY	10,300,000	35,920	Republic	Pres., Arpad Goncz	forint
Budapest	2,009,000	(93,033)		Prime min., Gyula Horn	111.94[29]
ICELAND	262,000	39,800	Republic	Pres., Vigdís Finnbogadottir	króna
Reykjavik	101,000	(103,000)		Prime min., David Oddsson	69.66
INDIA	911,600,000	1,269,346	Federal	Pres., Shankar Dayal Sharma	rupee
New Delhi	301,000	(3,287,593)	republic (C)	Prime min., P. V. Narasimha Rao	31.37[16]
INDONESIA[27]	199,700,000	741,100	Republic	Pres., Suharto	rupiah
Jakarta	8,222,500	(1,919,400)		Vice pres., Try Sustrisno	2,166.41
IRAN	61,200,000	636,372	Islamic	Pres., Hojatolislam Ali Akbar	rial
Tehran	6,042,600	(1,648,196)	republic	Hashemi Rafsanjani	1,749[18]
				Spiritual Guide, Ayatollah Ali Khameni	
IRAQ	19,900,000	169,235	Republic	Pres. and prime min., Saddam Hussein	dinar
Baghdad	3,844,600	(438,317)			0.3109
IRELAND	3,600,000	32,596	Republic	Pres., Mary Robinson	pound
Dublin	915,500[21]	(84,423)		Prime min., John Bruton	1.521

458

Revenue Expenditure in millions[3]	GDP in billions[4] GDP Per Capita	Imports Exports in millions[5]	Elementary Schools: Teachers Students	Secondary Schools: Teachers Students	Colleges and Universities: Teachers Students
$220,500	$1,348	$201,838	342,905	457,644	n.a.
$249,100	$19,500	$209,349	4,060,408	5,573,582	1,951,994
$1,300	$6.2	$884	4,782	n.a.	400
$1,500	$5,200	$2,273	210,000	51,348	4,000
$94	$0.376	$32	3,193	1,054	n.a.
$80	$850	$63	97,262	25,929	n.a.
n.a.	$2.3	n.a.	n.a.	n.a.	n.a.
n.a.	$1,700	n.a.	900,000[10]	—[10]	137,000
$918,000	$1,807	$326,981	n.a.	n.a.	218,410
$972,000	$20,800	$362,064	3,470,000	7,500,078	1,867,491
$1,000	$7.5	$1,273	66,068[28]	45,000	700
$905	$2,000	$1,018	1,796,490[28]	850,000	9,609
$325,500	$1,100.4	$205.390	229,100	300,000	89,500
$400,900	$17,300	$180,180	4,532,500	4,335,600	1,385,072
$28,300	$79.9	$23,220	42,485	57,975	14,207
$37,600	$8,000	$9,509	834,688	843,732	195,213
$78	$0.250[7]	$107	763	n.a.	n.a.
$51	$3,000[2]	$20	21,616	6,970	n.a.
$604	$11.2	$2,599	36,757	20,717	n.a.
$808	$3,700	$1,340	1,249,413	294,907	65,000
$449	$3.4	$768	8,577	4,684	n.a.
$708	$750	$622	421,869	106,811	n.a.
$33.6	$0.235	$62	n.a.	n.a.	n.a.
$44.8	$760	$16	79,035	n.a.	n.a.
$121	$0.417	$382	n.a.	n.a.	n.a.
$225	$2,300	$302	n.a.	n.a.	n.a.
$300	$2.6	$374	26,208[13]	9,500	n.a.
$416	$1,000	$103	555,433	185,000	n.a.
$1,400	$3.4	$1,130	23,872	8,507	3,500
$1,900	$2,100	$814	908,446	194,083	47,000
$19,200	$119[7]	$138,658	19,518	n.a.	6,027
$19,700	$21,500	$135,248	526,700	n.a.	88,950
$10,200	$35.7	$12,570	89,276	n.a.	17,743
$12,500	$6,100	$8,886	1,081,213	531,051	117,460
$1,800	$6.8	$1,349	n.a.	n.a.	n.a.
$1,900	$16,900	$1,399	n.a.	n.a.	6,161
$29,600	$290.4	$22,761	1,681,970	2,450,000	n.a.
$45,100	$1,250	$21.553	105,370,216	63,204,943	4,611,107
$32,800	$138.1	$28,086	1,276,217	770,774	135,462
$32,800	$3,200	$33,612	29,598,790	10,863,435	1,973,094
n.a.	$57.8[7]	$21,688	311,839	232,758	n.a.
n.a.	$4,900	n.a.	9,937,369	6,322,988	n.a.
n.a.	$17	$6,600	131,271	59,117	n.a.
n.a.	$2,000[1]	$10,400	2,857,467	1,144,938	n.a.
$16,000	$52.9	$21,386	15,775	21,371	5,929
$16,600	$12,600	$28,611	408,567	327,817	101,108

Nation Capital	Population[1]	Area of Country sq mi (sq km)	Type of Government	Heads of State and Government	Currency: Value of U.S. Dollar[2]
ISRAEL[26] Jerusalem	5,400,000 556,500	7,990 (20,700)	Republic	Pres., Ezer Weizman Prime min., Yitzhak Rabin	new shekel 3.052
ITALY Rome	57,200,000 2,723,300	116,320 (301,268)	Republic	Pres., Oscar Luigi Scalfaro Prem., Silvio Berlusconi	lira 1,570.50
IVORY COAST Yamoussoukro Abidjian (admin. cap)	13,900,000 120,000 2,534,000	124,518 (322,500)	Republic	Pres., Henri Konan Bedie Prime min., Kablan Duncan	CFA franc[23] 554.465
JAMAICA Kingston	2,500,000 587,800[21]	4,244 (10,991)	Parliamentary state (C)	Gov.-gen., Howard Cooke Prime min., P. J. Patterson	dollar 33.35[18]
JAPAN Tokyo	125,000,000 7,927,100	145,870 (377,801)	Constitutional monarchy	Head of state, Emperor Akihito Prime min., Tamiichi Murayama	yen 100.15
JORDAN Amman	4,200,000 1,272,000[21]	34,443 (89,206)	Constitutional monarchy	Head of state, King Hussein Prime min., Abd al-Salam al Majali	dinar 0.691
KAZAKHSTAN Almaty	17,100,000 1,151,000	1,049,160 (2,717,300)	Republic	Pres., Nursultan Nazarbayev Prime min., Sergei Tereshchenko	tenge n.a.
KENYA Nairobi	27,000,000 1,163,200	224,961 (582,646)	Republic (C)	Pres., Daniel arap Moi Vice pres., George Saitoti	shilling 56.1135
KIRIBATI Tarawa	72,300 25,200	280 (726)	Republic (C)	Speaker of Parliament, Beretitari Neeti	Australian dollar 1.37
KOREA, DEMOCRATIC PEOPLE'S REPUBLIC OF Pyongyang	23,100,000 2,639,400	46,540 (120,538)	Communist state	Leader, Kim Jong Il	won 2.15
KOREA, REPUBLIC OF Seoul	44,500,000 10,627,800	38,025 (98,484)	Republic	Pres., Kim Young Sam Prime min., Lee Hong Koo	won 806.20
KUWAIT Kuwait City	1,300,000 31,200	6,880 (17,818)	Constitutional monarchy	Emir, Jabir al-Ahmad al-Jabir al-Sabah Prime min., Saad al-Abdullah al-Salem al-Sabah	dinar 0.2963
KYRGYZSTAN Bishkek	4,500,000 641,400	76,640 (198,500)	Republic	Pres., Askar Akayev Prime min., Tursenbek Chyngyshev	som n.a.
LAOS Vientiane	4,700,000 377,400	91,430 (236,800)	Communist state	Pres., Nouhak Phoumsavan Prem., Khamtay Siphandone	kip 720.00
LATVIA Riga	2,500,000 910,200	24,600 (63,700)	Republic	Pres., Guntis Ulmanis Prime min., Valdis Birkavs	lats 0.56
LEBANON Beirut	3,600,000 1,500,000	4,015 (10,400)	Republic	Pres., Elias Hrawi Prime min., Rafiq al-Hariri	pound 1,681
LESOTHO Maseru	1,900,000 109,400	11,720 (30,355)	Constitutional monarchy (C)	Head of state, King Moshoeshoe II Prem., Ntsu Mokhehle	maloti 3.5982
LIBERIA Monrovia	2,900,000 425,000	38,250 (99,067)	Republic	Interim pres., Amos Sawyer	dollar 1.00
LIBYA Tripoli	5,100,000 990,700	679,362 (1,759,540)	Military dictatorship	Leader, Muammar al-Qaddafi	dinar 0.3574[29]
LIECHTENSTEIN Vaduz	30,000 4,900	62 (160)	Constitutional monarchy	Head of state, Prince Hans Adam Prem., Mario Frick	Swiss franc 1.3375

Revenue Expenditure in millions[3]	GDP in billions[4] GDP Per Capita	Imports Exports in millions[5]	Elementary Schools: Teachers Students	Secondary Schools: Teachers Students	Colleges and Universities: Teachers Students
$33,400	$69.6	$22,621	47,299	50,605	n.a.
$36,300	$15,000	$14,779	763,511	334,290	78,640
$302,000	$1,246	$188,450	251,621	579,690	58,359
$391,000	$18,000	$178,156	2,959,564	4,892,194	1,615,150
$2,300	$10.1	$5,347	39,057[13]	n.a.	n.a.
$3,600	$1,600	$6,220	1,447,785	n.a.	n.a.
$600	$3.1	$2,097	8,830[28]	n.a.	n.a.
$736	$4,000	$1,069	323,378[28]	225,240	23,220
$490,000	$3,761.5	$241,624	440,769	663,215	286,166
$579,000	$20,700	$362,244	8,947,226	10,676,866	2,899,143
$1,700	$5.2	$3,539	45,871[25]	9,022	4,014
$1,900	$5,600	$1,232	1,014,295	113,910	88,506
n.a.	$18.2	$358[19]	n.a.	n.a.	n.a.
n.a.	$4,300	$1,300[19]	n.a.	1,782,471	526,700
$2,400	$8.2	$1,711	172,117	n.a.	4,500
$2,800	$1,500	$1,336	5,392,319	n.a.	45,000
$29.9	$0.368	$33	545	237	n.a.
$16.3	$525	$4	16,020	3,357	428
$19,300	$20.8[6]	1,900	n.a.	n.a.	n.a
$19,300	$1,000[1,2]	1,300	n.a.	n.a.	n.a
$48,400	$319.5	$83,800	139,381	194,809	82,870
$48,400	$10,000	$82,236	4,336,252	4,479,463	1,858,568
$9,000	$24	$7,036	7,526	16,081	n.a.
$13,000	$15,400	$10,248	122,930	177,675	28,399
n.a.	$2.9	$100.4[19]	n.a.	n.a.	n.a.
n.a.	$2,600	$105.8[19]	949,000[10]	—[10]	100,700
$83	$1.3	$266	21,036	10,198	n.a.
$188.5	$2,000	$133	580,792	125,702	n.a.
n.a.	$1.6	n.a.	12,758	25,035	4,478
n.a.	$3,900	$429	133,846	242,644	41,138
$990	$6.3	$4,100	n.a.	n.a.	5,400
$1,980	$3,700	$925	345,662	248,097	85,495
$436	$0.625	$964	7,051	n.a.	490
$430	$2,100	$109	362,657	53,485	5,359
$242.1	$1.2	n.a.	n.a.	n.a.	n.a.
$435.4	$1,050	$460	n.a.	n.a.	n.a.
$8,100	$30.3	$5,361	99,623	18,501	n.a.
$9,800	$6,000	$11,235	1,238,986	215,508	72,899
$259	$0.630[7]	n.a.	409[10]	—[10]	n.a.[10]
$292	$22,300[2]	n.a.	3,354[10]	—[10]	n.a.[10]

Nation Capital	Population[1]	Area of Country sq mi (sq km)	Type of Government	Heads of State and Government	Currency: Value of U.S. Dollar[2]
LITHUANIA	3,700,000	25,170	Republic	Pres., Algirdas Brazauskas	litas
Vilnius	592,500	(65,200)		Prime min., Adolfas Slezevicius	4.00
LUXEMBOURG	395,000	998	Constitutional	Head of state, Grand Duke Jean	franc
Luxembourg	75,400	(2,586)	monarchy	Prime min., Jacques Santer	32.762
MACEDONIA	2,100,000	26,000	Republic	Pres., Kiro Gligorov	denar
Skopje	448,200	(67,000)		Prime min., Branko Crvenkovski	n.a.
MADAGASCAR	13,700,000	226,658	Republic	Pres. Albert Zafy	franc
Antananarivo	803,400	(587,041)		Prem., Francisque Ravony	3,605
MALAWI	9,500,000	45,747	Republic (C)	Pres., Muluzi Bakili	kwacha
Lilongwe	234,000[21]	(118,484)			7.2097
MALAYSIA	19,500,000	127,320	Federal constitutional monarchy (C)	Head of state, King Jaafar bin Abdul Rahman Prime min., Mahathir Mohamed	ringgit 2.587
Kuala Lumpur	1,145,000	(329,758)			
MALDIVES	238,000	115	Republic (C)	Pres., Abdul Gayoom	rufiyaa
Malé	55,100	(298)			11.39
MALI	9,100,000	479,000	Republic	Pres., Alpha Oumar Konare	CFA
Bamako	740,000	(1,240,000)		Prime min., Ibrahim Keita	franc[23] 554.465
MALTA	365,000	122	Republic (C)	Pres., Ugo Mifsud Bonnici	lira
Valletta	9,200	(316)		Prime min., Eddie Fenech Adami	2.6783
MARSHALL ISLANDS	46,000	70	Republic	Pres., Amata Kabua	U.S. dollar
Dalap-Uliga-Darrit	20,000	(181)			1.00
MAURITANIA	2,300,000	395,956	Islamic Republic	Head of state, Maaouiya Ould Sidi Ahmed Taya	ouguiya
Nouakchott	393,500[21]	(1,025,520)			122.44
MAURITIUS	1,100,000	788	Parliamentary state (C)	Pres., Cassam Uteem	rupee
Port Louis	143,400	(2,040)		Prime min., Aneerood Jugnauth	17.56
MEXICO	91,800,000	761,605	Federal republic	Pres., Ernesto Zedillo Ponce de León	new peso
Mexico City	8,237,000	(1,972,547)			4.70[29]
MICRONESIA	108,000	1,000	Republic	Pres., Bailey Olter	U.S. dollar
Palikir	5,500	(2,600)		Vice pres., Jacob Nena	1.00
MOLDOVA	4,400,000	13,010	Republic	Pres., Mircea Snegur	ruble
Chisinau	676,000	(33,700)		Prime min., Andrei Sangheli	1,971
MONACO	30,000	0.6	Constitutional monarchy	Head of state, Prince Rainier III	French
		(1.6)		Min. of state, Jacques Dupont	franc 5.5447
MONGOLIA	2,400,000	604,829	Republic	Pres., Punsalmaagiyn Ochirbat	tugrik
Ulan Bator	575,000	(1,566,500)		Prime min., Puntsagiyn Jasray	400.00[18]
MOROCCO	28,600,000	172,410	Constitutional monarchy	Head of state, King Hassan II	dirham
Rabat	1,472,000[21]	(446,550)		Prime min., Abdellatif Filali	8.9148
MOZAMBIQUE	15,800,000	308,642	Republic	Pres., Joaquim A. Chissano Prime min., Mário da Graça Machungo	metical 5,812
Maputo	1,098,000	(799,379)			
NAMIBIA	1,600,000	318,252	Republic (C)	Pres., Sam Nujoma	rand
Windhoek	125,000	(824,268)		Prime min., Hage Geingob	5.982
NAURU	8,100	8	Republic (C)	Pres., Bernard Dowiyogo	Australian dollar
Yaren	n.a.	21			1.37
NEPAL	22,100,000	56,827	Constitutional monarchy	Head of state, King Birenda Bir Bikram Shah Dev Prime min., Man Mohan Adhikary	rupee 49.26
Katmandu	419,000	(147,181)			

Revenue Expenditure in millions[3]	GDP in billions[4] GDP Per Capita	Imports Exports in millions[5]	Elementary Schools: Teachers Students	Secondary Schools: Teachers Students	Colleges and Universities: Teachers Students
$258.5	$2.9	n.a.	47,504	n.a.	n.a.
$270.2	$3,200	n.a.	207,522	337,890	65,600
$3,500	$12.4	—22	1,764	n.a.	n.a.
$3,500	$20,900		23,465	n.a.	1,163
n.a.	$1.9	$963	12,958	4,345	2,273
n.a.	$2,600	$889	261,540	73,381	26,405
$250	$3.1	$442	38,743	15,876	855
$265	$810	$305	1,490,317	312,939	42,681
$416	$2.1	$546	n.a.	n.a.	n.a.
$498	$750	$320	1,400,682	32,275	n.a.
$19,600	$61.2	$45,657	130,482	84,744	10,169
$18,000	$8,400	$47,122	2,652,397	1,566,790	121,412
$95	$0.14	$191	n.a.	n.a.	n.a.
$143	$620	$35	45,333	16,087	n.a.
$376	$3.1	$602	7,963	n.a.	701
$697	$600	$354	375,131	n.a.	6,703
$1,200	$2.9	$2,174	1,780	2,688	244
$1,200	6,900	$1,355	36,899	32,544	5,000
$55	$0.063[7]	$63	669	144	n.a.
n.a.	$1,500	$4	13,355	2,400	400
$280	$1.3	$639	4,276	2,236	250
$346	$1,450	$469	219,2589	43,034	5,850
$557	$3.3	$639	6,369	n.a.	414
$607	$13,400	$1,194	135,233	79,229	2,400
$58,100	$333.7	$50,147	486,686	412,789	134,424
$53,000	$7,800	$30,241	14,425,669	6,782,886	1,310,835
$165	$0.15[6]	$68	n.a.	n.a.	n.a.
$115	$1,500[1,2]	$2.3	n.a.	n.a.	1,028
n.a.	$4.1	$145[19]	16,853	35,000	n.a.
n.a.	$3,800	$108[19]	306,933	448,404	54,700
$424	$0.475	n.a.	60	n.a.	n.a.
$376	$16,000	n.a.	1,761	2,858	n.a.
n.a.	$0.339	$362	6,230	15,000	2,601
n.a.	$1,200	$381	154,600	275,000	28,209
$7,500	$29.8	$6,760	98,734	78,580	7,200
$7,700	$3,300	$3,991	2,727,833	1,207,734	240,000
$252	$1.2	$955	22,474	5,029	577
$607	$650	$132	1,199,476	162,486	3,482
$941	$2.6	$1,165	10,912	n.a.	331
$1,050	$2,600	$1,305	349,167	84,581	4,157
$69.7	$0.09[6]	$73	71	n.a.	n.a.
$51.5	10,000[1]	$93	1,451	n.a.	n.a.
$457	$3.1	$880	77,948	25,357	4,925
$725	$1,120	$390	3,034,710	855,137	110,239

Nation Capital	Population[1]	Area of Country sq mi (sq km)	Type of Government	Heads of State and Government	Currency: Value of U.S. Dollar[2]
NETHERLANDS, THE Amsterdam The Hague (seat of govt.)	15,400,000 719,900 444,700	16,133 (41,785)	Constitutional monarchy	Head of state, Queen Beatrix Prime min., Wim Kok	guilder 1.783
NEW ZEALAND Wellington	3,500,000 325,700	103,519 (268,112)	Parliamentary state (C)	Gov.-gen., Catherine Tizard Prime min., Jim Bolger	dollar 1.6922
NICARAGUA Managua	4,300,000 682,100	50,200 (130,000)	Republic	Pres., Violeta Chamorro Vice pres., Virgilio Godoy	gold cordoba 6.7022
NIGER Niamey	8,800,000 398,300	489,200 (1,267,000)	Republic	Pres., Mahamane Ousmane Prime min., Mahamadou Issoufou	CFA franc[23] 554.465
NIGERIA Abuja	98,100,000 305,900	356,669 (923,768)	Military rule (C)	Head of state, Sani Abacha	naira 22.00[9]
NORWAY Oslo	4,300,000 459,300	125,057 (323,895)	Constitutional monarchy	Head of state, King Harald V Prime min., Gro Harlem Brundtland	krone 6.9285
OMAN Muscat	1,900,000 380,000[21]	82,030 (212,457)	Monarchy	Sultan and prime min., Qaboos bin Said al-Said	rial 0.385
PAKISTAN Islamabad	126,400,000 201,000	307,374 (796,095)	Federal republic (C)	Pres., Farooq Leghari Prime min., Benazir Bhutto	rupee 30.65
PALAU Koror	16,000 9,500	196 (508)	Republic	Pres., Kuniwo Nakamura Vice pres., Tommy Remengesau, Jr.	—
PANAMA Panama City	2,500,000 584,800	29,762 (77,082)	Republic	Pres., Ernesto Perez Balladares Vice pres., Carlos Altamirano Duque	balboa 1.00
PAPUA NEW GUINEA Port Moresby	4,000,000 193,200	178,704 (462,840)	Parliamentary state (C)	Prime min., Julius Chan	kina 1.1848[29]
PARAGUAY Asunción	4,800,000 607,700	157,048 (406,752)	Republic	Pres., Juan Carlos Wasmosy	guarani 1,793[9]
PERU Lima	22,900,000 6,414,500[21]	496,225 (1,285,216)	Republic	Pres., Alberto Fujimori Prem., Efrain Goldenberg	new sol 2.19[9]
PHILIPPINES Manila	68,700,000 1,599,000	115,800 (300,000)	Republic	Pres., Fidel Ramos Vice pres., Joseph Estrada	peso 26.74
POLAND Warsaw	38,600,000 1,655,000	120,728 (312,683)	Republic	Pres., Lech Walesa Prime min., Waldemar Pawlak	zloty 22,554[18]
PORTUGAL Lisbon	9,900,000 830,500	35,672 (92,389)	Republic	Pres., Mário Soares Prime min., Aníbal Cavaco Silva	escudo 164.27
QATAR Doha	453,000 217,300	4,416 (11,437)	Constitutional monarchy	Emir and prime min., Khalifa bin Hamad al-Thani	riyal 3.639
ROMANIA Bucharest	22,700,000 2,064,500	91,700 (237,500)	Republic	Pres., Ion Iliescu Prime min., Nicolae Vacaroiu	leu 1,676
RUSSIA Moscow	147,800,000 8,957,000	6,592,850 (17,075,400)	Federal republic	Pres., Boris Yeltsin Prime min., Viktor S. Chernomyrdin	ruble 1,971
RWANDA Kigali	7,700,000 156,700	10,169 (26,338)	Transitional	Pres., Pasteur Bizimungu Prime min., Faustin Twagiramungu	franc 140.3099
SAINT KITTS AND NEVIS Basseterre	41,000 14,300	68 (176)	Parliamentary state (C)	Gov.-gen., Clement Athelston Arrindell Prime min., Kennedy Alphonse Simmonds	EC dollar[20] 2.70

Revenue Expenditure in millions[3]	GDP in billions[4] GDP Per Capita	Imports Exports in millions[5]	Elementary Schools: Teachers Students	Secondary Schools: Teachers Students	Colleges and Universities: Teachers Students
$109,900	$329.3	$126,557	64,700	86,000	41,348
$122,100	$18,900	$139,075	1,046,192	1,369,507	493,563
n.a.	$44.1	$9,636	19,583	23,000	12,096
n.a.	$15,200	$10,537	317,286	350,112	146,215
$375	$1.6	$892	18,901	5,200	2,130
$410	$2,650	$218	703,854	196,000	31,499
$193	$2.5	$355	8,835	2,775	n.a.
$355	$950	$312	368,732	76,758	n.a.
$9,000	$32.1	$8,119	384,212	141,491	n.a.
$10,800	$1,250	$11,886	14,805,937	3,600,620	n.a.
$45,300	$118	$23,956	50,614	n.a.	10,000
$51,800	$18,700	$31,853	309,432	380,916	166,499
$4,400	$12	$3,194	10,839	8,537	n.a.
$5,200	$10,200	$4,871	289,911	140,761	7,322
$9,400	$50.8	$9,500	218,300	209,195	36,100
$10,900	$2,150	$6,688	8,855,997	3,983,462	585,000
$41.05	n.a.	n.a.	n.a.	n.a.	1
n.a.	n.a.	n.a.	n.a.	n.a.	355
$1,800	$6.6	$2,188	15,249	9,754	3,300
$1,900	$6,000	$553	351,021	195,903	58,625
$1,330	$5	$1,299	14,117	3,293	n.a.
$1,490	$2,200	$2,491	443,552	69,596	7,736
$1,200	$5.4	$1,422	32,732	12,218	n.a.
$1,400	$3,800	$657	749,336	169,167	32,884
$2,000	$48.9	$4,901	135,502	87,624	45,241
$1,700	$3,400	$3,463	3,853,098	1,703,997	777,918
$11,500	$55	$18,757	294,485	89,063	70,000
$13,000	$2,600	$11,089	10,679,748	4,421,649	1,656,815
$24,300	$89.2	$18,834	308,873	105,214	n.a.
$27,100	$5,200	$14,143	5,231,769	2,030,842	584,177
$27,300	$85.7	$24,337	71,105	n.a.	14,500
$33,200	$8,800	$15,429	1,004,848	778,432	190,456
$2,500	$7.3	$1,720	4,917	5,016	605
$3,000	$16,000	n.a.	49,059	35,013	7,283
$19,000	$39.8	$6,522	57,104	165,311	18,123
$20,000	$2,900	$4,892	1,201,229	2,451,624	235,669
n.a.	$1,160[7]	$27,000	1,384,000[10]	n.a.[10]	247,000
n.a.	$7,800	$43,000	11,872,357	7,772,208	2,638,000
$350	$1.6	$260	18,937	3,413	n.a.
n.a.	$670	$67	1,104,902	94,586	n.a.
$85.7	$0.163	$100	350	294	51
$85.8	$4,000	$32	7,236	4,396	394

Nation Capital	Population[1]	Area of Country sq mi (sq km)	Type of Government	Heads of State and Government	Currency: Value of U.S. Dollar[2]
SAINT LUCIA Castries	136,000 53,900	238 (616)	Parliamentary state (C)	Gov.-gen., Stanislaus James Prime min., John George Melvin Compton	EC dollar[20] 2.70
SAINT VINCENT AND THE GRENADINES Kingstown	108,000 26,500[21]	150 (389)	Parliamentary state (C)	Gov.-gen., David Jack Prime min., James Mitchell	EC dollar[20] 2.70
SAN MARINO San Marino	24,000 4,300	24 (61)	Republic	Heads of state, captains-regent, two rotate every six months	Italian lira 1,570.50
SÃO TOMÉ AND PRÍNCIPE São Tomé	124,000 35,000	323 (837)	Republic	Pres., Miguel Trovoada Prime min., Evaristo Carvalho	dobra 240.00
SAUDI ARABIA Riyadh	18,000,000 2,000,000	830,000 (2,150,000)	Monarchy	Head of state and prem., King Fahd bin Abdalaziz al-Saud	riyal 3.7503
SENEGAL Dakar	8,200,000 1,571,600	75,750 (196,192)	Republic	Pres., Abdou Diouf Prime min., Habib Thiam	CFA franc[23] 554.465
SEYCHELLES Victoria	70,400 24,300[21]	175 (453)	Republic (C)	Pres., France Albert René	rupee 5.0291
SIERRA LEONE Freetown	4,600,000 469,800	27,699 (71,740)	Military rule (C)	Pres., Valentine Strasser	leone 560.00
SINGAPORE Singapore[24]	2,900,000	246 (636)	Republic (C)	Prs., Ong Teng Cheong Prime min., Goh Chok Tong	dollar 1.5268
SLOVAKIA Bratislava	5,300,000 440,400	18,933 (49,035)	Republic	Pres., Michal Kovac Prem., Vladimir Meciar	Slovak koruna 32.55
SLOVENIA Ljubljana	2,000,000 268,000	7,819 (20,251)	Republic	Pres., Milan Kucan Prime min., Janez Drnovsek	tolar 125.26
SOLOMON ISLANDS Honiara	350,000 33,700	10,953 (28,369)	Parliamentary state (C)	Gov.-gen., George Lepping Prime min., Francis Billy Hilly	dollar 3.2637
SOMALIA Mogadishu	9,800,000 1,000,000	246,200 (637,700)	None	—[17]	shilling 2,620.00[9]
SOUTH AFRICA Pretoria	41,200,000 443,100	472,359 (1,223,404)	Republic	State pres., Nelson Mandela	rand 3.5982[8]
SPAIN Madrid	39,200,000 2,909,800	194,885 (504,750)	Constitutional monarchy	Head of state, King Juan Carlos I Prime min., Felipe González	peseta 131.88
SRI LANKA Colombo	17,900,000 615,000	24,962 (64,652)	Republic (C)	Pres., Dingiri Banda Wijetunga Prime min., Chandrika Kumaratunga	rupee 49.18
SUDAN Khartoum	28,200,000 476,200	967,500 (2,506,000)	Republic	Head of state and prime min., Omar Hassan Ahmed al-Bashir	dinar 31.18,29
SURINAME Paramaribo	404,000 201,000	63,251 (163,820)	Republic	Pres., Ronald Venetiaan	guilder 330.5[29]
SWAZILAND Mbabane	681,000 38,300	6,704 (17,364)	Monarchy (C)	Head of state, King Mswati III Prime min., Prince Jameson Mbilini	lilangeni 3.5982
SWEDEN Stockholm	8,800,000 684,600	170,250 (440,945)	Constitutional monarchy	Head of state, King Carl XVI Gustaf Prime min., Ingvar Carlsson	krona 7.6652
SWITZERLAND Bern	7,000,000 134,600	15,943 (41,293)	Federal republic	Pres., Otto Stich Vice pres., Kaspar Villiger	franc 1.3375
SYRIA Damascus	14,000,000 1,497,000	71,498 (185,180)	Socialist republic	Pres., Hafez al-Assad Prime min., Mahmoud Zubi	pound 23.00[11]

Revenue Expenditure in millions[3]	GDP in billions[4] GDP Per Capita	Imports Exports in millions[5]	Elementary Schools: Teachers Students	Secondary Schools: Teachers Students	Colleges and Universities: Teachers Students
$121	$0.433	$313	1,181	514	n.a.
$127	$3,000	$123	32,622	9,419	n.a.
$62	$0.215[7]	$135	1,119	431	n.a.
$67	$2,000	$83	22,030	10,719	n.a.
$275	0.37[7]	n.a.	221	n.a.	n.a.
$275	$16,000[2]	n.a.	1,190	1,159	n.a.
$10.2	$0.05	$31	559	n.a.	n.a.
$36.8	$450	$5	19,822	n.a.	n.a.
$39,000	$125.5	$29,079	141,930	92,975	11,682
$50,000	$10,200	$47,797	2,025,948	1,073,361	163,688
$1,200	$6.3	$1,292	12,307	n.a.	949
$1,200	$2,000	$741	725,496	191,431	21,562
$172	$0.453	$89	548	735	171
$181	$3,900	$51	9,873	9,111	1,609
$68	$0.54	$147	10,850	5,969	600
$118	$750	$118	367,426	102,474	4,742
$11,900	$51.9	$85,234	10,006	10,000	n.a.
$10,500	18,700	$74,012	257,932	200,000	71,000
$4,500	$12	$5,950	15,859	48,340	n.a.
$5,200	$5,500	$5,130	350,604	657,010	66,002
n.a.	$12	$5,300	5,935	13,749	2,783
n.a.	$6,400	$5,100	104,441	211,426	39,264
$48	$0.9[7]	$101	2,490	364	n.a.
$107	$2,500	$94	53,320	6,363	n.a.
n.a.	$0.77	$249	n.a.	n.a.	n.a.
n.a.	$800	$58	n.a.	n.a.	n.a.
$26,300	$119	$20,017	n.a.	n.a.	16,861
$34,000	$5,900	$24,261	5,643,707	2,500,000	490,112
$97,700	$582	$78,626	125,828	294,438	70,410
$128,000	$13,400	$59,555	2,662,490	4,773,349	1,301,748
$2,300	$10.5	$3,991	69,965	108,489	n.a.
$3,600	$3,100	$2,859	2,059,203	2,185,277	51,883
$374.4	$6.5	n.a.	64,227	30,642	2,043
$1,200	$1,100	n.a.	2,168,180	718,298	59,824
$466	$1.9	$470	n.a.	n.a.	495
$716	$3,600	$420	n.a.	n.a.	4,319
$342	$2.3[7]	$680	5,504	n.a.	452
$410	$2,500	$565	180,285	n.a.	3,224
$45,100	$242.1	$42,681	60,022	65,410	n.a.
$73,100	$17,500	$49,857	594,891	602,703	207,265
$23,700	$246	$56,716	n.a.	n.a.	n.a.
$26,900	$22,300[2]	$58,687	420,089	561,470	146,266
$7,130	$26.7	$2,694	106,164	58,659	n.a.
$9,500	$6,000	$3,618	2,593,181	916,950	194,371

Nation Capital	Population[1]	Area of Country sq mi (sq km)	Type of Government	Heads of State and Government	Currency: Value of U.S. Dollar[2]
TAIWAN Taipei	21,100,000 2,718,000	13,900 (36,002)	Republic	Pres., Lee Teng-hui Prem., Lien Chan	dollar 26.39[18]
TAJIKISTAN Dushanbe	5,900,000 592,000	55,250 (143,100)	Republic	Pres., Imomali Rahmonov Prime min., Jamsed Karimov	ruble 1,971
TANZANIA Dodoma	29,800,000 203,800	364,900 (945,100)	Republic (C)	Pres., Ali Hassan Mwinyi Prime min., John Malecela	shilling 519.13
THAILAND Bangkok	59,400,000 5,876,000	198,115 (513,115)	Constitutional monarchy	Head of state, King Bhumibol Adulyadej Prime min., Chuan Leekpai	baht 25.04
TOGO Lomé	4,300,000 500,000	21,925 (56,785)	Republic	Pres., Gnassingbé Eyadéma Prime min., Edem Kodjo	CFA franc[23] 554.465
TONGA Nuku'alofa	103,000 29,000	290 (750)	Constitutional monarchy (C)	Head of state, King Taufa'ahau Tupou IV Prime min., Baron Vaea	pa'anga 1.3657
TRINIDAD AND TOBAGO Port of Spain	1,300,000 58,400	1,980 (5,128)	Republic (C)	Pres., Noor Mohammed Hassanali Prime min., Patrick A. M. Manning	dollar 5.575
TUNISIA Tunis	8,700,000 596,700	63,170 (163,610)	Republic	Pres., Zine al-Abidine Ben Ali Prime min., Hamed Karoui	dinar 1.005
TURKEY Ankara	61,800,000 2,541,900	300,948 (779,452)	Republic	Pres., Suleyman Demirel Prime min., Tansu Ciller	lira 32,118
TURKMENISTAN Ashgabat	4,100,000 411,000	186,460 (488,100)	Republic	Pres., Saparmuryad Niyazov	manat n.a.
TUVALU Funafuti	10,000 2,800	10 (26)	Parliamentary state (C)	Gov.-gen., Tomu Sione Prime min., Kamuta Laatsi	Australian dollar 1.37
UGANDA Kampala	19,800,000 773,500	93,104 (241,139)	Republic (C)	Pres., Yoweri Museveni Prime min., George C. Adyebo	shilling 1,042.00[15]
UKRAINE Kiev	51,500,000 2,616,000	233,090 (603,700)	Republic	Pres., Leonid Kuchma	karbovanets 108,600[29]
UNITED ARAB EMIRATES Abu Dhabi	1,700,000 243,000	32,280 (83,600)	Federal state	Pres., Zayed bin Sultan al-Nahyan Prime min., Maktoum bin Rashid al-Maktoum	dirham 3.671
UNITED STATES OF AMERICA Washington, DC	260,800,000 570,000	3,618,770 (9,372,570)	Federal republic	Pres., Bill Clinton Vice pres., Al Gore	dollar —
URUGUAY Montevideo	3,200,000 1,383,700	68,037 (176,215)	Republic	Pres., Luis Alberto Lacalle Herrera	peso Uruguayo 4.92[16]
UZBEKISTAN Tashkent	22,100,000 2,094,000	172,740 (447,400)	Republic	Pres., Islam A. Karimov Prime min., Abdulhashim Mutalov	sum n.a.
VANUATU Vila	154,000 19,400	4,707 (12,190)	Republic (C)	Pres., Jean Marie Leye Prime min., Maxime Carlot Korman	vatu 115.62
VENEZUELA Caracas	21,300,000 3,435,800[21]	352,145 (912,050)	Federal republic	Pres., Rafael Caldera	bolívar 196.30[9,29]
VIETNAM Hanoi	73,100,000 3,056,100	128,066 (331,689)	Communist state	Pres., Le Duc Anh Secy.-gen., Communist Party, Do Muoi	dong 10,971[18]

Revenue Expenditure in millions[3]	GDP in billions[4] GDP Per Capita	Imports Exports in millions[5]	Elementary Schools: Teachers Students	Secondary Schools: Teachers Students	Colleges and Universities: Teachers Students
$30,300	$220.1[6]	$77,099	84,304	87,206	42,584
$30,100	$10,700	$84,678	2,293,444	1,870,315	612,376
n.a.	$2.5	371[19]	25,000	62,700	n.a.
n.a.	$1,700	263[19]	519,100	652,700	68,800
$495	$2.8	$1,127	101,306	9,904	n.a.
$631	$500	$416	3,603,488	183,109	n.a.
$21,360	$115.8	$46,058	401,524	133,882	49,466
$22,400	$6,200	$36,800	6,813,151	2,397,262	1,156,174
$284	$1.7	$444	11,105	4,492	n.a.
$407	$1,300	$253	651,962	125,545	n.a.
$36.4	$0.2[7]	$61	784	876	n.a.
$68.1	$2,000	$16	16,658	14,825	n.a.
$1,600	$5.5	$1,448	7,512[28]	5,000	292
$1,600	$8,700	$1,612	196,333[28]	100,000	4,529
$4,300	$16.4	$6,215	56,154	36,535	5,360
$5,500	$5,200	$3,804	1,476,329	639,403	87,780
$36,500	$173.7	$29,174	234,961	170,611	38,468
$47,600	$4,800	$15,343	6,878,923	3,987,423	915,765
n.a.	$3.8	$1,200[19]	n.a.	n.a.	n.a.
n.a.	$3,900	$490[19]	842,000[10]	—[10]	75,400
$4.3	$0.006[6]	$4.4	72	31	0
$4.3	$700[1]	$0.2	1,485	345	0
$365	$3.2	$439	75,561[28]	n.a.	2,327
$545	$1,350	$142	2,632,764[28]	n.a.	21,489
n.a.	$54.2	$2,200[19]	501,900	n.a.	75,900
n.a.	$4,300	$3,000	4,102,100	3,281,500	890,192
$4,300	$36	$19,520	13,940	10,537	1,082
$4,800	$19,900	n.a.	238,469	129,683	10,405
$1,257,200	$6,374	$603,438	1,713,000	1,074,000	871,000
$1,460,600	$24,800	$464,773	31,638,000	15,561,000	14,359,000
$2,900	$11.9	$1,448	16,376	n.a.	6,500
$3,000	$7,700	$1,645	338,020	272,622	68,227
n.a.	$13.8	$947[19]	n.a.	n.a.	n.a.
n.a.	$2,500	$706[19]	4,700,000[10]	—[10]	591,800
$90	$0.142	$82	852[28]	n.a.	n.a.
$103	$1,050	$24	26,267[28]	4,184	n.a.
$9,800	$61.4	$12,200	183,298	32,572	46,137
$11,900	$9,100	$14,066	4,190,047	289,430	550,030
$1,900	$17.6[7]	$3,100	252,413	200,000	n.a.
$2,000	$800	$2,600	8,862,292	3,250,000	n.a.

469

Nation Capital	Population[1]	Area of Country sq mi (sq km)	Type of Government	Heads of State and Government	Currency: Value of U.S. Dollar[2]
WESTERN SAMOA Apia	157,000 32,200	1,600 (2,575)	Constitutional monarchy (C)	Head of state, Malietoa Tanumafili II Prime min., Tofilau Eti Alesana	talà n.a.
YEMEN Sana	12,900,000 500,000	186,400 (482,700)	Republic	Pres., Ali Abdullah Saleh Prime min., Abdul Aziz Abdul Ghani	rial 12.00
YUGOSLAVIA[14] Belgrade	10,500,000 1,168,500	34,449 (102,173)	Republic	Pres., Zoran Lilic Prem., Radoje Kontic	new dinar 1.5935
ZAIRE Kinshasa	42,500,000 2,796,000	905,568 (2,345,409)	Republic	Pres., Mobutu Sese Seko Prem., Leon Kengo wa Dondo	new zaire 249
ZAMBIA Lusaka	9,100,000 921,000	290,586 (752,714)	Republic (C)	Pres., Frederick Chiluba Vice pres., Levy Mwanawasa	kwacha 675.80
ZIMBABWE Harare	11,200,000 656,100	150,873 (390,759)	Republic (C)	Pres., Robert Mugabe	dollar 7.8293

[1]Mid-1994 estimates where available; some figures, particularly city populations, from earlier years.
[2]Unless otherwise noted, rates are as of June 24, 1994, and are middle rates of interbank bid and asked quotes.
[3]Latest data available.
[4]1993 where available; some figures from earlier years. Exchange rate conversion unless otherwise noted.
[5]1993 where available; some figures from earlier years. Imports CIF and exports FOB where available.
[6]Gross national product.
[7]Purchasing power equivalent.
[8]Commercial rate.
[9]Free market rate.
[10]Combined figure for elementary and secondary education.
[11]Nonessential imports.
[12]Data for both Greek and Turkish sectors.
[13]Includes preelementary teachers.
[14]Data for Serbia and Montenegro only.
[15]Priority rate.
[16]Banking rate.
[17]UN Secretary-General Boutros Boutros-Ghali in July 1992 declared Somalia to have no government.
[18]Official rate.
[19]Figures do not include trade among the successor states of the former Soviet Union.
[20]East Caribbean dollar.
[21]Metropolitan area.
[22]Combined data for Belgium and Luxembourg; trade between the two countries excluded.
[23]Communauté Financière Africaine franc.
[24]City-state.
[25]Grades 1 to 10.
[26]Entries exclude data for West Bank and Gaza Strip. Population of West Bank, 1,400,000; of Gaza Strip, 700,000. Area of West Bank, 2,270 sq. mi. (5,879 sq. km); of Gaza Strip, 146 sq. mi. (378 sq. km).
[27]Entries include East Timor's population of 700,000 and area of 5,763 sq. mi. (14,926 sq. km).
[28]Public education only.
[29]As of December 23, 1994.

Revenue Expenditure in millions[3]	GDP in billions[4] GDP Per Capita	Imports Exports in millions[5]	Elementary Schools: Teachers Students	Secondary Schools: Teachers Students	Colleges and Universities: Teachers Students
$95.3	$0.4[7]	$105	n.a.	n.a.	n.a.
$95.4	$2,000	$6	n.a.	n.a.	n.a.
n.a.	$7.7	$1,600	48,590	n.a.	1,800
n.a.	$1,300	$695	1,671,280	n.a.	53,082
n.a.	$9.5	$6,400	21,368	55,745	11,605
n.a.	$3,600	$4,400	473,902	831,506	143,268
n.a.	$7.8	$409	n.a.	n.a.	n.a.
n.a.	$450	$416	4,870,933	n.a.	n.a.
$665	$3.8	$948	n.a.	n.a.	n.a.
$767	$470	$745	1,461,206	n.a.	15,343
$1,700	$5.4	$2,055	52,415	25,225	3,076
$2,200	$1,900	$1,532	2,376,048	710,619	61,553

Principal Sources for Statistics of the World: Countries
Central Intelligence Agency, *The World Factbook 1994;* Europa Publications, *Europa World Year Book 1994; Facts on File;* International Institute for Strategic Studies, *The Military Balance 1994-1995;* International Monetary Fund, *International Financial Statistics, December 1994;* Population Reference Bureau, *1994 World Population Data Sheet; The Statesman's Year-Book 1994-1995;* Unesco, *Statistical Yearbook 1994;* United Nations; *Wall Street Journal.*

STATISTICS OF THE WORLD: UNITED STATES

State Capital	Population[1]	Area sq mi (sq km)	Governor Lieutenant-Governor	Revenue Expenditure in billions	Per Capita Personal Income
ALABAMA Montgomery	4,219,000 187,106	51,718 (133,949)	Gov., Jim Folsom, Jr. (D) Lt. gov., Vacant	$11.389 $10.242	$17,106
ALASKA Juneau	606,000 26,751	587,875 (1,522,589)	Gov., Walter J. Hickel (I) Lt. gov., John B. Coghill (I)	$7.358 $5.423	$23,008
ARIZONA Phoenix	4,075,000 983,403	114,006 (295,274)	Gov., Fife Symington (R) 	$10.843 $9.783	$18,119
ARKANSAS Little Rock	2,453,000 175,795	53,182 (137,741)	Gov., Jim Guy Tucker (D) Lt. gov., Mike Huckabee (R)	$6.446 $5.915	$15,994
CALIFORNIA Sacramento	31,431,000 369,365	158,647 (410,894)	Gov., Pete Wilson (R) Lt. gov., Leo McCarthy (D)	$108.222 $104.567	$21,884
COLORADO Denver	3,656,000 467,610	104,100 (269,618)	Gov., Roy Romer (D) Lt. gov., Mike Callihan (D)	$10.028 $8.673	$21,475
CONNECTICUT Hartford	3,275,000 139,739	5,006 (12,965)	Gov., Lowell P. Weicker, Jr. (I) Lt. gov., Eunice S. Groark (I)	$12.744 $12.507	$27,957
DELAWARE Dover	706,000 27,630	2,026 (5,247)	Gov., Tom Carper (D) Lt. gov., Ruth Ann Minner (D)	$2.876 $2.557	$21,735
DISTRICT OF COLUMBIA	570,000	68 (176)	Mayor, Sharon Pratt Kelly (D)	$3.376 $3.391	$29,836
FLORIDA Tallahassee	13,953,000 124,773	58,680 (151,980)	Gov., Lawton Chiles (D) Lt. gov., Buddy MacKay (D)	$33.216 $30.103	$20,710
GEORGIA Atlanta	7,055,000 394,017	58,929 (152,625)	Gov., Zell Miller (D) Lt. gov., Pierre Howard (D)	$16.585 $15.308	$19,203
HAWAII Honolulu	1,179,000 365,272	6,459 (16,729)	Gov., John Waihee (D) Lt. gov., Ben Cayetano (D)	$5.543 $5.606	$23,378
IDAHO Boise	1,133,000 125,738	83,574 (216,456)	Gov., Cecil D. Andrus (D) Lt. gov., C. L. ("Butch") Otter (R)	$3.406 $2.776	$17,540
ILLINOIS Springfield	11,752,000 105,227	54,343 (145,928)	Gov., Jim Edgar (R) Lt. gov., Bob Kustra (R)	$30.351 $28.132	$22,534
INDIANA Indianapolis	5,752,000 741,952	36,185 (93,719)	Gov., Evan Bayh (D) Lt. gov., Frank L. O'Bannon (D)	$14.653 $14.136	$19,161
IOWA Des Moines	2,829,000 193,187	56,276 (145,754)	Gov., Terry E. Branstad (R) Lt. gov., Joy Corning (R)	$8.224 $7.766	$18,324
KANSAS Topeka	2,554,000 119,883	82,282 (213,109)	Gov., Joan Finney (D) Lt. gov., James Francisco (D)	$6.730 $5.742	$19,874
KENTUCKY Frankfort	3,827,000 25,968	40,411 (104,664)	Gov., Brereton Jones (D) Lt. gov., Paul Patton (D)	$11.011 $10.543	$16,954
LOUISIANA Baton Rouge	4,315,000 219,531	47,719 (123,592)	Gov., Edwin Edwards (D) Lt. gov., Melinda Schwegmann (D)	$13.348 $12.893	$16,588
MAINE Augusta	1,240,000 21,325	33,128 (85,801)	Gov., John R. McKernan, Jr. (R) 	$3.926 $3.889	$18,775
MARYLAND Annapolis	5,006,000 33,187	10,455 (27,078)	Gov., William D. Schaefer (D) Lt. gov., Melvin Steinberg (D)	$14.842 $13.537	$23,920

The material in the following tables was the latest available. The symbol * indicates that the category is not applicable to the area mentioned or that the data were misleading for one reason or another; n.a. means that data were not available.

Public Roads miles	Railways[2] miles	Aircraft Departures	Daily News-papers	Public Elementary Schools (K-8): Teachers Students	Public Secondary Schools (9-12): Teachers Students	Colleges and Universities: Institutions Students
92,209	3,180	43,301	20	23,041 527,024	18,526 196,386	80 230,537
13,849	*	78,127	8	5,146 91,640	2,136 30,847	8 30,902
55,763	1,413	170,295	21	26,251 497,917	9,825 175,560	42 275,559
77,192	2,036	31,832	30	13,644 317,598	12,251 123,892	35 97,435
169,201	5,537	709,106	136	137,743 3,791,370	55,121 1,404,407	328 1,977,249
78,721	3,267	203,106	28	17,285 451,321	16,134 161,314	59 240,163
20,357	192	39,302	20	17,060 361,548	12,552 126,928	42 165,874
5,544	226	475	2	3,210 75,983	3,042 28,338	9 42,763
1,107	37	142,337	4	3,340 61,133	2,305 19,804	18 81,909
112,808	2,037	434,919	45	47,266 1,469,850	39,826 511,557	108 618,285
110,879	3,909	292,581	31	46,065 891,647	20,877 315,539	116 293,162
4,106	*	157,697	6	5,073 128,610	3,752 48,838	16 61,162
58,835	1,665	42,298	12	6,145 164,634	5,493 67,034	11 57,798
136,965	7,104	469,251	79	65,107 1,344,549	28,952 529,018	169 748,033
92,374	3,492	84,398	76	27,731 677,249	23,673 283,381	77 296,912
112,708	3,238	34,172	36	18,126 348,648	12,178 146,191	61 177,813
133,256	4,830	14,815	46	14,698 328,244	12,199 123,292	51 169,419
72,632	2,425	57,854	22	26,485 469,897	11,383 185,144	62 188,320
59,599	2,401	72,822	20	26,446 590,824	12,367 207,161	33 204,379
22,510	*	21,473	7	10,428 156,368	4,947 60,085	31 57,977
29,313	792	62,383	15	23,698 555,565	20,797 196,285	57 268,399

State Capital	Population[1]	Area sq mi (sq km)	Governor Lieutenant-Governor	Revenue Expenditure in billions	Per Capita Personal Income
MASSACHUSETTS Boston	6,041,000 574,283	8,262 (21,398)	Gov., William F. Weld (R) Lt. gov., Paul Cellucci (R)	$21.493 $21.557	$24,475
MICHIGAN Lansing	9,496,000 127,321	58,513 (151,548)	Gov., John Engler (R) Lt. gov., Connie Binsfeld (R)	$28.760 $27.051	$20,542
MINNESOTA St. Paul	4,567,000 272,235	84,397 (218,587)	Gov., Arne Carlson (R) Lt. gov., Joanell Dyrstad (R)	$16.245 $14.295	$21,017
MISSISSIPPI Jackson	2,669,000 196,637	47,695 (123,529)	Gov., Kirk Fordice (R) Lt. gov., Eddie Briggs (R)	$7.205 $6.235	$14,708
MISSOURI Jefferson City	5,278,000 35,481	69,709 (180,545)	Gov., Mel Carnahan (D) Lt. gov., Roger B. Wilson (D)	$12.559 $10.809	$19,559
MONTANA Helena	856,000 24,569	147,046 (380,847)	Gov., Marc Racicot (R) Lt. gov., Dennis Rehberg (R)	$3.023 $2.663	$17,413
NEBRASKA Lincoln	1,623,000 191,972	77,358 (200,356)	Gov., E. Benjamin Nelson (D) Lt. gov., Kim Robak (D)	$3.890 $3.823	$19,757
NEVADA Carson City	1,457,000 40,443	110,567 (286,367)	Gov., Bob Miller (D) Lt. gov., Sue Wagner (R)	$4.500 $4.051	$22,747
NEW HAMPSHIRE Concord	1,137,000 36,006	9,283 (24,043)	Gov., Stephen Merrill (R)	$3.011 $2.970	$22,169
NEW JERSEY Trenton	7,904,000 88,675	7,790 (20,176)	Gov., Christine Whitman (R)	$29.614 $28.923	$26,732
NEW MEXICO Santa Fe	1,654,000 98,928	121,598 (314,937)	Gov., Bruce King (D) Lt. gov., Casey Luna (D)	$6.303 $5.599	$16,333
NEW YORK Albany	18,169,000 292,594	49,112 (127,199)	Gov., Mario M. Cuomo (D) Lt. gov., Stan Lundine (D)	$78.209 $74.280	$24,771
NORTH CAROLINA Raleigh	7,070,000 207,951	52,672 (136,420)	Gov., James B. Hunt, Jr. (D) Lt. gov., Dennis A. Wicker (D)	$19.377 $16.916	$18,688
NORTH DAKOTA Bismarck	638,000 49,256	70,704 (183,122)	Gov. Edward T. Schafer (R) Lt. gov., Rosemarie Myrdal (R)	$2.288 $2.129	$17,123
OHIO Columbus	11,102,000 632,910	41,328 (107,039)	Gov., George Voinovich (R) Lt. gov., Mike DeWine (R)	$38.341 $31.685	$19,627
OKLAHOMA Oklahoma City	3,258,000 444,719	69,903 (181,048)	Gov., David Walters (D) Lt. gov., Jack Mildren (D)	$8.679 $8.272	$17,035
OREGON Salem	3,086,000 107,786	97,052 (251,363)	Gov., Barbara Roberts (D)	$10.826 $9.013	$19,447
PENNSYLVANIA Harrisburg	12,052,000 52,376	45,309 (117,350)	Gov., Robert P. Casey (D) Lt. gov., Mark Singel (D)	$37.779 $34.359	$21,241
RHODE ISLAND Providence	997,000 160,728	1,213 (3,142)	Gov., Bruce G. Sundlun (D) Lt. gov., Robert A. Weygand (D)	$3.765 $4.176	$21,203
SOUTH CAROLINA Columbia	3,664,000 98,052	31,117 (80,593)	Gov., Carroll Campbell, Jr. (R) Lt. gov., Nick Theodore (D)	$10.637 $10.386	$16,818
SOUTH DAKOTA Pierre	721,000 12,906	77,121 (199,742)	Gov., Walter Dale Miller (R) Lt. gov., Steve T. Kirby (R)	$1.942 $1.686	$17,977
TENNESSEE Nashville	5,175,000 510,784	42,146 (109,158)	Gov., Ned Ray McWherter (D) Lt. gov., John Wilder (D)	$11.864 $11.028	$18,415
TEXAS Austin	18,378,000 465,622	266,873 (691,198)	Gov., Ann W. Richards (D) Lt. gov., Bob Bullock (D)	$42.019 $39.091	$19,134
UTAH Salt Lake City	1,908,000 159,936	84,904 (219,900)	Gov., Mike Leavitt (R) Lt. gov., Olene S. Walker (R)	$5.348 $4.833	$16,138
VERMONT Montpelier	580,000 8,247	9,615 (24,903)	Gov., Howard Dean (D) Lt. gov., Barbara Snelling (R)	$1.953 $1.849	$19,442
VIRGINIA Richmond	6,552,000 203,056	40,598 (105,148)	Gov., George Allen (R) Lt. gov., Donald Beyer (D)	$16.307 $14.721	$21,544
WASHINGTON Olympia	5,343,000 33,840	68,127 (176,448)	Gov., Mike Lowry (D) Lt. gov., Joel Pritchard (R)	$19.930 $18.003	$21,773

Public Roads miles	Railways[2] miles	Aircraft Departures	Daily News- papers	Public Elementary Schools (K-8): Teachers Students	Public Secondary Schools (9-12): Teachers Students	Colleges and Universities: Institutions Students
30,563	441	166,140	45	20,905 629,649	28,625 230,299	117 422,976
117,659	2,458	192,544	53	32,761 1,164,829	39,492 438,731	106 559,729
129,959	4,509	144,100	24	23,273 569,298	21,777 224,226	98 272,920
72,834	1,463	13,722	20	16,729 370,006	10,381 136,662	47 123,754
121,787	4,669	265,519	46	28,180 621,712	24,804 237,645	98 296,617
69,768	2,266	45,136	11	6,731 115,315	3,404 44,696	20 39,644
92,702	3,810	24,699	19	10,968 202,501	8,337 79,975	33 122,603
45,778	1,352	136,207	7	6,465 165,348	4,234 57,626	9 63,877
14,938	*	20,433	10	8,096 133,182	3,558 48,065	30 63,924
35,097	957	144,990	24	45,999 817,661	26,373 312,899	61 342,446
60,812	1,893	41,747	16	10,353 217,418	4,473 98,250	32 99,276
111,882	2,413	353,960	85	88,304 1,893,303	62,774 796,383	314 1,069,772
96,028	2,614	224,163	50	38,471 810,576	23,916 303,507	122 383,453
86,727	3,276	12,194	8	5,242 84,569	2,552 34,165	20 40,470
113,823	4,543	228,254	90	70,593 1,282,466	35,150 513,952	156 573,183
112,467	2,886	58,321	29	18,582 438,796	15,835 158,300	46 182,105
96,036	2,361	121,734	20	15,156 365,416	9,392 144,706	44 167,415
117,038	3,606	271,912	91	45,421 1,215,974	43,691 501,639	219 629,832
6,057	*	21,835	8	4,577 105,677	4,165 38,121	14 79,165
64,158	2,184	33,007	17	25,404 460,260	11,891 173,159	59 171,443
83,305	1,173	11,592	11	5,570 97,882	2,371 36,691	20 37,596
85,037	2,199	175,947	27	30,249 612,188	11,659 233,430	78 242,970
294,142	10,315	769,797	83	118,719 2,628,714	103,187 907,157	178 938,526
40,508	1,396	89,780	8	9,726 329,883	7,133 133,987	16 133,083
14,166	*	7,926	9	2,995 73,865	2,827 24,693	22 37,377
68,429	3,261	51,175	28	37,845 757,847	26,335 274,078	87 354,172
79,428	2,767	228,559	28	23,948 651,743	16,820 244,732	62 276,484

State Capital	Population[1]	Area sq mi (sq km)	Governor Lieutenant-Governor	Revenue Expenditure in billions	Per Capita Personal Income
WEST VIRGINIA	1,822,000	24,231	Gov., W. Gaston Caperton (D)	$6.047	$16,148
Charleston	57,287	(62,758)		$5.943	
WISCONSIN	5,082,000	56,144	Gov., Tommy Thompson (R)	$18.677	$19,822
Madison	191,262	(145,412)	Lt. gov., Scott McCallum (R)	$14.621	
WYOMING	476,000	97,818	Gov., Mike Sullivan (D)	$2.181	$19,724
Cheyenne	50,008	(253,347)		$1.887	

[1]Mid-1994 estimates where available; some figures, particularly city populations, from earlier years.
[2]Class 1 railroads only.

OUTLYING AREAS OF THE UNITED STATES

Area Capital	Population[1]	Area sq mi (sq km)	Status	Governor Lieutenant-Governor	Revenue Expenditure in millions
AMERICAN SAMOA	55,223	77	Unincorporated	Gov., A. P. Lutali	$97
Pago Pago	3,500	(199)	territory	Lt. gov., Tauese P. Sunia	n.a.
GUAM	149,620	212	Unincorporated	Gov., Joseph F. Ada	$525
Agana	1,100	(549)	territory	Lt. gov., Frank F. Blas	$395
NORTHERN MARIANA	49,799	184	Commonwealth	Gov., Froilan Tenorio	$147
ISLANDS		(477)		Lt. gov., Benjamin	$127.7
Saipan	38,900			Manglona	
PUERTO RICO	3,797,100	3,515	Commonwealth	Gov., Pedro Rosselló	$7,617
San Juan	437,700	(9,104)			$7,617
VIRGIN ISLANDS	97,564	136	Unincorporated	Gov., Alexander A. Farrelly	$364.4
Charlotte Amalie	12,300	(352)	territory	Lt. gov., Derek M. Hodge	$364.4

[1]Mid-1994 estimates where available; some figures, particularly city populations, from earlier years.

476

Public Roads miles	Railways[2] miles	Aircraft Departures	Daily Newspapers	Public Elementary Schools (K-8): Teachers Students		Public Secondary Schools (9-12): Teachers Students		Colleges and Universities: Institutions Students	
35,045	2,700	7,608	23	9,923	219,037	7,495	99,259	28	90,252
110,978	1,765	74,696	37	33,358	588,447	18,801	240,968	64	307,902
37,642	1,785	6,990	5	2,884	71,798	2,937	28,515	9	31,548

Roads miles	Aircraft Departures	Radio and Television Stations	Newspapers	Public Elementary and Secondary School Teachers	Public School Students: Elementary Secondary		Higher Education: Institutions Students	
217	180	3	2	725	10,582	3,412	1	1,295
419	8,417	8	2	1,628	22,408	7,649	2	4,845
237	4,773	6	3	425	6,133	1,953	1	796
8,546	56,292	125	8	38,381	469,764	167,270	61	158,120
532	15,424	12	2	1,595	16,804	6,083	2	2,856

Principal Sources for Statistics of the World: United States and Outlying Areas
Census Bureau; Central Intelligence Agency, *The World Factbook 1994;* Commerce Department Bureau of Economic Analysis; Council of State Governments; Department of Education National Center for Education Statistics, *Digest of Education Statistics 1994;* Department of the Interior Office of Territorial and International Affairs, *Fact Sheets;* Office of the Budget of Washington, DC; Puerto Rico Federal Affairs Administration; Federal Aviation Administration, *FAA Statistical Handbook of Aviation 1994;* Gale Research Inc., *Gale Directory of Publications and Broadcast Media 1995;* Association of American Railroads, *Railroad Facts 1994.*

STATISTICS OF THE WORLD: CANADA

Province Capital	Population[1]	Area sq mi (sq km)	Government Leaders	Revenue Expenditure in millions
ALBERTA	2,716,200	255,285	Lt. gov., Gordon Towers	$14,397.4
Edmonton	839,900	(661,185)	Prem., Ralph Klein	$15,369.0
BRITISH COLUMBIA	3,668,400	365,950	Lt. gov., David C. Lam	$21,228.1
Victoria	287,900	(947,800)	Prem., Michael Harcourt	$22,725.7
MANITOBA	1,131,100	250,950	Lt. gov., W. Yvon Dumont	$6,484.8
Winnipeg	652,400	(649,950)	Prem., Gary Filmon	$6,889.0
NEW BRUNSWICK	759,300	28,354	Lt. gov., Norrie McCain	$4,469.2
Fredericton	71,900	(73,437)	Prem., Frank McKenna	$4,519.6
NEWFOUNDLAND AND LABRADOR	582,400	156,649 (405,720)	Lt. gov., Frederick Russell	$3,481.6
St. John's	171,900		Prem., Clyde Kirby Wells	$3,632.0
NORTHWEST TERRITORIES	64,300	1,322,910 (3,426,322)	Commissioner: Daniel L. Norris	$1,294.6
Yellowknife	15,200		Govt. leader: Nellie J. Cournoyea	$1,289.1
NOVA SCOTIA	936,700	21,425	Lt. gov., James Kinley	$4,542.0
Halifax	320,500	(55,490)	Prem., John P. Savage	$5,196.5
ONTARIO	10,927,800	412,582	Lt. gov., Henry N. R. Jackman	$49,387.8
Toronto	3,893,000	(1,068,582)	Prem., Bob Rae	$60,377.0
PRINCE EDWARD ISLAND	134,500	2,184 (5,657)	Lt. gov., Marion L. Reid	$808.4
Charlottetown			Prem., Catherine S. Callbeck	$830.3
QUEBEC	7,281,100	594,862	Lt. gov., Martial Asselin	$41,539.1
Québec	645,600	(1,540,687)	Prem., Jacques Parizeau	$46,548.2
SASKATCHEWAN	1,016,200	251,866	Lt. gov., J. E. N. Wiebe	$6,265.9
Regina	191,700	(652,330)	Prem., Roy Romanow	$6,510.0
YUKON TERRITORY	30,100	186,661	Commissioner: Kenneth McKinnon	$477.6
Whitehorse	17,900	(483,450)	Govt. leader: John Ostashek	$466.5

[1]City populations are 1991 census figures for metropolitan areas; other figures are latest estimates available.

The material in this table was the latest available. It should be noted that all dollar figures are in Canadian dollars.

Per Capita Personal Income	Motor Vehicle Registrations	Railways kilometers	Radio Stations Television Stations	Daily Newspapers	Elementary and Secondary Schools: Teachers Enrollment	Postsecondary Education: Institutions Enrollment
$22,679	1,910,612	4,454	55	9	27,893	27
			11		531,783	110,360
$23,164	2,659,642	6,660	87	20	32,707	26
			11		604,740	146,189
$19,996	787,184	2,874	27	4	13,303	15
			8		221,578	43,084
$18,101	510,454	1,091	22	4	8,320	13
			6		141,110	28,058
$17,451	309,921	240	25	2	7,805	13
			4		122,125	22,846
$21,381	26,723	—	6	—	1,084	1
			2		15,872	638
$18,959	625,812	704	23	6	10,340	22
			5		169,745	41,434
$23,757	6,231,948	13,436	155	47	120,545	53
			28		2,090,288	544,896
$18,159	90,537	—	5	3	1,370	3
			1		24,596	4,564
$20,809	3,705,902	4,593	111	11	63,399	102
			32		1,152,015	449,200
$19,068	699,870	3,712	30	4	10,815	5
			10		212,386	37,425
$24,688	27,436	—	3	1	385	1
			1		5,811	468

Principal Sources for Statistics of the World: Canada
Statistics Canada: *Education in Canada, Provincial Economic Accounts, Road Motor Vehicles,* and *Rail in Canada 1992; Corpus Administrative Index.*

KEY TO
SIGNED ARTICLES

Here is a list of contributors to this Yearbook. The initials at the end of an article are those of the author or authors of that article.

A.A., ALPHA ANDERSON, B.A. Writer and Editor.

A.A.F., ANN A. FLOWERS Instructor, Center for the Study of Children's Literature, Simmons College.

A.C., ANDY COHEN, B.A. General Manager, Curtis Publishing Company. Editor, *Football News.*

A.F., ANITA FINKEL, PH.D. Editor and Publisher, *The New Dance Review.* Former Associate Editor, *Ballet News.*

A.J.A., ALI JIMALE AHMED, PH.D. Assistant Professor of Comparative Literature, Queens College and the Graduate School and University Center of the City University of New York. President, Somali Studies Association of North America.

A.J.K.S., ALAN J. K. SANDERS Lecturer in Mongolian Studies, University of London. Author, *The People's Republic of Mongolia; Mongolia: Politics, Economics and Society.*

A.L.A., AUDREY L. ALTSTADT, B.A., A.M., PH.D. Assistant Professor of History, University of Massachusetts, Amherst. Author, *The Azerbaijani Turks: Power and Identity Under Russian Rule.*

A.L.R., ARTHUR L. ROBINSON, PH.D. Staff Scientist, Advanced Light Source, Lawrence Berkeley Laboratory.

A.N.M., ARUNA NAYYAR MICHIE, PH.D. Associate Professor of Political Science, Kansas State University.

A.P., AUDREY PAVIA, B.A. Editor, *Horse Illustrated* magazine.

A.S., ANWAR SYED, B.A., M.A., PH.D. Professor of Political Science, University of Massachusetts at Amherst. Author, *Pakistan: Islam, Politics and National Solidarity.*

A.W., ANTHONY WILSON-SMITH Ottawa Bureau Chief and Member, Board of Editors, *Maclean's* magazine.

B.A.A., BELINDA A. AQUINO, PH.D. Director, Center for Philippine Studies; Professor of Political Science and Asian Studies, University of Hawaii, Manoa.

B.A.B., BESS A. BROWN, B.A., M.A., PH.D. Senior Research Analyst, RFE/RL Research Institute.

B.C., BRIAN CLEARY, B.A. Staff Reporter, *Tennis Magazine.*

B.D., BENJAMIN DEAN, B.A., M.F.A. Writer and Editor.

B.H., BETSY HANSON, B.S., M.A. Former Reporter/Researcher, *Discover* magazine.

B.K., BOB KLAPISCH, B.A. Baseball Reporter, *New York Daily News.*

B.K.M., BRENDA K. MANUELITO Associate Director, Darcy McNickle Center for the History of the American Indian.

B.S., BILL STRICKLAND Managing Editor, *Bicycling* magazine.

B.V., BOB VERDI, A.B. Columnist, *Chicago Tribune.*

C.A.C., CARLOS A. CUNHA, PH.D. Professor of Political Science, Dowling College. Author, *The Portuguese Communist Party's Strategy for Power, 1921-1989.*

C.B., CRAIG BAXTER, B.S., M.A., PH.D. Professor of Politics and History, Juniata College. Coauthor, *Government and Politics in South Asia.*

C.C., CHARLES COOPER, B.A., M.A. Senior Editor, *Computer Shopper* magazine.

C.F.S., C. F. SCHUETZ, PH.D. Assistant Professor of Political Science, Carleton University, Ontario.

C.H.A., CALVIN H. ALLEN, JR. A.B., M.A., PH.D. Assistant Professor of History, University of Memphis. Author, *Oman: Modernization of the Sultanate.*

C.M., CIARAN McKEOWN, B.A. Subeditor, *Belfast Newsletter.* Author, *The Passion of Peace.*

C.M.C., CARL M. CANNON, B.A. White House Correspondent, *Baltimore Sun.*

C.R., CARL ROLLYSON, PH.D. Professor of Art, Baruch College, City University of New York.

C.S.L., CAROL SKALNIK LEFF, PH.D. Assistant Professor of Political Science, University of Illinois. Author, *National Conflict in Czechoslovakia.*

D.A., DAVID ARTER, B.A., M.A., PH.D. Professor of European Integration, Leeds Business School.

D.A.P., DOMINICK A. PISANO, B.A., M.S., PH.D. Curator/Deputy Chair, Aeronautics Department, National Air and Space Museum, Smithsonian Institution.

D.B., DON BOHNING, B.A. Latin America Editor, *The Miami Herald.*

D.B.G., DAVID B. GIVENS Director of Information, American Anthropological Association.

D.F.A., DONALD F. ANTHROP, PH.D. Professor of Environmental Studies, San Jose State University.

D.I.S., DAVID I. STEINBERG, B.A., M.A. Distinguished Professor of Korea Studies, School of Foreign Service, Georgetown University. Author, *The Future of Burma.*

D.J.P., DONALD J. PUCHALA, PH.D. Charles L. Jacobson Professor of Public Affairs and Director, Institute of International Studies, University of South Carolina.

D.L., DAVID LENNON, B.A. Sportswriter and Ski Columnist, *New York Newsday.*

D.Le., DANIEL LEWIS, M.A., PH.D. Instructor, History Department, San Bernardino Valley College.

D.N.C., DONALD N. CLARK, B.A., M.A., A.M., PH.D.
Professor of History, Trinity University. Editor, *Korea Briefing 1993.*

D.P.S., DAVID PATRICK STEARNS, B.S., M.A.
Classical Music and Theater Critic, *USA Today;* Contributing Editor, *Stereo Review.*

D.P.W., DAVID P. WERLICH, PH.D.
Professor of History, Southern Illinois University; author, *Peru: A Short History.*

D.V., DAVID VERSICAL, B.A., M.S.J.
National Editor, *Automotive News* magazine.

D.W., DENISE WILLIAMS, PH.D.
Assistant Professor in Behavioral Science Graduate Program, California State University, Dominguez Hills.

E.B., EDMUND BLAIR, B.A.
Staff Writer, *Middle East Economic Digest.*

E.C.R., EDWARD C. ROCHETTE
Former President, American Numismatic Association; Numismatic Writer, *Los Angeles Times* Syndicate.

E.J.F., ERIK J. FRIIS, B.S., M.A.
Editor and Publisher, *The Scandinavian-American Bulletin.*

E.K., EDMOND KELLER
Director, African Studies Center, University of California, Los Angeles.

E.L.N., ELEANOR LYNN NESMITH, B.A.
Writer, *Southern Living* magazine. Contributing Writer, *Washington Post Magazine, Architectural Record* magazine.

E.N.C., ELIZA NEWLIN CARNEY, M.S.
Staff Correspondent, *National Journal.*

E.S., ELAINE STUART, B.A.
Managing Editor, *Council of State Governments.*

E.S.E., ERIC S. EINHORN, PH.D.
Professor and Chairman of Political Science, University of Massachusetts, Amherst. Coauthor, *Modern Welfare States; Politics and Policy in Social Democratic Scandinavia.*

F.C.E., FREDERICK C. ENGELMANN, A.B., A.M., M.A., PH.D.
Professor Emeritus of Political Science, University of Alberta. Coauthor, *Canadian Political Parties: Origin, Character, Impact.*

F.G.E., F. GUNTHER EYCK, B.A., M.SC., M.A., PH.D.
Distinguished Adjunct Professor in Residence, School of International Service, American University. Author, *The Benelux Countries: An Historical Survey.*

F.H.L., FRED H. LAWSON, PH.D.
Associate Professor of Government, Mills College. Author, *The Social Origins of Egyptian Expansionism During the Muhammad Ali Period.*

F.L., FRANK LITSKY, B.S.
Sportswriter, *New York Times.* Author, *Superstars; The Winter Olympics; The New York Times Official Sports Record Book.*

G.B.H., GEOFFREY B. HAINSWORTH, PH.D.
Professor of Economics, University of British Columbia.

G.B.Ha., GARY B. HANSEN, PH.D.
Professor of Economics, Utah State University. Director, Utah Center for Productivity and Quality.

G.D.S., GUSTAV D. SPOHN, M.A.
Associate Editor, Religious News Service.

G.H., GEOFFREY HORN, M.A.
Freelance Writer and Editor.

G.H.L., GEORGE H. LAMSON, PH.D.
Professor of Economics, Carleton College.

G.S., GADDIS SMITH, PH.D.
Larned Professor of History, Yale University. Author, *Morality, Reason, and Power: American Diplomacy in the Carter Years.*

G.V.S., GARY VAN SICKLE, B.A.
Senior Writer, *Golf World* magazine.

I.S., INGRID STRAUCH, B.A.
Yearbook Supervising Editor.

J.A.K., JUDITH A. KESSLER, A.S.N., B.A.
Teaching Assistant in Sociology, University of Santa Barbara.

J.A.P., JOHN ANTHONY PETROPULOS, PH.D.
Professor of History, Amherst College. Author, *Politics and Statecraft in the Kingdom of Greece.*

J.B., JIM BUDD, B.A., M.S.
Freelance Writer.

J.C.W., JAMES C. WEBSTER
Editor, *The Webster Agricultural Letter.*

J.D., JOHN DAMIS, PH.D.
Professor of Political Science, Portland State University. Author, *Conflict in Northwest Africa.*

J.De., JAMES DEACON
Senior Editor, *Maclean's* magazine.

J.D.B., JOHN D. BELL, PH.D.
Professor of History, University of Maryland, Baltimore County.

J.D.M., JOHN D. MARTZ, PH.D.
Distinguished Professor of Political Science, Pennsylvania State University.

J.F.A., JOANN FAGOT AVIEL, M.A., L.L.D., PH.D.
Professor of International Relations, San Francisco State University.

J.F.C., JOHN FRANKLIN COPPER, PH.D.
Stanley J. Buckman Professor of International Studies, Rhodes College, Memphis.

J.G., JOSEPH GUSTAITIS, PH.D.
Yearbook Supervising Editor.

J.G.D., JOHN G. DEEDY, M.A.
Former Managing Editor, *Commonweal.* Contributor, *The New York Times.* Author, *Facts, Myths & Maybes: Everything You Know About Catholicism but Perhaps Don't.*

J.G.K., JIDLAPH G. KAMOCHE, PH.D.
Associate Professor of History, University of Oklahoma.

J.J.Z., JOSEPH J. ZASLOFF, PH.D.
Professor of Political Science, University of Pittsburgh. Specialist in Southeast Asian affairs.

J.K.B., JOHN K. BORCHARDT, PH.D.
Member-at-large on Board of Directors of the Professional Relations Division, American Chemical Society; research manager, Pulp and Paper Surfactants, Shell Development Company.

J.M., JOHN MUTTER, B.A.
Executive Editor, Bookselling, *Publishers Weekly.*

J.M.L., JEFFREY M. LADERMAN, M.S.
Senior Writer, *Business Week* magazine.

J.P.R., JAMES P. RAKOWSKI, PH.D.
Professor of Transportation and Business Logistics, University of Memphis.

J.R., JIM RUBIN, B.A.
Former Supreme Court Correspondent, Associated Press.

J.R.A., JAMES R. ASKER, B.A.
Senior Space Technology Editor, *Aviation Week & Space Technology.*

J.S., JOHN SCHMELTZER
Financial Writer, *Chicago Tribune.*

J.St., JAN STUART, B.A.
Theater Critic, *New York Newsday.*

J.Su., JUDY SUND, PH.D.
Associate Professor of Art History, Queens College, City University of New York.

J.T.S., JAMES T. SHERWIN
Former New York State, intercollegiate, and U.S. speed chess champion and international master.

J.Z.G., JOSÉ Z. GARCIA, PH.D.
Director, Center for Latin American Studies, New Mexico State University.

K.E.K., KAREN E. KRIGSMAN, B.A. *Yearbook* Editorial Assistant.

K.J.B., KIRK J. BEATTIE, M.A. Associate Professor of Political Science, Simmons College. Author, *Egypt During the Nasser Years.*

K.L., KEN LAWRENCE Secretary, American Philatelic Society. Columnist, *Linn's Stamp News, The American Philatelist* magazine. Author, *Linn's Plate Number Coil Handbook.*

K.L.S., KAREN LEE SCRIVO, M.A. Staff Writer, *Congressional Forecast.*

K.M., KENT MULLINER, B.S., M.A. Curator of International Collections and Assistant to the Dean, Ohio University Libraries.

K.M.S., KELLY MARTIN SKORA, PH.D. Adjunct Instructor, Department of Philosophy and Religion, American University.

K.S., KAARE STROM, PH.D. Associate Professor, University of California, San Diego. Author, *Minority Government and Majority Rule.*

K.W.G., KENNETH W. GRUNDY, PH.D. Professor of Political Science, Case Western Reserve University.

L.C.E., LESLIE C. ELIASON, PH.D. Assistant Professor of Public Affairs, University of Washington.

L.E., LARRY EDSALL, B.S. Managing Editor, *AutoWeek* magazine.

L.G., LOIS GOTTESMAN, M.A. Freelance Writer. Former Research Analyst, American Jewish Committee.

L.H., LINDA HIGGINS, B.A. Freelance Health and Medical Writer.

L.S.G., LOVETT S. GRAY, A.B. Freelance Writer and Consultant. Former Editor, National Council on Crime and Delinquency.

L.T.L., LARS T. LIH, B.A., H.PHIL. Research Fellow, Wellesley College.

M.A.N., MELINDA A. NEWMAN, B.A. Talent Editor, *Billboard* magazine.

M.B., MALIK BALLA, PH.D. Assistant Professor of Arabic, Michigan State University.

M.C.F., MAURA C. FLANNERY, PH.D. Professor of Biology, St. Vincent's College, St. John's University.

M.D., MICHAEL DIRDA, PH.D. Staff Writer and Editor, *Washington Post Book World.* Pulitzer Prize Winner in Criticism, 1993.

M.E.F., MARY ELLEN FISCHER, A.B., A.M., PH.D. Joseph C. Palamountain Professor of Government, Skidmore College. Author, *Nicolae Ceausescu: A Study in Political Leadership.*

M.G., MICHAEL GAWENDA, B.E. Deputy Editor, *The Age* (Melbourne).

M.G.B., MARY G. BIGGS, B.A., M.A., M.L.S., PH.D. Dean of the Library and Professor of English, Trenton State College.

M.G.G., M. GRANT GROSS Director, Chesapeake Research Consortium. Author, *Oceanography: A View of the Earth.*

M.J.C., MARTIN J. COLLO, PH.D. Associate Professor of Government and Politics, Widener University.

M.J.D., MARY-JANE DEEB, PH.D. Academic Director, Omani Program, School of International Service, American University. Author, *Libya's Foreign Policy in North Africa.*

M.M.M., MILANI M. MOHSEN, B.A. Associate Professor of Politics, Department of Government and International Affairs, University of South Florida, Tampa. Author, *The Making of Iran's Islamic Revolution.*

M.P., MARK PITSCH, B.A. Washington Editor, *Education Week.*

M.R., MARK ROSE, M.A. Managing Editor, *Archaeology* magazine.

M.S., MIKE SNIDER, B.S. Home Technology Reporter, *USA Today.*

M.W., MARGARET WILLY, F.R.S.L. Literary Scholar and Poet. Poetry collected in *The Invisible Sun; Every Star a Tongue.*

N.C.P., NICHOLAS C. PANO, M.A. Professor of History and Associate Dean, College of Arts and Sciences, Western Illinois University.

N.K., NELSON KASFIR, J.D., PH.D. Professor of Government, Dartmouth College.

N.P.N., NANCY PEABODY NEWELL, A.B. Research Associate, University of Nebraska. Coauthor, *The Struggle for Afghanistan.*

N.V., NICCOLÒ VIVARELLI, B.A. Special Correspondent, *Newsweek* magazine, Rome.

N.W.H., NOEL W. HOLSTON, M.B.A. Television Critic, Minneapolis-St. Paul *Star Tribune.* Coauthor, *Parents' Choice Guide to Children's Videos.*

O.K., OBRAD KESIC, M.A. Program Officer, Central and East European Programs, International Research and Exchanges Board.

P.B., PHYLLIS BENNIS, B.A. United Nations and Middle East Correspondent, Pacifica Radio. Author, *Altered States: A Reader in the New World Order.*

P.Bo., PAUL BODIN, PH.D. Assistant Professor, Center for Earthquake Research and Information, University of Memphis.

P.G., PAUL GARDNER Freelance Writer. Author, *The Simplest Game; Nice Guys Finish Last.* Columnist, *Soccer America;* commentator, NBC soccer telecasts.

P.G.K., PAUL G. KNIGHT, M.S. Instructor of Meteorology, Pennsylvania State University. Senior Forecaster, *New York Times.*

P.M., PHILIP MATTAR, PH.D. Executive Director, Institute for Palestine Studies. Associate Editor, *Journal of Palestine Studies.* Adjunct Professor, Georgetown University.

P.McL., PATRICIA McLAUGHLIN, B.A. Style Columnist, *Philadelphia Inquirer Magazine.*

P.Mo., PAUL MORAN, B.A. Racing Columnist, *New York Newsday.* Secretary-treasurer, New York Turf Writers Association.

P.M.L., PETER M. LEWIS, M.A. Assistant Professor, School of International Service, American University.

P.M.St.P., PAUL MATTHEW ST. PIERRE, PH.D. Assistant Professor, Department of English, Simon Fraser University, British Columbia.

P.P., PETER PASTOR, PH.D. Professor of History, Montclair State College. Editor, *Revolutions and Interventions in Hungary and Its Neighbor States, 1918-1919.*

P.W., PETER WINN, PH.D. Associate Professor of History, Tufts University. Senior Research Associate, Institute on Latin American and Iberian Studies, Columbia University.

R.A.S., RONALD A. SCHORN, PH.D. Planetary Astronomer and Historian, Intaglio, Inc. Former Chief, Ground-Based Planetary Astronomy, NASA.

R.C.O., ROBERT C. OBERST, PH.D. Associate Professor and Chairman of Political Science, Nebraska Wesleyan University. Coauthor, *Government and Politics in South Asia.*

482

R.E.K., ROGER E. KANET, PH.B., A.B., M.A., A.M., PH.D.
Professor of Political Science and Associate Vice Chancellor for Academic Affairs, University of Illinois at Urbana-Champaign. Coeditor, *The Cold War as Cooperation.*

R.H.H., ROBERT H. HEWSEN
Professor of Russian History, Rowan College of New Jersey. President, Society for the Study of Caucasia.

R.J.A., ROBERT J. ALEXANDER, PH.D.
Professor Emeritus, Rutgers University; Order of Condor of the Andes (Bolivia).

R.J.B., ROBERT J. BOWMAN
Senior Contributing Editor, *World Trade* magazine.

R.J.W., RICHARD J. WILLEY, PH.D.
Professor of Political Science, Vassar College. Author, *Democracy in the West German Trade Unions.*

R.M.G., ROBERT M. GARSSON, JR., M.A.
Washington Bureau Chief, *American Banker.*

R.O., ROBERT OLSON, PH.D.
Professor, Middle East and Islamic History, University of Kentucky. Author, *The Emergence of Kurdish Nationalism: 1880-1925.*

R.O.F., ROBERT OWEN FREEDMAN, PH.D.
Dean and Professor of Political Science, School of Graduate Studies, Baltimore Hebrew College. Author, *Soviet Policy Toward Israel Under Gorbachev; Moscow and the Middle East; The Intifada.*

R.R., ROBIN ROSENBERG, PH.D.
Deputy Director, North-South Center, University of Miami. Author, *Spain and Central America: Democracy and Foreign Policy.*

R.S., RAINER SCHULTE, PH.D.
Professor of Arts and Humanities and Director, Center for Translation Studies, University of Texas at Dallas. Editor, *Translation Review.* Author, *The Craft of Translation; Theories of Translation.*

R.S.N., RICHARD S. NEWELL, PH.D.
Professor of History and Asian Studies. Coordinator of International Studies, University of Northern Iowa. Coauthor, *The Struggle for Afghanistan.*

R.U., ROBERT URIU, B.A., M.I.A., M.PHIL., PH.D.
Assistant Professor of Political Science, East Asian Institute. Columbia University.

R.W., ROBERT WEISBROT, PH.D.
Professor of History, Colby College.

S.C.R., STEVE C. ROPP, PH.D.
Professor of Political Science, University of Wyoming. Author, *Panamanian Politics: From Guarded Nation to National Guard.*

S.G., SAM GOLDAPER
Retired Sports Reporter, *New York Times.* Recipient, Curt Gowdy Media Award, Basketball Hall of Fame.

S.H.P., SUSAN HARRINGTON PRESTON, M.A.
Yearbook Supervising Editor. Author, *Facing Change: Native Communities of the Peruvian Amazon.*

S.J., SUSANNE JONAS, PH.D.
Professor of Latin American and Latino Studies, University of California, Santa Cruz. Author, *The Battle for Guatemala: Rebels, Death Squads and U.S. Power.*

S.L., STEPHEN LEVINE, P.H.D.
Senior Lecturer, Department of Politics, Victoria University of Wellington.

S.P., STEPHEN PERLOFF
Exhibiting Photographer. Editor, *The Photo Review* magazine.

S.S., STEVENSON SWANSON
Environment Writer, *Chicago Tribune.*

S.W., STUART WEIR, B.A.
Senior Research Fellow, University of Essex. Freelance Journalist and Television Consultant. Founder, Charter 88.

T.D., THOMAS DEFRANK, M.A.
Deputy Bureau Chief and White House Correspondent, *Newsweek* magazine.

T.E.T., THOMAS E. TURNER, PH.D.
Author and Consultant.

T.J., TIM JONES, B.S.
Media Writer, Financial Desk, *Chicago Tribune.*

T.S., TAMARA SONN, PH.D.
Associate Professor, Department of Religious Studies, University of South Florida.

T.U.R., TOIVO U. RAUN, PH.D.
Professor of Central Eurasian Studies and Adjunct Professor of History, Indiana University, Bloomington. Author, *Estonia and the Estonians.*

T.W.R., THOMAS W. ROBINSON, B.S., M.A., PH.D.
Professor of China Studies, Government, and National Security; Chairperson, Asian and China Studies Course, Foreign Service Institute. President, American Asian Research Enterprises.

W.A.M., WILLIAM A. McGEVERAN, JR., M.A.
Yearbook Staff Editor.

W.D., WILLIAM DROZDIAK, B.S.
Paris Bureau Chief, *Washington Post.*

W.F.R., WILLIAM F. ROYCE, PH.D.
Professor Emeritus of Fisheries, University of Washington.

W.M., WILLIAM MINTER, PH.D.
Senior Research Fellow, Africa Policy Information Center. Visiting Scholar, American University. Author, *Apartheid's Contras: An Inquiry Into the Roots of War in Angola and Mozambique.*

W.M.W., W. MICHAEL WEIS, B.S., M.A., PH.D.
Associate Professor, Department of History, and Director, Divison of Social Studies, Illinois Wesleyan University. Author, *Cold Warriors and Coups d'Etat: Brazilian-American Relations, 1945-1964.*

W.W., WILLIAM WOLF, A.B.
Film Critic. Lecturer, New York University.

Z.E.K., ZENON E. KOHUT, PH.D.
Director, Canadian Institute of Ukrainian Studies. Author, *Russian Centralism and Ukrainian Autonomy: Imperial Absorption of the Hetmanate, 1760s-1830s.*

PICTURE CREDITS

2 Michael A. Schwarz **7** BUU Hires Ribeiro/Gamma-Liaison **8** *Top Left:* AP/Wide World Photos; *Top Right & Bottom:* Jeffrey Markowitz/Sygma **9** *Top:* Giboux/Gamma-Liaison; *Inset:* Ted Soqui/Sygma; *Bottom:* Cynthia Johnson/Gamma-Liaison **10** *Top Left & Right:* C. David Butow/Black Star; *Bottom:* Reuters/Bettmann Newsphotos **11** *Top & Bottom Right:* AP/Wide World Photos; *Bottom Left:* Bob Daemmrich/Sygma **12** *Top Left:* Thierry Orban/Sygma; *Top Right Pictures:* NASA; *Bottom:* Phil Humnick/The White House **13** *Top:* Robert Capa/Magnum; *Middle:* © 1994 Turnley/Newsweek/Black Star; *Bottom:* AP/Wide World Photos **14** *Top:* UPI/Bettmann Newsphotos; *Middle:* AP/Wide World Photos; *Bottom:* Dennis Brack/Black Star **15** *Top:* Gordon Hodge/Sygma; *Bottom:* AP/Wide World Photos **16** *Inset:* Roger Job/Gamma-Liaison; *Middle:* Reuters/Bettmann Newsphotos; *Bottom Left:* Gamma-Liaison; *Bottom Right:* AP/Wide World Photos **17** *Top Left:* Vladimir Pcholkin/Black Star; *Top Right:* Moshe Milner/Sygma; *Bottom:* Markel/Gamma-Liaison **18** *Top Left & Right:* AP/Wide World Photos; *Bottom:* Joan Marcus/Marc Bryan-Brown **19** *Inset:* Reuters/Bettmann Newsphotos; *Top:* David James; *Bottom Left & Right:* Sygma **20** *Top Left & Right:* Focus on Sports; *Bottom:* Sports Illustrated © Time Inc. **21** *Left, Middle, & Bottom:* AP/Wide World Photos; *Top Right:* © Duomo 1994 **22** *Top:* AP/Wide World Photos; *Bottom Left:* Focus on Sports; *Bottom Right:* Doug Beghtel/Sygma **24** The Granger Collection **25** Photo Researchers, Inc. **26** *Top:* The Granger Collection; *Bottom:* Scala/Art Resource **27** Art by Howard S. Friedman **28** Griffith Observatory **29** Art by Howard S. Friedman **31** University of Texas McDonald Observatory **32** *Top:* Hubble Space Telescope Comet Team and NASA **32** *Bottom* NASA/Reuters/Bettmann Newsphotos **33** both: MSSO, ANU/Science Photo Library/Photo Researchers, Inc. **34** NASA **35** Alan Levenson/Time Magazine **36** Dennis di Cicco **39** 24" x 36"/Acrylic on canvas © Peter Max 1993 **41** Jonathan Daniel/Allsport **42** *Top:* Shawn Botterill/Allsport; *Bottom:* AP/Wide World Photos **43** *Inset:* Shawn Botterill/Allsport; *Bottom:* Reuters/Bettmann Newsphotos **44** *Top:* Ben Radford/Allsport; *Bottom:* Reuters/Bettmann Newsphotos **45** Shawn Botterill/Allsport **46-47** Reuters/Bettmann Newsphotos **48** Shawn Botterill/Allsport **50** *Top:* Reuters/Bettmann Newsphotos; *Bottom:* Mike Hewitt/Allsport **53-64** Lionel Delevingne **66** Agence France-Presse **69** Reuters/Bettmann Newsphotos **71-72** Reuters/Bettmann Newsphotos **74** Courtesy Calgene **76** Farid Djaza/Sygma **79** Donald C. Johanson, Ph.D./Institute Of Human Origins **81** Noelle Soren **82** University of Wyoming **83** David Barnes/Stock Market **84** Gary Payne/Gamma-Liaison **85** Keith Bernstein/Gamma-Liaison **86** Collection of Udo and Anette Brandhorst, Cologne/The Museum of Modern Art **87** Virginia Museum of Fine Arts, Richmond/The Metropolitan Museum of Art **90** *Both:* JPL and NASA **92** Jonathan Marks/Australian Picture Library **93** Reuters/Bettmann Newsphotos **94** Ford Motor Co. **95** Chrysler Motors **97** Y. Hemsey/Gamma-Liaison **98-99** Reuters/Bettmann Newsphotos **100** Gilles Saussier/Gamma-Liaison **101** Stephen Crowley/NYT Pictures **103** Reuter **105** *All:* D. Perrett, K. Kay, S. Yoshikawa-University of St. Andrews/Photo Researchers, Inc. **106** AP/Wide World Photos **107** Henry Aldrich **108** Dr. Kenneth Lohmann/U. of N. Carolina **109** Charles Francis **112** *Both:* Courtesy of Alfred A. Knopf **113** *Left:* Courtesy of Warner Books; *Right:* Photos by Salle Merrill-Redfield/Courtesy of Warner Books **115** Saba **117** Reuter **118- 119** NBC **120** © Marko Shark **124-126** Reuter **127** © Nick Procaylo/Gamma-Liaison **128** Peter Bregg/Maclean's Magazine **129** Canapress Photo Service **131** Reuter **133** Agence France-Presse **135** Reuter **136** AP/Wide World Photos **138** Courtesy of Edward C. Rochette **139** Reuters/Bettmann Newsphotos **141** Courtesy of Bolt, Beranek and Newman **144** Reuters/Bettmann Newsphotos **146** *Top & Bottom Right:* AP/Wide World Photos; *Left:* Reuters/Bettmann Newsphotos **148** Reuter **150** Agence France-Presse **151** Sara Krulwich/NYT Pictures **152** © Johan Elbers 1995 **155** Reuters/Bettmann Newsphotos **156** *Right:* Reuter; *Left:* National Oceanic and Atmospheric Administration **157** AP/Wide World Photos **160-164** Reuters/Bettmann Newsphotos **166-168** Reuters/Bettmann Newsphotos **169** AP/Wide World Photos **170** Reuters/Bettmann Newsphotos **174** © 1994 Nintendo. Used courtesy Nintendo **175** Reuter **177** Agence France-Presse **179** Bettmann Newsphotos **180** John Gurzinski/NYT Pictures **181** AP/Wide World Photos **183** NTD, ODDR. Anderson/Photoreporters, Inc. **184** AP/Wide World Photos **186** Reuters/Bettmann Newsphotos **187** AP/Wide World Photos **188** Courtesy Embassy of Finland **189** Agence France-Presse **191** *All:* Courtesy Christian de Portzamparc **194** Reuter **195** DPA/Photoreporters, Inc. **196-197** Agence France-Presse **198** Geoff Wilkinson/Rex U.S.A. Ltd. **199** Gamma-Liaison **200** Bettmann Newsphotos **202** Agence France-Presse **203** AP/Wide World Photos **206** *Left:* Dr. Kari Lounatmaa/Science Photo Library/Photo Researchers, Inc.; *Right:* Yvonne Hemsey/Gamma-Liaison **209** Reuters/Bettmann Newsphotos **211** Agence France-Presse **212** Reuters/Bettmann Newsphotos **213** Agence France-Presse **215** *Top:* Roy Gumpel/NAMI; *Inset: Bottom Right & Left:* David Heald/NAMI **217-219** Reuter **221** Eslami Rad-Irib/Gamma-Liaison **222** Jaques Boissinot/Canapress **224** AP/Wide World Photos **226** Agence France-Presse **227** Reuters/Bettmann Newsphotos **229** Reuters/Bettmann Newsphotos **230** J. Rehg/Gamma-Liaison **234** J. Kaku Kurita/Gamma-Liaison **235-240** Reuters/Bettmann Newsphotos **241** Bilal Kabalan/Sipa Press **242** Reuter **244** Agence France-Presse **246** *Left:* © Rollie McKenna; *Right:* David Snodgress/Bloomington Herald-Times **248** *Left:* © Marion Ettlinger; *Right:* Penguin USA **250** Martyn Hayhow/Sipa Press **253** AP/Wide World Photos **254** *All:* Houghton Mifflin Company **255** Agence France-Presse **257** Don Renner **258** Reuters/Bettmann Newsphotos **259** Agence France-Presse **260** © Karim Daher/Gamma-Liaison **262** *Top:* Sergio Dorantes/Sygma; *Inset:* AP/Wide World Photos **264-266** Reuters/Bettmann Newsphotos **268-269** AP/Wide World Photos **271** Agence France-Presse **273** Photofest **275** Walt Disney Pictures/Shooting Star **276** *Top:* Miramax Films/Shooting Star; *Bottom:* Miramax Films **277** New Line Cinema/Shooting Star **279** Ken Schles/Reprise Records **280** © 1994 Todd Kaplan/Star File, Inc. **282** Bob Daemmrich/Sygma **283** Angel Records **286** Reuters/Bettmann Newsphotos **287** Reuter **288** Agence France-Presse **290** AP/Wide World Photos **292** Sygma **293** *Top:* Reuter; *Bottom:* AP/Wide World Photos **294** AP/Wide World Photos **295** © George Rose/Gamma-Liaison **296** Tracy Woodward/Gamma-Liaison **297** *Top:* The Kobal Collection; *Bottom:* S. Shipman-F.S.P/Gamma-Liaison **298** Sygma **299-300** AP/Wide World Photos **301** Gianni Giansanti/Sygma **302** Photofest **305** Agence France-Presse **306** AP/Wide World Photos **308** Dave Hartley/Rex USA Ltd. **309-311** Bettmann Newsphotos **312** *Both:* Steve Granitz/Retna Ltd. **313** AP/Wide World Photos **314** *Both:* Bettmann Newsphotos **315** © Sestini Agency/Gamma-Liaison **316** © Brad Markel/Gamma-Liaison **317** *Left:* Rex U.S.A. Ltd.; *Right:* © Berliner/Gamma-Liaison **318** AP/Wide World Photos **319** Rex U.S.A Ltd. **320-321** Reuters/Bettmann Newsphotos **322** AP/Wide World Photos **323** Lance Morrow/Barry Ament/Epic Records **324** *Left:* © Bill Wisser/Gamma-Liaison; *Right:* Photofest **325-329** AP/Wide World Photos **330** Cat Fanciers' Association **332** © Robert Frank/National Gallery of Art, Washington **335** Agence France-Presse **337** Vic DeLucia/NYT Pictures **340** *Left:* © 1994 Marty Katz; *Right:* Agence France-Presse **341** Reuter **342** Margaret Randall/W.W. Norton Co. **344** Agence France-Presse **346** Reuter **349** Reuter **350** © Duclos/Ribeiro/Gamma-Liaison **352** © Esaias Baitel/Gamma-Liaison **355** Reuters/Bettmann Newsphotos **357-358** AP/Wide World Photos **359** Map by Mapping Specialists **361** Reuter **363** AP/Wide World Photos **365** © Mike Persson/Gamma-Liaison **366** Map by Mapping Specialists **367** NASA **368** Gleb Kosorukov/NYT Pictures **369** Reuters/Bettmann Newsphotos **371** AP/Wide World Photos **372** Todd Rosenberg/Allsport **373-376** AP/Wide World Photos **377** Doug Pensinger/Allsport **378-379** AP/Wide World Photos **383** Reuters/Bettmann Newsphotos **384** Alan Zale/NYT Pictures **387** Reuters/Bettmann Newsphotos **388** Jeff Vinnick **389** *Left:* Reuter; *Right:* AP/Wide World Photos **390** Reuters/Bettmann Newsphotos **391** AP/Wide World Photos **392** Erich Schleger/Gamma-Liaison **393** Reuters/Bettmann Newsphotos **395** AP/Wide World Photos **396** Allsport **397** AP/Wide World Photos **400** Reuters/Bettmann Newsphotos **401** Reuter **402** Bill Pugliano/Gamma-Liaison **405** *Inset:* Robert Galbraith/Sipa Press; *Right:* AP/Wide World Photos **408- 409** Joan Marcus **410-414** Reuters/Bettmann Newsphotos **415** © Nelson Kasfir **417** Reuters/Bettmann Newsphotos **418** Agence France-Presse **421** © Cynthia Johnson/Gamma-Liaison **423** Frank Cammuso/Syracuse Herald-Journal **425** AP/Wide World Photos **432** Collection of the Supreme Court of the United States **434** Reuters/Bettmann Newsphotos **439** Sygma **440** San Francisco Chronicle/Sygma **441** Courtesy University of Pennsylvania **442** Reuter **444** Agence France-Presse **445** AP/Wide World Photos

INDEX TO THE 1995 YEARBOOK
EVENTS OF 1994

INTRODUCTION

This index is an alphabetical listing of persons, organizations, and events that are discussed in the 1995 Yearbook. Entries in **boldface** letters indicate subjects on which the Yearbook has an individual article. Entries in lightface type indicate individual references or sections within articles. In any entry, the letters a and b refer, respectively, to the left and right column of the page cited. If no letter follows a page number, the reference is to text that is printed in a different format. Usually only the first significant mention of a subject in a given article is included in the Index.

In a main entry such as **Australia,** 91b, the first number refers to the page on which the article begins. The succeeding page numbers refer to other text discussions in the volume. The first number in lightface entries, when these are not in numerical order, will similarly provide the most extensive information on the subject. Subentries following major entries refer to further references on the main subject, as in **Africa,** 70a; archaeology, 107b. The discussion of foreign relations of the United States in the United States of America article may be augmented by reference to separate articles on the countries and international organizations concerned.

When an entry uses the abbreviation **illus.,** the reference is to a caption and picture on the page mentioned. When a text mention and an illustration of the same subject fall within the same article, usually only the text location is included in the Index.

LIST OF ABBREVIATIONS USED IN THE INDEX
AIDS Acquired Immunodeficiency Syndrome
GATT General Agreement on Tariffs and Trade
Nafta North American Free Trade Agreement
NATO North Atlantic Treaty Organization
OPEC Organization of Petroleum Exporting Countries
PLO Palestine Liberation Organization
U.N. United Nations
U.S. United States

A

488

489

M

MacArthur Foundation awards, 342a
Macedonia, 256a, 462; Albania, 76a;
  Australia, 93a; Belgium, 107a;
  Greece, 201a
Madagascar, 462
Magazines and Newspapers, 257a,
  260a
magnetic field 110a, 334b
Mahfouz, Naguib, 73a
Maine, 472
Major, John, 319a, 196b, 198b, 222b;
  European Union, 199a
Major League Soccer (MLS), 51, 387b
Malawi, 71a, 462
Malaysia, 259a, 197b, 462
Maldives, 462
Mali, 462
Malle, Louis, 276a
malnutrition, 86a
Malta, 462
mammals, 108b
Mancini, Henry, 297a
Mandela, Nelson, 319b, 70a, 233b,
  364a, **illus.** 15
Manitoba, 478
Man of the Year (*Time* magazine),
  310b
Mantel, Hilary, 250a
Maori, 285b
Marlin, Sterling, 371b
Marshall Islands, 304a, 462
Maryland, 243a, 402b, 472
Masina, Giulietta, 297b
Massachusetts, 163a, 401b, 402b,
  474
masturbation, 324b, 345b, 424a
Masur, Kurt, 284a
materials science, 132a
Maupin, Armistead, 114b
Mauritania, 462
Mauritius, 462
May, Rollo, 297b
McCarthy, Cormac, 246a
McDougal, James, 422b
McEntire, Reba, 280a
McGraw, Tim, 279b
McKenzie, Kevin, 153a
McRae, Carmen, 297b
medicine. *See* Health and medicine
Menem, Carlos Saúl, 84b
Menendez, Lyle and Erik, 145b
mental diseases, 105b, 137a
Mercosur Treaty, 118b, 135a, 437a
Mercouri, Melina, 298a
mergers and acquisitions, aerospace
  industry, 96b; auto industry, 96a;
  broadcasting, 118b; Canada, 125b,
  129a; computer industry, 142b;
  defense industry, 266a; newspaper
  industry, 257a; railroad companies,
  411b; Switzerland, 405a
Merwin, W. S., 341a
Messier, Mark, 320b, 385a
meteorites, 156b
meteorology, 155a
Mexico, 260a, 218b, 462; banking
  industry, 103a; Costa Rica, 143a
Michael, George, 281a
Michel, Robert, 431a
Michelangelo, 86b
Michigan, 163b, 400a, 402b, 474
Micronesia, 462
Microsoft Corporation, 142a
Middle East. *See* specific country,
  e.g., Iran

Middle East/North Africa Economic
  Summit, 272b
Military and Naval Affairs, 263a;
  aviation, 96b; base closings, 433b;
  Bulgaria, 122b; China, 138a;
  Denmark/Belgium integration,
  285b; Estonia, 182b; India, 212b;
  Japan, 229b; Jordan, 232b;
  Nicaragua, 287a; North Korea,
  235a; Thailand, 408a
Miller, Arthur, 410b
Milosevic, Slobodan, 115b, 443b
Milutinovic, Bora, 45
Minnesota, 401a, 402b, 474
Minorities in the United States, 267a;
  environmental discrimination,
  176b; organized crime, 147b;
  television, 121a; voting, 433b
Mir (space station), 368a
Mississippi, 147b, 269a, 474
Missouri, 474
mites, 110b
Mitterand, Danielle, 331b
Mitterand, François, 189b, 190b,
  310b, 351a
Mitzelfeld, Jim, 341a
Mobutu, Sese Seko, 445a
modern dance, 153a
Moi, Daniel arap, 233a
Mojave Desert, 81a, 426b
Moldova, 270b, 354a, 462
molecular devices, 132a
Monaco, 462
Monet, Claude, 87a, 88b
money laundering, 102a, 327a
money markets, 102b, 196b
Mongolia, 271b, 462
monks, 353a
Montana, 432b, 474
Montenegro, 256a
Moorer, Michael, 378b
Moravcik, Jozef, 362a
Morgan, William, 298a
Morocco, 272a, 462
Motion Pictures, 272b
Mount Pinatubo, 331a
Mozambique, 277b, 71a, 336b, 462;
  Portugal, 336b
Mubarak, Hosni, 165b, 245a
Muhammad, Khalid Abdul, 351a
mummification, 80a
Munch, Edward, 89a
Munro, Alice, 248a
Murayama, Tomiichi, 228a
Murdoch, Rupert, 257a, 258
Murray, Anne, 62
Murray, Charles, 114a, 270a
museums and galleries, 89a; Boston,
  80b, 333a; France, 189b; New
  York City, 80b, 87a, 88a;
  photography, 332a
Music, 278b
musicals, 408b
Muslim-Croat federation, 115a, 417a
Muslim extremists. *See* Islamic
  extremism
Mussolini, Benito, 225b, 227a
mutual funds, 101a, 161b
Myanmar. *See* Burma (Myanmar)

N

NAACP. *See* National Association for
  the Advancement of Colored
  People (NAACP)

Nafta. *See* North American Free
  Trade Agreement (Nafta)
Nagorno-Karabakh, Republic of, 98a
Nairobi Declaration, 363a
Namibia, 462
Nano, Fatos, 75b
NASA, 97a
Nash, John F., 339b
Nasreen, Taslima, 100a, 99a, 352b
National Association for the
  Advancement of Colored People
  (NAACP), 267a, 269b
National Basketball Association
  (NBA), 375a
National Council of Churches, 345a,
  347a
National Football League (NFL), 380b
National Hockey League (NHL), 384b
nationalism, 257a, 351b, 353b, 413a
Nationalist Party, 99b, 369a, 406a
National Medal of Arts, 342b
National Organization for Women
  (NOW), 440b
National Rifle Association, 169a
National Weather Service, 210a
Native Americans. *See* Indians,
  American
NATO. *See* North Atlantic Treaty
  Organization (NATO)
natural gas, 337a, 220b, 328a, 414b
Nauru, 462
Navratilova, Martina, 311b, 388b
Nazarbayev, Nursultan, 232b
Nazis, 190a, 351a
Nebraska, 401b, 474
necrotizing fasciitis, 125b, **illus.** 206
Neeson, Liam, 313b
Nelson, Harriet, 298a
neo-Nazis, 130a, 195b, 256b, 351b
Nepal, 462
Netherlands, 285a, 331a, 464
Netherlands Antilles, 130b
Nevada, 474
Nevis. *See* Saint Kitts and Nevis
New Brunswick, 478
Newfoundland and Labrador, 478
New Hampshire, 474
New Jersey, 400a, 402a, 474
New Mexico, 402b, 474
newspapers. *See* Magazines and
  newspapers
New York, 169b, 433a, 474
New York City, ballet, 152b;
  corruption and fraud, 147a, 402a;
  domestic violence, 403a; Gay
  Games, 270b; history, 247a;
  libraries, 244a; music, 282b, 284a;
  Native Americans, 216a; terrorism,
  145b, 351b; tuberculosis, 207b
New York Stock Exchange, 158b
New York Times, 258a
New Zealand, 285b, 303a, 464
Nicaragua, 286b, 464
Nichols, Johanna, 81a
Niger, 464
Nigeria, 287b, 72b, 464
Nissan, 95b, 372a
Niue, 304a
Nixon, Richard (Milhous), 298b,
  114a, **illus.** 14, 309
Nobel Prizes, 339b, 133a, 224b,
  245b, 251b
Norman, Jessye, 284b
North, Oliver, 171a
North America, 107b, 247a
North American Free Trade
  Agreement (Nafta), 219b, 215b;

R

Rabin, Yitzhak, 223b, 225a, 232a, 306b
radioactive materials, 178a; dating, 79a, 80b; human experimentation, 210a, 340b; Indian lands, 215b; Kazakhstan, 233a; Marshall Islands, 304a; North Korea, 234a; smuggling 195a
Rafsanjani, Ali Akbar, 220a
railroads, 411b, 136a
rainstorms, 271b, 404b
Rako, Ronald, 146b
Ramey, Samuel, 283b
Ramirez, Michael P., 341a
Ramírez Sánchez, Ilich (Carlos the Jackal), 192b
Ramos, Fidel, 330b
Rao, Narasimha, 212b
rape and sexual assault, 127b, 145a, 379a
Raspberry, William, 341a
rats, 353b
Ray, Dixy Lee, 300a
Raye, Martha, 300a
Reagan, Nancy, 171b
Reagan, Ronald, 310a
Redfield, James, **illus.** 113
Redford, Robert, 273a
Redon, Odilon, 87b
Rehnquist, William, 165a, 432a
Reich, Robert, 176b
Reina, Carlos Roberto, 210a
Religion, 344a; American Indians, 216a; China, 136b; England, 200a; Ireland, 223a; Philippines, 331b; Poland, 335b; prize, 343a
religious cults, 126a, 130a, 404b
Remnick, David, 340a
Reno, Janet, 216a, 423a
Republican Party, Ecuador, 162a; El Salvador, 175b; Germany, 194a; United States. *See* Elections in the United States
retail trade, 160a
Reynolds, Albert, 197a, 222b, 223a
Reynolds, Mel, 169b
Reynolds, R.J., III, 300a
Rhode Island, 474
rice, 73a, 75a, 397b
Rice, Tim, 278b
Richards, Ann, 171a, 440b
Richardson, Bill, 216a
Richardson, Nolan, 375a
Richter, Sviatoslav, 284b
Rifkin, Joel, 145b
Rigg, Diana, 409a
Rio Group, 307a
Rivlin, Alice, 424a
Robb, Charles, 171a
Robbins, Tim, 274b
Robert F. Kennedy Human Rights Award, 342a
Roberts, Eugene, Jr., 258a
Robertson, Mary, 57
Robertson, Pat, 346b
Robinson, Glenn, 375b
Robinson, Henry Peach, 332a
Rocard, Michel, 190b
Rock, Allen 128a
Rock, Crissy, 274b
Rodbell, Martin, 340a
Rodham, Hugh, 171a
Roebling, Mary, 300a
Roland, Gilbert (Luis Antonio Damaso de Alonso), 300b

Roldán, Luis, 369b
Rolling Stones (rock group), 278b, 280b
Roman Catholic Church, 347a, 335b, 351a
Romania, 353b, 211b, 464
Romero, Cesar, 300b
Rostenkowski, Dan, 167b, 169a, 425b, **illus.** 8
Roth, Robert, 246b
Rothenberg, Alan, 387a
Roussin, Michel, 190b
Royal Danish Ballet, 152a
Rubin, Jerry, 300b
Rubio, Martiano, 369b
Rudolph, Wilma, 300b
Ruíz Massieu, José Francisco, 261a
Ruíz-Tagle, Eduardo Frei, 134a, **illus.** 135
Runyon, Marvin, 398a
Rushdie, Salman, 221a
Rusk, Dean, 301a
Russia, 354a, 464; Armenian-Azeri conflict, 86a, 98a; atomic smuggling, 195a; China, 137b; Estonia, 182a; European Union, 185b; Georgia, 193a; Iraq, 222a; Israel, 225a, 350b; Jewish community, 344a, 350b; Latvia, 241a; Lithuania, 256a; Malaysia, 260a; Moldova, 271b; oil spills, 178b; Poland, 335b; Romania, 354a; Tajikistan, 406b; Ukraine, 416b
Rutskoi, Aleksandr V., 355b
Rwanda, 358a, 464, **illus.** 16; Belgium, 106b; Burundi, 123b; churches, 347b; France, 192a; Japan, 231a; refugees, 70a, 72a, 286b, **illus.** 71; United Nations, 418b; Zanzibar, 407b

S

Saba, Umberto, 252b
Saint Kitts and Nevis, 131b, 464
Saint Lucia, 132a, 466
Saint Vincent and the Grenadines, 130b, 466
Saleh, Ali Abdullah, 443a
sales tax, 400a
Salinas de Gortari, Carlos, 260a, 263a
Salvi, John, 441b
Samper Pizano, Ernesto, 138b
Sampras, Pete, 388b, **illus.** 21
Samuel H. Scripps American Dance Festival Award, 342b
Sanguinetti, Julio, 436b
San Marino, 466
Santer, Jacques, 184, 199a, 256a
São Tomé and Príncipe, 466
Sarajevo Relief Fund, 391b, 396b
Saraswathi, Chandrashekhara, 353a
Saskatchewan, 478
Sasser, Jim, 170b
satellites, broadcasting, 119a; digital systems, 174b; U.S.-Russian cooperation, 368a; weather, 155a
Satmar Hasidim, 165a, 433a
Saudi Arabia, 360a, 466; Afghanistan, 69b; Jordan, 232b; Qatar, 328b
Savalas, Telly (Aristotle Savalas), 301a
Savimbi, Jonas, 77a
savings and loan industry, 101b
Say, Allen, 255b

Scalfaro, Oscar Luigi, 225b
Scarry, Richard, 301a
SCCA Trans-Am, 372b
Schaufuss, Peter, 152a
Schenkkan, Robert, 410b
Schluter, Paul, 153b
Schneerson, Menachem M., 301a, 351b
Scholastic Assessment Test, 164a
schools. *See* Public schools
School-to-Work Opportunities Act, 163b
Schuller, Gunther, 340b
Schumacher, Michael, 372a
Schwartz, Lloyd, 341a
Schwinger, Julian, 301a
secondary market law, 102b
Seeger, Pete, 342a, 342b
Seinfeld, Jerry, 324a
Seko, Sese, 73a
Seles, Monica, 389b
Selig, Bud, 372b
Selten, Reinhard, 339b
Senegal, 466
senior citizens, 59, 104a, 160a, 330b
Senna da Silva, Ayrton, 301a, 117b, 372a
Serbia, 122b, 256b
Serrano, Andre, 333a
Seselj, Vojislav, 444a
sex discrimination, 147b, 266b, 441b
sexual abuse, 223a; children, 278b, 433b; clergy, 348b
sexual assault. *See* Rape and sexual assault
sexual harassment, Australia, 94a; California, 441a; NAACP, 267b; Paula Jones, 308b, 423b; Tailhook scandal, 266b
sexual orientation, Australia, 92b; Canada, 129a; church, 223a, 345a; Gay Games, 270b; government protection, 171b; Great Britain, 200a; literature, 254a; magazines, 259a; military, 267a, 314b; Muslims, 352b
Seychelles, 466
Shakur, Tupac, 312b
Sharon, Ariel, 225b
Shear, Claudia, 411a
Sheehan, Patty, 382b
Sherry, Norman, 251a
Shevardnadze, Eduard, 193a
Shilts, Randy, 301b, 120b
Shoemaker-Levy 9 (comet), 35, 89b
Shore, Dinah (Frances Rose Shore), 301b
Short, Nigel, 133b
shrines, 213a, 220a, 353b
Shull, Clifford G., 340a
Shushkevich, Stanislau, 105a
Sierra Leone, 466
Sihanouk, Norodom, 125a
Silver, Nicky, 410b
Simon, Neil, 410b
Simon, Paul, 343b
Simpson, Nicole Brown, 145a
Simpson, O. J., 325a, 143b, **illus.** 9; books, 112b; cable TV, 122a; DNA testing, 145a; racial issues, 270a
Singapore, 361a, 466
Sinn Fein, 197a
Sirjani, Ali Akbar Saidi, 220b
Sistine Chapel, 86a
skiing, 386a
Slatkin, Leonard, 284a
Slovakia, 362a, 211b, 466